Introduction to
Finite Mathematics

Introduction to

Finite Mathematics

3rd edition

John G. Kemeny
President, Dartmouth College

J. Laurie Snell
Professor of Mathematics, Dartmouth College

Gerald L. Thompson
*Professor of Applied Mathematics and
Industrial Administration, Carnegie-Mellon University*

PRENTICE-HALL, INC.
Englewood Cliffs, New Jersey

Library of Congress Cataloging in Publication Data

KEMENY, JOHN G.
    Introduction to finite mathematics.

    Includes bibliographies.
    1. Mathematics—1961- 2. Social sciences—
Methodology. I. Snell, James Laurie, joint author.
II. Thompson, Gerald Luther, joint author.
III. Title.
QA39.2.K46 1974   510   73-16326
ISBN 0-13-483834-3

Introduction to Finite Mathematics

Third Edition

John G. Kemeny / J. Laurie Snell / Gerald L. Thompson

10 9 8 7 6 5 4 3 2 1

Printed in the United States of America

Prentice-Hall International, Inc., London
Prentice-Hall of Australia, Pty. Ltd., Sydney
Prentice-Hall of Canada, Ltd., Toronto
Prentice-Hall of India Private Limited, New Delhi
Prentice-Hall of Japan, Inc., Tokyo

Contents

Chapter 8   **APPLICATIONS TO THE**
BEHAVIORAL AND MANAGERIAL SCIENCES   **422**

INDEX   **481**

Preface
to the Third Edition

The term *Finite Mathematics* was first used in the title of the first edition of this book. Since that time it has been generally accepted to describe those topics in modern mathematics that do not depend upon limiting processes, derivatives, or other infinite concepts and that have important real-world applications.

The purpose of the first edition of this book was to introduce college students to the elementary theory of logic, sets, probability theory, and linear algebra and to treat a number of practical applications either from everyday situations or from applications to the biological and social sciences. This central idea has been retained in the third edition of the book; however, experience has shown the desirability of adding additional topics. We have therefore treated the original topics more concisely and added some new subjects and new treatments of old subjects.

The core material of the book consists of the first four chapters. Chapter 1 is a brief introduction to the elementary logic of statements. Chapter 2 contains the basic ideas of the theory of sets and also introduces some fundamental counting techniques. These two chapters constitute a condensed version of the first three chapters of the earlier editions. They contain all the material necessary for the later topics, but some of the more esoteric topics have been eliminated. Chapter 3 is an introduction to finite probability theory and Chapter 4 introduces vectors and matrices and the solution of simultaneous equations. This core material constitutes a self-contained unit which may be used as an introduction to finite mathematics. Or, it may be supplemented in a wide variety of ways by selecting topics from the later chapters. We will discuss several such options presently.

The use of computers was in its infancy when the first edition was published and wide-scale use of time-shared computers for educational purposes became a reality just after the publication of the second edition.

Since *Finite Mathematics* lends itself ideally to computer treatment, and since computers can make the study of *Finite Mathematics* more interesting and more meaningful, we have included an introduction to computer programming in Chapter 5. We have chosen for this purpose the general-purpose computer language BASIC which is widely used in time-sharing systems. The advantage of this language is that the student can start writing computer programs very quickly, and yet it is flexible enough to allow the writing of the most complex computer program. Chapter 5 has been so organized that much of the material and many of the exercises may be taken up even if computers are not available to the students. However, the full impact of the chapter cannot be realized without giving "hands-on" experience for students. Such experience in writing and debugging their own computer programs both provides students with greater mathematical power and helps to reinforce the understanding of fundamental concepts.

One of the shortcomings of the earlier editions of *Finite Mathematics* was the fact that while they contained a good introduction to probability theory, they included little or nothing about the applications of that theory to statistics. For this reason we have added, in Chapter 6, an introduction to finite statistics. This is a natural outgrowth of the core material and leads to a further wealth of practical applications.

Since the appearance of the first edition, linear programming and matrix game theory have received widespread use for a wide variety of applications. We have therefore included, in Chapter 7, a completely revised and expanded treatment of these two important topics. The key technique used in solving large-scale problems in these two areas is the simplex method, and the treatment included in this book is due to A. W. Tucker.

Chapter 8 is devoted entirely to applications. We have retained several of these from earlier editions, and have added three new topics. The first is an application to two linear economic models which depend on the same underlying mathematical model. The second is an application of linear programming to a governmental decision problem. The third discusses the branch-and-bound method for the solution of two combinatorial decision problems.

The problems at the end of each section of the core chapters, which have been widely used (and widely copied!), have been completely revised. As has been our custom, we have tried to give two of each kind of exercise wherever possible, one with and one without an answer printed in the text. We hope that this fresh problem material will come as welcome change for repeat users of the book. We have also updated a number of problems dealing with topics that have become irrelevant since 1957, when the first edition was published.

We believe that this book can be used in many different ways. The basic core material of the first four chapters (even with the omission of the asterisked sections) constitutes a self-contained unit. A course in finite mathematics with an introduction to computing is contained in Chapters 1–5. (The computer material may also be integrated with Chapters 2, 3, and 4 rather than waiting until the first four chapters are completed.) A course in finite mathematics with an introduction to statistics can be designed by covering Chapters 1–4 and the first five sections of Chapter 6. For a more technical introduction to statistics, including an introduction to computing, the first six chapters form a natural unit. An introduction to finite mathematics and linear programming and games is contained in Chapters 1–4 and Sections 1–4 and Sections 3 and 8–10 of Chapter 7. For a more technical introduction of the same topics, one needs an introduction to computation and therefore all of Chapters 1–5 and 7 should be included. Covering the book in its entirety gives a good introduction to the mathematics used in behavioral and social sciences; the same goal may be achieved somewhat more briefly by judicious selection of topics from the last four chapters.

We wish to thank our colleagues in many institutions who have read the material and made comments and suggestions. Professor Frank Deane has been especially helpful in this respect. We are particularly grateful to Professor A. W. Tucker for showing a strong and continuing interest in our work and for suggesting a new approach to the simplex method. We thank Messrs. Mike Vitale and Ross Kinderman for supplying most of the new problem material. We thank Mrs. Bonnie Clark for her assistance in the preparation of the manuscript. We also thank Mrs. Eleanor Balocik for her work in preparing the Solutions Manual. To Dartmouth College and Carnegie-Mellon University we offer our appreciation for providing facilities (including computer usage) which made the preparation of this book possible. And finally we thank the staff of Prentice-Hall for their careful attention to editorial details.

J.G.K., J.L.S., G.L.T.

Compound
Statements

1 PURPOSE OF THE THEORY

A *statement* is a verbal or written assertion which can be determined to be either true or false. In the English language such assertions are made by means of declarative sentences. For example, "It is snowing" and "I made a mistake in signing up for this course" are statements.

The reader should note that questions such as "Who killed cock robin?" or exhortations such as "Tread softly but carry a big stick!" are *not* statements in our sense since they do not have a truth value.

The two statements quoted in the first paragraph above are *simple statements*. A combination of two or more simple statements is a *compound statement*. For example, "It is snowing, and I wish that I were out of doors, but I made the mistake of signing up for this course" is a compound statement.

It might seem natural that one should make a study of simple statements first, and then proceed to the study of compound ones. However, the reverse order has proved to be more useful. Because of the tremendous variety of simple statements, the theory of such statements is very complex. It has been found in mathematics that it is often fruitful to assume for the moment that a difficult problem has been solved and then to go on to the next problem. Therefore we shall proceed as if we knew all about simple statements and study only the way they are compounded. The latter is a relatively easy problem.

While the first systematic treatment of such problems is found in the writings of Aristotle, mathematical methods were first employed by George Boole more than a hundred years ago. The more polished techniques now available are the product of twentieth-century mathematical logicians.

The fundamental property of any statement is that it is either true or

3

false (and that it cannot be both true and false). Naturally, we are interested in finding out which is the case. For a compound statement it is sufficient to know which of its components are true, since the truth values (i.e., the truth or falsity) of the components determine in a way to be described later the truth value of the compound.

Our problem then is twofold: (1) In how many different ways can statements be compounded? (2) How do we determine the truth value of a compound statement given the truth values of its components?

Let us consider ordinary mathematical statements. In any mathematical formula we find three kinds of symbols: *constants, variables,* and *auxiliary symbols.* For example, in the formula $(x + y)^2$ the plus sign and the exponent are constants, the letters x and y are variables, and the parentheses are auxiliary symbols. Constants are symbols whose meanings in a given context are fixed. Thus in the formula given above, the plus sign indicates that we are to form the sum of the two numbers x and y, while the exponent 2 indicates that we are to multiply $(x + y)$ by itself. Variables always stand for entities of a given kind, but they allow us to leave open just which particular entity we have in mind. In our example above the letters x and y stand for unspecified numbers. Auxiliary symbols function somewhat like punctuation marks. Thus if we omit the parentheses in the expression above we obtain the formula $x + y^2$, which has quite a different meaning than the formula $(x + y)^2$.

In this chapter we shall use variables of only one kind. We indicate these variables by the letters $p, q, r,$ etc., which will stand for unspecified statements. These statements frequently will be simple statements but may also be compound. In any case we know that, since each variable stands for a statement, it has an (unknown) truth value.

The constants that we shall use will stand for certain connectives used in the compounding of statements. We shall have one symbol for forming the negation of a statement and several symbols for combining two statements. It will not be necessary to introduce symbols for the compounding of three or more statements, since we can show that the same combination can also be formed by compounding them two at a time. In practice only a small number of basic constants are used and the others are defined in terms of these. It is even possible to use only a single connective! (See Section 2, Exercises 6–8.)

The auxiliary symbols that we shall use are, for the most part, the same ones used in elementary algebra. Any usage of a different symbol will be explained when it first occurs.

EXAMPLES   As examples of simple statements, let us take "The weather is nice" and "It is very hot." We will let p stand for the former and q for the latter.

Suppose we wish to make the compound statement that both are true. "The weather is nice *and* it is very hot." We shall symbolize this statement by $p \wedge q$. The symbol $\wedge$, which can be read "and," is our first connective.

In place of the strong assertion above we might want to make the weak (cautious) assertion that one or the other of the statements is true. "The weather is nice *or* it is very hot." We symbolize this assertion by $p \lor q$. The symbol $\lor$, which can be read "or," is the second connective which we shall use.

Suppose we believed that one of the statements above was false, for example, "It is *not* very hot." Symbolically we would write $\sim q$. Our third connective is then $\sim$, which can be read "not."

More complex compound statements can now be made. For example, $p \land \sim q$ stands for "The weather is nice *and* it is *not* very hot."

EXERCISES

1. The following are compound sentences or may be so interpreted. Find their simple components.
   (a) It is quite hot and I would like to go swimming.
   (b) It is raining or it is very humid.
   (c) Jones did not have time to go, but Smith went instead.
   [*Ans.* "Jones did have time to go"; "Smith went instead."]
   (d) The murderer is Jones or Smith.
   (e) Jack and Jill went up the hill.
   (f) Either Bill has not arrived or he left before we got here.
   (g) Neither the post office nor the bank is open today.
2. In Exercise 1 assign letters to the various components, and write the statements in symbolic form.   [*Ans.* (c) $\sim p \land q$.]
3. Write the following statements in symbolic form.
   (a) Fred likes George. (Statement p.)
   (b) George likes Fred. (Statement q.)
   (c) Fred and George like each other.
   (d) Fred and George dislike each other.
   (e) Fred likes George, but George does not reciprocate.
   (f) George is liked by Fred, but Fred is disliked by George.
   (g) Neither Fred nor George dislikes the other.
   (h) It is not true that Fred and George dislike each other.
4. Assume that Fred dislikes George and George likes Fred. Which of the eight statements in Exercise 3 are true?
5. Write the following statements in symbolic form, letting p be "Fred is smart" and q be "George is smart."
   (a) Fred is smart and George is not smart.
   (b) George is smart or George is not smart.
   (c) Neither Fred nor George is smart.
   (d) Either Fred is smart or George is not smart.
   (e) Fred is not smart, but George is smart.
   (f) It is not true that both Fred and George are not smart.
6. If Fred and George are both smart, which of the six compound statements in Exercise 5 are true?

7. For each statement in Exercise 5 give a condition under which it is false, if it is possible to do so.   [*Ans.* (a) George is smart.]

8. Let *p* be "Stock prices are high" and *q* be "Stocks are rising." Give a verbal translation for each of the following.
   (a) $p \vee q$.
   (b) $p \wedge q$.
   (c) $\sim p \vee \sim q$.
   (d) $\sim(p \wedge q)$.
   (e) $\sim(\sim p \vee q)$.
   (f) $\sim(\sim p \wedge \sim q)$.

9. Using your answers to Exercise 8, parts (d), (e), and (f), find simpler symbolic statements expressing the same idea. [*Ans.* (d) $\sim p \vee \sim q$.]

10. Let *p* be "I will win" and *q* be "You will lose." Using the methods of Exercises 8 and 9, find a simpler statement for

$$[\sim\sim q] \wedge \sim[\sim p \vee \sim q].$$

2   THE MOST COMMON CONNECTIVES

The truth value of a compound statement is determined by the truth values of its components. When discussing a connective we shall want to know just how the truth of a compound statement made from this connective depends upon the truth of its components. A very convenient way of tabulating this dependency is by means of a *truth table*.

Let us consider the compound $p \wedge q$. Statement *p* could be either true or false and so could statement *q*. Thus there are four possible pairs of truth values for these statements and we want to know in each case whether or not the statement $p \wedge q$ is true. The answer is straightforward: If *p* and *q* are both true, then $p \wedge q$ is true, and otherwise $p \wedge q$ is false. This seems reasonable since the assertion $p \wedge q$ says no more and no less than that *p* and *q* are both true.

Figure 1 gives the truth table which defines $p \wedge q$, the *conjunction* of *p* and *q*. The truth table contains all the information that we need to know about the connective $\wedge$, namely it tells us the truth value of the conjunction of two statements given the truth values of each of the statements.

We next look at the compound statement $p \vee q$, the *disjunction* of *p* and *q*. Here the assertion is that one or the other of these statements is true. Clearly, if one statement is true and the other false, then the disjunction

p	*q*	$p \wedge q$
T	T	T
T	F	F
F	T	F
F	F	F

Figure 1

p	*q*	$p \vee q$
T	T	?
T	F	T
F	T	T
F	F	F

Figure 2

p	q	$p \vee q$
T	T	T
T	F	T
F	T	T
F	F	F

Figure 3

p	q	$p \veebar q$
T	T	F
T	F	T
F	T	T
F	F	F

Figure 4

is true, while if both statements are false, then the disjunction is certainly false. Thus we can fill in the last three rows of the truth table for disjunction (see Figure 2).

Observe that one possibility is left unsettled, namely, what happens if both components are true? Here we observe that the everyday usage of "or" is ambiguous. Does "or" mean "one or the other or both" or does it mean "one or the other but not both"?

Let us seek the answer in examples. The sentence "This summer I will visit France or Italy" allows for the possibility that the speaker may visit both countries. However, the sentence "I will go to Dartmouth or to Princeton" indicates that only one of these schools will be chosen. "I will buy a TV set or a phonograph next year" could be used in either sense; the speaker may mean that he is trying to make up his mind which one of the two to buy, but it could also mean that he will buy *at least one* of these—possibly both. We see that sometimes the context makes the meaning clear, but not always.

A mathematician would never waste his time on a dispute as to which usage "should" be called the disjunction of two statements. Rather he recognizes two perfectly good usages, and calls one the *inclusive disjunction* (p or q or both) and the other the *exclusive disjunction* (p or q but not both). The symbol $\vee$ will be used for inclusive disjunction, and the symbol $\veebar$ will be used for exclusive disjunction. The truth tables for each of these are found in Figures 3 and 4. Unless we state otherwise, our disjunctions will be inclusive disjunctions.

The last connective which we shall discuss in this section is *negation*. If p is a statement, the symbol $\sim p$, called the negation of p, asserts that p is false. Hence $\sim p$ is true when p is false, and false when p is true. The truth table for negation is shown in Figure 5.

Besides using these basic connectives singly to form compound statements, several can be used to form a more complicated compound statement, in much the same way that complicated algebraic expressions can be formed by means of the basic arithmetic operations. For example, $\sim(p \wedge q)$, $p \wedge \sim p$, and $(p \vee q) \vee \sim p$ are all compound statements. They are to be read "from the inside out" in the same way that algebraic expressions are, namely, quantities inside the innermost parentheses are first grouped together, then these parentheses are grouped together, etc. Each compound statement has a truth table which can be constructed in a routine way. The following examples show how to construct truth tables.

p	$\sim p$
T	F
F	T

Figure 5

EXAMPLE 1 Consider the compound statement $p \vee \sim q$. We begin the construction of its truth table by writing in the first two columns the four possible pairs of truth values for the statements p and q. Then we write the proposition in question, leaving plenty of space between symbols so that we can fill in columns below. Next we copy the truth values of p and q in the columns below their occurrences in the proposition. This completes step 1 (see Figure 6).

p	q	p	$\vee$	$\sim q$
T	T	T		T
T	F	T		F
F	T	F		T
F	F	F		F
Step No.		1		1

Figure 6

Next we treat the innermost compound, the negation of the variable q, completing step 2 (see Figure 7).

p	q	p	$\vee$	$\sim$	q
T	T	T		F	T
T	F	T		T	F
F	T	F		F	T
F	F	F		T	F
Step No.		1		2	3

Figure 7

Finally we fill in the column under the disjunction symbol, which gives us the truth value of the compound statement for various truth values of its variables. To indicate this we place two parallel lines on each side of the final column, completing step 3 as in Figure 8.

p	q	p	$\vee$	$\sim$	q
T	T	T	T	F	T
T	F	T	T	T	F
F	T	F	F	F	T
F	F	F	T	T	F
Step No.		1	3	2	1

Figure 8

The next two examples show truth tables of more complicated compounds worked out in the same manner. There are only two basic rules which the student must remember when working these: first, work from the "inside out"; second, the truth values of the compound statement are found in the last column filled in during this procedure.

EXAMPLE 2 The truth table for the statement $(p \lor \sim q) \land \sim p$ together with the numbers indicating the order in which the columns are filled in appears in Figure 9.

p	q	$(p$	$\lor$	$\sim$	$q)$	$\land$	$\sim$	p
T	T	T	T	F	T	F	F	T
T	F	T	T	T	F	F	F	T
F	T	F	F	F	T	F	T	F
F	F	F	T	T	F	T	T	F
Step No.		1	3	2	1	4	2	1

Figure 9

Two compound statements having the same variables are said to be *equivalent* if and only if they have exactly the same truth table. It is always permissible, and sometimes desirable, to replace a given statement by an equivalent one.

EXAMPLE 3 Augustus DeMorgan was a well-known English mathematician and logician of the nineteenth century and was the first person to state two important equivalences, or "laws." The first of DeMorgan's laws asserts that the statements $\sim(p \land q)$ and $\sim p \lor \sim q$ are equivalent. The truth tables in Figure 10 show that this is indeed true. The reader will notice that we wrote

p	q	$\sim$	$(p \land q)$	$\sim p$	$\lor$	$\sim q$
T	T	F	T	F	F	F
T	F	T	F	F	T	T
F	T	T	F	T	T	F
F	F	T	F	T	T	T
Step No.		2	1	1	2	1

Figure 10

the truth tables for $p \land q$, $\sim p$, and $\sim q$ directly on the first step to shorten the work. Notice that the two columns marked on step 2 are identical, so that $\sim(p \land q)$ and $\sim p \lor \sim q$ are equivalent statements.

Let us give an interpretation of the equivalence just mentioned. Consider "It is false that business is good and stocks are high." The equivalent statement derived from DeMorgan's laws is: "Either business is bad or stocks are low." Intuitively the equivalence of these two compound statements is clear.

The other of DeMorgan's laws is that the statements $\sim(p \lor q)$ and $\sim p \land \sim q$ are equivalent. This law is discussed in Exercise 12.

EXAMPLE 4 The truth table for the statement $\sim[(p \wedge q) \vee (\sim p \wedge \sim q)]$ together with the numbers indicating the order in which the columns are filled appears in Figure 10a. We note that the compound statement has the same truth table as $p \veebar q$. These two statements are therefore equivalent.

p	q	$\sim$	$[(p$	$\wedge$	$q)$	$\vee$	$(\sim$	p	$\wedge$	$\sim$	$q)]$
T	T	F	T	T	T	T	F	T	F	F	T
T	F	T	T	F	F	F	F	T	F	T	F
F	T	T	F	F	T	F	T	F	F	F	T
F	F	F	F	F	F	T	T	F	T	T	F
Step No.		5	1	2	1	4	2	1	3	2	1

Figure 10a

To illustrate this equivalence, consider the statement "I will attend either Dartmouth or Princeton, but not both." This is equivalent to the *denial* of the statement "I will either attend both Dartmouth and Princeton [symbolized by $(p \wedge q)$] or I will attend neither Dartmouth nor Princeton [symbolized by $(\sim p \wedge \sim q)$]."

EXERCISES

1. Construct a truth table for each of the following:
    (a) $q \vee \sim q$.   [*Ans.* TT.]
    (b) $(p \wedge q) \vee \sim q$.
    (c) $\sim p \vee q$.
    (d) $[\sim(p \vee q) \wedge (\sim p \vee \sim q)]$.   [*Ans,* FFFT.]
2. Using only $\sim$, $\vee$, and $\wedge$, give a compound statement which symbolically states "p or q but not both."
3. Construct a truth table for your answer to Exercise 2, and compare it with Figure 4.
4. Let p stand for "Smith went skiing," and let q stand for "Smith broke his leg." Translate into symbolic form the statement "It is not the case that either Smith did not go skiing or Smith did not break his leg." Construct a truth table for this symbolic statement.
5. Find a simpler verbal statement about Smith whose symbolic form has the same truth table as the one in Exercise 4.
6. Let $p \downarrow q$ express that "both p and q are false." Write a symbolic expression for $p \downarrow q$ using $\sim$ and $\wedge$. Write a truth table for $p \downarrow q$.
7. Write a truth table for $p \downarrow p$.
8. Write a truth table for $(p \downarrow p) \downarrow (q \downarrow q)$.
9. Construct a truth table for each of the following:
    (a) $(\sim p \vee q) \wedge (p \vee \sim q)$.   [*Ans.* TFFT.]
    (b) $\sim(p \downarrow q)$.
    (c) $\sim(p \veebar \sim q)$.
    (d) $(p \wedge q) \vee (q \wedge p)$.

10. Construct symbolic statements, using only $\sim$, $\vee$, and $\wedge$, which have the following truth tables (a) and (b), respectively:

p	q	(a)	(b)
T	T	T	F
T	F	T	T
F	T	F	T
F	F	T	F

11. Using only $\sim$ and $\underline{\vee}$, construct a compound statement having the same truth table as:

(a) $(p \wedge q) \vee (\sim(p \vee q))$.   [*Ans.* $\sim(p \underline{\vee} q)$.]

(b) $p \vee q$.   [*Ans.* Impossible.]

(c) $\sim p \vee q$.

12. Use truth tables to show that $\sim(p \vee q)$ and $\sim p \wedge \sim q$ are equivalent.

3   OTHER CONNECTIVES

Suppose we did not wish to make an outright assertion but rather an assertion containing a condition. As examples, consider the following sentences. "If the weather is nice, I will take a walk." "If the following statement is true, then I can prove the theorem." "If the cost of living continues to rise, then the government will impose rigid curbs." Each of these statements is of the form *"if p then q."* The *conditional* is then a new connective which is symbolized by the arrow $\rightarrow$.

Of course the precise definition of this new connective must be made by means of a truth table. If both p and q are true, then to make logic coincide with ordinary usage $p \rightarrow q$ is certainly true, and if p is true and q false, then $p \rightarrow q$ is certainly false for the same reason. Thus the first two lines of the truth table can easily be filled in—see Figure 11a. Suppose now that p is false; how shall we fill in the last two lines of the truth table in Figure 11a? At first thought one might suppose that it would be best to leave it completely undefined. However, to do so would violate our basic principle that a statement is either true or false.

Therefore we make the completely arbitrary decision that the conditional, $p \rightarrow q$, is *true* whenever p is false, regardless of the truth value of q. This

p	q	$p \rightarrow q$
T	T	T
T	F	F
F	T	?
F	F	?

Figure 11a

p	q	$p \rightarrow q$
T	T	T
T	F	F
F	T	T
F	F	T

Figure 11b

decision enables us to complete the truth table for the conditional and it is given in Figure 11b. A glance at this truth table shows that the conditional $p \rightarrow q$ is considered false only if p is true and q is false. If we wished, we might rationalize the arbitrary decision made above by saying that if statement p happens to be false, then we give the conditional $p \rightarrow q$ the "benefit of the doubt" and consider it true. (For another reason, see Exercise 1.)

In everyday conversation it is customary to combine simple statements only if they are somehow related. Thus we might say "It is raining today and I will take an umbrella," but we would not say "I read a good book and I will take an umbrella." However, the rather ill-defined concept of relatedness is difficult to enforce. Concepts related to each other in one person's mind need not be related in another's. In our study of compound statements no requirement of relatedness is imposed on two statements in order that they be compounded by any of the connectives. This freedom sometimes produces strange results in the use of the conditional. For example, according to the truth table in Figure 11b, the statement "If $2 \times 2 = 5$, then black is white" is true, while the statement "If $2 \times 2 = 4$, then cows are monkeys" is false. Since we use the "if . . . then . . ." form usually only when there is a causal connection between the two statements, we might be tempted to label both of the above statements as nonsense. At this point it is important to remember that no such causal connection is intended in the usage of $\rightarrow$; the meaning of the conditional is contained in Figure 11b and nothing more is intended. This point will be discussed again in Section 6 in connection with implication.

Closely connected to the conditional connective is the *biconditional* statement, $p \leftrightarrow q$, which may be read *"p if and only if q."* The biconditional statement asserts that if p is true, then q is true, and if p is false, then q is false. Hence the biconditional is true in these cases and false in the others, so that its truth table can be filled in as in Figure 12.

p	q	$p \leftrightarrow q$
T	T	T
T	F	F
F	T	F
F	F	T

Figure 12

The biconditional is the last of the five connectives which we shall use in this chapter. The table below gives a summary of them together with the numbers of the figures giving their truth tables. Remember that the complete definition of each of these connectives is given by its truth table. The examples at the top of the next page show the use of the two new connectives.

Name	Symbol	Translated as	Truth Table
Conjunction	∧	"and"	Figure 1
Disjunction (inclusive)	∨	"or"	Figure 3
Negation	~	"not"	Figure 5
Conditional	→	"if . . . then . . ."	Figure 11b
Biconditional	↔	". . . if and only if . . ."	Figure 12

EXAMPLE 1   In Figures 13 and 14 the truth tables of two statements are worked out following the procedure of Section 2.

p	q	p	→	(p	∨	q)
T	T	T	T	T	T	T
T	F	T	T	T	T	F
F	T	F	T	F	T	T
F	F	F	T	F	F	F
Step No.		1	3	1	2	1

Figure 13

p	q	~	p	↔	(p	→	~	q)
T	T	F	T	T	T	F	F	T
T	F	F	T	F	T	T	T	F
F	T	T	F	T	F	T	F	T
F	F	T	F	T	F	T	T	F
Step No.		2	1	4	1	3	2	1

Figure 14

EXAMPLE 2   It is also possible to form compound statements from three or more simple statements. The next example is a compound formed from three simple

p	q	r	[p	→	(q	∨	r)]	∧	~	[p	↔	~	r]
T	T	T	T	T	T	T	T	T	T	T	F	F	T
T	T	F	T	T	T	T	F	F	F	T	T	T	F
T	F	T	T	T	F	T	T	T	T	T	F	F	T
T	F	F	T	F	F	F	F	F	F	T	T	T	F
F	T	T	F	T	T	T	T	F	F	F	T	F	T
F	T	F	F	T	T	T	F	T	T	F	F	T	F
F	F	T	F	T	F	T	T	F	F	F	T	F	T
F	F	F	F	T	F	F	F	T	T	F	F	T	F
Step No.			1	3	1	2	1	5	4	1	3	2	1

Figure 15

statements p, q, and r. Notice that there will be a total of eight possible triples of truth values for these three statements so that the truth table for our compound will have eight rows as shown in Figure 15.

EXAMPLE 3 It is interesting to consider statements that are equivalent to the conditional $p \to q$. In Exercise 14 you will be asked to show that the following statements have the same truth table as $p \to q$:

$$\sim p \lor q, \qquad \sim(p \land \sim q), \qquad \sim q \to \sim p.$$

It follows that the following English statements are equivalent:

If I win a prize then I must have bought a lottery ticket.
Either I didn't win or I bought a lottery ticket.
It is impossible to win a prize without buying a lottery ticket.
If I did not buy a lottery ticket then I won't win a prize.

Exercise 15 considers statements that are equivalent to the biconditional $p \leftrightarrow q$.

EXERCISES

1. One way of filling in the question-marked positions in Figure 11a is given in Figure 11b. There are three other possible ways.
   (a) Write the other three truth tables.
   (b) Show that each of these truth tables has an interpretation in terms of the connectives now available to us.
   (c) Show that the choice of Figure 11b is the only one possible so that $(p \land q) \to q$ is always true.
2. Construct truth tables for each of the following:
   (a) $(\sim p \lor q) \to r$.   [*Ans.* TFTTTFTF.]
   (b) $(p \land q) \to (p \lor q)$.
   (c) $[(p \lor q) \land (p \lor r)] \to p$.   [*Ans.* TTTTFTTT.]
   (d) $\sim(p \land q) \land \sim r$.
   (e) $(p \land (p \to q)) \to q$.   [*Ans.* TTTT.]
   (f) $\sim[(p \land q) \to r] \leftrightarrow [\sim(p \to r) \lor \sim(q \to r)]$.
3. The truth table for a statement compounded from two simple statements has four rows, and the truth table for a statement compounded from three simple statements has eight rows. How many rows would the truth table have for a statement compounded from four simple statements? From five? From n?
4. Let p stand for "He ate spinach," q stand for "He ate dessert," and r stand for "He read a logic book." Find a symbolic form for each of the following statements, and construct its truth table.
   (a) If he did not eat spinach, then he did not eat dessert.
   (b) He ate spinach but did not read a logic book.

    (c) If he read a logic book, then either he ate dessert or did not eat spinach.

    (d) He ate spinach if and only if he ate dessert and read a logic book.

5. Construct a truth table for each of the following:

    (a) $(p \rightarrow q) \vee \sim p$.

    (b) $((p \rightarrow q) \rightarrow q) \rightarrow q$.   *[Ans.* TFTT.*]*

    (c) $(p \leftrightarrow q) \leftrightarrow (p \leftrightarrow (p \leftrightarrow q))$.

    (d) $(\sim p \vee q) \leftrightarrow (\sim q \vee p)$.   *[Ans.* TFFT.*]*

6. Write truth tables for $q \vee p, q \wedge p, q \rightarrow p, q \leftrightarrow p$. Compare these with the truth tables in Figures 3, 1, 11b, and 12, respectively. When is it possible to interchange variables in a statement and get an equivalent statement?

7. Construct a truth table for $[((p \vee r) \rightarrow q) \wedge q] \rightarrow (p \vee r)$.

8. Find a simpler statement having the same truth table as the one found in Exercise 7.

9. Let p be "She will graduate," and let q be "She will find a job." Put each of the following into symbolic form, and construct the truth table for each symbolic statement.

    (a) If she graduates, then she will find a job.

    (b) If she graduates, then she will find a job, and if she finds a job, then she will graduate.

    (c) If she does not graduate, then she will not find a job.

    (d) Either she will graduate and find a job, or, if she does not graduate, then she will not find a job.

    (e) It is not the case that if she does not find a job then she will not graduate.

10. Construct the truth tables for:

    (a) $\sim(p \wedge q) \leftrightarrow (\sim r \vee \sim s)$.   *[Ans.* TFFFFTTTFTTTFTTT.*]*

    (b) $[\sim(p \rightarrow q) \vee (s \leftrightarrow (r \wedge p))] \wedge [p \rightarrow (q \rightarrow \sim r)]$.

                                     [Ans. FFFTTTTTFTFTFTFT.*]*

11. Using only $\wedge$, $\vee$, and $\sim$, write a statement which has the same truth table as:

    (a) $p \rightarrow q$

    (b) $\sim(p \rightarrow q)$

    (c) $p \leftrightarrow q$.

    Using only $\wedge$ and $\sim$, write a statement having the same truth table as $p \vee q$. What have we proved?

12. Look back at Exercises 6, 7, and 8 of Section 2. What compound statement has the same truth table as $p \downarrow p$? As $(p \downarrow p) \downarrow (q \downarrow q)$?

13. Using the results of Exercises 11 and 12, show that any truth table can be represented using only the single connective $\downarrow$. Using only that connective, write statements having the same truth table as:

    (a) $\sim p \wedge q$.   *[Ans.* $[(p \downarrow p) \downarrow (p \downarrow p)] \downarrow (q \downarrow q)$.*]*

    (b) $p \vee q$.

    (c) $p \rightarrow q$.

    (d) $q \rightarrow p$.

14. Show that $p \rightarrow q$, $\sim p \vee q$, $\sim(p \wedge \sim q)$, and $\sim q \rightarrow \sim p$ are all equivalent.

15. Show that the statements $p \leftrightarrow q$, $\sim p \leftrightarrow \sim q$, $(p \wedge q) \vee (\sim p \wedge \sim q)$, and $(\sim p \vee q) \wedge (\sim q \vee p)$ are all equivalent.

16. Let p be the statement "I win a prize" and q be the statement "I bought a lottery ticket." Give verbal equivalents of the statements in Exercise 15.

4 LOGICAL POSSIBILITIES

One of the most important contributions that mathematics can make to the solution of a scientific problem is to provide an exhaustive analysis of the logical possibilities for the problem. The role of science is then to discover facts which will eliminate all but one possibility. Or, if this cannot be achieved, at least science tries to estimate the probabilities of the various possibilities.

So far we have considered only a very special case of the analysis of logical possibilities, namely truth tables. We started with a small number of given statements, say p, q, and r, and we assumed that all the truth table cases were possible. This amounts to assuming that the three statements are logically unrelated. Then we could determine the truth or falsity of every compound statement formed from p, q, and r for every truth table case (every logical possibility).

But there are many more statements whose truth cannot be analyzed in terms of the eight truth table cases discussed above. For example, $\sim p \vee (q \wedge r \wedge \sim s)$ requires a finer analysis, a truth table with 16 cases.

Many of these ideas are applicable in a more general setting. Let us suppose that we have an analysis of logical possibilities. That is, we have a list of eventualities, such that one and only one of them can possibly be true. We know this partly from the framework in which the problem is considered, and partly as a matter of pure logic. We then consider *statements relative to this set of possibilities*. These are statements whose truth or falsity can be determined for each logical possibility. For example, the set of possibilities may be the eight truth table cases, and the statements relative to these possibilities are the compound statements formed from p, q, and r. But we should consider a more typical example.

EXAMPLE 1   Let us consider the following problem, which is of a type often studied in probability theory. "There are two urns; the first contains two black balls and one white ball, while the second contains one black ball and two white balls. Select an urn at random and draw two balls in succession from it. What is the probability that . . .?" Without raising questions of probability, let us ask what the possibilities are. Figures 16 and 17 give us two ways of analyzing the logical possibilities.

In Figure 16 we have analyzed the possibilities as far as colors of balls drawn was concerned. Such an analysis may be sufficient for many pur-

Case	Urn	First Ball	Second Ball
1	1	black	black
2	1	black	white
3	1	white	black
4	2	black	white
5	2	white	black
6	2	white	white

Figure 16

Case	Urn	First Ball	Second Ball
1	1	black no. 1	black no. 2
2	1	black no. 2	black no. 1
3	1	black no. 1	white
4	1	black no. 2	white
5	1	white	black no. 1
6	1	white	black no. 2
7	2	black	white no. 1
8	2	black	white no. 2
9	2	white no. 1	black
10	2	white no. 2	black
11	2	white no. 1	white no. 2
12	2	white no. 2	white no. 1

Figure 17

poses. In Figure 17 we have carried out a finer analysis, in which we distinguished between balls of the same color in an urn. For some purposes the finer analysis may be necessary.

It is important to realize that the possibilities in a given problem may be analyzed in many different ways, from a very rough grouping to a highly refined one. The only requirements on an analysis of logical possibilities are:

(1) That under any conceivable circumstances one and only one of these possibilities must be the case, and

(2) that the analysis is fine enough so that the truth value of each statement under consideration in the problem is determined in each case.

It is easy to verify that both analyses (Figures 16 and 17) satisfy the first condition. Whether the rougher analysis will satisfy the second condition depends on the nature of the problem. If we can limit ourselves to statements like "Two black balls are drawn from the first urn," then it suffices. But if we wish to consider "The first black ball is drawn after the second black ball from the first urn," then the finer analysis is needed.

Given the analysis of logical possibilities, we can ask for each assertion about the problem, and for each logical possibility, whether the assertion is true in this case. Normally, for a given statement there will be many cases in which it is true and many in which it is false. Logic will be able to do no more than to point out the cases in which the statement is true. In Example 1, the statement "One white ball and one black ball is drawn" is true (in Figure 16) in cases 2, 3, 4, and 5, and false in cases 1 and 6. However, there are two notable exceptions, namely, a statement that is true in every logically possible case, and one that is false in every case. Here logic alone suffices to determine the truth value.

A statement that is true in every logically possible case is said to be *logically true*. The truth of such a statement follows from the meaning of the words and the form of the statement, together with the context of the problem about which the statement is made. We shall see several examples of logically true statements below. A statement that is false in every logically possible case is said to be *logically false,* or to be a *self-contradiction*. For example, the conjunction of any statement with its own negation will always be a self-contradiction, since it cannot be true under any circumstances.

In Example 1, the statement "At most two black balls are drawn" is true in every case, in either analysis. Hence this statement is logically true. It follows from the very definition of the problem that we cannot draw more than two balls. Hence, also, the statement "Draw three white balls" is logically false.

What the logical possibilities are for a given set of statements will depend on the context, i.e., on the problem that is being considered. Unless we know what the possibilities are, we have not understood the task before us. This does not preclude that there may be several ways of analyzing the logical possibilities. In Example 1 above, for example, we gave two different analyses, and others could be found. In general, the question "How many cases are there in which p is true?" will depend on the analysis given. (This will be of importance in our study of probability theory.) However, note that a statement that is logically true (false) according to one analysis will be logically true (false) according to every other analysis of the given problem.

The truth table analysis is often the roughest possible analysis. There may be hundreds of logical possibilities, but if all we are interested in are compounds formed from p and q, we need only know when p and q are true or false. For example, a statement of the form $p \rightarrow (p \vee q)$ will have to be true in every conceivable case. We may have a hundred cases, giving varying truth values for p and q, but every such case must correspond to one of the four truth table cases, as far as the compound is concerned. In each of these four cases the compound is true, and therefore such a statement is logically true. An example of it is "If Jones is smart, then he is smart or lucky."

However, if the components are logically related, then a truth table analysis may not be adequate. Let p be the statement "Jim is taller than Bill," while q is "Bill is taller than Jim." And consider the statement "Either Jim is not taller than Bill or Bill is not taller than Jim," i.e., $\sim p \vee \sim q$. If we work the truth table of this compound, we find that it is false in the first case. But this case is not logically possible, since under no circumstances can p and q both be true! Our compound is logically true, but a truth table will not show this. Had we made a careful analysis of the possibilities as to the heights of the two men, we would have found that the compound statement is true in every case.

EXAMPLE 2   The Miracle Filter Company conducts an annual survey of the smoking habits of adult Americans. The results of the survey are organized into 25 files, corresponding to the 25 cases in Figure 18.

First, figures are kept separately for men and women. Secondly, the educational level is noted according to the following code:

0   did not finish high school
1   finished high school, no college
2   some college, but no degree
3   college graduate, but no graduate work
4   did some graduate work

Finally, there is a rough occupational classification: housewife, salaried professional, or salaried nonprofessional.

They have found that this classification is adequate for their purposes. For instance, to get figures on all adults in their survey who did not go beyond high school, they pull out the files numbered 1, 2, 3, 4, 11, 12, 13, 14, 15, and 16. Or they can locate data on male professional workers by looking at files 1, 3, 5, 7, and 9.

According to their analysis, the statement "The person is a housewife, professional, or nonprofessional" is logically true, while the statement "The person has educational level greater than 3, is neither professional nor nonprofessional, but not a female with graduate education" is a self-contradiction. The former statement is true about all 25 files, the latter about none.

Of course, they may at some time be forced to consider a finer analysis of logical possibilities. For instance, "The person is a male with annual income over $10,000" is *not* a statement relative to the given possibilities. We could choose a case—say case 6—and the given statement may be either true or false in this case. Thus the analysis is not fine enough.

Of all the logical possibilities, one and only one represents the facts as

Case	Sex	Educational Level	Occupation
1	male	0	prof.
2	male	0	nonprof.
3	male	1	prof.
4	male	1	nonprof.
5	male	2	prof.
6	male	2	nonprof.
7	male	3	prof.
8	male	3	nonprof.
9	male	4	prof.
10	male	4	nonprof.
11	female	0	housewife
12	female	0	prof.
13	female	0	nonprof.
14	female	1	housewife
15	female	1	prof.
16	female	1	nonprof.
17	female	2	housewife
18	female	2	prof.
19	female	2	nonprof.
20	female	3	housewife
21	female	3	prof.
22	female	3	nonprof.
23	female	4	housewife
24	female	4	prof.
25	female	4	nonprof.

Figure 18

they are. That is, for a given person, one and only one of the 25 cases is a correct description. To know which one, we need factual information. When we say that a certain statement is "true," without qualifying it, we mean that it is true in this one case. But, as we have said before, what the case actually is lies outside the domain of logic. Logic can tell us only what the circumstances (logical possibilities) are under which a statement is true.

EXERCISES

1. Prove that the negation of a logically true statement is logically false, and the negation of a logically false statement is logically true.
2. Prove that if p and $p \rightarrow q$ are logically true, then so is q.
3. Classify each of the following as logically true, logically false, or neither:
   (a) $(p \wedge (p \rightarrow q)) \rightarrow q$. [*Ans.* Logically true.]

      (b) $[(p \wedge q) \rightarrow r] \leftrightarrow [(p \rightarrow r) \wedge (q \rightarrow r)]$.

      (c) $p \rightarrow (q \vee \sim q)$.

      (d) $(p \rightarrow q) \wedge (q \rightarrow r) \wedge \sim (p \rightarrow r)$.

      (e) $((p \wedge q) \vee (p \wedge r)) \rightarrow p$.

      (f) $(p \vee q) \wedge (p \vee r)$.   [*Ans.* Neither.]

      (g) $(p \rightarrow q) \wedge \sim (\sim q \rightarrow \sim p)$.   [*Ans.* Logically false.]

4. Find all cases in Figure 18 about which the following statement is true: "The person is a nonprofessional and, if male, has had at least some college training."

5. In the example in Figure 18, give two logically true and two logically false statements (other than those in the text).

6. A hat is filled with slips numbered 1 through 20, and two slips are drawn. Which of the following analyses satisfy the first condition for logical possibilities? What is wrong with the others?

    The sum of the numbers on the slips is:

    (a) (1) even, (2) odd.

    (b) (1) prime, (2) greater than 37.

    (c) (1) less than 3, (2) even, (3) prime.

    (d) (1) divisible by 3, (2) not divisible by 3.

    (e) (1) less than 17, (2) 17, (3) greater than 17.

    (f) (1) greater than 2, (2) less than 40.

    (g) (1) 4, 8, 12, 16, or 20, (2) larger than 20, (3) smaller than 20 and odd.

7. In a college using grades A, B, C, D, and F how many logically possible report cards are there for a student taking four courses? What if the only grades are Pass and Fail?

8. A drive-in restaurant sells hamburgers for 35 cents, cheeseburgers for 45 cents, french fries for 20 cents, and milkshakes for 25 cents. How many logical possibilities are there for orders totaling 85 cents? What are they?   [*Partial Ans.* There are three possibilities.]

9. Concerning the answer to Exercise 8, which of the following are logically true? Which are logically false? Which are neither?

    (a) The order contains no french fries?   [*Ans.* Neither.]

    (b) The order contains more than one of some item.

    (c) The order contains two hamburgers.   [*Ans.* Logically false.]

    (d) The order contains french fries if and only if it contains a milkshake.

    (e) The order contains exactly two different types of food.

10. Suppose in Exercise 8 we are further told that the order is for a man who is on a diet and therefore cannot eat milkshakes. What can we conclude?

11. In Example 1, with the logical possibilities given by Figure 17, state the cases in which the following are true:

    (a) Exactly one white ball is drawn.

    (b) Either the first urn is selected and a white ball is chosen on the first draw, or two white balls are chosen.

    (c)   A white ball is drawn, and then a black ball.

    (d)   If the first ball is black, then the urn selected is not number 1 and the second ball is black.

    (e)   The balls are of the same color if and only if the first is black.

              [*Ans.* 1, 2, 5, 6, 9, 10.]

12.   A survey of families having three children is taken. The sex of each child is noted, beginning with the oldest. Construct a list of the logical possibilities. [*Hint:* There are eight cases.]

13.   In Exercise 12, in which cases is each statement below true?

    (a)   There are more girls than boys, but at least one boy.

    (b)   There is a boy if and only if there is a girl.

              [*Ans.* Every case *except* BBB and GGG.]

    (c)   The oldest child is a boy if the youngest is a girl.

14.   How does the list of possibilities in Exercise 12 change if we neglect the order in which the children were born?

5 TREE DIAGRAMS

A very useful tool for the analysis of logical possibilities is the drawing of a "tree." This device will be illustrated by several examples.

EXAMPLE 1   Consider again the survey of the Miracle Filter Company. They keep two large filing cabinets, one for men and one for women. Each cabinet has five drawers, corresponding to the five educational levels. Each drawer is subdivided according to occupations; drawers in the filing cabinet for men have two large folders, while in the other cabinet each drawer has three folders.

When a clerk files a new piece of information, he first has to find the right cabinet, then the correct drawer, and then the appropriate folder. This three-step process of filing is shown in Figure 19. For obvious reasons we shall call a figure like this, which starts at a point and branches out, a *tree*.

Observe that the tree contains all the information relevant to classifying a person interviewed. There are 25 ways of starting at the bottom and following a path to the top. The 25 paths represent the 25 cases in Figure

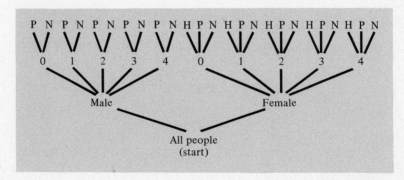

Figure 19

18. The order in which we performed the classification is arbitrary. We might as well have classified first according to educational level, then according to occupation, and then according to sex. We would still obtain a tree representing the 25 logical possibilities, but the tree would look quite different. (See Exercise 1.)

EXAMPLE 2   Next let us consider the example of Figure 16. This is a three-stage process; first we select an urn, then draw a ball and then draw a second ball. The tree of logical possibilities is shown in Figure 20. We note that six is the correct number of logical possibilities. The reason for this is: If we choose

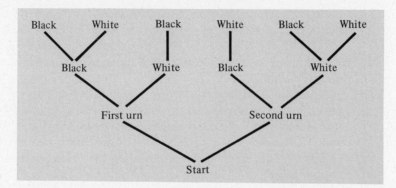

Figure 20

the first urn (which contains two black balls and one white ball) and draw from it a black ball, then the second draw may be of either color; however, if we draw a white ball first, then the second ball drawn is necessarily black. Similar remarks apply if the second urn is chosen.

EXAMPLE 3   As a final example, let us construct the tree of logical possibilities for the outcomes of a World Series played between the Pirates and the Orioles. In Figure 21 is shown half of the tree, corresponding to the case when the Pirates win the first game (the dotted line at the bottom leads to the other half of the tree). In the figure a "P" stands for a Pirate win and "O" for

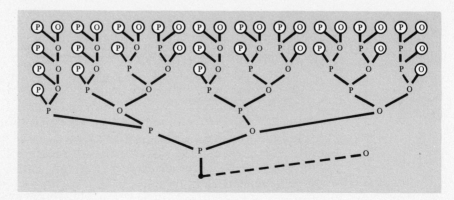

Figure 21

an Oriole win. There are 35 possible outcomes (corresponding to the circled letters) in the half-tree shown, so that the World Series can end in 70 ways.

This example is different from the previous two in that the paths of the tree end at different levels, corresponding to the fact that the World Series ends whenever one of the teams has won four games.

Not always do we wish as detailed an analysis as that provided in the examples above. If, in Example 2, we wanted to know only the color and order in which the balls were drawn and not which urn they came from, then there would be only four logical possibilities instead of six. Then in Figure 20 the second and fourth paths (counting from the left) represent the same outcome, namely, a black ball followed by a white ball. Similarly, the third and fifth paths represent the same outcome. Finally, if we cared only about the color of the balls drawn, not the order, then there are only three logical possibilities: two black balls, two white balls, or one black and one white ball.

A less detailed analysis of the possibilities for the World Series is also possible. For example, we can analyze the possibilities as follows: Pirates in four, five, six, or seven games, and Orioles in four, five, six, or seven games. The new classification reduced the number of possibilities from 70 to eight. The other possibilities have not been eliminated but merely grouped together. Thus the statement "Pirates in four games" can happen in only one way, while "Pirates in seven games" can happen in 20 ways (see Figure 21). A still less detailed analysis would be a classification according to the number of games in the series. Here there are only four logical possibilities.

You will find that it often requires several trials before the "best" way of listing logical possibilities is found for a given problem.

EXERCISES

1. Construct a tree for Example 1, if people are first classified according to educational level, then according to profession, and finally according to sex. Is the shape of the tree the same as in Figure 19? Does it represent the same possibilities?

2. We set up an experiment similar to that of Figure 20, but urn 1 contains two black balls and four white balls, while urn 2 has one white ball and five black balls. An urn is selected and three balls are drawn. Construct the tree of logical possibilities. How many cases are there?
   [*Ans.* 11.]

3. From the tree constructed in Exercise 2 answer the following questions.
   (a) In how many cases do we draw three white balls?
   (b) In how many cases do we draw three black balls?
   (c) In how many cases do we draw two white balls and a black ball?
   (d) How many cases does this leave? What cases are these?

4. In 1965 the Dodgers lost the first two games of the World Series, but won the series in the end. In how many ways can the Series go so that the winning team loses the first two games?   [*Ans.* 10.]

5. In how many ways can the World Series be played (see Figure 21) if the Pirates win the first game and
   (a) The Pirates win the series?   [*Ans.* 20.]
   (b) No team wins two games in a row?
   (c) The losing team wins three games in a row?
   (d) The losing team wins four games in a row?

6. The following is a typical process in genetics: Each parent has two genes for a given trait, AA or Aa or aa. The child will inherit one gene from each parent. What are the possibilities for a child if both parents are AA? What if one is AA and the other aa? What if one is AA and the other Aa? What if both are Aa? Construct a tree for each process. (Let stage 1 be the choice of a gene from the first parent, stage 2 from the second parent. Then see how many different types the resulting branches represent.)

7. It is often the case that types AA and Aa (see Exercise 6) are indistinguishable from the outside but easily distinguishable from type aa. What are the logical possibilities if the two parents are of noticeably different types?

8. A certain businessman has three favorite bars. After work he goes to one of these bars at which he orders either whiskey or scotch. If he likes the drink he goes directly home. If he does not like it, he goes to one of the other two bars and again orders either whiskey or scotch; he then goes home after the second drink. Draw the tree of logical possibilities, labeling the bars, A, B, and C. How many possibilities are there?

9. In Exercise 8, how many possibilities are there in which
   (a) He drinks only whiskey?   [*Ans.* 9.]
   (b) He visits bar B?
   (c) He visits bars A and B?
   (d) He visits Bar C and has both scotch and whiskey?

10. In Exercise 2 we wish to make a rougher classification of logical possibilities. What branches (in the tree there constructed) become identical if
   (a) We do not care about the order in which the balls are drawn?
   (b) We care neither about the order of balls, nor about the number of the urn selected?
   (c) We care only about what urn is selected, and whether the balls drawn are all the same color?

11. A menu lists a choice of soup, fruit, or orange juice for an appetizer; a choice of steak, chicken, or fish for the entree; and a choice of pie or cake for dessert. A complete dinner consists of one choice for each course. Draw a tree for the possible complete dinners.
   (a) How many different complete dinners are possible?   [*Ans.* 18.]

    (b) If a man refuses to eat chicken or cake, how many different complete dinners can be choose?

    (c) A certain customer eats pie for dessert if and only if he did not have fruit or orange juice for an appetizer. How many different complete meals are available to him?

12. A man is considering the purchase of one of four types of stocks. Each stock may go up, go down, or stay the same after his purchase. Draw the tree of logical possibilities.

13. For the tree constructed in Exercise 12 give a statement which

    (a) Is true in half the cases.

    (b) Is false in all but one case.

    (c) Is true in all but one case.

    (d) Is logically true.

    (e) Is logically false.

14. In how many different ways can 70 cents change be given, using quarters, dimes, and nickels? Draw a tree. [*Hint:* To eliminate duplication, require that larger coins be handed out before smaller ones. Let the branches of the tree be labeled with the number of coins of each type handed out.]   [*Ans.* 16.]

15. Redraw the tree of Exercise 14, requiring that smaller coins be handed out before larger ones.

16. What is the answer to Exercise 14 if only two dimes are available?

17. A college valedictorian plans to speak on brotherhood, integrity, or "the System" at commencement. The college president will speak on brotherhood, integrity, or the challenge of the future, but will not pick the same topic as the valedictorian. The college chaplain always speaks on brotherhood, unless the president does, in which case he chooses one of the other three topics.

    (a) Using a tree, determine the number of logical possibilities.

                                                          [*Ans.* 11.]

    (b) In how many of the different programs will there be a speech on "the System"?   [*Ans.* 6.]

    (c) How many different programs are there in which the audience will have to listen to more than one speech on the same topic?

18. In Exercise 17, how many logical possibilities are there if we take into account only speech topics and number of times a given topic is used and disregard the speakers and order of the speeches?

6 LOGICAL RELATIONS

Until now we have considered statements in isolation. Sometimes, however, we want to consider a relationship between pairs of statements. The most interesting such relation is that one statement (logically) *implies* another one. We *define* implication as follows: r implies s if s is true whenever r is true, i.e., if s is true in all the logically possible cases in which r is true. We shall use the notation $r \Rightarrow s$ for the relation r *implies* s.

If *p* implies *q* we also say that *q* follows from *p*, or that *q* is (logically) deducible from *p*. For example, in any mathematical theorem the hypothesis implies the conclusion.

Note that $r \Rightarrow s$ is a relation and *not a statement*. However, it follows from the definition that $r \Rightarrow s$ holds if and only if the conditional $r \rightarrow s$ is logically true.

For compound statements having the same components, truth tables provide a convenient method for testing this relation. In Figure 22 we

p	*q*	$p \leftrightarrow q$	$p \rightarrow q$	$p \lor q$
T	T	T	T	T
T	F	F	F	T
F	T	F	T	T
F	F	T	T	F

Figure 22

illustrate this method. Let us take $p \leftrightarrow q$ as our hypothesis *r*. Since it is true only in the first and fourth cases, and $p \rightarrow q$ is true in both these cases, we see that the statement $p \leftrightarrow q$ implies $p \rightarrow q$. On the other hand, the statement $p \lor q$ is false in the fourth case and hence it is not implied by $p \leftrightarrow q$. Again, a comparison of the last two columns of Figure 22 shows that the statement $p \rightarrow q$ does not imply and is not implied by $p \lor q$.

Let us now take up the "paradoxes" of the conditional. Conditional statements sound paradoxical when the components are not related. For example, it sounds strange to say that "If it is a nice day then chalk is made of wood" is true on a rainy day. It must be remembered that the conditional statement just quoted means no more and no less than that one of the following holds: (1) It is a nice day and chalk is made of wood, or (2) It is not a nice day and chalk is made of wood, or (3) It is not a nice day and chalk is not made of wood. (See Figure 11b.) And on a rainy day number (3) happens to be correct.

But it is by no means true that "It is a nice day" implies that "Chalk is made of wood." It is logically possible for the former to be true and for the latter to be false (indeed, this is the case on a nice day, with the usual method of chalk manufacture), hence the implication does not hold. Thus, while the conditional quoted in the previous paragraph is true on a given day, it is not logically true.

In common parlance "if ... then ..." is usually asserted on logical grounds. Hence any usage in which such an assertion happens to be true, but is not logically true, sounds paradoxical. Similar remarks apply to the common usage of "if and only if."

The second relation we shall consider is *equivalence*. We shall say that *r* is equivalent to *s*, denoted by $r \Leftrightarrow s$, if *r* is true whenever *s* is true and vice versa. In other words, $r \Leftrightarrow s$, if and only if $r \leftrightarrow s$ is logically true. We have already noted that equivalent statements have the same truth table.

p	q	$\sim p \wedge \sim q$	$\sim(p \vee q)$
T	T	F	F
T	F	F	F
F	T	F	F
F	F	T	T

Figure 23

Figure 23 establishes that $\sim p \wedge \sim q$ is equivalent to $\sim(p \vee q)$, which is one of *DeMorgan's laws.* (See Figure 10 for the other DeMorgan law.)

An implication $r \Rightarrow s$ or an equivalence $p \Leftrightarrow q$ can be established on purely logical grounds. From these we can construct valid arguments, as we shall see in Section 8. In Section 9 other ways of stating implications and equivalences will be discussed which are (sometimes) more convenient forms in which to carry out such arguments.

A third important relationship is that of inconsistency. Statements r and s are *inconsistent* if it is impossible for both of them to be true, in other words, if $r \wedge s$ is a self-contradiction. For example, the statements $p \wedge q$ and $\sim q$ are inconsistent (see Figure 24). An important use of logic is to check for inconsistencies in a set of assumptions or beliefs.

p	q	$p \wedge q$	$\sim q$
T	T	T	F
T	F	F	T
F	T	F	F
F	F	F	T

Figure 24

We conclude this section by listing several important implications and equivalences:

(1) $p \wedge q \Rightarrow p.$
(2) $p \wedge q \Rightarrow p \vee q.$
(3) $(p \leftrightarrow q) \Rightarrow (p \rightarrow q).$
(4) $p \wedge (p \rightarrow q) \Rightarrow q.$
(5) $(p \rightarrow q) \wedge \sim q \Rightarrow \sim p.$
(6) $(p \rightarrow q) \wedge (q \rightarrow r) \Rightarrow (p \rightarrow r).$
(7) $(p \leftrightarrow q) \wedge (q \leftrightarrow r) \Rightarrow (p \leftrightarrow r).$
(8) $(p \rightarrow q) \wedge (q \rightarrow p) \Leftrightarrow (p \leftrightarrow q).$

In the Exercises you will be asked to establish some of these relations.

EXERCISES

1. Show that $(p \leftrightarrow q) \rightarrow (p \rightarrow q)$ is logically true, but that $(p \leftrightarrow q) \rightarrow (p \lor q)$ is not logically true. Interpret this in terms of implications.

2. Is it true that $p \Rightarrow \sim p$? Explain why this does or does not tell us that $p \rightarrow \sim p$ is logically false.

3. If p is logically true, prove that
   (a) $p \lor q$ is logically true.
   (b) $\sim p \land q$ is logically false.
   (c) $p \land q$ is equivalent to q.
   (d) $\sim p \lor q$ is equivalent to q.

4. Construct truth tables for the following compounds and test for implications and equivalences.
   (a) $p \lor \sim q$.
   (b) $\sim p \leftrightarrow \sim q$.
   (c) $q \rightarrow p$.
   (d) $p \land \sim q$.
   (e) $\sim(p \rightarrow q)$.   [*Partial Ans.* (a) $\Leftrightarrow$ (c); (e) $\Rightarrow$ (a), (c), (d).]

5. Construct truth tables for the following compounds, and arrange them in order so that each compound implies all the following ones.
   (a) $\sim p \leftrightarrow q$.
   (b) $p \rightarrow (\sim p \rightarrow q)$.
   (c) $\sim[p \rightarrow (q \rightarrow p)]$.
   (d) $p \lor q$.
   (e) $\sim p \land q$.   [*Ans.* (c), (e), (a), (d), (b).]

6. Which of the following are equivalent: $p, \sim p, p \lor p, p \land p, p \rightarrow p, p \leftrightarrow p$? Prove (using truth tables) your answers. Which are inconsistent?

7. Construct a compound equivalent to $p \leftrightarrow q$ using only the connectives $\rightarrow$ and $\land$. Interpret your result in terms of equivalences and implications.
   [*Partial Ans.* Saying that two statements are equivalent is the same as saying that each implies the other.]

8. Show that $\sim p \land q \Leftrightarrow \sim(q \rightarrow p)$.

9. If p is logically true, q is logically false, and p and r are inconsistent, what is the status of $\sim p \Leftrightarrow \sim(q \lor r)$?

10. The statements r and s are compounds of p and q and have the following truth tables:

p	q	r	s	t
T	T	T	T	
T	F	F	F	
F	T	T	T	
F	F	T	F	

Find a statement t which is a compound of p and q satisfying each of the following properties:

    (a) $t \Leftrightarrow r$.   *[Ans. $p \to q$.]*

    (b) t is inconsistent with s.   *[Ans. $\sim q$.]*

    (c) $t \Leftrightarrow s$.

    (d) $t \leftrightarrow r$ is logically true.

    (e) $t \to s$ is neither logically true nor logically false.

    (f) $t \leftrightarrow s$ is logically false.

    (g) $r \Rightarrow t$.

    (h) $t \to r$ is logically false.

11.   In Exercise 10,

    (a)   What is the relation between r and s?   *[Ans. $s \Rightarrow r$.]*

    (b)   How many nonequivalent statements t which are compounds of p and q can be found which satisfy the condition that s implies t and t implies s? What are they?

12.   If r and s are compounds of p and q such that r is logically false and s is logically true, what compounds t will satisfy both the conditions $r \Rightarrow t$ and $t \Rightarrow s$.

13.   Pick out an inconsistent pair from among the following four compound statements.

    r: $p \to q$.

    s: q.

    t: $\sim(q \to p)$.

    u: $\sim p \leftrightarrow \sim q$.

14.   In Exercise 13 is there an inconsistent pair among r, s, and t? Is it possible that all three statements are true?

15.   What relation exists between two logically true statements? Between two self-contradictions?

16.   Show that the equivalences (1)–(4) hold.

17.   Show that the equivalences (5)–(8) hold.

18.   Let $p|q$ be defined as "p and q are not both true."

    (a)   Construct a truth table for $p|q$.   *[Ans. FTTT.]*

    (b)   Show that $(p|q)|(p|q)$ is equivalent to $p \wedge q$.

    (c)   Find a compound using only | which is equivalent to $\sim p$.

19.   We shall call a connective "adequate" if $\sim p$, $p \wedge q$, $p \vee q$, $p \leftrightarrow q$, and $p \to q$ can be expressed in terms of p, q, and that connective.

    (a)   Using the results of Exercise 11 in Section 3 and Exercise 18 above, show that the connective | is adequate.

    (b)   In Exercise 13, Section 3, it was shown that the connective $\downarrow$ is adequate. Could we define a third different connective such that it would also be adequate? (*Hint:* Consider the truth table that it must have. If we call the new connective $\updownarrow$, then $p \updownarrow p$ must be false if p is true, since otherwise any expression involving p and $\updownarrow$ would be true if p is true and we would not be able to express $\sim p$. Thus $p \updownarrow q$ is false if p and q are both true.)

*7 VALID ARGUMENTS

One of the most important tasks of a logician is the checking of *arguments*. By an argument we shall mean the assertion that a certain statement (the *conclusion*) follows from other statements (the *premises*). An argument will be said to be (logically) *valid,* if and only if the conjunction of the premises implies the conclusion; i.e., if the premises are all true, the conclusion *must* also be true.

It is important to realize that the truth of the conclusion is irrelevant as far as the test of the validity of the argument goes. A true conclusion is neither necessary nor sufficient for the validity of the argument. The two examples below show this, and they also show the form in which we shall state arguments, i.e., first we state the premises, then draw a line, and then state the conclusion.

EXAMPLE 1

If the United States is a democracy, then its
    citizens have the right to vote.
Its citizens do have the right to vote.
_____
Therefore the United States is a democracy.

The conclusion is, of course, true. However, the argument is not valid since the conclusion does not follow from the two premises, as we shall show later.

EXAMPLE 2

To pass this math course you must be a genius.
Every player on the football team has passed this course.
The captain of the football team is not a genius.
_____
Therefore the captain of the football team does not
    play on the team.

Here the conclusion is false, but the argument is valid since the conclusion follows from the premises. If we observe that the first premise is false, the paradox disappears. There is nothing surprising in the correct derivation of a false conclusion from false premises.

If an argument is valid, then the conjunction of the premises implies the conclusion. Hence if all the premises are ture, then the conclusion is also true. However, if one or more of the premises is false, so that the conjunction of all the premises is false, then the conclusion may be either true or false. In fact, all the premises could be false, the conclusion true, and the argument valid, as the following example shows.

EXAMPLE 3

All dogs have two legs.
All two-legged animals are carnivorous.
_____
Therefore, all dogs are carnivorous.

Here the argument is valid and the conclusion is true, but both premises are false!

Each of these examples underlines the fact that neither the truth value nor the content of the statements appearing in an argument affect the validity of the argument. In Figures 25a and 25b are two valid forms of arguments.

$$p \to q \qquad\qquad p \to q$$
$$\underline{ p } \qquad\qquad \underline{ \sim q }$$
$$\therefore q \qquad\qquad\qquad \therefore \sim p$$

Figure 25a   **Figure 25b**

The symbol $\therefore$ means "therefore." The truth tables for these argument forms appear in Figure 26.

p	q	$p \to q$	p	q	$p \to q$	$\sim q$	$\sim p$
T	T	T	T	T	T	F	F
T	F	F	T	F	F	T	F
F	T	T	F	T	T	F	T
F	F	T	F	F	T	T	T

Figure 26

For the argument of Figure 25a, we see in Figure 26 that there is only one case in which both premises are true, namely, the first case, and that in this case the conclusion is true, hence the argument is valid. Similarly, in the argument of Figure 25b, both premises are true in the fourth case only, and in this case the conclusion is also true; hence the argument is valid.

Another way of stating that the argument in Figure 25a is valid is that the implication $[(p \to q) \wedge q] \Rightarrow q$ is true. Similarly for Figure 25b we note that the implication $[(p \to q) \wedge \sim q] \Rightarrow \sim p$ is true. Actually any true implication gives rise to a valid argument and vice versa.

An argument that is not valid is called a *fallacy*. Two examples of fallacies are the following argument forms.

$$p \to q \qquad\qquad\qquad p \to q$$
$$\underline{ q } \quad \textit{Fallacies} \quad \underline{ \sim p }$$
$$\therefore p \qquad\qquad\qquad\qquad\qquad \therefore \sim q$$

In the first fallacy, both premises are true in the first and third cases of Figure 26, but the conclusion is false in the third case, so that the argument is invalid. (This is the form of Example 1.) Similarly, in the second fallacy we see that both premises are true in the last two cases, but the conclusion is false in the third case.

We say that an argument depends only upon its form in that it does not matter what the componenets of the argument are. The truth tables in Figure 26 show that if both premises are true, then the conclusions of the arguments in Figures 25a and 25b are also true. For the fallacies above, the truth tables show that it is possible to choose both premises true without making the conclusion true, namely, choose a false p and a true q.

EXAMPLE 4   Consider the following argument.

$$p \to q$$
$$\underline{q \to r}$$
$$\therefore p \to r$$

The truth table of the argument appears in Figure 27.

p	q	r	$p \to q$	$q \to r$	$p \to r$
T	T	T	T	T	T
T	T	F	T	F	F
T	F	T	F	T	T
T	F	F	F	T	F
F	T	T	T	T	T
F	T	F	T	F	T
F	F	T	T	T	T
F	F	F	T	T	T

Figure 27

Both premises are true in the first, fifth, seventh, and eighth rows of the truth table. Since in each of these cases the conclusion is also true, the argument is valid—that is, the implication $[(p \to q) \wedge (q \to r)] \Rightarrow (p \to r)$ is true. (Example 3 can be written in this form.)

Once we have discovered that a certain form of argument is valid, we can use it in drawing conclusions. It is then no longer necessary to compute truth tables. Presumably, this is what we do when we reason in everyday life; we apply a variety of valid forms known to us from previous experience. However, the truth table method has one great advantage: it is always applicable and purely automatic. We can even get a computer to test the validity of arguments involving compound statements.

EXERCISES

1. Test the validity of the following arguments:

(a) $p \leftrightarrow q$ (b) $p \vee q$ (c) $p \wedge q$
$$\underline{\quad p \quad}$$ $$\underline{\quad \sim p \quad}$$ $$\underline{\sim p \to q}$$
$$\therefore q$$ $$\therefore \quad q$$ $$\therefore \sim q$$

[*Ans.* (a), (b) are valid.]

2. Test the validity of the following arguments:

   (a) $$\begin{array}{c} p \rightarrow q \\ \underline{\sim q \rightarrow \sim r} \\ \therefore \quad r \rightarrow p \end{array}$$ (b) $$\begin{array}{c} p \rightarrow q \\ \underline{\sim r \rightarrow \sim q} \\ \therefore \sim r \rightarrow \sim p \end{array}$$

   [*Ans.* (b) is valid.]

3. Test the validity of the argument

$$\begin{array}{c} p \leftrightarrow q \\ q \vee r \\ \underline{\sim r} \\ \therefore \quad \sim p \end{array}$$

   [*Ans.* Not valid.]

4. Test the validity of the argument

$$\begin{array}{c} p \veebar q \\ \sim q \rightarrow r \\ \underline{\sim p \vee \sim r} \\ \therefore \quad \sim p \end{array}$$

5. Test the validity of the argument

$$\begin{array}{c} p \rightarrow q \\ \sim p \rightarrow \sim q \\ \underline{p \wedge \sim r} \\ \therefore \quad s \end{array}$$

6. Given are the premises $\sim p \rightarrow q$ and $\sim r \rightarrow \sim q$. We wish to find a valid conclusion involving p and r (if there is any).
   (a) Construct truth tables for the two premises.
   (b) Note the cases in which the conclusion must be true.
   (c) Construct a truth table for a combination of p and r only, filling in T wherever necessary.
   (d) Fill in the remainder of the truth table, making sure that you do not end up with a logically true statement.
   (e) What combination of p and r has this truth table? This is a valid conclusion.   [*Ans.* $p \vee r$.]

7. Translate the following argument into symbolic form, and test its validity.

> If this is a good course, then it is worth taking.
> Either the grading is lenient, or the course is not
>   worth taking.
> But the grading is not lenient.
> _____
> Therefore, this is not a good course.

   [*Ans.* Valid.]

8. Show that the following method may be used for testing the validity of an argument: Find the cases in which the conclusion is false, and show that in each case at least one premise is false.

9. Use the method of Exercise 8 to test Example 4.
10. Redo Exercise 1 using the method of Exercise 8.
11. Redo Exercise 4 using the method of Exercise 8.
12. Draw a valid conclusion from the following premises:

He is either a man or a mouse.
He has no skill in athletics.
To be a man it is necessary to command respect.
A man can command respect only if he has some athletic skill.

13. Draw a valid conclusion from the following premises:

Either he will go to graduate school or he will be drafted.
If he does not go to graduate school, he will get married.
If he gets married, he will need a good income.
He will not have a good income in the army.

14. Write the following argument in symbolic form, and test its validity.

"For the candidate to win, it is sufficient that he carry New York. He will carry New York only if he takes a strong stand on civil rights. He will not take a strong stand on civil rights. Therefore, he will not win."

15. Write the following argument in symbolic form and test its validity.

"Father praises me only if I can be proud of myself. Either I do well in sports or I cannot be proud of myself. If I study hard, then I cannot do well in sports. Therefore, if father praises me, then I do not study hard."

*8 VARIANTS OF THE CONDITIONAL

The conditional of two statements differs from the biconditional and from disjunctions and conjunctions of these two in that it lacks symmetry. Thus $p \vee q$ is equivalent to $q \vee p$, $p \wedge q$ is equivalent to $q \wedge p$, and $p \leftrightarrow q$ is equivalent to $q \leftrightarrow p$; but $p \to q$ is *not equivalent to* $q \to p$. The latter statement, $q \to p$, is called the *converse* of $p \to q$. Many of the most common fallacies in thinking arise from a confusion of a statement with its converse.

On the other hand, the conditional $p \to q$ is equivalent to the conditional $\sim q \to \sim p$, which is known as the *contrapositive*. The relationships among these three statements is demonstrated in Figure 28.

EXAMPLE 1   Let a be a positive real number, p the statement "$a < 7$," and q the statement "$a^2 < 100$." Then the conditional $p \to q$ is "If $a < 7$, then $a^2 < 100$." This is logically true, i.e., true for every positive real number. But the converse, "If $a^2 < 100$ then $a < 7$," is *not* logically true, and hence cannot be equivalent to the original statement. To show that it fails to be logically true, we must exhibit at least one logical possibility for which it is false. For example, if $a = 9$, then q is true ($9^2 < 100$) but p ($9 < 7$) is false.

The contrapositive is "If $a^2 \geq 100$, then $a \geq 7$," which *is* logically true.

		Conditional	Converse	Contra-positive
p	q	$p \rightarrow q$	$q \rightarrow p$	$\sim q \rightarrow \sim p$
T	T	T	T	T
T	F	F	T	F
F	T	T	F	T
F	F	T	T	T

Figure 28

Since a positive number a can have $a^2 \geq 100$ only if $a \geq 10$, it is necessarily true that $a \geq 7$.

A mathematical statement that one suspects to be true, but whose truth or falsity has not yet been established by a proof, is known as a *conjecture.* One then attempts one of two procedures. One may attempt to construct a proof, which establishes the logical truth of the proposition. Or one may attempt to construct a *counterexample,* that is, a single logically possible case for which the proposition is false, which shows that the statement is not logically true. In either case the conjecture is settled, either positively or negatively.

The use of conditionals seems to cause more trouble than the use of the other connectives, perhaps because of the lack of symmetry, but also perhaps because there are so many different ways of expressing conditionals. In many cases only a careful analysis of a conditional statement shows whether the person making the assertion means the given conditional or its converse. Indeed, sometimes he means both of these, i.e., he means the biconditional. (See Exercise 5.)

The statement "I will go for a walk only if the sun shines" is a variant of a conditional statement. A statement of the form "*p* only if *q*" is closely related to the statement "If *p* then *q*," but just how? Actually the two express the same idea. The statement "*p* only if *q*" states that "If $\sim q$ then $\sim p$" and hence is equivalent to "If *p* then *q*." Thus the statement at the beginning of the paragraph is equivalent to the statement "If I go for a walk, then the sun will be shining."

Other phrases, in common use by mathematicians, which indicate a conditional statement are: "a necessary condition" and "a sufficient condition." To say that *p* is a sufficient condition for *q* means that if *p* takes place, then *q* will also take place. Hence the sentence "*p* is a sufficient condition for *q*" is equivalent to the sentence "If *p* then *q*."

Similarly, the sentence "*p* is a necessary condition for *q*" is equivalent to "*q* only if *p*." Since we know that the latter is equivalent to "If *q* then *p*," it follows that the assertion of a necessary condition is the converse of the assertion of a sufficient condition.

Finally, if both a conditional statement and its converse are asserted, then effectively the biconditional statement is being asserted. Hence the assertion

Basic Statement	Equivalent Forms
If p then q	p only if q p is a sufficient condition for q
If q then p	q only if p p is a necessary condition for q
p if and only if q	p is a necessary and sufficient condition for q

Figure 29

"p is a necessary and sufficient condition for q" is equivalent to the assertion "p if and only if q."

These various equivalences are summarized in Figure 29.

EXAMPLE 1 (continued)   We can restate "If $a < 7$, then $a^2 < 100$" as follows:

$a < 7$ is a sufficient condition for $a^2 < 100$.
$a < 7$ only if $a^2 < 100$.
$a^2 < 100$ is a necessary condition that $a < 7$.

EXAMPLE 2   Let a be an integer, let p be the statement "a is odd," and let q be the statement "a^2 is odd." Then the biconditional $p \leftrightarrow q$ is the statement "Integer a is odd if and only if a^2 is odd," which can easily be proved to be true (see Section 9.) We can restate this as follows:

a is odd is necessary and sufficient that a^2 is odd.

Since $p \leftrightarrow q$ and $\sim p \leftrightarrow \sim q$ are equivalent, we can also state the theorem as:

a is even if and only if a^2 is even; or
a is even is necessary and sufficient that a^2 is even.

EXERCISES

1. Let p stand for "I will pass this course" and q for "I will do homework regularly." Put the following statements into symbolic form.
    (a)   I will pass the course only if I do homework regularly.
    (b)   Doing homework regularly is a necessary condition for me to pass this course.
    (c)   Passing this course is a sufficient condition for me to do homework regularly.
    (d)   I will pass this course if and only if I do homework regularly.
    (e)   Doing homework regularly is a necessary and sufficient condition for me to pass this course.

2. Take the statement in part (a) of the previous exercise. Form its converse, its contrapositive, and the converse of the contrapositive. For each of these give both a verbal and a symbolic form.

3. Let p stand for "It snows" and q for "The train is late." Put the following statements into symbolic form.

    (a) Snowing is a sufficient condition for the train to be late.

    (b) Snowing is a necessary and sufficient condition for the train to be late.

    (c) The train is late only if it snows.

4. Take the statement in part (a) of the previous exercise. Form its converse, its contrapositive, and the converse of its contrapositive. Give a verbal form of each of them.

5. Prove that the conjunction of a conditional and its converse is equivalent to the biconditional.

6. To what is the conjunction of the contrapositive and its converse equivalent? Prove it.

7. Prove that

    (a) $\sim\sim p$ is equivalent to p.

    (b) The contrapositive of the contrapositive is equivalent to the original conditional.

8. "For a matrix to have an inverse it is necessary that its determinant be different from zero." Which of the following statements follow from this? (No knowledge of matrices is required.)

    (a) For a matrix to have an inverse it is sufficient that its determinant be zero.

    (b) For its determinant to be different from zero it is sufficient for the matrix to have an inverse.

    (c) For its determinant to be zero it is necessary that the matrix have no inverse.

    (d) A matrix has an inverse if and only if its determinant is not zero.

    (e) A matrix has a zero determinant only if it has no inverse.

    [*Ans.* (b); (c); (e).]

9. "A function that is differentiable is continuous." This statement is true for all functions, but its converse is not always true. Which of the following statements are true for all functions? (No knowledge of functions is required.)

    (a) A function is differentiable only if it is continuous.

    (b) A function is continuous only if it is differentiable.

    (c) Being differentiable is a necessary condition for a function to be continuous.

    (d) Being differentiable is a sufficient condition for a function to be continuous.

    (e) Being differentiable is a necessary and sufficient condition for a function to be differentiable.   [*Ans.* (a); (d); (e).]

10. Prove that the negation of "p is a necessary and sufficient condition

for *q*" is equivalent to "*p* is a necessary and sufficient condition for $\sim q$."

11. Supply a conclusion to the following argument, making it a valid argument. [Adapted from Lewis Carroll.]

"If he goes to a party, he does not fail to brush his hair.
To look fascinating it is necessary to be tidy.
If he is an opium eater, then he has no self-command.
If he brushes his hair, he looks fascinating.
He wears white kid gloves only if he goes to a party.
Having no self-command is sufficient to make one look untidy.
Therefore. . . ."

*9 THE INDIRECT METHOD OF PROOF

A mathematical *theorem* is an implication of the form $p \Rightarrow q$, where p is the conjunction of hypotheses and q is the conclusion. A *proof* is an argument that shows the conditional statement $p \rightarrow q$ is logically true. Such an argument usually depends on axioms, known theorems, etc. The construction of mathematical proofs frequently requires great ingenuity.

Instead of showing that $p \rightarrow q$ is logically true it is sometimes more convenient to show that an equivalent statement is logically true. We call such arguments *indirect proofs*. For instance, if we show that the contrapositive

$$(1) \qquad \qquad \sim q \rightarrow \sim p$$

is logically true, then, since it is equivalent to $p \rightarrow q$, we have also proved the latter to be logically true.

EXAMPLE 1   Let x and y be positive integers.

Theorem   If xy is an odd number, then x and y are both odd.

Proof Suppose, on the contrary, that they are not both odd. Then one of them is even, say $x = 2z$. Then $xy = 2zy$ is an even number, contrary to hypothesis. Hence we have proved our theorem.

EXAMPLE 2   "He did not know the first name of the president of the Jones Corporation, hence he cannot be an employee of that firm. Why? Because every employee of that firm calls the boss by his first name (behind his back). Therefore, if he were really an employee of Jones, then he would know Jones's first name."

These are simple examples of a very common form of argument, frequently used both in mathematics and in everyday discussions. Let us try to unravel the form of the argument.

Given:	xy is an odd number.	He doesn't know Jones's first name.	p
To prove:	x and y are both odd numbers.	He doesn't work for Jones.	q
Suppose:	x and y are not both odd numbers.	He does work for Jones.	$\sim q$
Then:	xy is an even number.	He must know what Jones's first name is.	$\sim p$

In each case we assume the denial of the conclusion and derive, by a valid argument, the denial of the hypothesis. This is one form of the *indirect* method of proof.

There are several other important variants of this method of proof. It is easy to check that the following statements have the same truth table as—i.e., are equivalent to—the conditional $p \rightarrow q$.

(2) $$(p \wedge \sim q) \rightarrow \sim p.$$

(3) $$(p \wedge \sim q) \rightarrow q.$$

(4) $$(p \wedge \sim q) \rightarrow (r \wedge \sim r).$$

Statement (2) shows that in the indirect method of proof we may make use of the original hypothesis in addition to the contradictory assumption $\sim q$. Statement (3) shows that we may also use this double hypothesis in the direct proof of the conclusion q. Statement (4) shows that if, from the double hypothesis p and $\sim q$ we can arrive at a contradiction of the form $r \wedge \sim r$, then the proof of the original statement is complete. This last form of the method is often referred to as *reductio ad absurdum*.

These last forms of the method are very useful for the following reasons: First of all we see that we can always take $\sim q$ as a hypothesis in addition to p. Second we see that besides q there are two other conclusions. ($\sim p$ or a contradiction) which are just as good.

EXAMPLE 3 Let a and b be integers, p the statement "$a + b$ is odd and a is even," and q the conclusion "b is odd." We prove $p \rightarrow q$ by means of (2) as follows:

To prove:	$p \rightarrow q$	If $a + b$ is odd and a is even, then b is odd.
Suppose:	$p \wedge \sim q$	$a + b$ is odd, a is even, and b is even.
Then:	$\sim p$	$a + b$ is even (since the sum of two even numbers is even).

We can also illustrate (4) by starting the same way but ending with

Then:	$\sim p \wedge p$	$a + b$ is even (as above) and (by hypothesis) $a + b$ is odd.

EXAMPLE 4 Let p be the statement "$3a^3 - 2a + 4 = 0$" and q the statement "a is not 0." We use (3):

To prove:	$p \rightarrow q$	If $3a^3 - 2a + 4 = 0$, then $a \neq 0$.
Assume:	$p \wedge \sim q$	$3a^3 - 2a + 4 = 0$ and $a = 0$.
Then:	q	(Since $a = 0$, put $3a^3 = 0$ into the equation to get $-2a + 4 = 0$ or $a = 2$.) Hence $a \neq 0$.

We can also again illustrate (4) starting the same way but ending

Then:	$r \wedge \sim r$	(Put $3a^3 = 2a = 0$ into the equation, giving $4 = 0$.) Since we know $4 \neq 0$, we have the absurdity $(4 = 0) \wedge (4 \neq 0)$.

EXERCISES

1. Construct indirect proofs for the following assertions:
   (a) If x^2 is odd, then x is odd (x an integer).
   (b) If I am to pass this course, I must do homework regularly.
2. Give a symbolic analysis of the following argument:

   "If he is to succeed, he must be both competent and lucky. Because, if he is not competent, then it is impossible for him to succeed. If he is not lucky, something is sure to go wrong."
3. Construct indirect proofs for the following assertions.
   (a) If $p \vee q$ and $\sim q$, then p.
   (b) If $p \leftrightarrow q$ and $q \rightarrow \sim r$ and r, then $\sim p$.
4. Give a symbolic analysis of the following argument:

   "If Jones is the murderer, then he knows the exact time of death and the murder weapon. Therefore, if he does not know the exact time or does not know the weapon, then he is not the murderer."
5. Verify that forms (2), (3), and (4) given above are equivalent to $p \rightarrow q$.
6. Let x and y be integers. Construct indirect proofs for the following assertions.
   (a) If $x + y$ is even, then x and y are both odd or both even.
   (b) If $x + y$ is odd, then either x is odd and y even or x is even and y odd.
7. Consider the conditional $p \rightarrow (q \vee r)$ corresponding to a theorem in which the conclusion is a disjunction. Discuss the four forms of indirect proof for this statement. [*Hint:* Use Exercise 6 as an example.]
8. Give an example of an indirect proof of some statement in which a contradiction is derived from p and $\sim q$.
9. Give a statement equivalent to $(p \wedge q) \rightarrow r$ which is in terms of $\sim p$, $\sim q$, and $\sim r$. Show how this can be used in a proof where there are two hypotheses given.

10. Use the indirect method to establish the validity of the following argument.

$$p \ \underline{\vee} \ q$$
$$\sim p \rightarrow r$$
$$r \rightarrow s$$
$$\underline{q \rightarrow \sim s}$$
$$\therefore p$$

11. Use the indirect method on Exercise 7 of Section 7.

SUGGESTED READING

Church, A. *Introduction Mathematical Logic.* Princeton, N.J.: Princeton University Press, 1956.

Johnstone, H. W., Jr. *Elementary Deductive Logic.* New York: Crowell, 1954. Parts 1, 2, and 3.

Suppes, P. *Introduction to Mathematical Logic.* Princeton, N.J.: Van Nostrand, 1957.

Tarski, A. *Introduction to Logic.* 2nd rev. ed. New York: Oxford, 1946. Chapters I and II.

Sets and
Counting Problems

2

1 INTRODUCTION

A well-defined collection of objects is known as a *set*. This concept, in its complete generality, is of great importance in mathematics since all of mathematics can be developed by starting from it.

The various pieces of furniture in a given room form a set. So do the books in a given library, or the integers between 1 and 1,000,000 or all the ideas that mankind has had, or the human beings alive between 1 billion B.C. and A.D. 10 billion. These examples are all examples of *finite* sets, that is, sets having a finite number of elements. All the sets discussed in this book will be finite sets.

The collection of all tall people is *not* a well-defined set, because the word "tall" is not precisely defined. On the other hand the set of all people whose height is six feet or more *is* a well-defined set, because we can determine whether any given person belongs to the set simply by measuring his height.

There are two essentially different ways of specifying a set. One can give a rule by which it can be determined whether or not a given object is a member of the set, or one can give a complete list of the elements in the set. We shall say that the former is a *description* of the set and the latter is a *listing* of the set. For example, we can define a set of four people as (a) the members of the string quartet which played in town last night, or (b) four particular persons whose names are Jones, Smith, Brown, and Green. It is customary to use braces to surround the listing of a set; thus the set above should be listed {Jones, Smith, Brown, Green}.

We shall frequently be interested in sets of logical possibilities, since the analysis of such sets is very often a major task in the solving of a problem. Suppose, for example, that we were interested in the successes of three candidates who enter the presidential primaries (we assume there are no other entries). Suppose that the key primaries will be held in New Hampshire, Minnesota, Winsonsin, and California. Assume that candidate A enters all the primaries, that B does not contest in New Hampshire's primary, and C does not contest in Wisconsin's. A list of the logical possibilities is given in Figure 1. Since the New Hampshire and Wisconsin primaries can

Possibility Number	Winner in New Hampshire	Winner in Minnesota	Winner in Wisconsin	Winner in California
P1	A	A	A	A
P2	A	A	A	B
P3	A	A	A	C
P4	A	A	B	A
P5	A	A	B	B
P6	A	A	B	C
P7	A	B	A	A
P8	A	B	A	B
P9	A	B	A	C
P10	A	B	B	A
P11	A	B	B	B
P12	A	B	B	C
P13	A	C	A	A
P14	A	C	A	B
P15	A	C	A	C
P16	A	C	B	A
P17	A	C	B	B
P18	A	C	B	C
P19	C	A	A	A
P20	C	A	A	B
P21	C	A	A	C
P22	C	A	B	A
P23	C	A	B	B
P24	C	A	B	C
P25	C	B	A	A
P26	C	B	A	B
P27	C	B	A	C
P28	C	B	B	A
P29	C	B	B	B
P30	C	B	B	C
P31	C	C	A	A
P32	C	C	A	B
P33	C	C	A	C
P34	C	C	B	A
P35	C	C	B	B
P36	C	C	B	C

Figure 1

each end in two ways, and the Minnesota and California primaries can each end in three ways, there are in all $2 \cdot 2 \cdot 3 \cdot 3 = 36$ different logical possibilities as listed in Figure 1.

A set that consists of some members of another set is called a *subset* of that set. For example, the set of those logical possibilities in Figure 1 for which the statement "Candidate A wins at least three primaries" is true, is a subset of the set of all logical possibilities. This subset can also be defined by listing its members: {P1, P2, P3, P4, P7, P13, P19}.

In order to discuss all the subsets of a given set, let us introduce the following terminology. We shall call the original set the *universal set*, one-element subsets will be called *unit sets*, and the set which contains no members the *empty set*. We do not introduce special names for other kinds of subsets of the universal set. As an example, let the universal set $\mathcal{U}$ consist of the three elements {a, b, c}. The *proper subsets* of $\mathcal{U}$ are those sets containing some but not all of the elements of $\mathcal{U}$. The proper subsets here consist of three two-element sets—namely, {a, b}, {a, c}, and {b, c}—and three unit sets—namely, {a}, {b}, and {c}. To complete the picture, we also consider the universal set a subset (but not a proper subset) of itself, and we consider the empty set* $\mathcal{E}$, which contains no elements of $\mathcal{U}$, as a subset of $\mathcal{U}$. At first it may seem strange that we should include the sets $\mathcal{U}$ and $\mathcal{E}$ as subsets of $\mathcal{U}$, but the reasons for their inclusion will become clear later.

We saw that the three-element set above had $8 = 2^3$ subsets. In general, a set with n elements has 2^n subsets, as can be seen in the following manner. We form subsets P of $\mathcal{U}$ by considering each of the elements of $\mathcal{U}$ in turn and deciding whether or not to include it in the subset P. If we decide to put every element of $\mathcal{U}$ into P, we get the universal set, and if we decide to put no element of $\mathcal{U}$ into P, we get the empty set. In most cases we shall put some but not all the elements into P and thus obtain a proper subset of $\mathcal{U}$. We have to make n decisions, one for each element of the set, and for each decision we have to choose between two alternatives. We can make these decisions in $2 \cdot 2 \cdot \ldots \cdot 2 = 2^n$ ways, and hence this is the number of different subsets of $\mathcal{U}$ that can be formed. Observe that our formula would not have been so simple if we had not included the universal set and the empty set as subsets of $\mathcal{U}$.

In the example of the voting primaries above there are 2^{36} or about 70 billion subsets. Of course, we cannot deal with this many subsets in a practical problem, but fortunately we are usually interested in only a few of the subsets. The most interesting subsets are those which can be defined by means of a simple rule such as "the set of all logical possibilities in which C loses at least two primaries." It would be difficult to give a simple description for the subset containing the elements {P1, P4, P14, P30, P34}. On the other hand, we shall see in the next section how to define new subsets in terms of subsets already defined.

---

*Many books use ϕ to symbolize the empty set.

EXAMPLES   We illustrate the two different ways of specifying sets in terms of the primary voting example. Let the universal set $\mathcal{U}$ be the logical possibilities given in Figure 1.

1. What is the subset of $\mathcal{U}$ in which candidate B wins more primaries than either of the other candidates? *Answer:* {P11, P12, P17, P23, P26, P28, P29}.

2. What is the subset in which the primaries are split two and two? *Answer:* {P5, P8, P10, P15, P21, P30, P31, P35}.

3. Describe the set {P1, P4, P19, P22}. *Answer:* The set of possibilities for which A wins in Minnesota and California.

4. How can we describe the set {P18, P24, P27}? *Answer:* The set of possibilities for which C wins in California, and the other primaries are split three ways.

EXERCISES

1. In the primary example, list each of the following sets.
   (a) The set in which A and C win the same number of primaries.
   (b) The set in which the winner of the New Hampshire primary does not win another primary.
   (c) The set in which C wins all four primaries.

2. Again referring to the primary example, give simple descriptions of the following sets.
   (a) [P1, P4, P8, P11, P15, P18, P19, P22, P26, P29, P33, P36].
   (b) [P18, P22, P26].
   (c) [P1, P11, P19, P29].

3. The primaries are considered decisive if a candidate can win three primaries, or if he wins two primaries including California. List the set in which the primaries are decisive.

4. List the set of four-letter "words" formed by writing down the letters of the word *stop* in all possible ways. [*Hint:* The set has 24 elements.]

5. In Exercise 4, list the following subsets:
   (a) The set of English words.   [*Partial Ans.* There are 6.]
   (b) The set in which the letters are in alphabetical order either from left to right or from right to left.
   (c) The set in which *p* and *t* are next to each other.
   (d) The set in which only *s* is between *o* and *t*.
   (e) The set in which *t* and *s* are at the ends.

6. Find all pairs in Exercise 5 in which one set is a subset of the other.

7. A baker has four feet of display space to fill with some combination of bread, cake, and pie. A loaf of bread takes one-half foot of space, a cake takes one foot, and a pie takes two feet. Construct the set of possible distributions of shelf space, considering only the *total* space allotted to each kind of item.

8. In Exercise 7, list the following subsets.

(a) The set in which as much space is devoted to pie as to cake.

(b) The set in which equal space is given to two different items, and at least two different items are displayed.

(c) The set in which six or more items are displayed.

(d) The set in which at least two of the above conditions are satisfied.

9. A man has 65 cents in change, but he has no pennies and has at least as many dimes as nickels. Find the set of possibilities for his collection of coins.

10. In Exercise 9, list the following subsets.

(a) The set in which the man has exactly one quarter.

(b) The set in which the man has more half-dollars than quarters.

(c) The set in which the man has fewer than six coins.

(d) The set in which none of the above conditions is satisfied.

11. A set has 51 elements. How many subsets does it have? How many of the subsets have an even number of elements?   [*Ans.* 2^{51}, 2^{50}.]

12. Do Exercise 11 for the case of a set with 52 elements.

2 OPERATIONS ON SUBSETS

In Chapter 1 we considered the ways in which one could form new statements from given statements. Now we shall consider an analogous procedure, the formation of new sets from given sets. We shall assume that each of the sets that we use in the combination is a subset of some universal set, and we shall also want the newly formed set to be a subset of the same universal set. As usual, we can specify a newly formed set either by a description or by a listing.

If P and Q are two sets, we shall define a new set $P \cap Q$, called the *intersection* of P and Q as follows: $P \cap Q$ is the set which contains those and only those elements which belong to both P and Q. As an example, consider the logical possibilities listed in Figure 1. Let P be the subset in which candidate A wins at least three primaries, i.e., the set {P1, P2, P3, P4, P7, P13, P19}; let Q be the subset in which A wins the first two primaries, i.e., the set {P1, P2, P3, P4, P5, P6}. Then the intersection $P \cap Q$ is the set in which both events take place, i.e., where A wins the first two primaries *and* wins at least three primaries. Thus $P \cap Q$ is the set {P1, P2, P3, P4}.

If P and Q are two sets, we shall define a new set $P \cup Q$ called the *union* of P and Q as follows: $P \cup Q$ is the set that contains those and only those elements that belong either to P or to Q (or to both). In the example in the paragraph above, the union $P \cup Q$ is the set of possibilities for which either A wins the first two primaries *or* wins at least three primaries, i.e., the set {P1, P2, P3, P4, P5, P6, P7, P13, P19}.

To help in visualizing these operations we shall draw diagrams, called *Venn diagrams,** which illustrate them. We let the universal set be a rectangle and let subsets be circles drawn inside the rectangle. In Figure 2 we show

*Named after the English logician John Venn (1834–1923).

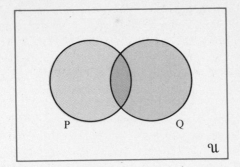

Figure 2

two sets P and Q as shaded circles, P shaded in color and Q in gray. Then the area shaded in both color and gray is the intersection $P \cap Q$ and the total shaded area is the union $P \cup Q$.

If P is a given subset of the universal set $\mathcal{U}$, we can define a new set $\tilde{P}$ called the *complement* of P as follows: $\tilde{P}$ is the set of all elements of $\mathcal{U}$ that are *not* contained in P. For example, if, as above, Q is the set in which candidate A wins the first two primaries, then $\tilde{Q}$ is the set $\{P7, P8, \ldots, P36\}$. The shaded area in Figure 3 is the complement of the set P. Observe that the complement of the empty set $\mathcal{E}$ is the universal set $\mathcal{U}$, and also that the complement of the universal set is the empty set.

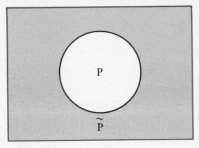

Figure 3

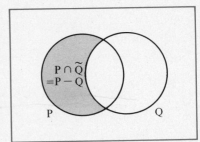

Figure 4

Sometimes we shall be interested in only part of the complement of a set. For example, we might wish to consider the part of the complement of the set Q that is contained in P, i.e., the set $P \cap \tilde{Q}$. The shaded area in Figure 4 is $P \cap \tilde{Q}$.

A somewhat more suggestive definition of this set can be given as follows: Let $P - Q$ be the *difference* of P and Q, that is, the set that contains those elements of P that do not belong to Q. Figure 4 shows that $P \cap \tilde{Q}$ and $P - Q$ are the same set. In the primary voting example above, the set $P - Q$ can be listed as $\{P7, P13, P19\}$.

The complement of a subset is a special case of a difference set, since we can write $\tilde{Q} = \mathcal{U} - Q$. If P and Q are nonempty subsets whose intersection is the empty set, i.e., $P \cap Q = \mathcal{E}$, then we say that they are *disjoint* subsets.

EXAMPLE 1   In the primary voting example let R be the set in which A wins the first three primaries, i.e., the set $\{P1, P2, P3\}$; let S be the set in which A wins the last two primaries, i.e., the set $\{P1, P7, P13, P19, P25, P31\}$. Then $R \cap S = \{P1\}$ is the set in which A wins the first three primaries and also the last two, that is, he wins all the primaries. We also have

$$R \cup S = \{P1, P2, P3, P7, P13, P19, P25, P31\},$$

which can be described as the set in which A wins the first three primaries or the last two. The set in which A does not win the first three primaries is $\tilde{R} = \{P4, P5, \ldots, P36\}$. Finally, we see that the difference set $R - S$ is the set in which A wins the first three primaries but not both of the last two. This set can be found by taking from R the element P1 which it has in common with S, so that $R - S = \{P2, P3\}$.

EXAMPLE 2   Let us give a step-by-step construction of the Venn diagram for the set $(P \cap Q) \cup (\tilde{P} \cap \tilde{Q})$. Figure 5 shows the set $P \cap Q$ which is the same as

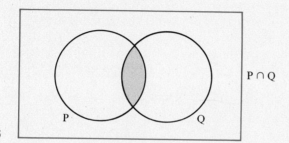

$P \cap Q$

Figure 5

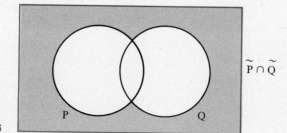

$\tilde{P} \cap \tilde{Q}$

Figure 6

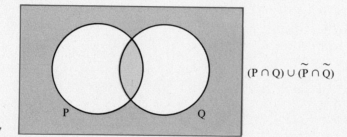

$(P \cap Q) \cup (\tilde{P} \cap \tilde{Q})$

Figure 7

the set of Figure 2 shaded in both color and gray; Figure 6 shows the set $\tilde{P} \cap \tilde{Q}$ which is the same as the complement of the shaded area in Figure 2. Finally, Figure 7 is the union of the two areas in Figures 5 and 6 and is the answer desired.

EXERCISES

1. Draw Venn diagrams for the following sets:
   (a) $P \cap Q$.
   (b) $\tilde{P} \cup Q$.
   (c) $P \cup \tilde{Q}$.
   (d) $\tilde{P} \cup \tilde{Q}$.

2. Give a step-by-step construction of the diagram for $((P \cup Q) - (P \cap Q)) \cap \tilde{Q}$.

3. Venn diagrams are also useful when three subsets are given. Construct such a diagram, given the subsets P, Q, and R. Identify each of the eight resulting areas in terms of P, Q, and R.

4. In assigning dormitory roomates, a college considers a student's sex, whether or not the student wants to live in a coed dorm, and whether the student is a freshman or an upperclassman. Draw a Venn diagram, and identify each of the eight areas.

5. Let F be the set of females, U the set of upperclassmen, and C the set of students desiring to live in a coed dorm. Define (symbolically) the following sets:
   (a) Upperclass males who do not want to live in a coed dorm.

   [*Ans.* $U \cap \tilde{F} \cap \tilde{C}$.]

   (b) Women who want to live in a coed dorm.
   (c) Male students who want to live in a coed dorm and are freshmen.
   (d) Women who are not freshmen and do not want to live in a coed dorm.

6. The college decides that two students can be roommates if both are of the same sex or if both are upperclassmen who want to live in a coed dorm. Identify the sets of students with the property that any two members of the set can be roommates.

7. The results of a survey of church attendance and golf playing are given in the following table:

Occupation	Golfs and Attends	Golfs and Doesn't Attend	Doesn't Golf and Attends	Doesn't Golf and Doesn't Attend
Doctor	15	20	3	2
Lawyer	10	9	9	6
CPA	8	0	11	7

Let D = doctor, L = lawyer, C = CPA, G = golfs, A = attends. Determine the number of people in each of the following classes.

(a) $D \cap G \cap \tilde{A}$.

(b) $\tilde{C} \cap \tilde{G} \cap A$.

(c) $(\overline{G \cup A}) \cap L$.

(d) $(D \cup L) \cap G$.   [*Ans.* 54.]

(e) $\tilde{L} \cap ((A \cap G) \cup (\tilde{A} \cap G))$.   [*Ans.* 43.]

8. In Exercise 7, which set of each of the following pairs has more members?

(a) $(D \cap G) - A$ or $\tilde{L} \cup (G \cap A)$?

(b) $\mathcal{E}$ or $C \cap \tilde{A} \cap G$?

(c) $(\overline{D \cup L})$ or C?

9. A college student hired to survey 1000 beer drinkers and record their age, sex, and educational level turned in the following figures: 700 males, 600 people over 25 years of age, 400 college graduates, 250 male college graduates, 225 college graduates over 25, 350 males over 25, and 150 male college graduates over 25. After turning in his results, he was fired. Why? [*Hint:* Draw a Venn diagram with three circles—for males, college graduates, and those over 25. Fill in the numbers in each of the eight areas, using the data given above. Start from the end of the list and work back.]

10. A survey of 110 lung cancer patients showed that 70 were cigarette smokers, 60 lived in urban areas, and 35 had hazardous occupations. Forty of the smokers lived in urban areas, 15 had hazardous occupations, and 5 were in both categories. Ten of the patients with hazardous occupations neither lived in an urban area nor smoked.

(a) How many of the patients living in urban areas had hazardous occupations?   [*Ans.* 15.]

(b) How many of those living in the urban areas neither smoked nor had hazardous occupations?   [*Ans.* 10.]

(c) How many patients smoke if and only if they live in an urban area?

(d) How many patients neither smoked, nor lived in an urban area, nor had a hazardous occupation?

11. A second survey of 100 patients had the following results: 45 smokers who lived in urban areas, 37 of whom did not have a hazardous occupation; 20 people with hazardous occupations, of whom 10 live in urban areas and 10 smoke; 75 smokers; and 10 who neither smoke, nor have a hazardous occupation, nor live in an urban area.

(a) How many patients with hazardous occupations neither smoke nor live in an urban area?   [*Ans.* 8]

(b) How many patients live in an urban area?

(c) How many patients smoke if and only if they do not have a hazardous occupation?

(d) How many patients smoke, have a hazardous occupation, and live in an urban area?

12. The following table summarizes the responses of 100 students asked what they thought about during math lectures:

Class and Status	Neither Food Nor Football	Only Food	Only Football	Food and Football
Senior Majors	20	12	4	6
Senior Nonmajors	8	10	15	0
Junior Majors	2	1	6	1
Junior Nonmajors	3	5	5	2

All the categories can be defined in terms of the following four: M (majors), S (seniors), F (food), and FT (football). How many students fall into each of the following categories?

(a) S

(b) $S - M$

(c) $M - S$

(d) $J \cap \tilde{M} \cap F \cap FT$

(e) $(J \cap F)$

(f) $\tilde{J} \cup \tilde{F}$ [*Ans.* 91.]

(g) $S \cap \tilde{M} \cap F$

(h) $(S \cup F) - \widetilde{FT}$ [*Ans.* 28.]

(i) $S \cap M \cap (\widetilde{F \cup FT})$ [*Ans.* 20.]

(j) $S \cup J$

3 THE RELATIONSHIP BETWEEN SETS AND COMPOUND STATEMENTS

The reader may have observed several times in the preceding sections that there was a close connection between sets and statements, and between set operations and compounding operations. In this section we shall formalize these relationships.

If we have a number of statements relative to a set of logical possibilities, there is a natural way of assigning a set to each statement. First we take the set of logical possibilities as our universal set. Then to each statement we assign the subset of logical possibilities of the universal set for which that statement is true. This idea is so important that we embody it in a formal definition.

Definition Let $\mathfrak{U}$ be a set of logical possibilities, let p be a statement relative to it, and let P be that subset of the possibilities for which p is true; then we call P the *truth set* of p.

If p and q are statements, then $p \vee q$ and $p \wedge q$ are also statements and hence must have truth sets. To find the truth set of $p \vee q$, we observe that it is true whenever p is true or q is true (or both). Therefore we must assign to $p \vee q$ the logical possibilities which are in P or in Q (or both); that is, we must assign to $p \vee q$ the set $P \cup Q$. On the other hand, the statement

$p \wedge q$ is true only when both p and q are true, so that we must assign to $p \wedge q$ the set $P \cap Q$.

Thus we see that there is a close connection between the logical operation of disjunction and the set operation of union, and also between conjunction and intersection. A careful examination of the definitions of union and intersection shows that the word "or" occurs in the definition of union and the word "and" occurs in the definition of intersection. Thus the connection between the two theories is not surprising.

Since the connective "not" occurs in the definition of the complement of a set, it is not surprising that the truth set of $\sim p$ is $\tilde{P}$. This follows since $\sim p$ is true when p is false, so that the truth set of $\sim p$ contains all logical possibilities for which p is false, that is, the truth set of $\sim p$ is $\tilde{P}$.

The truth sets of two propositions p and q are shown in Figure 8. Also marked on the diagram are the various logical possibilities for these two statements. The reader should pick out in this diagram the truth sets of the statements $p \vee q$, $p \wedge q$, $\sim p$, and $\sim q$.

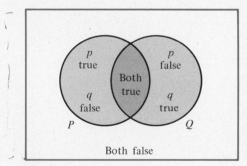

Figure 8

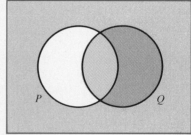

Figure 9

The connection between a statement and its truth set makes it possible to "translate" a problem about compound statements into a problem about sets. It is also possible to go in the reverse direction. Given a problem about sets, think of the universal set as being a set of logical possibilities and think of a subset as being the truth set of a statement. Hence we can "translate" a problem about sets into a problem about compound statements.

So far we have discussed only the truth sets assigned to compound statements involving $\vee$, $\wedge$, and $\sim$. All the other connectives can be defined in terms of these three basic ones, so that we can deduce what truth sets should be assigned to them. For example, we know that $p \rightarrow q$ is equivalent to $\sim p \vee q$. Hence the truth set of $p \rightarrow q$ is the same as the truth set of $\sim p \vee q$, that is, it is $\tilde{P} \cup Q$. The Venn diagram for $p \rightarrow q$ is shown in Figure 9, where the shaded area is the truth set for the statement. Observe that the unshaded area in Figure 9 is the set $P - Q = P \cap \tilde{Q}$, which is the truth set of the statement $p \wedge \sim q$. Thus the shaded area is the set $\widetilde{(P - Q)} = \widetilde{P \cap \tilde{Q}}$, which is the truth set of the statement $\sim[p \wedge \sim q]$. We have thus discovered the fact that $(p \rightarrow q)$, $(\sim p \vee q)$, and $\sim(p \wedge \sim q)$ are equivalent. It is always the case that two compound statements are equivalent if and only if they have the same truth sets. Thus we can test for equivalence by checking whether they have the same Venn diagram.

Suppose that p is a statement that is logically true. What is its truth set? Now p is logically true if and only if it is true in every logically possible case, so that the truth set of p must be $\mathcal{U}$. Similarly, if p is logically false, then it is false for every logically possible case, so that its truth set is the empty set $\mathcal{E}$.

Finally, let us consider the implication relation. Recall that p implies q if and only if the conditional $p \rightarrow q$ is logically true. But $p \rightarrow q$ is logically true if and only if its truth set is $\mathcal{U}$, that is, $(\widetilde{P - Q}) = \mathcal{U}$, or $(P - Q) = \mathcal{E}$. From Figure 4 we see that if $P - Q$ is empty, then P is contained in Q. We shall symbolize the containing relation as follows: $P \subset Q$ means "P is a subset of Q." We conclude that $p \Rightarrow q$ if and only if $P \subset Q$.

Figure 10 supplies a "dictionary" for translating from statement language to set language, and back. To each statement relative to a set of possibilities $\mathcal{U}$ there corresponds a subset of $\mathcal{U}$—namely, the truth set of the statement.

Statement Language	Set Language
r	R
s	S
$\sim r$	$\widetilde{R}$
$r \vee s$	$R \cup S$
$r \wedge s$	$R \cap S$
$r \rightarrow s$	$(\widetilde{R - S})$
$r \Rightarrow s$	$R \subset S$
$r \Leftrightarrow s$	$R = S$

Figure 10

This is shown in lines 1 and 2 of the figure. To each connective there corresponds an operation on sets, as illustrated in the next four lines. And to each relation between statements there corresponds a relation between sets, examples of which are shown in the last two lines of the figure.

EXAMPLE 1 Verify by means of a Venn diagram that the statement $[p \vee (\sim p \vee q)]$ is logically true. The assigned set of this statement is $[P \cup (\widetilde{P} \cup Q)]$, and its Venn diagram is shown in Figure 11. In that figure the set P is shaded in color, and the set $\widetilde{P} \cup Q$ is shaded in gray. Their union is the entire shaded area, which is $\mathcal{U}$, so that the compound statement is logically true.

Distributive Law?

EXAMPLE 2 Demonstrate by means of Venn diagrams that $p \vee (q \wedge r)$ is equivalent to $(p \vee q) \wedge (p \vee r)$. The truth set of $p \vee (q \wedge r)$ is the entire shaded area

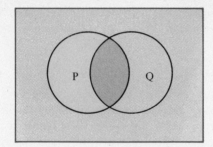

Figure 11

of Figure 12a, and the truth set of $(p \lor q) \land (p \lor r)$ is the area in Figure 12b shaded in both color and gray. Since these two sets are equal, we see that the two statements are equivalent.

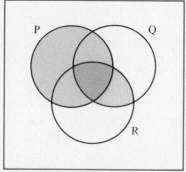

Figure 12a

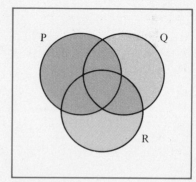

Figure 12b

EXAMPLE 3 Show by means of a Venn diagram that q implies $p \to q$. The truth set of $p \to q$ is the shaded area in Figure 9. Since this shaded area includes the set Q, we see that q implies $p \to q$.

EXERCISES

1. Use Venn diagrams to test the following statements for equivalences.
   (a) $\sim(p \lor q)$.
   (b) $\sim p \lor \sim q$.
   (c) $\sim(p \land q)$.
   (d) $\sim p \land \sim q$.
   (e) $q \to p$.
   (f) $\sim(\sim p \to q)$.

   [*Ans.* (a), (d), and (f) are equivalent; (b) $\Leftrightarrow$ (c).]

2. Use Venn diagrams to tell which of the following statements are logically true and which are logically false.
   (a) $p \land \sim p$.

(b) $(p \wedge q) \vee (\sim p \vee \sim q)$.   [*Ans.* Logically true.]

(c) $(p \wedge q) \vee (p \wedge \sim q)$.

(d) $\sim p \vee (q \to p)$.

(e) $p \to (q \to p)$.

(f) $\sim (p \to q) \wedge q$.

3. Derive a test for inconsistency of p and q, using Venn diagrams.

4. Three or more statements are said to be inconsistent if they cannot all be true. What does this say about their truth sets?

5. Use Venn diagrams for the following statements to test whether one implies the other.

(a) $p \wedge q$; $p \wedge \sim q$.   **(b)** $\sim (q \to p)$; $p \to q$.

(c) $p \wedge q$; $\sim p \vee q$.   **(d)** $\sim p \wedge q$; q.

(e) $p \vee q$; $p \to (\sim p \to q)$.   **(f)** $(p \to q) \wedge \sim q$; $q \to p$.

6. Find statements having each of the following as truth sets.

(a) $(P \cap Q) - R$.

(b) $(R - Q) \cup (Q - R)$.

(c) $P - (\widetilde{Q \cup R})$.

(d) $(\widetilde{P \cap Q}) \cup (P \cup R)$.

7. Use truth tables to find whether the following sets are all different.

(a) $(P \cap Q \cap \tilde{R}) \cup (P \cap \tilde{Q} \cap R) \cup (\tilde{P} \cap Q \cap R)$.

(b) $[P - (Q \cup R)] \cup (R \cap Q)$.

(c) $Q \cap \tilde{R}$.

(d) $(P \cap Q \cap \tilde{R}) \cup (\tilde{P} \cap Q \cap \tilde{R})$.

(e) $[(P \cap Q) \cup (P \cap R) \cup (r \cap Q)] - (p \cap Q \cap R)$.

(f) $[(P \cap \tilde{Q} \cap \tilde{R}) \cup [(\widetilde{Q \cup R}) - (Q \cap R)]] - (\tilde{P} \cap \tilde{Q} \cap \tilde{R})$.

8. Use truth tables to find whether each of the following sets is empty.

(a) $(P - Q) \cap (Q - P)$.   [*Ans.* Empty.]

(b) $(\tilde{P} \cup Q) \cap (\tilde{Q} \cup R) \cap (\widetilde{\tilde{P} \cup R})$.

(c) $(\widetilde{P \cap R}) \cap (\tilde{P} \cap \tilde{Q})$.   [*Ans.* Not empty.]

(d) $(\widetilde{P \cup R}) \cap \tilde{Q}$.

(e) $(P \cap Q) - P$.

(f) $(P \cap (Q - R)) - ((P \cap Q) - R)$.

9. Show, both by the use of truth tables and by the use of Venn diagrams, that $p \vee (q \wedge r)$ is equivalent to $(p \vee q) \wedge (p \vee r)$.

10. Use truth tables for the following pairs of sets to test whether one is a subset of the other.

(a) $P \cap Q$; $[R - (\widetilde{P \cup Q})]$.

(b) $(\tilde{P} \cap Q) \cap (\tilde{Q} \cup R)$; $\tilde{P} \cup R$.

(c) $P \cap (Q \cup R)$; $P \cap Q$.

(d) $P \cap \tilde{Q}$; $\tilde{P} \cap Q$.

(e) Q; $(\tilde{P} \cup Q) \cap P$.

(f) $P - (Q - R)$; $(P - Q) - R$.

11. The *symmetric difference* of P and Q is defined to be $(P - Q) \cup (Q - P)$. What connective corresponds to this set operation?

4 PERMUTATIONS

The first step in the analysis of a scientific problem is the determination of the set of logical possibilities. Next it is often necessary to determine how many different possible outcomes there are. We shall find this particularly important in probability theory. Hence it is desirable to develop general techniques for solving counting problems. In this section and the next we shall discuss the two most important cases in which it is possible to achieve formulas that solve the problem. When a formula cannot be derived, one must resort to certain other general counting techniques, tricks, or, in the last resort, complete enumeration of the possibilities.

As a first problem let us consider the number of ways in which a set of n different objects can be arranged. A *listing* of n different objects *in a certain order* is called a *permutation* of the n objects. We consider first the case of three objects, a, b, and c. We can exhibit all possible permutations of these three objects as paths of a tree, as shown in Figure 13. Each path

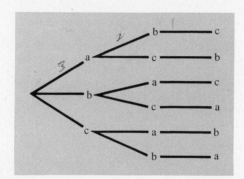

Figure 13

exhibits a possible permutation, and there are six such paths. We know there are six paths from the following argument: we have 3 choices for the first object; after this first choice we can choose the second object in 2 ways; then the last object must be listed; thus the total number of listings is $3 \cdot 2 \cdot 1 = 6$. We could also list these permutations as follows:

$$\begin{array}{ll} \text{abc,} & \text{bca,} \\ \text{acb,} & \text{cab,} \\ \text{bac,} & \text{cba.} \end{array}$$

If we were to construct a similar tree for n objects, we would find that the number of paths could be found by multiplying together the numbers $n, n - 1, n - 2$, continuing down to the number 1. The number obtained in this way occurs so often that we give it a symbol, namely $n!$, which is read *"n factorial."* Thus, for example, $3! = 3 \cdot 2 \cdot 1 = 6$, $4! = 4 \cdot 3 \cdot 2 \cdot 1 = 24$, and so on. For reasons that will be clear later, we define $0! = 1$. Thus we can say *there are n! different permutations of n distinct objects.*

EXAMPLE 1   Seven different machining operations are to be performed on a part, but they may be performed in any sequence. We may then consider $7! = 5040$ different orders in which the operations may be performed.

EXAMPLE 2   Ten workers are to be assigned to 10 different jobs. In how many ways can the assignments be made? The first worker may be assigned in 10 possible ways, the second in any of the 9 remaining ways, the third in 8, and so forth: there are $10! = 3,628,800$ possible ways of assigning the workers to the jobs.

EXAMPLE 3   A company has *n* directors. In how many ways can they be seated around a circular table at a board meeting, if two arrangements are considered different only if at least one person has a different person sitting on his right in the two arrangements? To solve the problem, consider one director in a fixed position. There are $(n - 1)!$ ways in which the other people may be seated. We have now counted all the arrangements we wish to consider different. Thus there are also $(n - 1)!$ possible seating arrangements.

For many counting problems it is not possible to give a simple formula for the number of possible cases. In many of these the only way to find the number of cases is to draw a tree and count them. In some problems, the following general principle is useful.

A General Principle   If one thing can be done in exactly *r* different ways, for each of these a second thing can be done in exactly *s* different ways, for each of the first two, a third can be done in exactly *t* ways, and so on, then the sequence of things can be done in $r \cdot s \cdot t \ldots$ ways.

EXAMPLE 4   Suppose we live in town X and want to go to town Z by passing through town Y. If there are three roads from X to Y, and two roads from Y to Z, in how many ways can we go from town X to town Z? By applying the general principle we see that there are $3 \cdot 2 = 6$ ways.

The validity of this general principle can be established by thinking of a tree representing all the ways in which the sequence of things can be done. There would be *r* branches from the starting position. From the ends of each of these *r* branches there would be *s* new branches, and from each of these *t* new branches, and so on. The number of paths through the tree would be given by the product $r \cdot s \cdot t \ldots$.

EXAMPLE 5   The number of permutations of n distinct objects is a special case of this principle. If we were to list all the possible permutations, there would be n possibilities for the first, for each of these $n - 1$ for the second, etc., until we came to the last object, and for which there is only one possibility. Thus there are $n(n - 1) \ldots 1 = n!$ possibilities in all.

EXAMPLE 6   An automobile manufacturer produces four different models; models A and B can come in any of four body styles—sedan, hardtop, convertible, and station wagon—while models C and D come only as sedans or hardtops. Each can can come in one of nine colors. Thus models A and B each have $4 \cdot 9 = 36$ distinguishable types, while C and D have $2 \cdot 9 = 18$ types, so that in all

$$2 \cdot 36 + 2 \cdot 18 = 108$$

different car types are produced by the manufacturer.

EXAMPLE 7   Suppose there are n applicants for a certain job. Three interviewers are asked independently to rank the applicants according to their suitability. It is decided that an applicant will be hired if he is ranked first by at least two of the three interviewers. What fraction of the possible reports would lead to the acceptance of some candidate? We shall solve this problem by finding the fraction of the reports that do not lead to an acceptance and subtract this answer from 1. Frequently an indirect attack of this kind is easier than the direct approach. The total number of reports possible is $(n!)^3$, since each interviewer can rank the men in $n!$ different ways. If a particular report does not lead to the acceptance of a candidate, it must be true that each interviewer has put a different man in first place. By our general principle, this can be done in $n(n - 1)(n - 2)$ different ways. For each possible first choice, there are $[(n - 1)!]^3$ ways in which the remaining men can be ranked by the interviewers. Thus the number of reports that do not lead to acceptance is

$$n(n - 1)(n - 2)[(n - 1)!]^3.$$

Dividing this number by $(n!)^3$, we obtain

$$\frac{(n - 1)(n - 2)}{n^2}$$

as the fraction of reports that fail to accept a candidate. The fraction that leads to acceptance is found by subtracting this fraction from 1, which gives

$$\frac{3n - 2}{n^2}.$$

For the case of three applicants, we see that $\frac{7}{9}$ of the possibilities lead to acceptance. Here the procedure might be criticized on the grounds that even if the interviewers are completely ineffective and are essentially guessing, there is a good chance that a candidate will be accepted on the basis of the reports. For n equal to ten, the fraction of acceptances is only .28, so that it is possible to attach more significance to the interviewers' ratings, if they reach a decision.

EXERCISES

1. A salesman is going to call on five customers. In how many different sequences can he do this if he
    (a) Calls on all five in one day?
    (b) Calls on three one day and two the next?
    [*Ans.* (a) 120; (b) 120.]

2. A machine shop has three milling machines, five lathes, six drill presses, and three grinders. In how many ways can a part be routed that must first be ground, then milled, then turned on a lathe, and then drilled? In how many ways can it be routed if these four operations can be performed in any order?

3. A department store wants to classify each of its customers having a charge account by using a three-character code consisting of n letters followed by $3 - n$ digits. How large must n be if there are 5000 charge accounts? What if there are 10,000? 20,000?

4. Modify Example 7 so that, to be accepted, an applicant must be first in two of the interviewers' ratings and must be either first or second in the third interviewer's rating. What fraction of the possible reports lead to acceptance in the case of three applicants? In the case of n?
    [*Ans.* $\frac{4}{9}$; $4/n^2$.]

5. A company has six officers and six directors; two of the directors are officers. List the possible memberships of a committee of four men who are either officers or directors in terms of the number of members who are (a) just officers, (b) just directors, and (c) both officers and directors.

6. In Exercise 5, how many ways are there of obtaining a committee of four consisting of
    (a) Three who are just officers and one who is officer and director?
    (b) One who is just an officer, one who is just a director, and two who are officers and directors?
    (c) At least two who are only directors and at least one who is officer and director?
    (d) At least two officers and at least two directors (assuming a man who is both officer and director satisfies both quotas)?
    [*Ans.* 160.]

7. Show the possible arrangement of machines A, B, C, and D in a circle. How many are there?

8. How many possible ways are there of seating six people A, B, C, D, E, and F at a circular table if
    (a) A must always have B on his right and C on his left?

(b)   A must always sit next to B?

(c)   A cannot sit next to B?

9. In seating *n* people around a circular table, suppose we distinguish between two arrangements only if at least one person has at least one different person sitting next to him in the two arrangements. That is, we do not regard two arrangements as different simply because the right-hand and left-hand neighbors of a person have interchanged places. Now how many distinguishable arrangements are there?

10. A certain symphony orchestra always plays one of the 41 Mozart symphonies, followed by one of 25 different modern works, followed by one of the 9 Beethoven symphonies.

(a)   How many different programs can it play?

(b)   How many different programs can be given if the pieces can be played in any order?

(c)   How many three-piece programs are possible if more than one piece from the same category can be played?

11. Find the number of arrangements of the five symbols that can be distinguished. (The same letters with different subscripts indicate distinguishable objects.)

(a) A_1, A_2, B_1, B_2, B_3.   [*Ans.* 120.]

(b) A, A, B_1, B_2, B_3.   [*Ans.* 60.]

(c) A, A, B, B, B.   [*Ans.* 10.]

12. Show that the number of distinguishable arrangements possible for *n* objects, n_1 of type 1, n_2 of type 2, and so on for *r* different types is

$$\frac{n!}{n_1!n_2! \cdots n_r!}.$$

13. A student takes a five-question multiple-choice test, each question having answer a, b, c, or d. If he knows that the answers to the test consist of two a's and one each of b, c, and d and he answers accordingly, in how many different ways can be answer the test? In what fraction of these will he get four or more right answers? In what fraction will he get three or more right?   [*Partial Ans.* 60.]

14. How many signals can a ship show if it has eight flags and a signal consists of five flags hoisted vertically on a rope?   [*Ans.* 6720.]

15. We must arrange four green, one red, and four blue books on a single shelf. All books are distinguishable.

(a)   In how many ways can this be done if there are no restrictions?

(b)   In how many ways if books of the same color must be grouped together?

(c)   In how many ways if, in addition to the restriction in (b) the red books must be to the left of the blue books?

(d)   In how many ways if, in addition to the restrictions in (b) and (c), the red and blue books must not be next to each other?

[*Ans.* 576.]

16. (a) How many five-digit numbers can be formed from the digits 1, 2, 3, 4, 5 using each digit only once?

   (b) How many of these numbers are less than 33,000?

17. A housewife who has just returned from shopping realizes that she has left her sunglasses at either the bank, the post office, the drugstore, or the grocery store, and so she must go back and search for them. Assume that when she returns to the building where she left them, she finds them and then goes directly home.

   (a) In how many different orders can all four places be searched?

   (b) Assume we now know that she found her glasses at the third place she returned to. How many different searches can she have made?

   (c) If we know only that her glasses were left at the bank, how many different searches can she have made?

5   LABELING PROBLEMS

The second general type of counting problem that we want to consider may be described as follows. We have n objects and we wish to label each of these objects with one of r different types of labels. To be more specific, we wish to determine the total number of ways that we can label the n objects with r labels if n_1 of the objects are to be given the first type of label, n_2 the second type, and so on, where $n_1, n_2, \ldots, n_r$ are given nonnegative integers such that $n_1 + n_2 + \cdots + n_r = n$.

As an example assume that we have eight customers, A, B, C, D, E, F, G, and H, and we wish to assign to each of them one of three salesmen, Brown, Jones, or Smith. And we want to make this assignment so that Brown is assigned to three customers, Jones to three, and Smith to two. Notice that we can interpret the problem as that of assigning a label—Brown, Jones, or Smith—to each of the eight customers. In how many ways can this assignment be made?

One way to assign the customers is to list them in some arbitrary order (that is, select a permutation of them) and then assign Brown to the first three, Jones to the next three, and Smith to the last two. There are 8! permutations or listings of the customers, but not all of these lead to different assignments. For instance, consider the following assignment:

$$|\,BCA\,|\,DFE\,|\,HG\,|.$$

Here, Brown is assigned to B, C, and A, Jones to D, F, and E, and Smith to H and G. Notice that another permutation such as

$$|\,ABC\,|\,DEF\,|\,GH\,|$$

gives the same customer assignments, since it differs only in the sequences for particular salesmen. There are $3! \cdot 3! \cdot 2!$ such listings, since we can arrange the three customers of Brown in 3! different ways, and for each of these, the customers of Jones in 3! different ways, and for each of these, the customers of Smith in 2! different ways. Since there are $3! \cdot 3! \cdot 2!$

different listings that lead to the same assignments and 8! listings in all, there are $8!/(3! \cdot 3! \cdot 2!)$ different assignments of customers to salesmen.

The same argument could be carried out for r salesmen and n customers with n_1 assigned to the first salesman, n_2 to the second, and so on. In fact there is really nothing special about the argument for this example, so we have the following basic result. Let $n_1, n_2, \ldots, n_r$ be nonnegative integers with $n_1 + n_2 + \cdots + n_r = n$. Then:

The number of ways that n objects can be labeled with r different types of labels, n_1 with the first type, n_2 with the second, and so on, is

$$\frac{n!}{n_1! n_2! \cdots n_r!}$$

We shall denote this number by the symbol

$$\binom{n}{n_1, n_2, \ldots, n_r}.$$

The special case when $r = 2$, meaning that there are just two types of labels, is particularly important. The problem is often stated in the following way. We are given a set of n elements; in how many ways can we choose a subset with j elements? If we interpret the problem to mean labeling each element as either "in the set" or "not in the set," we see that it is just a labeling problem whose answer is

$$\binom{n}{j, n-j} = \frac{n!}{j!(n-j)!};$$

and hence this is also the number of subsets with j elements. The notation $\binom{n}{j, n-j}$ is commonly shortened to $\binom{n}{j}$. These numbers are known as *binomial coefficients*.

Notice that every time we choose a subset of j elements to put in our subset we are also choosing a subset of $n - j$ elements to leave out. In this way we see that

$$\binom{n}{j} = \binom{n}{j, n-j} = \binom{n}{n-j}.$$

EXAMPLE 1   The aces and kings are removed from a bridge deck, and from the resulting eight-card deck a hand of two cards is dealt. How many such two-card hands are there? By the principle just stated we see that there are $\binom{8}{2} = \binom{8}{6} = 28$ such hands, since choosing a two-card hand is just the same as choosing the remaining six cards to keep in the deck. (The reader should enumerate the 28 possible two-card hands.)

EXAMPLE 2   A company buys a certain electronic component from three vendors. In how many ways can it place six orders, two with vendor A, three with vendor B, and one with vendor C? This is just the problem of labeling each of the six orders with one of three labels, A, B, or C. There are

$$\binom{6}{2,\,3,\,1} = \frac{6!}{2!3!1!} = 60$$

ways of carrying out the labeling.

EXAMPLE 3   On August 20, 1970, 1551 different stock issues were traded on the New York Stock Exchange. Of these, 701 advanced, 530 declined, and 320 closed unchanged from the previous day. In how many ways could this have happened? We must label each stock as "advanced," "declined," or "unchanged." There are

$$\frac{1551!}{701!530!320!}$$

different ways in which this particular result could occur. This number is approximately equal to $1.1 \cdot 10^{705}$.

EXAMPLE 4   This example will be important in probability theory, which we take up in the next chapter. If a coin is tossed six times, there are 2^6 possibilities for the outcome of the six throws, since each throw can result in either a head or a tail. How many of these possibilities result in four heads and two tails? We can interpret each assignment of outcomes to be a labeling of each integer from 1 to 6 with either H or T, corresponding to whether heads or tails came up on that toss. Since we required that four be labeled H and two T, the answer is $\binom{6}{4} = 15$. For n throws of a coin, a similar analysis shows that there are $\binom{n}{r}$ different sequences of H's and T's of length n that have exactly r heads and $n - r$ tails.

EXERCISES

  1. Compute the following numbers:

  (a) $\binom{8}{6}$.   [*Ans.* 28.]

  (b) $\binom{4}{2}$.

(c) $\binom{2}{1}$.

(d) $\binom{780}{779}$.   [*Ans.* 780.]

(e) $\binom{10}{0}$.

(f) $\binom{3}{2,0,1}$.

(g) $\binom{5}{2,2,1}$.   [*Ans.* 30.]

(h) $\binom{8}{4,1,3}$.

2. Show that
$$\binom{a}{b} = \frac{a \cdot (a-1) \cdot (a-2) \cdot \cdots \cdot (a-b+2) \cdot (a-b+1)}{b \cdot (b-1) \cdot (b-2) \cdot \cdots \cdot 2 \cdot 1},$$
where there are exactly b terms in both the numerator and the denominator.

3. A group of six workers is to be assigned to six of nine available jobs. If we are only interested in which jobs are assigned, and not the specific worker-job assignments and if all of the workers are assigned jobs, in how many ways can the jobs be assigned to the workers? How many possibilities are there for the unassigned jobs, if three of the jobs are sure to be assigned?   [*Ans.* 84, 20.]

4. Give an interpretation for $\binom{n}{0}$ and aso for $\binom{n}{n}$. Can you now give a reason for making $0! = 1$?

5. A hospital has just received eight chairs, four red and four blue. In how many different ways can these be distributed between two waiting rooms if each room must receive at least three chairs and at least one chair of each color? (Assume chairs of the same color are of different types, and thus distinguishable.)

6. From a lot containing six pieces, three good and three defective, a sample of three pieces is drawn. If we distinguish each piece, find the number of possible samples that can be formed
   (a) With no restrictions.   [*Ans.* 20.]
   (b) With three good pieces and no defectives.   [*Ans.* 1.]
   (c) With two good pieces and one defective.   [*Ans.* 9.]
   (d) With one good piece and two defectives.   [*Ans.* 9.]
   (e) With no good pieces and three defectives.   [*Ans.* 1.]
   What is the relation between your answer in part (a) and the answers to the remaining four parts?

7. Exercise 6 suggests that the following should be true:

$$\binom{2n}{n} = \binom{n}{0}\binom{n}{n} + \binom{n}{1}\binom{n}{n-1} +$$
$$\binom{n}{2}\binom{n}{n-2} + \cdots + \binom{n}{n}\binom{n}{0} = \binom{n}{0}^2 + \binom{n}{1}^2 + \cdots + \binom{n}{n}^2.$$

Show that it is true.

8. Consider a town with four plumbers, A, B, C, and D. On a certain day eight residents of the town telephone for a plumber. If each resident selects a plumber from the telephone directory, in how many ways can it happen that
    (a) Three residents call A, three call B, one calls C, and one calls D?
    (b) The distribution of calls to the plumbers is three, three, one, and one?   [*Ans.* 6720.]

9. In a class of 20 students, grades of A, B, C, D, and F are to be assigned. Omit arithmetic details in answering the following:
    (a) In how many ways can this be done if there are no restrictions?
    (b) In how many ways can this be done if the grades are assigned as follows: 2 A's, 3 B's, 10 C's, 3 D's, and 2 F's?
    (c) In how many ways can this be done if the following rules are to be satisfied: exactly 10 C's; the same number of A's as F's; the same number of B's and D's; always more B's than A's?

$$\left[Ans. \ \binom{20}{5,\,10,\,5} + \binom{20}{1,\,4,\,10,\,4,\,1} + \binom{20}{2,\,3,\,10,\,3,\,2}. \right]$$

10. In how many ways can a machine produce nine pieces, five of which are good and four of which are defective? In how many ways if no two consecutive pieces are both good or both defective?

11. Establish the identity

$$\binom{n}{r}\binom{r}{k} = \binom{n}{k}\binom{n-k}{r-k}$$

for $n \geq r \geq k$ in two ways, as follows:
    (a) Replace each expression by a ratio of factorials and show that the two sides are equal.
    (b) Consider the following problem: From a set of n people a committee or r is to be chosen, and from these r people a steering subcommittee of k people is to be selected. Show that the two sides of the identity give two different ways of counting the possibilities for this problem.

12. A brewing company contracts with a television station to show three spot commercials a week for 52 weeks. The commercials consist of a series of cartoons. It is decided that in no two weeks will exactly the same three cartoons be shown. What is the minimum number of cartoons that will accomplish this?

13. Twenty bridge players enter a tournament and form ten partnerships. Seven of the players are good bridge players, ten are mediocre, and three are terrible. How many possibilities are there for the winning partnership if we know that the winning partnership
   (a) Contained no terrible player?   [*Ans.* 136.]
   (b) Contained two good players?
   (c) Contained one good and one mediocre player?

14. Referring to Exercise 13, answer the following questions, omitting arithmetic computations.
   (a) How many possible sets of ten partnerships are there?
   (b) How many sets of ten partnerships are possible if no two terrible players play together?
   (c) How many sets of ten partnerships are possible if, in addition to restriction (b), no two good players play together and no two mediocre players play together?

15. A group of nine people is to be divided into three committees of two, three, and six members, respectively. The chairman of the group is to serve on all three committees and is the only member of the group who serves on more than one committee. In how many ways can the committee assignments be made?   [*Ans.* 168.]

16. A landlord decides to repaint two of his apartments, each having five rooms. Assuming that he uses only green, yellow, and blue paint and that each room is to be painted with only one color.
   (a) How many different ways are there of painting the apartments?
                                                               [*Ans.* 3^{10}.]
   (b) How many different ways are there of painting the apartments, given that no more than two colors are to be used in any one apartment?   [*Ans.* 8649.]

6 SOME PROPERTIES OF BINOMIAL COEFFICIENTS

The binomial coefficients $\binom{n}{j}$ introduced in Section 5 will play an important role in our future work. We give here some of the more important properties of these numbers.

A convenient way to obtain these numbers is given by the famous *Pascal triangle,* shown in Figure 14. To obtain the triangle we first write the 1's down the sides. Any of the other numbers in the triangle has the property that it is the sum of the two adjacent numbers in the row just above. Thus the next row in the triangle is 1, 6, 15, 20, 15, 6, 1. To find the binomial coefficient $\binom{n}{j}$ we look in the row corresponding to the number n and see where the diagonal line corresponding to the value of j intersects this row. For example, $\binom{4}{2} = 6$ is in the row marked $n = 4$ and on the diagonal marked $j = 2$.

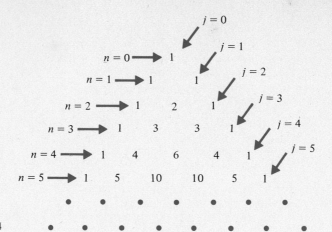

Figure 14

The property of the binomial coefficients upon which the triangle is based is

$$\binom{n+1}{j} = \binom{n}{j-1} + \binom{n}{j}.$$

This fact can be verified directly (see Exercise 5), but the following argument is interesting in itself. The number $\binom{n+1}{j}$ is the number of subsets with j elements that can be formed from a set of $n+1$ elements. Select one of the $n+1$ elements, x. Of the $\binom{n+1}{j}$ subsets some contain x, and some do not. The latter are subsets of j elements formed from n objects, and hence there are $\binom{n}{j}$ such subsets. The former are constructed by adding x to a subset of $j-1$ elements formed from n elements, and hence there are $\binom{n}{j-1}$ of them. Thus

$$\binom{n+1}{j} = \binom{n}{j-1} + \binom{n}{j}.$$

If we look again at the Pascal triangle, we observe that the numbers in a given row increase for a while, and then decrease. In fact, they increase to a unique maximum when n is even or to two equal maxima when n is odd.

An important application of binomial coefficients is in the expansion of products of the form $(x+y)^3$, $(a-2b)^{10}$, and so on. We shall derive a general formula for these by making use of the binomial coefficients.

Consider first the special case $(x+y)^3$. We write this as

$$(x+y)^3 = (x+y)(x+y)(x+y).$$

To perform the multiplication, we choose either an x or y from each of the three factors and multiply our choices together; we do this for all possible choices and add the results. To state this as a labeling problem, note that we want to label each of the three factors with the two labels x and y. In how many ways can we do this using two x labels and one y? The preceding section gives the answer $\binom{3}{2} = 3$. Hence the coefficient of x^2y in the expansion of the binomial is 3. More generally, the coefficient of the term of the form x^jy^{3-j} will be $\binom{3}{j}$ for $j = 0, 1, 2, 3$. Thus we can write the desired expansion as

$$(x + y)^3 = \binom{3}{3}x^3 + \binom{3}{2}x^2y + \binom{3}{1}xy^2 + \binom{3}{0}y^3$$
$$= x^3 + 3x^2y + 3xy^2 + y^3.$$

Binomial Theorem The expansion of $(x + y)^n$ is given by

$$(x + y)^n = \binom{n}{n}x^n + \binom{n}{n-1}x^{n-1}y + \binom{n}{n-2}x^{n-2}y^2$$
$$+ \cdots + \binom{n}{1}xy^{n-1} + \binom{n}{0}y^n.$$

EXAMPLE 1 Let us find the expansion for $(a - 2b)^3$. To fit this into the binomial theorem, we think of x as being a and y as being $-2b$. Then we have

$$(a - 2b)^3 = a^3 + 3a^2(-2b) + 3a(-2b)^2 + (-2b)^3$$
$$= a^3 - 6a^2b + 12ab^2 - 8b^3.$$

EXERCISES

1. Extend the Pascal triangle to $n = 16$. Save the result for later use.
2. **(a)** Show that a set with n elements has 2^n subsets. [*Hint:* Assume you have two different kinds of labels: "in the subset" and "not in the subset." In how many different ways can we label the n elements of the set?]
    (b) Prove that

    $$\binom{n}{0} + \binom{n}{1} + \binom{n}{2} + \cdots + \binom{n}{n} = 2^n,$$

    using the fact that a set with n elements has 2^n subsets.
3. Using the fact that

    $$\binom{n}{j+1} = \frac{n-j}{j+1}\binom{n}{j},$$

compute $\binom{27}{s}$ for $s = 1, 2, 3, 4, 5$ starting with the fact that $\binom{27}{0} = 1$.

4. For $n \leq m$ prove that

$$\binom{m}{0}\binom{n}{0} + \binom{m}{1}\binom{n}{1} + \binom{m}{2}\binom{n}{2} + \cdots + \binom{m}{n}\binom{n}{n} = \binom{m+n}{n}$$

by carrying out the following two steps:

   (a) Show that the left-hand side counts the number of ways of choosing equal numbers of men and women from sets of m men and n women.

   (b) Show that the right-hand side also counts the same number by showing that we can select equal numbers of men and women by selecting any subset of n persons from the whole set, and then combining the men selected with the women not selected.

5. Prove that

$$\binom{n+1}{j} = \binom{n}{j-1} + \binom{n}{j},$$

using only the fact that

$$\binom{n}{j} = \frac{n!}{j!\,(n-j)!}.$$

6. Expand by the binomial theorem:
   (a) $(x+1)^4$.   [*Ans.* $x^4 + 4x^3 + 6x^2 + 4x + 1$.]
   (b) $(2x+y)^3$.
   (c) $(x-2)^5$.
   (d) $(2a-x)^4$.
   (e) $(3x+4y)^3$.
   (f) $(100-2)^4$.

7. Using the binomial theorem, prove that

   (a) $\binom{n}{0} + \binom{n}{1} + \binom{n}{2} + \cdots + \binom{n}{n} = 2^n$.

   (b) $\binom{n}{0} - \binom{n}{1} + \binom{n}{2} - \binom{n}{3} + \cdots \pm \binom{n}{n} = 0$ for $n > 0$.

*7 APPLICATIONS OF COUNTING TECHNIQUES

One of the important areas in which finite mathematics is applied is in solving *combinatorial decision problems*. In such problems there are a finite number of ways in which a certain procedure can be carried out, and for each of these ways a cost or value can be calculated. We want to select a way of carrying out the procedure that has minimum cost or maximum value.

One method for solving combinatorial decision problems is to enumerate all the possible ways of carrying out the procedure and selecting the one that is most desirable. Although this is theoretically possible, it may be practically impossible since the number of alternatives frequently is too large to enumerate completely even with the aid of an electronic computer. Hence methods that do not require complete enumeration are needed to solve such problems.

We illustrate the use of counting techniques to help solve such problems.

EXAMPLE 1 Consider a city with a grid of streets as shown in Figure 15. Jones and Smith are at corner A and want to go to corner B, which is four blocks east and five blocks north of A. In how many ways can they make the journey and travel exactly nine blocks?

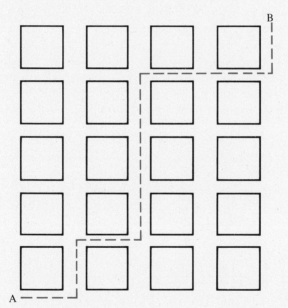

Figure 15

You may wish to try to count all possible ways, but if you try you are very likely to become tired and confused. This would be especially true if the distances were larger, say 100 blocks east and 100 blocks north! However we can reformulate the problem so that it is easy if we notice that all that Jones and Smith have to do is to make nine decisions, each decision being to go a block either east or north, with exactly four of the nine decisions being to go east and the remaining five to go north. For instance, one series of decisions, leading to the path shown dotted in Figure 15, is represented by the decisions

east, north, east, north, north, north, east, east, north.

Once we understand this reformulation of the problem, its solution is easy, since the number of ways we can choose four out of nine decisions to be east (or equally well five out of nine to be north) is clearly

$$\binom{9}{4} = \binom{9}{5} = \frac{6 \cdot 7 \cdot 8 \cdot 9}{1 \cdot 2 \cdot 3 \cdot 4} = 126 \text{ paths.}$$

The general problem is just as easy. If Jones and Smith are going h blocks east and k blocks north, the total number N of possible paths is given by

$$N = \binom{h + k}{h} = \binom{h + k}{k}.$$

Let us make this into a combinatorial decision problem by requiring that the number of corners turned on the path be a minimum. At least one corner must be turned. A little experimentation will show that two paths exist which turn at only one corner. These are (1) go four blocks east and five blocks north and (2) go five blocks north and four blocks east. These two answers solve the decision problem.

EXAMPLE 2   Suppose that point B is now three blocks east and five blocks north, and that the streets are alternate one-way east-west and north-south as indicated by the arrows in Figure 16. Smith is going to walk from A to B but Jones is going to take a taxi. We know that Smith must walk eight blocks and there are $\binom{8}{3} = 56$ possible paths he can take. After they arrive at B Jones and Smith compare notes. Smith said the taxi drove him ten blocks. Was the taxi driver honest?

The answer is yes, and it follows from the next theorem.

Figure 16   A

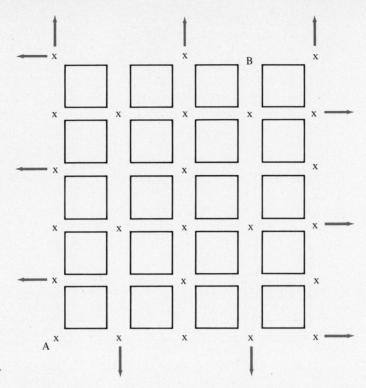

Figure 17

Theorem Consider a city with alternating one-way streets in both east-west and north-south directions. The shortest driving path between any two points A and B where B is northeast of A and the roads at A go east and north is either the same or exactly two blocks longer than the shortest walking path.

The proof is quite simple since we can easily show that, starting from A we can go to every corner of a four-block square except the center in exactly the same distance either by driving or walking (see the corners marked X in Figure 17.) To drive to the center of a four-block square (that is, to one of the corners not marked with an X in Figure 17) we drive first to an adjacent corner and then go to the center of the four-block square using the one-way streets. The latter step adds two additional blocks to the trip.

You may also wish to prove that if the roads at A go east and north and B is southwest of A, then the shortest driving path is either two or four blocks longer than the shortest walking path.

It is also true that the one-way-street pattern reduces the number of possible driving paths from A to B. In Exercise 1 you will be asked to show that there are six driving paths from A to B in Figure 16. Of these six there is only one that requires only two corners—and all the rest have more—so that the combinatorial decision problem now has a unique answer.

It often happens that a counting problem can be formulated in a number of different ways that sound quite different but that are in fact equivalent. And in one of these ways the answer may suggest itself readily. To illustrate how a reformulation can make a hard-sounding problem seem fairly easy, consider the following problem. Count the number of ways that n indistinguishable objects can be put into r cells. For instance, if there are three objects and three cells, the number of different ways can be enumerated as follows (using O for object and bars to indicate the sides of the cells):

```
| OOO |     |     |
| OO  | O   |     |
| OO  |     | O   |
| O   | OO  |     |
| O   | O   | O   |
| O   |     | OO  |
|     | OOO |     |
|     | OO  | O   |
|     | O   | OO  |
|     |     | OOO |
```

We see that in this case there are ten ways the task can be accomplished. But the answer for the general case is not clear.

If we look at the problem in a slightly different manner, the answer suggests itself. Instead of putting the objects *in* the cells, we imagine putting the cells *around* the objects. In the above case we see that three cells are constructed from four bars. Two of these bars must be placed at the ends. We think of the two other bars together with our three objects as occupying five intermediate positions. Of these five intermediate positions we must choose two of them for bars and three for the objects. Hence the total number of ways we can accomplish the task is $\binom{5}{2} = \binom{5}{3} = 10$, which is the answer we got by counting all the ways.

For the general case we can argue in the same manner. We have r cells and n objects. We need $r + 1$ bars to form the r cells, but two of these must be fixed on the ends. The remaining $r - 1$ bars together with the n objects occupy $r - 1 + n$ intermediate positions. And we must choose $r - 1$ of these for the bars and the remaining n for the objects. Hence our task can be accomplished in

$$\binom{n + r - 1}{r - 1} = \binom{n + r - 1}{n}$$

different ways.

EXAMPLE 3   Seven people enter an elevator that will stop at five floors. In how many different ways can the people leave the elevator if we are interested only in the number that depart at each floor, and do not distinguish among the people? According to our general formula, the answer is

$$\binom{7 + 5 - 1}{7} = \binom{11}{7} = 330.$$

Suppose we are interested in finding the number of such possibilities in which at least one person gets off at each floor. We can then arbitrarily assign one person to get off at each floor, and the remaining two can get off at any floor. They can get off the elevator in

$$\binom{2 + 5 - 1}{2} = \binom{6}{2} = 15$$

different ways.

EXERCISES

1.   In Figure 16 show that there are exactly six different driving paths from A to B.

2.   Find the unique path from A to B requiring only two corners in Figure 16.

3.   In Figure 15 suppose that point C is two blocks east and three blocks north of point A. How many ways are there of going from A to C and then to B by paths that are nine blocks long?   [*Ans.* 60.]

4.   In Figure 16 suppose that point C is one block east and one block north of A. How many driving paths are there for going from A to C and then to B that use the fewest number of blocks?

5.   Four partners in a game require a total score of exactly 20 points to win. In how many ways can they accomplish this? $\left[Ans. \ \binom{23}{3}. \right]$

6.   In how many ways can eight apples be distributed among four boys? In how many ways can this be done if each boy is to get at least one apple?

7.   Suppose we have n balls and r boxes with $n \geq r$. Show that the number of different ways that the balls can be put into the boxes which insures that there is at least one ball in every box is $\binom{n - 1}{r - 1}$.

8.   Identical prizes are to be distributed among five boys. It is observed that there are 15 ways that this can be done if each boy is to get at least one prize. How many prizes are there?   [*Ans.* 7.]

9.   By an ordered partition of n with r elements we mean a sequence of nonnegative integers, possibly some 0, written in a definite order, and having n as their sum. For instance, $\{1, 0, 3\}$ and $\{3, 0, 1\}$ are two

different ordered partitions of 4 with three elements. Show that the number of ordered partitions of n with r elements is $\binom{n+r-1}{n}$.

10. Show that the number of different possibilities for the outcomes of rolling n dice is $\binom{n+5}{n}$.

SUGGESTED READING

Breuer, Joseph. *Introduction to the Theory of Sets.* Englewood Cliffs, N.J.: Prentice-Hall, 1958.

Fraenkel, A. A. *Abstract Set Theory.* Amsterdam: North-Holland Publishing Co., 1953.

Goldberg, S. *Probability: An Introduction.* Englewood Cliffs, N.J.: Prentice-Hall, 1960.

Parzen, E. *Modern Probability Theory and Its Applications.* New York: John Wiley, 1960.

Whitworth, W. A. *Choice and Chance, with* 1000 *Exercises.* New York: Stechert, 1934.

Probability
Theory

3

1   INTRODUCTION

We often hear statements of the following kind: "It is likely to rain today," "I have a fair chance of passing this course," "There is an even chance that a coin will come up heads," etc. In each case our statement refers to a situation in which we are not certain of the outcome, but we express some degree of confidence that our prediction will be verified. The theory of probability provides a mathematical framework for such assertions.

Consider an experiment whose outcome is not known. Suppose that someone makes an assertion p about the outcome of the experiment, and we want to assign a probability to p. When statement p is considered in isolation, we usually find no natural assignment of probabilities. Rather, we look for a method of assigning probabilities to all conceivable statements concerning the outcome of the experiment. At first this might seem to be a hopeless task, since there is no end to the statements we can make about the experiment. However, we are aided by a basic principle:

Fundamental Assumption   Any two equivalent statements will be assigned the same probability.

As long as there are a finite number of logical possibilities, there are only a finite number of truth sets, and hence the process of assigning probabilities is a finite one. We proceed in three steps: (1) we first determine $\mathcal{U}$, the possibility set, that is, the set of all logical possibilities; (2) to each subset X of $\mathcal{U}$ we assign a number called the measure $m(X)$; (3) to each statement p we assign $m(P)$, the measure of its truth set, as a probability. The probability of statement p is denoted by $\Pr[p]$.

The first step, that of determining the set of logical possibilities, is one that we considered in the previous chapters. It is important to recall that there is no unique method for analyzing logical possibilities. In a given problem we may arrive at a very fine or a very rough analysis of possibilities, causing $\mathfrak{U}$ to have many or few elements.

Having chosen $\mathfrak{U}$, the next step is to assign a number to each subset X of $\mathfrak{U}$, which will in turn be taken to be the probability of any statement having truth set X. We do this in the following way.

Assignment of a Measure   Assign a positive number (weight) to each element of $\mathfrak{U}$, so that the sum of the weights assigned is 1. Then the measure of a set is the sum of the weights of its elements. The measure of the set $\mathcal{E}$ is 0.

EXAMPLE 1   An ordinary die is thrown. What is the probability that the number which turns up is less than four? Here the possibility set is $\mathfrak{U} = \{1, 2, 3, 4, 5, 6\}$. The symmetry of the die suggests that each face should have the same probability of turning up. To make this so, we assign weight $\frac{1}{6}$ to each of the outcomes.

In applications of probability to scientific problems, the analysis of the logical possibilities and the assignment of measures may depend upon factual information and hence can best be done by the scientist making the application.

Once the weights are assigned, to find the probability of a particular statement we must find its truth set and find the sum of the weights assigned to elements of the truth set. This problem, which might seem easy, can often involve considerable mathematical difficulty. The development of techniques to solve this kind of problem is the main task of probability theory.

EXAMPLE 1 (continued)   For the case of throwing an ordinary die we have already assigned equal weights to each outcome. Let us consider statements relative to $\mathfrak{U} = \{1, 2, 3, 4, 5, 6\}$. The truth set of the statement "The number that turns up is less than four" is $\{1, 2, 3\}$. Hence the probability of this statement is $\frac{3}{6} = \frac{1}{2}$, the sum of the weights of the elements in its truth set. Similarly, the truth set of the statement "The number that turns up is odd or is less than four" is $\{1, 2, 3, 5\}$. Hence the probability of this statement is $\frac{4}{6} = \frac{2}{3}$, which again is the sum of the weights assigned to elements in its truth set.

EXAMPLE 2   A man attends a race involving three horses A, B, and C. He feels that A and B have the same chance of winning but that A (and hence also B) is twice as likely to win as C is. What is the probability that A or C wins? We take as $\mathfrak{U}$ the set $\{A, B, C\}$. If we were to assign weight a to the outcome C, then we would assign weight $2a$ to each of the outcomes A and B. Since the sum of the weights must be 1, we have $2a + 2a + a = 1$, or $a = \frac{1}{5}$. Hence we assign weights $\frac{2}{5}, \frac{2}{5}, \frac{1}{5}$ to the outcomes A, B, and C, respectively. The truth set of the statement "Horse A or C wins" is $\{A, C\}$. The sum of the weights of the elements of this set is $\frac{2}{5} + \frac{1}{5} = \frac{3}{5}$. Hence the probability that A or C wins is $\frac{3}{5}$.

EXERCISES

1. Briefly explain the difference between the terms "weight," "measure," and "probability".

2. Let $\mathfrak{U} = \{a, b, c\}$. Assign weights to the three elements so that no two have the same weight, and find the measures of the eight subsets of $\mathfrak{U}$.

3. Give the possibility set $\mathfrak{U}$ for each of the following experiments:
   (a) A number from 1 to 7 is chosen at random.
   (b) A and B play a game of chess.
   (c) A student is asked for the month in which his birthday falls.
   (d) A die with all faces having the number six is thrown.

4. For which of the cases in Exercise 3 might it be appropriate to assign the same weight to each outcome?

5. In an election Jones has probability $\frac{3}{8}$ of winning, Smith has probability $\frac{1}{8}$, and Black has probability $\frac{1}{2}$.
   (a) Construct $\mathfrak{U}$.
   (b) Assign weights.
   (c) Find the measures of the eight subsets.
   (d) Give a pair of nonequivalent predictions which have the same probability.

6. A die is loaded in such a way that the probability of each face is proportional to the number of dots on that face. (For instance, a six is 3 times as probable as a two.) What is the probability of getting an even number in one throw?   [*Ans.* $\frac{4}{7}$.]

7. The owner of a certain hardware store places a sign stating "Back in 15 minutes" on his door at noon when he goes to lunch. Customers find that when this sign is posted the probabilities are .4 that he is back within 10 minutes, .45 that he returns in more than 10 but less than 20 minutes, and .145 that he returns after 20 minutes or more have elapsed.
   (a) What is the probability that he returns within 20 minutes?
                                                          [*Ans.* .85.]
   (b) What is the probability that he takes the rest of the day off and does not return at all?
   (c) Is it possible to determine the probability that he returns within 5 minutes?   [*Ans.* No.]

8. If a coin is thrown three times, list the eight possibilities for the outcomes of the three successive throws. A typical outcome can be written (HTH). Determine a probability measure by assigning an equal weight to each outcome. Find the probabilities of the following statements:
   r: The number of heads that occur is greater than the number of tails.   [*Ans.* $\frac{1}{2}$.]

s: Exactly two heads occur. [*Ans.* $\frac{3}{8}$.]

t: The same side turns up on every throw. [*Ans.* $\frac{1}{4}$.]

9. For the statements given in Exercise 8, which of the following equalities are true?
    (a) $\Pr[r \vee s] = \Pr[r] + \Pr[s]$.
    (b) $\Pr[s \vee t] = \Pr[s] + \Pr[t]$.
    (c) $\Pr[r \vee \sim r] = \Pr[r] + \Pr[\sim r]$.
    (d) $\Pr[r \vee t] = \Pr[r] + \Pr[t]$.

10. Which of the following pairs of statements (see Exercise 8) are inconsistent? (Recall that two statements are inconsistent if their truth sets have no element in common.)
    (a) r, s. (b) s, t.
    (c) $r, \sim r$. (d) r, t. [*Ans.* (b) and (c).]

11. State a property which is suggested by Exercises 9 and 10.

12. A number is chosen from the set $\{1, 2, 3\}$. If weights have been assigned to the three outcomes such that $\Pr[\text{a 1 or 2 is chosen}] = \frac{3}{5}$ and $\Pr[\text{a 2 or 3 is chosen}] = \frac{2}{3}$, find the weights. [*Ans.* $\frac{1}{3}, \frac{4}{15}, \frac{2}{5}$.]

13. Repeat Exercise 12 for each of the following cases
    (a) $\Pr[\text{a 1 or 2 is chosen}] = \frac{2}{5}$ and
        $\Pr[\text{a 2 or 3 is chosen}] = \frac{2}{5}$.
    (b) $\Pr[\text{a 2 is chosen}] = \frac{1}{3}$, and
        $\Pr[\text{a 1 or 2 is chosen}] = \frac{1}{2} \cdot \Pr[\text{a 2 or 3 is chosen}]$.

2 PROPERTIES OF A PROBABILITY MEASURE

Before studying special probability measures, we shall consider some general properties of such measures which are useful in computations and in the general understanding of probability theory.

Three basic properties of a probability measure are

(A) $m(X) = 0$ if and only if $X = \mathcal{E}$.

(B) $0 \leq m(X) \leq 1$ for any set X.

(C) For two sets X and Y,

$$m(X \cup Y) = m(X) + m(Y)$$

if and only if X and Y are disjoint, i.e., have no elements in common.

The proofs of properties (A) and (B) are left as an exercise (see Exercise 16). We shall prove (C).

We observe first that $m(X) + m(Y)$ is the sum of the weights of the elements of X added to the sum of the weights of Y. If X and Y are disjoint, then the weight of every element of $X \cup Y$ is added once and only once, and hence $m(X) + m(Y) = m(X \cup Y)$.

Assume now that X and Y are not disjoint. Here the weight of every element contained in both X and Y—i.e., in $X \cap Y$—is added twice in the sum $m(X) + m(Y)$. Thus this sum is greater than $m(X \cup Y)$ by an amount

$m(X \cap Y)$. By (A) and (B), if $X \cap Y$ is not the empty set, then $m(X \cap Y) > 0$. Hence in this case we have $m(X) + m(Y) > m(X \cup Y)$. Thus if X and Y are not disjoint, the equality in (C) does not hold. Our proof shows that in general we have

(C′) For any two sets X and Y,

$$m(X \cup Y) = m(X) + m(Y) - m(X \cap Y).$$

Since the probabilities for statements are obtained directly from the probability measure $m(X)$, any property of $m(X)$ can be translated into a property about the probability of statements. For example, the above properties become, when expressed in terms of statements,

(a) $\Pr[p] = 0$ if and only if p is logically false.
(b) $0 \leq \Pr[p] \leq 1$ for any statement p.
(c) The equality

$$\Pr[p \vee q] = \Pr[p] + \Pr[q]$$

holds if and only if p and q are inconsistent.
(c′) For any two statements p and q,

$$\Pr[p \vee q] = \Pr[p] + \Pr[q] - \Pr[p \wedge q].$$

Another property of a probability measure which is often useful in computation is

(D) $m(\widetilde{X}) = 1 - m(X)$,

or, in the language of statements,

(d) $\Pr[\sim p] = 1 - \Pr[p]$.

The proofs of (D) and (d) are left as an exercise (see Exercise 17).

It is important to observe that our probability measure assigns probability 0 only to statements which are logically false, i.e., which are false for every logical possibility. Hence, a prediction that such a statement will be true is certain to be wrong. Similarly, a statement is assigned probability 1 if and only if it is true in every case, i.e., logically true. Thus the prediction that a statement of this type will be true is certain to be correct. (While these properties of a probability measure seem quite natural, it is necessary, when dealing with infinite possibility sets, to weaken them slightly. We consider in this book only finite possibility sets.)

We shall now discuss the interpretation of probabilities that are not 0 or 1. We shall give only some intuitive ideas that are commonly held concerning probabilities. While these ideas can be made mathematically more precise, we offer them here only as a guide to intuitive thinking.

Suppose that, relative to a given experiment, a statement has been assigned probability p. From this it is often inferred that if a sequence of such experiments is performed under identical conditions, the fraction of experiments which yield outcomes making the statement true would be approximately p. The mathematical version of this is the "law of large numbers" of probability theory (which will be treated in Section 9). In cases where there is no natural way to assign a probability measure, the probability of a statement is estimated experimentally. A sequence of experiments is performed and the fraction of the experiments which make the statement true is taken as the approximate probability for the statement.

A second and related interpretation of probabilities is concerned with betting. Suppose that a certain statement has been assigned probability p. We wish to offer a bet that the statement will in fact turn out to be true. We agree to give r dollars if the statement does not turn out to be true, provided that we receive s dollars if it does turn out to be true. What should r and s be to make the bet fair? If it were true that in a large number of such bets we would win s a fraction p of the times and lose r a fraction $1 - p$ of the time, then our average winning per bet would be $sp - r(1 - p)$. To make the bet fair we should make this average winning 0. This will be the case if $sp = r(1 - p)$ or if $r/s = p/(1 - p)$. Notice that this determines only the ratio of r to s. Such a ratio, written $r:s$, is said to give *odds* in favor of the statement.

Definition   The *odds* in favor of an outcome are $r:s$ (r to s), if the probability of the outcome is p, and $r/s = p/(1 - p)$. Any two numbers having the required ratio may be used in place of r and s. Thus 6:4 odds are the same as 3:2 odds.

EXAMPLE   Assume that a probability of $\frac{3}{4}$ has been assigned to a certain horse winning a race. Then the odds for a fair bet would be $\frac{3}{4}:\frac{1}{4}$. These odds could be equally well written as $3:1$, $6:2$ or $12:4$, etc. A fair bet would be to agree to pay \$3 if the horse loses and receive \$1 if the horse wins. Another fair bet would be to pay \$6 if the horse loses and win \$2 if the horse wins.

EXERCISES

1.   Let p and q be statements such that $\Pr[p \vee q] = \frac{3}{4}$, $\Pr[p] = \frac{2}{3}$, and $\Pr[\sim q] = \frac{3}{4}$. Find $\Pr[p \wedge q]$.   [*Ans.* $\frac{1}{6}$.]

2.   Using the results of Exercise 1, find $\Pr[\sim p \vee \sim q]$.

3.   Let p and q be statements such that $\Pr[p] = \frac{1}{2}$ and $\Pr[q] = \frac{2}{3}$. Are p and q consistent?   [*Ans.* Yes.]

4.   Show that, if $\Pr[p] + \Pr[q] > 1$, then p and q are consistent.

5.   A student is worried about his grades in English and Art. He estimates that the probability of passing English is .4, that he will pass at least one course with probability .6, but that he has only probability .1 of

passing both courses. What is the probability that he will pass Art?
[*Ans.* .3.]

6. Given that a school has grades A, B, C, D, and F, and that a student has probability .9 of passing a course, and .6 of getting a grade lower than B, what is the probability that he will get a C or D? [*Ans.* $\frac{1}{2}$.]

7. State what odds a person should give on the following events:
   (a) That a card chosen at random from a 52-card deck is on ace.
   (b) That a four turns up when a dice is thrown.
   (c) That a coin which is flipped twice comes up heads both times.

8. Prove that if the odds in favor of a given statement are $r:s$, then the probability that the statement will be true is $r/(r + s)$.

9. Using the result of Exercise 8 and the definition of "odds," show that if the odds are $r:s$ that a statement is true, then the odds are $s:r$ that it is false.

10. A man is willing to give $3:1$ odds that the Democratic candidate will win the next presidential election. What must the probability of a Democratic victory be to make this a fair bet?

11. An American roulette wheel contains 38 slots (18 red, 18 black, and 2 green). What are the odds that red will turn up on a given spin?

12. A man offers $3:2$ odds that A will occur, and $1:2$ odds that B will occur. If he knows that A and B cannot both occur, what odds should he give that A or B will occur? [*Ans.* $14:1$.]

13. Suppose now the man offers $2:3$ odds that A will occur, and $2:1$ odds that B will occur. Again, he knows that A and B cannot both occur. What odds should he give that A or B will occur?

14. A man offers to bet "dollars to doughnuts" that a certain event will take place. Assuming that a doughnut costs a dime, what must the probability of the event be for this to be a fair bet? [*Ans.* $\frac{10}{11}$.]

15. If X and Y are two sets such that X is a subset of Y, prove that $m(X) \leq m(Y)$. Use this to prove that if p implies q then $\Pr[p] \leq \Pr[q]$.

16. Show from the definition of a probability measure that properties (A) and (B) of the text are true.

17. Prove property (D) of the text. Why does property (d) follow from this property?

18. Let X, Y, and Z be any three sets, the let m be any probability measure. Prove in two ways that $m(X \cup Y \cup Z) = m(X) + m(Y) + m(Z) - m(X \cap Y) - m(X \cap Z) - m(Y \cap Z) + m(X \cap Y \cap Z)$. Use a Venn diagram for the first proof. For the second, notice that $X \cup Y \cup Z = (X \cup Y) \cup Z$ and use property (C') of the text.

19. Suppose we assume that X, Y, and Z are *pairwise disjoint*—i.e., that $X \cap Y = X \cap Z = Y \cap Z = \mathcal{E}$. Show that $m(X \cup Y \cup Z) = m(X) + m(Y) + m(Z)$.

20. Suppose that we make the assumption (weaker than that in Exercise 19) that $X \cap Y \cap Z = \mathcal{E}$. Show by example that it is not necessarily the case that $m(X \cup Y \cup Z) = m(X) + m(Y) + m(Z)$.

21. Show that $m(X \cup Y \cup Z) \leq m(X) + m(Y) + m(Z)$.
22. Translate the result of Exercise 18 into a result concerning three statements p, q, and r.
23. Suppose $\Pr[p \wedge q] = \Pr[p \wedge r] = \Pr[q \cap r] = 0$ and $\Pr[p \vee q \vee r] = 1$. What can be said about the statements p, q, and r?
24. Suppose a card is drawn from a deck of playing cards. Let p be the statements "The card is an honor card. [i.e., an ace, king, queen, jack, or ten]" let q be the statement "The card is a spade," and let r be the statement "The card is either a heart or the king of clubs." Then $\Pr[p] = \frac{5}{13}$, $\Pr[q] = \frac{1}{4}$, $\Pr[r] = \frac{7}{26}$, $\Pr[p \wedge q] = \frac{5}{52}$, and $\Pr[p \wedge r] = \frac{3}{26}$. Find $\Pr[p \vee q \vee r]$. What is the probability that the card is neither a spade, a heart, nor an honor card?
25. The following is an alternative proof of property (C′) of the text. Give a reason for each step.
    (a) $X \cup Y = (X \cap \tilde{Y}) \cup (X \cap Y) \cup (Y \cap \tilde{X})$.
    (b) $m(X \cup Y) = m(X \cap \tilde{Y}) + m(X \cap Y) + m(\tilde{X} \cap Y)$.
    (c) $m(X \cup Y) = m(X) + m(Y) - m(X \cap Y)$.
26. Two women, A and B, go out to lunch. If the probability that A's check is exactly $3 is .25, the probability that B's check is exactly $3 is .35, and the probability that the larger of the two checks is exactly $3 is .05, what is the probability that the smaller check is exactly $3? [*Hint*: Enumerate the logical possibilities for the checks, and see which ones correspond to the quantities given above.]   [*Ans.* .55.]

3 THE EQUIPROBABLE MEASURE

We have already seen several examples where it was natural to assign the same weight to all possibilities in determining the appropriate probability measure. The probability measure determined in this manner is called the *equiprobable measure*. The measure of sets in the case of the equiprobable measure has a very simple form. In fact, if $\mathcal{U}$ has n elements and if the equiprobable measure has been assigned, then for any set X, $m(X)$ is r/n, where r is the number of elements in the set X. This is true since the weight of each element in X is $1/n$, and hence the sum of the weights of elements of X is r/n.

The particularly simple form of the equiprobable measure makes it easy to work with. In view of this, it is important to observe that a particular choice for the set of possibilities in a given situation may lead to the equiprobable measure, while some other choice will not. For example, consider the case of two throws of an ordinary coin. Suppose that we are interested in statements about the number of heads which occur. If we take for the possibility set the set $\mathcal{U} = \{HH, HT, TH, TT\}$ then it is reasonable to assign the same weight to each outcome, and we are led to the equiprobable measure. If, on the other hand, we were to take as possible outcomes the set $\mathcal{U} = \{no\ H, one\ H, two\ H\}$, it would not be natural to assign the same weight to each outcome, since one head can occur in two different ways, while each of the other possibilities can occur in only one way.

EXAMPLE 1   Suppose that we throw two ordinary dice. Each die can turn up a number from 1 to 6; hence there are $6 \cdot 6$ possibilities. We assign weight $\frac{1}{36}$ to each possibility. A prediction that is true in j cases will then have probability $j/36$. For example, "The sum of the dice is 5" will be true if we get $1 + 4$, $2 + 3, 3 + 2$, or $4 + 1$, that is, the sum can be 5 in four different ways. Hence the probability that the sum of the dice is 5 is $\frac{4}{36} = \frac{1}{9}$. The sum can be 12 in only one way, $6 + 6$. Hence the probability that the sum is 12 is $\frac{1}{36}$.

EXAMPLE 2   Suppose that two cards are drawn successively from a deck of cards. What is the probability that both are hearts? There are 52 possibilities for the first card, and for each of these there are 51 possibilities for the second. Hence there are $52 \cdot 51$ possibilities for the result of the two draws. We assign the equiprobable measure. The statement "The two cards are hearts" is true in $13 \cdot 12$ of the $52 \cdot 51$ possibilities. Hence the probability of this statement is $13 \cdot 12/52 \cdot 51 = \frac{1}{17}$.

EXAMPLE 3   Assume that, on the basis of a predictive index applied to students A, B, and C when entering college, it is predicted that after four years of college the scholastic record of A will be the highest, C the second highest, and B the lowest of the three. Suppose, in fact, that these predictions turn out to be exactly correct. If the predictive index has no merit at all and hence the predictions amount simply to guessing, what is the probability that such a prediction will be correct? There are $3! = 6$ orders in which the men might finish. If the predictions were really just guessing, then we would assign an equal weight to each of the six outcomes. In this case the probability is reasonably large, we would hesitate to conclude that the predictive index is in fact useful on the basis of this one experiment. Suppose, on the other hand, it predicted the order of six men correctly. Then a similar analysis would show that, by guessing, the probability is $1/6! = 1/720$ that such a prediction would be correct. Hence, we might conclude here that there is strong evidence that the index has some merit.

EXERCISES

1. A letter is chosen at random from the word "probability." What is the probability that it is a b? That it is a vowel?   [*Ans.* $\frac{2}{11}$; $\frac{4}{11}$.]
2. A card is drawn at random from a deck of playing cards.
    (a) What is the probability that it is either a heart or a king but not both?   [*Ans.* $\frac{15}{52}$.]
    (b) What is the probability that it is an honor card (ten, jack, queen, king, ace) and either a club or a spade?

3. An office building with ten floors has a broken elevator which lets people off at random floors. If a man starting on the first floor wants to go to the fourth floor,

    (a)   What is the probability that he ends up on the floor he wants?

    [*Ans.* $\frac{1}{10}$.]

    (b)   What is the probability that he ends up no closer to the fourth floor than when he started?

4. A word is chosen at random from the set of words $\mathcal{U} = \{$men, bird, ball, field, book$\}$. Let $p, q,$ and r be the statements:

    p: The word has two vowels.
    q: The first letter of the word is *b*.
    r: The word rhymes with cook.

    Find the probability of the following statements:

    (a) p.
    (b) q.
    (c) r.
    (d) $p \lor q$.
    (e) $\sim(p \land q) \land r$.
    (f) $p \to q$.   [*Ans.* $\frac{4}{5}$.]
    (g) $\sim p \leftrightarrow q$.

5. A single die is thrown. Find the probability that

    (a)   An odd number turns up.
    (b)   The number which turns up is greater than two.
    (c)   A seven turns up.

6. A single die is thrown twice. What value for the sum of the two outcomes has the highest probability? What value or values of the sum has the lowest probability of occurring?

7. In Exercise 6, what value or values for the product of the two outcomes has the highest probability of occurring?

8. A certain college has 500 students and it is known that

    250 read French.
    200 read German.
    100 read Russian.
     55 read French and Russian.
     35 read German and Russian.
     60 read German and French.
     20 read all three languages.

    If a student is chosen at random from the school, what is the probability that the student

    (a)   Reads two and only two languages?   [*Ans.* $\frac{9}{50}$.]
    (b)   Reads at least one language?

9. The letters of the word "connect" are scrambled and placed in a random order.

(a) What is the probability that they still spell "connect"?

[*Ans.* $\frac{1}{1260}$.]

(b) What is the probability that they are arranged in alphabetical order?

[*Ans.* $\frac{1}{1260}$.]

(c) What is the probability that the first and last letters are the same?

[*Ans.* $\frac{2}{21}$.]

10. Suppose that three people enter a restaurant which has a row of six seats. If they choose their seats at random, what is the probability that they sit with no seats between them? What is the probability that none of them is sitting in a seat next to somebody else?

11. Find the probability that a bridge hand will have suits of

(a) 5, 4, 3, and 1 cards.

$$Ans. \quad \frac{4!\binom{13}{5}\binom{13}{4}\binom{13}{3}\binom{13}{1}}{\binom{52}{13}} \cong .129.$$

(b) 6, 4, 2, and 1 cards.   [*Ans.* .047.]

(c) 4, 4, 3, and 2 cards.   [*Ans.* .216.]

(d) 4, 3, 3, and 3 cards.   [*Ans.* .105.]

12. There are $\binom{52}{13} = 6.35 \times 10^{11}$ possible bridge hands. Find the probability that a bridge hand dealt at random will be all of one suit. Estimate roughly the number of bridge hands dealt in the entire country in a year. Is it likely that a hand of all one suit will occur sometime during the year in the United States?

13. If ten people are seated at a circular table, what are the probabilities that

(a) A particular pair of people are seated next to each other?

[*Ans.* $\frac{2}{9}$.]

(b) Three particular people are sitting together?

14. A contestant on a TV quiz show is shown four pieces of merchandise and is given a list of four prices. She wins the grand prize if she matches each piece of merchandise with its correct pricetag. Assume she knows little about the current prices and assigns the prices randomly.

(a) What is the probability that she wins the grand prize?

[*Ans.* $\frac{1}{24}$.]

(b) What is the probability that she prices none of the items correctly?

15. A room contains a group of n people who are wearing badges numbered from 1 to n. If two people are selected at random, what is the probability that the larger badge number is 4? Answer this problem assuming that $n = 3, 4, 5, 6$.   [*Ans.* $0; \frac{1}{2}; \frac{3}{10}; \frac{1}{5}$.]

16. Find the probability of obtaining each of the following poker hands. (A poker hand is a set of five cards chosen at random from a deck of 52 cards.)

(a) Royal flush (ten, jack, queen, king, ace in a single suit).

$$\left[Ans.\ \frac{4}{\binom{52}{5}} = .0000015. \right]$$

(b) Straight flush (five in a sequence in a single suit, but not a royal flush).

$$\left[Ans.\ \frac{(40 - 4)}{\binom{52}{5}} = .000014. \right]$$

(c) Four of a kind (four cards of the same face value).

$$\left[Ans.\ \frac{624}{\binom{52}{5}} = .00024. \right]$$

(d) Full house (one pair and one triple of the same face value).

$$\left[Ans.\ \frac{3744}{\binom{52}{5}} = .0014. \right]$$

(e) Flush (five cards in a single suit but not a straight or royal flush).

$$\left[Ans.\ \frac{(5148 - 40)}{\binom{52}{5}} = .0020. \right]$$

(f) Straight (five cards in a row, not all of the same suit).

$$\left[Ans.\ \frac{(10,240 - 40)}{\binom{52}{5}} = .0039. \right]$$

(g) Straight or better. [*Ans.* 0076.]

17. Find the probability of not having a pair in a hand of poker.

18. Find the probability of a "bust" hand in poker. (A hand is a "bust" if there is no pair and it is neither a straight nor a flush.)

[*Ans.* .5012.]

19. In a survey, 100,000 people were interviewed. It was found that 65,832 of them had checking accounts, 43,971 of them had at least one credit card, and 32,348 of them had neither. What is the probability that a person selected at random from this sample has both a checking account and a credit card?

20. A certain French professor announces that he will select three out of eight pages of text to put on an examination and that each student can choose one of these three pages to translate. What is the minimum number of pages that a student should prepare in order to be certain of being able to translate a page that he has studied?

Smith decides to study only five of the eight pages. What is the probability that one of these five pages will appear on the examination? What is the smallest number of pages that Smith can study and still have probability greater than $\frac{3}{4}$ of being able to translate one page?

*4 TWO NONINTUITIVE EXAMPLES

There are occasions in probability theory when one finds a problem for which the answer, based on probability theory, is not at all in agreement with one's intuition. It is usually possible to arrange a few wagers that will bring one's intuition into line with the mathematical theory. A particularly good example of this is provided by the matching birthdays problem.

Assume that we have a room with r people in it and we propose the bet that there are at least two people in the room having the same birthday, i.e., the same month and day of the year. We ask for the value of r which will make this a fair bet. Few people will be willing to bet even money on this wager unless there were at least 100 people in the room. Most people would suggest 150 as a reasonable number. However, we shall see that with 150 people the odds are approximately, 4,100,000,000,000,000, to 1 in favor of two people having the same birthday, and that one should be willing to bet even money with as few as 23 people in the room.

Let us first find the probability that in a room with r people, no two have the same birthday. There are 365 possibilities for each person's birthday (neglecting February 29). There are, then, 365^r possibilities for the birthdays of r people. We assume that all these possibilities are equally likely. To find the probability that no two have the same birthday we must find the number of possibilities for the birthdays which have *no* day represented twice. The first person can have any of 365 days for his birthday. For each of these, if the second person is to have a different birthday, there are only 364 possibilities for his birthday. For the third man, there are 363 possibilities if he is to have a different birthday than the first two, etc. Thus the probability that no two people have the same birthday in a group of r people is

$$q_r = \frac{365 \cdot 364 \cdot \ldots \cdot (365 - r + 1)}{365^r}.$$

The probability that at least two people have the same birthday is then $p_r = 1 - q_r$. In Figure 1 the values of p_r and the odds for a fair bet, $p_r : (1 - p_r)$, are given for several values of r.

We consider now a second problem in which intuition does not lead to the correct answer. A hat-check girl has checked n hats, but they have become hopelessly scrambled. She hands back the hats at random. What is the probability that at least one man gets his own hat? For this problem some people's intuition would lead them to guess that for a large number of hats this probability should be small, while others guess that it should be large. Few people guess that the probability is neither large nor small and essentially independent of the number of hats involved.

Let p_j be the statement "the jth man gets his own hat back." We wish to find $\Pr[p_1 \vee p_2 \vee \ldots \vee p_n]$. A probability of this form can be found from the inclusion-exclusion formula as follows. We first add all proba-

Number of people in the room	Probability of at least two with same birthday	Approximate odds for a fair bet
5	.027	
10	.117	
15	.253	
20	.411	70:100
21	.444	80:100
22	.476	91:100
23	.507	103:100
24	.538	117:100
25	.569	132:100
30	.706	241:100
40	.891	819:100
50	.970	33:1
60	.994	170:1
70		1,200:1
80		12,000:1
90		160,000:1
100		3,300,000:1
125		31,000,000,000:1
150		4,100,000,000,000,000:1

Figure 1

bilities of the form $\Pr[p_i]$, then subtract the sum of all probabilities of the form $\Pr[p_i \wedge p_j]$, then add the sum of all probabilities of the form $\Pr[p_i \wedge p_j \wedge p_k]$, etc. However, each of these probabilities represents the probability that a particular set of men get their own hats back. These probabilities are very easy to compute.

Let us find the probability that out of n men some particular m of them get back their own hats. There are $n!$ ways that the hats can be returned. If a particular m of them are to get their own hats there are only $(n - m)!$ ways that it can be done. Hence the probability that a particular m men get their own hats back is

$$\frac{(n - m)!}{n!}$$

There are $\binom{n}{m}$ different ways we can choose m men out of n. Hence the mth group of terms contributes

$$\binom{n}{m} \cdot \frac{(n - m)!}{n!} = \frac{1}{m!}$$

Number of hats	Probability p_n that at least one man gets his own hat
2	.500000
3	.666667
4	.625000
5	.633333
6	.631944
7	.632143
8	.632118

Figure 2

to the alternating sum. Thus

$$\Pr[p_1 \vee p_2 \vee \ldots \vee p_n] = 1 - \frac{1}{2!} + \frac{1}{3!} - \frac{1}{4!} \cdots \pm \frac{1}{n!},$$

where the $+$ sign is chosen if n is odd and the $-$ sign if n is even. In Figure 2, these numbers are given for the first few values of n.

It can be shown that, as the number of hats increases, the probabilities approach a number $1 - (1/e) = .632121 \ldots$, where the number $e = 2.71828 \ldots$ is a number that plays an important role in many branches of mathematics.

EXERCISES

1. What odds should you be willing to give on a bet that at least two of the presidents of the United States have had the same birthday? Would you win the bet?
   [*Ans.* More than 4:1. Yes, Polk and Harding were both born on November 2.]

2. What odds should you be willing to give on the bet that at least two of the presidents of the United States have died on the same day of the year? Would you win the bet?
   [*Ans.* More than 2.7:1. Yes; Jefferson, Adams and Monroe all died on July 4.]

3. What odds should you be willing to give on a bet that at least two people in the United States Senate have the same birthday?

4. What is the probability that at least two members of the House of Representatives have the same birthday?

5. Find the probability that, in a group of r people, at least one pair has the same birthmonth. How large does r have to be for this probability to be greater than $\frac{1}{2}$? (Assume that the probability of being born in any month is the same.)

6. Show that the probability that, in a group of r people, *exactly* one pair

has the same birthday is

$$t_r = \binom{r}{2} \frac{365 \cdot 364 \cdot \ldots \cdot (365 - r + 2)}{365^r}.$$

7. Show that $t_r = \binom{r}{2} \dfrac{q_r}{366 - r}$, where t_r is defined in Exercise 6 and q_r is the probability that no pair has the same birthday.

8. Find a formula for the probability of having more than one coincidence of birthdays among r people, i.e., of having at least two pairs of identical birthdays, or of three or more people having the same birthday. [*Hint:* Express the answer in terms of t_r.]

9. Is it very surprising that there was more than one coincidence of the dates on which presidents died (see Exercise 2)?

10. A contest requires entrants to match the stage names of four movie stars with their real names. Assuming a contestant guesses at random, what is his probability of getting none right? Of getting exactly four right? Exactly three? Two? One?

11. In how many ways can 8 rooks be placed on a chessboard so that none can attack any of the others? What is the probability that, in such an arrangement of rooks, the black diagonal has no rooks on it? (Do not carry out the arithmetical details.) Would the probability change if we used 16 rooks and a 16×16 chess board?

12. A teacher has her class of 75 students correct their own homework. She collects the papers, shuffles them, and passes one to each student. What is the approximate probability that no student receives his own paper back?

13. The clubs are removed from a deck of playing cards, shuffled, and dealt face up on a table. The position of each of the thirteen cards is noted, and then they are picked up, shuffled, and again dealt face up on the table. What is the approximate probability that no card occupies the same position in both deals?

14. The integers 1, 2, and 3 are written down in an arbitrary order. What is the probability that no two adjacent integers are consecutive (i.e., that the patterns 12 and 23 do not occur)? Do the problem for 1, 2, 3, and 4.

5 CONDITIONAL PROBABILITY

Suppose that we have a given $\mathfrak{U}$ and that measures have been assigned to all subsets of $\mathfrak{U}$. A statement p will have probability $\Pr[p] = m(P)$. Suppose we now receive some additional information, say that statement q is true. How does this additional information alter the probability of p?

EXAMPLE 1 Suppose we throw an ordinary die, and we are interested in statement p, "A 3 turns up." By our usual analysis the probability of this statement is

$\frac{1}{6}$. Suppose now that someone looks at the die and tells us statement q, "An odd number turned up." How does knowing q change our probability for statement p? Clearly the possibility set has been reduced from $\{1, 2, 3, 4, 5, 6\}$ to $\{1, 3, 5\}$. Assigning equal weights to the new set gives the new probability that a 3 turns up as $\frac{1}{3}$.

The probability of p after the receipt of the information q is called its *conditional probability,* and it is denoted by $\Pr[p|q]$, which is read "the probability of p given q." In this section we shall construct a method of finding this conditional probability in terms of the measure m.

If we know that q is true, then the original possibility set $\mathfrak{U}$ has been reduced to Q and therefore we must define our measure on the subsets of Q instead of on the subsets of $\mathfrak{U}$. Of course, every subset X of Q is a subset of $\mathfrak{U}$, and hence we know $m(X)$, its measure before q was discovered. Since q cuts down on the number of possibilities, its new measure $m'(X)$ should be larger.

The basic idea on which the definition of m' is based is that, while we know that the possibility set has been reduced to Q, we have no new information about subsets of Q. If X and Y are subsets of Q, and $m(X) = 2 \cdot m(Y)$, then we will want $m'(X) = 2 \cdot m'(Y)$. This will be the case if the measures of subsets of Q are simply increased by a proportionality factor $m'(X) = k \cdot m(X)$, and all that remains is to determine k. Since we know that $1 = m'(Q) = k \cdot m(Q)$, we see that $k = l/m(Q)$ and our new measure on subsets of $\mathfrak{U}$ is determined by the formula

$$(1) \qquad\qquad m'(X) = \frac{m(X)}{m(Q)}.$$

How does this affect the probability of p? First of all, the truth set of p has been reduced. Because all elements of $\tilde{Q}$ have been eliminated, the new truth set of p is $P \cap Q$ and therefore

$$(2) \qquad \Pr[p|q] = m'(P \cap Q) = \frac{m(P \cap Q)}{m(Q)} = \frac{\Pr[p \wedge q]}{\Pr[q]}.$$

Note that if the original measure m is the equiprobable measure, then the new measure m' will also be the equiprobable measure on the set Q.

We must take care that the denominators in (1) and (2) be different from zero. Observe that $m(Q)$ will be zero if Q is the empty set, which happens only if q is self-contradictory. This is also the only case in which $\Pr[q] = 0$, and hence we make the obvious assumption that our information q is not self-contradictory.

EXAMPLE 2   In an election, candidate A has .4 chance of winning, B has .3 chance, C has .2 chance, and D has .1 chance. Just before the election, C withdraws. Now what are the chances of the other three candidates? Let q be the statement that C will not win, i.e., that A or B or D will win. Observe that $\Pr[q] = .8$, hence all the other probabilities are increased by a factor of $1/.8 = 1.25$. Candidate A now has .5 chance of winning, B has .375, and D has .125.

EXAMPLE 3 A family is chosen at random from the set of all families having exactly two children (not twins). What is the probability that the family has two boys, if it is known that there is a boy in the family? Without any information being given, we would assign the equiprobable measure on the set $\mathcal{U} = \{BB, BG, GB, GG\}$, where the first letter of the pair indicates the sex of the older child and the second that of the younger. The information that there is a boy causes $\mathcal{U}$ to change to $\{BB, BG, GB\}$, but the new measure is still the equiprobable measure. Thus the conditional probability that there are two boys given that there is a boy is $\frac{1}{3}$. If, on the other hand, we know that the first child is a boy, then the possibilities are reduced to $\{BB, BG\}$ and the conditional probability is $\frac{1}{2}$.

A particularly interesting case of conditional probability is that in which $\Pr[p|q] = \Pr[p]$. That is, the information that q is true has no effect on our prediction for p. If this is the case, we note that

$$(3) \qquad\qquad \Pr[p \wedge q] = \Pr[p]\Pr[q].$$

And the case $\Pr[q|p] = \Pr[q]$ leads to the same equation. Whenever equation (3) holds, we say that p and q are *independent*. Thus if q is not a self-contradiction, p and q are independent if and only if $\Pr[p|q] = \Pr[p]$.

EXAMPLE 4 Consider three throws of an ordinary coin, where we consider the eight possibilities to be equally likely. Let p be the statement "A head turns up on the first throw" and q be the statement "A tail turns up on the second throw." Then $\Pr[p] = \Pr[q] = \frac{1}{2}$ and $\Pr[p \wedge q] = \frac{1}{4}$ and therefore p and q are independent statements.

While we have an intuitive notion of independence, it can happen that two statements that may not seem to be independent are in fact independent. For example, let r be the statement "The same side turns up all three times." Let s be the statement "At most one head occurs." Then r and s are independent statements (see Exercise 10).

An important use of conditional probabilities arises in the following manner. A set of statements $q_1, q_2, \ldots, q_n$ is said to be a *complete set of alternatives* if one and only one statement can be true. We wish to find the probability of a statement p, given a complete set of alternatives $q_1, q_2, \ldots, q_n$ such that the probability $\Pr[q_i]$ as well as the conditional probabilities $\Pr[p|q_i]$ can be found for every i. Then in terms of these we can find $\Pr[p]$ by

$$\Pr[p] = \Pr[q_1]\Pr[p|q_1] + \Pr[q_2]\Pr[p|q_2] + \ldots + \Pr[q_n]\Pr[p|q_n].$$

The proof of this assertion is left as an exercise (see Exercise 13).

EXAMPLE 5   A psychology student once studied the way mathematicians solve problems and contended that at times they try too hard to look for symmetry in a problem. To illustrate this she asked a number of mathematicians the following problem: Fifty balls (25 white and 25 black) are to be put in two urns, not necessarily the same number of balls in each. How should the balls be placed in the urns so as to maximize the chance of drawing a black ball, if an urn is chosen at random and a ball drawn from this urn? A quite surprising number of mathematicians answered that you could not do any better than $\frac{1}{2}$, by the symmetry of the problem. In fact one can do a good deal better by putting one black ball in urn 1, and all the 49 other balls in urn 2. To find the probability in this case let p be the statement "A black ball is drawn," q_1 the statement "Urn 1 is drawn" and q_2 the statement "Urn 2 is drawn." Then q_1 and q_2 are a complete set of alternatives, so

$$\Pr[p] = \Pr[q_1]\Pr[p|q_1] + \Pr[q_2]\Pr[p|q_2].$$

But $\Pr[q_1] = \Pr[q_2] = \frac{1}{2}$ and $\Pr[p|q_1] = 1$, $\Pr[p|q_2] = \frac{24}{49}$. Thus

$$\Pr[p] = \frac{1}{2} \cdot 1 + \frac{1}{2} \cdot \frac{24}{49} = \frac{73}{98} \approx .745.$$

When told the answer, a number of the mathematicians that had said $\frac{1}{2}$ replied that they thought there had to be the same number of balls in each urn. However, since this had been carefully stated not to be necessary, they also had fallen into the trap of assuming too much symmetry.

EXERCISES

1. A card is drawn at random from a pack of playing cards. What is the probability that it is a 6 or a king, given that it is between 5 and 9 inclusive?

2. A die is loaded in such a way that the probability of a given number turning up is proportional to that number (e.g., a six is 3 times as likely to turn up as a two).
   (a) What is the probability of rolling an odd number, given that a six does not turn up?   [*Ans.* $\frac{3}{5}$.]
   (b) What is the probability of rolling a six, given that an even number turns up?   [*Ans.* $\frac{1}{2}$.]

3. Suppose we arrange the letters of the word "random" in a random order.
   (a) Find the probability that the letters are in alphabetical order given that the new arrangement begins with a and ends with r.
                                                                      [*Ans.* $\frac{1}{24}$.]
   (b) Which is greater, the probability that the two vowels are not together or the probability that the two vowels are not together and the new arrangement begins with d?

4. Referring to Exercise 8 in Section 3, what is the probability that the man selected studies German if
   (a) He studies French?

(b) He studies French and Russian?

(c) He studies neither French nor Russian?

5. A student takes a five-question true-false exam. What is the probability that he will get all answers correct if

(a) He is only guessing?

(b) He knows that the instructor puts more true than false questions on his exams?

(c) He knows, in addition to (b), that the instructor never puts three questions in a row with the same answer?

(d) He knows, in addition to (b) and (c), that the first and last questions must have the opposite answer?

(e) He knows, in addition to (b), (c), and (d), that the answer to the second problem is "false"?

6. A die is thrown twice. What is the probability that the sum of the faces which turn up is 7, 8, or 9, given that one of them is a 4? Given that the first throw is a 4? [*Ans.* $\frac{5}{11}$; $\frac{1}{2}$.]

7. If $\Pr[q] = \frac{2}{5}$ and $\Pr[\sim p | \sim q] = \frac{1}{3}$, find $\Pr[p \lor q]$. [*Ans.* $\frac{4}{5}$.]

8. A certain motorist knows that before he reaches his destination the road forks four times, giving 16 possible paths. However, he does not remember which way he should turn at each of the forks. He decides that at each fork he will pick randomly which direction to go; thus each of the 16 possible patterns is equally likely. Unfortunately, after the four turns he realizes that he is in the wrong place.

(a) What is the probability that he made a wrong turn at the first fork?

(b) Given that he made the correct first turn, what is the probability that his second turn was incorrect? [*Ans.* $\frac{4}{7}$.]

(c) Given that he made at least two correct turns, what is the probability that his first turn was correct?

9. Three persons, A, B, and C, are placed at random in a straight line. Let r be the statement "B is on the left" and let s be the statement "C is on the right."

(a) What is $\Pr[r \land s]$?

(b) Are r and s independent? [*Ans.* No.]

10. Prove that statements r and s in Example 4 are independent.

11. Let a deck of cards consist of the jacks and queens chosen from a bridge deck, and let two cards be drawn from the new deck. Find

(a) The probability that the cards are both jacks, given that one is a jack. [*Ans.* $\frac{3}{11} = .27$.]

(b) The probability that the cards are both jacks, given that one is a red jack. [*Ans.* $\frac{5}{13} = .38$.]

(c) The probability that the cards are both jacks, given that one is the jack of hearts. [*Ans.* $\frac{3}{7} = .43$.]

12. Which is greater, $\Pr[$a bridge hand contains 4 aces $|$ it contains 1 ace$]$ or $\Pr[$a bridge hand contains 4 aces $|$ it contains the ace of spades$]$?

13. Let p be any statement and q_1, q_2, q_3 be a complete set of alternatives.

Prove that

$$\Pr[p] = \Pr[q_1]\Pr[p|q_1] + \Pr[q_2]\Pr[p|q_2] + \Pr[q_3]\Pr[p|q_3].$$

14. The following example shows that r may be independent of p and q without being independent of $p \wedge q$ and $p \vee q$. We throw a coin twice. Let p be "The first toss comes out heads," q be "The second toss comes out heads," and r be "The two tosses come out different." Compute $\Pr[r]$, $\Pr[r|p]$, $\Pr[r|q]$, $\Pr[r|p \wedge q]$, $\Pr[r|p \vee q]$.   [*Ans.* $\frac{1}{2}, \frac{1}{2}, \frac{1}{2}, 0, \frac{2}{3}$.]

15. Assume that p and q are independent statements relative to a given measure. Prove that each of the following pairs of statements are independent relative to this same measure.
    (a) p and $\sim q$.
    (b) $\sim q$ and p.
    (c) $\sim p$ and $\sim q$.

16. Prove that for any three statements p, q and r,

$$\Pr[p \wedge q \wedge r] = \Pr[p] \cdot \Pr[q|p] \cdot \Pr[r|p \wedge q].$$

17. **(a)** What is true about $\Pr[p|q]$ and $\Pr[q|p]$ if p and q are inconsistent?
    (b) Under what other circumstances will it be true that $\Pr[p|q] = \Pr[q|p]$?

18. A card is drawn at random from a deck of playing cards. Are the following pairs of statements independent?
    (a) p: A jack is drawn.
          q: A black card is drawn.
    (b) p: A black jack, queen, or king is drawn.
          q: A spade which is not a 2, 3, or 4 is drawn.

19. A multiple-choice-test question lists four alternative answers, of which just one is correct. If a student has done his homework, then he is certain to identify the correct answer; otherwise he chooses an answer at random. Let p be the statement "A student does his homework" and q the statement "He answers the question correctly." Let $\Pr[p] = a$.
    (a) Find a formula for $\Pr[p|q]$ in terms of a.
    (b) Show that $\Pr[p|q] \geq \Pr[p]$ for all values of a. When does the equality hold?

20. A simple genetic model for the color of a person's eyes is the following: There are two kinds of color-determining genes, B and b, and each person has two color-determining genes. If both are b, he has blue eyes; otherwise he has brown eyes. Assume that one-quarter of the people have two B genes, one-quarter of the people have two b genes, and the rest have one B gene and one b gene.
    (a) If a man has brown eyes, what is the probability that he has two B genes?
    Assume that a man has brown eyes and that his wife has brown eyes. A child born to this couple will get one gene from the man and one

from his wife, the selection in each case being a random selection from the parent's two genes.

(b) What is the probability that the child will have blue eyes?

(c) If the child has brown eyes, what is the probability that both of the parents have two B genes? [*Ans.* $\frac{1}{8}$.]

21. Two unfair coins, labeled A and B, are tossed. If Pr [A and B come up heads] $= \frac{1}{8}$ and Pr [A and B come up heads | at least one of them comes up heads] $= \frac{3}{14}$, find Pr [A comes up heads] and Pr [B comes up heads]. Assume that A has the greater probability of coming up heads and that the statements "A comes up heads" and "B comes up heads" are independent.

22. Three red, three green, and three blue balls are to be put into three urns, with at least two balls in each urn. Then an urn is selected at random and two balls withdrawn.

(a) How should the balls be put in the urns in order to maximize the probability of drawing two balls of different color? What is the probability? [*Partial Ans.* 1.]

(b) How should the balls be put in the urns in order to maximize the probability of withdrawing a red and a green ball? What is the maximum probability? [*Partial Ans.* $\frac{7}{10}$.]

23. A man who is extremely worried about having the plane in which he is flying blown up nevertheless always carries a bomb with him when he flies, because he has read that the probability of *two* people on the same plane having bombs is very low. Is his reasoning correct?

6 FINITE STOCHASTIC PROCESSES

We consider here a very general situation which we shall specialize in later sections. We deal with a sequence of experiments where the outcome on each particular experiment depends on some chance element. Any such sequence is called a *stochastic process*. (The Greek word *stochos* means "guess.") We shall assume a finite number of experiments and a finite number of possibilities for each experiment. We assume that, if all the outcomes of the experiments which precede a given experiment were known, then both the possibilities for this experiment and the probability that any particular possibility will occur would be known. We wish to make predictions about the process as a whole. For example, in the case of repeated throws of an ordinary coin we would assume that on any particular experiment we have two outcomes, and the probabilities for each of these outcomes is one-half regardless of any other outcomes. We might be interested, however, in the probabilities of statements of the form, "More than two-thirds of the throws result in heads," or "The number of heads and tails which occur is the same," etc. These are questions which can be answered only when a probability measure has been assigned to the process as a whole. In this section we show how probability measure can be assigned, using the given information. In the case of coin tossing, the probabilities

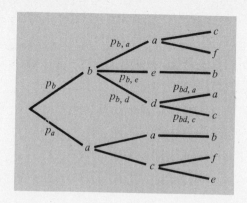

Figure 3

(hence also the possibilities) on any given experiment do not depend upon the previous results. We shall not make any such restriction here since the assumption is not true in general.

We shall show how the probability measure is constructed for a particular example, and the procedure in the general case is similar.

We assume that we have a sequence of three experiments, the possibilities for which are indicated in Figure 3. The set of all possible outcomes which might occur on any of the experiments is represented by the set $\{a, b, c, d, e, f\}$. Note that if we know that outcome b occurred on the first experiment, then we know that the possibilities on experiment two are $\{a, e, d\}$. Similarly, if we know that b occurred on the first experiment and a on the second, then the only possibilities for the third are $\{c, f\}$. We denote by p_a the probability that the first experiment results in outcome a, and by p_b the probability that outcome b occurs in the first experiment. We denote by $p_{b,d}$ the probability that outcome d occurs on the second experiment, which is the probability computed on the assumption that outcome b occurred on the first experiment. Similarly for $p_{b,a}, p_{b,e}, p_{a,a}, p_{a,c}$. We denote by $p_{bd,c}$ the probability that outcome c occurs on the third experiment, the latter probability being computed on the assumption that outcome b occurred on the first experiment and d on the second. Similarly for $p_{ba,c}, p_{ba,f}$, etc. We have assumed that these numbers are given and the fact that they are probabilities assigned to possible outcomes would mean that they are positive and that

$$p_a + p_b = 1, \quad p_{b,a} + p_{b,e} + p_{b,d} = 1, \quad \text{and} \quad p_{bd,a} + p_{bd,c} = 1, \text{ etc.}$$

It is convenient to associate each probability with the branch of the tree that connects the branch point representing the predicted outcome. We have done this in Figure 3 for several branches. The sum of the numbers assigned to branches from a particular branch point is one, e.g.,

$$p_{b,a} + p_{b,e} + p_{b,d} = 1.$$

A possibility for the sequence of three experiments is indicated by a path through the tree. We define now a probability measure on the set of all paths. We call this a *tree measure*. To the path corresponding to outcome b on the first experiment, d on the second, and c on the third, we assign the weight $p_b \cdot p_{b,d} \cdot p_{bd,c}$. That is the *product* of the probabilities associated with each branch along the path being considered. We find the probability for each path through the tree.

Before showing the reason for this choice, we must first show that it determines a probability measure—in other words, that the weights are positive and the sum of the weights is one. The weights are products of positive numbers and hence positive. To see that their sum is one we first find the sum of the weights of all paths corresponding to a particular outcome, say b, on the first experiment and a particular outcome, say d, on the second. We have

$$p_b \cdot p_{b,d} \cdot p_{bd,a} + p_b \cdot p_{b,d} \cdot p_{bd,c} = p_b \cdot p_{b,d}[p_{bd,a} + p_{bd,c}] = p_b \cdot p_{b,d}.$$

For any other first two outcomes we would obtain a similar result. For example, the sum of the weights assigned to paths corresponding to outcome a on the first experiment and c on the second is $p_a \cdot p_{a,c}$. Notice that when we have verified that we have a probability measure, this will be the probability that the first outcome results in a and the second experiment results in c.

Next we find the sum of the weights assigned to all the paths corresponding to the cases where the outcome of the first experiment is b. We find this by adding the sums corresponding to the different possibilities for the second experiment. But by our preceding calculation this is

$$p_b \cdot p_{b,a} + p_b \cdot p_{b,e} + p_b \cdot p_{b,d} = p_b [p_{b,a} + p_{b,e} + p_{b,d}] = p_b.$$

Similary, the sum of the weights assigned to paths corresponding to the outcome a on the first experiment is p_a. Thus the sum of all weights is $p_a + p_b = 1$. Therefore we do have a probability measure. Note that we have also shown that the probability that the outcome of the first experiment is a has been assigned probability p_a in agreement with our given probability.

To see the complete connection of our new measure with the given probabilities, let $X_j = z$ be the statement "The outcome of the jth experiment was z." Then the statement $[X_1 = b \wedge X_2 = d \wedge X_3 = c]$ is a compound statement that has been assigned probability $p_b \cdot p_{b,d} \cdot p_{bd,c}$. The statement $[X_1 = b \wedge X_2 = d]$ we have noted has been assigned probability $p_b \cdot p_{b,d}$ and the statement $[X_1 = b]$ has been assigned probability p_b. Thus

$$\Pr[X_3 = c \,|\, X_2 = d \wedge X_1 = b] = \frac{p_b \cdot p_{b,d} \cdot p_{bd,c}}{p_b \cdot p_{b,d}} = p_{bd,c}$$

$$\Pr[X_2 = d \,|\, X_1 = b] = \frac{p_b \cdot p_{b,d}}{p_b} = p_{b,d}.$$

Thus we see that our probabilities, computed under the assumption that previous results were known, become the corresponding conditional probabilities when computed with respect to the tree measure. It can be shown that the tree measure which we have assigned is the only one which will lead to this agreement. We can now find the probability of any statement concerning the stochastic process from our tree measure.

EXAMPLE 1   Suppose that we have two urns. Urn 1 contains two black balls and three white balls. Urn 2 contains two black balls and one white ball. An urn is chosen at random and a ball chosen from this urn at random. What is the probability that a white ball is chosen? A hasty answer might be $\frac{1}{2}$, since there are an equal number of black and white balls involved and everything is done at random. However, it is hasty answers like this (which is wrong) which show the need for a more careful analysis.

We are considering two experiments. The first consists in choosing the urn and the second in choosing the ball. There are two possibilities for the first experiment, and we assign $p_1 = p_2 = \frac{1}{2}$ for the probabilities of choosing the first and the second urn, respectively. We then assign $p_{1,W} = \frac{3}{5}$ for the probability that a white ball is chosen, under the assumption that urn 1 is chosen. Similarly we assign $p_{1,B} = \frac{2}{5}, p_{2,W} = \frac{1}{3}, p_{2,B} = \frac{2}{3}$. We indicate these probabilities on the possibility tree in Figure 4. The probability that a white

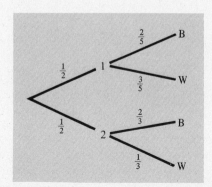

Figure 4

ball is drawn is then found from the tree measure as the sum of the weights assigned to paths which lead to a choice of a white ball. This is $\frac{1}{2} \cdot \frac{3}{5} + \frac{1}{2} \cdot \frac{1}{3} = \frac{7}{15}$.

EXAMPLE 2   Suppose that a man leaves a bar which is on a corner which he knows to be one block from his home. He is unable to remember which street leads to his home. He proceeds to try each of the streets at random without ever choosing the same street twice until he goes on the one which leads to his home. What possibilities are there for his trip home, and what is the probability for each of these possible trips? We label the streets A, B, C, and Home. The possibilities together with typical probabilities are given in Figure 5. The probability for any particular trip, or path, is found by taking the product of the branch probabilities.

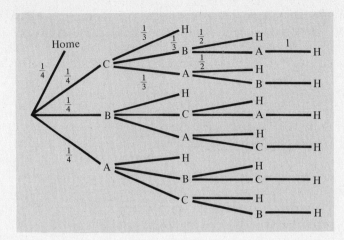

Figure 5

EXAMPLE 3 Assume that you are presented with two slot machines, A and B. Each machine pays the same fixed amount when it pays off. Machine A pays off each time with probability $\frac{1}{2}$, and machine B with probability $\frac{1}{4}$. You are not told which machine is A. Suppose that you choose a machine at random and win. What is the probability that you chose machine A? We first construct the tree (Figure 6) to show the possibilities and assign branch

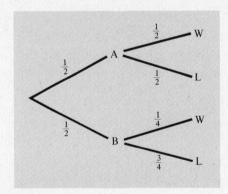

Figure 6

probabilities to determine a tree measure. Let p be the statement "Machine A was chosen" and q be the statement "The machine chosen paid off." Then we are asked for

$$\Pr[p\,|\,q] = \frac{\Pr[p \wedge q]}{\Pr[q]}.$$

The truth set of the statement $p \wedge q$ consists of a single path which has been assigned weight $\frac{1}{4}$. The truth set of the statement q consists of two paths, and the sum of the weights of these paths is $\frac{1}{2} \cdot \frac{1}{2} + \frac{1}{2} \cdot \frac{1}{4} = \frac{3}{8}$.

Thus $\Pr[p|q] = \frac{2}{3}$. Thus if we win, it is more likely that we have machine A than B and this suggests that next time we should play the same machine. If we lose, however, it is more likely that we have machine B than A, and hence we would switch machines before the next play. (See Exercise 9.)

EXERCISES

1. Construct a tree measure to represent the possibilities for four throws of an ordinary coin. Assume that the probability of a head on any toss is $\frac{1}{2}$ regardless of any information about other throws.

2. Using the tree constructed in Exercise 1, find the probability of the following events:
   (a) Two heads and two tails occur. [*Ans.* $\frac{3}{8}$.]
   (b) The third toss is heads, given that the first two were tails.
   [*Ans.* $\frac{1}{2}$.]
   (c) The first and third tosses are the same, given that the second and third tosses are the same. [*Ans.* $\frac{1}{2}$.]

3. A man has found through long experience with a certain soda machine that after depositing his money he will receive a soda with probability .8, his money will be returned with probability .1, and the machine will take the money with probability .1. If his money is returned, he deposits it again. If the machine takes his money, he kicks it, so that when he deposits more money the possible outcomes and their probabilities are soda, .85; return, 0; and take money, .15. After the second try he gives up. Construct a tree measure to represent the possible outcomes of the man's encounter with the soda machine.

4. In Exercise 3 find the probability of the following events:
   (a) The man gets a soda.
   (b) The man loses some money.
   (c) The man gets a soda on his second try.
   (d) The man gets a soda, given that he tried twice.

5. A man wins a certain tournament if he can win two consecutive games out of three played alternately with two opponents A and B. A is a better player than B. The probability of winning a game when B is the opponent is $\frac{2}{3}$. The probability of winning a game when A is his opponent is only $\frac{1}{3}$. Construct a tree measure for the possibilities for three games, assuming that he plays alternately but plays A first. Do the same assuming that he plays B first. In each case find the probability that he will win two consecutive games. Is it better to play two games against the stronger player or against the weaker player?
   [*Ans.* $\frac{10}{27}$; $\frac{8}{27}$; better to play strong player twice.]

6. A manufacturing plant makes a certain part on two different machines. Of the parts made by machine A, 80 percent are good and 20 percent defective; machine B is older and produces good parts only 75 percent of the time. Construct a tree measure for the experiment of picking a machine at random, then choosing two pieces of its output and

inspecting them. What is the probability that both pieces are good? What is the probability that the pieces are good, given that they came from machine A? What is the probability that the pieces came from machine B, given that both are defective?

7. A cancer researcher has observed that 60 percent of young men begin to smoke cigarettes. Once someone begins to smoke, he quits with probability .25. Smokers develop lung cancer with probability .15, while one-time smokers who have quit get lung cancer with probability .1. Those men who have never smoked get lung cancer with probability .025. Construct a tree measure which illustrates this data. What is the probability that a man gets lung cancer? Given that he gets lung cancer, what is the probability that he once smoked cigarettes?

8. An urn contains three coins. One coin is fair, one falls heads with probability .6, and the other falls heads with probability .4. Construct a tree measure, and find the probability that a coin chosen from the urn at random and flipped will come up heads. Find the probability that the coin chosen was the fair one, given that it came up tails.
    [*Ans.* $\frac{1}{2}$; $\frac{1}{3}$.]

9. In Example 3, assume that the player makes two plays. Find the probability that he wins at least once under the assumption that
    (a) He plays the same machine twice.   [*Ans.* $\frac{19}{32}$.]
    (b) He plays the same machine the second time if and only if he won the first time.   [*Ans.* $\frac{20}{32}$.]

10. An urn initially contains two red and two blue balls. A ball is drawn from the urn, and it and two more balls of the same color are replaced in the urn. This process is carried out again, and finally a single ball is drawn. Construct a tree measure for the possible outcomes of the experiment. What is the probability that all three balls drawn are of the same color? What is the probability that the third ball is blue, given that the first two are red? What is the probability that the first two balls have the same color?   [*Partial Ans.* $\frac{1}{2}$.]

11. A chess player plays three successive games of chess. His psychological makeup is such that the probability of his winning a given game is $(\frac{1}{2})^{k+1}$, where k is the number of games he has won so far. (For instance, the probability of his winning the first game is $\frac{1}{2}$, the probability of his winning the second game *if he has already won the first game* is $\frac{1}{4}$, etc.) What is the probability that he will win at least two of the three games.   [*Ans.* $\frac{9}{32}$.]

12. Two defective lightbulbs have become mixed with three good bulbs. The bulbs are chosen one by one and tested until it is discovered which bulbs are defective. What is the least possible number of draws necessary? What is the greatest possible number of draws necessary? What is the probability that at most three draws are needed? Exactly three draws? Given that four draws are needed, what is the probability that the second and fourth bulbs are defective?

13. A composer of aleatory (random) music writes his works in three-note

sections. The first note of each section is randomly chosen from A, C, and F. If the first note is A, the second is F with probability $\frac{1}{2}$ and B with probability $\frac{1}{2}$. If the first note is C, the second is B with probability $\frac{1}{4}$ and D with probability $\frac{3}{4}$. If the first note is F, the second is E with probability $\frac{1}{3}$ and A with probability $\frac{2}{3}$. The third note is the same as the first with probability $\frac{3}{8}$ and is one note higher than the first with probability $\frac{5}{8}$ (ignore sharps and flats). What is the probability that a given 3-note section contains a B? What is the probability that it contains a B, given that it contains no note twice? (Musical notes are arranged in ascending alphabetical order; thus B is one note higher than A, etc.)

14. Before a political convention, a political expert has assigned the following probabilities. The probability that the President will be willing to run again is $\frac{1}{2}$. If he is willing to run, he and his Vice-President are sure to be nominated and have probability $\frac{3}{5}$ of being elected again. If the President does not run, the present Vice-President has probability $\frac{1}{10}$ of being nominated, and any other presidential candidate has probability $\frac{1}{2}$ of being elected. What is the probability that the present Vice-President will be re-elected as either Vice-President or President?

[*Ans.* $\frac{13}{40}$.]

15. A and B, finalists in a table tennis tournament, agree to play a best-of-three series for the championship. A has probability .6 of winning each game. What is the probability that A wins the championship? What is the probability that exactly three games are needed? What is the probability that the player who wins the first game goes on to win the championship?

16. In a room there are three chests, each chest contains two drawers, and each drawer contains one coin. In one chest each drawer contains a gold coin; in the second chest each drawer contains a silver coin; and in the last chest one drawer contains a gold coin and the other contains a silver coin. A chest is picked at random and then a drawer is picked at random from that chest. When the drawer is opened, it is found to contain a gold coin. What is the probability that the other drawer of that same chest will also contain a gold coin?   [*Ans.* $\frac{2}{3}$.]

17. Four slips of paper, marked with the integers 1 through 4, are placed in a hat. What is the probability that the numbers on two slips drawn at random from the hat are in ascending (not necessarily consecutive) order?

18. A survey revealed that 75 percent of all mathematicians are eldest sons. Given that 90 percent of mathematicians are male, and the average family has three children, are the results surprising? (Assume that male and female children are equally likely.)

19. A student claims to be able to distinguish beer from ale. He is given a series of three tests. In each test he is given two glasses of beer and one of ale and asked to pick out the ale. If he gets two or more correct we shall admit his claim. Draw a tree to represent the possibilities

(either he guesses right or he guesses wrong) for his answers. Construct the tree measure corresponding to his guessing and find the probability that his claim will be established if he guesses on every trial.

20. Urn A contains two red balls and one black ball; urn B contains one ball of each color. An urn is selected at random and a ball drawn from it. If the ball is black, it is returned to the urn; if it is red, it is placed in the other urn. Then another ball is drawn, this one from the other urn. Find the probability that the second ball drawn is black. What is the probability that both balls are the same color? Given that both balls drawn are red, what is the probability that the first urn chosen was A?

7 BAYES'S PROBABILITIES

The following situation often occurs. Measures have been assigned in a possibility space $\mathcal{U}$. A complete set of alternatives, $p_1, p_2, \ldots, p_n$ has been singled out. Their probabilities are determined by the assigned measure. (Recall that a complete set of alternatives is a set of statements such that for any possible outcome one and only one of the statements is true.) We are now given that a statement q is true. We wish to compute the new probabilities for the alternatives relative to this information. That is, we wish the conditional probabilities $\Pr[p_j|q]$ for each p_j. We shall give two different methods for obtaining these probabilities.

The first is by a general formula. We illustrate this formula for the case of four alternatives: p_1, p_2, p_3, p_4. Consider $\Pr[p_2|q]$. From the definition of conditional probability,

$$\Pr[p_2|q] = \frac{\Pr[p_2 \wedge q]}{\Pr[q]}.$$

But since p_1, p_2, p_3, p_4, are a complete set of alternatives,

$$\Pr[q] = \Pr[p_1 \wedge q] + \Pr[p_2 \wedge q] + \Pr[p_3 \wedge q] + \Pr[p_4 \wedge q].$$

Thus

$$\Pr[p_2|q] = \frac{\Pr[p_2 \wedge q]}{\Pr[p_1 \wedge q] + \Pr[p_2 \wedge q] + \Pr[p_3 \wedge q] + \Pr[p_4 \wedge q]}.$$

Since $\Pr[p_j \wedge q] = \Pr[p_j]\Pr[q|p_j]$, we have the desired formula

$$\Pr[p_2|q]$$
$$= \frac{\Pr[p_2] \cdot \Pr[q|p_2]}{\Pr[p_1] \cdot \Pr[q|p_1] + \Pr[p_2] \cdot \Pr[q|p_2] + \Pr[p_3] \cdot \Pr[q|p_3] + \Pr[p_4] \cdot \Pr[q|p_4]}.$$

Similar formulas apply for the other alternatives, and the formula generalizes in an obvious way to any number of alternatives. In its most general form it is called *Bayes's theorem*.

EXAMPLE 1   Suppose that a freshman must choose among mathematics, physics, chemistry, and botany as his science course. On the basis of the interest he expressed, his adviser assigns probabilities of .4, .3, .2, and .1 to his choosing each of the four courses, respectively. His adviser does not hear which course he actually chose, but at the end of the term the adviser hears that he received A in the course chosen. On the basis of the difficulties of these courses the adviser estimates the probability of the student getting an A in mathematics to be .1, in physics .2, in chemistry .3, and in botany .9. How can the adviser revise his original estimates as to the probabilities of the student taking the various courses? Using Bayes's theorem we get

Pr [He took math | He got an A]

$$= \frac{(.4)(.1)}{(.4)(.1) + (.3)(.2) + (.2)(.3) + (.1)(.9)} = \frac{4}{25} = .16.$$

Similar computations assign probabilities of .24, .24, and .36 to the other three courses. Thus the new information, that he received an A, had little effect on the probability of his having taken physics or chemistry, but it has made it much less likely that he took mathematics, and much more likely that he took botany.

It is important to note that knowing the conditional probabilities of q relative to the alternatives is not enough. Unless we also know the probabilities of the alternatives at the start, we cannot apply Bayes's theorem. However, in some situations it is reasonable to assume that the alternatives are equally probable at the start. In this case the factors Pr $[p_1], \ldots,$ Pr $[p_4]$ cancel from our basic formula, and we get the special form of the theorem:

If   Pr $[p_1] =$ Pr $[p_2] =$ Pr $[p_3] =$ Pr $[p_4],$ then

$$\text{Pr} [p_2|q] = \frac{\text{Pr} [q|p_2]}{\text{Pr} [q|p_1] + \text{Pr} [q|p_2] + \text{Pr} [q|p_3] + \text{Pr} [q|p_4]}.$$

EXAMPLE 2   In a sociological experiment the subjects are handed four sealed envelopes, each containing a problem. They are told to open one envelope and try to solve the problem in ten minutes. From past experience, the experimenter knows that the probability of their being able to solve the hardest problem is .1. With the other problems, they have probabilities of .3, .5, and .8. Assume the group succeeds within the allotted time. What is the probability that they selected the hardest problem? Since they have no way of knowing which problem is in which envelope, they choose at random, and we assign equal probabilities to the selection of the various problems. Hence the above simple formula applies. The probability of their having selected the hardest problem is

$$\frac{.1}{.1 + .3 + .5 + .8} = \frac{1}{17}.$$

The second method of computing Bayes's probabilities is to draw a tree, and then to redraw the tree in a different order. This is illustrated in the following example.

EXAMPLE 3 There are three urns. Each urn contains one white ball. In addition, urn I contains one black ball, urn II contains two, and urn III contains three. An urn is selected and one ball is drawn. The probability for selecting the three urns is $\frac{1}{6}, \frac{1}{2}$, and $\frac{1}{3}$, respectively. If we know that a white ball is drawn, how does this alter the probability that a given urn was selected?

First we construct the ordinary tree and tree measure (Figure 7).

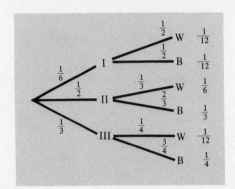

Figure 7

Next we redraw the tree, using the ball drawn as stage 1, and the urn selected as stage 2. We have the same paths as before, but in a different order. So the path weights are read off from the previous tree. The probability of drawing a white ball is

$$\tfrac{1}{12} + \tfrac{1}{6} + \tfrac{1}{12} = \tfrac{1}{3}.$$

This leaves the branch weights of the second stage to be computed (see Figure 8). But this is simply a matter of division. For example, the branch

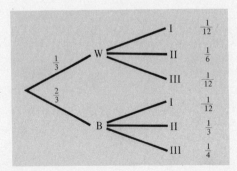

Figure 8

weights for the branches starting at "W" must be $\frac{1}{4}, \frac{1}{2}, \frac{1}{4}$ to yield the correct path weights. Thus, if a white ball is drawn, the probability of having selected urn I has increased to $\frac{1}{4}$, the probability of having picked urn III has fallen to $\frac{1}{4}$, while the probability of having chosen urn II is unchanged (see Figure 9).

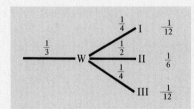

Figure 9

This method is particularly useful when we wish to compute all the conditional probabilities. We shall apply the method next to Example 1. The tree and tree measure for this example in the natural order is shown in Figure 10. In that figure the letters M, P, C, and B stand for mathematics, physics, chemistry, and botany, respectively.

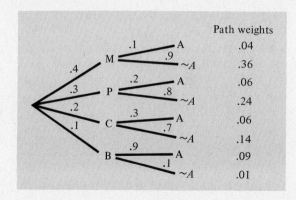

Figure 10

The tree drawn in reverse order is shown in Figure 11.

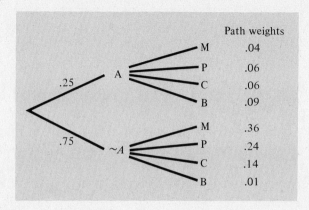

Figure 11

Each path in this tree corresponds to one of the paths in the original tree. Therefore the path weights for this new tree are the same as the weights assigned to the corresponding paths in the first tree. The two branch weights at the first level represent the probability that the student receives an A or that he does not receive an A. These probabilities are also easily obtained from the first tree. In fact,

$$\Pr[A] = .04 + .06 + .06 + .09 = .25$$

and

$$\Pr[\sim A] = 1 - .25 = .75.$$

We have now enough information to obtain the branch weights at the second level, since the product of the branch weights must be the path weights. For example, to obtain $p_{A,M}$ we have

$$.25 \cdot p_{A,M} = .04 \quad \text{or} \quad p_{A,M} = .16.$$

But $p_{A,M}$ is also the conditional probability that the student took math given that he got an A. Hence this is one of the new probabilities for the alternatives in the event that the student received an A. The other branch probabilities are found in the same way and represent the probabilities for the other alternatives. By this method we obtain the new probabilities for all alternatives under the hypothesis that the student receives an A as well as the hypothesis that the student does not receive an A. The results are shown in the completed tree in Figure 12.

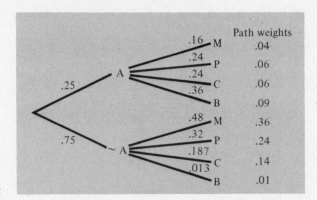

Figure 12

EXERCISES

1. A certain New England state has fair weather 20 percent of the time and foul weather 80 percent of the time. If a given day is fair, the probability that the next day is fair is .25; if a given day is foul, the next day is also foul with probability .75. If it is fair today, what is the probability that it was fair yesterday?

2. A survey showed that 25 percent of American cars are compacts, 40 percent are intermediates, and 35 percent are standard size. If a compact car is involved in an accident, the probability that its occupants are seriously injured is .6. For an intermediate car the probability is .5, and for standard size car it is .4. Given that the occupants of a car were seriously injured in an accident, what is the probability that the car was a compact? What is the probability that the car was an intermediate? A standard?

3. For Exercise 2, construct the tree measure and the tree drawn in reverse order.

4. On a multiple-choice exam there are four possible answers for each question. Therefore, if a student knows the right answer, he has probability 1 of choosing correctly; if he is guessing, he has probability $\frac{1}{4}$ of choosing correctly. Let us further assume that a good student will know 90 percent of the answers, a poor student only 50 percent. If a good student chooses the right answer, what is the probability that he was only guessing? Answer the same question about a poor student, if the poor student chooses the right answer.   [*Ans.* $\frac{1}{37}, \frac{1}{5}$.]

5. At a small coeducational college, 50 percent of the students are majoring in liberal arts, 10 percent in nursing, 10 percent in performing arts, and 30 percent in education. The proportion of women in the various majors is 40, 90, 60, and 50 percent respectively. Find the probability that a given male student is enrolled in each of the majors.

6. Of 200 people attending an office picnic, 150 eat one helping of potato salad, 30 eat two helpings, and 20 eat three helpings. Later many of those who attended the picnic became sick, and it is discovered that the potato salad was the cause. A doctor estimates that the probability of becoming sick is .3 times the number of servings of potato salad eaten. Find the probability that a person who became sick ate one, two, or three helpings. Do the same for a person who did not get sick.

7. Three men, A, B, and C, are in jail, and one of them is to be hanged the next day. The jailor knows which man will hang, but must not announce it. Man A says to the jailor, "Tell me the name of one of the two who will not hang. If both are to go free, just toss a coin to decide which to say. Since I already know that at least one of them will go free, you are not giving away the secret." The jailor thinks a moment and then says, "No, this would not be fair to you. Right now you think the probability that you will hang is $\frac{1}{3}$; but if I tell you the name of one of the others who is to go free, your probability of hanging increases to $\frac{1}{2}$. You would not sleep as well tonight." Was the jailor's reasoning correct?   [*Ans.* No.]

8. A machine for testing radio tubes will detect a defective tube with probability .95, but will show that a good tube is defective with probability .1. A technician knows that one tube in a radio with ten tubes is defective. He selects a tube at random, tests it, and finds that the machine indicates the tube is defective. What is the probability that

the tube actually is defective? Suppose the machine says the tube is good. What is now the probability that the tube is in fact defective?

9. (This problem should be done both with and without using Bayes's theorem.) A deck contains three cards. One is black on both sides, another is red on both sides, and the third has one red side and one black side. A card is selected from the deck at random and dealt onto a table; the face showing is black. What is the probability that the other face is also black?

10. One coin in a collection of 8 million coins has two heads. The rest are fair coins. A coin chosen at random from the collection is tossed ten times and comes up heads every time. What is the probability that it is the two-headed coin?

11. Referring to Exercise 10, assume that the coin is tossed n times and comes up heads every time. How large does n have to be to make the probability approximately $\frac{1}{2}$ that you have the two-headed coin?
[*Ans.* 23.]

12. A musicologist is attempting to determine the composer of a newly discovered baroque ditty. He thinks it equally likely to be Archangelo Spumani or his lesser-known brother Pistachio. Unfortunately both composed only in the keys of A major and F minor; Archangelo used the former 60 percent of the time, while Pistachio used the latter in 80 percent of his compositions. If the musicologist discovers that the work is in F minor, what is the probability that it was written by Archangelo? By Pistachio?

13. One-third of the subjects in a test of cold remedies are given vitamin C, $\frac{1}{2}$ are given antibiotics, and $\frac{1}{6}$ are given a placebo. The colds of $\frac{1}{4}$ of the vitamin-C group, $\frac{1}{2}$ of the antibiotic group, and $\frac{3}{5}$ of the placebo group are cured. What is the probability that a subject whose cold was *not* cured was given vitamin C? What is the probability that a subject whose cold was cured was given a placebo?

14. The manager of an office employing 15 women and 5 men discovers that the men are equally likely to use a paper clip as a nail cleaner, as a paper fastener, or as ammunition for a rubber-band slingshot. The women never shoot paper clips, but use them as nail cleaners with probability .75 and as paper fasteners with probability .25. If a paper clip is used as a nail cleaner, what is the probability that it was used by a woman? What is the probability that a clip shot across the office was shot by a man?

8 INDEPENDENT TRIALS WITH TWO OUTCOMES

In the preceding section we developed a way to determine a probability measure for any sequence of chance experiments where there are only a finite number of possibilities for each experiment. While this provides the framework for the general study of stochastic processes, it is too general to be studied in complete detail. Therefore, in probability theory we look for simplifying assumptions which will make our probability measure easier to work with. It is desired also that these assumptions be such as to apply to a variety of experiments which would occur in practice. In this book we shall limit ourselves to the study of two types of processes. The first, the independent trials process, will be considered in the present section. This process was the first one to be studied extensively in probability theory. The second, the Markov chain process, is a process that is finding increasing application, particularly in the social and biological sciences, and will be considered in Section 12.

A process of independent trials applies to the following situation. Assume that there is a sequence of chance experiments, each of which consists of a repetition of a single experiment, carried out in such a way that the results of any one experiment in no way affect the results in any other experiment. We label the possible outcome of a single experiment by $a_1, \ldots, a_r$. We assume that we are also given probabilities $p_1, \ldots, p_r$ for each of these outcomes occurring on any single experiment, the probabilities being independent of previous results. The tree representing the possibilities for the sequence of experiments will have the same outcomes from each branch point, and the branch probabilities will be assigned by assigning probability p_j to any branch leading to outcome a_j. The tree measure determined in this way is the measure of an *independent trials process*. In this section we shall consider the important case of two outcomes for each experiment. The more general case is studied in Section 10.

In the case of two outcomes we arbitrarily label one outcome "success" and the other "failure." For example, in repeated throws of a coin we might call heads success, and tails failure. We assume there is given a probability p for success and a probability $q = 1 - p$ for failure. The tree measure for a sequence of three such experiments is shown in Figure 13. The weights assigned to each path are indicated at the end of the path.

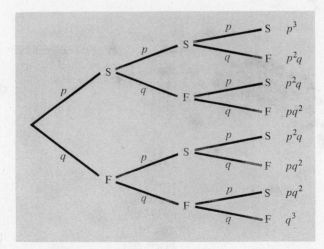

Figure 13

The question which we now ask is the following. Given an independent trials process with two outcomes, what is the probability of *exactly x* successes in *n* experiments? We denote this probability by $f(n, x; p)$ to indicate that it depends upon *n, x,* and *p*.

Assume that we had a tree for this general situation, similar to the tree in Figure 13 for three experiments, with the branch points labeled *S* for success and *F* for failure. Then the truth set of the statement "Exactly *x* successes occur" consists of all paths which go through *x* branch points labeled *S* and $n - x$ labeled *F*. For instance, in Figure 13 suppose $x = 2$ so that we are interested in the probability that "exactly two successes" occur. We look for all the paths that go through two branch points labeled S and $(3 - 2)$ or one branch point labeled F. (There are three paths of this type.) To find the probability of this statement we must add the weights for all such paths. We are helped first by the fact that our tree measure assigns the same weight to any such path, namely $p^x q^{n-x}$. The reason for this is that every branch leading to an *S* is assigned probability *p*, and every branch leading to *F* is assigned probability *q*, and in the product there will be *x p*'s and $(n - x) q$'s. To find the desired probability we need only find the number of paths in the truth set of the statement "Exactly *x* successes occur." But that is just the number of ways we can label *x* branch points with *S* and $n - x$ branch points with *F*. We found in Chapter 2 that this labeling could be done in $\binom{n}{x}$ ways. Thus we have proved:

In an independent trials process with two outcomes the probability of exactly x successes in n experiments is given by

$$f(n, x; p) = \binom{n}{x} p^x q^{n-x}.$$

EXAMPLE 1   Consider *n* throws of an ordinary coin. We label heads "success" and tails "failure," and we assume that the probability is $\frac{1}{2}$ for heads on any one throw independently of the outcome of any other throw. Then the probability that exactly *x* heads will turn up is

$$f(n, x; \tfrac{1}{2}) = \binom{n}{x}\left(\frac{1}{2}\right)^n.$$

For example, in 100 throws the probability that exactly 50 heads will turn up is

$$f(100, 50; \tfrac{1}{2}) = \binom{100}{50}\left(\frac{1}{2}\right)^{100},$$

which is approximately .08. Thus we see that it is quite unlikely that exactly one-half of the tosses will result in heads. On the other hand, suppose that we ask for the probability that nearly one-half of the tosses will be heads. To be more precise, let us ask for the probability that the number of heads which occur does not deviate by more than 10 from 50. To find this we must add

$$f(100, x; \tfrac{1}{2}) \quad \text{for} \quad x = 40, 41, \ldots, 60.$$

If this is done, we obtain a probability of approximately .96. Thus, while it is unlikely that exactly 50 heads will occur, it is very likely that the number of heads which occur will not deviate from 50 by more than 10.

EXAMPLE 2 Assume that we have a machine which, on the basis of data given, is to predict the outcome of an election as either a Republican victory or a Democratic victory. If two identical machines are given the same data, they should predict the same result. We assume, however, that any such machine has a certain probability q of reversing the prediction that it would ordinarily make, because of a mechanical or electrical failure. To improve the accuracy of our prediction we give the same data to r identical machines, and choose the answer which the majority of the machines give. To avoid ties we assume that r is odd. Let us see how this decreases the probability of an error due to a faulty machine.

Consider r experiments, where the jth experiment results in success if the jth machine produces the prediction which it would make when operating without any failure of parts. The probability of success is then $p = 1 - q$. The majority decision will agree with that of a perfectly operating machine if we have more than $r/2$ successes. Suppose, for example, that we have five machines, each of which has a probability of .1 of reversing the prediction because of a parts failure. Then the probability for success is .9, and the probability that the majority decision will be the desired one is

$$f(5, 3; 0.9) + f(5, 4; 0.9) + f(5, 5; 0.9),$$

which is found to be approximately .991 (see Exercise 3).

Thus the above procedure decreases the probability of error due to machine failure from .1 in the case of one machine to .009 for the case of five machines.

EXERCISES

1. Compute for $n = 4$, $n = 6$, and $n = 8$ the probability of obtaining heads exactly half the time when an ordinary coin is thrown.
2. Do Exercise 1 for a loaded coin which has probability $\tfrac{3}{4}$ of coming up heads. How do the answers compare with those in Exercise 1?
   [*Ans.* .211, .132, .087.]
3. Verify that the probability .991 given in Example 2 is correct.
4. A machine produces light bulbs that are good with probability .95 and defective with probability .05. What is the probability that a sample of ten bulbs selected at random from the machine's output contains at most one defective bulb? (Do not carry out the computation.)

5. Suppose an unprepared student takes a five-question multiple-choice exam. Each question has four possible answers, only one of which is correct. What is the probability that he can attain a passing grade of 80 percent by guessing?

6. A coin is to be thrown eight times. What is the most probable number of heads that will occur? What is the number having the highest probability, given that the first four throws result in heads?

7. A die is made by marking the faces of a regular dodecahedron with the numbers 1 through 12. What is the probability that on exactly three out of six throws of the die, a number larger than 8 turns up?

8. Suppose a coin is flipped six times. What is the probability that more than half of the tosses come up tails? Answer the same for seven throws, and for 17,219 throws.

9. Suppose seven coins are flipped eleven times each. What is the probability that more than half of the coins come up heads more than one-half of the time?
   [*Ans.* $\frac{1}{2}$.] [*Hint:* Use the result of Exercise 8 twice.]

10. A small factory has ten workers. The workers eat their lunch at one of two diners, and they are just as likely to eat at one as in the other. If the proprietors want to be more than .95 sure of having enough seats, how many seats must each of the diners have?   [*Ans.* Eight seats.]

11. Suppose we have a computer routine to produce random digits. What is the probability that in ten trials of the routine, more than two zeros are output?

12. A trapper has found through experience that he can expect a given trap to catch an animal once every three weeks. How many traps should he set to have probability at least .7 of catching at least two animals a week?

13. In a certain board game players move around the board, and each turn consists of a player's rolling a pair of dice. If a player is on the square marked "Park Bench," he must roll a seven or doubles before he is allowed to move out.
    (a) What is the probability that a player stuck on "Park Bench" will be allowed to move out on his next turn?
    (b) A player stuck on "Park Bench" has probability greater than $\frac{3}{4}$ of getting out after how many rolls?   [*Ans.* (a) $\frac{1}{3}$; (b) 4.]

14. A machine produces small electrical parts which are perfect with probability .8, defective but usable with probability .15, and useless with probability .05. Find the probability that a sample of ten parts made by the machine contains exactly eight perfect parts. (Do not carry out the computation.)

15. Find the probability that the sample in Exercise 14 contains seven perfect parts, two defective but usable parts, and one useless part.

16. Show that $f(n, x; p) = \dfrac{(n - x + 1)p}{x \cdot q} f(n, x - 1; p)$.

17. For given n and p, find the k such that $f(n, k; p)$ is the largest. [*Hint:* We want $f(n, k; p) \geq f(n, k - 1; p)$ and $f(n, k; p) \geq f(n, k + 1; p)$; use the result of Exercise 16.]

18. Without actually computing the probabilities, find the value of x for which $f(20, x; .3)$ is largest.

19. A restaurant orders five pieces of apple pie and five pieces of cherry pie. Assume that the restaurant has ten customers, and the probability that a customer will ask for apple pie is $\frac{3}{4}$ and for cherry pie is $\frac{1}{4}$.
  (a) What is the probability that the ten customers will all be able to have their first choice? (Do not carry out the computation.)
  (b) What number of each kind of pie should the restaurant order if it wishes to order ten pieces of pie and wants to maximize the probability that the ten customers will all have their first choice?

20. Suppose a computer routine for generating random digits is operated 1000 times. What is the most likely number of times the digit 7 appears?

9   THE LAW OF LARGE NUMBERS

In this section we shall study some further properties of the independent trials process with two outcomes. In Section 8 we saw that the probability for x successes in n trials is given by

$$f(n, x; p) = \binom{n}{x} p^x q^{n-x}.$$

In Figure 14 we show these probabilities graphically for $n = 8$ and $p = \frac{3}{4}$.

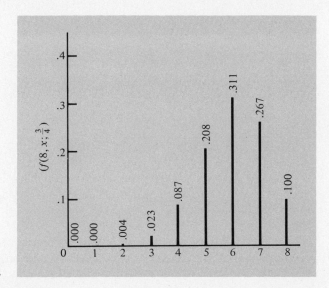

Figure 14

In Figure 15 we have done similarly for the case of $n = 7$ and $p = \frac{3}{4}$.

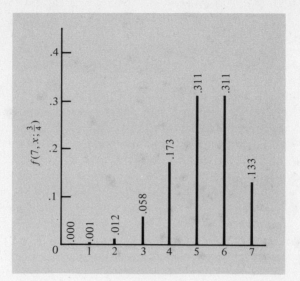

Figure 15

We see in the first case that the values increase up to a maximum value at $x = 6$ and then decrease. In the second case the values increase up to a maximum value at $x = 5$, have the same value for $x = 6$, and then decrease. These two cases are typical of what can happen in general.

Consider the ratio of the probability of $x + 1$ successes in n trials to the probability of x successes in n trials, which is

$$\frac{\binom{n}{x+1}p^{x+1}q^{n-x-1}}{\binom{n}{x}p^x q^{n-x}} = \frac{n-x}{x+1} \cdot \frac{p}{q}.$$

This ratio will be greater than one as long as $(n - x)p > (x + 1)q$ or as long as $x < np - q$. If $np - q$ is not an integer, the values $\binom{n}{x}p^x q^{n-x}$ increase up to a maximum value, which occurs at the first integer greater than $np - q$, and then decrease. In case $np - q$ is an integer, the values $\binom{n}{x}p^x q^{n-x}$ increase up to $x = np - q$, are the same for $x = np - q$ and $x = np - q + 1$, and then decrease.

Thus we see that, in general, values near np will occur with the largest probability. It is not true that one particular value near np is highly likely to occur, but only that it is relatively more likely than a value further from np. For example, in 100 throws of a coin, $np = 1000 \cdot \frac{1}{2} = 50$. The probability of exactly 50 heads is approximately .08. The probability of exactly 30 is approximately .00002.

More information is obtained by studying the probability of a given deviation of the proportion of successes x/n from the number p; that is, by studying for $\epsilon > 0$,

$$\Pr\left[|\frac{x}{n} - p| < \epsilon\right].$$

For any fixed n, p, and ϵ, the latter probability can be found by adding all the values of $f(n, x; p)$ for values of x for which the inequality $p - \epsilon < x/n < p + \epsilon$ is true. In Figure 16 we have given these probabilities for the case $p = .3$ with various values for ϵ and n. In the first column we have the case $\epsilon = .1$. We observe that as n increases, the probability that the fraction of successes deviates from .3 by less than .1 tends to the value 1. In fact, to four decimal places the answer is 1.0000 after $n = 400$. In the second column we have the same probabilities for the smaller value of $\epsilon = .05$. Again the probabilities are tending to 1 but not so fast. In the third column we have given these probabilities for the case $\epsilon = .02$. We see now that even after 1000 trials there is still a reasonable chance that the fraction x/n is not within .02 of the value of $p = .3$. It is natural to ask if we can expect these probabilities also to tend to 1 if we increase n sufficiently. The answer is yes and this is assured by one of the fundamental theorems of probability called the *law of large numbers*. This theorem asserts that, for any $\epsilon > 0$,

$$\Pr\left[|\frac{x}{n} - p| < \epsilon\right]$$

tends to 1 as n increases indefinitely.

$$\Pr\left[|\frac{x}{n} - p| < \epsilon\right] \quad \text{for} \quad p = .3 \quad \text{and} \quad \epsilon = .1, .05, .02.$$

n	$\Pr\left[|\frac{x}{n} - .3| < .10\right]$	$\Pr\left[|\frac{x}{n} - .3| < .05\right]$	$\Pr\left[|\frac{x}{n} - .3| < .02\right]$
20	.5348	.1916	.1916
40	.7738	.3945	.1366
60	.8800	.5184	.3269
80	.9337	.6068	.2853
100	.9626	.6740	.2563
200	.9974	.8577	.4107
300	.9998	.9326	.5116
400	1.0000	.9668	.5868
500	1.0000	.9833	.6461
600	1.0000	.9915	.6944
700	1.0000	.9956	.7345
800	1.0000	.9977	.7683
900	1.0000	.9988	.7970
1000	1.0000	.9994	.8216

Figure 16

It is important to understand what this theorem says and what it does not say. Let us illustrate its meaning in the case of coin tossing.

We are going to toss a coin n times and we want the probability to be very high, say greater than .99, that the fraction of heads which turn up will be very close, say within .001, of the value .5. The law of large numbers assures us that we can have this if we simply choose n large enough. The theorem itself gives us no information about how large n must be. Let us, however, consider this question.

To say that the fraction of the times success results is near p is the same as saying that the actual number of successes x does not deviate too much from the expected number np. To see the kind of deviations which might be expected we can study the value of $\Pr[|x - np| \geq d]$. A table of these values for $p = .3$ and various values of n and d are given in Figure 17. Let us ask how large d must be before a deviation as large as d could be considered surprising. For example, let us see for each n the value of d which makes $\Pr[|x - np| \geq d]$ about .04. From the table, we see that d should be 7 for $n = 50$, 9 for $n = 80$, 10 for $n = 100$, etc. To see deviations which might be considered more typical we look for the values of d which make $\Pr[|x - np| \geq d]$ approximately $\frac{1}{3}$. Again from the table, we see that d should be 3 or 4 for $n = 50$, 4 or 5 for $n = 80$, 5 for $n = 100$, etc. The answers to these two questions are given in the last two columns of the table. An examination of these numbers shows us that deviations which we would consider surprising are approximately $\sqrt{n}$ while those which are more typical are about one half as large or $\sqrt{n}/2$.

This suggests that $\sqrt{n}$, or a suitable multiple of it, might be taken as a unit of measurement for deviations. Of course, we would also have to study how $\Pr[|x - np| \geq d]$ depends on p. When this is done, one finds that $\sqrt{npq}$ is a natural unit; it is called a *standard deviation*. It can be shown that for large n the following approximations hold:

$$\Pr[|x - np| \geq \sqrt{npq}] \approx .3174$$
$$\Pr[|x - np| \geq 2\sqrt{npq}] \approx .0455$$
$$\Pr[|x - np| \geq 3\sqrt{npq}] \approx .0027.$$

That is, a deviation from the expected value of one standard deviation is rather typical, while a deviation of as much as two standard deviations is quite surprising and three very surprising. For values of p not too near 0 or 1, the value of $\sqrt{pq}$ is approximately $\frac{1}{2}$. Thus these approximations are consistent with the results we observed from our table.

For large n, $\Pr[x - np \geq k\sqrt{npq}]$ or $\Pr[x - np \leq -k\sqrt{npq}]$ can be shown to be approximately the same. Hence these probabilities can be estimated for $k = 1, 2$, and 3 by taking $\frac{1}{2}$ the values given above.

EXAMPLE 1   In throwing an ordinary coin 10,000 times, the expected number of heads is 5000, and the standard deviation for the number of heads is $\sqrt{10,000(\frac{1}{2})(\frac{1}{2})} = 50$. Thus the probability that the number of heads which

$$p = 3; \qquad \Pr[|x - np| \geq d].$$

n\d	1	2	3	4	5	6	7	8	9	10	11	12	13	14	15	16	17	Pr near to .04	Pr near to $\frac{1}{3}$
50	.878	.644	.441	.280	.164	.088	.043	.020	.008									7	3–4
80	.903	.715	.542	.393	.272	.179	.112	.066	.037	.020	.010							9	4–5
100	.913	.744	.586	.445	.326	.230	.155	.101	.063	.037	.021	.012						10	5
120	.921	.765	.619	.486	.370	.273	.195	.135	.090	.058	.036	.022	.012					11	5–6
140	.927	.782	.645	.519	.407	.310	.230	.166	.116	.079	.052	.033	.021	.012				12	6
170	.933	.802	.676	.558	.451	.357	.276	.209	.154	.111	.078	.054	.036	.024	.015	.009		13	6
200	.939	.817	.700	.589	.488	.396	.316	.247	.189	.142	.105	.076	.053	.037	.025	.017	.011	14	7

Figure 17

turn up deviates from 5000 by as much as one standard deviation, or 50, is approximately .317. The probability of a deviation of as much as two standard deviations, or 100, is approximately .046. The probability of a deviation of as much as three standard deviations, or 150, is approximately .003.

EXAMPLE 2 Assume that in a certain large city, 900 people are chosen at random and asked if they favor a certain proposal. Of the 900 asked, 550 say they favor the proposal and 350 are opposed. If, in fact, the people in the city are equally divided on the issue, would it be unlikely that such a large majority would be obtained in a sample of 900 of the citizens? If the people were equally divided, we would assume that the 900 people asked would form an independent trials process with probability $\frac{1}{2}$ for a "yes" answer and $\frac{1}{2}$ for a "no" answer. Then the standard deviation for the number of "yes" answers in 900 trials is $\sqrt{900(\frac{1}{2})(\frac{1}{2})} = 15$. Then it would be very unlikely that we would obtain a deviation of more than 45 from the expected number of 450. The fact that the deviation in the sample from the expected number was 100, then, is evidence that the hypothesis that the voters were equally divided is incorrect. The assumption that the true proportion is any value less than $\frac{1}{2}$ would also lead to the fact that a number as large as 550 favoring in a sample of 900 is very unlikely. Thus we are led to suspect that the true proportion is greater than $\frac{1}{2}$. On the other hand, if the number who favored the proposal in the sample of 900 were 465, we would have only a deviation of one standard deviation, under the assumption of an equal division of opinion. Since such a deviation is not unlikely, we could not rule out this possibility on the evidence of the sample.

EXAMPLE 3 A certain Ivy League college would like to admit 800 students in their freshman class. Experience has shown that if they accept 1250 students they will have acceptances from approximately 800. If they admit as many as 50 too many students they will have to provide additional dormitory space. Let us find the probability that this will happen assuming that the acceptances of the students can be considered to be an independent trials process. We take as our estimate for the probability of an acceptance $p = \frac{800}{1250} = .64$. Then the expected number of acceptances is 800 and the standard deviation for the number of acceptances is $\sqrt{1250 \times .64 \times .36} \approx 17$. The probability that the number accepted is three standard deviations or 51 from the mean is approximately .0027. This probability takes into account a deviation above the mean or below the mean. Since in this case we are only interested in a deviation above the mean, the probability we desire is half of this or approximately .0013. Thus we see that it is highly unlikely that the college will have to have new dormitory space under the assumptions we have made.

We finish this discussion of the law of large numbers with some final remarks about the interpretation of this important theorem.

Of course no matter how large n is we cannot prevent the coin from coming up heads every time. If this were the case we would observe a fraction of heads equal to 1. However, this is not inconsistent with the theorem, since the probability of this happening is $(\frac{1}{2})^n$ which tends to 0 as n increases. Thus a fraction of 1 is always possible, but becomes increasingly unlikely.

The law of large numbers is often misinterpreted in the following manner. Suppose that we plan to toss the coin 1000 times and after 500 tosses we have already obtained 400 heads. Then we must obtain less than one-half heads in the remaining 500 tosses to have the fraction come out near $\frac{1}{2}$. It is tempting to argue that the coin therefore owes us some tails and it is more likely that tails will occur in the last 500 tosses. Of course this is nonsense, since the coin has no memory. The point is that something very unlikely has already happened in the first 500 tosses. The final result can therefore also be expected to be a result not predicted before the tossing began.

We could also argue that perhaps the coin is a biased coin, but this would make us predict more heads than tails in the future. Thus the law of averages, or the law of large numbers, should not give you great comfort if you have had a series of very bad hands dealt you in your last 100 poker hands. If the dealing is fair, you have the same chance as ever of getting a good hand.

Early attempts to define the probability p that success occurs on a single experiment sounded like this. If the experiment is repeated indefinitely, the fraction of successes obtained will tend to a number p, and this number p is called the probability of success on a single experiment. While this fails to be satisfactory as a definition of probability, the law of large numbers captures the spirit of this frequency concept of probability.

EXERCISES

1. In 64 tosses of an ordinary coin, what is the expected number of heads that turn up? What is the standard deviation for the number of heads that occur? [*Ans.* 32, 4.]

2. A die is loaded so that the probability of any face turning up is proportional to the number on that face. If the die is rolled 150 times, what is the expected number of times a three will turn up? What is the standard deviation for the number of threes that turn up?
[*Ans.* $\frac{150}{7}$, $\frac{30}{7}$.]

3. Suppose the die in Exercise 2 is tossed 75 times. What is the expected number of times a three or a six will turn up? What is the standard deviation for the number of such throws?

4. An unknown coin is tossed 10,000 times and comes up heads 5100 times? Is it likely that the coin is fair?

5. In a large number of independent trials with probability p for success, what is the approximate probability that the number of successes will

deviate from the expected number by more than one standard deviation but less than two standard deviations?   [*Ans.* .272.]

6. A farmer has found that, on the average, 1 percent of his 1000 apple trees die and must be replaced each year. The year after an atomic power plant begins operating nearby, 19 of the farmer's trees die. Should he suspect that his trees are dying due to other than natural causes?

7. Consider *n* independent trials with probability *p* for success. Let *r* and *s* be numbers such that $p < r < s$. What does the law of large numbers say about

$$\Pr\left[r < \frac{x}{n} < s\right]$$

as we increase *n* indefinitely? Answer the same question in the case that $r < p < s$.

8. Although 10 percent of those receiving Ph.D's in mathematics each year are women, all ten people hired by the mathematics department of a small college over the past five years have been men. Is there reason to suspect that the department is discriminating against women?

9. A researcher studying the effects of diet on heart disease notes that 15 percent of all men over 55 have heart disease, and 47 men out of a sample of 500 men over 55 on a low-cholesterol diet have heart disease. Is it reasonable for him to hypothesize that a low-cholesterol diet may reduce the incidence of heart disease?

10. What is the approximate probability that, in 10,000 throws of an ordinary coin, the number of heads which turn up lies between 4850 and 5150? What is the probability that the number of heads lies in the same interval, given that in the first 1900 throws there were 1600 heads?

11. Suppose we want to be 95 percent sure that the fraction of heads that turn up when a fair coin is tossed *n* times does not differ from $\frac{1}{2}$ by more than .01. How large should *n* be?

[*Ans.* Approximately 10,000.]

12. A small college found that, while it was all female, 2 percent of its students majored in mathematics. After it became coeducational, the college had 10 math majors in its first mixed graduating class of 400 students. Is it likely that coeducation had some effect on the number of students electing to major in mathematics?

13. A preelection poll indicates that 55 percent of the voters will choose candidate A. When the election is over, candidate A has received 5200 of the 9900 votes cast. How accurate was the poll?

14. Suppose that for each roll of a fair die you lose $1 when an odd number comes up and win $1 when an even number comes up. Then after 40,000 rolls you can, with approximately 84 percent confidence, expect to have lost not more than how many dollars?

15. The Dartmouth computer, having nothing better to do, flipped a coin 1,000,000 times. It obtained 499,452 heads. Is this number reasonable?

*10   INDEPENDENT TRIALS WITH MORE THAN TWO OUTCOMES

By extending the results of Section 8, we shall study the case of independent trials in which we allow more than two outcomes. We assume that we have an independent trials process where the possible outcomes are $a_1, a_2, \ldots, a_k$, occurring with probabilities $p_1, p_2, \ldots, p_k$, respectively. We denote by

$$f(r_1, r_2, \ldots, r_k; p_1, p_2, \ldots, p_k)$$

the probability that, in

$$n = r_1 + r_2 + \ldots + r_k$$

such trials, there will be r_1 occurences of a_1, r_2 or a_2, etc. In the case of two outcomes this notation would be $f(r_1, r_2; p_1, p_2)$. In Section 8 we wrote this as $f(n, r; p) = f(n, r_1; p_1)$ since r_2 and p_2 are determined from n, r_1, and p_1. We shall indicate how this probability is found in general, but carry out the details only for a special case. We choose $k = 3$, and $n = 5$ for purposes of illustration. We shall find $f(1, 2, 2; p_1, p_2, p_3)$.

We show in Figure 18 enough of the tree for this process to indicate the branch probabilities for a path (heavy lines) corresponding to the outcomes a_2, a_3, a_1, a_2, a_3. The tree measure assigns weight $p_2 \cdot p_3 \cdot p_1 \cdot p_2 \cdot p_3 = p_1 \cdot p_2^2 \cdot p_3^2$ to this path.

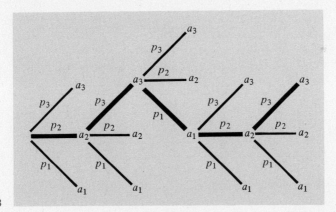

Figure 18

There are, of course, other paths through the tree corresponding to one occurrence of a_1, two of a_2, and two of a_3. However, they would all be assigned the same weight $p_1 \cdot p_2^2 \cdot p_3^2$, by the tree measure. Hence to find $f(1, 2, 2; p_1, p_2, p_3)$, we must multiply this weight by the number of paths having the specified number of occurrences of each outcome.

We note that the path a_2, a_3, a_1, a_2, a_3 can be specified by labeling the numbers 1 to 5 with the outcomes a_1, a_2, a_3. Thus trial 3 is labeled with outcome a_1, trials 1 and 4 are labeled with outcome a_2, and trials 2 and 5 are labeled with outcome a_3. Conversely, any such labeling of the numbers 1 to 5 which uses label a_1 once and labels a_2 and a_3 twice each corresponds to a unique path of the desired kind. Hence the number of such paths is the number of such labelings. But this is

$$\binom{5}{1, 2, 2} = \frac{5!}{1! \, 2! \, 2!}$$

(see Chapter 2, Section 5), so that the probability of one occurrence of a_1, two of a_2, and two of a_3 is

$$\binom{5}{1, 2, 2} \cdot p_1 \cdot p_2^2 \cdot p_3^2.$$

The above argument carried out in general leads, for the case of independent trials with outcomes $a_1, a_2, \ldots, a_k$ occurring with probabilities $p_1, p_2, \ldots, p_k$, to the following.

The probability for r_1 occurrences of a_1, r_2 occurrences of a_2, etc., is given by

$$f(r_1, r_2, \ldots, r_k; p_1, p_2, \ldots, p_k) = \binom{n}{r_1, r_2, \ldots, r_k} p_1^{r_1} \cdot p_2^{r_2} \cdots p_k^{r_k}.$$

EXAMPLE 1 A die is thrown 12 times. What is the probability that each number will come up twice? Here there are six outcomes, $1, 2, 3, 4, 5, 6$ corresponding to the six sides of the die. We assign each outcome probability $\frac{1}{6}$. We are then asked for

$$f(2, 2, 2, 2, 2, 2; \tfrac{1}{6}, \tfrac{1}{6}, \tfrac{1}{6}, \tfrac{1}{6}, \tfrac{1}{6}, \tfrac{1}{6}),$$

which is

$$\binom{12}{2, 2, 2, 2, 2, 2} \left(\frac{1}{6}\right)^2 \left(\frac{1}{6}\right)^2 \left(\frac{1}{6}\right)^2 \left(\frac{1}{6}\right)^2 \left(\frac{1}{6}\right)^2 \left(\frac{1}{6}\right)^2 = .0034....$$

EXAMPLE 2 Suppose that we have an independent trials process with four outcomes a_1, a_2, a_3, a_4 occurring with probability p_1, p_2, p_3, p_4, respectively. It might be that we are interested only in the probability that r_1 occurrences of a_1 and r_2 occurrences of a_2 will take place with no specification about the number of each of the other possible outcomes. To answer this question we simply consider a new experiment where the outcomes are $a_1, a_2, \bar{a}_3$. Here $\bar{a}_3$ corresponds to an occurrence of either a_3 or a_4 in our original experiment. The corresponding probabilities would be $p_1, p_2,$ and $\bar{p}_3$ with $\bar{p}_3 = p_3 + p_4$. Let $\bar{r}_3 = n - (r_1 + r_2)$. Then our question is answered by finding the probability in our new experiment for r_1 occurrences of a_1, r_2 or a_2, and $\bar{r}_3$ of $\bar{a}_3$, which is

$$\binom{n}{r_1, r_2, \bar{r}_3} p_1^{r_1} p_2^{r_2} \bar{p}_3^{\bar{r}_3}.$$

The same procedure can be carried out for experiments with any number of outcomes where we specify the number of occurrences of such particular outcomes. For example, if a die is thrown ten times the probability that a one will occur exactly twice and a three exactly three times is given by

$$\binom{10}{2,3,5}\left(\frac{1}{6}\right)^2\left(\frac{1}{6}\right)^3\left(\frac{4}{6}\right)^5 = .043. \ldots$$

EXERCISES

1. Gypsies sometimes toss a thick coin for which heads and tails are equally likely, but which also has probability $\frac{1}{5}$ of standing on edge (i.e., neither heads nor tails). What is the probability of exactly two heads and three tails in five tosses of a gypsy coin? [*Ans.* $\frac{64}{625}$.]

2. Three horses, A, B, and C, compete in four races. Assuming that each horse has an equal chance in each race, what is the probability that A wins two races and B and C win one each? What is the probability that the same horse wins all four races? [*Ans.* $\frac{4}{27}$, $\frac{1}{27}$.]

3. Three children go into a restaurant where each gets either an ice-cream cone, a sundae, or a milkshake. Assuming that each gets an ice-cream cone twice as often as a milkshake and a sundae twice as often as an ice-cream cone, what is the probability that at least two of them order the same thing?

4. Assume that in a certain large college 40 percent of the students are freshmen, 30 percent are sophomores, 20 percent are juniors, and 10 percent are seniors. A committee of eight is chosen at random from the student body. What is the probability that there are equal numbers from each class on the committee?

5. If four dice are thrown, find the probability that there are 2 twos and 2 threes, given that all the outcomes are less than four. [*Ans.* $\frac{2}{27}$.]

6. Let us assume that when a batter comes to bat, he has probability .6 of being put out, .1 of getting a walk, .2 of getting a single, .1 of getting an extra-base hit. If he comes to bat five times in a game, what is the probability that
   (a) He gets a walk and a single (and three outs)? [*Ans.* $\frac{54}{625}$.]
   (b) He has a perfect day (no outs)? [*Ans.* $\frac{32}{3125}$.]
   (c) He gets a single, two extra base hits, and a walk (and one out)?

7. Assume that a single torpedo has a probability $\frac{1}{2}$ of sinking a ship, probability $\frac{1}{4}$ of damaging it, and probability $\frac{1}{4}$ of missing. Assume further that two damaging shots are sufficient to sink a ship. What is the probability that four torpedoes will succeed in sinking a ship? [*Ans.* $\frac{251}{256}$.]

8. A hiker is planning to make a three-day trip to the mountains. He estimates that on a given day it is clear with probability $\frac{1}{3}$, is cloudy with probability $\frac{1}{2}$, and rains with probability $\frac{1}{6}$. He will consider the trip enjoyable if he does not get rained on and if he has at least two clear days. Assuming the weather on a given day is independent of previous weather,
   (a) Find the probability that he enjoys the trip.

(b) Given that at least one day was not clear, what is probability that he enjoyed the trip?

9. Let us assume that in a World Series game a batter has probability $\frac{1}{4}$ of getting no hits, $\frac{1}{2}$ of getting one hit, and $\frac{1}{4}$ of getting two hits, assuming that the probability of getting more than two hits is negligible. In a four-game World Series, find the probability that the batter gets

(a) Exactly two hits.

(b) Exactly three hits.

(c) Exactly four hits.

(d) Exactly five hits.

(e) Fewer than two hits or more than five.

[*Ans.* $\frac{7}{64}$; $\frac{7}{32}$; $\frac{35}{128}$; $\frac{7}{32}$; $\frac{23}{128}$.]

10. Jones, Smith, and Green live in the same house. The mailman has observed that on the average Jones receives twice as much mail as Green and three times as much as Smith. If he has four letters for this house, what is the probability that each man receives at least one letter?

11. Assume that in a certain course the probability that a student chosen at random will get an A is .1, that he will get a B is .2, that he will get a C is .4, that he will get a D is .2, and that he will get an E is .1. What distribution of grades is most likely in the case of four students? [*Ans.* One B, two C's, one D.]

12. A professor decides that he will fail any student who misses more than two classes in a given week or is absent or walks in late every day in a given week. The class meets four times a week. A particular student's sleeping habits are such that he misses class $\frac{1}{5}$ of the time, walks in late $\frac{3}{10}$ of the time, and arrives before the start of class $\frac{1}{2}$ of the time.

(a) What is the probability that he is failed during the first week of the course?

(b) What is the probability that he is failed during the first two weeks of the course? (Note that when he begins the second week, his performance the first week does not matter any more.)

[*Ans.* .151.]

11 EXPECTED VALUE

In this section we shall discuss the concept of expected value. Although it originated in the study of gambling games, it enters into almost any detailed probabilistic discussion.

Definition If in an experiment the possible outcomes are numbers, $a_1, a_2, \ldots, a_k$, occurring with probability $p_1, p_2, \ldots, p_k$, then the *expected value* is defined to be

$$E = a_1 p_1 + a_2 p_2 + \ldots + a_k p_k.$$

The term "expected value" is not to be interpreted as the value that will necessarily occur on a single experiment. For example, if a person bets $1 that a head will turn up when a coin is thrown, he may either win $1 or lose $1. His expected value is $(1)(\frac{1}{2}) + (-1)(\frac{1}{2}) = 0$, which is not one of the possible outcomes. The term "expected value" had its origin in the following consideration. If we repeat an experiment with expected value E a large number of times, and if we expect a_1 a fraction p_1 of the time, a_2 a fraction p_2 of the time, etc., then the average that we expect per experiment is E. In particular, in a gambling game E is interpreted as the average winning expected in a large number of plays. Here the expected value is often taken as the value of the game to the player. If the game has a positive expected value, the game is said to be favorable; if the game has expected value zero it is said to be fair; and if it has negative expected value it is described as unfavorable. These terms are not to be taken too literally, since many people are quite happy to play games that, in terms of expected value, are unfavorable. For instance, the buying of life insurance may be considered an unfavorable game which most people choose to play.

EXAMPLE 1   For the first example of the application of expected value we consider the game of roulette as played at Monte Carlo. There are several types of bets which the gambler can make, and we consider two of these.

The wheel has the number 0 and the numbers from 1 to 36 marked on equally spaced slots. The wheel is spun and a ball comes to rest in one of these slots. If the player puts a stake, say $1, on a given number, and the ball comes to rest in this slot, then he receives from the croupier 36 times his stake, or $36. The player wins $35 with probability $\frac{1}{37}$ and loses $1 with probability $\frac{36}{37}$. Hence his expected winnings are

$$\tfrac{35}{37} - 1 \cdot \tfrac{36}{37} = -\tfrac{1}{37} = -.027.$$

This can be interpreted to mean that in the long run he can expect to lose about 2.7 percent of his stakes.

A second way to play is the following. A player may bet on "red" or "black." The numbers from 1 to 36 are evenly divided between the two colors. If a player bets on "red" and a red number turns up, he receives twice his stake. If a black number turns up, he loses his stake. If 0 turns up, then the wheel is spun until it stops on a number different from 0. If this is black, the player loses; but if it is red, he receives only his original stake, not twice it. For this type of play, the gambler wins $1 with probability $\frac{18}{37}$, breaks even with probability $\frac{1}{2} \cdot \frac{1}{37} = \frac{1}{74}$, and loses $1 with probability $\frac{18}{37} + \frac{1}{2} \cdot \frac{1}{37} = \frac{37}{74}$. Hence his expected winning is

$$1 \cdot \tfrac{18}{37} + 0 \cdot \tfrac{1}{74} - 1 \cdot \tfrac{37}{74} = -.0135.$$

In this case the player can expect to lose about 1.35 percent of his stakes in the long run. Thus the expected loss in this case is only half as great as in the previous case.

EXAMPLE 2 A player rolls a die and receives a number of dollars corresponding to the number of dots on the face which turns up. What should the player pay for playing, to make this a fair game? To answer this question, we note that the player wins 1, 2, 3, 4, 5 or 6 dollars, each with probability $\frac{1}{6}$. Hence, his expected winning is

$$1(\tfrac{1}{6}) + 2(\tfrac{1}{6}) + 3(\tfrac{1}{6}) + 4(\tfrac{1}{6}) + 5(\tfrac{1}{6}) + 6(\tfrac{1}{6}) = 3\tfrac{1}{2}.$$

Thus if he pays \$3.50, his expected winnings will be zero.

EXAMPLE 3 What is the expected number of successes in the case of four independent trials with probability $\frac{1}{3}$ for success? We know that the probability of x successes is $\binom{4}{x}\left(\frac{1}{3}\right)^{x}\left(\frac{2}{3}\right)^{4-x}$. Thus

$$E = 0 \cdot \binom{4}{0}\left(\frac{1}{3}\right)^{0}\left(\frac{2}{3}\right)^{4} + 1 \cdot \binom{4}{1}\left(\frac{1}{3}\right)^{1}\left(\frac{2}{3}\right)^{3} + 2 \cdot \binom{4}{2}\left(\frac{1}{3}\right)^{2}\left(\frac{2}{3}\right)^{2}$$

$$+ 3 \cdot \binom{4}{3}\left(\frac{1}{3}\right)^{3}\left(\frac{2}{3}\right)^{1} + 4 \cdot \binom{4}{4}\left(\frac{1}{3}\right)^{4}\left(\frac{2}{3}\right)^{0}$$

$$= 0 + \frac{32}{81} + \frac{48}{81} + \frac{24}{81} + \frac{4}{81} = \frac{108}{81} = \frac{4}{3}.$$

In general, it can be shown that in n trials with probability p for success, the expected number of successes is np.

EXAMPLE 4 In the game of craps a pair of dice is rolled by one of the players. If the sum of the spots shown is 7 or 11, he wins. If it is 2, 3, or 12, he loses. If it is another sum, he must continue rolling the dice until he either repeats the same sum or rolls a 7. In the former case he wins, in the latter he loses. Let us suppose that he wins or loses \$1. Then the two possible outcomes are $+1$ and -1. We shall compute the expected value of the game. First we must find the probability that he will win.

We represent the possibilities by a two-stage tree shown in Figure 19. While it is theoretically possible for the game to go on indefinitely, we do not consider this possibility. This means that our analysis applies only to games which actually stop at some time.

The branch probabilities at the first stage are determined by thinking of the 36 possibilities for the throw of the two dice as being equally likely and taking in each case the fraction of the possibilities which correspond to the branch as the branch probability. The probabilities for the branches at the second level are obtained as follows. If, for example, the first outcome was a 4, then when the game ends, a 4 or 7 must have occurred. The possible outcomes for the dice were

$$\{(3, 1), (1, 3), (2, 2), (4, 3), (3, 4), (2, 5), (5, 2), (1, 6), (6, 1)\}.$$

Again we consider these possibilities to be equally likely and assign to the branch considered the fraction of the outcomes which correspond to this

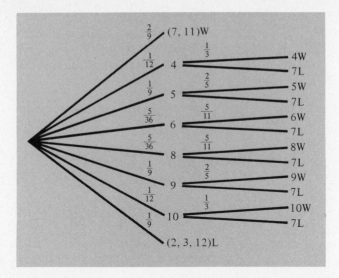

Figure 19

branch. Thus to the 4 branch we assign a probability $\frac{3}{9} = \frac{1}{3}$. The other branch probabilities are determined in a similar way. Having the tree measure assigned, to find the probability of a win we must simply add the weights of all paths leading to a win. If this is done, we obtain $\frac{244}{495}$. Thus the player's expected value is

$$1 \cdot \left(\tfrac{244}{495}\right) + (-1) \cdot \left(\tfrac{251}{495}\right) = -\tfrac{7}{495} = -.0141.$$

Hence he can expect to lose 1.41 percent of his stakes in the long run. It is interesting to note that this is just slightly less favorable than his losses in betting on "red" in roulette.

EXERCISES

1. If 13 coins are thrown, what is the expected number of heads that will turn up?   [*Ans.* $\frac{13}{2}$.]

2. An urn contains two black and three white balls. Balls are successively drawn from the urn without replacement until a white ball is obtained. Find the expected number of draws required. Do the same for the case of four black and six white balls.

3. Suppose that A tosses three coins and receives $8 if three heads appear, $4 if two heads appear, $2 if one head appears, and $1 if no heads appear. What is the expected value of the game to him? [*Ans.* $3\frac{3}{8}$.]

4. Two players, A and B, play the following dice game. A shakes a die that has three 2's and three 3's on the faces, while B shakes a die painted with four 1's and two 6's. Find A's expected winning (or loss) for each of the following sets of rules.

    (a) The player that shakes the lower number pays the other player $2.   [*Ans.* $\frac{2}{3}$.]

(b) The player that shakes the lower number pays the other player a number of dollars equal to the difference between the two outcomes.

(c) The player that shakes the lower number pays the other player a number of dollars equal to the number shaken by the other player.

5. A coin is thrown until the second time a head comes up or until three tails in a row occur. Find the expected number of times the coin is thrown. [*Ans.* $\frac{105}{32}$.]

6. A man wishes to purchase a five-cent newspaper. He has in his pocket one dime and five pennies. The newsman offers to let him have the paper in exchange for one coin drawn at random from the customer's pocket.

(a) Is this a fair proposition and, if not, to whom is it favorable? [*Ans.* Favorable to man.]

(b) Answer the same questions as in (a) assuming that the newsman demands two coins drawn at random from the customer's pocket. [*Ans.* Fair proposition.]

7. Referring to Exercise 17 of Chapter 1, Section 5, assuming that each speaker chooses his topic at random from those available to him,

(a) Find the expected number of speeches on brotherhood during a given program.

(b) Find the smallest number of programs that we would have to attend in order that the expected value of the number of speeches on integrity that we hear is to be at least five.

8. Prove that if the expected value of a given experiment is *E,* and if a constant c is added to each of the outcomes, the expected value of the new experiment is $E + c$.

9. Prove that, if the expected value of a given experiment is *E,* and if each of the possible outcomes is multiplied by a constant k, the expected value of the new experiment is $k \cdot E$.

10. A bets x cents against B's 78 cents that, if two cards are dealt from a shuffled pack of ordinary playing cards, both cards will be of the same color. What value of x will make this bet fair?

11. Betting on "red" in roulette can be described roughly as follows. We win with probability .49, get our money back with probability .01, and lose with probability .50. Draw the tree for three plays of the game, and compute (to three decimals), the probability of each path. What is the probability that we are ahead at the end of three bets? [*Ans.* .485.]

12. Assume that the odds are $r:s$ that a certain statement will be true. If a man receives s dollars if the statement turns out to be true, and gives r dollars if not, what is his expected winning?

13. In the World Series, we assume that the stronger team has probability .6 of winning each game. In this case the probabilities of the series

lasting 4, 5, 6, or 7 games are .16, .27, .30, and .28, respectively. What is the expected length of the World Series?   [*Ans.* 5.75.]

14. An office worker buys root beer from a defective machine which gives him orange soda instead of root beer $\frac{1}{5}$ of the time. He keeps buying soda until he gets his root beer or runs out of dimes. How many dimes must he carry with him every day if he wants to be able to expect to get root beer on at least 99 out of 100 days he uses the machine?
[*Ans.* 3.]

15. Suppose that in roulette at Monte Carlo we place 50 cents on "red" and 50 cents on "black." What is the expected value on the game? Is this better or worse than placing $1 on "red"? Which of the two games would it be more desirable to play?

16. Suppose that we modify the game of craps as follows: On a 7 or 11 the player wins $1; on a 2, 3, or 12 he loses $x; otherwise the game is as usual, all losses being $x. Find the expected value of the new game, and determine the value of x for which it becomes a fair game.

17. A gambler is given the choice of playing one of the following games. Either he pays $10 and throws three dice, receiving in return the number of dollars equal to the sum of the three outcomes, or he pays $12 and throws two dice, receiving in return the number of dollars equal to the product of the two outcomes. Which game should he play?

18. A pair of dice is rolled. Each die has the number 1 on two opposite faces, the number 2 on two opposite faces, and the number 3 on two opposite faces. The "roller" wins a dollar
    (i) if the sum of 4 occurs on the first roll; or
    (ii) if the sum of 3 or 5 occurs on the first roll and the same sum occurs on a subsequent roll before the sum of 4 occurs.
    Otherwise he loses a dollar.
    (a) What is the probability that the person rolling the dice wins?
    (b) What is the expected value of the game?   [*Ans.* (a) $\frac{23}{45}$; (b) $\frac{1}{45}$.]

12 MARKOV CHAINS

In this section we shall study a more general kind of process than the ones considered in the last three sections.

We assume that we have a sequence of experiments with the following properties. The outcome of each experiment is one of a finite number of possible outcomes $a_1, a_2, \ldots, a_r$. It is assumed that the probability of outcome a_j on any given experiment is not necessarily independent of the outcomes of previous experiments but depends at most upon the outcome of the immediately preceding experiment. We assume that there are given numbers p_{ij} which represent the probability of outcome a_j on any given experiment, given that outcome a_i occurred on the preceding experiment. The outcomes $a_1, a_2, \ldots, a_r$ are called *states,* and the numbers p_{ij} are called *transition probabilities.* If we assume that the process begins in some partic-

ular state, then we have enough information to determine the tree measure
for the process and can calculate probabilities of statements relating to the
overall sequence of experiments. A process of the above kind is called a
Markov chain process.

The transition probabilities can be exhibited in two different ways. The
first way is that of a square array. For a Markov chain with states $a_1, a_2,$
and a_3, this array is written as

$$P = \begin{pmatrix} p_{11} & p_{12} & p_{13} \\ p_{21} & p_{22} & p_{23} \\ p_{31} & p_{32} & p_{33} \end{pmatrix}.$$

Such an array is a special case of a *matrix*. Matrices are of fundamental
importance to the study of Markov chains as well as being important in
the study of other branches of mathematics. They will be studied in detail
in the next chapter.

A second way to show the transition probabilities is by a *transition
diagram*. Such a diagram is illustrated for a special case in Figure 20. The
arrows from each state indicate the possible states to which a process can
move from the given state.

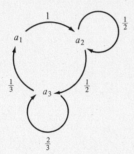

Figure 20

The matrix of transition probabilities which corresponds to this diagram
is the matrix

$$P = \begin{array}{c} a_1 \\ a_2 \\ a_3 \end{array} \begin{pmatrix} \begin{array}{ccc} a_1 & a_2 & a_3 \end{array} \\ 0 & 1 & 0 \\ 0 & \frac{1}{2} & \frac{1}{2} \\ \frac{1}{3} & 0 & \frac{2}{3} \end{pmatrix}.$$

An entry of 0 indicates that the transition is impossible.

Notice that in the matrix P the sum of the elements of each row is 1.
This must be true in any matrix of transition probabilities, since the elements
of the ith row represent the probabilities for all possibilities when the process
is in state a_i.

The kind of problem in which we are most interested in the study of
Markov chains is the following. Suppose that the process starts in state i.

What is the probability that after n steps it will be in state j? We denote this probability by $p_{ij}^{(n)}$. Notice that we do *not* mean by this the nth power of the number p_{ij}. We are actually interested in this probability for all possible starting positions i and all possible terminal positions j. We can represent these numbers conveniently again by a matrix. For example, for n steps in a three-state Markov chain we write these probabilities as the matrix

$$P^{(n)} = \begin{pmatrix} p_{11}^{(n)} & p_{12}^{(n)} & p_{13}^{(n)} \\ p_{21}^{(n)} & p_{22}^{(n)} & p_{23}^{(n)} \\ p_{31}^{(n)} & p_{32}^{(n)} & p_{33}^{(n)} \end{pmatrix}.$$

EXAMPLE 1   Let us find for a Markov chain with transition probabilities indicated in Figure 20 the probability of being at the various possible states after three steps, assuming that the process starts at state a_1. We find these probabilities by constructing a tree and a tree measure as in Figure 21.

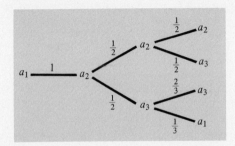

Figure 21

The probability $p_{13}^{(3)}$, for example, is the sum of the weights assigned by the tree measure to all paths through our tree which end at state a_3. That is,

$$1 \cdot \tfrac{1}{2} \cdot \tfrac{1}{2} + 1 \cdot \tfrac{1}{2} \cdot \tfrac{2}{3} = \tfrac{7}{12}.$$

Similarly,

$$p_{12}^{(3)} = 1 \cdot \tfrac{1}{2} \cdot \tfrac{1}{2} = \tfrac{1}{4} \quad \text{and} \quad p_{11}^{(3)} = 1 \cdot \tfrac{1}{2} \cdot \tfrac{1}{3} = \tfrac{1}{6}.$$

By constructing a similar tree measure, assuming that we start at state a_2, we could find $p_{21}^{(3)}$, $p_{22}^{(3)}$, and $p_{23}^{(3)}$. The same is true for $p_{31}^{(3)}$, $p_{32}^{(3)}$, and $p_{33}^{(3)}$. If this is carried out (see Exercise 7) we can write the results in matrix form as follows:

$$P^{(3)} = \begin{matrix} & \begin{matrix} a_1 & a_2 & a_3 \end{matrix} \\ \begin{matrix} a_1 \\ a_2 \\ a_3 \end{matrix} & \begin{pmatrix} \tfrac{1}{6} & \tfrac{1}{4} & \tfrac{7}{12} \\ \tfrac{7}{36} & \tfrac{7}{24} & \tfrac{37}{72} \\ \tfrac{4}{27} & \tfrac{7}{18} & \tfrac{25}{54} \end{pmatrix} \end{matrix}.$$

Again the rows add up to 1, corresponding to the fact that if we start at a given state we must reach some state after three steps. Notice now that all the elements of this matrix are positive, showing that it is possible to reach any state from any state in three steps. In the next chapter we shall develop a simple method of computing $P^{(n)}$.

EXAMPLE 2   Suppose that we are interested in studying the way in which a given state votes in a series of national elections. We wish to make long-term predictions and so shall not consider conditions peculiar to a particular election year. We shall base our predictions only on past history of the outcomes of the elections, Republican or Democratic. It is clear that a knowledge of these past results would influence our predictions for the future. As a first approximation, we assume that the knowledge of the past beyond the last election would not cause us to change the probabilities for the outcomes on the next election. With this assumption we obtain a Markov chain with two states R and D and matrix of transition probabilities

$$\begin{array}{c} \\ R \\ D \end{array} \begin{pmatrix} \overset{\displaystyle R}{1-a} & \overset{\displaystyle D}{a} \\ b & 1-b \end{pmatrix}.$$

The numbers a and b could be estimated from past results as follows. We could take for a the fraction of the previous years in which the outcome has changed from Republican in one year to Democratic in the next year, and for b the fraction of reverse changes.

We can obtain a better approximation by taking into account the previous two elections. In this case our states are RR, RD, DR, and DD, indicating the outcome of two successive elections. Being in state RR means that the last two elections were Republican victories. If the next election is a Democratic victory, we will be in state RD. If the election outcomes for a series of years is $DDDRDRR$, then our process has moved from state DD to DD to DR to RD to DR, and finally to RR. Notice that the first letter of the state to which we move must agree with the second letter of the state from which we came, since these refer to the same election year. Our matrix of transition probabilities will then have the following form:

$$\begin{array}{c} RR \\ DR \\ RD \\ DD \end{array} \begin{pmatrix} \overset{\displaystyle RR}{1-a} & \overset{\displaystyle DR}{0} & \overset{\displaystyle RD}{a} & \overset{\displaystyle DD}{0} \\ b & 0 & 1-b & 0 \\ 0 & 1-c & 0 & c \\ 0 & d & 0 & 1-d \end{pmatrix}.$$

Again the numbers a, b, c, and d would have to be estimated. The study of this example is continued in Chapter 4, Section 7.

EXAMPLE 3   The following example of a Markov chain has been used in physics as a
simple model for diffusion of gases. We shall see later that a similar model
applies to an idealized problem in changing populations.

We imagine n black balls and n white balls which are put into two urns
so that there are n balls in each urn. A single experiment consists in choosing
a ball from each urn at random and putting the ball obtained from the
first urn into the second urn, and the ball obtained from the second urn
into the first. We take as state the number of black balls in the first urn.
If at any time we know this number, then we know the exact composition
of each urn. That is, if there are j black balls in urn 1, there must be $n - j$
black balls in urn 2, $n - j$ white balls in urn 1, and j white balls in urn
2. If the process is in state j, then after the next exchange it will be in state
$j - 1$, if a black ball is chosen from urn 1 and a white ball from urn 2.
It will be in state j if a ball of the same color is drawn from each urn.
It will be in state $j + 1$ if a white ball is drawn from urn 1 and a black
ball from urn 2. The transition probabilities are then given by (see Exercise 12)

$$p_{jj-1} = \left(\frac{j}{n}\right)^2 \qquad j > 0$$

$$p_{jj} = \frac{2j(n - j)}{n^2}$$

$$p_{jj+1} = \left(\frac{n - j}{n}\right)^2 \quad j < n$$

$$p_{jk} = 0 \qquad\qquad \text{otherwise.}$$

A physicist would be interested, for example, in predicting the composition
of the urns after a certain number of exchanges have taken place. Certainly
any predictions about the early stages of the process would depend upon
the initial composition of the urns. For example, if we started with all black
balls in urn 1, we would expect that for some time there would be more
black balls in urn 1 than in urn 2. On the other hand, it might be expected
that the effect of this initial distribution would wear off after a large number
of exchanges. We shall see later, in Chapter 4, Section 7, that this is indeed
the case.

EXERCISES

1. Draw a transition diagram for the Markov chains with transition
    probabilities given by the following matrices:

$$\begin{pmatrix} \frac{1}{2} & 0 & \frac{1}{2} \\ 0 & 1 & 0 \\ \frac{1}{3} & 0 & \frac{2}{3} \end{pmatrix}, \quad \begin{pmatrix} \frac{1}{3} & \frac{1}{6} & \frac{1}{2} \\ \frac{1}{6} & \frac{1}{2} & \frac{1}{3} \\ \frac{1}{2} & \frac{1}{3} & \frac{1}{6} \end{pmatrix}, \quad \begin{pmatrix} 0 & 1 \\ \frac{1}{2} & \frac{1}{2} \end{pmatrix}, \quad \begin{pmatrix} 0 & 1 & 0 & 0 \\ 1 & 0 & 0 & 0 \\ 1 & 0 & 0 & 0 \\ \frac{1}{12} & \frac{1}{6} & \frac{1}{4} & \frac{1}{2} \end{pmatrix}.$$

2. Give the matrix of transition probabilities corresponding to the following transition diagrams:

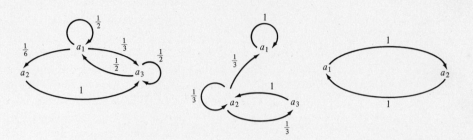

3. What is the matrix of transition probabilities for the Markov chain in Example 3, for the case of two white balls and two black balls?

4. Find the matrix $P^{(2)}$ for the Markov chain determined by the matrix of transition probabilities

$$P = \begin{pmatrix} \frac{1}{4} & \frac{3}{4} \\ \frac{1}{3} & \frac{2}{3} \end{pmatrix}. \qquad \left[Ans. \begin{pmatrix} \frac{5}{16} & \frac{11}{16} \\ \frac{11}{36} & \frac{25}{36} \end{pmatrix}. \right]$$

5. Find the matrices $P^{(2)}$, $P^{(3)}$, $P^{(4)}$ for the Markov chain determined by the transition probabilities

$$\begin{pmatrix} 1 & 0 & 0 \\ 0 & 1 & 0 \\ 0 & 0 & 1 \end{pmatrix}.$$

Find the same for the Markov chain determined by the matrix

$$\begin{pmatrix} 0 & 0 & 1 \\ 0 & 1 & 0 \\ 1 & 0 & 0 \end{pmatrix}.$$

6. (a) What is the relationship between independent trials processes and Markov chains?

> [*Ans.* Every independent trials process, given a particular starting state, is a Markov chain.]

(b) Set up a transition diagram and matrix for tossing a fair coin. Find $P^{(2)}$ and $P^{(3)}$.

(c) Repeat part (b) for a coin that comes up heads with probability $\frac{3}{4}$.

7. Referring to the Markov chain with transition probabilities indicated in Figure 21, construct the tree measures and determine the values of

$$p_{21}^{(3)}, p_{22}^{(3)}, p_{23}^{(3)} \quad \text{and} \quad p_{31}^{(3)}, p_{32}^{(3)}, p_{33}^{(3)}.$$

8. Suppose that a Markov chain has two states, a_1 and a_2, and transition probabilities given by the matrix

$$\begin{pmatrix} \frac{1}{2} & \frac{1}{2} \\ \frac{1}{4} & \frac{3}{4} \end{pmatrix}.$$

By means of a separate chance device we choose a state in which to start the process. This device chooses a_1 with probability $\frac{1}{2}$ and a_2 with probability $\frac{1}{2}$. Find the probability that the process is in state a_1 after the first step. Answer the same question in the case that the device chooses a_1 with probability $\frac{1}{3}$ and a_2 with probability $\frac{2}{3}$.   [*Ans.* $\frac{3}{8}$; $\frac{1}{3}$.]

9. A certain calculating machine uses only the digits 0 and 1. It is supposed to transmit one of these digits through several stages. However, at every stage there is a probability p that the digit which enters this stage will be changed when it leaves. We form a Markov chain to represent the process of transmission by taking as states the digits 0 and 1. What is the matrix of transition probabilities?

10. For the Markov chain in Exercise 9, draw a tree and assign a tree measure, assuming that the process begins in state 1 and moves through three stages of transmission. What is the probability that the machine after three stages produces the digit 1, i.e., the correct digit? What is the probability that the machine changed the digit from 1 but ended up with a 1 after three stages?

11. A student has a class that meets on Monday, Wednesday, and Friday. He decides on any one of these days to go to class with a probability that depends only on whether or not he went to the last class. If he did go to class on one day, he goes to the next class with probability $\frac{1}{2}$. If he did not go to one class, he goes to the next class with probability $\frac{3}{4}$. Set up the matrix of transition probabilities and find the probability that if he went to class on Monday, he will also attend the class on Friday of that week.

12. Explain why the transition probabilities given in Example 3 are correct.

13. Assume that a man's profession can be classified as professional, skilled laborer, or unskilled laborer. Assume that of the sons of professional men 80 percent are professionals, 15 percent are skilled laborers, and 5 percent are unskilled laborers. In the case of sons of skilled laborers, 50 percent are skilled laborers, 25 percent are professionals, and 25 percent are unskilled laborers. Finally, in the case of unskilled laborers, 40 percent of the sons are unskilled laborers and 30 percent each are in the other two categories. Assume that every man has a son, and form a Markov chain by following a given family through several generations. Set up the matrix of transition probabilities. Find the probability that the grandson of a skilled laborer is a professional man.

[*Ans.* .4.]

14. In Exercise 13 we assumed that every man has a son. Assume instead

that the probability a man has a son is .75. Form a Markov chain with four states. The first three states are as in Exercise 13, and the fourth state is such that the process enters it if a man has no son, and that the state cannot be left. This state represents families whose male line has died out. Find the matrix of transition probabilities and find the probability that a skilled laborer has a grandson who is a professional man.   [*Ans.* .225.]

15. In another model for diffusion, it is assumed that there are two urns which together contain N balls numbered from 1 to N. Each second a number from 1 to N is chosen at random, and the ball with the corresponding number is moved to the other urn. For $N = 4$ set up a Markov chain by taking as state the number of balls in urn 1. Find the transition matrix.

16. In a two-player game, each player starts out with three chips. Two dice are then tossed. If the sum of the numbers tossed is less than 7, player A gets a chip from player B. If the total is greater than 7, B gets a chip from A. If a 7 is tossed, either the player with less chips gets one from the other player or, if the players are even, they remain even. The game continues until one player runs out of chips. Using as states the number of chips that A has, set up the transition matrix. (Assume that once A gets to the state 0 or 6 he stays there with probability 1 next time.)

17. In Exercise 16, find the following:

   (a) The probability that B loses in three turns. $\left[Ans. \dfrac{125}{1728}. \right]$

   (b) The probability that B loses in three turns starting with two chips left.

   (c) $P_{24}^{(3)}$.

   (d) The probability that A loses in five or less turns.

   $$\left[Ans. \frac{34{,}625}{12^5} \approx .139. \right]$$

*13   GAMBLER'S RUIN

In this section we shall study a particular Markov chain, which is interesting in itself and has far-reaching applications. Its name, "gambler's ruin," derives from one of its many applications. In the text we shall describe the chain from the gambling point of view, but in the exercises we shall present several other applications.

   Let us suppose that you are gambling against a professional gambler or gambling house. You have selected a specific game to play, on which you have probability p of winning. The gambler has made sure that the game is favorable to him, so that $p < \frac{1}{2}$. However, in most situations p will be close to $\frac{1}{2}$. (The cases $p = \frac{1}{2}$ and $p > \frac{1}{2}$ are considered in the exercises.)

At the start of the game you have A dollars, and the gambler has B dollars. You bet \$1 on each game, and play until one of you is ruined. What is the probability that you will be ruined? Of course, the answer depends on the exact values of p, A, and B. We shall develop a formula for the ruin-probability in terms of these three given numbers.

First we shall set the problem up as a Markov chain. Let $N = A + B$, the total amount of money in the game. As states for the chain we choose the numbers $0, 1, 2, \ldots, N$. At any one moment the position of the chain is the amount of money *you* have. The initial position is shown in Figure 22.

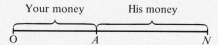

Figure 22

If you win a game, your money increases by \$1, and the gambler's fortune decreases by \$1. Thus the new position is one state to the right of the previous one. If you lose a game, the chain moves one step to the left. Thus at any step there is probability p of moving one step to the right, and probability $q = 1 - p$ of one step to the left. Since the probabilities for the next position are determined by the present position, it is a Markov chain.

If the chain reaches 0 or N, we stop. When 0 is reached, you are ruined. When N is reached, you have all the money, and you have ruined the gambler. We shall be interested in the probability of *your* ruin, i.e., the probability of reaching 0.

Let us suppose that p and N are fixed. We actually want the probability of ruin when we start at A. However, it turns out to be easier to solve a problem that appears much harder: Find the ruin-probability for every possible starting position. For this reason we introduce the notation x_i, to stand for the probability of your ruin if you start in position i (that is, if you have i dollars).

Let us first solve the problem for the case $N = 5$. We have the unknowns x_0, x_1, x_2, x_3, x_4, and x_5. Suppose that we start at position 2. The chain moves to 3, with probability p, or to 1, with probability q. Thus

$$\Pr[\text{ruin}|\text{start at } 2] = \Pr[\text{ruin}|\text{start at } 3] \cdot p + \Pr[\text{ruin}|\text{start at } 1] \cdot q,$$

using the conditional probability formula, with a set of two alternatives. But once it has reached state 3, a Markov chain behaves just as if it had been started there. Thus

$$\Pr[\text{ruin}|\text{start at } 3] = x_3.$$

And, similarly,

$$\Pr[\text{ruin}|\text{start at } 1] = x_1.$$

We obtain the key relation

$$x_2 = px_3 + qx_1.$$

We can modify this as follows: using $p + q = 1$, we have

$$x_2 = (p + q)x_2 = px_3 + qx_1$$
$$p(x_2 - x_3) = q(x_1 - x_2)$$
$$x_1 - x_2 = r(x_2 - x_3),$$

where $r = p/q$, and hence $r < 1$. When we write such an equation for each of the four "ordinary" positions, we obtain

(1)
$$x_0 - x_1 = r(x_1 - x_2)$$
$$x_1 - x_2 = r(x_2 - x_3)$$
$$x_2 - x_3 = r(x_3 - x_4)$$
$$x_3 - x_4 = r(x_4 - x_5).$$

We must still consider the two extreme positions. Suppose that the chain reaches 0. Then you are ruined, hence the probability of your ruin is 1. While if the chain reaches $N = 5$, the gambler drops out of the game, and you can't be ruined. Thus

(2)
$$x_0 = 1, \qquad x_5 = 0.$$

If we substitute the value of x_5 in the last equation of (1), we have $x_3 - x_4 = rx_4$. This in turn may be substituted in the previous equation, etc. We thus have the simpler equations

(3)
$$x_4 = 1 \cdot x_4$$
$$x_3 - x_4 = rx_4$$
$$x_2 - x_3 = r^2 x_4$$
$$x_1 - x_2 = r^3 x_4$$
$$x_0 - x_1 = r^4 x_4.$$

Let us add all the equations. We obtain

$$x_0 = (1 + r + r^2 + r^3 + r^4)x_4.$$

From (2) we have that $x_0 = 1$. We also use the simple identity

$$(1 - r)(1 + r + r^2 + r^3 + r^4) = 1 - r^5,$$

which implies

$$1 + r + r^2 + r^3 + r^4 = \frac{1 - r^5}{1 - r}.$$

And then we solve for x_4:

$$x_4 = \frac{1 - r}{1 - r^5}.$$

If we add the first two equations in (3), we have that $x_3 = (1 + r)x_4$. Similarly, adding the first three equations, we solve for x_2, and adding the

Ruin-probabilities for $p = .45, .48, .49, .495.$

$p = .45$

A \ B	1	5	10	20	50
1	.550	.905	.973	.997	1
5	.260	.732	.910	.988	1
10	.204	.666	.881	.984	1
20	.185	.638	.868	.982	1
50	.182	.633	.866	.982	1

$p = .48$

A \ B	1	5	10	20	50
1	.520	.865	.941	.981	.999
5	.202	.599	.788	.923	.994
10	.131	.472	.690	.878	.990
20	.095	.381	.606	.832	.985
50	.078	.334	.555	.801	.982

$p = .49$

A \ B	1	5	10	20	50
1	.510	.850	.926	.969	.994
5	.184	.550	.731	.871	.972
10	.110	.402	.599	.788	.951
20	.069	.287	.472	.690	.921
50	.045	.204	.363	.586	.881

$p = .495$

A \ B	1	5	10	20	50
1	.505	.842	.918	.961	.989
5	.175	.525	.699	.838	.948
10	.100	.367	.550	.731	.905
20	.058	.242	.402	.599	.839
50	.031	.143	.259	.438	.731

Figure 23

first four equations we obtain x_1. We now have our entire solution:

$$(4) \qquad x_1 = \frac{1-r^4}{1-r^5}, \quad x_2 = \frac{1-r^3}{1-r^5}, \quad x_3 = \frac{1-r^2}{1-r^5}, \quad x_4 = \frac{1-r}{1-r^5}.$$

The same method will work for any value of N. And it is easy to guess from (4) what the general solution looks like. If we want x_A, the answer is a fraction like those in (4). In the denominator the exponent of r is always N. In the numerator the exponent is $N - A$, which equals B. Thus the ruin-probability is

$$(5) \qquad\qquad x_A = \frac{1-r^B}{1-r^N}.$$

We recall that A is the amount of money you have, B is the gambler's stake, $N = A + B$, p is your probability of winning a game, and $r = p/(1-p)$.

In Figure 23 we show some typical values of the ruin-probability. Some of these are quite startling. If the probability of p is as low as .45 (odds against you on each game 11:9) and the gambler has $20 to put up, you are almost sure to be ruined. Even in a nearly fair game, say $p = .495$, with each of you having $50 to start with, there is a .731 chance for your ruin.

It is worth examining the ruin-probability formula, (5), more closely. Since the denominator is always less than 1, your probability of ruin is at least $1 - r^B$. This estimate does not depend on how much money you have, only on p and B. Since r is less than 1, by making B large enough we can make r^B practically 0, and hence make it almost certain that you will be ruined.

Suppose, for example, that a gambler wants to have probability .999 of ruining you. (You can hardly call him a gambler under those circumstances!) He must make sure that $r^B < .001$. For example, if $p = .495$, the gambler needs $346 to have probability .999 of ruining you, even if you are a millionaire. If $p = .48$, he needs only $87. And even for the almost fair game with $p = .499$, $1727 will suffice.

There are two ways that gamblers achieve this goal. Small gambling houses will fix the odds quite a bit in their favor, making r much less than 1. Then even a relatively small bank of B dollars suffices to assure them of winning. Larger houses, with B quite sizable, can afford to let you play nearly fair games.

EXERCISES

1. Suppose you are playing the "shell game" with a gambler. (In this game, the gambler hides a pea under one of three cups and shuffles them around, and you guess which cup it is.) If you guess correctly, you win $1; if you guess wrong, you lose $1. Suppose you each start out with $2 and play until someone is ruined. What is your probability of losing all your money?

2. Verify that the proof of the text is still correct when $p > \frac{1}{2}$. Interpret formula (5) for this case.

3. Show that if $p > \frac{1}{2}$ and both parties have a substantial amount of money, your probability of ruin is approximately $1/r^A$.

4. Suppose that both the gambler and the player in Exercise 1 start with $10. Find the approximate probability of the *gambler* being ruined. (Use Exercise 3.)

5. Modify the proof in the text to apply to the case $p = \frac{1}{2}$. What is the probability of your ruin?   [*Ans. B/N.*]

6. Suppose the game in Exercise 1 is being played with two cups, and you start with $10, the gambler with $15. What is your probability of being ruined?

7. A man leaves a bar in a state of intoxication, and starts to walk randomly. Fifty steps to the left of the bar is the subway entrance, and 50 steps to the right of the bar is the police station. What is the probability that the man makes it to the subway before arriving at the police station if:
   (a) He is equally likely to take a step to the right as to the left?
   (b) He has probability .52 of taking a step to the left?
   (c) He has probability .55 of taking a step to the right?

8. A demon operates a gate between two halves of a box. Initially each side of the box contains 20 molecules. The demon attempts to operate the gate in such a way that all the molecules end up on the left side of the box. Since the inside of the box is quite dark, however, he succeeds only 51 percent of the time; on the other occasions when he opens the gate, a molecule escapes from left to right. (The gate shuts so quickly that only one molecule passes through it each time it is opened.) Suppose the demon operates the gate until all the molecules are on one side or the other. What is the probability that all will be on the left side?   [*Ans. .690.*]

9. What is the approximate value of x_A if you are rich and the gambler starts with $1? Assume the game is weighted so the gambler has the advantage.

10. Suppose you are playing the shell game of Exercise 1 with a poverty-stricken gambler who has only $1, while you are a millionaire. What, approximately, is the probability that you will be ruined?

11. Consider a simple model for evolution. On a small island there is room for 1000 members of a certain species. One year a favorable mutant appears. We assume that in each subsequent generation either the mutants take one place from the regular members of the species, with probability .6, or the reverse happens. Thus for example, the mutation disappears in the very first generation with probability .4. What is the probability that the mutants eventually take over? [*Hint:* See Exercise 9.]   [*Ans.* $\frac{1}{3}$.]

12. After a single crystal of the (fictional) substance ice-eight is added to a container of water, there is probability .9 that one molecule of water

changes to ice-eight every minute, and probability .1 that a crystal of ice-eight changes back to water. What is the approximate probability that the entire contents of the container will eventually consist of ice-eight?

13. You are in the following hopeless situation: You are playing the shell game of Exercise 1, in which you have only $\frac{1}{3}$ chance of winning. You have \$1, and your opponent has \$15. What is the probability of your winning all his money if
    (a) You bet \$1 each time?
    (b) You bet all your money each time?   [*Ans.* $\frac{1}{81}$.]
14. Repeat Exercise 13 for the case of a fair game, where you have probability $\frac{1}{2}$ of winning.

    NOTE: Exercises 15–18 deal with the following win problem: A and B are playing a game in which A has probability .6 of winning. They play until A wins three games or B wins two games.

15. Set up the process as a Markov chain in which the states are (a, b), where A has won a games and B has won b games.
16. For each state (a, b), find the probability that A wins.
17. What is the probability that A will achieve his goal first? [*Ans.* $\frac{297}{625}$.]
18. Suppose that payments are made as follows: If A wins three games, he receives \$1; if B wins two games then A pays \$1. What is the expected value of A's winnings, to the nearest penny?

SUGGESTED READING

Dwass, M. *Probability: Theory and Applications.* New York: W. A. Benjamin, 1969.

Feller, W. *An Introduction to Theory and its Applications.* New York: John Wiley, 1950.

Goldberg, S. *Probability: An Introduction.* Englewood Cliffs, N.J.: Prentice-Hall, 1960.

Mosteller, F. *Fifty Challenging Problems in Probability with Solutions.* Reading, Mass.: Addison-Wesley, 1960.

Mosteller, F.; Rourke, Robert E. K.; and **Thomas, G. B.** *Probability with Statistical Applications.* Reading, Mass.: Addison-Wesley, 1970.

Parzen, E. *Modern Probability Theory and Its Applications.* New York: John Wiley, 1960.

Vectors
and Matrices

1 COLUMN AND ROW VECTORS

A *column vector* is an ordered collection of numbers written in a column. Examples of such vectors are

$$\begin{pmatrix} 1 \\ -2 \end{pmatrix}, \quad \begin{pmatrix} .6 \\ .4 \end{pmatrix}, \quad \begin{pmatrix} 0 \\ 0 \\ 0 \end{pmatrix}, \quad \begin{pmatrix} 3 \\ -4 \\ 0 \end{pmatrix}, \quad \begin{pmatrix} 1 \\ -1 \\ 2 \\ 4 \end{pmatrix}.$$

The individual numbers in these vectors are called *components,* and the number of components a vector has is one of its distinguishing characteristics. Thus the first two vectors above have two components; the next two have three components; and the last has four components. When talking more generally about n-component column vectors we shall write

$$u = \begin{pmatrix} u_1 \\ u_2 \\ \vdots \\ u_n \end{pmatrix}.$$

Analogously, a *row vector* is an ordered collection of numbers written in a row. Examples of row vectors are

$$(1, 0), \quad (-2, 1), \quad (2, -3, 4, 0), \quad (-1, 2, -3, 4, -5).$$

Each number appearing in the vector is again called a *component* of the vector, and the number of components a row vector has is again one of its important characteristics. Thus the first two examples are two-component, the third a four-component, and the fourth a five-component vector. The vector $v = (v_1, v_2, \ldots, v_n)$ is an n-component row vector.

Two row vectors, or two column vectors, are said to be *equal* if and only if corresponding components of the vector are equal. Thus for the vectors

$$u = (1, 2), \qquad v = \begin{pmatrix} 1 \\ 2 \end{pmatrix}, \qquad w = (1, 2), \qquad x = (2, 1)$$

we see that $u = w$ but $u \neq v$, and $u \neq x$.

If u and v are three-component column vectors, we shall define their sum $u + v$ by componentwise addition as follows:

$$u + v = \begin{pmatrix} u_1 \\ u_2 \\ u_3 \end{pmatrix} + \begin{pmatrix} v_1 \\ v_2 \\ v_3 \end{pmatrix} = \begin{pmatrix} u_1 + v_1 \\ u_2 + v_2 \\ u_3 + v_3 \end{pmatrix}.$$

Similarly, if u and v are three-component row vectors, their sum is defined to be

$$\begin{aligned} u + v &= (u_1, u_2, u_3) + (v_1, v_2, v_3) \\ &= (u_1 + v_1, u_2 + v_2, u_3 + v_3). \end{aligned}$$

Note that the sum of two three-component vectors yields another three-component vector. For example,

$$\begin{pmatrix} 1 \\ -1 \\ 2 \end{pmatrix} + \begin{pmatrix} 2 \\ 3 \\ -1 \end{pmatrix} = \begin{pmatrix} 3 \\ 2 \\ 1 \end{pmatrix}$$

and

$$(4, -7, 12) + (3, 14, -14) = (7, 7, -2).$$

The sum of two n-component vectors (either row or column) is defined by componentwise addition in an analogous manner, and yields another n-component vector. Observe that we do not define the addition of vectors unless they are both row or both column vectors having the same number of components.

Because the order in which two numbers are added does not affect the answer, it is also true that the order in which vectors are added does not matter; that is,

$$u + v = v + u,$$

where u and v are both row or both column vectors. This is the so-called *commutative law of addition*. A numerical example is

$$\begin{pmatrix} 1 \\ -1 \\ 2 \end{pmatrix} + \begin{pmatrix} 2 \\ 3 \\ -1 \end{pmatrix} = \begin{pmatrix} 3 \\ 2 \\ 1 \end{pmatrix} = \begin{pmatrix} 2 \\ 3 \\ -1 \end{pmatrix} + \begin{pmatrix} 1 \\ -1 \\ 2 \end{pmatrix}$$

Once we have the definition of the addition of two vectors, we can easily see how to add three or more vectors by grouping them in pairs as in the addition of numbers. For example,

$$\begin{pmatrix}1\\0\\0\end{pmatrix}+\begin{pmatrix}0\\2\\0\end{pmatrix}+\begin{pmatrix}0\\0\\3\end{pmatrix}=\begin{pmatrix}1\\0\\0\end{pmatrix}+\begin{pmatrix}0\\2\\3\end{pmatrix}=\begin{pmatrix}1\\2\\3\end{pmatrix}=\begin{pmatrix}1\\2\\0\end{pmatrix}+\begin{pmatrix}0\\0\\3\end{pmatrix}=\begin{pmatrix}1\\2\\3\end{pmatrix}$$

and

$$(1,0,0)+(0,2,0)+(0,0,3)=(1,2,0)+(0,0,3)=(1,2,3)$$
$$=(1,0,0)+(0,2,3)=(1,2,3).$$

In general, the sum of any number of vectors (row or column), each having the same number of components, is the vector whose first component is the sum of the first components of the vectors, whose second component is the sum of the second components, and so on.

The multiplication of a number a times a vector v is defined by componentwise multiplication of a times the components of v. For the three-component case we have

$$au = a\begin{pmatrix}u_1\\u_2\\u_3\end{pmatrix}=\begin{pmatrix}au_1\\au_2\\au_3\end{pmatrix}$$

for column vectors and

$$av = a(v_1, v_2, v_3) = (av_1, av_2, av_3)$$

for row vectors. If u is an n-component vector (row or column), then au is defined similarly by componentwise multiplication. This operation is sometimes called *scalar multiplication* of a vector, where *scalar* is another name for a number.

If u is any vector, we define its negative $-u$ to be the vector $-u = (-1)u$. Thus in the three-component case for row vectors we have

$$-u = (-1)(u_1, u_2, u_3) = (-u_1, -u_2, -u_3).$$

Once we have the negative of a vector it is easy to see how to subtract vectors: we simply add "algebraically." For the three-component column-vector case we have

$$u - v = \begin{pmatrix}u_1\\u_2\\u_3\end{pmatrix}-\begin{pmatrix}v_1\\v_2\\v_3\end{pmatrix}=\begin{pmatrix}u_1-v_1\\u_2-v_2\\u_3-v_3\end{pmatrix}.$$

Specific examples of subtraction of vectors occur in the exercises at the end of this section.

An important vector is the zero vector, all of whose components are zero. For example, three-component zero vectors are

$$0=\begin{pmatrix}0\\0\\0\end{pmatrix}\qquad\text{and}\qquad 0=(0,0,0).$$

When there is no danger of confusion we shall use the symbol 0, as above, to denote the zero (row or column) vector. The meaning will be clear from the context. The zero vector has the important property that, if u is any vector, then $u + 0 = u$. A proof for the three-component column-vector case is as follows:

$$u + 0 = \begin{pmatrix} u_1 \\ u_2 \\ u_3 \end{pmatrix} + \begin{pmatrix} 0 \\ 0 \\ 0 \end{pmatrix} = \begin{pmatrix} u_1 + 0 \\ u_2 + 0 \\ u_3 + 0 \end{pmatrix} = \begin{pmatrix} u_1 \\ u_2 \\ u_3 \end{pmatrix} = u.$$

One of the chief advantages of the vector notation is that we can denote a whole collection of numbers by a single letter such as $u, v, \ldots$, and treat such a collection as if it were a single quantity. By using the vector notation we can state very complicated relationships in a simple manner. The student will see many examples of this in the remainder of the present chapter and in the three succeeding chapters.

EXERCISES

1. Compute the quantities below for the vectors

$$u = \begin{pmatrix} 2 \\ 1 \\ 8 \\ 6 \end{pmatrix}, \quad v = \begin{pmatrix} 3 \\ -5 \\ 2 \\ 0 \end{pmatrix}, \quad w = \begin{pmatrix} 6 \\ 6 \\ -6 \\ -6 \end{pmatrix}.$$

(a) $u + w$. $\left[Ans. \begin{pmatrix} 8 \\ 7 \\ 2 \\ 0 \end{pmatrix}. \right]$

(b) $5w$.

(c) $v - u$.

(d) $3u + 7v - 2w$. $\left[Ans. \begin{pmatrix} 15 \\ -44 \\ 50 \\ 30 \end{pmatrix}. \right]$

(e) $\frac{1}{2}w + \frac{3}{4}u$.

(f) $u - w - v$.

(g) $-2u + 3v - 100w$.

2. Compute (a) through (g) of Exercise 1 if the vectors u, v, and w are

$$u = (7, 0, -3), \qquad v = (2, 1, -5), \qquad w = (1, -1, 0).$$

3. (a) Show that the zero vector is not changed when multiplied by any number.

   (b) If u is any vector, show that $0 + u = u$.

4. If $2u - v = 0$, what is the relationship between the components of u and those of v?   [*Ans.* $v_i = 2u_i$.]

5. When possible, compute the following sums; when not possible, give reasons.

   (a) $(2, 3) + 2\begin{pmatrix}1\\5\end{pmatrix} = ?$

   (b) $0(5, 1, 7) + 3(6, 2, 6) = ?$

   (c) $\begin{pmatrix}3\\1\\2\end{pmatrix} + 5 + \begin{pmatrix}6\\2\\6\end{pmatrix} = ?$ [*Ans.* Not possible.]

   (d) $\begin{pmatrix}21\\22\\23\\24\end{pmatrix} + 32\begin{pmatrix}1\\2\\0\\1\end{pmatrix} = ?$ [*Ans.* $\begin{pmatrix}53\\86\\23\\56\end{pmatrix}$.]

6. If $\begin{pmatrix}6\\6\\0\end{pmatrix} + \begin{pmatrix}u_1\\u_2\\u_3\end{pmatrix} = \begin{pmatrix}5\\-5\\5\end{pmatrix}$, find u_1, u_2, and u_3.   [*Ans.* $-1, -11, 5$.]

7. If $8\begin{pmatrix}v_1\\v_2\\v_3\end{pmatrix} = \begin{pmatrix}7\\-16\\0\end{pmatrix}$, find the components of v.

8. Find three vectors $u, v,$ and w such that $w = 3u$, $v = 2u$, and
$$2u + 3v + 4w = \begin{pmatrix}20\\10\\-25\end{pmatrix}.$$

9. If $\begin{pmatrix}0\\0\\0\end{pmatrix} + \begin{pmatrix}u_1\\u_2\\u_3\end{pmatrix} = \begin{pmatrix}0\\0\\0\end{pmatrix}$, what can be said concerning the components u_1, u_2, u_3?

10. If $0\begin{pmatrix}u_1\\u_2\\u_3\end{pmatrix} = \begin{pmatrix}0\\0\\0\end{pmatrix}$, what can be said concerning the components u_1, $u_2\ u_3$?

11. If $(u_1 + u_2 + u_3 + u_4)\begin{pmatrix}u_1\\u_2\\u_3\\u_4\end{pmatrix} = \begin{pmatrix}1\\3\\5\\7\end{pmatrix}$, what are $u_1, u_2, u_3,$ and u_4?

12. (a) Show that the vector equation
$$x\begin{pmatrix}5\\7\end{pmatrix} + y\begin{pmatrix}3\\-10\end{pmatrix} = \begin{pmatrix}-16\\77\end{pmatrix}$$
represents two simultaneous linear equations for the two variables x and y.

(b)   Solve the equations for x and y from (a) and substitute into the vector equation above to check your work.

13.   Write the following simultaneous linear equations in vector form:

$$ax + by = e$$
$$cx + dy = f.$$

[*Hint:* Follow the form given in Exercise 12.]

14.   Suppose that we associate with each person a three-component row vector having the following entries: age, height, and weight. Would it make sense to add together the vectors associated with two different persons? Would it make sense to multiply one of these vectors by a constant?

15.   Suppose that we associate with each person leaving a supermarket a row vector whose components give the quantities of each available item that he has purchased. Answer the same questions as those in Exercise 14.

16.   Let us associate with each supermarket a column vector whose entries give the prices of each item in the store. Would it make sense to add together the vectors associated with two different supermarkets? Would it make sense to multiply one of these vectors by a constant? Discuss the differences in the situations given in Exercises 14, 15, and 16.

17.   Consider the vectors

$$x = \begin{pmatrix} x_1 \\ x_2 \end{pmatrix}, \qquad y = \begin{pmatrix} y_1 \\ y_2 \end{pmatrix}.$$

Show that the vector

$$\tfrac{1}{2}(x + y)$$

has components that are the averages of the components of x and y. Generalize this result to the case of n vectors.

18.   Would the concept of averages, as discussed in Exercise 17, be applicable to the vectors mentioned in Exercises 14, 15, and 16? How would the averages be interpreted?

19.   In a certain school students take four courses each semester. At the end of the semester the registrar records the grades of each student as a row vector. He then gives the student 4 points for each A, 3 points for each B, 2 points for each C, 1 point for each D, and 0 for each F. The sum of these numbers, divided by 4, is the student's grade point average.

(a)   If a student has a 4.0 average, what are the logical possibilities for his grade vector? [*Hint:* Each grade vector will have five components.]

(b)   What are the possibilities if he has a 3.0 average?

(c)   What are the possibilities if he has a 2.0 average?

20. Let $x = \begin{pmatrix} x_1 \\ x_2 \end{pmatrix}$. Define $x \geq 0$ to be the conjunction of the statements $x_1 \geq 0$ and $x_2 \geq 0$. Define $x \leq 0$ analogously. If $(x_1 + x_2) x \geq 0$, what must be true of x?

21. Using the definition in Exercise 20, define $x \geq y$ to mean $x - y \geq 0$, where x and y are vectors of the same shape. Consider the following four vectors:

$$x = \begin{pmatrix} 3 \\ 5 \\ -1 \end{pmatrix}, \qquad y = \begin{pmatrix} 6 \\ 5 \\ 6 \end{pmatrix}, \qquad u = \begin{pmatrix} 0 \\ 0 \\ -2 \end{pmatrix}, \qquad v = \begin{pmatrix} 4 \\ 2 \\ 0 \end{pmatrix}.$$

   (a) Show that $x \geq u$.
   (b) Show that $v \geq u$.
   (c) Is there any relationship between x and v?
   (d) Show that $y \geq x$, $y \geq u$, and $y \geq v$.

22. (a) If $x^{(1)}, x^{(2)}, \ldots, x^{(n)}$ is a set of n vectors, show how to find a vector u such that $u \geq x^{(i)}$ for all i. Also show how to find a vector v such that $v \leq x^{(i)}$ for all i.

   (b) Apply the results of part (a) to the vectors in Exercise 21.

   (c) Let $u = \begin{pmatrix} 630 \\ 520 \\ 310 \end{pmatrix}$, $v = \begin{pmatrix} 960 \\ 200 \\ 400 \end{pmatrix}$, and $w = \begin{pmatrix} 600 \\ 750 \\ 490 \end{pmatrix}$. If $x = \begin{pmatrix} -4 \\ -5 \\ -2 \end{pmatrix}$, find the largest number n such that $nx \geq u$, $nx \geq v$, and $nx \geq w$. [*Ans.* -235.]

2 THE PRODUCT OF VECTORS; EXAMPLES

The reader may wonder why it is necessary to introduce both column and row vectors when their properties are so similar. This question can be answered in several different ways. First, in many applications two kinds of quantities are studied simultaneously, and it is convenient to represent one of them as a row vector and the other as a column vector. Second, there is a way of combining row and column vectors that is very useful for certain types of calculations. To bring out these points let us look at the following simple economic example.

EXAMPLE 1   Suppose a man named Smith goes into a grocery store to buy a dozen each of peaches and oranges, a half-dozen each of apples and pears, and three lemons. Let us represent his purchases by means of the following row vector:

$$x = [6 \text{ (apples)}, 12 \text{ (peaches)}, 3 \text{ (lemons)}, 12 \text{ (oranges)}, 6 \text{ (pears)}]$$
$$= (6, 12, 3, 12, 6).$$

Suppose that apples are 4 cents each, peaches 6 cents, lemons 9 cents, oranges 5 cents, and pears 7 cents. We can then represent the prices of these items as a column vector:

$$y = \begin{pmatrix} 4 \\ 6 \\ 9 \\ 5 \\ 7 \end{pmatrix} \begin{matrix} \text{cents per apple} \\ \text{cents per peach} \\ \text{cents per lemon} \\ \text{cents per orange} \\ \text{cents per pear.} \end{matrix}$$

The obvious question is: What is the total amount that Smith must pay for his purchases? We would like to multiply the quantity vector x by the price vector y, and we would like the result to be Smith's bill. We see that our multiplication should have the following form:

$$x \cdot y = (6, 12, 3, 12, 6) \begin{pmatrix} 4 \\ 6 \\ 9 \\ 5 \\ 7 \end{pmatrix}$$

$$\begin{aligned} &= 6 \cdot 4 + 12 \cdot 6 + 3 \cdot 9 + 12 \cdot 5 + 6 \cdot 7 \\ &= 24 + 72 + 27 + 60 + 42 \\ &= 225 \text{ cents} \quad \text{or} \quad \$2.25. \end{aligned}$$

This is, of course, the computation that the cashier performs in figuring Smith's bill.

We shall adopt in general the above definition of multiplication of row times column vectors.

Definition   Let u be a row vector and v a column vector each having the same number n of components; then we shall define the produce $u \cdot v$ to be

$$u \cdot v = u_1 v_1 + u_2 v_2 + \ldots + u_n v_n.$$

Notice that we always write the row vector first and the column vector second, and this is the only kind of vector multiplication that we consider. Some examples of vector multiplication are

$$(2, 1, -1) \cdot \begin{pmatrix} 3 \\ -1 \\ 4 \end{pmatrix} = 2 \cdot 3 + 1 \cdot (-1) + (-1) \cdot 4 = 1,$$

$$(1, 0) \cdot \begin{pmatrix} 0 \\ 1 \end{pmatrix} = 1 \cdot 0 + 0 \cdot 1 = 0 + 0 = 0.$$

Note that the result of vector multiplication is always a *number*.

EXAMPLE 2   Consider an oversimplified economy that has three industries, which we call coal, electricity, and steel, and three consumers 1, 2, and 3. Suppose that each consumer uses some of the output of each industry and also that each industry uses some of the output of each other industry. We assume that the amounts used are positive or zero, since using a negative quantity has no immediate interpretation. We can represent the needs of each consumer and industry by a three-component demand (row) vector, the first component measuring the amount of coal needed by the consumer or industry; the second component the amount of electricity needed; and the third component the amount of steel needed, in some convenient units. For example, the demand vectors of the three consumers might be

$$d_1 = (3, 2, 5), \qquad d_2 = (0, 17, 1), \qquad d_3 = (4, 6, 12)$$

and the demand vectors of each of the industries might be

$$d_C = (0, 1, 4), \qquad d_E = (20, 0, 8), \qquad d_S = (30, 5, 0),$$

where the subscript C stands for coal, the subscript E for electricity, and the subscript S for steel. Then the total demand for these goods by the consumers is given by the sum

$$d_1 + d_2 + d_3 = (3, 2, 5) + (0, 17, 1) + (4, 6, 12) = (7, 25, 18).$$

Also, the total industrial demand for these goods is given by the sum

$$d_C + d_E + d_S = (0, 1, 4) + (20, 0, 8) + (30, 5, 0) = (50, 6, 12).$$

Therefore the total overall demand is given by the sum

$$(7, 25, 18) + (50, 6, 12) = (57, 31, 30).$$

Suppose now that the price of coal is \$1 per unit, the price of electricity is \$2 per unit, and the price of steel is \$4 per unit. Then these prices can be represented by the column vector

$$p = \begin{pmatrix} 1 \\ 2 \\ 4 \end{pmatrix}.$$

Consider the steel industry: it sells a total of 30 units of steel at \$4 per unit, so that its total income is \$120. Its bill for the various goods is given by the vector product

$$d_S \cdot p = (30, 5, 0) \cdot \begin{pmatrix} 1 \\ 2 \\ 4 \end{pmatrix} = 30 + 10 + 0 = \$40.$$

Hence the profit of the steel industry is \$120 − \$40 = \$80. (In the exercises the profits of the other industries will be found.)

This model of an economy is unrealistic in two senses. First, we have not chosen realistic numbers for the various quantities involved. Second, and more important, we have neglected the fact that the more an industry produces the more inputs it requires.

EXAMPLE 3   Consider the rectangular coordinate system in the plane shown in Figure 1. A two-component row vector $x = (a, b)$ can be regarded as a point in

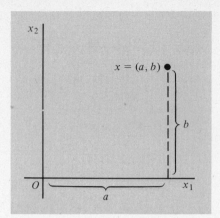

Figure 1

the plane located by means of the coordinate axes as shown. The point x can be found by starting at the origin of coordinates O and moving a distance a along the x_1 axis; then moving a distance b along a line parallel to the x_2 axis. If we have two such points, say $x = (a, b)$ and $y = (c, d)$, then the points $x + y, -x, -y, x - y, y - x, -x -y$ have the geometric significance shown in Figure 2.

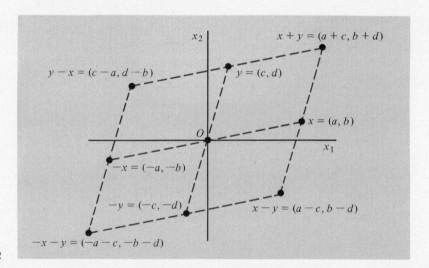

Figure 2

The idea of multiplying a row vector by a number can also be given a geometric meaning. In Figure 3 we have plotted the point corresponding to the vector $x = (1, 2)$, and $2x, \frac{1}{2}x, -x,$ and $-2x$. Observe that all these points lie on a line through the origin of coordinates. Another vector quantity that has geometrical significance is the vector $z = ax + (1 - a)y$,

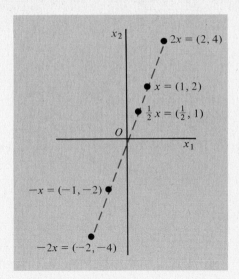

Figure 3

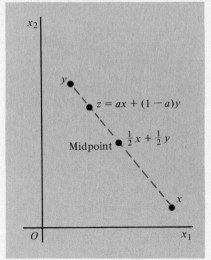

Figure 4

where a is any number between 0 and 1. Observe in Figure 4 that the points z all lie on the line segment between the points x and y. If $a = \frac{1}{2}$, the corresponding point on the line segment is the midpoint of the segment. Thus, if $x = (a, b)$ and $y = (c, d)$, then the point

$$\tfrac{1}{2}x + \tfrac{1}{2}y = \tfrac{1}{2}(a, b) + \tfrac{1}{2}(c, d)$$

$$= \left(\frac{a + c}{2}, \frac{b + d}{2} \right)$$

is the midpoint of the line segment between x and y.

EXERCISES

1. Let $u = (2, -1, 3)$, $v = (5, 0, 2)$, $x = \begin{pmatrix} -7 \\ 1 \\ 2 \end{pmatrix}$, and $y = \begin{pmatrix} 0 \\ 8 \\ 3 \end{pmatrix}$.

   Compute the following:
   (a) $(u + v) \cdot (x + y)$.
   (b) $((3u \cdot x) \cdot v) \cdot y$.
   (c) $u \cdot x - 4v \cdot y$.
   (d) $u \cdot x + 3u \cdot y - v \cdot y$. [*Ans.* -12.]
   (e) $(2(v + u) \cdot y) - 5uy$.
   (f) $4u \cdot x + 6[v \cdot (3x - y)]$. [*Ans.* -630.]

2. If $x = (5, -4, 2)$ and $y = (1, 8, 1)$ are points in space, what is the midpoint of the line segment joining x to y? [*Ans.* $(3, 2, \frac{3}{2})$.]

3. Let $x = (-1, 3)$ and $y = (4, 1)$ be row vectors. Plot the points corresponding to x and y, and compute and plot the following vectors:

(a) $\frac{1}{2}x + \frac{1}{2}y.$ (d) $2x - y.$
(b) $x + y.$ (e) $y + 4x.$
(c) $\frac{2}{3}x + \frac{1}{3}y.$ (f) $x - y.$

4. Prove that vector multiplication satisfies the following two properties:

(i) $u \cdot (av) = a(u \cdot v),$
(ii) $u \cdot (v + w) = u \cdot v + u \cdot w,$

where u is a three-component row vector, v and w are three-component column vectors, and a is a number.

5. If u is a three-component row vector, v is a three-component column vector having the same number of components, and a is a number, prove that $a(u \cdot v) = u \cdot (av).$

6. A certain football stadium has three gates. After one game, the ticket-taker at gate 1 reported admitting 275 adults, 300 students, and 15 children; the ticket-taker at gate 2 admitted 200 adults, 107 students, and 40 children; and 65 adults, 250 students, and 60 children were admitted at gate 3.
(a) Write the numbers of people admitted through each gate as a three-component row vector.
(b) Use vector addition to find how many people in each category attended the game.
(c) Suppose that adults pay $3.00 to attend the game, students pay $2.00, and children pay 50¢. Assuming that each person buys his ticket at the gate, calculate the value of the tickets sold at each gate.
(d) Compute in two different ways the total value of tickets sold.

7. Perform the following calculations for Example 2.
(a) Compute the amount that each industry and each consumer has to pay for the goods it receives.
(b) Compute the profit made by each of the industries.
(c) Find the total amount of money that is paid out by all the industries and consumers.
(d) Find the proportion of the total amount of money found in (c) paid out by the industries. Find the proportion of the total money that is paid out by the consumers.

8. A farmer intends to plant 40 acres of corn, 25 acres of wheat, and 30 acres of rye. Write a three-component row vector whose components give the number of acres of each grain he wants to plant. Suppose an acre of corn requires an hour to plant, an acre of wheat 45 minutes, and an acre of rye one-half hour. Write a column vector whose components give the number of minutes needed to plant an acre of each crop. Use vector multiplication to find the total time required for planting.

9. In Exercise 8, suppose the seed for an acre of corn cost $40, for an acre of wheat $15, and for an acre of rye $10. Find the total amount

the farmer must spend on seed. If an acre of corn brings the farmer a *profit* of $19, an acre of wheat $15, and an acre of rye $4, find the total profit the farmer will make.

10. The production of a book involves several steps: first it must be set into type, then it must be printed, and finally it must be supplied with covers and bound. Suppose the typesetter charges $6 an hour, paper costs $\frac{1}{4}$ cent per sheet, the printer charges 11 cents for each minute that his press runs, the cover costs 28 cents, and the binder charges 15 cents to bind each book. Suppose now that a publisher wishes to print a book that requires 300 hours of work by the typesetter, 220 sheets of paper per book, and 5 minutes of press time per book.

   (a) Write a five-component row vector that gives the requirements for the first book. Write another row vector that gives the requirements for the second, third, . . . copies of the book. Write a five-component column vector whose components give the prices of the various requirements for each book, in the same order as they are listed in the requirement vectors above.

   (b) Using vector multiplication, find the cost of publishing one copy of a book.   [*Ans.* $1801.53.]

   (c) Using vector addition and multiplication, find the cost of printing a first-edition run of 5000 copies.   [*Ans.* $9450.]

   (d) Assuming that the printing plates from the first edition are used again, find the cost of printing a second edition of 5000 copies.
                                                                      [*Ans.* $7650.]

11. Let $x = \begin{pmatrix} x_1 \\ x_2 \end{pmatrix}$, and let a and b be the vectors $a = (-1, 4)$, $b = (2, -7)$. If $ax = 1$ and $bx = 2$, find x_1 and x_2.
                                                        [*Ans.* $x_1 = 15, x_2 = 4$.]

12. Let $x = \begin{pmatrix} x_1 \\ x_2 \end{pmatrix}$, and let a and b be the vectors $a = (3, 3)$, $b = (-1, 4)$. If $ax = x_1$ and $bx = x_2$, find x_1 and x_2.

13. Consider the vectors

$$a = (a_1, a_2), \qquad b = (b_1, b_2), \qquad x = \begin{pmatrix} x_1 \\ x_2 \end{pmatrix}$$

and two numbers c_1 and c_2. Show that the equations

$$ax = c_1, \qquad bx = c_2$$

represent two simultaneous equations in two unknowns.

14. Show that every set of two simultaneous equations in two unknowns can be written as in Exercise 13.

15. Consider an experiment in which there are two outcomes: we win $10 with probability $\frac{1}{5}$ and lost $5 with probability $\frac{4}{5}$. Let $a = (10, -5)$ and $p = \begin{pmatrix} \frac{1}{5} \\ \frac{4}{5} \end{pmatrix}$. Show that the expected outcome of the experiment is ap.

16. A gambling game works as follows. Two dice are rolled. If no sixes turn up, we lose $1; if one six turns up, we win $1; if two sixes turn up we win $10. Set up a row vector representing the various outcomes and a column vector representing the probability of those outcomes. Use vector multiplication to find the expected outcomes. Is the game fair?

17. If an experiment has outcomes $a_1, a_2, \ldots, a_n$ occurring with probabilities $p_1, p_2, \ldots, p_n$, define the vectors

$$a = (a_1, \ldots, a_n) \quad \text{and} \quad p = \begin{pmatrix} p_1 \\ p_2 \\ \vdots \\ p_n \end{pmatrix}$$

Show that the expected outcome is ap.

18. Consider the vectors $x = (1, 5)$, $y = (3, 1)$, and $f = \begin{pmatrix} 1 \\ 1 \end{pmatrix}$.

(a) Compute $\frac{1}{2}xf$ and $\frac{1}{2}yf$, and show that these numbers are the averages of the components of x and y, respectively. [Partial Ans. 3, 2.]

(b) Compute $\frac{1}{4}(x + y)f$, and give an interpretation for this number. [Partial Ans. $2\frac{1}{2}$.]

19. Let x and y be two n-component row vectors, and let f be an n-component column vector all of whose entries are 1's.

(a) Compute $(1/n)xf$ and $(1/n)yf$ and interpret the result.

(b) Compute $(\frac{1}{2}n)(x + y)f$ and interpret the result. [Hint: Exercise 18 is a special case.]

20. How would the results of Exercise 19 change if we used three vectors: x, y, and z?

3   MATRICES AND THEIR COMBINATION WITH VECTORS

A matrix is a rectangular array of numbers written in the form

$$A = \begin{pmatrix} a_{11} & a_{12} & \cdots & a_{1n} \\ a_{21} & a_{22} & \cdots & a_{2n} \\ \cdot & \cdot & \cdots & \cdot \\ a_{m1} & a_{m2} & \cdots & a_{mn} \end{pmatrix}.$$

Here the letters a_{ij} stand for real numbers and m and n are integers. Observe that m is the number of rows and n is the number of columns of the matrix. For this reason we call it an $m \times n$ matrix. If $m = n$, the matrix is *square*. The following are examples of matrices:

$$(1, 2, 3), \quad \begin{pmatrix} 1 \\ 2 \\ 3 \end{pmatrix}, \quad \begin{pmatrix} 1 & -1 \\ -2 & 2 \end{pmatrix};$$

$$\begin{pmatrix} 1 & 0 & 0 & 0 \\ 0 & 1 & 0 & 0 \\ 0 & 0 & 1 & 0 \\ 0 & 0 & 0 & 1 \end{pmatrix}; \begin{pmatrix} 1 & 7 & -8 & 9 & 10 \\ 3 & -1 & 14 & 2 & -6 \\ 0 & 3 & -5 & 7 & 0 \end{pmatrix}.$$

The first example is a row vector which is a 1×3 matrix; the second is a column vector which is a 3×1 matrix; the third example is a 2×2 square matrix; the fourth is a 4×4 square matrix; and the last is a 3×5 matrix.

Two matrices having the same shape (i.e., having the same number of rows and columns) are said to be equal if and only if the corresponding entries are equal.

Recall that in Chapter 3, Section 12, we found that a matrix arose naturally in the consideration of a Markov chain process. To give another example of how matrices occur in practice and are used in connection with vectors, we consider the following example.

EXAMPLE 1 Suppose that a building contractor has accepted orders for five ranch-style houses, seven Cape Cod houses, and twelve colonial-style houses. We can represent his orders by means of a row vector $x = (5, 7, 12)$. The contractor is familiar, of course, with the kinds of "raw materials" that go into each type of house. Let us suppose that these raw materials are steel, wood, glass, paint, and labor. The numbers in the matrix below give the amounts of each raw material going into each type of house, expressed in convenient units. (The numbers are put in arbitrarily, and are not meant to be realistic.)

$$
\begin{array}{l}
 & \text{Steel} & \text{Wood} & \text{Glass} & \text{Paint} & \text{Labor} \\
\text{Ranch:} & 5 & 20 & 16 & 7 & 17 \\
\text{Cape Cod:} & 7 & 18 & 12 & 9 & 21 \\
\text{Colonial:} & 6 & 25 & 8 & 5 & 13
\end{array} = R.
$$

Observe that each row of the matrix is a five-component row vector which gives the amounts of each raw material needed for a given kind of house. Similarly, each column of the matrix is a three-component column vector which gives the amounts of a given raw material needed for each kind of house. Clearly, a matrix is a very succinct way of summarizing this information.

Suppose now that the contractor wishes to compute how much of each raw material to obtain in order to fulfill his contracts. Let us denote the matrix above by R; then he would like to obtain something like the product xR, and he would like the product to tell him what orders to make out. The product should have the following form:

$$
xR = (5, 7, 12) \begin{pmatrix} 5 & 20 & 16 & 7 & 17 \\ 7 & 18 & 12 & 9 & 21 \\ 6 & 25 & 8 & 5 & 13 \end{pmatrix}
$$

$$
\begin{aligned}
= (\ & 5 \cdot 5 + 7 \cdot 7 + 12 \cdot 6, \quad 5 \cdot 20 + 7 \cdot 18 + 12 \cdot 25, \\
& 5 \cdot 16 + 7 \cdot 12 + 12 \cdot 8, \quad 5 \cdot 7 + 7 \cdot 9 + 12 \cdot 5, \\
& 5 \cdot 17 + 7 \cdot 21 + 12 \cdot 13) \\
= (\ & 146, 526, 260, 158, 388).
\end{aligned}
$$

Thus we see that the contractor should order 146 units of steel, 526 units of wood, 260 units of glass, 158 units of paint, and 388 units of labor. Observe that the answer we get is a five-component row vector and that each entry in this vector is obtained by taking the vector product of x times the corresponding column of the matrix R.

The contractor is also interested in the prices that he will have to pay for these materials. Suppose that steel costs $15 per unit, wood costs $8 per unit, glass costs $5 per unit, paint costs $1 per unit, and labor costs $10 per unit. Then we can write the cost as a column vector as follows:

$$y = \begin{pmatrix} 15 \\ 8 \\ 5 \\ 1 \\ 10 \end{pmatrix}.$$

Here the product Ry should give the costs of each type of house, so that the multiplication should have the form

$$Ry = \begin{pmatrix} 5 & 20 & 16 & 7 & 17 \\ 7 & 18 & 12 & 9 & 21 \\ 6 & 25 & 8 & 5 & 13 \end{pmatrix} \begin{pmatrix} 15 \\ 8 \\ 5 \\ 1 \\ 10 \end{pmatrix}$$

$$= \begin{pmatrix} 5 \cdot 15 + 20 \cdot 8 + 16 \cdot 5 + 7 \cdot 1 + 17 \cdot 10 \\ 7 \cdot 15 + 18 \cdot 8 + 12 \cdot 5 + 9 \cdot 1 + 21 \cdot 10 \\ 6 \cdot 15 + 25 \cdot 8 + 8 \cdot 5 + 5 \cdot 1 + 13 \cdot 10 \end{pmatrix}$$

$$= \begin{pmatrix} 492 \\ 528 \\ 465 \end{pmatrix}.$$

Thus the cost of materials for the ranch style house is $492, for the Cape Cod house is $528, and for the Colonial house $465.

The final question which the contractor might ask is what is the total cost of raw materials for all the houses he will build. It is easy to see that this is given by the vector xRy. We can find it in two ways as shown below.

$$xRy = (xR)y = (146, 526, 260, 158, 388) \cdot \begin{pmatrix} 15 \\ 8 \\ 5 \\ 1 \\ 10 \end{pmatrix} = 11{,}736$$

$$xRy = x(Ry) = (5, 7, 12) \cdot \begin{pmatrix} 492 \\ 528 \\ 465 \end{pmatrix} = 11{,}736.$$

The total cost is then $11,736.

We shall adopt, in general, the above definitions for the multiplication of a matrix times a row or a column vector.

Definition Let A be an $m \times n$ matrix, let x be an m-component row vector, and let u be an n-component column vector; then we define the products xA and Au as follows:

$$xA = (x_1, x_2, \cdots, x_m) \begin{pmatrix} a_{11} & a_{12} & \cdots & a_{1n} \\ a_{21} & a_{22} & \cdots & a_{2n} \\ & & \cdots & \\ a_{m1} & a_{m2} & \cdots & a_{mn} \end{pmatrix}$$

$$= (x_1 a_{11} + x_2 a_{21} + \cdots + x_m a_{m1}, \quad x_1 a_{12} + x_2 a_{22} + \cdots + x_m a_{m2},$$
$$\cdots, \quad x_1 a_{1n} + x_2 a_{2n} + \cdots + x_m a_{mn});$$

$$Au = \begin{pmatrix} a_{11} & a_{12} & \cdots & a_{1n} \\ a_{21} & a_{22} & \cdots & a_{2n} \\ & & \cdots & \\ a_{m1} & a_{m2} & \cdots & a_{mn} \end{pmatrix} \begin{pmatrix} u_1 \\ u_2 \\ \vdots \\ u_n \end{pmatrix} = \begin{pmatrix} a_{11}u_1 + a_{12}u_2 + \cdots + a_{1n}u_n \\ a_{21}u_1 + a_{22}u_2 + \cdots + a_{2n}u_n \\ \cdots \\ a_{m1}u_1 + a_{m2}u_2 + \cdots + a_{mn}u_n \end{pmatrix}.$$

The reader will find these formulas easy to work with if he observes that each entry in the products xA or Au is obtained by vector multiplication of x or u by a column or row of the matrix A. Notice that in order to multiply a row vector times a matrix, the number of rows of the matrix must equal the number of components of the vector, and the result is another row vector; similarly, to multiply a matrix times a column vector, the number of columns of the matrix must equal the number of components of the vector, and the result of such a multiplication is another column vector.

Some numerical examples of the multiplication of vectors and matrices are:

$$(1, 0, -1) \begin{pmatrix} 3 & 1 \\ 2 & 3 \\ 2 & 8 \end{pmatrix} = (1 \cdot 3 + 0 \cdot 2 - 1 \cdot 2, 1 \cdot 1 + 0 \cdot 3 - 1 \cdot 8)$$

$$= (1, -7);$$

$$\begin{pmatrix} 3 & 1 & 2 \\ 2 & 3 & 8 \end{pmatrix} \begin{pmatrix} 1 \\ -1 \\ 2 \end{pmatrix} = \begin{pmatrix} 3 - 1 + 4 \\ 2 - 3 + 16 \end{pmatrix} = \begin{pmatrix} 6 \\ 15 \end{pmatrix};$$

$$\begin{pmatrix} 3 & 2 & -1 \\ 1 & 0 & 2 \\ 0 & 3 & 1 \\ 5 & -4 & 7 \\ -3 & 2 & -1 \end{pmatrix} \begin{pmatrix} 1 \\ 0 \\ -2 \end{pmatrix} = \begin{pmatrix} 5 \\ -3 \\ -2 \\ -9 \\ -1 \end{pmatrix}.$$

Observe that if x is an m-component row vector and A is $m \times n$, then xA is an n-component row vector; similarly, if u is an n-component column vector, then Au is an m-component column vector. These facts can be observed in the examples above.

EXAMPLE 2   Consider a Markov chain with transition matrix

$$P = \begin{pmatrix} \frac{1}{3} & \frac{2}{3} \\ \frac{1}{2} & \frac{1}{2} \end{pmatrix}.$$

Choose the initial state by a random device that selects states a_1 and a_2 each with probability $\frac{1}{2}$. Let us indicate the choice of initial state by the vector $p^{(0)} = (\frac{1}{2}, \frac{1}{2})$ where the first component gives the probability of choosing state a_1 and the second the probability of choosing state a_2. Let us compute the product $p^{(0)}P$. We have

$$p^{(0)}P = (\tfrac{1}{2}, \tfrac{1}{2}) \begin{pmatrix} \frac{1}{3} & \frac{2}{3} \\ \frac{1}{2} & \frac{1}{2} \end{pmatrix} = (\tfrac{1}{6} + \tfrac{1}{4}, \tfrac{1}{3} + \tfrac{1}{4}) = (\tfrac{5}{12}, \tfrac{7}{12}).$$

Using the methods of Chapter 3, one can show that after one step there is probability $\frac{5}{12}$ that the process will be in state a_1 and probability $\frac{7}{12}$ that it will be in state a_2. Let $p^{(1)}$ be the vector whose first component gives the probability of the process being in state a_1 after one step and whose second component gives the probability of it being in state a_2 after one step. In our example we have $p^{(1)} = (\frac{5}{12}, \frac{7}{12}) = p^{(0)}P$.

In general, the formula $p^{(1)} = p^{(0)}P$ holds for any Markov process with transition matrix P and initial probability vector $p^{(0)}$.

EXAMPLE 3   In Example 1 of Section 2 assume that Smith has two stores at which he can make his purchases, and let us assume that the prices charged at these two stores are slightly different. Let the price vector at the second store be

$$y = \begin{pmatrix} 5 \\ 5 \\ 10 \\ 4 \\ 6 \end{pmatrix} \begin{array}{l} \text{cents per apple} \\ \text{cents per peach} \\ \text{cents per lemon} \\ \text{cents per orange} \\ \text{cents per pear.} \end{array}$$

Smith now has the option of buying all his purchases at store 1, all at store 2, or buying just the lower-priced items at the store charging the lower price. To help him decide, we form a price matrix as follows:

	Prices, Store 1	Prices, Store 2	Minimum Price
	4	5	4
	6	5	5
$P =$	9	10	9
	5	4	4
	7	6	6

The first column lists the prices of store 1, the second column lists the price of store 2, and the third column lists the lower of these two prices. To compute Smith's bill under the three possible ways he can make his purchases, we compute the produce xP, as follows:

$$xP = (6, 12, 3, 12, 6) \begin{pmatrix} 4 & 5 & 4 \\ 6 & 5 & 5 \\ 9 & 10 & 9 \\ 5 & 4 & 4 \\ 7 & 6 & 6 \end{pmatrix} = (225, 204, 195).$$

We thus see that if Smith buys only in store 1, his bill will be $2.25; if he buys only in store 2, his bill will be $2.04; but if he buys each item in the cheaper of the two stores (apples and lemons in store 1, and the rest in store 2), his bill will be $1.95.

Exactly what Smith will, or should, do depends upon circumstances. If both stores are equally close to him, he will probably split his purchases and obtain the smallest bill. If store 1 is close and store 2 is very far away, he may buy everything at store 1. If store 2 is closer and store 1 is far enough away so that the 9 cents he would save by splitting his purchases is not worth the travel effort, he may buy everything at store 2.

The problem just cited is an example of a *decision problem*. In such problems it is necessary to choose one of several courses of action, or *strategies*. For each such course of action or strategy, it is possible to compute the cost or *worth* of such a strategy. The decision maker will choose a strategy with maximum worth.

Sometimes the worth of an outcome must be measured in psychological units and we then say that we measure the *utility* of an outcome. For the purposes of this book we shall always assume that the utility of an outcome is measured in monetary units, so that we can compare the worths of two different outcomes to the decision maker.

EXAMPLE 4   As a second example of a decision problem, consider the following. An urn contains five red, three green, and one white ball. One ball will be drawn at random, and then payments will be made to holders of three kinds of lottery tickets, A, B, and C, according to the following schedule:

$$M = \begin{array}{c} \text{Red} \\ \text{Green} \\ \text{White} \end{array} \begin{pmatrix} \begin{array}{ccc} \text{Ticket A} & \text{Ticket B} & \text{Ticket C} \\ 1 & 3 & 0 \\ 4 & 1 & 0 \\ 0 & 0 & 16 \end{array} \end{pmatrix}.$$

Thus, if a red ball is selected, holders of ticket A will get $1, holders of ticket B will get $3, and holders of ticket C will get nothing. If green is chosen, the payments are 4, 1, and 0, respectively. If white is chosen, holders of ticket C get $16, and the others nothing. Which ticket would we prefer to have?

Our decision will depend upon the concept of expected value discussed in the preceding chapter. The statements "draw a red ball," "draw a green ball," and "draw a white ball" have probabilities $\frac{5}{9}$, $\frac{3}{9}$, and $\frac{1}{9}$, respectively.

From these probabilities we can calculate the expected value of holding each of the lottery tickets as described in the last chapter. However, a compact way of performing all these calculations is to compute the product pM, where p is the probability vector

$$p = (\tfrac{5}{9}, \tfrac{3}{9}, \tfrac{1}{9}).$$

From this we have

$$pM = (\tfrac{5}{9}, \tfrac{3}{9}, \tfrac{1}{9}) \begin{pmatrix} 1 & 3 & 0 \\ 4 & 1 & 0 \\ 0 & 0 & 16 \end{pmatrix}$$

$$= (1 \cdot \tfrac{5}{9} + 4 \cdot \tfrac{3}{9} + 0 \cdot \tfrac{1}{9}, \quad 3 \cdot \tfrac{5}{9} + 1 \cdot \tfrac{3}{9} + 0 \cdot \tfrac{1}{9}, \quad 0 \cdot \tfrac{5}{9} + 0 \cdot \tfrac{3}{9} + 16 \cdot \tfrac{1}{9})$$

$$= (\tfrac{17}{9}, \tfrac{18}{9}, \tfrac{16}{9}).$$

It is easy to see that the three components of pM give the expected values of holding lottery tickets A, B, and C, respectively. From these numbers we can see that ticket B is the best, A is the next best, and C is third best.

If we have to pay for the tickets, then the cost of the tickets will determine which is the best buy. If each ticket costs \$3 we would be better off by not buying any ticket, since we would then expect to lose money. If each ticket costs \$1 then we should buy ticket B, since it would give us a net expected gain of \$2 − \$1 = \$1. If the first two tickets cost \$2.10, and the third cost \$1.50, we should buy ticket C since it is the only one for which we would have a positive net expectation.

EXERCISES

1. Perform the following multiplications:

   (a) $\begin{pmatrix} 7 & 6 \\ -3 & 2 \end{pmatrix}\begin{pmatrix} 1 \\ -3 \end{pmatrix} = ?$ $\qquad\qquad$ [*Ans.* $\begin{pmatrix} -11 \\ -9 \end{pmatrix}$.]

   (b) $(2, -2)\begin{pmatrix} -3 & 2 \\ -1 & 0 \end{pmatrix} = ?$

   (c) $\begin{pmatrix} 0 & 3 & 1 \\ 3 & -1 & 7 \\ -5 & 14 & -8 \\ 7 & 2 & 9 \\ 0 & -6 & 10 \end{pmatrix}\begin{pmatrix} 6 \\ 1 \\ -1 \end{pmatrix} = ?$

   (d) $(5, 5)\begin{pmatrix} 1 & -1 \\ -1 & 1 \end{pmatrix} = ?$ $\qquad\qquad$ [*Ans.* $(0, 0)$.]

   (e) $\begin{pmatrix} 1 & -1 \\ -1 & 1 \end{pmatrix}\begin{pmatrix} 12 \\ 12 \end{pmatrix} = ?$

   (f) $(0, 1, -5)\begin{pmatrix} 3 & 1 & 2 & 0 & -8 \\ 6 & 8 & 2 & 1 & 14 \\ 2 & 15 & 2 & 0 & -5 \end{pmatrix} = ?$

(g) $(x_1, x_2)\begin{pmatrix} a & b \\ c & d \end{pmatrix} = ?$ *[Ans. $ax_1 + cx_2, bx_1 + dx_2$.]*

(h) $\begin{pmatrix} w & x \\ y & z \end{pmatrix}\begin{pmatrix} p_1 \\ p_2 \end{pmatrix} = ?$

(i) $\begin{pmatrix} 1 & 0 & 0 & 0 \\ 0 & 1 & 0 & 0 \\ 0 & 0 & 1 & 0 \\ 0 & 0 & 0 & 1 \end{pmatrix}\begin{pmatrix} u_1 \\ u_2 \\ u_3 \\ u_4 \end{pmatrix} = ?$

(j) $(x_1, x_2, x_3, x_4)\begin{pmatrix} 1 & 0 & 0 & 0 \\ 0 & 1 & 0 & 0 \\ 0 & 0 & 1 & 0 \\ 0 & 0 & 0 & 1 \end{pmatrix} = ?$

2. What number does the matrix in parts (i) and (j) of Exercise 1 resemble?

3. Notice that in Exercise 1(d), above, the product of a row vector none of whose components is zero and a matrix none of whose components is zero is the zero row vector. Find a second example, this time using a 3×3 matrix, which is similar to this one. Answer the analogous question for Exercise 1(e).

4. Consider the matrices

$$A = \begin{pmatrix} a_{11} & a_{12} \\ a_{21} & a_{22} \end{pmatrix}, \qquad x = \begin{pmatrix} x_1 \\ x_2 \end{pmatrix}, \qquad b = \begin{pmatrix} b_1 \\ b_2 \end{pmatrix}.$$

(a) Show that the equation $Ax = b$ represents two simultaneous equations in two unknowns.

(b) Show that every set of two simultaneous equations in two unknowns can be written in this form for the proper choice of A and b.

5. When possible, solve for the indicated quantities.

(a) $(x_1, x_2)\begin{pmatrix} 6 & 8 \\ -9 & 0 \end{pmatrix} = (-45, 72)$. Find the vector x.

(b) $(6, 9)\begin{pmatrix} a & b \\ c & d \end{pmatrix} = (12, -15)$. Find the matrix $\begin{pmatrix} a & b \\ c & d \end{pmatrix}$.

In this case can you find more than one solution?

(c) $\begin{pmatrix} 5 & -5 \\ -5 & 5 \end{pmatrix}\begin{pmatrix} u_1 \\ u_2 \end{pmatrix} = \begin{pmatrix} 7 \\ 0 \end{pmatrix}$. Find the vector u.

(d) $\begin{pmatrix} 3 & -7 \\ -12 & 28 \end{pmatrix}\begin{pmatrix} u_1 \\ u_2 \end{pmatrix} = \begin{pmatrix} -1 \\ 4 \end{pmatrix}$. Find u. How many solutions can you find?

$$\left[Ans. \text{ Infinitely many solutions, all of the form } u = \begin{pmatrix} k \\ \dfrac{3k + 1}{7} \end{pmatrix}. \right]$$

6. Solve for the indicated quantities below and give an interpretation for each.

(a) $(1, -1)\begin{pmatrix} 0 & 2 \\ -2 & 4 \end{pmatrix} = a(1, -1)$; find a.   [*Ans. a = 2.*]

(b) $\begin{pmatrix} 1 & 2 \\ 2 & 4 \end{pmatrix}\begin{pmatrix} u_1 \\ u_2 \end{pmatrix} = 5\begin{pmatrix} u_1 \\ u_2 \end{pmatrix}$; find u. How many answers can you find?

$$\left[Ans.\ u = \begin{pmatrix} k \\ 2k \end{pmatrix} \text{ for any number } k.\right]$$

(c) $\begin{pmatrix} 3 & 3 \\ 6 & 10 \end{pmatrix}\begin{pmatrix} u_1 \\ u_2 \end{pmatrix} = \begin{pmatrix} u_1 \\ u_2 \end{pmatrix}$; find u. How many answers are there?

7. In Example 1 of this section, assume that the contractor is to build eight ranch-style, four Cape Cod, and four colonial-type houses. Recompute, using matrix multiplication, the total cost of raw materials, in two different ways, as in the example.

8. In Example 2 use tree measures to show that $p^{(2)} = p^{(1)}P$.

9. In Example 2 of this section, assume that the initial probability vector is $p^{(0)} = (\frac{1}{6}, \frac{5}{6})$. Find the vector $p^{(1)}$.   [*Ans.* $(\frac{17}{36}, \frac{19}{36})$.]

10. Consider the Markov chain with two states whose transition matrix is

$$P = \begin{pmatrix} a & 1 - a \\ 1 - b & b \end{pmatrix},$$

where a and b are nonnegative numbers less than 1. Suppose the initial probability vector for the process is $p^{(0)} = (p_1^{(0)}, p_2^{(0)})$, where $p_1^{(0)}$ is the initial probability of choosing state 1 and $p_2^{(0)}$ is the initial probability of choosing state 2. Derive the formulas for the components of the vector $p^{(1)}$.   [*Ans.* $p^{(1)} = ap_1^{(0)} + (1 - b)p_2^{(0)}, (1 - a)p_1^{(0)} + bp_2^{(0)}.$]

11. Suppose that $\begin{pmatrix} a & b & c \\ d & e & f \\ g & h & i \end{pmatrix}$ is the transition matrix of a three-state

Markov chain. Find $(x, y, z)\begin{pmatrix} a & b & c \\ d & e & f \\ g & h & i \end{pmatrix}\begin{pmatrix} 1 \\ 1 \\ 1 \end{pmatrix}$.   [*Ans. x + y + z.*]

12. The following matrix gives the vitamin contents of three food items, in conveniently chosen units:

Vitamin:	A	B	C	D
Food I:	.5	.5	0	0
Food II:	.3	0	.2	.1
Food III:	.1	.1	.2	.5

If we eat 11 units of food I, 6 units of food II, and 4 units of food III, how much of each type of vitamin have we consumed? If we pay only for the vitamin content of each food, paying 10 cents, 20 cents, 25 cents, and 50 cents, respectively, for units of the four vitamins, how much does a unit of each type of food cost? Compute in two ways the total cost of the food we ate.   [*Partial Ans.* $3.75.]

13. In Example 3, by how much would store 1 have to reduce the price of apples to make Smith's total purchases less expensive there than at store 2?

14. In Example 3, find the store at which the total cost to Smith is the least when he wishes to purchase
    (a) $x = (4, 1, 2, 0, 1)$.   [*Ans.* Store 1; cost 47 cents.]
    (b) $x = (1, 3, 2, 4, 0)$.
    (c) $x = (2, 2, 2, 0, 2)$.

15. In Example 4, let us assume that an individual chooses ticket 1 with probability r_1, ticket 2 with probability r_2, and ticket 3 with probability r_3. Let $r = \begin{pmatrix} r_1 \\ r_2 \\ r_3 \end{pmatrix}$. Give an interpretation for pMr. Compute this for $r_1 = \frac{1}{4}$, $r_2 = \frac{1}{4}$, and $r_3 = \frac{1}{2}$.
    [*Ans.* $pMr = \frac{67}{36}$, which is the expected return.]

16. A game room contains three pinball machines. Either a game on one of these machines terminates normally, or else the machine refunds enough money for one or two games. A game also ends if the machine is tilted. The probability of each of these events is given by the following matrix:

	Normal	Refunds 1 Game	Refunds 2	Tilt
Machine 1	.8	.09	.01	.1
$M =$ Machine 2	.75	.045	.005	.2
Machine 3	.9	.04	.01	.05

    Assume that $n = (25, 20, 30)$ represents the number of games played on machines 1, 2, and 3, respectively. Compute and interpret nM.

17. In Exercise 16, Suppose it costs 10¢ to play one game.
    (a) Construct a column vector with entries being the profit per game made by the owner of the machines for each of the different outcomes.
    (b) What is the expected profit made by the owner if 100 people play machine 1, 80 play machine 2, and 120 play machine 3.
    (c) Due to space limitations the owner must sell one of the machines. Which one should he sell?

18. (a) Consider the matrices
    $$P = \begin{pmatrix} \frac{1}{3} & \frac{2}{3} \\ \frac{3}{4} & \frac{1}{4} \end{pmatrix} \quad \text{and} \quad f = \begin{pmatrix} 1 \\ 1 \end{pmatrix}.$$
    Show that $Pf = f$. The vector f is called a fixed vector on the right of P.
    (b) Let $w = (\frac{9}{17}, \frac{8}{17})$ and let P be the matrix in part (a). Show that $wP = w$. For this reason w is called a fixed vector on the left of P.

19. Let P be the matrix of transition probabilities for a Markov chain having n states, and let f be a column matrix all of whose entries

are 1's. Show that $Pf = f$. [*Hint:* Exercise 18 provides a special case.]

20. Let A, B, and C be matrices of the same shape, and let h and k be numbers. Use the ordinary rules for numbers plus the definitions of this section to show that the following laws hold:

(a1) $A + B = B + A$ (commutative law of addition).

(a2) $A + (B + C) = (A + B) + C$ (associative law of addition).

(a3) If 0 is the zero matrix of the same shape, then $A + 0 = A$ (additive identity law).

(a4) Define $-A = (-1)A$; then $A + (-A) = 0$ (additive inverse law).

(s1) $h(kA) = (hk)A$ (mixed associative law).

(s2) $1A = A$ for all A (unity law).

(s3) $h(A + B) = hA + hB$ (first distributive law).

(s4) $(h + k)A = hA + kA$ (second distributive law).

21. A company is considering which of three methods of production it should use in producing three goods, A, B, and C. The amount of each good produced by each method is shown in the matrix:

$$R = \begin{pmatrix} \overset{\text{A}}{2} & \overset{\text{B}}{3} & \overset{\text{C}}{1} \\ 1 & 2 & 3 \\ 2 & 4 & 1 \end{pmatrix} \begin{matrix} \text{Method 1} \\ \text{Method 2} \\ \text{Method 3.} \end{matrix}$$

Let p be a vector whose components represent the profit per unit for each of the goods. What does the vector Rp represent? Find three different vectors p such that under each of these profit vectors a different method would be most profitable.

[*Partial Ans.* For $p = \begin{pmatrix} 10 \\ 8 \\ 7 \end{pmatrix}$ method 3 is most profitable.]

4 THE ADDITION AND MULTIPLICATION OF MATRICES

Two matrices of the same shape—that is, having the same number of rows and columns—can be added together by adding corresponding components. For example, if A and B are two 2×3 matrices, we have

$$A + B = \begin{pmatrix} a_{11} & a_{12} & a_{13} \\ a_{21} & a_{22} & a_{23} \end{pmatrix} + \begin{pmatrix} b_{11} & b_{12} & b_{13} \\ b_{21} & b_{22} & b_{23} \end{pmatrix}$$

$$= \begin{pmatrix} a_{11} + b_{11} & a_{12} + b_{12} & a_{13} + b_{13} \\ a_{21} + b_{21} & a_{22} + b_{22} & a_{23} + b_{23} \end{pmatrix}.$$

Observe that the addition of vectors (row or column) is simply a special case of the addition of matrices. Numerical examples of the addition of matrices are

$$(1, 0, -2) + (0, 5, 0) = (1, 5, -2);$$

$$\begin{pmatrix} 1 & 0 \\ 0 & 1 \end{pmatrix} + \begin{pmatrix} -1 & 0 \\ 0 & -1 \end{pmatrix} = \begin{pmatrix} 0 & 0 \\ 0 & 0 \end{pmatrix};$$

$$
\begin{pmatrix} 7 & 0 & 0 \\ -3 & 1 & -6 \\ 4 & 0 & 7 \\ 0 & -2 & -2 \\ 1 & 1 & 1 \end{pmatrix} + \begin{pmatrix} -8 & 0 & 1 \\ 4 & 5 & -1 \\ 0 & 3 & 0 \\ -1 & 1 & -1 \\ 0 & -4 & 2 \end{pmatrix} = \begin{pmatrix} -1 & 0 & 1 \\ 1 & 6 & -7 \\ 4 & 3 & 7 \\ -1 & -1 & -3 \\ 1 & -3 & 3 \end{pmatrix}.
$$

Other examples occur in the exercises. The reader should observe that we do *not* add matrices of different shapes.

If A is a matrix and k is any number, we define the matrix kA as

$$
kA = k \begin{pmatrix} a_{11} & a_{12} & \cdots & a_{1n} \\ a_{21} & a_{22} & \cdots & a_{2n} \\ \vdots & \vdots & \cdots & \vdots \\ a_{m1} & a_{m2} & \cdots & a_{mn} \end{pmatrix} = \begin{pmatrix} ka_{11} & ka_{12} & \cdots & ka_{1n} \\ ka_{21} & ka_{22} & \cdots & ka_{2n} \\ \vdots & \vdots & \cdots & \vdots \\ ka_{m1} & ka_{m2} & \cdots & ka_{mn} \end{pmatrix}.
$$

Observe that this is merely entrywise multiplication, as was the analogous concept for vectors. Examples of multiplication of matrices by constants are

$$
-2 \begin{pmatrix} 7 & -2 & 8 \\ 0 & 5 & -1 \end{pmatrix} = \begin{pmatrix} -14 & 4 & -16 \\ 0 & -10 & 2 \end{pmatrix};
$$

$$
6 \begin{pmatrix} 1 & 0 \\ 0 & 1 \\ 3 & -4 \end{pmatrix} = \begin{pmatrix} 6 & 0 \\ 0 & 6 \\ 18 & -24 \end{pmatrix}.
$$

The multiplication of a vector by a number is a special case of the multiplication of a matrix by a number.

Under certain conditions two matrices can be multiplied together to give a new matrix. As an example, let A be a 2×3 matrix and B be a 3×2 matrix. Then the product AB is found to be

$$
AB = \begin{pmatrix} a_{11} & a_{12} & a_{13} \\ a_{21} & a_{22} & a_{23} \end{pmatrix} \begin{pmatrix} b_{11} & b_{12} \\ b_{21} & b_{22} \\ b_{31} & b_{32} \end{pmatrix}
$$

$$
= \begin{pmatrix} a_{11}b_{11} + a_{12}b_{21} + a_{13}b_{31} & a_{11}b_{12} + a_{12}b_{22} + a_{13}b_{32} \\ a_{21}b_{11} + a_{22}b_{21} + a_{23}b_{31} & a_{21}b_{12} + a_{22}b_{22} + a_{23}b_{32} \end{pmatrix}.
$$

Observe that the product is a 2×2 matrix. Also notice that each entry in the new matrix is the product of one of the rows of A times one of the columns of B; for example, the entry in the second row and first column is found as the product

$$
(a_{21} \quad a_{22} \quad a_{23}) \begin{pmatrix} b_{11} \\ b_{21} \\ b_{31} \end{pmatrix} = a_{21}b_{11} + a_{22}b_{21} + a_{23}b_{31}.
$$

The following definition holds for the general case of matrix multiplication:

Definition   Let A be an $m \times k$ matrix and B be a $k \times n$ matrix; then the product matrix $C = AB$ is an $m \times n$ matrix whose components are

$$c_{ij} = (a_{i1} \quad a_{i2} \quad \cdots \quad a_{ik}) \begin{pmatrix} b_{1j} \\ b_{2j} \\ \vdots \\ b_{kj} \end{pmatrix}$$

$$= a_{i1}b_{1j} + a_{i2}b_{2j} + \cdots + a_{ik}b_{kj}.$$

The important things to remember about this definition are: first, in order to be able to multiply matrix A times matrix B, the number of columns of A must be equal to the number of rows of B; second, the product matrix $C = AB$ has the same number of rows as A and the same number of columns as B; finally, to get the entry in the ith row and jth column of AB we multiply the ith row of A times the jth column of B. Notice that the product of a vector times a matrix is a special case of matrix multiplication.

Below are several examples of matrix multiplication:

$$\begin{pmatrix} 2 & -1 \\ 0 & 3 \end{pmatrix}\begin{pmatrix} 7 & 0 \\ -2 & -3 \end{pmatrix} = \begin{pmatrix} 16 & 3 \\ -6 & -9 \end{pmatrix};$$

$$\begin{pmatrix} 3 & 0 & 1 & 1 \\ -1 & 2 & 0 & 0 \\ 0 & 0 & 2 & 1 \end{pmatrix}\begin{pmatrix} 0 & 0 \\ -1 & 0 \\ 1 & 1 \end{pmatrix} = \begin{pmatrix} 4 & 1 & 1 \\ -1 & -2 & 0 \\ 2 & 2 & 2 \end{pmatrix};$$

$$\begin{pmatrix} 3 & 1 & 4 \\ 2 & 0 & 5 \end{pmatrix}\begin{pmatrix} 1 & 3 & 0 & 0 \\ 1 & 1 & 0 & 0 \\ 0 & 0 & 1 & 1 \end{pmatrix} = \begin{pmatrix} 4 & 10 & 4 & 4 \\ 2 & 6 & 5 & 5 \end{pmatrix}.$$

We next ask how we multiply more than two matrices together. Let A be an $m \times h$ matrix, let B be an $h \times k$ matrix, and let C be a $k \times n$ matrix. Then we can certainly define the products $(AB)C$ and $A(BC)$. It turns out that these two products are equal, and we define the product ABC to be their common value; that is,

$$ABC = A(BC) = (AB)C.$$

The rule expressed in the above equation is called the *associative law* for multiplication. We shall not prove the associative law here, although the student will be asked to check an example of it in Exercise 5.

If A and B are square matrices of the same size, then they can be multiplied in either order. It is not true, however, that the product AB is necessarily equal to the product BA. For example, if

$$A = \begin{pmatrix} 1 & 1 \\ 0 & 0 \end{pmatrix} \quad \text{and} \quad B = \begin{pmatrix} 1 & 0 \\ 1 & 0 \end{pmatrix},$$

then we have

$$AB = \begin{pmatrix} 1 & 1 \\ 0 & 0 \end{pmatrix}\begin{pmatrix} 1 & 0 \\ 1 & 0 \end{pmatrix} = \begin{pmatrix} 2 & 0 \\ 0 & 0 \end{pmatrix},$$

whereas

$$BA = \begin{pmatrix} 1 & 0 \\ 1 & 0 \end{pmatrix}\begin{pmatrix} 1 & 1 \\ 0 & 0 \end{pmatrix} = \begin{pmatrix} 1 & 1 \\ 1 & 1 \end{pmatrix},$$

and it is clear that $AB \neq BA$.

EXERCISES

1. Perform the following matrix operations:

   (a) $\begin{pmatrix} 3 & 2 \\ 1 & 4 \\ 5 & 3 \end{pmatrix} - \begin{pmatrix} 0 & 7 \\ -3 & -3 \\ 8 & 1 \end{pmatrix} = ?$ $\left[Ans. \begin{pmatrix} 3 & -5 \\ 4 & 7 \\ -3 & 2 \end{pmatrix}.\right]$

   (b) $3\begin{pmatrix} 1 & 0 & 4 \\ 3 & 1 & -2 \\ 2 & 1 & -1 \end{pmatrix} + \begin{pmatrix} 2 & 0 & 2 \\ 5 & 0 & 1 \\ 3 & 5 & 2 \end{pmatrix} = ?$

   (c) $\begin{pmatrix} 1 & 8 \\ -3 & 0 \end{pmatrix}\begin{pmatrix} 2 & 1 \\ -1 & 2 \end{pmatrix} = ?$

   (d) $\begin{pmatrix} 0 & 10 \\ 3 & 6 \end{pmatrix}\begin{pmatrix} 8 & 1 & 3 \\ -6 & -1 & 2 \end{pmatrix} = ?$

   (e) $\begin{pmatrix} 8 & -6 \\ 1 & -1 \\ 3 & 2 \end{pmatrix}\begin{pmatrix} 0 & 3 \\ 10 & 6 \end{pmatrix} = ?$

   (f) $\begin{pmatrix} 1 & 3 \\ 1 & 5 \end{pmatrix}\left[\begin{pmatrix} 3 & 6 \\ 4 & 4 \end{pmatrix} - 8\begin{pmatrix} 5 & 4 \\ 0 & 3 \end{pmatrix}\right] = ?$

   (g) $\begin{pmatrix} 1 & -2 \\ 1 & -1 \end{pmatrix}\begin{pmatrix} 2 \\ 1 \end{pmatrix} = ?$

   (h) $\begin{pmatrix} 7 & 9 & 2 \\ 4 & 9 & 6 \\ 5 & 6 & 0 \end{pmatrix}\begin{pmatrix} 3 & 3 & 5 \\ 3 & 9 & 4 \\ 4 & 5 & 7 \end{pmatrix} = ?$ $\left[Ans. \begin{pmatrix} 56 & 112 & 85 \\ 63 & 123 & 98 \\ 33 & 69 & 49 \end{pmatrix}.\right]$

   (i) $\left[2\begin{pmatrix} 6 & 0 & 1 \\ 1 & -3 & 2 \end{pmatrix} + \begin{pmatrix} 4 & 0 & -4 \\ 2 & 1 & -1 \end{pmatrix}\right]\begin{pmatrix} 3 & 0 & 1 \\ -1 & 2 & 0 \\ 0 & 0 & 2 \end{pmatrix} = ?$

   (j) $\begin{pmatrix} 1 & -1 \\ -1 & 1 \end{pmatrix}\begin{pmatrix} 1 & -1 \\ -1 & 1 \end{pmatrix} = ?$

2. Consider the matrices $A = \begin{pmatrix} -19 & 2 \\ 14 & -10 \\ 5 & 0 \end{pmatrix}$, $B = \begin{pmatrix} 7 & 2 & 19 \\ 4 & 26 & -2 \\ 13 & 0 & 7 \end{pmatrix}$,

   $C = \begin{pmatrix} 4 & 1 & -1 \\ 6 & 3 & -5 \end{pmatrix}$, and $D = \begin{pmatrix} 10 & -7 \\ 4 & 15 \end{pmatrix}$. Their shapes are 3×2, $3 \times$

   3, 2×3, and 2×2, respectively. What is the shape of:
   (a) AC?

    (b) *CB*?

    (c) *DC*?   [*Ans.* 2×3.]

    (d) *ACB*?

    (e) *BAC*?

    (f) *DCB*?

    (g) *DCBA*?

    (h) *ADCB*?   [*Ans.* 3×3.]

3. In Exercise 2, find the component:

    (a) In the second row and second column of *AC*.   [*Ans.* -16.]

    (b) In the first row and the third column of *CB*.

    (c) In the last row and last column of *AC*.

    (d) In the last row and last column of *CA*.   [*Ans.* -18.]

    (e) In the second row and first column of *DC*.

4. Let *A* be any 3×3 matrix and let *I* be the matrix

$$I = \begin{pmatrix} 1 & 0 & 0 \\ 0 & 1 & 0 \\ 0 & 0 & 1 \end{pmatrix}.$$

Show that $AI = IA = A$. The matrix *I* acts for the products of matrices in the same way that the number 1 acts for products of numbers. For this reason it is called the *identity matrix*.

5. Verify the associative law for the special case when

$$A = \begin{pmatrix} -1 & 3 & 3 \\ 6 & 5 & 1 \end{pmatrix}, B = \begin{pmatrix} 4 & -3 & 3 \\ 8 & 0 & 5 \\ 5 & -4 & 3 \end{pmatrix}, \text{ and } C = \begin{pmatrix} 9 & 4 \\ 7 & -4 \\ 0 & 1 \end{pmatrix}.$$

6. The commutative law for addition is

$$A + B = B + A$$

for any two matrices *A* and *B* of the same shape. Prove that the commutative law for addition is true from the definition of matrix addition and from the fact that it is true for ordinary numbers.

7. Show that there is *not* a commutative law for matrix multiplication by finding two 2×2 matrices *A* and *B* different than the ones in the text such that $A \cdot B \neq B \cdot A$.

8. The distributive law for numbers and matrices is

$$k(A + B) = kA + kB$$

for any number *k* and any two matrices *A* and *B* of the same shape. Prove that this law holds from the definitions of numerical multiplication of matrices, addition of matrices, and the ordinary rules for numbers.

9. The distributive laws for matrices are

$$(A + B)C = AC + BC,$$

$$C(A + B) = CA + CB,$$

where A, B, and C are matrices of suitable shapes. Show that these laws hold from the definitions of matrix multiplication and addition, and the ordinary rules for numbers.

10. Let A be any 3×3 matrix and let 0 be the matrix

$$0 = \begin{pmatrix} 0 & 0 & 0 \\ 0 & 0 & 0 \\ 0 & 0 & 0 \end{pmatrix}.$$

Show that $A0 = 0A = 0$ for any A. Also show that $A + 0 = 0 + A = A$ for any A. The matrix 0 acts for matrices in the same way that the number 0 acts for numbers. For this reason it is called the *zero matrix*.

11. Show that for any square matrix A there is a matrix B of the same shape as A such that $A + B = 0$. (B is called the *additive inverse* of A.)

12. Find the additive inverse of each of the following matrices:

(a) $\begin{pmatrix} 1 & 1 \\ 2 & -1 \end{pmatrix}$.

(b) $\begin{pmatrix} -3 & 2 \\ 6 & 1 \end{pmatrix}$.

(c) $\begin{pmatrix} -3 & 2 & 4 \\ 0 & 8 & 3 \\ 5 & 4 & -7 \end{pmatrix}$.

13. If $A = \begin{pmatrix} 0 & 0 \\ 0 & 1 \end{pmatrix}$ and $B = \begin{pmatrix} 1 & 0 \\ 0 & 0 \end{pmatrix}$, show that $AB = \begin{pmatrix} 0 & 0 \\ 0 & 0 \end{pmatrix}$. Thus the product of two matrices can be the zero matrix even though neither of the matrices is itself zero. Find another example that illustrates this point.

14. If A is a square matrix, it can be multiplied by itself; hence we can define (using the associative law)

$$A^2 = A \cdot A$$
$$A^3 = A^2 \cdot A = A \cdot A \cdot A$$
$$\cdots$$
$$A^n = A^{n-1} \cdot A = A \cdot A \cdot \cdots \cdot A \quad (n \text{ factors}).$$

These are naturally called "powers" of the matrix A, A^2 being called the square of A, A^3 the cube of A, etc.

(a) Compute A^2, A^3, and A^4 for $A = \begin{pmatrix} 2 & 0 \\ 3 & -1 \end{pmatrix}$.

(b) If I and 0 are the matrices defined in Exercises 4 and 10, find I^2, I^3, I^n, 0^2, 0^3, and 0^n.

(c) If $A = \begin{pmatrix} 1 & 1 \\ 1 & 1 \end{pmatrix}$, find A^n.

(d)　If $A = \begin{pmatrix} 0 & 1 & 2 \\ 0 & 0 & -1 \\ 0 & 0 & 0 \end{pmatrix}$, find A^2, A^3, and A^n.

15.　Find the matrices $P^{(2)}$ and $P^{(3)}$ for the Markov chain whose transition matrix is $P = \begin{pmatrix} \frac{1}{2} & \frac{1}{2} \\ \frac{2}{3} & \frac{1}{3} \end{pmatrix}$. Compute P^2 and P^3 and compare the results.

16.　Cube the matrix

$$\begin{pmatrix} 0 & 1 & 0 \\ 0 & \frac{1}{2} & \frac{1}{2} \\ \frac{1}{3} & 0 & \frac{2}{3} \end{pmatrix}.$$

Compare your answer with the matrix $P^{(3)}$ in Example 1, Chapter 3, Section 12, and comment on the result.

17.　Consider a two-state Markov process whose transition matrix is

$$P = \begin{pmatrix} p_{11} & p_{12} \\ p_{21} & p_{22} \end{pmatrix}.$$

(a)　Assuming that the process starts in state 1, draw the tree and set up tree measures for three stages of the process. Do the same, assuming that the process starts in state 2.

(b)　Using the trees drawn in (a), compute the quantities $p_{11}^{(3)}, p_{12}^{(3)}, p_{21}^{(3)}, p_{22}^{(3)}$. Write the matrix $P^{(3)}$.

(c)　Compute the cube $P^{(3)}$ of the matrix P.

(d)　Compare the answers you found in parts (b) and (c) and show that $P^{(3)} = P^3$.

18.　Let $A = \begin{pmatrix} 1 & 0 \\ 1 & 2 \end{pmatrix}$.

(a)　Find a matrix B such that $AB = \begin{pmatrix} 1 & 0 \\ 0 & 1 \end{pmatrix}$. Show that $BA = \begin{pmatrix} 1 & 0 \\ 0 & 1 \end{pmatrix}$ as well.

(b)　Find a matrix C such that $AC = \begin{pmatrix} 1 & 1 \\ 1 & 3 \end{pmatrix}$. What is CA?

19.　A diagonal matrix is square and its only nonzero entries are on the main diagonal. For instance, the matrices

$$A = \begin{pmatrix} 1 & 0 \\ 0 & 4 \end{pmatrix}, \qquad B = \begin{pmatrix} 3 & 0 \\ 0 & 2 \end{pmatrix}$$

are 2×2 diagonal matrices.

(a)　Show that A and B commute, i.e., $AB = BA$.

(b)　Show that any pair of diagonal matrices of the same size commute when multiplied together.

20.　A *scalar matrix* is a diagonal matrix in which all the entries on the main diagonal are equal. For instance, the matrices $A = \begin{pmatrix} 3 & 0 \\ 0 & 3 \end{pmatrix}$ and $B = \begin{pmatrix} -7 & 0 \\ 0 & -7 \end{pmatrix}$ are 2×2 scalar matrices.

(a) Show that A commutes with *any* 2×2 matrix.
(b) Show that any scalar matrix A can be written as kI, where k is a number and I is the identity matrix of the appropriate size.
(c) Show that any scalar matrix commutes with *any* other matrix of the same size.

21. In Example 1 of Section 3 assume that the contractor wishes to take into account the cost of transporting raw materials to the building site as well as the purchasing cost. Suppose the costs are as given in the matrix below:

	Purchase	Transport	
	15	4.5	Steel
	8	2	Wood
$Q =$	5	3	Glass
	1	0.5	Paint
	10	0	Labor

Referring to the example:

(a) By computing the product RQ find a 3×2 matrix whose entries give the purchase and transportation costs of the materials for each kind of house.
(b) Find the product xRQ, which is a two-component row vector whose first component gives the total purchase price and second component gives the total transportation cost.
(c) Let $z = \begin{pmatrix} 1 \\ 1 \end{pmatrix}$ and then compute $xRQz$, which is a number giving the total cost of materials and transportation for all the houses being built.   [*Ans.* 14,304.]

22. A candy company packages four sizes of assorted chocolates: the Sampler, Sweetheart, Matinee, and Jumbo boxes. The Sampler contains 3 almond creams, 4 chocolate nougats, 5 caramel creams, and 3 nut clusters. The Sweetheart contains 6 almond creams, 4 chocolate nougats, 8 caramel creams, and 7 nut clusters. In the Matinee box are 10 almond creams, 15 chocolate nougats, 5 caramel creams, and 5 nut clusters. The Jumbo assortment has 10 almond creams, 15 chocolate nougats, 15 caramel creams, and 10 nut clusters. The company uses as ingredients in its manufacturing process chocolate, nuts, and cream filling. An almond cream contains 1 unit of chocolate, 2 units of nuts, and 2 units of cream filling; a chocolate nougat, 2 units each of chocolate and cream filling; a caramel cream, 4 units of cream filling; and a nut cluster, 3 units of nuts and 2 units of chocolate. Suppose a unit of chocolate costs 1¢, a unit of nuts 1.6¢, and a unit of cream filling 2¢.

If the company packages 50 Samplers, 75 Sweethearts, 40 Matinees, and 100 Jumbos,
  (a) What is the total number of each type of candy produced?
  (b) What is the total number of units of each ingredient used to make all the candy?
  (c) What is the total cost of the candy in each box?
  (d) What is the total cost of all the candy in all the boxes?

[*Ans.* $651.50.]

5 THE SOLUTION OF LINEAR EQUATIONS

There are many occasions when the simultaneous solutions of linear equations is important. In this section we shall develop methods for finding out whether a set of linear equations has solutions, and for finding all such solutions.

EXAMPLE 1 Consider the following example of three linear equations in three unknowns:

(1) $$x_1 + 4x_2 + 3x_3 = 1$$
(2) $$2x_1 + 5x_2 + 4x_3 = 4$$
(3) $$x_1 - 3x_2 - 2x_3 = 5.$$

Equations such as these, containing one or more variables, are called *open statements*. Statement (1) is true for some values of the variables (for instance, when $x_1 = 1$, $x_2 = 0$, and $x_3 = 0$), and false for other values of the variables (for instance, when $x_1 = 0$, $x_2 = 1$, and $x_3 = 0$). The truth set of (1) is the set of all vectors $\begin{pmatrix} x_1 \\ x_2 \\ x_3 \end{pmatrix}$ for which (1) is true. Similarly, the truth set of the three simultaneous equations (1), (2), and (3) is the set of all vectors $\begin{pmatrix} x_1 \\ x_2 \\ x_3 \end{pmatrix}$ which make true their conjunction

$$(x_1 + 4x_2 + 3x_3 = 1) \wedge (2x_1 + 5x_2 + 4x_3 = 4) \wedge (x_1 - 3x_2 - 2x_3 = 5).$$

When we say that we solve a set of simultaneous equations, we mean that we determine the truth set of their conjunction.

Before we discuss the solution of these equations we note that they can be written as a single equation in matrix form as follows:

$$\begin{pmatrix} 1 & 4 & 3 \\ 2 & 5 & 4 \\ 1 & -3 & -2 \end{pmatrix} \begin{pmatrix} x_1 \\ x_2 \\ x_3 \end{pmatrix} = \begin{pmatrix} 1 \\ 4 \\ 5 \end{pmatrix}.$$

One of the uses of vector and matrix notation is in writing a large number of linear equations in a single simple matrix equation such as the one above. It also leads to the detached coefficient form of solving simultaneous equations that we shall discuss at the end of the present section and in the next section.

The method of solving the linear equations above is the following. First we use equation (1) to eliminate the variable x_1 from equations (2) and (3); i.e., we subtract 2 times (1) from (2) and then subtract (1) from (3), giving

(1′) $$x_1 + 4x_2 + 3x_3 = 1$$
(2′) $$-3x_2 - 2x_3 = 2$$
(3′) $$-7x_2 - 5x_3 = 4.$$

By *pivoting* we shall mean the operation of using an equation to eliminate a variable from the other equations. The *pivot* is the coefficient of the variable being eliminated. In this case the pivot is 1. Next we pivot on -3 in (2′): divide equation (2′) through by the coefficient of x_2, namely, -3, obtaining $x_2 + \frac{2}{3}x_3 = -\frac{2}{3}$. We use this equation to eliminate x_2 from each of the other two equations. In order to do this we subtract 4 times this equation from (1′) and add 7 times this equation to (3′), obtaining

(1″) $$x_1 + 0 + \tfrac{1}{3}x_3 = \tfrac{11}{3}$$
(2″) $$x_2 + \tfrac{2}{3}x_3 = -\tfrac{2}{3}$$
(3″) $$-\tfrac{1}{3}x_3 = -\tfrac{2}{3}.$$

The last step is to pivot on $-\frac{1}{3}$ by dividing through (3″) by $-\frac{1}{3}$, which is the coefficient of x_3, obtaining the equation $x_3 = 2$; we use this equation to eliminate x_3 from the first two equations as follows:

(1‴) $$x_1 + 0 + 0 = \quad 3$$
(2‴) $$x_2 + 0 = -2$$
(3‴) $$x_3 = \quad 2.$$

The solution can now be read from these equations as $x_1 = 3$, $x_2 = -2$, and $x_3 = 2$. The reader should substitute these values into the original equations (1), (2), and (3) above to see that the solution has actually been obtained.

In the example just discussed we saw that there was only one solution to the set of three simultaneous equations in three variables. Example 2 will be one in which there is *more* than one solution, and Example 3 will be one in which there are *no* solutions to a set of three simultaneous equations in three variables.

EXAMPLE 2   Consider the following linear equations:

(4) $$x_1 - 2x_2 - 3x_3 = 2$$
(5) $$x_1 - 4x_2 - 13x_3 = 14$$
(6) $$-3x_1 + 5x_2 + 4x_3 = 0.$$

Let us proceed as before and use equation (4) to eliminate the variable x_1 from the other two equations. Pivoting on the 1 coefficient of x_1 in (4), we have

(4')
$$x_1 - 2x_2 - 3x_3 = 2$$

(5')
$$-2x_2 - 10x_3 = 12$$

(6')
$$-x_2 - 5x_3 = 6.$$

Proceeding as before, we divide equation (5') by -2, obtaining the equation $x_2 + 5x_3 = -6$. We use this equation to eliminate the variable x_2 from each of the other equations—namely, we add twice this equation to (4') and then add the equation to (6'):

(4'')
$$x_1 + 0 + 7x_3 = -10$$

(5'')
$$x_2 + 5x_3 = -6$$

(6'')
$$0 = 0.$$

Observe that we have eliminated the last equation completely! We also see that the variable x_3 can be chosen completely arbitrarily in these equations. To emphasize this, we move the terms involving x_3 to the right-hand side, giving

(4''')
$$x_1 = -10 - 7x_3$$

(5''')
$$x_2 = -6 - 5x_3.$$

The reader should check, by substituting these values of x_1 and x_2 into equations (4), (5), and (6), that they are solutions regardless of the value of x_3. Let us also substitute particular values for x_3 to obtain numerical solutions. Thus, if we let $x_3 = 1, 0, -2$, respectively, and compute the resulting numbers, using (4''') and (5'''), we obtain the following numerical solutions:

$$x_1 = -17, \qquad x_2 = -11, \qquad x_3 = 1$$
$$x_1 = -10, \qquad x_2 = -6, \qquad x_3 = 0$$
$$x_1 = 4, \qquad x_2 = 4, \qquad x_3 = -2.$$

The reader should also substitute these numbers into (4), (5), and (6) to show that they are solutions. To summarize, our second example has an infinite number of solutions, one for each numerical value of x_3 which is substituted into equations (4''') and (5''').

EXAMPLE 3   Suppose that we modify equation (6) by changing the number on the right-hand side to 2. Then we have

(7)
$$x_1 - 2x_2 - 3x_3 = 2$$

(8)
$$x_1 - 4x_2 - 13x_3 = 14$$

(9)
$$-3x_1 + 5x_2 + 4x_3 = 2.$$

If we carry out the same procedure as before and use (7) to eliminate x_1 from (8) and (9), we obtain

(7') $x_1 - 2x_2 - 3x_3 = 2$

(8') $-2x_2 - 10x_3 = 12$

(9') $-x_2 - 5x_3 = 8.$

We divide (8') by -2, the coefficient of x_2, obtaining, as before, $x_2 + 5x_3 = -6$. Using this equation to eliminate x_2 from the other two equations, we have

(7'') $x_1 + 0 + 7x_3 = -10$

(8'') $x_2 + 5x_3 = -6$

(9'') $0 = 2.$

Observe that the last equation is *logically false,* that is, false for all values of x_1, x_2, x_3. Because our elimination procedure has led to a false result we conclude that the equations (7), (8), and (9) have *no* solution. The student should always keep in mind that this possibility exists when considering simultaneous equations.

In the examples above the equations we considered had the same number of variables as equations. The next example has more variables than equations and the last has more equations than variables.

EXAMPLE 4   Consider the following two equations in three variables:

(10) $-4x_1 + 3x_2 + 2x_3 = -2$

(11) $5x_1 - 4x_2 + x_3 = 3.$

Using the elimination method outlined above, we divide (10) by -4, and then subtract 5 times the result from (11), obtaining

(10') $x_1 - \frac{3}{4}x_2 - \frac{1}{2}x_3 = \frac{1}{2}$

(11') $-\frac{1}{4}x_2 + \frac{7}{2}x_3 = \frac{1}{2}.$

Multiplying (11') by -4 and using it to eliminate x_2 from (10'), we have

(10'') $x_1 + 0 - 11x_3 = -1$

(11'') $x_2 - 14x_3 = -2.$

We can now let x_3 take on any value whatsoever and solve these equations for x_1 and x_2. We emphasize this fact by rewriting them as in Example 2 as

(10''') $x_1 = 11x_3 - 1$

(11''') $x_2 = 14x_3 - 2.$

The reader should check that these are solutions and also, by choosing specific values for x_3, find numerical solutions to these equations.

EXAMPLE 5   Let us consider the other possibility suggested by Example 4, namely, the case in which we have more equations than variables. Consider the following equations:

(12) $-4x_1 + 3x_2 = 2$

(13) $5x_1 - 4x_2 = 0$

(14) $2x_1 - x_2 = a,$

where a is an arbitrary number. Using equation (12) to eliminate x_1 from the other two we obtain

(12′) $x_1 - \frac{3}{4}x_2 = -\frac{1}{2}$

(13′) $-\frac{1}{4}x_2 = \frac{5}{2}$

(14′) $\frac{1}{2}x_2 = a + 1.$

Next we use (13′) to eliminate x_2 from the other equations, obtaining

(12″) $x_1 + 0 = -8$

(13″) $x_2 = -10$

(14″) $0 = a + 6.$

These equations remind us of the situation in Example 3, since we shall be led to a false result unless $a = -6$. We see that equations (12), (13), and (14) have the solution $x_1 = -8$ and $x_2 = -10$ only if $a = -6$. If $a \neq -6$, then there is *no* solution to these equations.

The examples above illustrate all the possibilities that can occur in the general case. There may be no solutions, exactly one solution, or an infinite number of solutions to a set of simultaneous equations.

The procedure that we have illustrated above is one that turns any set of linear equations into an equivalent set of equations from which the existence of solutions and the solutions can be easily read. A student who learned other ways of solving linear equations may wonder why we use the above procedure—one which is not always the quickest way of solving equations. The answer is that we use it because it always works, that is, it is a *canonical* procedure to apply to *any* set of linear equations. The faster methods usually work only for equations that have solutions, and even then may not find all solutions.

The computational process illustrated above is summarized in the flow diagram of Figure 5. In that diagram the instructions encircled by dotted lines are either beginning or ending instructions; those enclosed in solid rectangles are intermediate computational steps; and those enclosed in ovals ask questions, the answers to which determine which of two paths the computational process will follow.

The direction of the process is always indicated by arrows. The flow diagram of Figure 5 can easily be turned into a computer program for

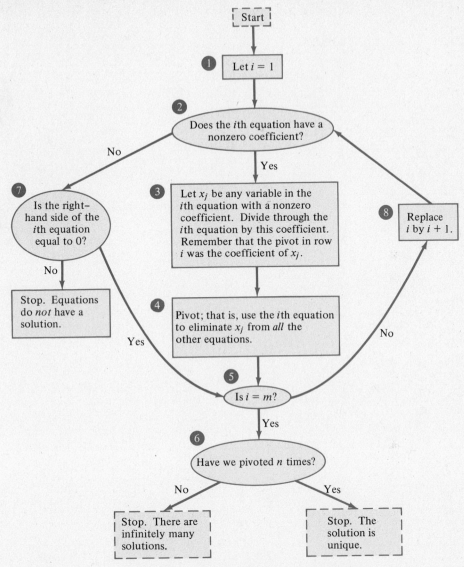

Figure 5   Flow diagram for solving m equations in n variables.

solving m linear equations in n variables. Students having access to a computer will find it a useful exercise to write such a program.

Let us return again to the equations of Example 1. Note that the variables, coefficients, and equals signs are in columns at the beginning of the solution and are always kept in the same column. It is obvious that the *location* of the coefficient is sufficient identification for it and that it is unnecessary to keep writing the variables. We can start with the format or *tableau*

(15) $$\begin{pmatrix} 1 & 4 & 3 & 1 \\ 2 & 5 & 4 & 4 \\ 1 & -3 & -2 & 5 \end{pmatrix}.$$

Note that the coefficients of x_1 are found in the first column, the coefficients of x_2 in the second column, of x_3 in the third column, and the constants on the right-hand side of the equation all occur in the fourth column. The vertical line represents the equals signs in the equations.

The tableau of (15) will be called the *detached coefficient tableau* for simultaneous linear equations. We now show how to solve simultaneous equations using the detached coefficient tableau.

EXAMPLE 6 Starting with the tableau of (15) we carry out exactly the same calculations as in Example 1, which lead to the following series of tableaus:

$$(16) \qquad \begin{pmatrix} 1 & 4 & 3 & \bigm| & 1 \\ 0 & -3 & -2 & \bigm| & 2 \\ 0 & -7 & -5 & \bigm| & 4 \end{pmatrix}$$

$$(17) \qquad \begin{pmatrix} 1 & 0 & \frac{1}{3} & \bigm| & \frac{11}{3} \\ 0 & 1 & \frac{2}{3} & \bigm| & -\frac{2}{3} \\ 0 & 0 & -\frac{1}{3} & \bigm| & -\frac{2}{3} \end{pmatrix}$$

$$(18) \qquad \begin{pmatrix} 1 & 0 & 0 & \bigm| & 3 \\ 0 & 1 & 0 & \bigm| & -2 \\ 0 & 0 & 1 & \bigm| & 2 \end{pmatrix}.$$

From the tableau of (18) we can easily read the answer $x_1 = 3$, $x_2 = -2$, and $x_3 = 2$, which is the same as before.

The correspondence between the calculations of Example 1 and of the present example is as follows:

(1), (2), and (3)	correspond to	(15).
(1′), (2′), and (3′)	correspond to	(16).
(1″), (2″), and (3″)	correspond to	(17).
(1‴), (2‴), and (3‴)	correspond to	(18).

Note that in the tableau form we are always careful to keep zero coefficients in each column when necessary.

EXAMPLE 7 Suppose that we have two sets of simultaneous equations to solve and that they differ only in their right-hand sides. For instance, suppose we want to solve

$$(19) \qquad \begin{pmatrix} 1 & 4 & 3 \\ 2 & 5 & 4 \\ 1 & -3 & -2 \end{pmatrix} \begin{pmatrix} x_1 \\ x_2 \\ x_3 \end{pmatrix} = \begin{pmatrix} 1 \\ 4 \\ 5 \end{pmatrix} \quad \text{and} \quad = \begin{pmatrix} -1 \\ 0 \\ 2 \end{pmatrix}.$$

It is obvious that the calculations on the left-hand side will be the same regardless of the numbers appearing on the right-hand side. Therefore it is possible to solve both sets of simultaneous equations at once. We shall illustrate this in the following series of tableaus:

$$(20) \quad \begin{pmatrix} 1 & 4 & 3 & | & 1 & -1 \\ 2 & 5 & 4 & | & 4 & 0 \\ 1 & -3 & -2 & | & 5 & 2 \end{pmatrix}$$

$$(21) \quad \begin{pmatrix} 1 & 4 & 3 & | & 1 & -1 \\ 0 & -3 & -2 & | & 2 & 2 \\ 0 & -7 & -5 & | & 4 & 3 \end{pmatrix}$$

$$(22) \quad \begin{pmatrix} 1 & 0 & \frac{1}{3} & | & \frac{11}{3} & \frac{5}{3} \\ 0 & 1 & \frac{2}{3} & | & -\frac{2}{3} & -\frac{2}{3} \\ 0 & 0 & -\frac{1}{3} & | & -\frac{2}{3} & -\frac{5}{3} \end{pmatrix}$$

$$(23) \quad \begin{pmatrix} 1 & 0 & 0 & | & 3 & 0 \\ 0 & 1 & 0 & | & -2 & -4 \\ 0 & 0 & 1 & | & 2 & 5 \end{pmatrix}.$$

We find the answers

$$x_1 = 3, \qquad x_2 = -2, \qquad x_3 = 2$$

to the first set of equations and the answers

$$x_1 = 0, \qquad x_2 = -4, \qquad x_3 = 5.$$

to the second set of equations. The reader should check these answers by substituting into the original equations.

EXERCISES

1. Find all solutions to the following simultaneous equations:
   (a) $x_1 + 2x_2 + 3x_3 = 4$
   $4x_1 + 5x_2 + 6x_3 = -2$ [*Ans.* $x_1 = -7$, $x_2 = 4$, $x_3 = 1$.]
   $7x_1 + 8x_2 + 27x_3 = 10.$
   (b) $-x_1 \quad\quad + 3x_3 = 16$
   $2x_1 + 7x_2 + 3x_3 = -6$ [*Ans.* No solution.]
   $-x_1 + 7x_2 + 12x_3 = 41.$
   (c) $-x_1 \quad\quad + 3x_3 = 8$
   $2x_1 + 7x_2 + 3x_3 = -3$
   $-x_1 + 7x_2 + 12x_3 = 21.$
   [*Ans.* $x_1 = 3x_3 - 8$, $x_2 = \frac{1}{7}(13 - 9x_3)$, $x_3 =$ any real number.]
2. Find all solutions of the following simultaneous equations:
   (a) $x_1 + 5x_2 + 3x_3 = 2$
   $x_1 + x_2 + x_3 = -2$
   $13x_1 + 4x_2 + 7x_3 = 4.$
   (b) $5x_1 + 3x_2 - x_3 = -2$
   $2x_1 - 2x_2 + 3x_3 = 3$
   $3x_1 \quad\quad + x_3 = 0.$
   (c) $2x_1 + 3x_2 - x_3 = 0$
   $\quad\quad -4x_2 + x_3 = 0$
   $8x_1 \quad\quad - x_3 = 0.$

3. Rework Examples 2–4 using the detached coefficient tableau.
4. Find all solutions of the following equations using all the detached coefficient tableau:

(a) $2x_1 + 2x_2 - x_3 = -4$
$-x_2 + 2x_3 = -2$

$\dfrac{x_1}{2} + x_2 + x_3 = 1.$

(b) $5x_1 + 3x_2 + 3x_3 = 7$
$-2x_1 + 4x_2 + 8x_3 = -3$
$-x_1 + 3x_2 + 4x_3 = 2.$

(c) $3x_1 + 6x_2 - x_3 = -7$
$x_1 + 5x_2 = 0$
$2x_2 + x_3 = 14.$

5. Find all solutions of the following equations:

(a) $-x_1 + x_2 - x_3 + x_4 = 13$
$2x_2 - 6x_3 + 7x_4 = 0$
$-2x_1 + x_2 + x_3 + 5x_4 = -13$
$3x_1 - 2x_2 + 2x_3 + x_4 = 26.$

(b) $x_1 + 2x_2 + 3x_3 + 4x_4 = 10$
$2x_1 - x_2 + x_3 - x_4 = 1$
$3x_1 + x_2 + 4x_3 + 3x_4 = 11$
$-2x_1 + 6x_2 + 4x_3 + 10x_4 = 18.$

6. Solve the following four simultaneous sets whose right-hand sides are listed under (a), (b), (c), and (d) below. Use the detached coefficient tableau.

	(a)	(b)	(c)	(d)
$3x_1 + 6x_2 + 4x_3 =$	−4	2	1	−1
$4x_1 + 8x_2 + 5x_3 =$	8	2	1	−1
$4x_1 + 3x_3 =$	0	2	1	1.

[*Ans.* (a) $x_1 = 30$, $x_2 = 11$, $x_3 = -40$.]

7. Solve the following four sets of simultaneous equations, which differ only in their right-hand sides:

	(a)	(b)	(c)	(d)
$-x_1 + 2x_3 =$	−2	−2	4	1
$2x_1 + 7x_2 + 3x_3 =$	4	2	−1	12
$-x_1 + 7x_2 + 11x_3 =$	0	4	1	17.

[*Ans.* (d) $x_1 = x_2 = x_3 = 1$.]

8. Solve the following four sets of simultaneous equations:

	(a)	(b)	(c)	(d)
$x_1 + 6x_2 + x_3 =$	12	12	0	−9
$-x_1 - 2x_2 - 9x_3 =$	−9	0	12	0
$3x_2 + 3x_3 =$	0	−9	−9	12.

[*Ans.* (a) $x_1 = 10\frac{3}{4}$, $x_2 = \frac{1}{4}$, $x_3 = -\frac{1}{4}$.]

9. A man is ordered by his doctor to take 10 units of vitamin A, 9 units of vitamin D, and 19 units of vitamin E each day. The man can choose from three brands of vitamin pills. Brand X contains two units of vitamin A, three units of vitamin D, and five units of vitamin E; brand Y has 1, 3, and 4 units, respectively; and brand Z has 1 unit of vitamin A, 1 of vitamin E, and none of vitamin D.

   (a) Find all possible combinations of pills that will provide exactly the required amounts of vitamins.

   (b) If brand X costs 1¢ a pill, brand Y 6¢, and brand Z 3¢, is there a solution costing exactly 15¢ a day?

   (c) What is the least expensive solution? The most expensive?

10. Show that the equations

$$4x_1 - 4x_2 + ax_3 = c$$
$$3x_1 - 2x_2 + bx_3 = d$$

   always have a solution for all values of a, b, c, and d.

11. Find conditions on a, b, and c in order that the equations

$$3x_1 + 2x_2 = a$$
$$-4x_1 + x_2 = b$$
$$2x_1 + 5x_2 = c$$

   have a solution.

12. For what value of the constant k does the following system have a unique solution? Find the solution in this case. What is the case if k does not take on this value?

$$2x \qquad + 4z = \quad 6$$
$$3x + y + z = -1$$
$$2y - z = -2$$
$$x - y + kz = -5.$$

   [*Ans.* $k = -2$; $x = -1$, $y = 0$, $z = 2$; no solution.]

13. Let $x = (x_1, x_2, x_3)$, let $A = \begin{pmatrix} a \\ b \\ c \end{pmatrix}$, and let d be any number. What can you say about the truth set of the statement $xA = d$ in the following cases:

   (a) $A \neq 0$?

   (b) $A = 0$, $d = 0$?

   (c) $A = 0$, $d \neq 0$?

   What can you conclude?

14. Let P be the matrix $P = \begin{pmatrix} \frac{1}{2} & \frac{1}{2} \\ \frac{1}{4} & \frac{3}{4} \end{pmatrix}$, and let $x = (x_1, x_2)$.

   (a) Find all solutions of the equation $xP = x$.

   (b) Choose the solution(s) for which $x_1 + x_2 = 1$.

15. Let P be the matrix $P = \begin{pmatrix} \frac{1}{2} & \frac{1}{2} & 0 \\ \frac{1}{3} & \frac{1}{3} & \frac{1}{3} \\ \frac{1}{4} & \frac{1}{2} & \frac{1}{4} \end{pmatrix}$, and let $x = (x_1, x_2, x_3)$.

   (a) Find all solutions of the equation $xP = x$.
   (b) Choose the solution(s) for which $x_1 + x_2 + x_3 = 1$.

16. Let P be as in Exercise 15, and let $x = \begin{pmatrix} x_1 \\ x_2 \\ x_3 \end{pmatrix}$. Redo the exercise, using the equation $Px = x$.

17. Let x be as in Exercise 15, and let A be the matrix

$$\begin{pmatrix} 2 & 0 & 3 \\ 0 & 1 & 5 \\ -3 & 0 & 1 \end{pmatrix}.$$

   (a) Find all solutions of the equation $xA = x$.
   (b) Choose the solution(s) for which $x_1 + x_2 + x_3 = 1$.
       [*Ans.* $x_1 = \frac{15}{11}, x_2 = -\frac{9}{11}, x_3 = \frac{5}{11}.$]

18. (a) Show that the simultaneous linear equations

$$3x_1 - 5x_2 + 3x_3 = 9$$
$$4x_1 + 4x_2 - 7x_3 = 0$$

   can be interpreted as a single-matrix-times–column-vector equation of the form

$$\begin{pmatrix} 3 & -5 & 3 \\ 4 & 4 & -7 \end{pmatrix} \begin{pmatrix} x_1 \\ x_2 \\ x_3 \end{pmatrix} = \begin{pmatrix} 9 \\ 0 \end{pmatrix}.$$

   (b) Show that any set of simultaneous linear equations may be interpreted as a matrix equation of the form $Ax = b$, where A is an $m \times n$ matrix, x is an n-component column vector, and b is an m-component column vector.

19. (a) Show that the equations of Exercise 18(a) can be interpreted as a row-vector-times–matrix equation of the form

$$(x_1, x_2, x_3) \begin{pmatrix} 3 & 4 \\ -5 & 4 \\ 3 & -7 \end{pmatrix} = 90.$$

   (b) Show that any set of simultaneous linear equations may be interpreted as a matrix equation of the form $xA = b$, where A is an $m \times n$ matrix, x is an m-component row vector, and b is an n-component row vector.

20. (a) Show that the simultaneous linear equations of Exercise 18(a) can be interpreted as asking for all possible ways of expressing the column vector $\begin{pmatrix} 9 \\ 0 \end{pmatrix}$ in terms of the column vectors $\begin{pmatrix} 3 \\ 4 \end{pmatrix}, \begin{pmatrix} -5 \\ 4 \end{pmatrix}$ and $\begin{pmatrix} 3 \\ -7 \end{pmatrix}.$

(b) Show that any set of linear equations may be interpreted as asking for all possible ways of expressing a column vector in terms of given column vectors.

21. Redo Exercise 20, using Exercise 19(a) and *row* vectors.

22. Consider the following set of simultaneous equations:

$$x_1 - x_2 = a$$
$$x_3 + x_4 = b$$
$$x_2 - x_4 = c$$
$$x_1 + x_3 = d.$$

(a) For what conditions on a, b, c, and d will these equations have a solution?

(b) Give a set of balues for a, b, c, and d for which the equations do not have a solution.

(c) Show that if there is one solution to these equations, then there are infinitely many solutions.

23. Which of the following statements are true and which false concerning the solution of m simultaneous linear equations in n unknowns written in the form $Ax = b$?

(a) If there are infinitely many solutions, then $n > m$.

(b) If the solution is unique, then $n = m$.

(c) If $m = n$, then the solution is unique.

(d) If $n > m$, then there cannot be a unique solution.

(e) If $b = 0$, then there is always at least one solution.

(f) If $b = 0$, then there are always infinitely many solutions.

(g) If $b = 0$, and $x^{(1)}$ and $x^{(2)}$ are solutions, then $x^{(1)} + x^{(2)}$ is also a solution.   [*Ans.* (d), (e), and (g) are true.]

6 THE INVERSE OF A SQUARE MATRIX

If A is a square matrix and B is another square matrix of the same size having the property that $BA = I$ (where I is the identity matrix), then we say that B is the *inverse* of A. When it exists, we shall denote the inverse of A by the symbol A^{-1}. To give a numerical example, let A and A^{-1} be the following:

(1)
$$A = \begin{pmatrix} 4 & 0 & 5 \\ 0 & 1 & -6 \\ 3 & 0 & 4 \end{pmatrix}$$

(2)
$$A^{-1} = \begin{pmatrix} 4 & 0 & -5 \\ -18 & 1 & 24 \\ -3 & 0 & 4 \end{pmatrix}.$$

Then we have

$$A^{-1}A = \begin{pmatrix} 4 & 0 & -5 \\ -18 & 1 & 24 \\ -3 & 0 & 4 \end{pmatrix} \cdot \begin{pmatrix} 4 & 0 & 5 \\ 0 & 1 & -6 \\ 3 & 0 & 4 \end{pmatrix} = \begin{pmatrix} 1 & 0 & 0 \\ 0 & 1 & 0 \\ 0 & 0 & 1 \end{pmatrix} = I.$$

If we multiply these matrices in the other order, we also get the identity matrix; thus

$$AA^{-1} = \begin{pmatrix} 4 & 0 & 5 \\ 0 & 1 & -6 \\ 3 & 0 & 4 \end{pmatrix} \cdot \begin{pmatrix} 4 & 0 & -5 \\ -18 & 1 & 24 \\ -3 & 0 & 4 \end{pmatrix} = \begin{pmatrix} 1 & 0 & 0 \\ 0 & 1 & 0 \\ 0 & 0 & 1 \end{pmatrix} = I.$$

In general it can be shown that if A is a square matrix with inverse A^{-1}, then the inverse satisfies the equation

$$A^{-1}A = AA^{-1} = I.$$

Next we show that a square matrix can have only one inverse. For suppose that in addition to A^{-1} we also have a B such that

$$BA = I.$$

Then we see that

$$B = BI = B(AA^{-1}) = (BA)A^{-1} = IA^{-1} = A^{-1}.$$

Finding the inverse of a matrix is analogous to finding the reciprocal of an ordinary number, but the analogy is not complete. Every nonzero number has a reciprocal, but there are matrices, not the zero matrix, which have no inverse. For example, if

$$A = \begin{pmatrix} 1 & -1 \\ -1 & 1 \end{pmatrix} \quad \text{and} \quad B = \begin{pmatrix} 1 & 1 \\ 1 & 1 \end{pmatrix},$$

then

$$AB = \begin{pmatrix} 1 & -1 \\ -1 & 1 \end{pmatrix} \cdot \begin{pmatrix} 1 & 1 \\ 1 & 1 \end{pmatrix} = \begin{pmatrix} 0 & 0 \\ 0 & 0 \end{pmatrix} = 0.$$

From this we shall show that neither A nor B can have an inverse. To show that A does not have an inverse, let us assume that A had an inverse A^{-1}. Then

$$B = (A^{-1}A)B = A^{-1}(AB) = A^{-1}0 = 0,$$

contradicting the fact that $B \neq 0$. The proof that B cannot have an inverse is similar.

Let us now try to calculate the inverse of the matrix A in (1). Specifically, let's try to calculate the first column of A^{-1}. Let

$$x = \begin{pmatrix} x_1 \\ x_2 \\ x_3 \end{pmatrix}$$

be the desired entries of the first column. Then from the equation $AA^{-1} = I$ we see that we must solve

$$\begin{pmatrix} 4 & 0 & 5 \\ 0 & 1 & -6 \\ 3 & 0 & 4 \end{pmatrix} \begin{pmatrix} x_1 \\ x_2 \\ x_3 \end{pmatrix} = \begin{pmatrix} 1 \\ 0 \\ 0 \end{pmatrix}.$$

Similarly, to find the second and third columns of A^{-1} we want to solve the additional sets of equations,

$$\begin{pmatrix} 4 & 0 & 5 \\ 0 & 1 & -6 \\ 3 & 0 & 4 \end{pmatrix} \begin{pmatrix} x_1 \\ x_2 \\ x_3 \end{pmatrix} = \begin{pmatrix} 0 \\ 1 \\ 0 \end{pmatrix} \quad \text{and} \quad = \begin{pmatrix} 0 \\ 0 \\ 1 \end{pmatrix},$$

respectively. We thus have three sets of simultaneous equations that differ only in their right-hand sides. This is exactly the situation described in Example 7 of the previous section.

To solve them, we start with the tableau

(3)
$$\begin{pmatrix} 4 & 0 & 5 & | & 1 & 0 & 0 \\ 0 & 1 & -6 & | & 0 & 1 & 0 \\ 3 & 0 & 4 & | & 0 & 0 & 1 \end{pmatrix}$$

and carry out the calculations as described in the last section. This gives rise to the following series of tableaus. In (3) divide the first row by 4, copy the second row, and subtract 3 times the new first row from the old third row, which yields the tableau

(4)
$$\begin{pmatrix} 1 & 0 & \frac{5}{4} & | & \frac{1}{4} & 0 & 0 \\ 0 & 1 & -6 & | & 0 & 1 & 0 \\ 0 & 0 & \frac{1}{4} & | & -\frac{3}{4} & 0 & 1 \end{pmatrix}.$$

Next we multiply the third row of (4) by 4, multiply the new third row by 6 and add to the old second row, and multiply the new third row by $\frac{5}{4}$ and subtract from the old first row. We have the final tableau:

(5)
$$\begin{pmatrix} 1 & 0 & 0 & | & 4 & 0 & -5 \\ 0 & 1 & 0 & | & -18 & 1 & 24 \\ 0 & 0 & 1 & | & -3 & 0 & 4 \end{pmatrix}.$$

We see that the inverse A^{-1} which is given in (2) appears to the right of the vertical line in the tableau of (5).

The procedure just illustrated will find the inverse of any square matrix A, *providing A has an inverse.* We summarize it as follows:

Rule for Inverting a Matrix   Let A be a matrix that has an inverse. To find the inverse of A start with the tableau

$$(A|I)$$

and change it by row transformations (as described in Section 5) into the tableau

$$(I|B).$$

The resulting matrix B is the inverse A^{-1} of A.

Even if A has no inverse, the procedure just outlined can be started. At some point in the procedure a tableau will be found that is not of the desired final form and from which it is impossible to change by row transformations of the kind described.

EXAMPLE 1   Show that the matrix

$$A = \begin{pmatrix} 4 & 0 & 8 \\ 0 & 1 & -6 \\ 2 & 0 & 4 \end{pmatrix}$$

has no inverse.

We set up the initial tableau as follows:

(6)
$$\begin{pmatrix} 4 & 0 & 8 & 1 & 0 & 0 \\ 0 & 1 & -6 & 0 & 1 & 0 \\ 2 & 0 & 4 & 0 & 0 & 1 \end{pmatrix}.$$

Carrying out one set of row transformations, we obtain the second tableau as follows:

(7)
$$\begin{pmatrix} 1 & 0 & 2 & \frac{1}{4} & 0 & 0 \\ 0 & 1 & -6 & 0 & 1 & 0 \\ 0 & 0 & 0 & -\frac{1}{2} & 0 & 1 \end{pmatrix}.$$

It is clear that we cannot proceed further since there is a row of zeros to the left of the equals sign on the third set of equations. Hence we conclude that A has no inverse.

Because of the form of the final tableau in (7), we see that it is impossible to solve the equations

$$\begin{pmatrix} 4 & 0 & 8 \\ 0 & 1 & -6 \\ 2 & 0 & 4 \end{pmatrix} \begin{pmatrix} x_1 \\ x_2 \\ x_3 \end{pmatrix} = \begin{pmatrix} 0 \\ 0 \\ 1 \end{pmatrix},$$

since these equations are inconsistent as is shown by the tests developed in Section 5. In other words, it is not possible to solve for the third column of the inverse matrix.

It is clear that an $n \times n$ matrix A has an inverse if and only if the following sets of simultaneous equations—

$$Ax = \begin{pmatrix} 1 \\ 0 \\ \vdots \\ 0 \end{pmatrix}, \qquad Ax = \begin{pmatrix} 0 \\ 1 \\ \vdots \\ 0 \end{pmatrix}, \qquad \dots, \qquad Ax = \begin{pmatrix} 0 \\ 0 \\ \vdots \\ 1 \end{pmatrix}$$

—can all be uniquely solved. And these sets of simultaneous equations, since they all share the same left-hand sides, can be solved uniquely if and only if the transformation of the rule for inverting a matrix can be carried out. Hence we have proved the following theorem.

Theorem A square matrix A has an inverse if and only if the tableau

$$(A \mid I)$$

can be transformed by row transformations into the tableau

$$(I \mid A^{-1}).$$

EXAMPLE 2 Let us find the inverse of the matrix

$$A = \begin{pmatrix} 1 & 4 & 3 \\ 2 & 5 & 4 \\ 1 & -3 & -2 \end{pmatrix}.$$

The initial tableau is

$$\left(\begin{array}{ccc|ccc} 1 & 4 & 3 & 1 & 0 & 0 \\ 2 & 5 & 4 & 0 & 1 & 0 \\ 1 & -3 & -2 & 0 & 0 & 1 \end{array} \right).$$

Transforming it by row transformations, we obtain the following series of tableaus:

$$\left(\begin{array}{ccc|ccc} 1 & 4 & 3 & 1 & 0 & 0 \\ 0 & -3 & -2 & -2 & 1 & 0 \\ 0 & -7 & -5 & -1 & 0 & 1 \end{array} \right)$$

$$\left(\begin{array}{ccc|ccc} 1 & 0 & \frac{1}{3} & -\frac{5}{3} & \frac{4}{3} & 0 \\ 0 & 1 & \frac{2}{3} & \frac{2}{3} & -\frac{1}{3} & 0 \\ 0 & 0 & -\frac{1}{3} & \frac{11}{3} & -\frac{7}{3} & 1 \end{array} \right)$$

$$\left(\begin{array}{ccc|ccc} 1 & 0 & 0 & 2 & -1 & 1 \\ 0 & 1 & 0 & 8 & -5 & 2 \\ 0 & 0 & 1 & -11 & 7 & -3 \end{array} \right).$$

The inverse of A is then

$$A^{-1} = \begin{pmatrix} 2 & -1 & 1 \\ 8 & -5 & 2 \\ -11 & 7 & -3 \end{pmatrix}.$$

The reader should check that $A^{-1}A = AA^{-1} = I$.

EXAMPLE 3 A cookie recipe requires 4 cups of sugar and 2 cups of flour while a cake recipe needs 3 cups of sugar and 4 cups of flour. If we have 40 cups of sugar and 30 cups of flour on hand, how many recipes of each can we make? In order to answer this question let x be the number of cookie recipes and y the number of cake recipes to be made. Then the sugar and flour requirements give rise to the following two equations:

$$4x + 3y = 40 \quad \text{(Sugar equation)}$$
$$2x + 4y = 30 \quad \text{(Flour equation)}.$$

Let us rewrite these equations in matrix form as

$$\begin{pmatrix} 4 & 3 \\ 2 & 4 \end{pmatrix}\begin{pmatrix} x \\ y \end{pmatrix} = \begin{pmatrix} 40 \\ 30 \end{pmatrix}.$$

If we can invert the matrix we can solve the problem as

$$\begin{pmatrix} x \\ y \end{pmatrix} = \begin{pmatrix} 4 & 3 \\ 2 & 4 \end{pmatrix}^{-1}\begin{pmatrix} 40 \\ 30 \end{pmatrix}.$$

The initial tableau of the matrix inversion problem is

$$\left(\begin{array}{cc|cc} 4 & 3 & 1 & 0 \\ 2 & 4 & 0 & 1 \end{array}\right).$$

Pivoting on the 4 in the upper left-hand corner gives

$$\left(\begin{array}{cc|cc} 1 & \frac{3}{4} & \frac{1}{4} & 0 \\ 0 & \frac{5}{2} & -\frac{1}{2} & 1 \end{array}\right).$$

Finally, pivoting on the $\frac{5}{2}$ term we obtain

$$\left(\begin{array}{cc|cc} 1 & 0 & \frac{2}{5} & -\frac{3}{10} \\ 0 & 1 & -\frac{1}{5} & \frac{2}{5} \end{array}\right),$$

and so the inverse of the original matrix appears on the right. The solution to our problem is, then,

$$\begin{pmatrix} x \\ y \end{pmatrix} = \begin{pmatrix} \frac{2}{5} & -\frac{3}{10} \\ -\frac{1}{5} & \frac{2}{5} \end{pmatrix}\begin{pmatrix} 40 \\ 30 \end{pmatrix} = \begin{pmatrix} 7 \\ 4 \end{pmatrix}.$$

In other words, we can make 7 batches of cookies and 4 cakes from the materials we have.

EXERCISES

1. Compute the inverse of each of the following matrices:

$$A = \begin{pmatrix} 3 & -1 \\ -1 & 2 \end{pmatrix}, \qquad B = \begin{pmatrix} -5 & 1 & 10 \\ 9 & -2 & -17 \\ -4 & 1 & 8 \end{pmatrix},$$

$$C = \begin{pmatrix} 3 & 1 & 0 \\ 2 & 2 & 2 \\ 11 & 3 & 1 \end{pmatrix}, \qquad D = \begin{pmatrix} 1 & -7 & 3 & 2 \\ 0 & -1 & 7 & 3 \\ 0 & 0 & -1 & 2 \\ 0 & 0 & 0 & 1 \end{pmatrix}.$$

$$\left[Partial\ ans.\ A^{-1} = \begin{pmatrix} .4 & .2 \\ .2 & .6 \end{pmatrix}, \qquad B^{-1} = \begin{pmatrix} 1 & 2 & 3 \\ -4 & 0 & 5 \\ 1 & 1 & 1 \end{pmatrix}. \right]$$

2. Let B and C be the matrices of Exercise 1; let $x = \begin{pmatrix} x_1 \\ x_2 \\ x_3 \end{pmatrix}$ and

$y = (y_1, y_2, y_3)$; let a, b, c, d, and e be the following vectors:

$$a = \begin{pmatrix} -1 \\ 0 \\ 2 \end{pmatrix}, \qquad b = \begin{pmatrix} 4 \\ -1 \\ 3 \end{pmatrix}, \qquad c = (1, 5, 3),$$

$$d = (1, 1, 1), \quad \text{and} \quad e = \begin{pmatrix} 1 \\ 1 \\ 1 \end{pmatrix}.$$

Uses the inverses computed in Exercise 1 to solve the following equations:
  (a) $Bx = a$.
  (b) $yB = d$.
  (c) $Cx = e$.
  (d) $Bx = b$.
  (e) $yB = c$.
  (f) $yC = c$.

3. Show that each of the following matrices fails to have an inverse.

$$A = \begin{pmatrix} 4 & 2 \\ 6 & 3 \end{pmatrix}, \qquad B = \begin{pmatrix} 3 & 1 & 0 \\ 8 & 2 & 1 \\ 11 & 3 & 1 \end{pmatrix},$$

$$C = \begin{pmatrix} -3 & -1 & 1 \\ 4 & 3 & -2 \\ -7 & 1 & 1 \end{pmatrix}, \qquad D = \begin{pmatrix} 2 & 1 & 1 & 1 \\ 1 & -3 & 5 & -2 \\ 0 & 3 & -4 & 2 \\ 2 & 0 & 1 & -1 \end{pmatrix}.$$

4. For each of the matrices in Exercise 3 find a nonzero vector whose product with the given matrix is 0.

5. Solve the following four sets of simultaneous equations by first writing them in the form $Ax = B$, where B is a 3×4 matrix, and finding the inverse of A.

$$
\begin{array}{cccccc}
 & & \text{(a)} & \text{(b)} & \text{(c)} & \text{(d)} \\
4x_1 & + 5x_3 = & 1 & 1 & 0 & 8 \\
x_2 & - 6x_3 = & 2 & 0 & 0 & 1 \\
3x_1 & + 4x_3 = & 3 & 0 & 1 & 0.
\end{array}
$$

[*Ans.* (a) $x_1 = -11$, $x_2 = 56$, $x_3 = 9$.]

6. Let A be a square matrix. Show that if A has no inverse, then neither do any of its positive powers A^k. Show that if A has an inverse, then the inverse of A^2 is $(A^{-1})^2$. What is the inverse of A^3? Of A^n?

7. The formula $(A^{-1})^{-1} = A$ states that if A has an inverse A^{-1}, then A^{-1} itself has an inverse and this inverse is A. Prove both parts of this statement.

8. Expand the formula $(AB)^{-1} = B^{-1}A^{-1}$ into a two-part statement analogous to the one in Exercise 7. Then prove both parts of your statement.

9. Give a criterion for deciding whether the 2×2 matrix $\begin{pmatrix} a & b \\ c & d \end{pmatrix}$ has an inverse.   [*Ans. ad $\neq$ bc.*]

10. Give a formula for $\begin{pmatrix} a & b \\ c & d \end{pmatrix}^{-1}$, when it exists.

11. If $\begin{pmatrix} a & b \\ c & d \end{pmatrix}$ has an inverse and has integer components, what condition must it fulfill in order that $\begin{pmatrix} a & b \\ c & d \end{pmatrix}^{-1}$ have integer components?

12. Let A be the matrix $\begin{pmatrix} 5 & 3 \\ 3 & 2 \end{pmatrix}$.

    (a) Use Exercise 10 to find A^{-1}.

    (b) Use the result of (a) to solve the equations $Ax = b$ and $A^2x = c$, where $x = \begin{pmatrix} x_1 \\ x_2 \end{pmatrix}$, $b = \begin{pmatrix} -1 \\ 0 \end{pmatrix}$, and $c = \begin{pmatrix} 1 \\ 1 \end{pmatrix}$.

13. **(a)** Show that $(AB)^{-1} \neq A^{-1}B^{-1}$ for the matrices $A = \begin{pmatrix} 2 & -5 \\ -1 & 3 \end{pmatrix}$ and $B = \begin{pmatrix} -1 & 0 \\ 2 & 1 \end{pmatrix}$.

    (b) Find $(AB)^{-1}$ in two ways. [*Hint:* Use Exercises 10 and 8.]

14. Solve the following problems by first inverting the matrix involved.

    (a) An automobile factory produces two models. The first requires 1 man-hour to paint and $\frac{1}{2}$ man-hour to polish; the second requires 1 man-hour for each process. During each hour that the assembly line is operating, there are 100 man-hours available for painting and 80 man-hours for polishing. How many of each model can be produced each hour if all the man-hours available are to be utilized?

    (b) Suppose each car of the first type requires 10 widgets and 14 shims, and each car of the second type requires 7 widgets and 10 shims. The factory can obtain 800 widgets and 1130 shims each hour. How many cars of each model can it produce while utilizing all the parts available? [*Ans.* 45, 50.]

15. Solve the following problem by first inverting the matrix. (Assume $ad \neq bc$.) If a grinding machine is supplied x pounds of meat and y pounds of scraps (meat scraps and fat) per day, then it will produce $ax + by$ pounds of ground meat and $cx + dy$ pounds of hamburger per day. In other words, its production vector is

$$\begin{pmatrix} a & b \\ c & d \end{pmatrix} \begin{pmatrix} x \\ y \end{pmatrix}.$$

What inputs are necessary in order to get 25 pounds of ground meat and 70 pounds of hamburger? In order to get 20 pounds of ground meat and 100 pounds of hamburger?

16. A square matrix is *lower-triangular* if it has zeros on and above its main diagonal. For instance, $Q = \begin{pmatrix} 0 & 0 & 0 \\ -1 & 0 & 0 \\ 4 & 3 & 0 \end{pmatrix}$ is lower-triangular.

(a) Compute Q^2.

(b) Compute Q^3.

(c) Show that $Q^k = 0$ for $k \geq 3$.

17. Let Q be as in Exercise 16.

(a) Show that $(I - Q)(I + Q + Q^2) = I - Q^3 = I$.

(b) Show that, because of (a), $I + Q + Q^2 = (I - Q)^{-1}$.

(c) Use (b) to compute $(I - Q)^{-1}$.

(d) Let $w = (w_1, w_2, w_3)$, $d = (-1, 5, 3)$. Use (c) to solve the equation $w = wQ + d$.

18. (a) Show that the sum of any two lower-triangular matrices is lower-triangular.

(b) Show that the product of any two lower-triangular matrices is lower-triangular.

19. Let Q be an $n \times n$ lower-triangular matrix.

(a) Show that $Q^k = 0$ for $k \geq n$.

(b) Show that $(I - Q)(I + Q + \cdots + Q^{n-1}) = I - Q^n = I$.

(c) Show that $(I - Q)^{-1} = I + Q + \cdots + Q^{n-1}$.

(d) Show that all entries above the main diagonal of $(I - Q)^{-1}$ are 0.

(e) Show that if Q has nonnegative *integer* entries, then so does $(I - Q)^{-1}$.

20. Find $(I - Q)^{-1}$ for each of the following:

(a) $\begin{pmatrix} 0 & 0 \\ 0 & 0 \end{pmatrix}$.

(b) $\begin{pmatrix} 0 & 0 & 0 \\ 3 & 0 & 0 \\ -1 & 2 & 0 \end{pmatrix}$.

(c) $\begin{pmatrix} 0 & 0 & 0 & 0 \\ 5 & 0 & 0 & 0 \\ 4 & -1 & 0 & 0 \\ -2 & 1 & 3 & 0 \end{pmatrix}$.

(d) $\begin{pmatrix} 0 & 0 & 0 & 0 & 0 \\ 3 & 0 & 0 & 0 & 0 \\ 0 & -1 & 0 & 0 & 0 \\ 1 & 5 & 4 & 0 & 0 \\ -2 & 1 & 2 & -3 & 0 \end{pmatrix}$.

7 APPLICATIONS OF MATRIX THEORY TO MARKOV CHAINS

In this section we shall show applications of matrix theory to Markov chains. For simplicity we shall confine our discussion to three-state Markov chains, but a similar procedure will work for any other Markov chain.

In Section 12 of Chapter 3, we noted that to each Markov chain there was a matrix of transition probabilities. For example, if there are three states, a_1, a_2, and a_3, then

$$P = \begin{array}{c} \\ a_1 \\ a_2 \\ a_3 \end{array} \begin{array}{ccc} a_1 & a_2 & a_3 \\ \left(\begin{array}{ccc} p_{11} & p_{12} & p_{13} \\ p_{21} & p_{22} & p_{23} \\ p_{31} & p_{32} & p_{33} \end{array} \right) \end{array}$$

Is the transition matrix for the chain. Recall that the *row sums* of P are all equal to 1. Such a matrix is called a transition matrix.

Definition A *transition matrix* is a square matrix with nonnegative entries such that the sum of the entries in each row is 1.

In order to obtain a Markov chain we must specify how the process starts. Suppose that the initial state is chosen by a chance device that selects state a_j with probability $p_j^{(0)}$. We can represent these initial probabilities by means of the vector $p^{(0)} = (p_1^{(0)}, p_2^{(0)}, p_3^{(0)})$. As in Exercise 17 of Section 4, we can construct a tree measure for as many steps of the process as we wish to consider. Let $p_j^{(n)}$ be the probability that the process will be in state a_j after n steps. Let the vector of these probabilities be $p^{(n)} = (p_1^{(n)}, p_2^{(n)}, p_3^{(n)})$.

Definition A row vector p is called a *probability vector* if it has nonnegative components whose sum is 1.

Obviously the vectors $p^{(0)}$ and $p^{(n)}$ are probability vectors. Also each row of a transition matrix is a probability vector.

By means of the tree measure it can be shown that these probabilities satisfy the following equations:

$$\begin{aligned} p_1^{(n)} &= p_1^{(n-1)}p_{11} + p_2^{(n-1)}p_{21} + p_3^{(n-1)}p_{31}, \\ p_2^{(n)} &= p_1^{(n-1)}p_{12} + p_2^{(n-1)}p_{22} + p_3^{(n-1)}p_{32}, \\ p_3^{(n)} &= p_1^{(n-1)}p_{13} + p_2^{(n-1)}p_{23} + p_3^{(n-1)}p_{33}. \end{aligned}$$

It is not hard to give intuitive meanings to these equations. The first one, for example, expresses the fact that the probability of being in state a_1 after n steps is the sum of the probabilities of being at each of the three possible states after $n - 1$ steps and then moving to state a_1 on the nth step. The interpretation of the other equations is similar.

If we recall the definition of the product of a vector times a matrix, we can write the equations above as

$$p^{(n)} = p^{(n-1)}P.$$

If we substitute values of n, we get the equations: $p^{(1)} = p^{(0)}P$; $p^{(2)} = p^{(1)}P = p^{(0)}P^2$; $p^{(3)} = p^{(2)}P = p^{(0)}P^3$; and so on. In general, it is evident that

$$p^{(n)} = p^{(0)}P^n.$$

Thus we see that, if we multiply the vector $p^{(0)}$ of initial probabilities by the nth power of the transition matrix P, we obtain the vector $p^{(n)}$, whose components give the probabilities of being in each of the states after n steps.

In particular, let us choose $p^{(0)} = (1, 0, 0)$, which is equivalent to letting the process start in state a_1. From the equation above we see that then $p^{(n)}$ is the first row of the matrix P^n. Thus the elements of the first row of the matrix P^n give us the probabilities that after n steps the process will be in a given one of the states, under the assumption that it started in state a_1. In the same way, if we choose $p^{(0)} = (0, 1, 0)$, we see that the second row of P^n gives the probabilities that the process will be in one of the various states after n steps, given that it started in state a_2. Similarly the third row gives these probabilities, assuming that the process started in state a_3.

In Section 12 of Chapter 3, we considered special Markov chains that started in given fixed states. There we arrived at a matrix $P^{(n)}$ whose ith row gave the probabilities of the process ending in the various states, given that it started at state a_i. By comparing the work that we did there with what we have just done, we see that the matrix $P^{(n)}$ is merely the nth power of P, that is, $P^{(n)} = P^n$. (Compare Exercise 17 of Section 4.) Matrix multiplication thus gives a convenient way of computing the desired probabilities.

Definition   The probability vector w is a *fixed point* of the matrix P, if $w = wP$.

EXAMPLE 1   Consider the transition matrix

$$P = \begin{pmatrix} \frac{2}{3} & \frac{1}{3} \\ \frac{1}{2} & \frac{1}{2} \end{pmatrix} = \begin{pmatrix} .667 & .333 \\ .500 & .500 \end{pmatrix}.$$

If $w = (.6, .4)$, then we see that

$$wP = (.6, .4)\begin{pmatrix} \frac{2}{3} & \frac{1}{3} \\ \frac{1}{2} & \frac{1}{2} \end{pmatrix} = (.6, .4) = w,$$

so that w is the fixed point of the matrix P.

If we had happened to choose the vector w as our initial probability vector $p^{(0)}$, we would have had $p^{(n)} = p^{(0)}P^n = wP^n = w = p^{(0)}$. In this case the probability of being at any particular state is the same at all steps of the process. Such a process is in *equilibrium*.

As seen above, in the study of Markov chains we are interested in the powers of the matrix P. To see what happens to these powers, let us further consider the example.

EXAMPLE 1
(continued)   Suppose that we compute powers of the matrix P in the example above. We have

$$P^2 = \begin{pmatrix} .611 & .389 \\ .583 & .417 \end{pmatrix}, \qquad P^3 = \begin{pmatrix} .602 & .398 \\ .597 & .403 \end{pmatrix}, \qquad \text{and so on.}$$

It looks as if the matrix P^n is approaching the matrix

$$W = \begin{pmatrix} .6 & .4 \\ .6 & .4 \end{pmatrix};$$

and, in fact, it can be shown that this is the case. (When we say that P^n approaches W we mean that each entry in the matrix P^n gets close to the corresponding entry in W.) Note that each row of W is the fixed point w of the matrix P.

Definition A transition matrix is said to be *regular* if some power of the matrix has only positive components.

Thus the matrix in the example is regular, since every entry in it is positive, so that the first power of the matrix has all positive entries. Other examples occur in the exercises.

Theorem If P is a regular transition matrix, then

   i. the powers P^n approach a matrix W;
  ii. each row of W is the same probability vector w;
 iii. the components of w are positive.

We omit the proof of this theorem;* however, we can prove the next theorem.

Theorem If P is a regular transition matrix, and W and w are given by the previous theorem, then

  a. if p is any probability vector, pP^n approaches w;
  b. the vector w is the unique fixed-point probability vector of P.

Proof First let us consider the vector pW. The first column of W has a w_1 in each row. Hence in the first component of pW each component of p is multiplied by w_1, and therefore we have w_1 times the sum of the components of p, which is w_1. Doing the same for the other components, we note that pW is simply w. But pP^n approaches pW; hence it approaches w. Thus if any probability vector is multiplied repeatedly by P, it approaches the fixed point w. This proves part (a).

Since the powers of P approach W, $P^{n+1} = P^n P$ approaches W, but it also approaches WP; hence $WP = W$. Any one row of this matrix equation states that $wP = w$; hence w is a fixed point (and by the previous theorem a probability vector). We must still show that it is unique. Let u be any probability-vector fixed point of P. By part a of the theorem we know that uP^n approaches w. But since u is a fixed point, $uP^n = u$. Hence u remains fixed but "approaches" w. This is possible only if $u = w$. Hence w is the only probability-vector fixed point. This completes the proof of part b.

---

*For an elementary proof see John G. Kemeny and J. Laurie Snell, *Finite Markov Chains*, Princeton, N.J., Van Nostrand, 1960.

The following is an important consequence of the above theorem. If we take as p the vector $p^{(0)}$ of initial probabilities, then the vector $pP^n = p^{(n)}$ gives the probabilities after n steps, and this vector approaches w. Therefore no matter what the initial probabilities are, if P is regular, then after a large number of steps the probability that the process is in state a_j will be very nearly w_j.

We noted for an independent trials process that if p is the probability of a given outcome a, then this may be given an alternate interpretation by means of the law of large numbers: in a long series of experiments the fraction of outcomes in which a occurs is approximately p, and the approximation gets better and better as the number of experiments increases. For a regular Markov chain the components of the vector w play the analogous role. That is, the fraction of times that the chain is in state a_i approaches w_i, no matter how one starts.

EXAMPLE 1 (continued) Let us take $p^{(0)} = (.1, .9)$ and see how $p^{(n)}$ changes. Using P as in the example above, we have that $p^{(1)} = (.5167, .4833)$, $p^{(2)} = (.5861, .4139)$, and $p^{(3)} = (.5977, .4023)$. Recalling that $w = (.6, .4)$, we see that these vectors do approach w.

EXAMPLE 2 As an example let us derive the formulas for the fixed point of a 2×2 transition matrix with positive components. Such a matrix is of the form

$$P = \begin{pmatrix} 1 - a & a \\ b & 1 - b \end{pmatrix},$$

where $0 < a < 1$ and $0 < b < 1$. Since P is regular, it has a unique probability-vector fixed point $w = (w_1, w_2)$. Its components must satisfy the equations

$$w_1(1 - a) + w_2 b = w_1,$$
$$w_1 a + w_2(1 - b) = w_2.$$

Each of these equations reduces to the single equation $w_1 a = w_2 b$. This single equation has an infinite number of solutions. However, since w is a probability vector, we must also have $w_1 + w_2 = 1$, and the new equation gives the point $[b/(a + b), a/(a + b)]$ as the unique fixed-point probability vector of P.

EXAMPLE 3 Suppose that the President of the United States tells person A his intention either to run or not to run in the next election. Then A relays the news to B, who in turn relays the message to C, and so on, always to some new person. Assume that there is a probability $p > 0$ that any one person, when he gets the message, will reverse it before passing it on to the next person. What is the probability that the nth man to hear the message will be told that the President will run? We can consider this as a two-state Markov chain, with states indicated by "yes" and "no." The process is in state "yes" at time n if the nth person to receive the message was told that the President would run. It is in state "no" if he was told that the President would not run. The matrix P of transition probabilities is then

$$
\begin{array}{c}
 \quad\quad\quad \text{yes} \quad\quad \text{no} \\
\begin{array}{c} \text{yes} \\ \text{no} \end{array}
\begin{pmatrix} 1 - p & p \\ p & 1 - p \end{pmatrix}.
\end{array}
$$

Then the matrix P^n gives the probabilities that the nth man is given a certain answer, assuming that the President said "yes" (first row) or assuming that the President said "no" (second row). We know that these rows approach w. From the formulas of the last example, we find that $w = (\frac{1}{2}, \frac{1}{2})$. Hence the probabilities for the nth man's being told "yes" or "no" approach $\frac{1}{2}$ independently of the initial decision of the President. For a large number of people, we can expect that approximately one-half will be told that the President will run and the other half that he will not, independently of the actual decision of the President.

Suppose now that the probability a that a person will change the news from "yes" to "no" when transmitting it to the next person is different from the probability b that he will change it from "no" to "yes." Then the matrix of transition probabilities becomes

$$
\begin{array}{c}
 \quad\quad\quad \text{yes} \quad\quad \text{no} \\
\begin{array}{c} \text{yes} \\ \text{no} \end{array}
\begin{pmatrix} 1 - a & a \\ b & 1 - b \end{pmatrix}.
\end{array}
$$

In this case $w = [b/(a + b), a/(a + b)]$. Thus there is a probability of approximately $b/(a + b)$ that the nth person will be told that the President will run. Assuming that n is large, this probability is independent of the actual decision of the president. For n large we can expect, in this case, that a proportion approximately equal to $b/(a + b)$ will have been told that the President will run, and a proportion $a/(a + b)$ will have been told that he will not run. The important thing to note is that, from the assumptions we have made, it follows that it is not the President but the people themselves who determine the probability that a person will be told "yes" or "no," and the proportion of people in the long run that are given one of these predictions.

EXAMPLE 4   For this example, we continue the study of Example 2 in Chapter 3, Section 12. The first approximation treated in that example leads to a two-state Markov chain, and the results are similar to those obtained in Example 1 above. The second approximation led to a four-state Markov chain with transition probabilities given by the matrix

$$
\begin{array}{c}
\quad\quad\quad \text{RR} \quad\quad \text{DR} \quad\quad \text{RD} \quad\quad \text{DD} \\
\begin{array}{c} \text{RR} \\ \text{DR} \\ \text{RD} \\ \text{DD} \end{array}
\begin{pmatrix}
1 - a & 0 & a & 0 \\
b & 0 & 1 - b & 0 \\
0 & 1 - c & 0 & c \\
0 & d & 0 & 1 - d
\end{pmatrix}.
\end{array}
$$

If a, b, c, and d are all different from 0 or 1, then the square of the matrix has no zeros, and hence the matrix is regular. The fixed probability vector is found in the usual way (see Exercise 18) and is

$$\left(\frac{bd}{bd + 2ad + ca}, \frac{ad}{bd + 2ad + ca}, \frac{ad}{bd + 2ad + ca}, \frac{ca}{bd + 2ad + ca}\right).$$

Note that the probability of being in state RD after a large number of steps is equal to the probability of being in state DR. This shows that in equilibrium a change from R to D must have the same probability as a change from D to R.

From the fixed vector we can find the probability of being in state R in the far future. This is found by adding the probability of being in state RR and DR, giving

$$\frac{bd + ad}{bd + 2ad + ca}.$$

Notice that, to find the probability of being in state R on the election preceding some election far in the future, we should add the probabilities of being in states RR and RD. That we get the same result corresponds to the fact that predictions far in the future are essentially independent of the particular period being predicted. In other words, the process is acting as if it were in equilibrium.

EXERCISES

1. Which of the following matrices are regular?

(a) $\begin{pmatrix} \frac{1}{2} & \frac{1}{2} \\ \frac{1}{2} & \frac{1}{2} \end{pmatrix}$.

(b) $\begin{pmatrix} 0 & 1 \\ \frac{1}{4} & \frac{3}{4} \end{pmatrix}$.   [*Ans.* Regular.]

(c) $\begin{pmatrix} 1 & 0 \\ \frac{1}{3} & \frac{2}{3} \end{pmatrix}$.

(d) $\begin{pmatrix} \frac{1}{5} & \frac{4}{5} \\ 1 & 0 \end{pmatrix}$.   [*Ans.* Regular.]

(e) $\begin{pmatrix} \frac{1}{2} & \frac{1}{2} \\ 0 & 1 \end{pmatrix}$.

(f) $\begin{pmatrix} 0 & 1 \\ 1 & 0 \end{pmatrix}$.   [*Ans.* Not regular.]

(g) $\begin{pmatrix} \frac{1}{2} & \frac{1}{2} & 0 \\ 0 & \frac{1}{2} & \frac{1}{2} \\ \frac{1}{3} & \frac{1}{3} & \frac{1}{3} \end{pmatrix}$.

(h) $\begin{pmatrix} \frac{1}{3} & 0 & \frac{2}{3} \\ 0 & 1 & 0 \\ 0 & \frac{1}{5} & \frac{4}{5} \end{pmatrix}$.   [*Ans.* Not regular.]

2. Show that the 2×2 matrix

$$P = \begin{pmatrix} 1 - a & a \\ b & 1 - b \end{pmatrix}$$

is the regular transition matrix if and only if either

    i. $0 < a \leq 1$ and $0 < b < 1$;   or
    ii. $0 < a < 1$ and $0 < b \leq 1$.

3. Let P be a transition matrix in which all the entries that are not zero have been replaced by x's. Devise a method of raising such a matrix to powers in order to check for regularity. Illustrate your method by showing that

$$P = \begin{pmatrix} 0 & 1 & 0 \\ 0 & 0 & 1 \\ \frac{1}{2} & \frac{1}{2} & 0 \end{pmatrix}$$

is regular.

4. Use the method developed in Exercise 3 to test the following matrix for regularity:

$$P = \begin{pmatrix} 0 & 0 & \frac{1}{10} & 0 & \frac{9}{10} \\ 1 & 0 & 0 & 0 & 0 \\ 0 & \frac{1}{6} & \frac{1}{2} & \frac{1}{3} & 0 \\ 0 & 0 & 0 & 0 & 1 \\ 0 & \frac{3}{7} & 0 & \frac{4}{7} & 0 \end{pmatrix}.$$

5. **(a)** Give a probability theory interpretation to the condition of regularity.
   (b) Consider a Markov chain such that it is possible to go from any state a_i to any state a_j and such that p_{kk} is not 0 for at least one state a_k. Prove that the chain is regular. [*Hint:* Consider the times that it is possible to go from a_i to a_j via a_k.]

6. Find the fixed point for the matrix in Exercise 2 for each of the cases listed there. [*Hint:* Most of the cases were covered in the text above.]

7. Find the fixed point w for each of the following regular matrices:

   (a) $\begin{pmatrix} \frac{1}{3} & \frac{2}{3} \\ \frac{5}{6} & \frac{1}{6} \end{pmatrix}$.   [*Ans.* $\frac{5}{9}, \frac{4}{9}$.]

   (b) $\begin{pmatrix} .37 & .63 \\ .63 & .37 \end{pmatrix}$.

   (c) $\begin{pmatrix} \frac{3}{8} & \frac{5}{8} \\ \frac{3}{8} & \frac{5}{8} \end{pmatrix}$.

   (d) $\begin{pmatrix} \frac{1}{2} & \frac{1}{4} & \frac{1}{4} \\ \frac{1}{3} & \frac{2}{3} & 0 \\ 0 & \frac{1}{4} & \frac{3}{4} \end{pmatrix}$.   [*Ans.* $(\frac{2}{7}, \frac{3}{7}, \frac{2}{7})$.]

(e) $\begin{pmatrix} \frac{5}{7} & \frac{2}{7} \\ \frac{1}{9} & \frac{8}{9} \end{pmatrix}$.

8. Let $p^0 = (\frac{1}{2}, \frac{1}{2})$ and compute $p^{(1)}$, $p^{(2)}$, and $p^{(3)}$ for the matrices in Exercises 7(a), (b), and (c). Do they approach the fixed points of these matrices?

9. Consider the two-state Markov chain with transition matrix

$$P = \begin{array}{c} \\ a_1 \\ a_2 \end{array} \begin{array}{c} a_1 \quad a_2 \\ \begin{pmatrix} 0 & 1 \\ 1 & 0 \end{pmatrix} \end{array}.$$

What is the probability that after n steps the process is in state a_1, if it started in state a_2? Does this probability become independent of the initial position for large n? If not, the theorem of this section must not apply. Why? Does the matrix have a unique fixed-point probability vector?

10. Compute the first five powers of the matrix

$$P = \begin{pmatrix} .7 & .3 \\ .3 & .7 \end{pmatrix}.$$

From these, guess the fixed-point vector w. Check by computing what w is.

11. Prove that, if a regular 3×3 transition matrix has the property that its column sums are 1, its fixed-point probability vector is $(\frac{1}{3}, \frac{1}{3}, \frac{1}{3})$. State a similar result for $n \times n$ transition matrices having column sums equal to 1.

12. The Land of Oz is blessed by many things, but not good weather. They never have two nice days in a row. If they have a nice day they are just as likely to have snow as rain the next day. If they have snow (or rain), they have an even chance of having the same the next day. If there is a change from snow or rain, only half of the time is this a change to a nice day. Set up a three-state Markov chain to describe this situation. Find the long-range probability for rain, for snow, and for a nice day. What fraction of the days does it rain in the Land of Oz?   [*Ans.* The probabilities are: nice, $\frac{1}{5}$; rain, $\frac{2}{5}$; snow, $\frac{2}{5}$.]

13. A professor tries not to be late for class too often. If he is late one day, he is 95 percent sure to be on time next time. If he is on time, then the next day there is a 25 percent chance of his being late. In the long run, how often is he late for class?

14. Consider the three-state Markov chain with transition matrix

$$P = \begin{pmatrix} \frac{1}{4} & \frac{1}{2} & \frac{1}{4} \\ \frac{2}{5} & \frac{3}{5} & 0 \\ 1 & 0 & 0 \end{pmatrix}.$$

(a) Show that the matrix has a unique fixed probability vector.
          [*Ans.* $(\frac{2}{5}, \frac{1}{2}, \frac{1}{10})$.]

    (b) Approximately what is the entry in the third column of the first row of P^{100}?

    (c) What is the interpretation of the entry estimated in (b)?

15. A carnival man moves a pea among three shells, A, B, and C. Whenever the pea is under A, he moves it with equal probability to A or B. When it is under B, he is sure to move it to C. When it is under C, he is sure to put it next time under C or B, but is twice as likely to put it under C as B.

Set up a Markov chain taking as states the letters of the shells under which the pea appears after a move. Give the matrix of transition probabilities. Assume that the pea is initially under shell A. Which of the following statements are logically true?

    (a) After the first move, the pea is under A or B.

    (b) After the second move, the pea is under shell B or C.

    (c) If the pea appears under B, it will eventually appear under A again if the process goes on long enough.

    (d) If the pea appears under C, it will not appear under A again.

                             [*Ans.* (a) and (d) are logically true.]

16. In Exercise 15, assume that when the pea is under C, the carnival man is sure to put it next time under C or A, but twice as likely to put it under C as A. If you arrive on the scene after he has been playing for a long time, and bet even money that next time it will turn up under a certain shell, which shell should you bet on,

    (a) Given that you have not seen the previous play?

    (b) Given that the last time the pea was under A?

Which of the above bets would be fair?

17. Let P be the matrix

$$P = \begin{pmatrix} 1 & 0 \\ \frac{1}{2} & \frac{1}{2} \end{pmatrix}.$$

Compute the unique probability-vector fixed point of P, and use your result to prove that P is not regular.

18. Show that the vector given in Example 4 is the fixed vector of the transition matrix.

19. Show that the matrix

$$P = \begin{pmatrix} 1 & 0 & 0 \\ \frac{1}{2} & 0 & \frac{1}{2} \\ 0 & 0 & 1 \end{pmatrix}$$

has more than one probability-vector fixed point. Find the matrix that P^n approaches, and show that it is not a matrix all of whose rows are the same.

20. A businessman goes to a convention in Chicago once a year. While there, he stays at one of four hotels. Two of them, hotels 1 and 2, are expensive. The other two are very expensive. Assuming that he goes to a given hotel one year, the hotel he goes to the next year is determined by the following matrix of probabilities:

$$
\begin{array}{c}
 \\
1 \\
2 \\
3 \\
4
\end{array}
\begin{array}{cccc}
1 & 2 & 3 & 4 \\
\end{array}
\left(
\begin{array}{cccc}
\frac{1}{4} & 0 & \frac{3}{4} & 0 \\
\frac{2}{5} & 0 & \frac{3}{5} & 0 \\
0 & \frac{1}{2} & 0 & \frac{1}{2} \\
0 & \frac{1}{3} & 0 & \frac{2}{3}
\end{array}
\right).
$$

    (a)   If he stays at hotel 1 one year, what is the probability that he stays in very expensive hotels for at least two of the next three conventions?

    (b)   Find the long-run probabilities for staying in each of the hotels.

21. For Exercise 20, compute the following:

    (a)   Given that in 1970 and 1973 he stayed in hotel 1, what is the probability that he stayed in a very expensive hotel during either 1971 or 1972?

    (b)   If in 1970 he stayed in hotel 1 and in 1972 he was in a very expensive hotel, what is the probability that in 1973 he stayed in an expensive hotel?   [*Ans.* $\frac{7}{18}$.]

22. A professor has three pet questions, one of which occurs on every test he gives. The students know his habits well. He never uses the same question twice in a row. If he used question 1 last time, he tosses a coin, and uses question 2 if a head comes up. If he used question 2, he tosses two coins and switches to question 3 if at least one comes up heads. If he used question 3, he tosses three coins and switches to question 1 if at least one comes up heads. In the long run, which question does he use most often and how frequently is it used?

23. In some cases it makes sense to form a new Markov chain from an old one by condensing two or more states into one.

    (a)   Show that this can be done for the Land of Oz example (Exercise 12), using as the two new states nice and bad (rain or snow). Set up the matrix of transition probabilities and compute the fixed vector.   [*Partial ans.* $(\frac{1}{5}, \frac{4}{5})$.]

    (b)   Compare the fixed vector obtained in part (a) to that obtained in Exercise 12.

    (c)   Would it make sense to condense states in the hotel example (Exercise 20), using as new states expensive (1 or 2) and very expensive (3 or 4)? Explain your answer.   [*Partial ans.* No.]

24. A certain company decides each year to add *a* new workers to its payroll, to remove *b* workers from its payroll, or to leave its workforce unchanged. There is probability $\frac{3}{4}$ that the action taken in the given year will be the same as the action taken in the previous year. The president of the company has ruled that they should never fire workers the year after they added some, and that they should never hire workers the year after they fired some. Moreover, if no workers were added or fired in the previous year, the company is twice as likely to add workers as to fire them.

(a) Set up the problem as a Markov chain with three states.

(b) Show that it is regular.

(c) Find the long-run probability of each type of action.

(d) For what values of a and b will the company tend to increase in size? To decrease? To stay the same?

[*Ans.* (d) $a > b/2$; $a < b/2$; $a = b/2$.]

8 ABSORBING MARKOV CHAINS

In this section we shall consider a kind of Markov chain quite different from regular chains.

Definition A state in a Markov chain is an *absorbing state* if it is impossible to leave it. A Markov chain is *absorbing* if (1) it has at least one absorbing state, and (2) from every state it is possible to go to an absorbing state (not necessarily in one step).

EXAMPLE 1 A particle moves on a line; each time it moves one unit to the right with probability $\frac{1}{2}$, or one unit to the left. We introduce barriers so that if it ever reaches one of these barriers it stays there. As a simple example, let the states be $0, 1, 2, 3, 4$. States 0 and 4 are absorbing states. The transition matrix is then

$$P = \begin{array}{c} \\ 0 \\ 1 \\ 2 \\ 3 \\ 4 \end{array} \begin{array}{ccccc} 0 & 1 & 2 & 3 & 4 \\ \left(\begin{array}{ccccc} 1 & 0 & 0 & 0 & 0 \\ \frac{1}{2} & 0 & \frac{1}{2} & 0 & 0 \\ 0 & \frac{1}{2} & 0 & \frac{1}{2} & 0 \\ 0 & 0 & \frac{1}{2} & 0 & \frac{1}{2} \\ 0 & 0 & 0 & 0 & 1 \end{array} \right) \end{array}.$$

The states $1, 2, 3$ are all nonabsorbing states, and from any of these it is possible to reach the absorbing states 0 and 4. Hence the chain is an absorbing chain. Such a process is usually called a *random walk*.

When a process reaches an absorbing state we shall say that it is *absorbed*.

Theorem In an absorbing Markov chain the probability that the process will be absorbed is 1.

We shall indicate only the basic idea of the proof of the theorem. From each nonabsorbing state a_j it is possible to reach an absorbing state. Let n_j be the minimum number of steps required to reach an absorbing state, starting from state a_j. Let p_j be the probability that, starting from state a_j, the process will *not* reach an absorbing state in n_j steps. Then $p_j < 1$. Let

n be the largest of the n_j and let p be the largest of the p_j. The probability of not being absorbed in n steps is less than p, in $2n$ steps is less than p^2, and so on. Since $p < 1$, these probabilities tend to zero.

For an absorbing Markov chain we consider three interesting questions: (a) What is the probability that the process will end up in a given absorbing state? (b) On the average, how long will it take for the process to be absorbed? (c) On the average, how many times will the process be in each nonabsorbing state? The answer to all these questions depends, in general, on the state from which the process starts.

Consider then an arbitrary absorbing Markov chain. Let us renumber the states so that the absorbing states come first. If there are r absorbing states and s nonabsorbing states, the transition matrix will have the following *canonical* (or standard) *form.*

(1)
$$P = \begin{array}{c} r \\ s \end{array}\left(\begin{array}{c|c} \overset{r \text{ states}}{I} & \overset{s \text{ states}}{O} \\ \hline R & Q \end{array}\right).$$

Here I is an r-by-r identity matrix, O is an r-by-s zero matrix, R is an s-by-r matrix, and Q is an s-by-s matrix. The first r states are absorbing and the last s states are nonabsorbing.

In Section 7 we saw that the entries of the matrix P^n gave the probabilities of being in the various states starting from the various states. It is easy to show that P^n is of the form

(2)
$$P^n = \begin{pmatrix} I & O \\ * & Q^n \end{pmatrix},$$

where the asterisk stands for the s-by-r matrix in the lower left-hand corner of P^n, which we do not compute here. The form of P^n shows that the entries of Q^n give the probabilities for being in each of the nonabsorbing states after n steps for each possible nonabsorbing starting state. (After zero steps the process must be in the same nonabsorbing state in which it started. Hence $Q^0 = I$.) By our first theorem, the probability of being in the nonabsorbing states after n steps approaches zero. Thus every entry of Q^n must approach zero as n approaches infinity; that is, $Q^n \to 0$.

Consider then the infinite series

$$I + Q + Q^2 + Q^3 + \ldots .$$

Suppose that Q were a nonnegative number x instead of a nonnegative matrix. To correspond to the fact that $Q^n \to O$ we take x to be less than 1. Then

$$1 + x + x^2 + \ldots = (1 - x)^{-1}.$$

It can be proved that the matrix series behaves in exactly the same way. That is,

$$I + Q + Q^2 + \ldots = (I - Q)^{-1}.$$

The matrix $(I - Q)^{-1}$ will be called the *fundamental matrix* for the given absorbing chain. It has the following important interpretation:

Let n_{ij} be the mean number of times that the chain is in state a_j if it starts in state a_i, for nonabsorbing states a_i and a_j. Let N be the matrix whose components are n_{ij}. We shall show that $N = (I - Q)^{-1}$. If we take into account the contribution of the original state (which is 1 if $i = j$ and 0 otherwise), we may write the equation

$$n_{ij} = d_{ij} + (p_{i,r+1}n_{r+1,j} + p_{i,r+2}n_{r+2,j} + \ldots + p_{i,r+s}n_{r+s,j}),$$

where d_{ij} is 1 if $i = j$ and 0 otherwise. (Note that the sum in parentheses is merely the sum of the products $p_{ik}n_{kj}$ for k running over the nonabsorbing states.) This equation may be written in matrix form:

$$N = I + QN.$$

Then $(I - Q)N = I$, and hence $N = (I - Q)^{-1}$, as was to be shown. Thus we have found a probabilistic interpretation for our fundamental matrix; its i, j entry is the mean number of times that the chain is in state a_j if it starts at a_i. The fact that $N = I + Q + Q^2 + \ldots$ also has a probabilistic interpretation. Since the i, j entry of Q^n is the probability of being in a_j on the nth step if we start at a_i, we have shown that the mean of the number of times in state a_j may be written as the sum of the probabilities of being there on particular steps. Thus we have answered question (c) as follows:

Theorem Let $N = (I - Q)^{-1}$ be the fundamental matrix for an absorbing chain. Then the entries of N give the mean number of times in each nonabsorbing state for each possible nonabsorbing starting state.

EXAMPLE 1 (continued) In Example 1 the transition matrix in canonical form is

$$
\begin{array}{c c}
 & \begin{array}{ccccc} 0 & 4 & 1 & 2 & 3 \end{array} \\
\begin{array}{c} 0 \\ 4 \\ 1 \\ 2 \\ 3 \end{array} &
\left(\begin{array}{cc|ccc}
1 & 0 & 0 & 0 & 0 \\
0 & 1 & 0 & 0 & 0 \\
\hline
\frac{1}{2} & 0 & 0 & \frac{1}{2} & 0 \\
0 & 0 & \frac{1}{2} & 0 & \frac{1}{2} \\
0 & \frac{1}{2} & 0 & \frac{1}{2} & 0
\end{array}\right).
\end{array}
$$

From this we see that the matrix Q is

$$Q = \begin{pmatrix} 0 & \frac{1}{2} & 0 \\ \frac{1}{2} & 0 & \frac{1}{2} \\ 0 & \frac{1}{2} & 0 \end{pmatrix}$$

and

$$I - Q = \begin{pmatrix} 1 & -\frac{1}{2} & 0 \\ -\frac{1}{2} & 1 & -\frac{1}{2} \\ 0 & -\frac{1}{2} & 1 \end{pmatrix}.$$

Computing $(I - Q)^{-1}$, we find

$$
N = (I - Q)^{-1} = \begin{matrix} & \begin{matrix} 1 & 2 & 3 \end{matrix} \\ \begin{matrix} 1 \\ 2 \\ 3 \end{matrix} & \begin{pmatrix} \frac{3}{2} & 1 & \frac{1}{2} \\ 1 & 2 & 1 \\ \frac{1}{2} & 1 & \frac{3}{2} \end{pmatrix} \end{matrix}.
$$

Thus, starting at state 2, the mean number of times in state 1 before absorption is 1, in state 2 it is 2, and in state 3 it is 1.

We next answer question (b). If we add all the entries in a row, we shall have the mean number of times in any of the nonabsorbing states for a given starting state—that is, the mean time required before being absorbed. This may be described as follows:

Theorem Consider an absorbing Markov chain with s nonabsorbing states. Let c be an s-component column vector with all entries 1. Then the vector $t = Nc$ has as components the mean number of steps before being absorbed for each possible nonabsorbing starting state.

EXAMPLE 1
(continued)   For Example 1 we have

$$
t = Nc = \begin{matrix} & \begin{matrix} 1 & 2 & 3 \end{matrix} \\ \begin{matrix} 1 \\ 2 \\ 3 \end{matrix} & \begin{pmatrix} \frac{3}{2} & 1 & \frac{1}{2} \\ 1 & 2 & 1 \\ \frac{1}{2} & 1 & \frac{3}{2} \end{pmatrix} \end{matrix} \begin{pmatrix} 1 \\ 1 \\ 1 \end{pmatrix}
$$

$$
= \begin{matrix} \begin{matrix} 1 \\ 2 \\ 3 \end{matrix} & \begin{pmatrix} 3 \\ 4 \\ 3 \end{pmatrix} \end{matrix}.
$$

Thus the mean number of steps to absorption starting at state 1 is 3, starting at state 2 it is 4, and starting at state 3 it is again 3. Since the process necessarily moves to 1 or 3 from 2, it is clear that it requires one more step starting from 2 than from 1 or 3.

We now consider question (a). That is, what is the probability that an absorbing chain will end up in a particular absorbing state? It is clear that this probability will depend upon the starting state and be interesting only for the case of a nonabsorbing starting state. We write as usual our matrix in the canonical form

$$
P = \left(\begin{array}{c|c} I & O \\ \hline R & Q \end{array} \right).
$$

Theorem Let b_{ij} be the probability that an absorbing chain will be absorbed in state a_j if it starts in the nonabsorbing state a_i. Let B be the matrix with entries b_{ij}. Then

$$B = NR,$$

where N is the fundamental matrix and R is as in the canonical form.

Proof Let a_i be a nonabsorbing state and a_j be an absorbing state. If we compute b_{ij} in terms of the possibilities on the outcome of the first step, we have the equation

$$b_{ij} = p_{ij} + \sum_k p_{ik}b_{kj},$$

where the summation is carried out over all nonabsorbing states a_k. Writing this in matrix form gives

$$B = R + QB$$
$$(I - Q)B = R$$

and hence
$$B = (I - Q)^{-1}R = NR.$$

EXAMPLE 1 (continued) In the random-walk example we found that

$$N = \begin{pmatrix} \frac{3}{2} & 1 & \frac{1}{2} \\ 1 & 2 & 1 \\ \frac{1}{2} & 1 & \frac{3}{2} \end{pmatrix}.$$

From the canonical form we find that

$$R = \begin{pmatrix} \frac{1}{2} & 0 \\ 0 & 0 \\ 0 & \frac{1}{2} \end{pmatrix}.$$

Hence

$$B = NR = \begin{pmatrix} \frac{3}{2} & 1 & \frac{1}{2} \\ 1 & 2 & 1 \\ \frac{1}{2} & 1 & \frac{3}{2} \end{pmatrix} \begin{pmatrix} \frac{1}{2} & 0 \\ 0 & 0 \\ 0 & \frac{1}{2} \end{pmatrix}$$

$$= \begin{matrix} 1 \\ 2 \\ 3 \end{matrix} \begin{pmatrix} \frac{3}{4} & \frac{1}{4} \\ \frac{1}{2} & \frac{1}{2} \\ \frac{1}{4} & \frac{3}{4} \end{pmatrix}.$$

Thus, for instance, starting from a_1, there is probability $\frac{3}{4}$ of absorption in a_0 and $\frac{1}{4}$ for absorption in a_4.

Let us summarize our results. We have shown that the answers to questions (a), (b), and (c) can all be given in terms of the fundamental matrix $N = (I - Q)^{-1}$. The matrix N itself gives us the mean number of times in each state before absorption depending upon the starting state. The column vector $t = Nc$ gives us the mean number of steps before absorption, depending upon the starting state. The matrix $B = NR$ gives us the probability of absorption in each of the absorbing states, depending upon the starting state.

EXERCISES

1. Which of the following transition matrices are from absorbing chains?

   (a) $P = \begin{pmatrix} \frac{1}{3} & \frac{2}{3} \\ 0 & 1 \end{pmatrix}$.

   (b) $P = \begin{pmatrix} \frac{1}{2} & 0 & \frac{1}{2} \\ 0 & 1 & 0 \\ \frac{1}{4} & 0 & \frac{3}{4} \end{pmatrix}$.

   (c) $P = \begin{pmatrix} 1 & 0 & 0 & 0 & 0 \\ 1 & 0 & 0 & 0 & 0 \\ 0 & 0 & \frac{1}{2} & \frac{1}{2} & 0 \\ 0 & 0 & 0 & 0 & 1 \\ 0 & \frac{3}{7} & 0 & \frac{4}{7} & 0 \end{pmatrix}$.   [*Ans.* Absorbing.]

   (d) $P = \begin{pmatrix} 1 & 0 & 0 & 0 \\ 0 & \frac{1}{2} & \frac{1}{2} & 0 \\ \frac{1}{10} & \frac{2}{10} & \frac{3}{10} & \frac{4}{10} \\ 0 & 0 & 0 & 1 \end{pmatrix}$.

   (e) $P = \begin{pmatrix} \frac{1}{2} & 0 & 0 & \frac{1}{2} \\ 0 & 1 & 0 & 0 \\ 0 & 0 & 1 & 0 \\ \frac{5}{8} & 0 & \frac{1}{4} & \frac{1}{8} \end{pmatrix}$.

2. Consider the three-state transition matrix

$$P = \begin{pmatrix} 1 & 0 & 0 \\ a & \frac{1}{2} & b \\ c & 0 & d \end{pmatrix}.$$

   For what choices of $a, b, c,$ and d do we not obtain an absorbing chain?

3. In the random-walk example (Example 1) of the present section, assume that the probability of a step to the right is $\frac{3}{4}$ and a step to the left is $\frac{1}{4}$. Find N, t, and B. Compare these with the results for probability $\frac{1}{2}$ for a step to the right and $\frac{1}{2}$ to the left.

4. In the hotel example of Exercise 20, Section 7, let us assume that the man is so impressed with the service at hotel 2 that, once he goes there, he refuses to go to any of the other hotels again. This gives

$$
\begin{array}{c}
\begin{array}{cccc} & 1 & 2 & 3 & 4 \end{array} \\
\begin{array}{c} 1 \\ 2 \\ 3 \\ 4 \end{array}
\begin{pmatrix} \frac{1}{4} & 0 & \frac{3}{4} & 0 \\ 0 & 1 & 0 & 0 \\ 0 & \frac{1}{2} & 0 & \frac{1}{2} \\ 0 & \frac{1}{3} & 0 & \frac{2}{3} \end{pmatrix}.
\end{array}
$$

(a) Find the fundamental matrix N, and also T and B. What is the interpretation of these quantities?

(b) Given that in 1970 and 1973 he stayed in hotel 1, what is the probability that he stayed in a very expensive hotel during either 1971 or 1972?

5. A rat is put into the maze of the figure below. Each time period, it chooses at random one of the doors in the compartment it is in and moves into another compartment.

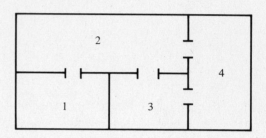

(a) Set up the process as a Markov chain (with states being the compartments) and identify it.   [*Ans*. Regular.]

(b) In the long run, what fraction of his time will the rat spend in compartment 2?   [*Ans*. $\frac{3}{8}$.]

(c) What is the relation between the number of entrances to a given compartment and the fraction of the time the rat will spend in that compartment?

(d) Make compartment 4 into an absorbing state by assuming the rat will stay in it once it reaches it. Set up the new process, and identify it as a kind of Markov chain.   [*Ans*. Absorbing.]

(e) In part (d), if the rat starts in compartment 2, how many steps will it take him, on the average, to reach compartment 4?

6. An analysis of a recent hockey game between Dartmouth and Princeton showed the following facts: If the puck was in the center (C) the probabilities that it next entered Princeton territory (P) or Dartmouth territory (D) were .4 and .6, respectively. From D it went back to C with probability .95 or into the Dartmouth goal ($\bar{D}$) with probability .05 (Princeton scores one point). From P it next went to C with probability .9 and to Princeton's goal ($\bar{P}$) with probability .1 (Dartmouth scores one point). Assuming that the puck begins in C after each point, find the transition matrix of this five-state Markov chain. Calculate the probability that Dartmouth will score.   [*Ans*. $\frac{4}{7}$.]

7. The following is an alternative method of finding the probability of absorption in a particular state, say a_j. Find the column vector d such that the jth component of d is 1, all other components corresponding to absorbing states are 0, and $Pd = d$. There is only one such vector. Component d_i is the probability of absorption in a_j if the process starts

in a_i. Use this method to find the probability of absorption in state 0 in the random-walk example given in this section.

8. The following is an alternative method for finding the mean number of steps to absorption. Let t_i be the mean number of steps to absorption starting at state a_i. This must be the same as taking one more step and then adding $p_{ij}t_j$ for every nonabsorbing state a_j.

  (a) Give reasons for the claim above that

$$t_i = 1 + \sum_j p_{ij}t_j,$$

  where the summation is over the nonabsorbing states.

  (b) Solve for t for the random-walk example.

  (c) Verify that the solution agrees with that found in the text.

9. A man is in jail and needs \$400 for bail. Once he is out, he can recover his million-dollar loot. In jail he can make a sequence of bets in which, if he bets X dollars, he wins X dollars with probability $\frac{1}{3}$ and loses X dollars with probability $\frac{2}{3}$. He can bet any amount he wishes as long as he can pay if he loses. He has \$100. He decides to try the bold strategy of betting as much as he has each time or at least enough to get his \$400—that is, to bet \$100 if he has \$100, \$200 if he has \$200, and \$100 if he has \$300. To assess his chances of getting out now, he sets up the transition matrix:

$$
P = \begin{array}{c} 0 \\ 400 \\ 100 \\ 200 \\ 300 \end{array}
\begin{array}{c} \begin{array}{ccccc} 0 & 400 & 100 & 200 & 300 \end{array} \\
\left(\begin{array}{cc|ccc}
1 & 0 & 0 & 0 & 0 \\
0 & 1 & 0 & 0 & 0 \\
\frac{2}{3} & 0 & 0 & \frac{1}{3} & 0 \\
\frac{2}{3} & \frac{1}{3} & 0 & 0 & 0 \\
0 & \frac{1}{3} & 0 & \frac{2}{3} & 0
\end{array} \right) = \left(\begin{array}{c|c} I & O \\ \hline R & Q \end{array} \right).
\end{array}
$$

  (a) Find the matrix $N = (I - Q)^{-1}$.

  (b) Find the expected number of bets that he will make under this bold strategy.   [*Ans.* $\frac{4}{3}$.]

  (c) Find the probability that he will get his bail money under this strategy.

  (d) Repeat parts (a), (b), and (c) assuming that he uses a more timid strategy of betting \$100 each time. Which strategy provides a longer expected game? Which strategy gives him the better chance of recovering his loot?

10. A number is chosen at random from the integers 1, 2, 3, 4, 5. If x is chosen, then another number is chosen from the set of integers less than or equal to x. This process is continued until the number 1 is chosen. Form a Markov chain by taking as states the largest number

that can be chosen. Show that

$$N = \begin{array}{c} \\ 2 \\ 3 \\ 4 \\ 5 \end{array} \begin{array}{cccc} 2 & 3 & 4 & 5 \\ \left(\begin{array}{cccc} 1 & 0 & 0 & 0 \\ 1 & \frac{1}{2} & 0 & 0 \\ 1 & \frac{1}{2} & \frac{1}{3} & 0 \\ 1 & \frac{1}{2} & \frac{1}{3} & \frac{1}{4} \end{array} \right) \end{array} + I,$$

where I is the 4×4 identity matrix. What is the mean number of draws?   [*Ans.* $\frac{37}{12}$.]

11. Using the result of Exercise 10, make a conjecture for the form of the fundamental matrix if we start with integers from 1 to n. What would the mean number of draws be if we started with numbers from 1 to 10?

12. Peter and Paul are matching pennies, and each player flips his (fair) coin before revealing it. They initially have four pennies between them and the game ends whenever one of them has all the pennies. Let the states be labeled with the number of pennies that Peter has.
    (a) Write the transition matrix.
    (b) What kind of a Markov chain is it?
    (c) If Peter initially has two pennies, what is the probability that he will win the game?

13. A certain college which is trying to pass several liberal measures is plagued by the problem of conservative alumni. It is determined that if an alumnus votes for a liberal policy, he will with probability $\frac{5}{6}$ vote in favor of the next policy and will with probability $\frac{1}{6}$ turn conservative. Once he turns conservative he will continue to vote against all liberal policies. Assume there are 20,000 alumni, 4000 of whom voted conservatively before the college starts trying to pass these measures. If all the alumni vote and if 12,000 opposing votes are needed to defeat a policy which the college is trying to pass, how many of its new liberal policies can the college expect to pass?

14. Three tanks fight a three-way duel. Tank A has probability $\frac{1}{2}$ of destroying the tank it fires at. Tank B has probability $\frac{1}{3}$ of destroying its target tank, and tank C has probability $\frac{1}{6}$ of destroying its target tank. The tanks fire together and each tank fires at the strongest opponent not yet destroyed. Form a Markov chain by taking as state the tanks which survive any one round. Find N, t, B, and interpret your results.

15. Consider the following model. A man buys a store. The profits of the store vary from month to month. For simplicity we assume that he earns either $5000 or $2000 a month ("high" or "low"). The man may sell his store at any time; there is a 10 percent chance of his selling during a high-profit month and a 40 percent chance during a low-profit month. If he does not sell, with probability $\frac{2}{3}$ the profits will be the same the next month, and with probability $\frac{1}{3}$ they will change.

(a) Set up the transition matrix.

$$\begin{array}{c} \text{Sell} \\ [Ans. \ \text{High} \\ \text{Low} \end{array} \begin{pmatrix} 1 & 0 & 0 \\ \frac{1}{10} & \frac{3}{5} & \frac{3}{10} \\ \frac{2}{5} & \frac{1}{5} & \frac{2}{5} \end{pmatrix}.]$$

(b) Compute N, Nc, and NR and interpret each.

(c) Let $f = \begin{pmatrix} 5000 \\ 2000 \end{pmatrix}$ and compute the vector $g = Nf$.

$$\left[Ans. \ g = \begin{pmatrix} 20{,}000 \\ 10{,}000 \end{pmatrix}. \right]$$

(d) Show that the components of g have the following interpretation: g_i is the expected amount that he will gain before selling, given that he started in state i.

SUGGESTED READING

Beaumont, R. A. *Linear Algebra.* New York: Harcourt, Brace and World, 1965.

Birkhoff, G., and Maclane, S. *A Survey of Modern Algebra.* 3rd ed. New York: Macmillan, 1965.

Fraleigh, John B. *First Course in Abstract Algebra.* Reading, Mass.: Addison-Wesley, 1967.

Hadley, G. *Linear Algebra.* Reading, Mass.: Addison-Wesley, 1961. Chapters 1–5.

Hohn, Franz E. *Elementary Matrix Algebra.* 2nd ed. New York: Macmillan, 1964.

Johnson, R. E. *First Course in Abstract Algebra.* Englewood Cliffs, N.J.: Prentice-Hall, 1953.

Kemeny, John G., and Snell, J. Laurie. *Finite Markov Chains.* Princeton, N.J.: Van Nostrand, 1960.

Noble, Ben. *Applied Linear Algebra.* Englewood Cliffs, N.J.: Prentice-Hall, 1969.

Weiss, Marie J., and Dubisch, R. *Higher Algebra for the Undergraduate.* 2nd ed. New York: John Wiley, 1962.

Computer
Programming

5

1 INTRODUCTION

Modern high-speed computers have made all forms of computation vastly easier. Calculations that used to take several days to complete can now be carried out in a few seconds. The availability of a modern computer can take a great deal of drudgery out of mathematical computations and makes possible large-scale computations that would otherwise be impossible. This is particularly true in the area of finite mathematics, since each of the branches of mathematics introduced in this book is well suited to computer applications.

It is the purpose of this chapter to give a first introduction to the use of high-speed computers. A computer is an electronic device designed to carry out arithmetical operations and to follow a long list of instructions as to what calculations should be carried out. A computer does no more and no less than a human user instructs it to do; however, it can carry out tasks at tremendous speed and with great accuracy. The key to the use of a computer is learning how to write a set of instructions. Such a set of instructions is called a *program*, and the art of writing such instructions is known as *programming*. This chapter will give a number of examples of programs for high-speed computers designed to carry out calculations in finite mathematics. Although only elementary programming techniques will be illustrated, they will be sufficient to carry out many significant mathematical tasks.

The chapter is written so that it may profitably be studied without having a computer available. However, being able to try out examples on a computer will significantly improve the learning experience. Each section will include many exercises that do not require the use of the computer and also some exercises that must be completed on a computer.

In order to communicate with a human being, it is necessary to understand the language he speaks. Similarly, a user must learn a suitable language for communicating with a computer. Fortunately, there are several easily learned languages that most computers "speak." One language widely used, particularly in educational uses, is BASIC. The present chapter provides a brief introduction to the language BASIC. The reader interested in more sophisticated applications, including many further applications to finite mathematics, is referred to the book *Basic Programming*, which is listed in the suggested readings at the end of the chapter.

Since the language BASIC is almost self-explanatory, it is simplest to learn it by looking at some actual programs. The program EXAMPLE1 is designed to compute several factorials—specifically, 4!, 6!, and 10!. The program consists of five lines, each of which contains one instruction for the computer. It will be noted that each line starts with a line number. These numbers are required in BASIC to make it easy to enter corrections to a given program. For example, if a user wishes to correct a given line, he simply retypes that line with the same line number and the correction is automatically made by the computer. Or, if it is desired to insert a line between, say, lines 20 and 30, one may type the new instruction with any number between 20 and 30 and a correction is automatically made. Thus it is good practice to choose line numbers with gaps between them (for example, multiples of 10) to allow for the insertion of additional instructions. An additional use of line numbers will be explained in the next section.

Most of the variables in this chapter are represented by capital letters, since many computer terminals print only capitals.

Look now at EXAMPLE1. Line 10 in EXAMPLE1 instructs the computer to compute 4!, i.e., $1 \times 2 \times 3 \times 4$. To avoid the ambiguity between the dot as a multiplication sign and as a decimal point, BASIC uses an asterisk (*) to indicate multiplication. Specifically, the LET command in line 10 tells the machine to compute $1 \times 2 \times 3 \times 4$ and to call the answer "X.") Thus after the computer has carried out the instruction in line 10, X will equal 24. This quantity may now be used in the rest of the program. In line 20 the computer is asked to take X and multiply it by 5 and then by 6, and to call the result Y. Thus Y will equal 6! or 720. Similarly, on line 30 the previous result is multiplied by 7, 8, 9, and 10, thus obtaining 10!, and calling the result Z. The instruction LET is designed to carry out a wide variety of computations. The format for the LET command is always to put on the right-hand side of the equals sign the computation that is to be carried out and to indicate the name of the result on the left-hand side of the equals sign.

Computations are useless unless the user can see the result. In a long program there are many partial results that are of no interest to the user and that would take too long to be typed, so that we don't want to print every result. Therefore there is an instruction in BASIC called PRINT which tells the computer to print or type only the desired results. Line 40 instructs the computer to type out X, Y, and Z. It is up to the programmer to

■ EXAMPLE1

```
10 LET X = 1*2*3*4
20 LET Y = X*5*6
30 LET Z = Y*7*8*9*10
40 PRINT X,Y,Z
50 END
READY

RUN

EXAMPLE1

 24                  720                 3628800

0.062 SEC.
READY
```

remember that the results stand for 4!, 6!, and 10!, respectively. The final instruction, in line 50, is **END**. In all programs the last instruction must be an **END** statement. This line both indicates the physical end of the program and tells the computer to stop.

Immediately after the program we show the results that are printed as the program is executed or "**RUN**." Three numbers are printed which are the desired results. It is important to note that the computations took only a small fraction of a second.*

Many interesting and useful programs can be written with the minimal vocabulary of **LET**, **PRINT**, and **END**. A more sophisticated example is shown in **EXAMPLE2**. Line 10 carries out a subtraction and an addition. Line 20 shows one decimal fraction being divided by the sum of two other decimal fractions. Note that parentheses are inserted as usual. Line 30 requires an additional word of explanation. One usually communicates with a computer through a typewriterlike terminal device, and this imposes certain limitations on the way formulas are typed. Specifically, each formula must be contained on a single line. This was already illustrated by the form of division on line 20. Since it is not possible to type an exponent on a higher line, an upward arrow ($\uparrow$) is used to indicate an exponent. Thus line 30 asks the computer to raise the number 2.15 to the sixth power and to let the answer be **Z**.

Line 40 illustrates some additional options available for the **PRINT** instruction. In **EXAMPLE1** a comma (,) separated the variables, which is the signal to BASIC to line up the answers in predetermined columns (also called fields), normally up to five columns per line. If one is not interested

---

*The reader will note that in the computer output zeros appear as '0'. This is done to distinguish the number zero from the letter 'O'. Unfortunately, different conventions for this are used on different computer terminals.

■ EXAMPLE2

```
10 LET X = 397-128+511
20 LET Y = .57/(.23+.82)
30 LET Z = 2.15↑6
40 PRINT X;Y;Z;2*X;Y*Z
50 END
READY

RUN

EXAMPLE2

 780   0.542857   98.7713   1560   53.6187

0.059 SEC.
READY
```

in a special format but would simply like to have answers printed one after the other, the answers are separated by semicolons (;), as shown in **EXAMPLE2**. This example also shows that computation instructions may take place within a **PRINT** statement. In addition to printing X, Y, and Z, we have also asked the computer to **PRINT** 2∗X and Y∗Z. Recall that an asterisk (∗) is used to denote multiplication to the computer. The results are again shown.

These examples illustrate the fact that once the user masters a simple language for entering requests to the computer, all the hard work can be left to the machine. One of the nice features of modern computers is the fact that one can become quite expert in their use without necessarily having any understanding of how computers work. This is similar to the fact that millions of people use telephones and drive automobiles without having any understanding of the nature of telephone-switching networks or of automobile engines. That is why in this chapter we are concentrating entirely on the art of programming and not on the operation of computers. The following sections will introduce, step by step, some more powerful commands in the language BASIC which will enable the reader to use the computer for more complex calculations.

EXERCISES

Only Exercises 7–11 require the use of a computer.

1. Write a program that will compute and print the sum of the first three positive integers, of the first five positive integers, and of the first ten positive integers.

2. Write a program to compute the cube root of 100. (You will need to recall that a cube root is the same as the $\frac{1}{3}$ power.)

3. Write a two-instruction program to compute $\binom{7}{3}$.

4. The following program contains three *illegal* instructions, that is, instructions not satisfying the rules we have prescribed. Identify them.

```
10   LET X = .12345/.54321
20   LET Y = X↑Z
30   LET U = XY
40   LET X = X − X
50   PRINT X,Y,U + Z
60   PRINT X,Y,Z²
70   END
80   LET X = Y + Z
```

5. Without using a computer, figure out what would be printed when the following program is run.

```
10   LET X = 2
20   LET Y = 7 − 4
30   LET Z = Y↑X
40   LET Z = Z − 2*Y + X
50   PRINT Z/X
60   END
```
                                                                    [*Ans.* 2.5.]

6. Without using a computer, figure out what would be printed when the following program is run.

```
10   LET X = 20/5
20   LET Y = X↑(1/2)
30   LET Z = 1*2*3
40   LET U = Z − 3*Y
50   PRINT U
60   END
```

7. Try the program of Exercise 4 on a computer to see what error messages are printed.

8. Run the program of Exercise 2 on a computer. What is the cube root of 100?   [*Ans.* 4.64159.]

9. Use a computer to compute
(.54321/.12345)*(40/37)↑3.

10. Using a computer, employ a trial-and-error method to find the smallest integer whose fifth power is greater than 1,000,000.

11. Use a computer to compute $\binom{20}{7}$ [*Ans.* 77520.]

2 MORE ON THE LANGUAGE BASIC

The programs in Section 1 are not typical in that each instruction is carried out only once by the computer. Such calculations could easily be done with a desk calculator. To make the best use of the great speed of high-speed computers it is desirable to give short programs which result in hundreds, thousands, or even millions of computer operations. One technique for this is the application of the same instructions to many different sets of data. This will be illustrated in the present section. An even more powerful technique will be shown in next section.

Let us suppose that we wish to carry out a number of divisions. Instead of writing a separate instruction for each operation, we can write a single instruction and use it over and over again, as shown in the program DI-VIDE. Line 20 instructs the computer to PRINT the numbers A,B and their quotient. The trick is to specify various pairs A,B. This is accomplished by storing on line 40 a set of data and instructing the computer on line 10 to pick off two of these numbers. The READ statement instructs the computer to pick the next two numbers on the DATA line and call the first number A and the second number B.

Thus the first time line 10 is executed, A will equal 12 and B will equal 4, and thus on line 20 this pair of numbers will be printed as will their quotient $A/B = 3$. The next time line 10 is executed, A will equal 144 and B will equal 12. This will continue until all the data has been used up.

After reading a pair of numbers and printing the result, we would like the computer to go back and do the same two instructions over again. This is accomplished by a GOTO statement. Line 30 instructs the machine to GOTO 10—that is, to go to line 10, which in this case happens to be the beginning of the program. This is another important use of line numbers.

```
DIVIDE

10 READ A,B
20 PRINT A,B,A/B
30 GOTO 10
40 DATA 12,4,144,12,10,3.45,19782,345
50 END
READY

RUN

DIVIDE

12                4                3
144               12               12
10                3.45             2.89855
19782             345              57.3391
OUT OF DATA AT 10

STOP
0.079 SEC.
READY
```

```
40 DATA 169,13,2.97,1.23,-200,-50,12345,1289
RUN

DIVIDE

 169              13            13
 2.97            1.23           2.41463
-200             -50            4
 12345          1289           9.57719
OUT OF DATA AT 10

STOP
0.080 SEC.
READY


5 PRINT "FIRST NO.","SECOND NO.","QUOTIENT"
RUN

DIVIDE

FIRST NO.       SECOND NO.      QUOTIENT
 169             13             13
 2.97           1.23            2.41463
-200            -50             4
 12345         1289            9.57719
OUT OF DATA AT 10

STOP
0.090 SEC.
READY
```

We include with a listing of the program the results that are obtained. It will be noted that the four pairs of numbers are printed on separate lines with the quotient in each case printed in the third column. This run also illustrates that there are two different ways of terminating a computer program. One is by reaching an END instruction; the other is for some condition to occur under which the computer can no longer proceed. In this particular case the fifth time it is asked to READ numbers A and B, it finds that there are no numbers left and therefore it prints the OUT OF DATA message. This is a perfectly legitimate way of terminating a program.

The advantage of writing a program with READ and DATA statements is twofold. First, it shortens the program significantly. Second, if the user wishes to reuse the program with different pairs of numbers, he only has to change line 40 and the rest of the program is still valid. If one retypes line 40 with different data and types "RUN" again, the new results will be obtained. This is shown as a second RUN of the program DIVIDE.

We would like to illustrate one more capability of the PRINT instruction.

It is often convenient to label the output of a computer program. A PRINT instruction will PRINT any label contained between quotation marks exactly as you typed it. We can add labels to the program DIVIDE as follows:

5 PRINT "FIRST NO.", "SECOND NO.", "QUOTIENT".

Making the line number "5" indicates to the computer that the instruction should be inserted at the beginning of the program (i.e., before line 10). The three labels will be printed exactly as indicated. The fact that the labels are separated by commas indicates to the machine that they should be typed in separate columns and they will automatically line up with the three columns of output. A new RUN is shown. Such labels may be inserted anywhere in a PRINT statement, as will be seen in the next program.

 A simple computer program will allow us to convert a probability to odds. We recall (see Chapter 3, Section 2) that if the probability that an event will occur is P, and $Q = 1 - P$, then the odds in favor of the event may be expressed as P/Q to 1. This is carried out in the program ODDS.

 A set of probabilities is provided on line 90. Line 10 reads one of these probabilities and calls it P. Line 15 computes Q. Line 20 does double duty, both computing the odds and printing the answers. Note that in line 20

ODDS

```
5   PRINT "PROBABILITY"," ODDS "
10  READ P
15  LET Q = 1-P
20  PRINT P,P/Q;"TO 1"
30  GOTO 10
90  DATA .5,.75,.6,.3333333,.1
99  END
READY

RUN

ODDS

PROBABILITY          ODDS
 0.5                  1 TO 1
 0.75                 3 TO 1
 0.6                  1.5 TO 1
 0.333333             0.5 TO 1
 0.1                  0.111111  TO 1
OUT OF DATA AT 10

STOP
0.083 SEC.
READY
```

P is followed by a comma so that the probability will occur in one column and the odds in a separate column. After P/Q we have inserted a semicolon (;) so that the quotient is immediately followed by the phrase "TO 1." The effect of this PRINT format is clearly shown in the RUN. Line 30 simply instructs the program to go back and carry out the computations for the next probability.

As we look at the output we notice that while the first three lines look very clear, the last two are somewhat unnatural. One does not usually say that the odds are 0.5 to 1 in favor of an event; rather one would prefer to say that the odds are 1 to 2 in favor, or 2 to 1 against the event. To achieve this one must have one output format if the odds are in favor of the event (i.e., P greater than Q), and another format if they are not. We must be able to tell the computer that if a certain relationship holds then one thing should happen, and that otherwise something else should happen. This is provided for in BASIC by the IF . . . THEN instruction.

In the program ODDS2 we have inserted a test at line 17. If P is less

ODDS2

```
5   PRINT "PROBABILITY"," ODDS "
10  READ P
15  LET  Q = 1-P
17  IF P<Q THEN 40
20  PRINT P,P/Q;"TO 1"
30  GOTO 10
40  PRINT P," 1 TO";Q/P
50  GOTO 10
90  DATA .5,.75,.6,.3333333,.1
99  END
READY

RUN

ODDS2

PROBABILITY         ODDS
 0.5                1 TO 1
 0.75               3 TO 1
 0.6                1.5 TO 1
 0.333333           1 TO 2.
 0.1                1 TO 9
OUT OF DATA AT 10

STOP
0.090 SEC.
READY
```

than Q then the computer is instructed to skip to line 40 and use the alternate output format. But if $P \geq Q$ the computer goes on to line 20. On line 40 we compute the odds as 1 to Q/P rather than the form used on line 20. A RUN of the modified program is shown and the reader will note that the odds are now in both a simpler and a more natural form.

The significance of the IF . . . THEN statement is that the computer can be instructed to go in one of two different directions. And where it goes depends on the result of previous computations. In those cases where P turns out to be greater than or equal to Q, the computer proceeds with lines 20 and 30. However, if P is less than Q then the computer skips to lines 40 and 50. Thus the same computer program can handle both cases, and uses a simple test to distinguish between them.

The general form of this instructions is:

$$\text{IF [relationship] THEN [line number]}.$$

The line number may be any line number in the program. For the relationship we may use six relational symbols: $=$ (equals), $<$ (is less than), $>$ (is greater than), $<=$ (is less than or equal to), $>=$ (is greater than or equal to), and $<>$ (is not equal to). A more complex example is the following:

$$\text{IF } (X*Y + 3) <= Z \text{ THEN 35}.$$

If the current value of $X*Y + 3$ is less than or equal to the current value of Z, the program takes line 35 as its next instruction. If not, it will proceed in the normal order.

EXERCISES

Only Exercises 10–14 require the use of a computer.

1. Write a program that will READ a list of numbers and compute and print their fifth powers.

2. There are many ways of avoiding the "OUT OF DATA" message. One is to have a dummy number at the end of the DATA (say −99999) and to have the computer terminate when that number is READ. Modify the program of Exercise 1 by adding an IF statement so that it will terminate in this manner.

3. Modify the program ODDS2 so that instead of "1 TO 9" it will print "9 TO 1 AGAINST."

4. Modify the program ODDS2 to avoid the "OUT OF DATA" message.

5. If the DATA in the program ODDS contains an illegal probability (i.e., a negative number of a probability greater than 1), the result will be meaningless. Insert a test to make sure that P is between 0 and 1.

6. Write a program that will read a list of numbers from DATA and find its largest element. You will have to avoid the "OUT OF DATA" termination. (See Exercise 2.)

7. Modify the program of Exercise 6 to find the smallest element.

8. The absolute value Y of a number X may be computed in BASIC by writing **LET Y = ABS (X)**. Design a test to check whether two numbers A and B are within 0.001 of each other.

9. In BASIC, INT(X) is the greatest integer less than or equal to the number X. For example, INT(6.235) = 6, INT(10.999) = 10, INT(15) = 15, and INT(-3.52) = -4. Design a test to check whether an integer X is an even number.

10. By means of the **IF . . . THEN** statement we can remove the trial-and-error method from Exercise 10, Section 1. Design and **RUN** a program that will **READ** a number A (A $>$ 0), and find the smallest integer N whose fifth power is greater than A.

11. Try out the program of Exercise 6 on a computer. Does it work correctly when all the numbers in the **DATA** are negative?

12. In BASIC, SQR(X) is the square root of X. Use a computer to print a table of square roots for the first ten integers.

13. Modify the program of Exercise 12 to print the square roots of every fifth number between 100 and 200 (i.e., 100, 105, 110, . . . , 200).

14. There is a fast computational technique for finding the square root of a number A without using the "built-in" **SQR** function. One lets X be a guess at the square root. (For example, X = 1 is all right.) Let Y = A/X. If X is the correct square root, then Y = X. If not, one uses the average of X and Y as the next guess, and repeats the process until X and Y differ by less than a predetermined small error—say 0.000001. (See Exercise 8.) Write and **RUN** a program which carries out this technique. Check the answers by means of **SQR**.

3 LOOPS

Let us return to the problem of computing factorials. To compute 10! it is possible to proceed as in **EXAMPLE1**, or to write a single instruction:

$$\text{LET } X = 1*2*3*4*5*6*7*8*9*10.$$

However, this is a nuisance even for 10! and becomes very inconvenient for 25!. It also means that if we wish to compute several different factorials we have to write a different line for each one. We would instead like to write a simple set of instructions which say roughly, "Take the numbers from 1 to 10 and multiply them together." This can be accomplished by the pair of instructions **FOR** and **NEXT**.

The heart of the program **FCTRL** is contained in the "loop" on lines 30–50. The letter K will consecutively stand for the integers 1 through 10. The letter F will contain all the partial results and will eventually equal 10!. To understand line 40 we must remember that in a **LET** instruction the computer first computes the right-hand side and then lets the letter on the left equal the result. Thus F is multiplied by the current value of K and this becomes the new value of F. Line 50 instructs the computer to go on to the next value of K until all ten numbers have been used up.

```
█   FCTRL

20 LET F = 1
30 FOR K = 1 TO 10
40 LET F = F*K
50 NEXT K
60 PRINT F
99 END
READY

RUN

FCTRL

 3628800

0.052 SEC.
READY
```

Before starting the loop we must tell the computer what the "initial value" of F should be. In computing a product the initial value must always be 1. If we were computing a sum we would start with 0 (see Exercise 6). After the loop is completed we PRINT the final answer on line 60 and then

Line no.	Result
20	F = 1
30	K = 1
40	F = 1*1 = 1
50	GOES BACK TO 30
30	K = 2
40	F = 1*2 = 2
50	GOES BACK TO 30
30	K = 3
40	F = 2*3 = 6
50	GOES BACK TO 30
	•
	•
	•
30	K = 10
40	F = (362880)*10 = 3628800
50	K EXHAUSTED, DOES NOT GO BACK
60	PRINT VALUE OF 10!
99	STOPS

Figure 1

line 99 instructs the computer to stop. Figure 1 shows what actually happens as each step in the computation is performed.

It is easy to modify this program to compute the factorial of an arbitrary number. In FCTRL2 we first PRINT labels and then READ the number N whose factorial we are trying to compute. In line 30 K now goes from 1 to N. In line 60 we have elected to PRINT both N and its factorial. Line 70 instructs the program to go back and read the next number. Line 90 contains five different values for N. The RUN shows the factorials of these five numbers.

Two comments are in order concerning the output. First, 20! is a number too large for all of the digits to be printed out. Therefore the computer prints it in "scientific notation." The abbreviation $E + 18$ stands for 10^{18}. In other words, the answer is 2.4329×10^{18}. It is also worth noting that 0! came out to be 1 without any special instruction to the computer. This is one more way of showing that $0! = 1$ is the "natural convention."

FCTRL2

```
5 PRINT "NUMBER","FACTORIAL"
10 READ N
20 LET F = 1
30 FOR K = 1 TO N
40 LET F = F*K
50 NEXT K
60 PRINT N,F
70 GOTO 10
90 DATA 4,7,10,20,0
99 END
READY

RUN

FCTRL2

NUMBER              FACTORIAL
 4                  24
 7                  5040
10                  3628800
20                  2.4329 E+18
 0                  1
OUT OF DATA AT 10

STOP
0.082 SEC.
READY
```

As our next illustration of loops we shall write a short program that computes an expected value. We recall from Chapter 3, Section 11, that an expected value is computed for an experiment whose possible outcomes are numbers by multiplying the numerical outcome A with the probability P of the outcome for each possible outcome, and adding up the results. This is carried out in the program EXPECT.

■ EXPECT

```
10 LET E = 0
20 FOR K = 1 TO 5
30 READ A,P
40 LET E = E + A*P
50 NEXT K
60 PRINT E
90 DATA 1,.3,2,.2,5,.05,-1,.25,-2,.2
99 END
READY

RUN

EXPECT

 0.3

 0.059 SEC.
READY
```

Since the expected value E is computed as a sum, its initial value is set to 0. In the loop of lines 20–50, for each of the five possible outcomes we first read the numerical value A and the probability P. We then add to the previous value of E the quantity A*P. This will become the new value of E. After the loop is completed (by going through all five cases) E will be the expected value. This is printed by line 60. Note that the variable K acts as a counter only and does not otherwise enter the computation.

We see that the expected value in this simple illustration is 0.3. Of course in this case the answer could have been obtained more easily by hand computation. However, if the number of cases were significantly larger and the numbers were not as nice, the computer would indeed be useful.

Let us now turn to an application for which a computer is indispensable. We shall write a computer program for the "birthday problem" treated in Chapter 3, Section 4. (This example should be skipped by those who have not read that section.)

The problem was to compute the probability that among R people there are at least two with the same birthday. The trick was to compute first the probability Q that all the birthdays are different, given by a formula in Section 4 of Chapter 3; then the probability we desire will be $P = 1 - Q$. In the program BIRTHDAY lines 15–45 carry out this computation in five simple instructions. The remaining lines are designed to allow us to compute

■■ BIRTHDAY

```
5   PRINT "PEOPLE","PROBABILITY"
10  READ R
15  LET Q = 1
20  FOR K = 1 TO R
30  LET Q = Q * (366-K)/365
40  NEXT K
45  LET P = 1-Q
50  PRINT R,P
60  GOTO 10
90  DATA 10,20,22,23,30,50
99  END
READY

RUN

BIRTHDAY

PEOPLE             PROBABILITY
 10                0.116948
 20                0.411438
 22                0.475695
 23                0.507297
 30                0.706316
 50                0.970374
OUT OF DATA AT 10

STOP
0.100 SEC.
READY
```

the answer for several different values of R and to PRINT the answers. The reader is invited to compare the results with those given in Figure 1 of Chapter 3. That the results agree (except for the fact that these numbers are rounded to three places in Figure 1) is not surprising since they were originally obtained by means of a computer. This is a good example in which a simple computer program and one-tenth of a second of computer time can save hours of laborious hand calculations.

The question is often raised: What is the probability of having more than one coincidence of birthdays in a given group? That is, what are the chances that there will be three people with the same birthday or two pairs of identical birthdays or even larger coincidences? This probability can be computed in two steps. One first computes (as above) the probability of having some kind of coincidence. Then one computes separately the probability of having precisely one pair of people with the same birthday. The difference of these two quantities will give the probability of a multiple coincidence.

▮ BIRTH2

```
5   PRINT "PEOPLE","PROBABILITY"
10  READ R
15  LET Q = 1
20  FOR K = 1 TO R
30  LET Q = Q * (366-K)/365
40  NEXT K
45  LET P = 1-Q
50  LET E = 1
60  FOR K = 1 TO R-1
65  LET E = E * (366-K)/365
70  NEXT K
75  LET E = E/365
77  LET E = E*R*(R-1)/2
80  PRINT R,P-E
85  GOTO 10
90  DATA 20,25,30,35,36,40,50
99  END
READY

RUN

BIRTH2

PEOPLE              PROBABILITY
 20                 8.82398 E-2
 25                 0.189257
 30                 0.326101
 35                 0.480722
 36                 0.511803
 40                 0.630989
 50                 0.855524
OUT OF DATA AT 10

STOP
0.134 SEC.
READY
```

The program **BIRTH2** is designed to compute this probability for various numbers of people. The quantities **Q** and **P** are computed as before. The quantity **E** will stand for the probability of exactly one pair with the same birthday. Let us first calculate the probability that the first two people have a specific birthday, say October 26, and that all the other people have different birthdays. This probability is $\frac{1}{365} \times \frac{1}{365} \times \frac{364}{365} \times \frac{363}{365} \times \ldots$. However, the same two people could have had a coincidence of birthdays on any of 365 days, and therefore we must multiply the answer by 365. This will cancel the first factor of $\frac{1}{365}$. This calculation is carried out in **BIRTH2**, lines 50–75. We must still correct this answer since we have so far assumed that it is the first two people who have a coincidence of birthdays. Such a coincidence may occur for any pair from among the R people, and therefore we must multiply the answer by $\binom{R}{2} = \frac{R \times (R - 1)}{2}$, which is carried out in line 77. You should "step through" the program **BIRTH2** by hand to see that it is actually carrying out the calculations described above.

The program prints the probability of a multiple coincidence for several different numbers of people. We notice that for 25 people—a number for which we already have a better-than-even chance of having some coincidence—the probability of a greater coincidence is less than .2. The smallest number of people for which a multiple coincidence has better than an even chance is 36. We note that for 50 people the probability of a multiple coincidence is very high.

We have now discussed nine instructions in BASIC. It is significant that these nine instructions are sufficient to write many interesting programs. They are summarized in Figure 2 for the reader's convenience.

Instructions for nine-word BASIC

Instruction	Example	Purpose
LET	LET X $= 2+3$	Carries out computations
PRINT	PRINT X,Y,X$+$Y	Prints results
END	END	Terminates computation
READ	READ A,B	Enters numbers from DATA
DATA	DATA 5,-2,3.4	Stores data
GOTO	GOTO 20	Transfers program control
IF . . . THEN	IF X$>$3 THEN 20	Performs a test
FOR	FOR N $= 1$ TO 8	Starts a loop
NEXT	NEXT N	Closes a loop

Figure 2

EXERCISES

Only Exercises 9–14 require the use of a computer.

1. Use **FOR** and **NEXT** to write a program that will compute the seventh powers of the first ten positive integers.

2. Write a program that will compute the cube roots of the integers from 1 to 20.

3. A loop need not run through all the integers specified in the FOR statement. For example, the instruction

    FOR N = 1 TO 15 STEP 2

    will run through the odd numbers from 1 to 15. Write a program to compute the cube roots of the multiples of 10 from 10 to 100.

4. Write a program to print the fifth powers of the even integers up to 30.

5. If we know how many numbers there are on the DATA list, we may avoid the OUT OF DATA message by reading the data within a loop. Modify DIVIDE in this manner. [*Hint:* Remember that a pair of numbers is READ each time.]

6. Write a program to compute the sum of the first 100 integers. What must the initial value of the sum be?

7. Modify the program of Exercise 6 to READ a number N and then to compute the sum of the first N integers.

8. Write a program to compute the sum of an arithmetic series. READ only the numbers A, D, N, and have the computer construct the sum of the series with N terms, starting with A, and increasing by D each time. I.e., the series is

    $$A + (A + D) + (A + 2D) + \cdots + (A + (N-1)D).$$

9. RUN the program of Exercise 7 for several values of N. Check that the answer is always $N(N+1)/2$.

10. In BASIC, LOG(X) is the natural logarithm of X. Print a table of natural logarithms for the first ten integers.

11. RUN the program of Exercise 3 on a computer.

12. Write a program that computes the sum of the first N odd integers. RUN it for several values of N, and guess what the general formula for the sum is.

13. The technique described in Exercise 5 is not the best one, since when the number of DATA elements is changed, the loop must also be changed. This may be avoided by starting DATA with a single number that tells us how many times we have to go through the loop. Say this is N. Then we start our loop with

    FOR K = 1 TO N.

    Modify DIVIDE accordingly, and RUN it.

14. In the Land of Oz the calendar year has 534 days. Modify the programs BIRTHDAY and BIRTH2 accordingly.
    (a) How many people should we have in order to have a better-than-even chance of a coincidence?   [*Ans.* 28.]
    (b) How many for a better-than-even chance of a multiple coincidence?

4 LISTS AND TABLES

In many applications we wish to work with an entire array of numbers at the same time. For this BASIC provides "lists" and "tables." A list can be used to store a sequence of numbers, while a table contains a two-dimensional array of numbers. We shall see in the next section that lists can also be used as vectors and tables also as matrices, in the sense of Chapter 4, allowing us to carry out matrix operations.

We have had previous arrays of numbers contained in our DATA statement. However, in each case we READ the numbers one or two at a time, and once we made use of them, we could afford to forget them. A list becomes important when the entire array must be remembered. For example, if we wish merely to read a sequence of numbers, multiply each one by 5, and print the results, there is no need to employ a list. However, an application as simple as reading a sequence of numbers and printing them out in the opposite order requires the use of a list. This is shown in the program BACK.

BACK

```
10 FOR I = 1 TO 8
20 READ L(I)
30 NEXT I
40 FOR I = 8 TO 1 STEP -1
50 PRINT L(I);
60 NEXT I
90 DATA 1,3,6,10,15,21,28,36
99 END
READY

RUN

BACK

   36   28   21   15   10   6   3   1

0.066 SEC.
READY
```

BASIC allows one list or table for each letter of the alphabet. For example, if the letter L is used to designate a list, then L(3) will stand for the third element of the list, while L(7) will stand for the seventh element. It would be more common mathematical notation to write these as L_3 and L_7. However, these cannot be typed on the devices one uses to communicate with computers. Lists and tables are nonetheless often referred to as "subscripted variables" because of the more usual mathematical notations for them.

We have found it convenient in earlier chapters of this book to refer to an arbitrary element of a list of numbers by a notation such as L_i. The analog in BASIC is to write the formula L(I). Then as I runs through the numbers $1, 2, \ldots$, the quantity of L(I) will run through the various elements of the list. We take advantage of this possibility in the program BACK as lines 10–30 read the entire list of eight elements. The first time through the loop I equals 1 and therefore on line 20 we read L(1); thus the data element "1" on line 90 becomes the first element of the list. The second time $I = 2$ and therefore we read L(2) and thus the data element "3" becomes the second element of the list. Finally, the data element "36" will become L(8).

To print out the list in reverse order we can again employ a three-instruction loop. We want to print each L(I); however, we want $I = 8, 7, \ldots, 1$. Line 40 shows an additional flexibility of the FOR instruction. One can specify any step size by which the program proceeds. (If no step is specified, the computer assumes that the step size is 1.) In this case we specify STEP $- 1$; thus $I = 8$ the first time, then 7, then 6, etc.

The semicolon (;) on line 50 will assure that the numbers are printed one after the other without any extra space. If instead of a semicolon we had used a comma (,) the numbers would be printed in columns. If we had used no punctuation at the end of the line, each component would have been printed on a new line.

The program DICE computes the probability of winning in the game of craps (see Chapter 3, Section 11). We shall use the list P to store the probabilities for various possible sums when two dice are rolled. For example. P(5) will be the probability of shooting a 5, which we know to be $\frac{4}{36}$. Whenever a list is used in BASIC, space is automatically allocated in the computer for up to ten elements. Similarly for any table, BASIC will allocate for a table of size up to a 10×10. If larger lists and tables are desired, one must specify this through the use of a DIM or dimension statement. Thus in the program DICE we indicate the list P will have 12 elements. In case several different uses are contemplated for the same list, one must specify a DIM large enough to accommodate the longest list.

Lines 20–40 set up the probabilities for rolling a 2 through a 7. We leave to the reader the verification of these formulas. Lines 50 through 70 take advantage of the symmetry of the problem; e.g. the probability of an 8 is the same as the probability of a 6. At the end of this loop all the various probabilities for different totals on a single roll have been computed and the next step is to compute the probability W for winning in the game of craps.

You will recall that if a 7 or 11 turns up on the first roll, we win immediately. This is reflected in line 100. To this probability we must add the probability of "making our point." That is, if the initial roll is 4, 5, 6, 8, 9, or 10, then we must keep rolling until we either repeat that number (in

■ DICE

```
10 DIM P(12)
20 FOR K = 2 TO 7
30 LET P(K) = (K-1)/36
40 NEXT K
50 FOR K = 8 TO 12
60 LET P(K) = P(14-K)
70 NEXT K
100 LET W = P(7) + P(11)
110 FOR K = 4 TO 10
112 IF K=7 THEN 130
115 LET C = P(K)/(P(K)+P(7))
120 LET W = W + P(K)*C
130 NEXT K
170 PRINT W
180 PRINT 244/495
199 END
READY

RUN

DICE

 0.492929
 0.492929

0.076 SEC.
READY
```

which case we win) or until a 7 turns up.

This calculation is carried out in the loop on lines 110–130. Since our "point" may be 4, 5, 6, 8, 9, or 10, we allow the loop to run from 4 to 10. However we must exclude 7 as a possibility and this is the reason for line 112: if K is 7, we jump to the end of the loop—in other words, we eliminate this possibility. Line 115 computes the conditional probability that the number K will be repeated given that we shall get either K or a 7. This is the simplest way of computing the probability of getting a K before we get a 7. On line 120 we add to our previous winning probability the probability that we both have K as our initial point and that we win with it. By the time the loop is completed W will equal the probability of winning at craps. This is printed on line 170. We had calculated this probability in Chapter 3 as $\frac{244}{495}$ and we also print this quantity for comparison. We note from the RUN that the two answers are identical.

Let us now consider the use of tables. If T stands for a table, we must indicate which row and which column in the table we are looking at. Thus T(3,5) will stand for the table entry in row 3 and column 5. As usual the arguments (or subscripts) may be variables. Thus T(I,J) will stand for the entry in row I and column J, which is more usually indicated by T_{ij}. As an illustration we shall recompute one of the tables previously computed in the book. This will be the table of binomial coefficients, usually known as the Pascal triangle. We shall compute the quantities $\binom{N}{J}$ for the values $N = 0, 1, 2, \ldots, 30$ and all possible values of J, namely $J = 0, 1, \ldots, N$. Only two facts are needed to compute the Pascal triangle. One is the fact that $\binom{N}{0} = \binom{N}{N} = 1$. The other is the fact that any entry "inside" the triangle is equal to the sum of the two entries immediately above it.

BINOMC

```
10 DIM B(30,30)
20 FOR N = 0 TO 30
30 LET B(N,0) = 1
40 LET B(N,N) = 1
50 FOR J = 1 TO N-1
60 LET B(N,J) = B(N-1,J-1) + B(N-1,J)
70 NEXT J
80 NEXT N
90
100 PRINT " N"," J","BINOM"
110 FOR K = 1 TO 4
120 READ N,J
130 PRINT N,J,B(N,J)
140 NEXT K
190 DATA 10,5,15,3,25,10,30,15
199 END
READY

RUN

BINOMC
```

N	J	BINOM
10	5	252
15	3	455
25	10	3268760
30	15	1.55118 E+8

```
0.188 SEC.
READY
```

In the program BINOMC, line 10 saves enough space for a 30×30 table. The entry B(N,J) will stand for $\binom{N}{J}$. The entire calculation of the triangle is carried out on lines 20–80. We let N run from 0 through 30. For each given N we first fill in the $\binom{N}{0}$ and $\binom{N}{N}$ on lines 30 and 40. Then we start the loop on J in which J runs from 1 through $N-1$ to compute the "inside" entries. Line 60 simply states that a given entry of B is the sum of two entries on the previous row. Lines 70 and 80 close the two loops.

This is our first example of a "double loop." Such a double loop is legal as long as one loop is completely contained within the other one. The interpretation is very simple: the computer picks a first value for N and then runs through all the indicated values of J; it then picks the next value of N and repeats the procedure; and so on. Note that in this example the

■ BINOMPR

```
10  DIM B(30,30)
20  FOR N = 0 TO 30
30  LET B(N,0) = 1
40  LET B(N,N) = 1
50  FOR J = 1 TO N-1
60  LET B(N,J) = B(N-1,J-1) + B(N-1,J)
70  NEXT J
80  NEXT N
90
100 PRINT " N"," J"," P"," PROB."
110 FOR K = 1 TO 3
120 READ N,J,P
130 PRINT N,J,P,B(N,J)*P↑J*(1-P)↑(N-J)
140 NEXT K
190 DATA 10,5,.3,15,7,.4,30,15,.5
199 END
READY

RUN

BINOMPR
```

N	J	P	PROB.
10	5	0.3	0.102919
15	7	0.4	0.177084
30	15	0.5	0.144464

```
0.185 SEC.
READY
```

range of the second loop depends on the value of **N** in the first loop (see line 50). It is in this way that we fill out a triangle. If we were instead filling out a rectangle or a square, the possible values of **J** would not depend on the value **N**.

Just to show that the calculations are correct, we end up by printing four binomial coefficients. It is worth noting that the entire calculation of nearly 500 binomial coefficients—including some very large ones, as can be seen on the last line of the output—took only about two-tenths of a second. The same calculation by paper and pencil is a formidable task.

Some additional comments are in order. Line 90 is blank. This has no effect on the computations, but it separates the two major portions of the program for easier reading. On line 100 we **PRINT** appropriate labels. It should be noted that since we use commas both here and on line 130, the outputs automatically line up. The loop on lines 110–150 is employed to avoid the "OUT OF DATA" message.

Once we have binomial coefficients computed, they can be used for the solution of many kinds of problems. As an illustration we have included the program **BINOMPR** which computes binomial probabilities. Lines 10–90 are identical with the previous program since these simply compute the Pascal triangle. In the rest of the program we read the value of **N, J, P**, and compute the probability of precisely **J** successes in **N** trials with probability **P** for success on each trial. In line 130 we print **N, J**, and **P** and then compute and print the binomial probability by the well-known formula (see Chapter 3, Section 8). For example, the second line of the output shows that if we have 15 experiments with probability .4 for success on each experiment, then the probability of precisely 7 successes is about .177. (See previous page.)

EXERCISES

Only Exercises 8–12 require the use of a computer.

1. We wish to read **N** numbers from a **DATA** list and perform a task on them. Which of the following tasks require that the numbers be stored in a list?
    (a) Find the largest number.
    (b) Print the even-numbered entries.
    (c) Print first the even-numbered and then the odd-numbered entries.
    (d) Find the sum of the numbers.
    (e) Find the sum of the first and last entries.
    (f) Arrange the numbers in order.   [*Ans.* (c) and (f).]
2. To use the same program for tables of different dimensions, one should read first the dimensions of the table, and then read the table. (Otherwise one does not know how many rows and columns to read.) Write such a program.
3. Write a program that will read a table and compute the row sums.
4. Write a program to read a list of four entries and a list of seven entries

and construct a table T so that T(I,J) is the product of the Ith entry of the first list and Jth entry of the second list.

5. Write a program to read a list and arrange the numbers in increasing order.

6. Modify the program of Exercise 5 to arrange the numbers in decreasing order.

7. Write a program to calculate the probability of winning in the dice game of Chapter 3, Section 11, Exercise 18.

8. Use the program **DICE** to compute the expected value of the game if $1 is bet each time.

9. Use **DICE** to compute the expected value of the game if we win $2 on 7 or 11, lose $3 on 2, 3, or 12, and win or lose $1 for making or failing to make our point.

10. Compute the row sums of the Pascal triangle for N = 0, 1, . . . , 10. Use the binomial theorem to explain the results.

11. For N = 0, 1, . . . , 10 compute the sum of $\binom{N}{J} 2^J$. Use the binomial theorem to explain the results.

12. This is an exercise in modular arithmetic. For I,J = 1, 2, . . . , 6 let T(I,J) be I*J reduced by 7's. That is, if the product is 7 or greater, keep subtracting 7 until the result is less than 7. Print the table. What pattern do you observe?

5 VECTORS AND MATRICES

A natural use of lists and tables is to use them for vectors and matrices and to carry out matrix operations with them. BASIC recognizes this use by having a special set of instructions that enable one to carry out the matrix operation in a single step. We shall illustrate this by writing two programs for the addition of vectors, one not using the special instructions and one using them.

In the program VECADD the calculations are accomplished in four triples of instructions (loops). The first three instructions read a seven-component vector A, the second triple reads a similar vector B, and the third triple of instructions computes the vector sum letting the vector C stand for the answer. Finally, lines 100–120 print the answer.

▰▰ VECADD

```
10 FOR I = 1 TO 7
20 READ A(I)
30 NEXT I
40 FOR I = 1 TO 7
50 READ B(I)
60 NEXT I
70 FOR I = 1 TO 7
```

```
80 LET C(I) = A(I) + B(I)
90 NEXT I
100 FOR I = 1 TO 7
110 PRINT C(I);
120 NEXT I
190 DATA 1,2,3,4,5,6,7
191 DATA 5,8,2,0,-1,-3,-7
199 END
READY

RUN

VECADD

 6  10  5  4  4  3  0

0.083 SEC.
READY
```

In the program VECADD2 we have replaced each triple of instructions (each loop) by a single special instruction. One signals to BASIC that an instruction is a special matrix instruction by starting with "MAT." The first two instructions each read a seven-component vector, the third instruction carries out the vector addition, and the fourth instruction prints the vector.

█ VECADD2

```
10 MAT READ A(7)
40 MAT READ B(7)
70 MAT C = A + B
100 MAT PRINT C;
190 DATA 1,2,3,4,5,6,7
191 DATA 5,8,2,0,-1,-3,-7
199 END
READY

RUN

VECADD2


 6  10  5  4  4  3  0

0.076 SEC.
READY
```

The comparison of the two programs will show exactly what the MAT instructions accomplish. Clearly the second program is simpler and shorter. The saving is even greater when we are dealing with a matrix or if we want to do more complicated matrix operations.

The next program, MATSUB, is similar to VECADD2 except that we are dealing with matrices and we perform a subtraction of two matrices. We have arranged the data for the two 3×4 matrices A and B on lines 50-52 and 60-62, respectively. This was done purely for the convenience of the

■ MATSUB

```
10 MAT READ A(3,4)
20 MAT READ B(3,4)
30 MAT C = A - B
40 MAT PRINT C;
49
50 DATA 1,2,3,4
51 DATA 5,6,7,8
52 DATA 7,6,5,4
59
60 DATA 4,3,2,1
61 DATA 0,-1,-2,-3
62 DATA -2,-3,-2,-1
69
99 END
READY

RUN

MATSUB


-3  -1   1   3
 5   7   9  11
 9   9   7   5

0.084 SEC.
READY
```

reader, so that he may easily check the computed answer. One could have listed the data all on one line, or divided it among several lines in an arbitrary way, as long as the data appeared in the order in which the program calls for it. However, it is usually good practice to arrange the data in a neat format for easier proofreading.

The next program, MATMPY, carries out a matrix multiplication. It reads a 3 × 4 matrix A and a 4 × 2 matrix B and computes the product, a 3 × 2 matrix C = AB. The program MATMPY should be self-explanatory.

■ MATMPY

```
10 MAT READ A(3,4)
20 MAT READ B(4,2)
30 MAT C = A*B
40 MAT PRINT C;
49
50 DATA 1,2,3,4
51 DATA 5,6,7,8
52 DATA 7,6,5,4
59
60 DATA 2,1
61 DATA 3,2
62 DATA -1,0
63 DATA -3,-4
69
99 END
READY

RUN

MATMPY


-7 -11
-3 -15
 15  3


0.079 SEC.
READY
```

The single most powerful instruction in BASIC is the one-line command that inverts a matrix. This is illustrated on line 20 of the program MATINV. Line 10 reads a 3 × 3 matrix A. In line 20 we let $B = A^{-1}$. We then PRINT the inverse. The data in the program is taken from Example 2, Section 6 or Chapter 4. Naturally, we obtain the same result as in that section.

Since matrix inversion is available, it provides a convenient method of solving N equations in N unknowns. We know that we can write equations in the form AX = B. Here A contains the $n \times n$ matrix of coefficients of the left-hand sides of the equations while B is a vector containing the right-hand sides of the equations. The vector X contains the unknowns. If the matrix A has an inverse, then the solution may be written in the form $X = A^{-1}B$. This is carried out in the program EQU. To make the program

■ MATINV

```
10 MAT READ A(3,3)
20 MAT B = INV(A)
30 MAT PRINT B;
39
40 DATA 1,4,3
41 DATA 2,5,4
42 DATA 1,-3,-2
49
99 END
READY

RUN

MATINV


  2.  -1.   1.
  8.  -5.   2.
-11.   7.  -3.

0.082 SEC.
READY
```

more general, we first read the value of N. This will enable us to solve
different numbers of equations in different numbers of unknowns by simply
changing the data. We then read the matrix A and the vector B, compute
the inverse of A, and compute the solution X on line 50. The answers are
printed on line 60. The reader can easily verify that the solution is correct.

■ EQU

```
10 READ N
20 MAT READ A(N,N)
30 MAT READ B(N)
40 MAT I = INV(A)
50 MAT X = I*B
60 MAT PRINT X;
69
70 DATA 4
79
80 DATA 4,2,6,8
81 DATA 1,2,3,4
82 DATA 4,3,2,1
```

```
83 DATA 8,6,2,4
89
90 DATA -12,-5,5,12
99 END
READY

RUN

EQU


 1   2.  -2.  -1.

0.087 SEC.
READY
```

If the reader has ever attempted to solve four equations in four unknowns, he will be happy to see that the same solution may be obtained on a computer in a small fraction of a second. Indeed, the same program will yield the solution of 50 equations in 50 unknowns in roughly 6 seconds! Although we illustrate programming techniques in terms of very simple examples, it is important to remember that the same techniques work on problems much too large to do by hand and often take only a few seconds to do on the computer.

One word of warning is in order for the last two programs. Not all matrices have inverses, and therefore one should really insert in the program a test as to whether the matrix does have an inverse. Such a test exists in BASIC but it is beyond the scope of our present treatment.

EXERCISES

Only Exercises 8–12 require the use of a computer.

1. Write a program that will add two matrices without using MAT instructions.
2. Write a program that will compute the tenth power of a square matrix P.
3. In BASIC, a vector of all 1's, say of five components, may be constructed by means of the instruction

$$MAT \ X = CON(5).$$

Write a program to read a 7×5 matrix A and compute AX (where X is the vector of all 1's). Interpret AX.
4. In BASIC a vector or a matrix may be multiplied by a number as follows:

$$MAT \ Y = (5.2)*X.$$

Then $Y = 5.2X$. Write a program to read two five-component vectors X and Y and to compute

(a) 3Y.

(b) $X + 2Y$.

(c) $5.2X - 3.17Y$.

5. Write a program that will read two 3×4 matrices A and B and compute

(a) $A - 3B$.

(b) $5.07A + 7.98B$.

6. Write a program that will read a 3×3 matrix A, compute its inverse A^{-1}, and compute the product AA^{-1}.

7. Write a program that will check for two 4×4 matrices A and B whether $AB = BA$. It should print "YES" if they are equal.

8. Set up DATA for a 3×4 matrix A, a 4×2 matrix B, and a 2×3 matrix C. Compute:

(a) ABC.

(b) BCA.

(c) CAB.

(d) BAC.

9. Set up DATA for a 10×10 matrix all of whose components are zeroes or ones. Attempt to invert it. [*Hint:* Make sure that no row and no column consists entirely of zeroes.]

10. Use the computer to verify that $(AB)^{-1} = B^{-1}A^1$.

11. RUN the program of Exercise 6. How close is the final matrix to an identity matrix? (In general one expects some round-off errors.)

12. Try the program of Exercise 7 for several examples. Can you find examples where $AB = BA$?

6 APPLICATIONS TO MARKOV CHAINS

Let us illustrate the first theorem of Chapter 4, Section 7. It states that if P is a regular transition matrix, its powers approach a matrix whose rows are identical, each row being a probability vector with positive components. This can be illustrated by taking such a transition matrix and raising it to higher and higher powers. To speed up the process we shall square the matrix each time, so that we shall compute the powers P^2, P^4, P^8, P^{16}, and P^{32}.

In the program OZ we have chosen Exercise 12 in Section 7 of Chapter 4, dealing with the weather in the Land of Oz. We have arranged the transition matrix so that the first row corresponds to "nice," the next to "rain," and the final row to "snow." We first read the 3×3 transition matrix. Then in the loop in lines 15–50 we square this matrix five times. Line 20 carries out the actual squaring and line 30 prints the new matrix. On line 40 we let S take the place of P so that when we go through the loop again it is the new matrix that is squared.

Looking at the output we have a dramatic demonstration of the funda-

■ OZ

```
10 MAT READ P(3,3)
15 FOR T = 1 TO 5
20 MAT S = P*P
30 MAT PRINT S;
40 MAT P = S
50 NEXT T
90 DATA 0,.5,.5
91 DATA .25,.5,.25
92 DATA .25,.25,.5
99 END
READY

RUN

OZ


 0.25   0.375   0.375
 0.1875   0.4375   0.375
 0.1875   0.375   0.4375

 0.203125   0.398437   0.398437
 0.199219   0.402344   0.398437
 0.199219   0.398437   0.402344

 0.200012   0.399994   0.399994
 0.199997   0.400009   0.399994
 0.199997   0.399994   0.400009

 0.2   0.4   0.4
 0.2   0.4   0.4
 0.2   0.4   0.4

 0.2   0.4   0.4
 0.2   0.4   0.4
 0.2   0.4   0.4

0.139 SEC.
READY
```

mental theorem. By the third squaring—that is, when we look at P^8—the rows of the matrix are almost identical and have nearly assumed their limiting values. In the next two printed matrices, P^{16} and P^{32}, we see that, to the accuracy to which results are printed, we have the limiting probabilities of .2 for nice, .4 for rain, and .4 for snow.

We shall next turn to absorbing Markov chains as treated in Chapter 4, Section 8. We shall show how easy it is to compute the basic quantities N, T, and B on a computer.

In order to specify an absorbing chain, we need to know the number of transient states* (K) and the number of absorbing states (L). We need also to specify the two submatrices R and Q. This is accomplished in lines 10 and 20 of the program TRANS and in the DATA statements. The computation and printing of all the other quantities is accomplished in lines 30–90. Lines 30 and 40 illustrate two additional MAT commands. We can set up an identity matrix of specified size and a constant vector (vector of all 1's) in single instructions. We then let $D = I - Q$ and compute the inverse $N = (I - Q)^{-1}$. Similarly, we compute T and B. We have thus translated the three main theorems on absorbing chains into six instructions in BASIC. Finally, on line 90 we print the matrices N, T, and B. The data used in TRANS is taken from Example 1 of Section 8 in Chapter 4. The output may be compared with that example.

Of course, this is too small an example to make it worth using a computer.

*Nonabsorbing states are commonly called *transient* states.

■■■■   TRANS

```
10  READ K,L
20  MAT READ R(K,L),Q(K,K)
25
30  MAT I = IDN(K,K)
40  MAT C = CON(K)
50  MAT D = I-Q
60  MAT N = INV(D)
70  MAT T = N*C
80  MAT B = N*R
90  MAT PRINT N,T,B
95
100 DATA 3,2
105
110 DATA .5,0
111 DATA 0,0
112 DATA 0,.5
115
120 DATA 0,.5,0
121 DATA .5,0,.5
122 DATA 0,.5,0
125
199 END
READY

RUN
```

TRANS

1.5	1	0.5
1	2	1
0.5	1	1.5

3	4	3

0.75	0.25
0.5	0.5
0.25	0.75

0.116 SEC.
READY

Therefore we change the data to run a more substantial example. Our large example will be a random walk with ten transient states and with probability .7 of taking a step to the right. This chain is symbolically indicated in Figure 3. To find the fundamental matrix for this chain we have to invert a 10×10 matrix, and therefore we have a more substantial challenge for the computer. It is important to note that the main part of the program does not have to be changed at all. The only changes needed are in the DATA statements. (If there were more than ten transient states, one would also have to insert a DIM statement.) We also elected to omit the printing of the matrix N, since it is very large and not particularly interesting.

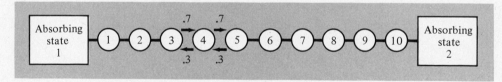

Figure 3

We show the new data statements and the run of the program TRANS2. Looking first at the second half of the output, the matrix B, we note that for most of the states we are almost certain to end up in the second absorbing state (i.e., at the right-hand end). It is surprising that even if one starts in transient state 1, way over on the left, one has a better-than-even chance of ending up on the right. The vector T, containing the expected number of steps before being absorbed, is also quite interesting. If we start near the right-hand endpoint, absorption takes place very fast, as may be expected. However, the result is not obvious on the left-hand side. For example, if one starts in transient state 1, there is probability .3 of being absorbed in a single step. On the other hand, it is more likely that absorption will take place at the right-hand endpoint, which will take a considerable

```
100  DATA  10,2
110  DATA  .3,0
111  DATA  0,0
112  DATA  0,0
113  DATA  0,0
114  DATA  0,0
115  DATA  0,0
116  DATA  0,0
117  DATA  0,0
118  DATA  0,0
119  DATA  0,.7
120  DATA  0,.7,0,0,0,0,0,0,0,0
121  DATA  .3,0,.7,0,0,0,0,0,0,0
122  DATA  0,.3,0,.7,0,0,0,0,0,0
123  DATA  0,0,.3,0,.7,0,0,0,0,0
124  DATA  0,0,0,.3,0,.7,0,0,0,0
125  DATA  0,0,0,0,.3,0,.7,0,0,0
126  DATA  0,0,0,0,0,.3,0,.7,0,0
127  DATA  0,0,0,0,0,0,.3,0,.7,0
128  DATA  0,0,0,0,0,0,0,.3,0,.7
129  DATA  0,0,0,0,0,0,0,0,.3,0
199  END

READY

RUN
```

TRANS2

```
13.22   17.45   17.84   16.57   14.60
12.33    9.93    7.47    4.99    2.50

0.4285    0.5715
0.1836    0.8164
0.0786    0.9214
0.0336    0.9664
0.0144    0.9856
0.0061    0.9939
0.0026    0.9974
0.0010    0.9990
0.0004    0.9996
0.0001    0.9999

0.288 SEC.
READY
```

amount of time. We find that the longest time to absorption, 17.84 steps, is from transient state 3.

For our final application in this section we consider a "Markov chain game." Any absorbing Markov chain can be turned into a game as follows. First assign a "value" to each absorbing state. A positive value may be interpreted as a prize one wins if one reaches this state while a negative value is a penalty to be paid if that state is reached. A player starts at a given transient state and moves from state to state in accordance with the transition probabilities of the Markov chain until an absorbing state is reached, where he receives a payoff or pays a penalty. The interesting question is what the expected payoff is for various different possible starting transient states. If the values are collected into a vector V with as many components as there are absorbing states, then it is very easy to see that the expected payoff for different starting states is given by the vector BV.

As an illustration we shall consider a game based on a two-dimensional random walk as shown in Figure 4. There are ten transient states. From

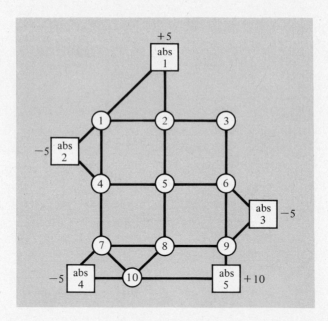

Figure 4

each of these the player moves to any of the states to which it is connected with equal probabilities. Thus from state 4 there is probability $\frac{1}{4}$ of moving to states 1, 5, or 7 or to absorbing state 2. There are five absorbing states, and one receives a prize of $5 at the first one and $10 at the last one and loses $5 at the other three absorbing states. The payoffs balance out, but it is intuitively clear that it is advantageous to start at some states and disadvantageous to start at others. However, if one is offered the chance to play this game with state 5 as the starting state, should one accept?

To solve this problem we have modified the program **TRANS** by changing the data and by adding three additional lines. Line 25 will read the vector V from the data in line 130. And line 81 computes the payoff vector P as B∗V. Also, we print only the vector P. When we run the resulting program TRANS3 we find that there are some favorable starting states—notably state 2, where the expected payoff is $1.08—and some highly unfavorable states, the worst being state 4, where the expected loss is $1.78. We find

```
25 MAT READ V(L)

81 MAT P = B*V

100 DATA 10,5
110 DATA .25,.25,0,0,0
111 DATA .25,0,0,0,0
112 DATA 0,0,0,0,0
113 DATA 0,.25,0,0,0
114 DATA 0,0,0,0,0
115 DATA 0,0,.25,0,0
116 DATA 0,0,0,.25,0
117 DATA 0,0,0,0,0
118 DATA 0,0,.25,0,.25
119 DATA 0,0,0,.25,.25
120 DATA 0,.25,0,.25,0,0,0,0,0,0
121 DATA .25,0,.25,0,.25,0,0,0,0,0
122 DATA 0,.5,0,0,0,.5,0,0,0,0
123 DATA .25,0,0,0,.25,0,.25,0,0,0
124 DATA 0,.25,0,.25,0,.25,0,.25,0,0
125 DATA 0,0,.25,0,.25,0,0,0,.25,0
126 DATA 0,0,0,.25,0,0,0,.25,0,.25
127 DATA 0,0,0,0,.25,0,.25,0,.25,.25
128 DATA 0,0,0,0,0,.25,0,.25,0,0
129 DATA 0,0,0,0,0,0,.25,.25,0,0
130 DATA +5,-5,-5,-5,+10

READY

RUN

TRANS3

-0.17   +1.08   -0.02   -1.78   -0.46
-1.13   -1.48   -0.03   +0.96   +0.87

0.292 SEC.
READY
```

that in state 5 one almost but not quite breaks even. There is an overall expected loss of 46 cents; thus one should *not* agree to play the game starting at state 5.

Although we gave this application an interpretation as a game, there are many other interpretations of a Markov chain game. There are processes in nature that are described by absorbing Markov chains where one can in a natural way assign a "value" to ending up at a given terminal. Here the expected payoff has a natural interpretation. There is also a method for computing voltages in a simple electric circuit using this technique. (See *Finite Mathematics with Business Applications*.) In recent years Markov chains have acquired considerable importance in applications to many sciences. It is therefore interesting to see how easy it is to compute fundamental quantities for Markov chains by means of a high-speed computer.

EXERCISES

Only Exercises 5–12 require the use of a computer.

1. Vectors in BASIC are column vectors, but a matrix of one row may be used as a row vector. Write a program to read a row vector and a column vector, of four components each, and to compute their product.

2. If **A** is probability row vector, and if it is repeatedly multiplied on the right by a regular transition matrix **P**, it will approach the fixed vector. (See Chapter 4, Section 7.) Write a program to carry out this process.

3. For a transient chain, N may be computed as the sum of the infinite series

$$N = I + Q + Q^2 + Q^3 + \ldots .$$

   Write a program to compute the first 21 terms of this series.

4. Write a program which, for an absorbing Markov chain, will compute Q and R from N and B. [*Hint:* Compute N^{-1}.]

5. Compute powers of the transition matrix

$$P = \begin{pmatrix} .1 & .2 & .3 & .4 \\ .4 & .3 & .2 & .1 \\ .3 & .1 & .4 & .2 \\ .2 & .4 & .1 & .3 \end{pmatrix}$$

   to find the fixed vector.

6. Compute powers of the transition matrix

$$P = \begin{pmatrix} 0 & .3 & 0 & .7 \\ .5 & 0 & .5 & 0 \\ 0 & .6 & 0 & .4 \\ .2 & 0 & .8 & 0 \end{pmatrix}$$

   and explain the result.

7. Let h be an arbitrary column vector of three components. Multiply it repeatedly by the OZ transition matrix and observe that it tends to a constant vector. Interpret the constant.

8. Try out the program of Exercise 2 for the Land of Oz.

9. RUN the program of Exercise 4 to verify that it produces Q and R correctly.

10. Apply the program TRANS to Exercise 6 of Chapter 4, Section 8.

11. Modify the program TRANS to verify the identity $QB = B - R$.

12. Design your own Markov chain game and compute the expected values for various starting positions.

7   LINEAR EQUATIONS

The purpose of this section is to translate the flow diagram of Figure 5 in Section 5 of Chapter 4 for the solution of linear equations into a computer program. We shall first do this in a straightforward manner and show that the program reproduces the results of Chapter 4, Section 5. However, we shall then note that the program is inadequate; this will give us an opportunity to consider one of the deeper problems of computer programming— namely, the question of numerical accuracy. We shall assume that there is no variable all of whose coefficients are 0.

The program LINEQU is designed to follow Figure 5 (Chapter 4). Boxes 1–6 correspond to blocks of instructions starting at lines 100, 200, 300, 400, 500, and 600. Box 7 is combined with box 2, and box 8 with box 5. For easy identification each block of instructions starts with a REM (or "remark") statement. Such a REM statement is for the convenience of the programmer and is ignored by the computer. LINEQU is designed to solve M equations in N unknowns. We start by saving space for our list and table, reading M and N, and then reading the tableau T of coefficients. It should be noted that T has N + 1 columns since it contains not only the coefficients of the left-hand side of the equations but also the numbers on the right-hand side.

In the remainder of the program I and J will be the subscripts corresponding to the pivot. The auxiliary variables I1 and J1 are used as running subscripts for rows and columns. The process consists of choosing a pivot in each row and operating with it; this loop starts at line 100 and ends at line 500. Lines 200–220 search for a nonzero element in row I. If such an element is found, we jump to line 300. It should be noted that as we jump out of the loop of lines 200–220, the subscript J is correctly set for the pivot. If we complete the entire loop, then the left-hand side of the equation is zero. In line 230 we check whether the right-hand side is also zero. If it is not, we jump to line 900 and type out "THERE IS NO SOLUTION."

At line 300 we note what the pivot is. We also put into the list P the subscript of the variable we pivoted on. This will make it much easier to identify the solution of the problem. It should be noted that if the equation was identically equal to zero, and hence could be ignored, then at line 240

■   LINEQU

```
5   DIM T(20,21),P(20)
10  READ M,N
20  MAT READ T(M,N+1)
29
100 REM   START MAIN LOOP
110 FOR I = 1 TO M
120
200 REM   FIND PIVOT
205 FOR J = 1 TO N
210 IF T(I,J) <> 0 THEN 300
220 NEXT J
230 IF T(I,N+1) <> 0 THEN 900
240 LET P(I) = 0
250 GOTO 500
260
300 REM   DIVIDE BY PIVOT
302 LET P = T(I,J)
305 LET P(I) = J
310 FOR J1 = 1 TO N+1
320 LET T(I,J1) = T(I,J1)/P
330 NEXT J1
340
400 REM   SUBTRACT MULTIPLES OF ROW
405 FOR I1 = 1 TO M
410 IF I1 = I THEN 460
420 LET C = T(I1,J)
430 FOR J1 = 1 TO N+1
440 LET T(I1,J1) = T(I1,J1) - C*T(I,J1)
450 NEXT J1
460 NEXT I1
470
500 REM   CLOSE MAIN LOOP
510 NEXT I
520
600 REM   PRINT ANSWERS
605 FOR I = 1 TO M
610 LET P = P(I)
620 IF P = 0 THEN 790
625 LET B = T(I,N+1)
630 PRINT "X";STR$(P);" = ";STR$(B);
640 FOR J = 1 TO N
645 IF J = P THEN 690
650 LET C = T(I,J)
660 IF C = 0 THEN 690
```

```
665 IF C<Ø THEN 680
670 PRINT " - ";
675 GOTO 687
680 LET C = -C
685 PRINT " + ";
687 PRINT STR$(C);"*";"X";STR$(J);
690 NEXT J
700 PRINT
790 NEXT I
800 GOTO 999
900 PRINT "THERE IS NO SOLUTION."
905

910 DATA 3,3
920 DATA 1,4,3,1
921 DATA 2,5,4,4
922 DATA 1,-3,-2,5
999 END

READY

RUN

LINEQU

X1 = 3.
X2 = -2.
X3 = 2.

Ø.166 SEC.
READY
```

we entered a zero into the list of pivots. Lines 310–330 complete this particular box of the flow diagram by dividing all coefficients in this row of the tableau by the pivot P.

We must now subtract suitable multiples of the pivotal row from the other rows. This is accomplished in lines 400–460. The subscript I1 will run through all the rows; however, on line 410 we make sure that we skip over the pivotal row. C is equated to the appropriate multiplier and the subtraction is carried out in the loop in lines 430–450. When this double loop is completed, on line 500 we go on to the next row. It should be noted that the entire heart of the program is contained in lines 100–500, a total of only 20 instructions in BASIC.

The answers are printed in the loop of lines 600–790. This piece of code could be much simpler except for two complications: First, we want to have a nice format for the answer. Second, we want to handle not only the case of a unique solution but find all possible solutions in case there are infinitely many of them. To obtain a nice-looking form for the answers, we need to introduce an additional feature of BASIC. (It should be noted that there are many other advanced features of BASIC not covered in this book.) When BASIC prints the numerical value of a variable, it either starts with a minus sign or a blank and places a blank after the number. This is very convenient when we simply want to print a list of numbers one after the other. However, it spoils the output when we want to print, for example, "X5." But writing the string command "STR$(P)" will print a numerical value of P without initial or trailing blanks. (This command is not available in all versions of BASIC.)

If the solution were always unique, the output would be accomplished by the six instructions in lines 600–630 and 790. We look at each equation once, and look up in the list of pivots what the subscript P of the pivot was. If this is 0, then the equation is identically 0 and therefore can be ignored. Otherwise B is the value of the variable and, on line 630, we print out an answer that may look like "X5 = 3.2." Here is where we see the advantage of having remembered the element we pivoted on. Its coefficient ends up being 1, and hence the right-hand side of the equation is its value.

The loop in lines 640–690 handles the case of infinitely many solutions. If the solution is not unique, then variables other than the pivot are left over with nonzero coefficients. These variables may be given arbitrary values. We usually indicate this by "bringing the variable to the right-hand side." Thus we search in the loop to see whether any variable other than the pivot has a nonzero coefficient. If it does, we print it with a suitable coefficient after the value we have already printed on the right-hand side. It should be noted that we had to test on line 665 whether the coefficient was positive or negative and the two cases are treated separately. It is left as an exercise for the reader to step through this part of the program by hand.

```
920 DATA 1,-2,-3,2
921 DATA 1,-4,-13,14
922 DATA -3,5,4,0

READY

RUN

LINEQU2

X1 = -10 - 7*X3
X2 = -6 - 5*X3

0.153 SEC.
READY
```

The data in LINEQU is taken from Example 1 in Section 5 of Chapter 4. The printed answer agrees with the answer found earlier.

To show that the program also works in the case of infinitely many solutions or no solutions, we change the data to those of Examples 2 and 3 (of Section 5 in Chapter 4) respectively. These are shown in LINEQU2 and LINEQU3. It should be noted that the output format for the case of infinitely many solutions is very easily readable. It shows that X3 may take on any value and it indicates what the corresponding values of X1 and X2 must be.

```
922 DATA -3,5,4,2

READY

RUN

██████  LINEQU3

THERE IS NO SOLUTION.

0.167 SEC.
READY
```

Next we try out the program with a larger data base. In LINEQU4 we have four equations in five unknowns. The result seems reasonable; indeed,

```
910 DATA 4,5
920 DATA 3,2,1,2,3,11
921 DATA -1,-1,-2,1,1,-6
922 DATA 1,2,3,4,5,3
923 DATA 2,2,0,8,10,2

READY

RUN

██████  LINEQU4

X1 =  4.5 + 3.5*X4
X2 = -1. - 7.5*X4
X3 =  1 + 2.5*X4
X5 = -0.5

0.179 SEC.
READY
```

if we check it all the indicated solutions are correct. However, a more careful check will show that we have failed to find all the solutions! We have run into one of the subtleties of computer programming: a program that to all appearances is correct produces incorrect results. The problem is one of round-off errors. When this happens, one must do troubleshooting on the computer program, or as it is commonly phrased, one must "debug" it. A very useful procedure is to ask the computer to print out not just the final solution but also the intermediate steps. This may be accomplished by replacing line 500 by:

500   MAT PRINT T;

With this change the tableau will be printed after each iteration. A look at the output would indicate that something went wrong between the third and fourth iterations. The last line in the third iteration would appear as follows:

$$2 \times 10^{-7} \times X5 = -1 \times 10^{-7}.$$

From this the computer concludes that X5 equals -0.5. However, the very small numbers appearing in this equation represent round-off errors and should actually be zero. The reason for round-off errors is the fact that a computer can only carry a fraction to a limited number of decimal places (usually six to nine). Furthermore, it works with a number system to base 2. Whether a rounding is necessary depends on the base. Therefore one must anticipate that in hand calculations where no round-off error appears, one may appear on the computer, or vice versa. In this particular case this very minute round-off error changes the whole nature of the solution. The equation should actually be $0 = 0$, and therefore X5 should be available as a variable whose value may be chosen arbitrarily. Therefore, due to a minute error, we lost infinitely many available solutions.

The lesson that we learn is that if a variable's value was computed through complicated calculation, we cannot assume that a 0 will come out to be exactly 0. This forces us to modify lines 210, 230, and 660. We shall assume that any sufficiently small number is produced by a round-off error and should really be a 0. Of course, the question is just what does "sufficiently small" mean? This is a deep and difficult question, and there is no universally satisfactory answer to it. For any proposed solution to this problem one can find a set of equations for which the program will produce the wrong results. We shall, however, show one quite common solution to this dilemma that will handle "normal" cases. Our assumption will be that any coefficient that turns out to be less than 10^{-6} is a round-off error and should be 0.

Thus on line 660 instead of asking whether the coefficient C is equal to 0, we shall ask whether its absolute value is less than 10^{-6}. In BASIC one computes the absolute value of C by writing "ABS(C)." The corresponding corrections must also be made on line 210 and line 230. We show these corrections and the corrected run in LINEQU5. This time we have found all the solutions to the problem.

```
210 IF ABS(T(I,J)) > 1E-6 THEN 300

230 IF ABS(T(I,N+1)) > 1E-6 THEN 900

660 IF ABS(C) < 1E-6 THEN 690

READY

RUN
```

LINEQU5

```
X1 = 6.5 + 3.5*X4 + 4.*X5
X2 = -5.5 - 7.5*X4 - 9.*X5
X3 = 2.5 + 2.5*X4 + 3.*X5

0.202 SEC.
READY
```

The resulting program is of quite general use in solving linear equations. The exercises will show modifications of this program that may be used for other purposes—e.g., inverting a matrix. We again see that a relatively short BASIC program, and surprisingly short computing times, can solve important practical problems.

This section has also given the reader a first taste of the complex field of finding numerical solutions to mathematical problems. This field is known as *numerical analysis*. It treats the wide variety of difficulties one runs into in finding numerical solutions, and also searches for the most efficient numerical methods of solving a variety of problems.

EXERCISES

Only Exercises 4–10 require the use of a computer.

1. Modify the program LINEQU5 to solve simultaneously two sets of equations with identical left sides but different right sides.
2. If the coefficients of the left side of a set of equations form an $n \times n$ matrix A, and if one successfully pivots on every row (no left side becomes identically zero), then A^{-1} exists. This is true irrespective of the right side of the equation. Modify LINEQU5 to serve as a test of whether a given square matrix has an inverse.
3. Write a program to invert a square matrix using the method of Section 6 in Chapter 4.
4. Use LINEQU5 to solve the equations of Exercise 5 in Section 5 of Chapter 4.

5. Use **LINEQU5** to solve the following equations:

$$4X_1 - 3X_2 + 2X_3 - X_4 + 5X_5 = -10$$
$$X_1 - 2X_2 + 3X_3 + X_4 - X_5 = 12$$
$$2X_1 + X_2 - X_3 + 2X_4 + 5X_5 = -1$$
$$3X_1 - 2X_2 + X_3 - X_4 + 2X_5 = -6$$
$$2X_1 - X_2 + 2X_3 - X_4 + X_5 = 0.$$

[*Ans.* $1, 2, 3, 4, -2$.]

6. Use **LINEQU5** on Exercise 12 of Section 5 in Chapter 4 for several values of k. Check the answer there given.

7. **RUN** the program of Exercise 1 using the **DATA** of **LINEQU2** and **LINEQU3**.

8. Apply the program of Exercise 2 to the matrices in Exercise 3 of Section 6 in Chapter 4.

9. Apply the program of Exercise 3 to the matrices in Exercise 1 of Section 6 in Chapter 4.

10. Use the program of Exercise 3 to invert the following matrix:

$$A = \begin{pmatrix} .9 & -.1 & -.2 & -.3 & -.1 \\ -.2 & .8 & -.1 & 0 & -.2 \\ -.2 & -.2 & .7 & -.1 & -.1 \\ -.1 & 0 & -.2 & .8 & -.3 \\ -.1 & -.3 & -.2 & -.1 & .9 \end{pmatrix}.$$

SUGGESTED READING

Barrodale, Ian, et al. *Elementary Computer Applications.* New York: John Wiley, 1971.

Gross, Jonathan L., and Brainerd, Walter S. *Fundamental Programming Concepts.* New York: Harper and Row, 1972.

Kemeny, John G., A. S. Schleifer, Jr., J. Laurie Snell, and Gerald L. Thompson. *Finite Mathematics with Business Applications.* 2nd ed. Englewood Cliffs, N.J.: Prentice-Hall, 1972.

Kemeny, John G., and Kurtz, Thomas E. *Basic Programming.* 2nd ed. New York: John Wiley, 1972.

Statistics

6

1 INTRODUCTION

In the study of probability theory, we assign a probability measure to the possible outcomes of an experiment. We then make probability predictions relating to the experiment. For example, a coin is tossed ten times. We assign an equal weight to all possible sequences of heads and tails. We then compute the probability that exactly six heads turn up. We find that this probability is $\binom{10}{6} \cdot (\frac{1}{2})^{10} = .205$. Statistics deals with the inverse problem. We do not know the basic probability measure, but we are able to carry out certain chance experiments, from which we obtain information about the underlying measure.

As an example, assume that in a large population each person holds an opinion on the question of legalizing marijuana. They either favor this or are opposed. We choose at random 20 people and ask them their opinions. Choosing "at random" means that we have an equal chance of obtaining any group of 20 people from the entire population. If the size of the population is large, the effect of knowing certain of the opinions will not significantly change the chance that the next person sampled will say "yes." Thus it is reasonable to assume that the underlying chance model is an independent trials model with probability p for success (answer "yes") on each trial, where p is the proportion in the entire population that favor legalizing marijuana.

On the basis of the sample we would like to estimate p. The intuitive estimate for the parameter p would be simply the fraction $\bar{p}$ of persons in the sample that say "yes." In Figure 1 we show the result of drawing ten samples of 20 each in a case where $p = .4$. While our estimates are in general near the true value .4, our worst estimate is .2, only half the true value.

Experiment number	Number of "yes" answers	Fraction $\bar{p}$
1	6	.3
2	8	.4
3	9	.45
4	4	.2
5	7	.35
6	6	.3
7	6	.3
8	9	.45
9	5	.25
10	7	.35

Figure 1

From the binomial measure (see Chapter 3, Section 8) we can calculate the exact probability that the observed fraction $\bar{p}$ will lie in a given range. For example, the values of $f(20, x; .4)$ for x between 6 and 10 add up to .747. Thus with probability .747 our estimate will be between .3 and .5.

We recall from our study of independent trials that the expected number of successes in a sample of size n is np and the standard deviation for the number of successes is $\sqrt{npq}$ (see Chapter 3, Section 9). Further, the probability of a deviation of more than 3 standard deviations from the expected number is very unlikely (.001). Thus if we increase the sample size to 2400 the expected number of "yes" responses would be 960 and the standard deviation $\sqrt{2400 \times .4 \times .6} = 24$. Thus our estimate would with high probability lie between $\frac{960 - 72}{2400} = .37$ and $\frac{960 + 72}{2400} = .43$, in the interval [.37, .43].

This suggests that when p is unknown we should try to estimate from the sample an interval within which we believe the true p lies. We shall show in Section 4 that this can indeed be done.

In some situations we need to make a choice between two estimates for p. For example, the incidence of colds may be known and we wish to test the claim that this can be decreased if people take large doses of vitamin C. Thus we have to determine whether the incidence of colds among those taking vitamin C is the same as for the whole population or a smaller value. Or a manufacturer may assume that his production process is operating correctly if it produces no more than 1 percent defective items but is not operating correctly if it produces as many as 5 percent defective items. He is interested in devising a test to see if the system is operating correctly.

Perhaps the largest statistical test ever conducted was the test designed in the early '50s to see if the vaccine developed by Jonas Salk would effectively cut down the incidence of polio. The average incidence of polio at that time was about 50 per 100,000 persons. It was not expected that the vaccine would be 100 percent effective, but it was hoped that it would cut down the incidence of polio by at least 50 percent. Thus we can view the experiment as a test of the hypothesis that a person vaccinated will have a significantly lower probability of being afflicted with polio than a person not vaccinated. This type of hypothesis testing will be studied in Section 3.

In applying probability models, predictions from the model are only reliable if the assumptions made in describing the model are reasonably met. Similarly, our statistical inferences are based upon certain assumptions. We have already mentioned the assumption of randomness in a sample. There are many pitfalls that one can fall into if care is not taken. Perhaps the most famous example of this is the celebrated prediction of the *Literary Digest* that Alfred Landon would defeat Franklin Roosevelt in the 1936 presidential election. In this poll the sample was chosen from names obtained from telephone books and car registrations. In 1936 this was not at all a "random sample" and the prediction was badly in error. Opinion polls are still trying to recover from this blunder. We shall discuss this and other pitfalls in more detail in Section 5.

Before we continue our discussion of statistics we shall need one important result from probability theory called the central limit theorem. This will be studied in the next section.

For use in the exercises and in later sections we show the probabilities for ten independent trials and various values of p in Figure 2.

Table of values of $f(10, x; p)$

x	0.1	0.25	0.4	0.5	0.6	0.75	0.9
0	0.349	0.056	0.006	0.001	0	0	0
1	0.387	0.188	0.040	0.010	0.002	0	0
2	0.194	0.282	0.121	0.044	0.011	0	0
3	0.057	0.250	0.215	0.117	0.042	0.003	0
4	0.011	0.146	0.251	0.205	0.111	0.016	0
5	0.001	0.058	0.201	0.246	0.201	0.058	0.001
6	0	0.016	0.111	0.205	0.251	0.146	0.011
7	0	0.003	0.042	0.117	0.215	0.250	0.057
8	0	0	0.011	0.044	0.121	0.282	0.194
9	0	0	0.002	0.010	0.040	0.188	0.387
10	0	0	0	0.001	0.006	0.056	0.349

Figure 2

EXERCISES

1. A random sample of ten persons is chosen in New York City at a time when 60 percent are in favor of Kelly for mayor and 40 percent are in favor of McGrath. What is the probability that the sample will show less than 50 percent in favor of Kelly?   [*Ans.* .166.]

2. An independent trials experiment is repeated ten times with six suc-

cesses. Which value of p in Figure 2 gives the highest probability of obtaining the outcome of six successes—i.e., the observed outcome?

3. In Exercise 1 assume that the sample size is increased to 9600. Find the expected number and the standard deviation for the number of those in favor of Kelly. What could we say about the range of our estimates if the number of "yes" responses does not deviate by more than three standard deviations from the expected number?

4. In a city there are 100,000 persons who are going to vote on the question of legalizing marijuana. Of these, 90,000 are under 50 years of age and 10,000 are 50 or over. Assume that 75 percent of those under 50 favor legalizing marijuana and of those 50 or older only 20 percent are in favor. What is the probability that a person chosen at random will favor legalizing marijuana? In a sample of 100 chosen at random what is the expected number that will answer "yes"? What is the expected number if a random sample of 100 is chosen, 50 from each of the two groups?

5. In an experiment where the probability distribution depends on a single number, or parameter, the following is a standard method of estimating this parameter. Choose the value of the parameter which gives the highest probability of obtaining the observed result. This method is called the method of *maximum likelihood*. On the basis of the result of Exercise 2, what would you guess to be the maximum likelihood estimator for an independent trials experiment for the probability p of success when x successes are observed in n trials?

6. A box has ten items, eight good and two defective. A sample of five is chosen with replacement—that is, after each item is chosen and inspected it is replaced (i.e., put back) before the next item is drawn. Find the probability that the sample has exactly one defective item.
[*Ans.* .410.]

7. Answer the same question as in Exercise 6 if the sampling is done without replacement. That is, a set of five is chosen at random from all possible subsets of five items of the box. Find the probability that the sample has exactly one defective item and compare your answer to that obtained in Exercise 6.

$$[Ans. \frac{\binom{2}{1}\binom{8}{4}}{\binom{10}{5}} = .556.]$$

8. A sample of three items is chosen from a box of 1000 of which 80 percent are defective. Show that the probability of obtaining exactly one defective item is essentially the same whether we sample with or without replacement.

9. Assume that the incidence of lung cancer among smokers is estimated to be 20 per 100,000 and among heavy smokers to be 200 per 100,000.

Estimate the probability that a person who smokes will *not* get lung cancer and compare this with the estimate for a heavy smoker.

[*Ans.* .9998, .998.]

10.   A hardware store receives boxes of 50 bolts. Experience has shown that they occasionally get a bad lot. When they get a box they choose two bolts at random and if either is defective they return the box. Assume that a box has five defective bolts. What is the probability that the box will be sent back?

11.   Referring to Exercise 10, assume that the store receives shipments of ten boxes each with 50 bolts. It combines the 500 bolts and then chooses two bolts at random; if either is defective it sends back the entire lot. If the shipment contains 50 defectives in all, is the probability of the lot being returned larger than, equal to, or smaller than the probability in Exercise 10 of a single box with five defectives being returned?

12.   Toss a coin 100 times. In each group of ten tosses count the number of heads. Compare the results with Figure 2.

13.   Toss a pair of coins 100 times. In each group of ten tosses count the number of times two heads turn up. Compare the results with Figure 2.

2   THE CENTRAL LIMIT THEOREM

As we have indicated, to go further in our discussion of statistics we shall need an important theorem of probability theory called the *central limit theorem*. While this is a very general theorem, we shall discuss it in this section only as it applies to independent trials processes.

As usual, let p be the probability of success on a trial and $f(n, p; x)$ the probability of exactly x successes in n trials.

In Figure 3 we have plotted bar graphs which represent $f(n, .3; x)$ for $n = 10, 50, 100,$ and 200. We note first of all that the graphs are drifting off to the right. This is not surprising, since their peaks occur at np, which is steadily increasing. We also note that while the total area is always 1, this area becomes more and more spread out.

We want to redraw these graphs in a manner that prevents the drifting and the spreading out. First of all, we replace x by $x - np$, assuring that our peak always occurs at 0. Next we introduce a new unit for measuring the deviation, which depends on n, and which gives comparable scales. As we saw in Chapter 3, Section 9, the standard deviation $\sqrt{npq}$ is such a unit.

We must still insure that probabilities are represented by areas in the graph. In Figure 3 this is achieved by having a unit base for each rectangle, and having the probability $f(n, p; x)$ as height. Since we are now representing a standard deviation as a single unit on the horizontal axis, we must take $f(n, p; x) \sqrt{npq}$ as the heights of our rectangles. The resulting curves for $n = 50$ and $n = 200$ are shown in Figures 4 and 5, respectively.

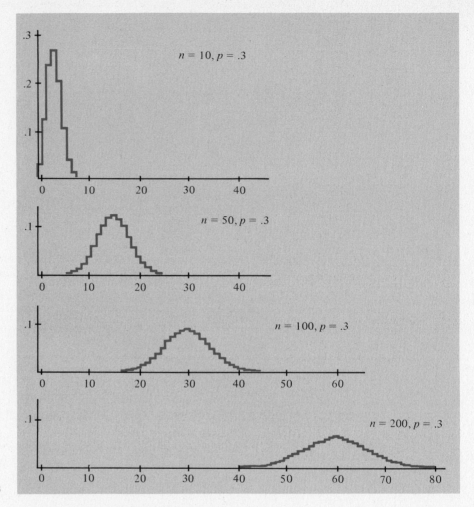

Figure 3

We note that the two figures look very much alike. We have also shown in Figure 5 that it can be approximated by a bell-shaped curve. This curve represents the function*

$$f(x) = \frac{1}{\sqrt{2\pi}}\, e^{-x^2/2},$$

and is known as the *normal curve.* It is a fundamental theorem of probability theory that as n increases, the appropriately rescaled bargraphs more and more closely approach the normal curve. The theorem is known as the *central limit theorem,* and we have illustrated it graphically.

More precisely, the theorem states that for any two numbers a and b, with $a < b$,

*The number e is the base of natural logarithms and its numerical value is 2.71828182.... Its derivation and most important properties are discussed in most calculus books.

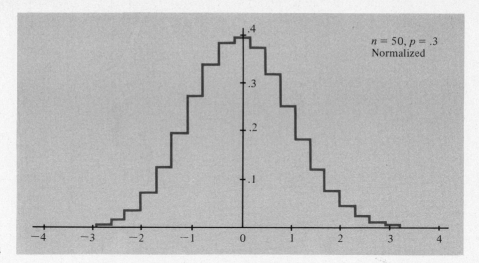

Figure 4

$$\Pr\left[a < \frac{x - np}{\sqrt{npq}} < b\right]$$

approaches the area under the normal curve between a and b, as n increases. This theorem is particularly interesting in that the normal curve is symmetric about 0, while $f(n, p; x)$ is symmetric about the expected value np only for the case $p = \frac{1}{2}$. It should also be noted that we always arrive at the same normal curve, no matter what the value of p is.

In Figure 6 we give a table for the area under the normal curve between 0 and d. Since the total area is 1, and since it is symmetric about the origin, we can compute arbitrary areas from this table. For example, suppose that

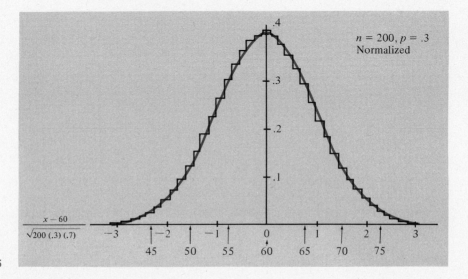

Figure 5

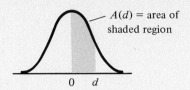

$A(d)$ = area of shaded region

d	$A(d)$	d	$A(d)$	d	$A(d)$	d	$A(d)$
.0	.000	1.1	.364	2.1	.482	3.1	.4990
.1	.040	1.2	.385	2.2	.486	3.2	.4993
.2	.079	1.3	.403	2.3	.489	3.3	.4995
.3	.118	1.4	.419	2.4	.492	3.4	.4997
.4	.155	1.5	.433	2.5	.494	3.5	.4998
.5	.191	1.6	.445	2.6	.495	3.6	.4998
.6	.226	1.7	.455	2.7	.497	3.7	.4999
.7	.258	1.8	.464	2.8	.497	3.8	.49993
.8	.288	1.9	.471	2.9	.498	3.9	.49995
.9	.316	2.0	.477	3.0	.4987	4.0	.49997
1.0	.341					5.0	.49999997

Figure 6

we wish the area between -1 and $+2$. The area between 0 and 2 is given in the table as .477. The area between -1 and 0 is the same as between 0 and 1, and hence is given as .341. Thus the total area is .818. The area outside the interval $(-1, 2)$ is then $1 - .818 = .182$.

EXAMPLE 1   Let us find the probability that s differs from the expected value np by as much as d standard deviations.

$$\Pr\left[|x - np| \geq d\sqrt{npq}\right] = \Pr\left[\left|\frac{x - np}{\sqrt{npq}}\right| \geq d\right],$$

and hence the approximate answer should be the area outside the interval $(-d, d)$ under the normal curve. For $d = 1, 2, 3$ we obtain

$$1 - (2 \times .341) = .318, \qquad 1 - (2 \times .477) = .046$$

and

$$1 - (2 \times .4987) = .0026,$$

respectively. These agree with the values given in Chapter 3, Section 9, to within rounding errors. In fact, the central limit theorem is the basis of those estimates.

EXAMPLE 2   In Chapter 3, Section 9, we considered the example of tossing a coin 10,000 times. The expected number of heads that turn up is 5000, and the standard deviation is $\sqrt{10,000 \cdot \frac{1}{2} \cdot \frac{1}{2}} = 50$. We observed that the probability of a deviation of more than two standard deviations (or 100) is very unlikely.

On the other hand, consider the probability of a deviation of less than .1 standard deviation—that is, of a deviation of less than 5. The area from 0 to .1 under the normal curve is .040, and hence the probability of a deviation from 5000 of less than 5 is approximately .08. Thus, while a deviation of 100 is very unlikely, it is also very unlikely that a deviation of less than 5 will occur.

EXAMPLE 3   The normal approximation can be used to estimate the individual probability $f(n, x; p)$ for large n. For example, let us estimate $f(200, 65; .3)$. The graph of the probabilities $f(200, x; .3)$ was given in Figure 5 together with the normal approximation. The desired probability is the area of the bar corresponding to $x = 65$. An inspection of the graph suggests that we should take the area under the normal curve between 64.5 and 65.5 as an estimate for this probability. In normalized units this is the area between

$$\frac{4.5}{\sqrt{200(.3)(.7)}} \quad \text{and} \quad \frac{5.5}{\sqrt{200(.3)(.7)}},$$

or between .6944 and .8487. Our table is not fine enough to find this area, but from more complete tables, or by machine computation, this area may be found to be .046 to three decimal places. The exact value to three decimal places is .045. This procedure gives us a good estimate.

If we check all of the values of $f(200, x; .3)$ we find in each case that we would make an error of at most .001 by using the normal approximation. There is unfortunately no simple way to estimate the error caused by the use of the central limit theorem. The error will clearly depend upon how large n is, but it also depends upon how near p is to 0 or 1. The greatest accuracy occurs when p is near $\frac{1}{2}$.

EXERCISES

1. Let x be the number of successes in n trials of an independent trials process with probability p for success. Let $x^* = \dfrac{x - np}{\sqrt{npq}}$. For large n estimate the following probabilities:
    (a) Pr $[x^* < -2.5]$.   [*Ans.* .006.]
    (b) Pr $[x^* < 2.5]$.
    (c) Pr $[x^* \geq -.5]$.
    (d) Pr $[-1.5 < x^* < 1]$.   [*Ans.* .774.]

2. A coin is biased in such a way that a head comes up with probability .8 on a single toss. Use the normal approximation to estimate the probability that in a million tosses there are more than 800,400 heads.

3. Plot a graph of the probabilities $f(10, x; .5)$. Plot a graph also of the normalized probabilities as in Figures 4 and 5.

4. An ordinary coin is tossed 1 million times. Let x be the number of heads which turn up. Estimate the following probabilities:

    (a)   Pr $[499{,}500 \leq x \leq 500{,}500]$.

    (b)   Pr $[499{,}000 \leq x \leq 501{,}000]$.

    (c)   Pr $[498{,}500 \leq x \leq 501{,}500]$.

          [*Ans.* .682; .954; .997 (approximate answers).]

5. Assume that a baseball player has probability .37 of getting a hit each time he comes to bat. Find the probability of getting an average of .388 or better if he comes to bat 300 times during the season. (In 1957 Ted Williams had a batting average of .388 and Mickey Mantle had an average of .353. If we assume this difference is due to chance, we may estimate the probability of a hit as the combined average, which is about .37.)   [*Ans.* .242.]

6. A true-false examination has 48 questions. Assume that the probability that a given student knows the answer to any one question is $\frac{3}{4}$. A passing score is 30 or better. Estimate the probability that the student will fail the exam.

7. In Example 3 of Section 9 in Chapter 3, assume that the school decides to admit 1296 students. Estimate the probability that they will have to have additional dormitory space.   [*Ans.* Approximately .115.]

8. Peter and Paul each have 20 pennies. They each toss a coin and Peter wins a penny if his coin matches Paul's, otherwise he loses a penny; they do this 400 times, keeping score but not paying until the 400 matches are over. What is the probability that one of the players will not be able to pay? Answer the same question for the case in which Peter has 10 pennies and Paul has 30.

9. In tossing a coin 100 times, the probability of getting 50 heads is, to three decimal places, .080. Estimate this same probability using the central limit theorem.   [*Ans.* .080.]

10. A standard medicine has been found to be effective in 80 percent of the cases where it is used. A new medicine for the same purpose is found to be effective in 90 of the first 100 patients on which the medicine is used. Could this be taken as good evidence that the new medication is better than the old?

11. Two railroads are competing for the passenger traffic of 1000 passengers by operating similar trains at the same hour. If a given passenger is equally likely to choose one train as the other, how many seats should the railroad provide if it wants to be sure that its seating capacity is sufficient in 99 out of 100 cases?   [*Ans.* 537.]

3 TEST OF HYPOTHESES

We turn now to our first typical statistical problem. As we indicated in the introductory section, our problem is often to decide between two or more competing probability measures. We shall illustrate this in terms of an example.

EXAMPLE Smith claims that he has the ability to distinguish ale from beer and has bet Jones a dollar to that effect. Now Smith does not mean that he can distinguish beer from ale with 100 percent accuracy, but rather that he believes that he can distinguish them a proportion of the time which is significantly greater than $\frac{1}{2}$.

Assume that it is possible to assign a number p which represents the probability that Smith can pick out the ale from a pair of glasses, one containing ale and one beer. We identify $p = \frac{1}{2}$ with his having no ability, $p > \frac{1}{2}$ with his having some ability, and $p < \frac{1}{2}$ with his being able to distinguish, but having the wrong idea which is the ale. If we knew the value of p, we would award the dollar to Jones if p were $\leq \frac{1}{2}$, and to Smith if p were $> \frac{1}{2}$. As it stands, we have no knowledge of p and thus cannot make a decision. We perform an experiment and make a decision as follows.

Smith is given a pair of glasses, one containing ale and the other beer, and is asked to identify which is the ale. This procedure is repeated ten times, and the number of correct identifications is noted. If the number correct is at least eight, we award the dollar to Smith, and if it is less than eight, we award the dollar to Jones.

We now have a definite procedure and shall examine this procedure from both Jones's and Smith's points of view. We can make two kinds of errors. We may award the dollar to Smith when in fact the appropriate value of p is $\leq \frac{1}{2}$, or we may award the dollar to Jones when the appropriate value for p is $> \frac{1}{2}$. There is no way that these errors can be completely avoided. We hope that our procedure is such that each of the bettors will be convinced that, if he is right, he will very likely win the bet.

Jones believes that the true value of p is $\frac{1}{2}$. We shall calculate the probability of Jones winning the bet if this is indeed true. We assume that the individual tests are independent of each other and all have the same probability $\frac{1}{2}$ for success. (This assumption will be unreasonable if the glasses are too large.) We have then an independent trials process with $p = \frac{1}{2}$ to describe the entire experiment. The probability that Jones will win the bet is the probability that Smith gets fewer than eight correct. From the table in Figure 2 we compute that this probability is approximately .945. Thus Jones sees that, if he is right, it is very likely that he will win the bet.

Smith, on the other hand, believes that p is significantly greater than $\frac{1}{2}$. If he believes that p is as high as .9, we see from Figure 2 that the probability of his getting eight or more correct is .930. Then both men will be satisfied by the bet.

Suppose, however, that Smith thinks the value of p is only about .75. Then the probability that he will get eight or more correct and thus win the bet is .526. There is then only an approximately even chance that the experiment will discover his abilities, and he probably will not be satisfied with this. If Smith really thinks his ability is represented by a p value of about $\frac{3}{4}$, we would have to devise a different method of awarding the dollar. We might, for example, propose that Smith win the bet if he gets seven or more correct. Then, if he has probability $\frac{3}{4}$ of being correct on a single trial, the probability that he will win the bet is approximately .776. If $p = \frac{1}{2}$, the probability that Jones will win the bet is about .828 under this new arrangement. Jones's chances of winning are thus decreased, but Smith may be able to convince him that it is a fairer arrangement than the first procedure.

In the theory of hypothesis testing it is common to refer to one hypothesis, say $p = \frac{1}{2}$, as the null hypothesis H_0, and an alternate hypothesis as H_1.

In the above example, it was possible to make two kinds of errors. The probability of making these errors depended on the way we designed the experiment and the method we used for the required decision. In some cases we are not too worried about the errors and can make a relatively simple experiment. In other cases, errors are very important, and the experiment must be designed with that fact in mind. For example, the possibility of error is certainly important in the case that a vaccine for a given disease is proposed and the statistician is asked to help in deciding whether or not it should be used. In this case it might be assumed that there is a certain probability p that a person will get the disease if not vaccinated and a probability r that he will get it if he is vaccinated. If we have some knowledge of the approximate value of p, we are then led to construct an experiment to decide whether r is greater than p, equal to p, or less than p. The first case would be interpreted to mean that the vaccine actually tends to produce the disease, the second that it has no effect, and the third that it prevents the disease; so that we can make three kinds of errors. We could recommend acceptance when it is actually harmful, we could recommend acceptance when it has no effect, or finally we could reject it when it actually is effective. The first and third might result in the loss of lives, the second in the loss of time and money of those administering the test. Here it would certainly be important that the probability of the first and third kinds of errors be made small. To see how it is possible to make the probability of both errors small, we return to the case of Smith and Jones.

EXAMPLE (continued)   Suppose that, instead of demanding that Smith make at least eight correct identifications out of ten trials, we insist that he make at least 60 correct identifications out of 100 trials. (The glasses must now be very small.) Then, if $p = \frac{1}{2}$, the probability that Jones wins the bet is about .98; so that we are extremely unlikely to give the dollar to Smith when in fact it should go to Jones. (If $p < \frac{1}{2}$, it is even more likely that Jones will win.) If $p > \frac{1}{2}$, we can also calculate the probability that Smith will win the bet. These probabilities are shown in the graph in Figure 7. The dashed curve gives for comparison the corresponding probabilities for the test requiring eight out of ten correct. Note that with 100 trials, if p is $\frac{3}{4}$, the probability that Smith wins the bet is nearly 1, while in the case of eight out of ten, it was only about $\frac{1}{2}$. Thus in the case of 100 trials, it would be easy to convince

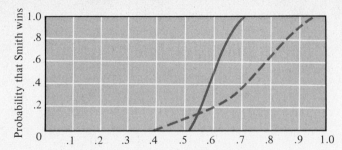

Figure 7

both Smith and Jones that whichever one is correct is very likely to win the bet.

Thus we see that the probability of both types of errors can be made small at the expense of having a large number of experiments.

In applications it is important to have some estimate of the number of experiments that are necessary to reduce the probabilities of errors to acceptable levels. Assume, for example, that we are trying to decide for an independent trials process whether the true probability is p_0 or p_1. Assume that $p_0 < p_1$. We want to design a test so that the probability of error under either hypothesis is at most a. We choose a number s so that the area under the normal curve beyond s is a. We perform n experiments. If p_0 is correct, the probability of the number of successes x exceeding the expected number np_0 by s standard deviations is a. That is, if p_0 is correct, then

$$\Pr\left[x > np_0 + s\sqrt{np_0q_0}\right] = a.$$

On the other hand, if p_1 is correct, the probability that the number of successes will be more than s standard deviations below the expected value of np_1 is also a. That is, if p_1 is correct, then

$$\Pr\left[x < np_1 - s\sqrt{np_1q_1}\right] = a.$$

Assume, then, that we can choose n so that

$$np_0 + s\sqrt{np_0q_0} < np_1 - s\sqrt{np_1q_1}.$$

Then we can choose a value t greater than the first number but such that $t - 1$ is less than the second number. We accept p_0 if $x \leq t - 1$ and p_1 if $x \geq t$. The test will have a probability of error of at most a under either hypothesis. We can achieve this inequality if

$$\sqrt{n}p_0 + s\sqrt{p_0q_0} < \sqrt{n}p_1 - s\sqrt{p_1q_1}$$

or

$$s\left[\frac{\sqrt{p_0q_0} + \sqrt{p_1q_1}}{p_1 - p_0}\right] < \sqrt{n}$$

or

$$n > s^2 \left[\frac{\sqrt{p_0 q_0} + \sqrt{p_1 q_1}}{p_1 - p_0} \right]^2.$$

For example, in our beer and ale example, assume that $p_0 = .5$ and $p_1 = .75$. We would like to be 90 percent certain of being correct. Then from Figure 6 (Section 2) we see that $s = 1.3$. Thus we must have

$$n > (1.3)^2 \left[\frac{\sqrt{.5 \times .5} + \sqrt{.75 \times .25}}{.75 - .5} \right]^2 = 23.5.$$

We would need only a moderate number of experiments, namely 24. Then $np_0 + s\sqrt{np_0 q_0} = 15.18$ and $np_1 - s\sqrt{np_1 q_1} = 15.24$. Jones is 90 percent sure that Smith will have fewer than 16 correct guesses, while Smith is 90 percent sure that he will have more than 15 correct guesses. Thus we award the bet to Smith if he guesses correctly at least 16 times out of 24 experiments.

Consider, however, the Salk vaccine experiment. In this experiment we want to test $p_0 = .00025$ against $p_1 = .00050$—that is, whether the vaccine will reduce the incidence of polio from 50 to 25 per 100,000. We would want a great deal of reliability for such a test. Let us choose s so that the probability of error is less than .001. We can have this by choosing $s = 3.1$. Then we must have

$$n \geq (3.1)^2 \times \left[\frac{\sqrt{.00025 \times .99975} + \sqrt{.0005 \times .9995}}{.00025} \right] = 223,956.$$

In one of the major parts of the Salk vaccine experiment the vaccine was given to 200,000 students. Of these vaccinated students 57 contracted polio. In Exercise 10 you are asked to design an experiment to test the hypothesis $p_1 = .00050$ against the hypothesis $p_0 = .00025$.

EXERCISES

1. Assume that in the beer and ale experiment Jones agrees to pay Smith if Smith gets at least nine out of ten correct.
   (a) What is the probability of Jones paying Smith even though Smith cannot distinguish beer and ale, and guesses?   [*Ans.* .011.]
   (b) Suppose that Smith can distinguish with probability .9. What is the probability of his not collecting from Jones?   [*Ans.* .264.]

2. Suppose that in the beer and ale experiment Jones wishes the probability to be less than .1 that Smith will be paid if, in fact, he guesses. How many of ten trials must he insist that Smith get correct to achieve this?

3. In the analysis of the beer and ale experiment, we assume that the various trials were independent. Discuss several ways that error can enter, because of the nonindependence of the trials, and how this error

can be eliminated. (For example, the glasses in which the beer and ale were served might be distinguishable.)

4. Consider the following two procedures for testing Smith's ability to distinguish beer from ale.

   (a) Four glasses are given at each trial, three containing beer and one ale, and he is asked to pick out the one containing ale. This procedure is repeated ten times. He must guess correctly seven or more times.

   (b) Ten glasses are given him, and he is told that five contain beer and five ale, and he is asked to name the five which he believes contain ale. He must choose all five correctly.

   In each case, find the probability that Smith establishes his claim by guessing. Is there any reason to prefer one test over the other?

   [*Ans.* (a) .003; (b) .004.]

5. A testing service claims to have a method for predicting the order in which a group of freshmen will finish in their scholastic record at the end of college. The college agrees to try the method on a group of five students, and says that it will adopt the method if, for these five students, the prediction is either exactly correct or can be changed into the correct order by interchanging one pair of *adjacent* men in the predicted order. If the method is equivalent to simply guessing, what is the probability that it will be accepted?   [*Ans.* $\frac{1}{24}$.]

6. The standard treatment for a certain disease leads to a cure in $\frac{1}{4}$ of the cases. It is claimed that a new treatment will result in a cure in $\frac{3}{4}$ of the cases. The new treatment is to be tested on ten people having the disease. If seven or more are cured, the new treatment will be adopted. If three or fewer people are cured, the treatment will not be considered further. If the number cured is four, five, or six, the results will be called inconclusive, and a further study will be made. Find the probabilities for each of these three alternatives first, under the assumption that the new treatment has the same effectiveness as the old, and second, under the assumption that the claim made for the treatment is correct.

7. Three upperclassmen debate the intelligence of the freshmen class. One claims that most freshmen (say 90 percent of them) are intelligent. A second claims that very few (say 10 percent) of them are intelligent, while a third one claims that a freshman is just as likely to be intelligent as not. They administer an intelligence test to ten freshmen, classifying them as intelligent or not. They agree that the first man wins the bet if eight or more are intelligent, the second if two or fewer, the third in all other cases. For each man, calculate the probability that he wins the bet, if he is right.   [*Ans.* .930, .930, .890.]

8. Ten men take a test with ten problems. Each man on each question has probability $\frac{1}{2}$ of being right, if he does not cheat. The instructor determines the number of students who get each problem correct. If he finds on four or more problems there are fewer than three or more

than seven correct, he considers this convincing evidence of communication between the students. Give a justification for the procedure. [*Hint:* The table in Figure 2 must be used twice, once for the probability of fewer than three or more than seven correct answers on a given problem, and the second time to find the probability of this happening on four or more problems.]

9. An instructor claims that a certain student knows only 70 percent of the material. The student claims that he knows 85 percent. Design a test that will settle the argument with probability .9.

[*Ans.* 50 questions, student must get 40 correct answers.]

10. Assume that the Salk vaccine is to be given to 225,000 students. It is claimed that the probability of getting polio is $\leq .00025$ if vaccinated and .00050 if not vaccinated. Design a test to decide between these two alternatives. In the actual experiment there were 28 cases per 100,000 of polio among the 200,000 vaccinated. This would suggest 63 cases in 225,000 students. Would your test establish the claim that the Salk vaccine was effective, if this few cases of polio occurred in the experiment?

4 CONFIDENCE INTERVALS

Consider n independent trials with probability p for success on each trial. We assume that we do not know p but want to make, on the basis of our observations, some estimate of p. Let a be any number between 0 and 1. Then from Figure 6 we can find a number s such that the area under the normal curve beyond s is $a/2$. For example, if $a = .05$ then we can choose $s = 2$. By the central limit theorem, if x is the number of successes, then

$$\Pr\left[\left|\frac{x - np}{\sqrt{npq}}\right| \leq s\right] \approx 1 - a.$$

This is the same as saying that

$$\Pr\left[\left|\frac{x/n - p}{\sqrt{pq/n}}\right| \leq s\right] \approx 1 - a.$$

Putting $\bar{p} = x/n$, we have

$$\Pr\left[|\bar{p} - p| \leq s\sqrt{pq/n}\right] \approx 1 - a.$$

Using the fact that $pq \leq \frac{1}{4}$ for all p (see Exercise 9), we have

$$\Pr\left[|\bar{p} - p| \leq s/2\sqrt{n}\right] \geq 1 - a.$$

Thus, no matter what p is, with probability at least $1 - a$, the true value will not deviate from $\bar{p}$ by more than $s/2\sqrt{n}$. We say then that

$$\bar{p} - \frac{s}{2\sqrt{n}} \leq p \leq \bar{p} + \frac{s}{2\sqrt{n}}$$

with confidence $1 - a$. We call the interval

$$\left[\bar{p} - \frac{s}{2\sqrt{n}}, \ \bar{p} + \frac{s}{2\sqrt{n}}\right]$$

a $100(1 - a)$ percent confidence interval. For example, the 95 percent confidence interval requires $s = 2$, and hence is $\left[p - \dfrac{1}{\sqrt{n}}, \ p + \dfrac{1}{\sqrt{n}}\right]$.

For example, if in 400 trials a drug is found effective 124 times or .31 of the time, the 95 percent confidence interval for p is

$$\left[.31 - \frac{1}{20}, \ .31 + \frac{1}{20}\right],$$

or [.26, .36]. The 99 percent confidence interval would be found by using $s = 2.6$. This gives

$$\left[.31 - \frac{2.6}{40}, \ .31 + \frac{2.6}{40}\right],$$

or [.245, .375]. Of course, as we demand more confidence our prediction is more conservative, i.e., the interval is larger.

It is important to realize that the interval obtained depends upon the value of $\bar{p}$, which in turn depends upon the value of x. Thus $\bar{p}$ is a chance quantity. We are assuming that the true value p, though unknown, is not a chance quantity. Thus our confidence interval itself is a chance quantity which may or may not cover the true value p. When we choose a 95 percent confidence interval we mean that the probability is .95 that the interval will cover the true value p. Thus by the law of large numbers we expect this to be the case about 95 percent of the time.

In Figure 8 we give the results of computing the 95 percent confidence intervals based upon several experiments with $n = 100$ trials for a true value of $p = .7$. We carried out this experiment 20 times. It will be noted that in each case the interval does include the true value, though sometimes just barely. We should not have been surprised if in one or two cases it did not.

The use of the inequality $pq \leq \frac{1}{4}$ was for convenience and simplicity of our computations. It results in slightly larger confidence intervals than are necessary for a given confidence level. Without making this approximation it is possible to transform the first inequality into an inequality about $\bar{p}$ to obtain a more exact confidence interval (see Exercise 14).

As a second example of confidence intervals consider the following problem. In a small town lottery tickets numbered from 1 to N are being sold weekly and a prize is given to the person who holds the ticket having the lucky number drawn at random from the numbers from 1 to N. The value of N is not publicly announced, but is the same every week. A man buys lottery tickets for ten weeks, receiving numbers $27, 46, 77, 85, 34, 24, 34, 46, 34$, and 89. Before buying a ticket the following week, he wants to

.63	.83
.59	.79
.67	.87
.65	.85
.59	.79
.65	.85
.61	.81
.51	.71
.61	.81
.57	.77
.58	.78
.59	.79
.61	.81
.60	.80
.68	.88
.68	.88
.66	.86
.56	.76
.60	.80
.63	.83

Figure 8

n	$\dfrac{1}{(.05)^{1/n}}$
5	1.821
6	1.648
7	1.534
8	1.454
9	1.395
10	1.349

Figure 9

M	$M/(.05^{.1})$
100	134
96	129
89	120
88	118
99	133
93	125
97	130
85	114
74	99
99	133
82	110
98	132
97	130
91	122
93	125
96	129
97	130
90	121
91	122
98	132

Figure 10

estimate his chance of winning; i.e., he wants to estimate N. Of course he knows that N is at least 89, the highest number that he has drawn.

Let us see how we would obtain confidence intervals for the unknown "parameter" N. The man has in effect drawn a number from the N possible numbers n times. Let M be the maximum of the numbers drawn. Then for fixed n and N, M may be considered a chance quantity. For any A,

$$\Pr[M \le A] = \left(\frac{A}{N}\right)^n.$$

As before, let a be any number between 0 and 1. We can choose A so that $A = a^{1/n}N$. Then

$$\Pr[M \le a^{1/n}N] = \frac{(a^{1/n}N)^n}{N^n} = a$$

or

$$\Pr\left[\frac{M}{a^{1/n}} \le N\right] = a.$$

That is,

$$\Pr\left[N < \frac{M}{a^{1/n}}\right] = 1 - a.$$

Since $M \le N$, we can write this as

$$\Pr\left[M \le N < \frac{M}{a^{1/n}}\right] = 1 - a.$$

Thus the interval $[M, M/a^{1-n}]$ has probability $1 - a$ of covering N and hence is a $100(1 - a)$ percent confidence interval for N. In any given example, for a 95 percent confidence interval, we choose $a = .05$ and hence $M/a^{1/n} = 89/(.5)^{1/10} = 120.1$. Hence the man can be 95 percent sure that there are at most 120 lottery tickets.

For such calculations the table in Figure 9 is useful.

In Figure 10 we have indicated the result of twenty experiments with N equal in each case to 100 and $n = 10$. We have computed the 95 percent confidence intervals. In this case we see that one interval does not include the true value of N. Thus the intervals include the true value of N precisely 95 percent of the time.

EXAMPLE The Fish and Game Department is interested in estimating the number of trout in a pond (which contains only trout). They take out a sample of 1000 fish and mark them. Later they take another sample of 1600 and find that 120 of them are marked. What is a reasonable estimate for the total number of trout?

Let n be the unknown total. Since 1000 of them were marked, there is probability $p = 1000/n$ that a fish in the second sample will be marked.

The observed fraction is $\bar{p} = 120/1600$, and the 95 percent confidence interval yields

$$\frac{120}{1600} - \frac{1}{\sqrt{1600}} \leq p \leq \frac{120}{1600} + \frac{1}{\sqrt{1600}},$$

or

$$\frac{3}{40} - \frac{1}{40} \leq p \leq \frac{3}{40} + \frac{1}{40},$$

or

$$\frac{1}{20} \leq p \leq \frac{1}{10}.$$

Hence

$$\frac{1}{20} \leq \frac{1000}{n} \leq \frac{1}{10},$$

and we obtain the estimate $10{,}000 \leq n \leq 20{,}000$.

EXERCISES

1. A prospective college student visits a college and sits in on a class of 50 students. She notes that there are 39 men and 10 women in the class. She decides to compute the 95 percent confidence interval for the proportion of girls in the school. She will reject the school if this interval excludes the possibility that $\frac{1}{3}$ of the students are women. Does she reject the school for this reason?

2. A young ballplayer in his first season is at bat 400 times and gets 100 hits for a batting average of .250. Find 90 percent confidence limits for his batting average based upon his first season. Is it reasonable to believe that he may in fact be a .300 batter?

   [*Ans.* [.209, .291]; maybe, next year.]

3. A large company has as many as a million accounts. It wishes to estimate the number that are at least three months delinquent in their payments. A thousand accounts are randomly selected and of these it is observed that 30 are at least three months delinquent. Find the 95 percent confidence limits for the proportion of customers that are at least three months behind in their payments.

4. Opinion pollsters in election years usually poll about 3000 voters. Suppose that in an election year 51 percent favor candidate A and 49 percent favor candidate B in a poll. Construct 95 percent confidence limits on the true percentage of the population in favor of A.

   [*Ans.* .492, .528.]

5. An experimenter has an independent trials process and she has a hypothesis that the true value of p is p_0. She decides to carry out a number of trials, and from the observed $\bar{p}$ calculate the 95 percent

confidence interval of p. She will reject p_0 if it does not fall within these limits. What is the probability that she will reject p_0 when in fact it is correct? Should she accept p_0 if it does fall within the confidence interval?

6. A coin is tossed 100 times and turns up heads 61 times. Using the method of Exercise 5, test the hypothesis that the coin is a fair coin.
[*Ans.* Reject.]

7. In an experiment with independent trials we are going to estimate p by the fraction $\bar{p}$ of successes. We wish our estimate to be within .02 of the correct value with probability .95. Show that 2500 observations will always suffice. Show that if it is known that p is approximately .1, then 900 observations would be sufficient.

8. In the Weldon dice experiment, 12 dice were thrown 26,306 times and the appearance of a 5 or a 6 was considered to be a success. The mean number of successes observed was, to four decimal places, 4.0524. Is this result significantly different from the expected average number of 4?
[*Ans.* Yes.]

9. Prove that $pq \leq \frac{1}{4}$. [*Hint:* write $p = \frac{1}{2} + x$.]

10. Suppose that out of 1000 persons interviewed 650 said that they would vote for Mr. Big for mayor. Construct the 99 percent confidence interval for p, the proportion in the city that would vote for Mr. Big.

11. In a pond 400 fish are marked. If in a subsequent sample of 225 there are 45 marked fish, find the 90 percent confidence interval for the total number of fish.

12. In a large city each taxi is assigned a number. A man observes the numbers 125, 135, 356, 344, 25, 299, and 320 on seven occasions that he takes a cab. On the basis of this, compute the 95 percent confidence limits for the number of cabs in the city. If he knows that the number of cabs is a multiple of 100, can be determine the total?

13. Suppose that the man in Exercise 12 takes three more cabs numbered 76, 421, and 211. Can he be 95 percent sure of the total?
[*Ans.* Yes.]

14. In this section we have approximated confidence limits on p such that $\Pr\left[|\bar{p} - p| \leq s\sqrt{\dfrac{pq}{n}}\right] = 1 - a$. The expression inside the brackets is equivalent to $(\bar{p} - p)^2 \leq s^2\left(\dfrac{p(1-p)}{n}\right)$. Substituting equality for inequality we obtain a quadratic equation which can be solved for p in terms of $\bar{p}$, s, and n. There will be two roots r_1 and r_2, where $r_1 \leq r_2$ and the above inequality will be satisfied for all p such that $r_1 \leq p \leq r_2$. Use this information to obtain more exact confidence intervals than that obtained by setting $pq = \frac{1}{4}$.

15. A hundred names are picked at random out of a large telephone book. It is found that 70 of these names have eight letters or less. Place 95 percent confidence limits on the fraction of names in that telephone book containing eight letters or less:

(a) Using the estimate developed in the text.

(b) Using the limits developed in exercise 14.   [*Ans.* .602, .783.]

(c) Suppose we were using the method of Exercise 5 to test the hypothesis that 79 percent of the names have eight or less letters. Which of the above intervals would be better?

5 SOME PITFALLS

Statistics properly used is a very powerful tool. If it is not properly used it can lead to incorrect predictions and thereby cause considerable distrust in its methods. We have already mentioned the example of the poll of the *Literary Digest* in the 1936 presidential election between Roosevelt and Landon. In this poll about 10 million postcards were sent to persons whose names were obtained from telephone directories and car registrations. Several million cards were returned, with 40.9 percent in favor of Franklin Roosevelt. A few weeks later in the actual election, Roosevelt obtained 60.7 percent of the vote.

There are two obvious flaws in the above procedure. The first, and the one which is normally blamed for the error, is that people who had telephones or cars at that time were not truly representative of the voting population as a whole. The second is the possibility that people change their minds between the time a poll is taken and the election takes place. They may even deliberately tell the poll taker one thing and vote another. Of course, with many millions of people it is difficult to choose a truly random sample. However, let us assume that there were in fact 60.7 percent of the people in favor of Roosevelt at the time of the poll and that we could choose a random sample of only 10,000 voters. In Figure 11 we indicate the result of simulating 30 such samples and determining the 99 percent confidence intervals. We see that in every case we would have picked Roosevelt to win. This is on the basis of only 10,000 samples rather than the millions which led to a wrong answer. Thus if statistics can be properly used it is a very powerful tool.

.586	.618
.591	.623
.594	.626
.59	.622
.594	.626
.598	.63
.591	.623
.591	.623
.592	.625
.595	.627
.59	.622
.583	.616
.588	.62
.591	.623
.603	.635
.59	.622
.592	.624
.597	.629
.595	.627
.588	.62

Figure 11

Because of the difficulties indicated above there is still, with some justice, skepticism of polls. However, there is also some danger in refusing to use statistical methods. For example, assume that an all-male college wishes to know the opinion of its alumni on the question of becoming a coeducational institution. Assume that there are 30,000 alumni and in fact 60 percent are in favor of the college admitting women. This is a situation in which any person not asked could conceivably challenge the poll. Assume then that it is decided to poll by mail *all* the alumni. Also assume that a proportion p of those who favor coeducation will respond to the query and a proportion $2p$ of those who oppose will respond because they feel more strongly about the matter. Then the expected number of yes answers would be 18,000p and the no answers would be 24,000p. Thus, neglecting sampling errors, the vote would be 18,000p/42,000p = .43 in favor, and coeducation would be defeated. On the other hand, as we have seen, a relatively small random sample in which the response of each person sampled was recorded would give a much more reliable indication of the true feelings of the alumni. For example, a sample of 1000 was taken in such a poll and a 95 percent confidence interval of (.559, .621) was obtained. Here is a situation where one could also use the method of hypothesis testing discussed in Section 3.

As we have indicated previously, a number of precautions had to be taken in the experiment to test the effectiveness of Salk vaccine. First, although initially the incidence of polio was only about 50 per 100,000, there was considerable variability from year to year and from region to region. So a reduction from 50 to 25 in a sample of 100,000 could easily be caused by reasons having nothing to do with the effectiveness of the vaccine. Thus it was decided to have control groups. In one part of the experiment a population of students was divided into two groups of about 200,000 each. All were inoculated at the same time. The first group received the Salk vaccine and the second a harmless and useless salt solution (a "placebo"). The decision as to which students received the real vaccine was made randomly, and the knowledge of whether a student was given the vaccine or the placebo was not made known to the student or to the physician observing the student. The reason for this is that in such experiments knowledge of whether the subject has been treated or not has been found to introduce a bias in the diagnosis and in the behavior of the subject. As indicated earlier, the test did show a significantly lower rate among those vaccinated. The test led to further development of vaccines and the virtual elimination of polio in the United States.

There have been a large number of statistical studies to determine if smoking is injurious to one's health. It is now widely believed that this is the case. However, the problem of establishing this has been exceedingly difficult, and there are still statisticians who feel that more testing must be done. In the case of the polio vaccine it was possible to select two groups and randomly give one half the vaccine and the other half a placebo. Random selection eliminates the effect of biases which can creep in, such as differences in age, place of residence, economic status, etc. To do the corresponding experiment for smoking would require one randomly selected group to become heavy smokers and the rest to abstain. This is clearly not possible, and many of the studies have had to rely on choosing groups in a less random way and studying their smoking and health patterns. In the exercises some of these methods are briefly mentioned and you are asked to consider possible pitfalls. While statisticians who criticize these tests or refuse to accept their conclusions are often accused of being overly cautious, their criticisms have led to the development of more careful methods of statistical tests in these very difficult areas. It should be emphasized that demonstrating that more heavy smokers than nonsmokers get lung cancer does not demonstrate that smoking is a cause of lung cancer. It seems likely that there will still be controversy about this question until more knowledge is obtained as to what is the essential cause of cancer.

In the *Literary Digest* poll the particular people that responded to the postcard inquiry was a chance quantity. In effect, the *size* of the sample was random. While pollsters do not intentionally take advantage of this, the results under such circumstances can be distorted. We illustrate this in an extreme case where the experimenter deliberately tries to take advantage of the randomness of the size of the experiment.

Assume that Mr. Esp claims that he has extrasensory perception. An experiment is arranged in which he is to tell, when a card is placed face down, whether it has a circle or a square on it. Of course we would want to run a large number of experiments, but for the point we are trying to make we can take a small number, say four. If Mr. Esp is just guessing, we can find his expected score (percentage correct) in the usual manner. The tree and tree measure are shown in Figure 12, and his expected score is $1 \times \frac{1}{16} + \frac{3}{4} \times \frac{4}{16} + \frac{1}{2} \times \frac{6}{16} + \frac{1}{4} \times \frac{4}{16} + 0 \times \frac{1}{16} = \frac{1}{2}$.

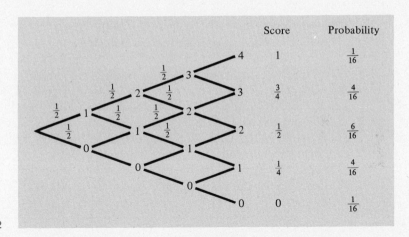

Figure 12

Assume now that the experimenter, eager to find a good subject, stops the experiment the first time (if any) that Mr. Esp's score is greater than $\frac{1}{2}$. Then the new tree measure, still assuming guessing, is shown in Figure 13. We see now that his expected score is

$$1 \times \frac{1}{2} + \frac{2}{3} \times \frac{1}{8} + \frac{1}{2} \times \frac{1}{8} + \frac{1}{4} \times \frac{3}{16} + 0 \times \frac{1}{16} = \frac{133}{192} = .69,$$

which is considerably better than before.

It is extremely important in designing a statistical test to decide upon the criteria for acceptance or rejection before the test is carried out. Of course, we should not be surprised if we find some unlikely feature of an experiment by looking after the fact for something of small probability. A local expert on probability theory would occasionally be roused from bed at one in the

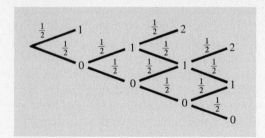

Figure 13

morning to have an excited colleague ask, "What is the probability of being dealt a hand of all hearts in bridge." He would answer, "The same as any other hand," and then go back to sleep.

EXERCISES

1. In the tests of the Salk vaccine 400,000 students volunteered to be vaccinated. Half were vaccinated and half given placebo. Among these 400,000 people 199 got polio. Assuming that a person who had polio was equally likely to be in either of the groups, place 99 percent confidence limits on the number of people in the vaccinated group that got polio. Does the fact that of the 199 reported cases 142 were in the placebo group suggest that the vaccine was effective?

2. Referring to Exercise 1, data was taken also on 340,000 students who did not volunteer to be inoculated. Assuming that these people had the same probability of getting polio as those who received the placebo, place 99 percent confidence limits on the number of people among this group to get polio. What does the fact that among this group there were 157 polio cases suggest? How might we explain this result?

3. In many of the major studies of smoking and health the samples are obtained by interviewing whomever happens to be at home when the interviewer calls. This person answers questions relating to everyone in the family over 21. Comment on some possible defects in this method of sampling.

4. In one major study of smoking and health two groups were compared, one that had lung cancer and another that was chosen by virtue of having similar backgrounds to the group that had cancer. Comment on this technique of sampling.

5. This exercise is designed to show that optional stopping in sampling can significantly change the results. Consider the following game. A box contains five balls, three of which are red and two blue. If a red ball is drawn we lose a dollar, if a blue ball we win a dollar.
   (a) Find the expected value of the game if one ball is drawn.

   [*Ans.* −20 cents.]

   (b) Show that the game becomes increasingly unfavorable if two, three, four, or five balls are drawn.
   (c) Show that the game is favorable if you are allowed to stop at any

time. Use the following strategy: If the first draw is blue, stop. Otherwise, play until you are even or until all five balls are drawn.

[*Partial ans*. Value is +20 cents.]

6. In a certain college 25 out of 324 faculty members with Ph.D.'s are women. Nationally approximately 20 percent of all Ph.D.'s are awarded to women. Test the hypothesis that the faculty members were picked from the national pool without regard to sex.

7. In regarding the significance of Exercise 6 as evidence of discrimination, what other factors would have to be taken into account? For example, is it sufficient to know the present percentage of women among Ph.D.'s? And should one know something about the distribution among disciplines?

8. The President of the United States announces a major policy decision. His mail the following week contains 25,000 irate letters and 10,000 favoring his decision. Would it be reasonable to conclude that a majority of people oppose his decision?

6   COMPUTER APPLICATIONS

In many problems in statistics the theory is straightforward but the computations are very difficult. This makes statistics an important area for computer applications. We shall first illustrate this by the computation of confidence intervals considered earlier in this chapter, then we shall introduce the important technique of *simulation*.

In Section 4, for the example of the lottery ticket, the only difficulty in computing the confidence interval for the total number of tickets is the necessity of raising a decimal fraction to the $1/n$ power. This is simply done in BASIC. In the program LOTTERY we supply N (the number of tickets bought), M (the largest number observed), and C (the percentage confidence

```
LOTTERY


10  READ N,M,C
20  LET A = 1-C
30  PRINT M, M/A↑(1/N)
90  DATA 10,89,.95
99  END
READY


RUN


LOTTERY


 89                    120.086


0.060 SEC.
READY
```

desired). The entire computation is carried out in two instructions. The RUN shows the 95 percent confidence interval if among ten tickets bought the highest number was 89.

The program **CONFIDE** computes three confidence intervals for an independent trials experiment in which we observed x successes in n trials. The

███ CONFIDE

```
10 READ X,N
20 LET P = X/N
30 LET D = 2*SQR(N)
40 FOR K = 1 TO 3
50 READ S
60 PRINT P-S/D,P+S/D
70 NEXT K
80 DATA 61,100
90 DATA 1.65,2,2.6
99 END
READY

RUN

CONFIDE

    0.5275          0.6925
    0.51            0.71
    0.48            0.74

0.070 SEC.
READY
```

DATA in Line 90 supplies the number of standard deviations for 90, 95, and 99 percent confidence. The rest of this simple program is a direct translation of the formula obtained in Section 4. The RUN shows that if we observe 61 successes in 100 trials we can be 90 percent sure that the true value of p is below .7, but we cannot be 95 percent sure. It also shows that we can be 95 percent sure that $p > .5$, but not 99 percent sure.

Other formulas in this chapter may similarly be translated into simple computer programs. (See the Exercises.)

Probabilistic models prevail in the social sciences. While many of them can, in principle, be treated by the methods studied in this book, in practice they frequently are much too complicated to obtain precise theoretical results. In such cases, simulation by a high-speed computer may be a powerful tool.

Simulation is a process during which the computer acts out a situation from real life. Typically, the relevant facts about an experiment are supplied to the computer, and it is instructed to run through a large series of experiments, perhaps under varying conditions. This enables the scientist to carry out in an hour a series of experiments that would otherwise take years, and at the same time all the important information is automatically tabulated by the computer.

Of course, the computer cannot duplicate the exact circumstances of an experiment. The facts fed to it are based on a model (or theory) formed by the scientist, and the value of the simulation depends on the accuracy of the model. Thus the main significance of simulation is that it enables a scientist to study the kind of behavior predicted by his model. For very complicated models this may be the only procedure open to him.

In addition to the use of simulation for theoretical studies, there are two very important types of pragmatic uses of simulation: (1) It can be used as a planning device. If there are various alternative courses of action open, the computer is asked to try out the various alternatives under different conditions, and report the advantages and disadvantages of each course. (2) Simulation may be used as a training device. For example, business schools are making increasing use of "business games" in which fledgling executives may try their skill at decision making under realistic circumstances.

We shall first discuss how computers simulate stochastic processes, and then illustrate simulation in terms of examples previously considered in this book. Simulation depends on the generation of so-called *random numbers*. In BASIC this is achieved by an instruction using "RND," such as

LET X = RND.

Every time this instruction is executed, BASIC generates a real number between 0 and 1 by a process that is reasonably random.

Actually, the computer is forced to cheat, in that it has only a finite capacity for expressing numbers. Thus it may in reality divide the unit interval into a million (or more) numbers, and give them in a quite random order. When its supply is exhausted, it will start again giving the same numbers in the same order. However, if one needs only 100,000 numbers, or even a million numbers, the results are highly satisfactory.

We illustrate this by means of the program RANDOM, which generates 30 random numbers. In looking at the output the reader should recall that E-2 indicates multiplication by 10^{-2}; thus 8.5 E-2 = .085. The distribution is reasonably random. For example, 6 out of 30 numbers lie between .3 and .5, which is what we would expect. However, there are "too many" numbers between .2 and .3. Whether this is statistically significant needs to be checked (see Exercise 5).

Very often instead of random numbers we need random integers. For example, to simulate the roll of a die we need random integers from 1 to 6. We show the process for generating these in the other two RUNSs of

```
RANDOM

10 FOR I = 1 TO 30
20 LET X = RND
30 PRINT X,
40 NEXT I
99 END
READY

RUN

RANDOM

0.406533      0.272549      0.850262      0.595677      0.421672
0.597993      0.251284      0.365032      0.779619      0.692297
0.757194      8.53103 E-2   0.244524      0.259585      0.612122
0.240634      0.540498      0.363964      2.01594 E-2   0.275084
0.351612      0.929495      0.145359      0.592702      0.321399
0.840201      0.111732      0.557491      5.53524 E-2   0.940065

0.097 SEC.
READY
```

```
20 LET X = 6*RND
RUN

RANDOM

2.4392      1.63529     5.10157     3.57406     2.53003
4.18799     1.5077      2.19019     4.67771     4.15373
4.54316     0.511862    1.46714     1.55751     3.67273
1.4438      3.24299     2.18379     0.120957    1.6505
2.10967     5.57697     0.872151    3.55621     1.9314
5.04121     0.670392    3.34495     0.332114    5.64039

0.095 SEC.
READY

20 LET X = INT(6*RND)+1
RUN

RANDOM

3       2       6       4       3
5       2       3       5       5
5       1       2       2       4
2       4       3       1       2
3       6       1       4       2
6       1       4       1       6

0.090 SEC.
READY
```

RANDOM. First we print out 6 times the random numbers. They are now spread evenly on the interval $(0, 6)$. Thus if we take their integer parts, the numbers 0, 1, 2, 3, 4, 5 will turn up with equal probabilities, at random. By taking integer parts and adding one, we obtain the "roll of a die."

One common use of random numbers is to simulate an independent trials process. Such a process with $p = .3$ may be simulated as follows:

> 100 IF RND < .3 THEN 200
> 100 PRINT "FAILURE"
> . . .
> 200 PRINT "SUCCESS"

It is in the nature of the process that generates random numbers that the probability of RND $< .3$ is precisely .3. Of course any other probability may be used in place of .3.

EXAMPLE 1   *Craps.* Let us simulate the game of shooting craps. This is carried out by the program CRAPS, which closely follows the flow diagram in Figure 14, on page 304.

CRAPS

```
5    FOR N = 1 TO 10
10   LET D1 = INT(6*RND)+1
20   LET D2 = INT(6*RND)+1
30   LET D = D1 + D2
35   PRINT D;
40   IF D < 4 THEN 300
50   IF D = 12 THEN 300
60   IF D = 7 THEN 200
70
100  REM   TRY TO MAKE POINT
110  LET X = D
120  LET D1 = INT(6*RND)+1
130  LET D2 = INT(6*RND)+1
140  LET D = D1 + D2
150  PRINT D;
160  IF D = X THEN 200
170  IF D = 7 THEN 300
180  GOTO 120
190
200  REM   PLAYER WINS
210  PRINT "YOU WIN"
220  GOTO 400
230
```

```
300 REM   PLAYER LOSES
310 PRINT "YOU LOSE"
320
400 REM   START OVER
420 NEXT N
430
999 END
READY

RUN

CRAPS

 5  10   8   5 YOU WIN
10   6   4   6   7 YOU LOSE
 3 YOU LOSE
 9   5   8   5   7 YOU LOSE
 4   2  11   7 YOU LOSE
 8   4   8 YOU WIN
 7 YOU WIN
 2 YOU LOSE
 5   5 YOU WIN
 7 YOU WIN

0.117 SEC.
READY
```

One may consider running a program like CRAPS a large number of times, keeping count of the amount won or lost, and use it to estimate the expected value of the game. (In Chapter 3, Section 11, this was found to be $-.0141$.) Let us suppose that we try to simulate 10,000 games. How good an estimate can we expect? We know that the 95 percent confidence interval for a probability near .5 is $1/\sqrt{n}$. But if the fraction of successes is high by that amount, the fraction of losses will be low by the same amount, and vice versa. Thus we should expect errors up to $2/\sqrt{n}$ on either side of the expected value. For $n = 10,000$ this is an error of .02. In five such simulations the values obtained were: $-.0238$, $-.0298$, $-.0090$, $+.0016$, and $-.0084$. All are within the 95 percent confidence interval, but one simulation shows a loss twice the expected size and one actually shows a profit.

Thus, while a simulation provides an easy rough approximation to the answer, a good approximation requires a substantial computer effort. A simulation of 250,000 games requires about three minutes of computing time, much longer than the other examples we have shown in this book. Two such RUNs produced values of $-.0115$ and $-.0154$, which are much closer to the real value (see Exercise 4).

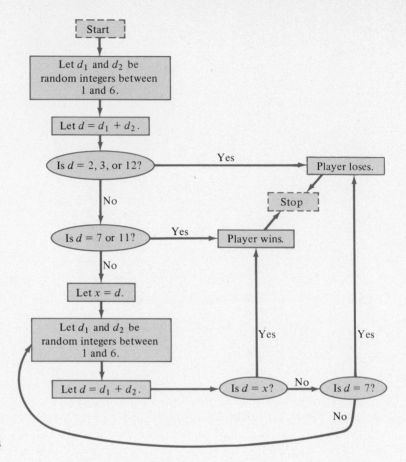

Figure 14

EXAMPLE 2 *Poker.* In the exercises of Section 3 in Chapter 3 we computed the probabilities for various poker hands. Let us obtain estimates for the same by simulation.

Our problem here amounts to selecting five cards at random from a deck of 52 cards. We first number the cards from 1 to 52, in any convenient manner. Then we select one card by generating a random integer from the set 1 through 52. (This can be achieved by computing INT(52*RND + 1).) Next we select one of the 51 remaining cards at random, etc. When we have five cards, we determine how good a hand we drew.

This simulation was carried out for 10,000 poker hands on the Dartmouth Computer. The results were as in Figure 15.

You will be asked, in the exercises, to compare these figures with the expected values.

EXAMPLE 3 *Land of Oz.* Models in the social sciences often depend on Markov chain processes. While there are powerful theoretical tools for treating Markov chains, sufficiently complex models may have to be simulated. We shall

Type of hand	Number of times
Bust	5046
One pair	4169
Two pairs	508
Three of a kind	191
Straight	43
Flush	11
Full house	25
Four of a kind	6
Straight flush	1

Figure 15

illustrate this for a simple Markov chain, which we have already treated theoretically.

Consider the Land of Oz (Chapter 4, Section 7, Exercise 12). Suppose that we wished to find the fraction of times that the weather is "nice," "rain," or "snow," by simulation. We would first pick a starting state, say "rain." We then know that the probability of "rain" is $\frac{1}{2}$, of "nice" $\frac{1}{4}$, and of "snow" $\frac{1}{4}$. We can achieve this by generating an RND; if it is less than $\frac{1}{2}$ we decide on "rain," if it is between $\frac{1}{2}$ and $\frac{3}{4}$ then "nice" is next, while if RND $> \frac{3}{4}$ then "snow" is next.

The program RANDOMOZ carries out 1000 simulations for each starting state. After reading the transition probabilities, it starts a loop on S, the starting state. S1 is the current state. The list N is used for counting—e.g., N(1) is the total number of nice days. The only other comment needed is the explanation of line 90. Suppose that the probabilities of stepping into the three states is currently .25, .5, and .25. Then we should compare the random number successively with .25, .25 + .5 = .75, and .25 + .5 + .25 = 1. The same result may more simply be achieved by successive subtraction of .25, .5, and .25 until the number turns negative.

The program prints the number of times in each state for each starting state. While the values are reasonably close to the expected values of 200, 400, and 400, they are not close enough to be convincing. We show a second RUN with 10,000 simulations for each starting state and this time the fractions are much closer to the limiting probabilities .2, .4, and .4.

EXAMPLE 4   *Central Limit Theorem.* By simulating an independent trials process a large number of times we can hope to obtain an approximation of the central limit theorem. The program CLTH uses this method to approximate four values in Figure 6. Since the same distribution is obtained for any value of P, its choice is not crucial. The program uses P = .3. It carries out 100 experiments and counts the number of successes, noting how many standard deviations we are off the expected value. It repeats this 1000 times to get a frequency distribution.

▮ RANDOMOZ

```
10 MAT READ P(3,3)
20 DATA 0,.5,.5
21 DATA .25,.5,.25
22 DATA .25,.25,.5
30 FOR S = 1 TO 3
40 LET S1 = S
50 LET N(1)=N(2)=N(3)=0
60 FOR N = 1 TO 1000
70 LET X = RND
80 FOR I = 1 TO 3
90 LET X = X-P(S1,I)
100 IF X<0 THEN 120
110 NEXT I
120 LET N(I) = N(I)+1
130 LET S1 = I
140 NEXT N
150 PRINT N(1);N(2);N(3)
160 NEXT S
999 END
READY

RUN

RANDOMOZ

 211   391   398
 186   420   394
 199   378   423

1.019 SEC.
READY

60 FOR N = 1 TO 10000
RUN

RANDOMOZ

 2006   3997   3997
 1976   3982   4042
 2068   3973   3959

9.286 SEC.
READY
```

CLTH starts by setting up P, N, the expected value E, and the standard deviation S. Then the loop of 1000 repetitions is started. For each repetition, X, the number of successes, is initially set to 0. Lines 50–80 count the number of successes in 100 trials. On line 60, if RND $>$ .3 we have a failure, and hence the next line is skipped. For a success, X is increased by 1. Line 90 computes the number of standard deviations. We shall keep track only whether it is between 0 and 1, between 1 and 2, etc. This is accomplished on lines 100 and 110. When all 1000 repetitions are completed, we wish

■■■   CLTH

```
10 LET P = .3
20 LET N = 100
25 LET E = N*P
30 LET S = SQR(N*P*(1-P))
40 FOR I = 1 TO 1000
45 LET X = 0
50 FOR J = 1 TO N
60 IF RND > .3 THEN 80
70 LET X = X+1
80 NEXT J
90 LET Y = ABS((X-E)/S)
100 LET K = INT(Y)+1
110 LET N(K) = N(K)+1
120 NEXT I
130 PRINT "STD'S","AREA"
140 FOR D = 1 TO 4
150 LET A = A+N(D)/2000
160 PRINT D,A
170 NEXT D
199 END
READY

RUN

CLTH

STD'S          AREA
 1             0.334
 2             0.4795
 3             0.4975
 4             0.5

5.466 SEC.
READY
```

to print the approximate areas. A comment concerning line 150 is in order. We wish to compute the cumulative areas, as in Figure 5; hence we keep adding the new area to the previous value of A. The reason for dividing the total number of occurrences N(D) by 2000 rather than 1000 is that we want the area on one side of the expected value, while our counting method lumped the two sides together.

We note that the computed values agree quite well with the true values. The true values are .341, .477, .4987, .49997.

EXAMPLE 5   *Baseball.* The game of baseball is a good example of a game having a model for which a complete theoretical treatment is not practical, and hence much can be gained from simulation.

How would we build a simulation model for a given team, in order to study the way they produce runs? Fortunately, some very detailed statistics are kept, over long periods, which are ideal for building such a model. Let us suppose that a given batter comes to bat. We know from past experience what the probabilities are for his making an out, getting a walk, or getting a hit of various kinds. We simply generate an RND, and use it to decide what the batter did.

For example, if he has probabilities .1 for a walk, .64 for an out, .2 for a single, .03 for a double, .01 for a triple, and .02 for a home run, we can generate a random integer from 1 through 100, and interpret it as in Figure 16.

Range	Result	Probability
1–10	Walk	.1
11–74	Out	.64
75–94	Single	.2
95–97	Double	.03
98	Triple	.01
99–100	Home run	.02

Figure 16

We can then bring the next batter to bat, and arrive at a result based on *his* past performance. The running on the bases may be simulated similarly. For example, we can feed into the machine the probability that a man on first reaches third on a single. Just how realistic we wish to make the model depends entirely on how much work we are willing to do.

It should be noted that we are simulating only the batting of *one* team. We do not here consider the batting of the other team, or questions of defensive play.

Such a model would be most useful in training young managers. The computer could make all decisions (many of them stochastic) having to do with the performance of the players, while the manager could make all decisions normally open to managers. For example, he could call for a hit-and-run play, and the machine would simulate the results. He could call for a steal, or send in a pinch hitter, or tell a batter to try to hit a long fly ball.

By the use of a computer a new manager could gain an entire season's experience in a few days—and he would not be learning at the expense of his team.

The model is also useful for planning purposes, as we shall illustrate here. One important task of the manager is to decide on his batting order. He could feed a variety of batting orders to the computer, have it try each for a season's games (or more), and report back the results.

This was actually done on the Dartmouth Computer.

The team used in the simulation was the starting line-up of the 1963 world champion Los Angeles Dodgers. The line-up of Figure 17 was used throughout.

Line-up	Batting average	Slugging average
1. Wills	.302	.349
2. Gilliam	.282	.383
3. W. Davis	.245	.365
4. T. Davis	.326	.457
5. Howard	.273	.518
6. Fairly	.271	.388
7. McMullen	.236	.339
8. Roseboro	.236	.351
9. Pitcher (average)	.117	.152

Figure 17

An entire season of 162 games was simulated, keeping detailed records for each player. Of course, this simulation differed from the normal year in a few respects. For instance, the first eight players played every inning of every game. Since only the batting was simulated, no allowance was made for defensive play, nor did the game stop after eight innings if the home team was ahead. Games were not called on account of rain, and there were no extra-inning games. But many important features concerning batting were recreated quite realistically. We shall cite a few of the more interesting results.

Seven of the batters ended up with batting averages close to their actual ones, but two did not. Tommy Davis, the league's leading hitter, had an even more spectacular year during simulation: he batted an even .350 (compared with .326 in 1963). On the other hand, Fairly, who had batted .271 in actuality, had a bad simulated year, batting only .250. This shows how much a batting average can change due to purely random factors.

Howard was far ahead in home runs, with 54. This is much higher than the 28 he had in actuality, but he was only used part-time in 1963, while in the simulated year he played all the time. Two of the home runs were hit by pitchers—just as in real life. In one game Howard hit three home runs. But mostly it was the balance of the Dodger team that showed up; there were ten games in which three different players hit home runs.

There were no really spectacular slumps, though Gilliam once went 15 consecutive at-bats without getting a hit. The total number of runs scored was 652, in excellent agreement with the actual 640. On the other hand, the 1352 men left on base compared very poorly with the Dodgers' league-leading performance of leaving only 1034 men on base. Two factors in this were the absence of double-plays and pinch hitters in the simulation model. But there is probably some other relevant attribute of the team that was missed in the model.

Perhaps the most interesting result is the number of shutouts (*of the* Dodgers, of course). There were 11 in the simulation, as compared to the league-leading performance of only 8 shutouts. In the simulation, two of the shutouts occurred in the final two games. Thus, if the season ended in 160 games, the simulation would have been off by only one shutout. This shows how hard it is to get an accurate estimate for a small probability through simulation! And there was a four-game stretch late in the season in which three of the games ended in shutouts. If this had happened in real life, all the Los Angeles papers would have carried headlines about a Dodger batting slump.

To compare various possible batting orders, several line-ups were simulated for ten entire seasons. The seven line-ups are shown in the first column of Figure 18, and the results in the second column. The standard deviation of the average number of runs per game was about .07. Since the difference between the best and the worst line-ups is over three standard deviations, one is tempted to conclude that the batting order really makes a difference —though not very much of a difference.

However, this simulation—though time-consuming—is not conclusive. We may still entertain the hypothesis that any line-up averages about 3.95 runs per game, and all seven outcomes are within two standard deviations of this. We are forced into an even more substantial simulation run.

The simulation was repeated; this time every line-up had seven sets of ten entire seasons simulated. The newly computed averages are shown in the third column of Figure 18, while the maximum and minimum values obtained for a set of ten seasons are shown in the last column. Since we have simulated seven times as many games for each line-up, the standard deviation is reduced by a factor of $\sqrt{7}$, to less than .03. The differences in the averages now look more significant. Also, we note that the ranges obtained for the first five line-ups don't overlap (or hardly overlap) the ranges for the last two line-ups. We may therefore conclude that we have five "good" and two "poor" line-ups. And this hypothesis stands up under more sophisticated tests.

What characterizes the poor line-ups? Most noticeably, the pitcher is first, rather than being last. But also we note that the Dodgers had three weak

| | Average number of runs per game | | |
Line-up	10 seasons	7 × 10 seasons	Range
1, 2, 3, 4, 5, 6, 7, 8, 9	4.06	4.00	3.91–4.06
1, 4, 2, 5, 6, 3, 8, 7, 9	4.07	4.02	3.92–4.07
4, 5, 6, 1, 2, 3, 7, 8, 9	4.00	3.98	3.90–4.04
2, 1, 3, 5, 4, 6, 8, 7, 9	3.98	4.01	3.95–4.08
1, 4, 7, 2, 5, 8, 3, 6, 9	3.90	3.98	3.90–4.05
9, 8, 7, 6, 5, 4, 3, 2, 1	3.89	3.82	3.72–3.89
9, 6, 3, 8, 5, 2, 7, 4, 1	3.83	3.83	3.76–3.92

Figure 18

hitters (numbers 3, 7, and 8), and two of these are near the top of the bad line-ups. We therefore conclude that poor hitters should be near the end of the line-up. But little else can be concluded.

We should also note that the difference between best and worst is surprisingly little, and drastic changes in the "best" have practically no effect. Thus we conclude that the importance of the batting order has been greatly exaggerated.

One additional remark may be of interest: The first line-up in Figure 18 is, of course, the one actually chosen by the manager. The last five are simply permutations chosen according to simple patterns. However, the second line-up was chosen by one of the authors, a Dodger fan, as his attempt to "manage" the team. He was most pleased that it turned out best! Of course, .02 is only $\frac{2}{3}$ of a standard deviation, which represents about three runs per year, and is not significant.

EXERCISES

1. Use the RUN of RANDOM to simulate an independent trials process with probability .4 of success, for 30 trials. How many successes do you obtain?   [*Ans.* 15.]

2. Simulate three games of craps as follows. To imitate the roll of a pair of dice choose pairs of outcomes of the last RUN of RANDOM reading from left to right in successive rows and then proceed according to the rules of craps.
    [*Partial Ans.* On first game player rolls a 5 and wins.]

3. From Chapter 3, Section 3, Exercises 16, 17, and 18, compute the expected number of bust, straight, flush, and full house hands in 10,000 poker hands. Also compute the standard deviation for each. Do the figures given in Example 2 for the simulation look reasonable?
    [*Partial Ans.* Bust: expect 5012; off by less than one standard deviation.]

4. What would be reasonable 95 percent confidence limits for the deviation from the expected number of wins in 250,000 games of craps?

Do the simulated results of $-.0115$ and $-.0154$ mentioned in the text fall within these limits?

5. Using the data of the 30 random numbers between 0 and 1 generated by **RANDOM**, test the hypothesis that the probability that a random number generated this way has probability .1 of falling between .2 and .3.

6. Use the random numbers produced by the program **RANDOM** to simulate 30 days' weather in the Land of Oz, following a rainy day; see Example 3.

7. Change the random numbers generated by **RANDOM** between 0 and 1 to random numbers between 1 and 100.

8. Suppose that we have a baseball team whose batters each performs according to the simulation scheme in Figure 16. Use the random integers obtained in Exercise 7 to simulate the performance of the first 30 batters on one team. How does the team stand after 30 men have come to bat?   [*Ans.* End of six innings; four runs scored.]

9. In 1951, Gil Hodges of the Brooklyn Dodgers was officially at bat 582 times and hit 40 home runs. Estimate his probability of hitting a home run each time he was at bat. How large a fluctuation in his annual home-run output is attributable to pure chance?

10. From 1949 through 1959, Gil Hodges had the following number of home runs: $23, 32, 40, 32, 31, 42, 27, 32, 27, 22, 25$. Is there a case for his having had "good" and "bad" years, or may we assign the differences entirely to chance fluctuations: [*Hint:* Estimate the expected value from the data and use Exercise 10.]

               [*Ans.* Explainable as chance fluctuations.]

11. In Exercise 14 of Section 4, you were asked to derive the more exact confidence intervals

$$\frac{1}{1 + s^2/n}\left[\bar{p} + \frac{s^2}{2n} \pm s\left(\frac{\bar{p}(1 - \bar{p})}{n} + \frac{s^2}{4n^2}\right)^{1/2}\right].$$

Write a program to compute these more exact intervals given $n, \bar{p}$, and s.

12. Use the program of Exercise 11 to rework Exercises 2 and 6 of Section 4. Also rework each of these exercises using the program **CLTH** given in this section. For each exercise give one possible value for p which is ruled out by the more exact confidence interval but is not ruled out by the approximation used in the program in this section.

13. Write a program to test the hypothesis p_0 against p_1, given p_0, p_1, and s. Have the program print both the number of experiments needed and the number of those experiments that must be successful in order to accept hypothesis p_1.

14. Use the program of Exercise 13 to rework Exercises 9 and 11 of Section 3.

15. Write a program which, given p, simulates 100 tosses of a coin which comes up heads with probability p. Combine this with the program for confidence intervals given in the text and compute 95 percent

confidence limits for p, given the simulated data, and see whether p is within the confidence interval. Do the same using the more exact confidence limits which the program of Exercise 11 computes.

16. Run the program of Exercise 15 a total of 500 times and find, for each method, what fraction of the time p lies within the confidence interval.

SUGGESTED READING

Blackwell, David. *Basic Statistics*. New York: McGraw-Hill, 1969.

Hodges, J. L., Jr., and Lehmann, E. L. *Basic Concepts of Probability and Statistics*. 2nd ed. San Francisco: Holden-Day, 1971.

Kurtz T. E. *Basic Statistics*. Englewood Cliffs, N.J.: Prentice-Hall, 1963.

Mosteller, F.: Rourke, Robert E. K.; and Thomas, G. B. *Probability with Statistical Applications*. Reading, Mass.: Addison-Wesley, 1970.

Tanur, Judith, et al., eds. *Statistics: A Guide to the Unknown*. San Francisco: Holden-Day, 1972.

Linear Programming
and the Theory of Games

7

1 POLYHEDRAL CONVEX SETS

Recall that an equation containing one or more variables is called an *open statement*. For instance,

(a) $$-2x_1 + 3x_2 = 6$$

is an example of an open statement. If we let $A = (-2, 3)$, $x = \begin{pmatrix} x_1 \\ x_2 \end{pmatrix}$, and $b = 6$, we can write (a) in matrix form as

$$Ax = (-2, 3)\begin{pmatrix} x_1 \\ x_2 \end{pmatrix} = -2x_1 + 3x_2 = 6 = b.$$

For some two-component vectors x the statement $Ax = b$ is true and for others it is false. For instance, if $x = \begin{pmatrix} 3 \\ 4 \end{pmatrix}$, it is true, since $-2 \cdot 3 + 3 \cdot 4 = 6$; and if $x = \begin{pmatrix} 2 \\ 4 \end{pmatrix}$, it is false, since $-2 \cdot 2 + 3 \cdot 4 = 8$. The set of all two-component vectors x that make the open statement $Ax = b$ true is defined to be the *truth set* of the open statement.

EXAMPLE 1   In plane geometry it is usual to picture in the plane the truth sets of open statements such as (a). Thus we can regard each two-component vector x as being the components of a point in the plane in the usual way. Then the truth set or *locus* (which is the geometric term for truth set) of (a) is

For a nontechnical introduction to linear programming the reader should cover the first three sections; for a more technical exposition including the simplex method, cover the first six sections. For a nontechnical introduction to the theory of games, cover just Sections 8, 9, and 10; and for a technical introduction, cover the whole chapter.

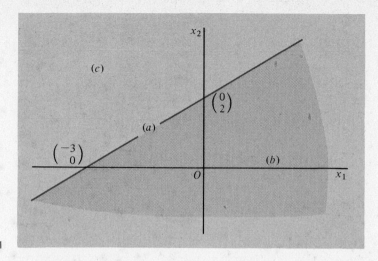

Figure 1

the straight line plotted in Figure 1. Points on this line may be obtained by assuming values for one of the variables and computing the corresponding values for the other variable. Thus, setting $x_1 = 0$, we find $x_2 = 2$, so that the point $x = \begin{pmatrix} 0 \\ 2 \end{pmatrix}$ lies on the locus; similarly, setting $x_2 = 0$, we find $x_1 = -3$, so that the point $\begin{pmatrix} -3 \\ 0 \end{pmatrix}$ lies on the locus; and so on.

In the same way inequalities of the form $Ax \leq b$ or $Ax < b$ or $Ax \geq b$ or $Ax > b$ are open statements and possess truth sets. And in the case that x is a two-component vector, these can be plotted in the plane.

EXAMPLE 2   Consider the inequalities (b) $Ax < b$, (c) $Ax > b$, (d) $Ax \leq b$, and (e) $Ax \geq b$, where A, x, and b are as in Example 1. They may be written as

(b) $-2x_1 + 3x_2 < 6,$

(c) $-2x_1 + 3x_2 > 6,$

(d) $-2x_1 + 3x_2 \leq 6,$

(e) $-2x_1 + 3x_2 \geq 6.$

Consider (b) first. What points $\begin{pmatrix} x_1 \\ x_2 \end{pmatrix}$ satisfy this inequality? By trial and error we can find many points on the locus. Thus the point $\begin{pmatrix} 1 \\ 2 \end{pmatrix}$ is on it, since $-2 \cdot 1 + 3 \cdot 2 = 4 < 6$; on the other hand, the point $\begin{pmatrix} 1 \\ 3 \end{pmatrix}$ is not on the locus, because $-2 \cdot 1 + 3 \cdot 3 = -2 + 9 = 7$, which is not less than 6.

In between these two points we find $\begin{pmatrix} 1 \\ \frac{8}{3} \end{pmatrix}$, which lies on the boundary—that

is, on the locus of (a). We note that, starting with $\begin{pmatrix} 1 \\ \frac{8}{3} \end{pmatrix}$ on locus (a), by

increasing x_2 we went outside the locus (b); by decreasing x_2 we came into
the locus (b) again. This holds in general. Given a point on the locus of
(a), by increasing its second coordinate we get more than 6, but by decreasing
the second coordinate we get less than 6, and hence the latter gives a point
in the truth set of (b). Thus we find that the locus of (b) consists of all
points of the plane *below* the line (a)—in other words, the shaded area in
Figure 1. The area on one side of a straight line is called an *open half-plane*.

We can apply exactly the same analysis to show that the locus of (c) is
the open half-plane above the line (a). This can also be deduced from the
fact that the truth sets of statements (a), (b), and (c) are disjoint and have
as union the entire plane.

Since (d) is the disjunction of (a) and (b), the truth set of (d) is the union
of the truth sets of (a) and (b). Such a set, which consists of an open
half-plane together with the points on the line that define the half-plane,
is called a *closed half-plane*. Obviously, the truth set of (e) consists of the
union of (a) and (c) and therefore is also a closed half-plane.

Frequently we want to assert several different open statements at once—
that is, we want to assert the conjunction of several such statements. The
easy way to do this is to let A be an $m \times n$ matrix, x an n-component column
vector, and b an m-component column vector. Then the statement $Ax \leq b$
is the conjunction of the m statements $A_i x \leq b_i$, where A_i *is the* ith row
of A and b_i is the ith entry of b.

EXAMPLE 3   A box manufacturer makes small and large boxes from a single kind of
cardboard. The small boxes require 2 square feet of cardboard each and
the large boxes 3 square feet each. If the manufacturer has 60 square feet
of cardboard on hand, what are the possible combinations of small and large
boxes that he can make?

In order to set up this problem let x_1 be the number of small boxes and
x_2 the number of large boxes to be made. Since it is impossible to make
negative numbers of boxes, we have the obvious constraints

(f) $$x_1 \geq 0,$$
(g) $$x_2 \geq 0.$$

Also, because of the constraint on the total amount of cardboard on hand,
we have

(h) $$2x_1 + 3x_2 \leq 60.$$

If we now want to state these three inequality constraints simultaneously
in the form $Ax \leq b$, we must first change (f) and (g) into $\leq$ constraints.

This can be done by multiplying through by -1, so that (f) becomes $-x_1 \leq 0$ and (g) becomes $-x_2 \leq 0$. If we now define

$$A = \begin{pmatrix} -1 & 0 \\ 0 & -1 \\ 2 & 3 \end{pmatrix}, \qquad x = \begin{pmatrix} x_1 \\ x_2 \end{pmatrix}, \qquad b = \begin{pmatrix} 0 \\ 0 \\ 60 \end{pmatrix},$$

we see that $Ax \leq b$ is a matrix way of asserting the conjunction of (f), (g), and (h). The truth set of $Ax \leq b$ is the intersection of the three individual truth sets. The truth set of (f) is the right half-plane; the truth set of (g) is the upper half-plane; and the truth set of (h) is the half-plane below and on the line $2x_1 + 3x_2 = 60$. The intersection of these is the triangle (including the sides and corners) shaded in Figure 2. The area shaded in Figure 2 contains all those and only those points that simultaneously satisfy (f), (g), and (h), or, equivalently, $Ax \leq b$.

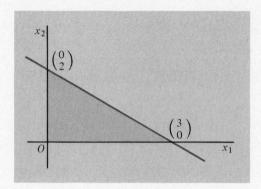

Figure 2

In the examples considered so far we have restricted ourselves to open statements with two variables. Such statements have truth sets that can be sketched in the plane. In the same way, open statements with three variables have truth sets that can be visualized in three-dimensional space. Open statements with four or more variables have truth sets in four or more dimensions, which we can no longer visualize. However, applied problems frequently lead to such statements. Fortunately, we shall develop methods (in Section 5) for handling them without having to visualize the truth sets geometrically.

In order to have a notation that will enable us to talk in general about conjunctions of several open statements in any number of dimensions, we shall, for the remainder of this chapter, consider b to be an m-component column vector, x an n-component column vector, and A an $m \times n$ matrix. The ith row of A will be denoted by A_i. Similarly, the ith component of b will be denoted by b_i. Of course, A_i is an n-component row vector and b_i is a number. We shall let $\mathfrak{X}_n$ denote the set of all n-component column vectors x. Thus in Example 3 we had $m = 3$ and $n = 2$. A was a 3×2

matrix, x a two-component column vector, and b a three-component column vector. The set of all two-component column vectors x is denoted by $\mathfrak{X}_2$.

We now set up some definitions that will be used in the later exposition.

Definition The truth set of $A_i x = b_i$ is called a *hyperplane* in $\mathfrak{X}_n$. The truth sets of inequalities of the form $A_i x < b_i$ or $A_i x > b_i$ are called *open half-spaces*, while the truth sets of the inequalities $A_i x \leq b_i$ or $A_i x \geq b_i$ are called *closed half-spaces* in $\mathfrak{X}_n$.

When we assert the conjunction of several open statements, the resulting truth set is the intersection of the truth sets of the individual open statements. Thus in Example 3 we have the conjunction of $m = 3$ open statements in $\mathfrak{X}_2$. In Figure 2 we show this geometrically as the intersection of $m = 3$ closed half-spaces (-planes) in $n = 2$ dimensions. Such intersections of closed half-spaces are of special importance.

Definition The intersection of a finite number of closed half-spaces is a *polyhedral convex set*.

Theorem Any polyhedral convex set is the truth set of an inequality statement of the form $Ax \leq b$.

Proof A closed half-space is the truth set of an inequality of the form $A_i x \leq b_i$. (An inequality of the form $A_i x \geq b_i$ can be converted into one of this form by multiplying by -1.) Now a polyhedral convex set is the truth set of the conjunction of several such statements. Since A is the matrix whose ith row is A_i and b is the column vector with components b_i, then the inequality statement $Ax \leq b$ is a succinct way of stating the conjunction of the inequalities $A_1 x \leq b_1, \ldots, A_m x \leq b_m$. This completes the proof.

The terminology polyhedral *convex* sets is used because these sets are special examples of convex sets. A convex set C is a set such that whenever u and v are points of C, the entire line segment between u and v also belongs to C. This is equivalent to saying that all points of the form $z = au + (1 - a)v$ for $0 \leq a \leq 1$ belong to C whenever u and v do. In this chapter we shall be concerned primarily with polyhedral convex sets.

EXERCISES

1. Draw pictures of the truth sets of $Ax \leq b$, where A and b are as given below. (Construct the truth sets of the individual statements first and then take their intersection.)

(a) $A = \begin{pmatrix} 1 & 0 \\ 0 & 1 \\ -2 & -3 \end{pmatrix}$, $b = \begin{pmatrix} 3 \\ 2 \\ 0 \end{pmatrix}$.

(b) $A = \begin{pmatrix} -2 & -3 \\ -1 & 1 \\ 1 & 1 \end{pmatrix}$, $b = \begin{pmatrix} -6 \\ 2 \\ 3 \end{pmatrix}$.

(c) $A = \begin{pmatrix} 2 & 3 \\ -1 & 1 \\ 1 & 1 \end{pmatrix}$, $b = \begin{pmatrix} 6 \\ 2 \\ 3 \end{pmatrix}$.

(d) $A = \begin{pmatrix} 0 & -1 \\ -1 & 0 \\ 1 & 0 \end{pmatrix}$, $b = \begin{pmatrix} 0 \\ 0 \\ 2 \end{pmatrix}$.

(e) $A = \begin{pmatrix} 1 & 0 \\ -1 & 0 \\ 0 & 1 \\ 0 & -1 \end{pmatrix}$, $b = \begin{pmatrix} 2 \\ 2 \\ 3 \\ 3 \end{pmatrix}$.

(f) $A = \begin{pmatrix} 3 & 2 \\ 3 & 2 \end{pmatrix}$, $b = \begin{pmatrix} -6 \\ 6 \end{pmatrix}$.

(g) $A = \begin{pmatrix} -3 & -2 \\ 3 & 2 \end{pmatrix}$, $b = \begin{pmatrix} -6 \\ 6 \end{pmatrix}$.

(h) $A = \begin{pmatrix} -1 & 1 \\ 1 & 1 \end{pmatrix}$, $b = \begin{pmatrix} 0 \\ 0 \end{pmatrix}$.

(i) $A = \begin{pmatrix} 1 & 0 \\ -1 & 0 \end{pmatrix}$, $b = \begin{pmatrix} 2 \\ -5 \end{pmatrix}$.

(j) $A = \begin{pmatrix} -3 & -2 \\ -2 & -3 \\ -1 & 0 \\ 0 & -1 \end{pmatrix}$, $b = \begin{pmatrix} -6 \\ -6 \\ 0 \\ 0 \end{pmatrix}$.

(k) $A = \begin{pmatrix} -2 & -1 \\ 1 & 0 \\ 0 & 1 \end{pmatrix}$, $b = \begin{pmatrix} -7 \\ 0 \\ 0 \end{pmatrix}$.

2.   In the cardboard-box problem of Example 3 consider the following additional constraints:

(a)   "At least as many small as large boxes should be made." Write a constraint involving x_1 and x_2 that expresses this and find A and b. Draw the picture of the resulting convex set.
   [*Partial ans.* $-x_1 + x_2 \le 0$.]

(b)   In addition to the constraints above add a constraint expressing; "at most 20 small boxes should be made." Find A and b and sketch the convex set.   [*Partial ans.* $x_1 \le 20$.]

3.   Of the polyhedral convex sets constructed in Exercise 1, which have a finite area and which have infinite area?
   [*Partial ans.* (c), (d), (f), (h), and (j) are of infinite area; (g) is a line; (i) and (k) are empty.]

4. For each of the following half-planes give an inequality of which it is the truth set.
    (a) The open half-plane above the x_1 axis.   [*Ans.* $x_2 > 0$.]
    (b) The closed half-plane on and above the straight line making angles of 45 degrees with the positive x_1 and x_2 axis.

Exercises 5 through 9 refer to a situation in which a retailer is trying to decide how many units of items X and Y he should keep in stock. Let x be the number of units of X and y be the number of units of Y. X costs \$4 per unit and Y costs \$3 per unit.

5. One cannot stock a negative number of units of either X or Y. Write these conditions as inequalities and draw their truth sets.
6. The maximum demand over the period for which the retailer is contemplating holding inventory will not exceed 600 units of X or 600 units of Y. Modify the set found in Exercise 5 to take this into account.
7. The retailer is not willing to tie up more than \$2400 in inventory altogether. Modify the set found in Exercise 6.
8. The retailer decides to invest at least twice as much in inventory of item X as he does in inventory of item Y. Modify the set of Exercise 7.
9. Finally, the retailer decides that he wants to invest \$900 in inventory of item Y. What possibilities are left?   [*Ans.* None.]

10. Assume that a pound of meat contains 80 units of protein and 10 units of calcium while a quart of milk contains 15 units of protein and 60 units of calcium. If an adult's minimum daily requirements are 40 units of protein and 30 units of calcium, what consumption quantities of meat and milk will yield at least these minimum daily requirements? A convenient way to summarize the data is by the following *data box:*

Food	Protein	Calcium
Meat	$80 \dfrac{\text{units protein}}{\text{lb meat}}$	$10 \dfrac{\text{units calcium}}{\text{lb meat}}$
Milk	$15 \dfrac{\text{units protein}}{\text{qt milk}}$	$60 \dfrac{\text{units calcium}}{\text{qt milk}}$
Requirements	$40 \dfrac{\text{units protein}}{\text{day}}$	$30 \dfrac{\text{units calcium}}{\text{day}}$

(a) Let w_1 be the number of pounds of meat and w_2 be the number of quarts of milk consumed per day, and let $w = (w_1, w_2)$. Write inequality constraints that will solve the above problem. Find A and c so that they can be written $wA \geq c$.

(b) Sketch the set of feasible vectors. Show that it is unbounded (that it has infinite area).

(c) Show that another way of indicating units is as in the data box that follows:

	Protein	Calcium	
Meat	80	10	(per pound)
Milk	15	60	(per quart)
Requirements	40	30	(per day)
	(units)	(units)	

2 EXTREME POINTS; MAXIMA AND MINIMA OF LINEAR FUNCTIONS

In the present section we first discuss the problem of finding the extreme points of a bounded convex polyhedral set. Then we find out how to compute the maximum and minimum values of a linear function defined on such a set.

We use the following notation: the polyhedral convex set C is the truth set of the statement $Ax \leq b$, where A is an $m \times n$ matrix, x is an n-component column vector, and b is an m-component column vector. We let $A_1, A_2, \ldots, A_m$ denote the rows of A. Hence A_i is an n-component row vector and

$$A = \begin{pmatrix} A_1 \\ A_2 \\ \vdots \\ A_m \end{pmatrix}.$$

The statement $Ax \leq b$ is then the conjunction of the statements

$$A_1x \leq b_1, \quad A_2x \leq b_2, \quad \ldots, \quad A_mx \leq b_m.$$

Definition We shall call the truth set of the statement $A_ix = b_i$ the bounding hyperplane of the half space $A_ix \leq b_i$.

Thus, in Figure 1 of the preceding section the slanting line (a) is the bounding hyperplane of the half-space (b).

We found in the previous section that a convex set C is the intersection of a finite number of half-spaces. The bounding hyperplanes of these half-spaces that also contain points of C are called *bounding hyperplanes* of C. Thus in Example 3 of Section 1 the bounding hyperplanes of the polyhedral convex set given there are the three boundary lines of the triangle shaded in Figure 2. Note that these lines intersect in pairs in three points, the vertices of the triangle.

Definition Let C be the polyhedral convex set defined by $Ax \leq b$, where x is an n-component vector. Then a point T is an *extreme* (or *corner*) *point* of C if it

a. belongs to C, and
b. is the intersection of n bounding hyperplanes of C.

EXAMPLE 1 Find the extreme points of the polyhedral convex set $Ax \leq b$, where

$$A = \begin{pmatrix} 2 & 3 \\ -2 & -1 \\ 0 & -1 \end{pmatrix}, \qquad x = \begin{pmatrix} x_1 \\ x_2 \end{pmatrix}, \qquad b = \begin{pmatrix} 60 \\ -32 \\ -2 \end{pmatrix}.$$

The corresponding inequalities are:

$$\begin{aligned} 2x_1 + 3x_2 &\leq 60, \\ 2x_1 + x_2 &\geq 32, \\ x_2 &\geq 2. \end{aligned}$$

The last two inequalities have been multiplied through by -1, and can be regarded as managerial constraints added to the box-manufacturer problem of Example 3 of Section 1. A sketch of the three half-planes (Figure 3)

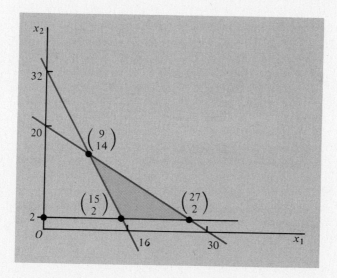

Figure 3

shows that the set of feasible solutions is a triangle. Hence we can find the extreme points by changing the inequalities to equalities in pairs and solving three sets of simultaneous equations. We obtain in this way the points

$$\begin{pmatrix} 9 \\ 14 \end{pmatrix}, \qquad \begin{pmatrix} 15 \\ 2 \end{pmatrix}, \qquad \begin{pmatrix} 27 \\ 2 \end{pmatrix},$$

which are the extreme points of the set.

We can now give an interpretation for the various points of the polyhedral convex set in terms of the system of inequalities. An extreme point lines on two boundaries, which means that two of the inequalities are actually equalities. A point on a side, other than an extreme point, lies on one boundary and hence one inequality is an equality. An interior point of the polygon must, by a process of elimination, correspond to the case where the inequalities are all strict inequalities—that is, not only $\leq$ but $<$ holds.

There is a mechanical (but lengthy) method for finding all the extreme points of a polyhedral convex set C defined by $Ax \leq b$. Consider the bounding hyperplanes $A_1x = b_1, \ldots, A_mx = b_m$ of the half-spaces that determine C. Select a subset of n of these hyperplanes and solve their equations simultaneously. If the result is a unique point x^0, then (and only then) check to see whether x^0 belongs to C. If it does, by the above definition, x^0 is an extreme point of C. Moreover, all extreme points of C can be found in this manner.

EXAMPLE 2   Let

$$A = \begin{pmatrix} -1 & 0 \\ 0 & -1 \end{pmatrix} \quad \text{and} \quad b = \begin{pmatrix} 0 \\ 0 \end{pmatrix}.$$

Then the polyhedral convex set C defined by $Ax \leq b$ is the first quadrant of the x_1, x_2 plane, shaded in Figure 4. The only extreme point is the origin, which is the intersection of the lines $x_1 = 0$ and $x_2 = 0$. This is an example of an *unbounded* polyhedral convex set.

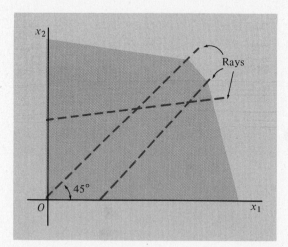

Figure 4

Notice that the set C in Example 2 contains the *ray* or half-line that starts at the origin of coordinates and extends upward to the right making a 45-degree angle with the axes. This ray is dotted in Figure 4. Of course, this set also contains many other rays; two others are shown in the figure.

We shall say that a polyhedral convex set is *bounded* if it does not contain a ray. A set, such as the one in Figure 4, that does contain rays will be called *unbounded*. For simplicity we shall restrict our discussion in most of this chapter to bounded convex sets.

EXAMPLE 3 Consider the box-manufacturer problem of Example 3 of Section 1, and suppose that the manufacturer makes a profit of $1 on small and $2 on large boxes. Hence, if he makes x_1 small and x_2 large boxes, his profit function is $x_1 + 2x_2$, and the inequalities limiting the choice of x_1 and x_2 are given in Example 1. What is the most and what the least profit he can make?

We must find the maximum and the minimum value of $x_1 + 2x_2$ for point (x_1, x_2) in the triangle shaded in Figure 3. Let us first try the extreme points. At $(15, 2)$ we have a profit of 19, at $(27, 2)$ a profit of 31, and at $(9, 14)$ a profit of 37. The last extreme point is most profitable. But what can we say about the remainder of the triangle? If we start at $(9, 14)$ and try to move to other points in the triangle, the best thing to do is to move along the bounding hyperplane $2x_1 + 3x_2 = 60$, since in this way we can get the most favorable tradeoff between x_1 and x_2. However, for each unit we decrease x_2 along this line we can increase x_1 by only $\frac{3}{2}$ units, with a net loss of profit. Hence the maximum profit is taken on at the extreme point $(9, 14)$. A similar argument shows that the minimum profit is taken on at the extreme point $(15, 2)$. Thus for this example the maximum and minimum profits are observed at extreme points. We shall show that this is true in general.

Given a convex polyhedral set C and a linear function

$$cx = c_1x_1 + c_2x_2 + \ldots + c_nx_n,$$

where $c = (c_1, c_2, \ldots, c_n)$, we want to show in general that the maximum and minimum values of the function cx always occur at extreme points of C. We shall carry out the proof for the planar case in which $n = 2$, but our results are true in general.

First, we shall show that the values of the linear function $c_1x_1 + c_2x_2$ on any line segment lie *between* the values the function has at the two endpoints (possibly equal to the value at one endpoint). We represent the points as column vectors $\begin{pmatrix} x_1 \\ x_2 \end{pmatrix}$ and then we see that our linear function is represented by the row vector (c_1, c_2). Let the endpoints of the segment be

$$p = \begin{pmatrix} x_1' \\ x_2' \end{pmatrix} \quad \text{and} \quad q = \begin{pmatrix} x_1'' \\ x_2'' \end{pmatrix}.$$

We have seen in Chapter 4 (see Figure 4) that the points in between p and q can be represented as $tp + (1 - t)q$, with $0 \leq t \leq 1$. If the values of the function at the points p and q are P and Q, respectively (assume that $P \geq Q$), then at a point in between the value will be $tP + (1 - t)Q$, since the function is linear. This value can also be written as

$$tP + (1 - t)Q = Q + (P - Q)t,$$

which (for $0 \leq t \leq 1$) is at least Q and at most P.

We are now in a position to prove the result illustrated in Example 3.

Theorem A linear function cx defined over a convex polyhedral set C takes on its maximum (and minimum) value at an extreme point of C.

Proof The proof of the theorem is illustrated in Figure 5. We shall suppose that at the extreme point p the function takes on a value P greater than or equal to the value at any other extreme point, and at the extreme point

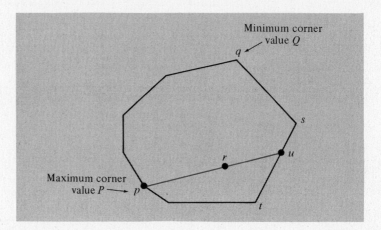

Figure 5

q it takes on its smallest extreme-point value, Q. Let r be any point of the polygon. Draw a straight line between p and r and continue it until it cuts the polygon again at a point u lying on an edge of the polygon, say the edge between the corner points s and t. (The line may even cut the edge at one of the points s and t; the analysis remains unchanged.) By hypothesis the value of the function at any corner point must lie between Q and P. By the above result the value of the function at u must lie between its values at s and t, and hence must also lie between Q and P. Again by the above result the value of the function at r must lie between its values at p and u, and hence must also lie between Q and P. Since r was any point of the polygon, our theorem is proved.

Suppose that in place of the linear function $c_1x_1 + c_2x_2$ we had considered the function $c_1x_1 + c_2x_2 + k$. The addition of the constant k merely changes every value of the function, including the maximum and minimum values of the function, by that amount. Hence the analysis of where the maximum and minimum values of the function are taken on is unchanged. Therefore, we have the following theorem.

Theorem The function $cx + k$ defined over a convex polyhedral set C takes on its maximum (and minimum) value at an extreme point of C.

A method of finding the maximum or minimum of the function $cx + k$ defined over a convex set C is then the following: Find the extreme points of the set; there will be a finite number of them; substitute the coordinates of each into the function; the largest of the values so obtained will be the maximum of the function and the smallest value will be the minimum of the function. The method was illustrated previously in Example 3.

In Section 5 we shall describe the so-called *simplex method*, which is considerably more efficient for solving the problem in Example 3.

EXERCISES

1. Consider the cardboard-box problem of Exercise 2 of Section 1. Assuming that both constraints stated in (a) and (b) are in effect and the profit function is $x_1 + 2x_2$, find the extreme point (or points) that give maximum and minimum profit.

2. Rework Exercise 1 with profit function $2x_1 + 3x_2$. Show that in this case there is more than one solution for maximum profit.

3. Consider the diet problem of Exercise 10 of Section 1. Suppose that meat costs $1 per pound and milk costs 30 cents per quart. Find the lowest-cost diet that will meet minimum requirements.
    [*Ans.* $w = (\frac{13}{31}, \frac{40}{93})$, cost is $\$\frac{17}{31}$.]

4. The owner of an oil truck with a capacity of 500 gallons hauls gasoline and oil products from city to city. On any given trip he wishes to load his truck with at least 200 gallons of regular gasoline, at least 100 gallons of high-test gasoline, and at most 150 gallons of kerosene. Assuming that he always fills his truck to capacity, find the convex set of ways that he can load his truck. Interpret the extreme points of the set. [*Hint:* There are four extreme points.]

5. An advertiser wishes to sponsor a half-hour television comedy and must decide on the composition of the show. The advertiser insists that there be at least three minutes of commercials, while the television network requires that the commercial time be limited to at most 15 minutes. The comedian refuses to work more than 22 minutes each half-hour show. If a band is added to play while neither the comedian nor the commercials are on, construct the convex set C of possible assignments of time to the comedian, the commercials, and the band that use up the 30 minutes. Find the extreme points of C.
    [*Ans.* if x_1 is the comedian time, x_2 the commercial time, and $30 - x_1 - x_2$ the band time, the extreme points are

$$\binom{0}{3}, \binom{22}{3}, \binom{22}{8}, \binom{15}{15} \text{ and } \binom{0}{15}.]$$

6. In Exercise 4 suppose that the oil truck operator gets 3 cents per gallon for delivering regular gasoline, 2 cents per gallon for high-test, and 1 cent per gallon for kerosene. Write the expression that gives the total amount he will get paid for each possible load that he carries. How should he load his truck in order to earn the maximum amount? [*Ans.* He should carry 400 gallons of regular gasoline, 100 gallons of high test, and no kerosene.]

7. In Exercise 6, if he gets 3 cents per gallon for regular and 2 cents per gallon for high-test gasoline, how high must his payment for kerosene become before he will load it on his truck in order to make a maximum profit?

    [*Ans.* He must get paid at least 3 cents per gallon of kerosene.]

8. In Exercise 5 let x_1 be the number of minutes the comedian is on and x_2 the number of minutes the commercial is on the program. Suppose the comedian costs \$200 per minute, the commercials cost \$50 per minute, and the band is free. How should the advertiser choose the composition of the show in order that its costs be a minimum?

9. Consider the polyhedral convex set P defined by the inequalities

    $$-1 \le x_1 \le 4,$$
    $$0 \le x_2 \le 6.$$

    Find four different sets of conditions on the constants a and b that the function $\mathbf{F}(x) = ax_1 + bx_2$ should have its maximum at one and only one of the four corner points of P. Find conditions that $\mathbf{F}$ should have its minimum at each of these points.

    [*Ans.* For example, the maximum is at $\binom{4}{6}$ if $a > 0$ and $b > 0$.]

10. A well-known nursery rhyme goes, "Jack Sprat could eat no fat, his wife could eat no lean. . . ." Suppose Jack wishes to have at least one pound of lean meat per day, while his wife (call her Jill) needs at least .4 pound of fat per day. Assume they buy only beef having 10 percent fat and 90 percent lean, and pork having 40 percent fat and 60 percent lean. Jack and Jill want to fulfill their minimal diet requirements at the lowest possible cost.

    (a) Let x be the amount of beef and y the amount of pork they purchase per day. Construct the convex set of points in the plane representing purchases that fulfill both persons' minimum diet requirements.

    (b) Suggest necessary restrictions on the purchases that will change this set into a convex polygon.

    (c) If beef costs \$1 per pound, and pork costs 50 cents per pound, show that the diet of least cost has only pork, and find the minimum cost.   [*Ans.* \$.83.]

    (d) If beef costs 75 cents and pork costs 50 cents per pound, show that there is a whole-line segment of solution points and find the minimum cost.   [*Ans.* \$.83.]

(e) If beef and pork each cost $1 a pound, show that the unique minimal cost diet has both beef and pork. Find the minimum cost.
[*Ans.* $1.40.]

(f) Show that the restriction made in part (b) did not alter the answers given in (c)–(e).

11. In Exercise 10(d) show that for all but one of the minimal-cost diets Jill has more than her minimum requirement of fat, while Jack always gets exactly his minimal requirement of lean. Show that all but one of the minimal-cost diets contains some beef.

12. In Exercise 10(e) show that Jack and Jill each get exactly their minimal requirements.

13. In Exercise 10 if the price of pork is fixed at $1 a pound, how low must the price of beef fall before Jack and Jill will eat only beef?
[*Ans.* $.25.]

14. In Exercise 10 suppose that Jack decides to reduce his minimal requirement to .6 pound of lean meat per day. How does the convex set change? How do the solutions in 3(c), (d), and (e) change?

3 LINEAR PROGRAMMING PROBLEMS

An important class of practical problems are those that require the determination of the maximum or the minimum of a linear function $cx + k$ defined over a polyhedral convex set of points C. We illustrate these so-called *linear programming problems* by means of the following examples. In Section 5 we shall discuss the simplex method for solving these examples.

EXAMPLE 1 An automobile manufacturer makes automobiles and trucks in a factory that is divided into two shops. Shop 1, which performs the basic assembly operation, must work 5 man-days on each truck but only 2 man-hours on each automobile. Shop 2, which performs finishing operations, must work 3 man-hours for each automobile or truck that it produces. Because of men and machine limitations shop 1 has 180 man-hours per week available while shop 2 has 135 man-hours per week. If the manufacturer makes a profit of $300 on each truck and $200 on each automobile, how many of each should he produce to maximize his profit?

Before proceeding, let us summarize the problem in the *data box* of Figure 6. (The term *data box* is due to A. W. Tucker.) Notice that the numbers introduced above appear in the data box with their physical dimensions attached. When doing dimensional analysis, in the sense of physics, we may manipulate these dimension quantities just like algebraic quantities. We shall see in Section 6 that we can obtain interpretations for dual variables by means of dimensional analysis. The reader is strongly advised to set up a similar data box for every linear programming example he works.

An alternate and slightly more elegant way of indicating the units in the data box is shown in Figure 7. The reader should compare it with Figure

	Trucks	Autos	Capacities
Shop 1	$5 \dfrac{\text{S1-manhr}}{\text{truck}}$	$2 \dfrac{\text{S1-manhr}}{\text{auto}}$	$180 \dfrac{\text{S1-manhr}}{\text{week}}$
Shop 2	$3 \dfrac{\text{S2-manhr}}{\text{truck}}$	$3 \dfrac{\text{S2-manhr}}{\text{auto}}$	$135 \dfrac{\text{S2-manhr}}{\text{week}}$ ·
Profits	$300 \dfrac{\$}{\text{truck}}$	$200 \dfrac{\$}{\text{auto}}$	

Figure 6

	Trucks	Autos	Capacities	
Shop 1	5	2	180	(Man-hours)
Shop 2	3	3	135	(Man-hours)
Profits	300	200		($)
	(per truck)	(per auto)	(per week)	

Figure 7

6 to see the correspondence between them. When in doubt, use the more explicit indications of Figure 6.

A dimensional fraction such as "S1-manhr/truck" is read "shop 1 man-hours per truck." Suppose we now introduce two variables x_1 with dimensions "trucks/week," which will become the number of trucks per week we should produce, and x_2 with dimensions "autos/week." Then the first constraint of the data box of Figure 6 becomes:

$$\left(5 \frac{\text{S1-manhr}}{\text{truck}}\right)\left(x_1 \frac{\text{trucks}}{\text{week}}\right) + \left(2 \frac{\text{S1-manhr}}{\text{auto}}\right)\left(x_2 \frac{\text{autos}}{\text{week}}\right) \leq 180 \frac{\text{S1-manhr}}{\text{week}}.$$

Now, by canceling the common term "truck" from numerator and denominator of the first term, and similarly canceling the common dimension "auto" from the numerator and denominator of the second term, we see that the resulting dimensions of each term are "S1-manhr/week"—the same as the dimensions of the capacity term on the right-hand side of the inequality. A similar dimensional analysis can be carried out for the second capacity constraint. Dropping dimensions, we have the following restrictions:

$$5x_1 + 2x_2 \leq 180,$$
$$3x_1 + 3x_2 \leq 135,$$

together with the obviously necessary nonnegative constraints $x_1 \geq 0$ and $x_2 \geq 0$.

Subject to these constraints we want to maximize the profit function:

$$\left(300 \frac{\$}{\text{truck}}\right)\left(x_1 \frac{\text{trucks}}{\text{week}}\right) + \left(200 \frac{\$}{\text{auto}}\right)\left(x_2 \frac{\text{autos}}{\text{week}}\right).$$

Canceling out the common terms, we see that the dimensions of this function are simply "\$/week."

In order to state the problem as a linear programming problem we define the quantities:

$$A = \begin{pmatrix} 5 & 2 \\ 3 & 3 \end{pmatrix}, \quad b = \begin{pmatrix} 180 \\ 135 \end{pmatrix}, \quad \text{and} \quad c = (300, 200),$$

which are immediately evident from the data boxes in Figure 6 and 7. Then our problem is:

Maximum problem: Determine the vector $x = \begin{pmatrix} x_1 \\ x_2 \end{pmatrix}$ so that the weekly profit, given by the quantity cx, is a maximum subject to the inequality constraints $Ax \le b$ and $x \ge 0$. The inequality constraints insure that the weekly number of available man-hours is not exceeded and that nonnegative quantities of automobiles and trucks are produced.

The graph of the convex set of possible x vectors is pictured in Figure 8. This is a problem of the kind discussed in the previous section.

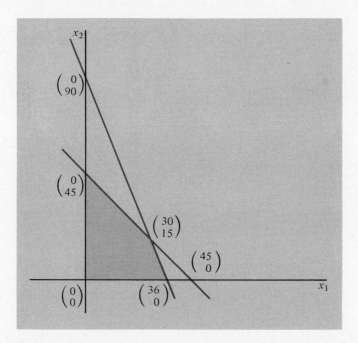

Figure 8

The extreme points of the convex set C are

$$T_1 = \begin{pmatrix} 0 \\ 0 \end{pmatrix}, \quad T_2 = \begin{pmatrix} 36 \\ 0 \end{pmatrix}, \quad T_3 = \begin{pmatrix} 0 \\ 45 \end{pmatrix}, \quad \text{and} \quad T_4 = \begin{pmatrix} 30 \\ 15 \end{pmatrix}.$$

Following the solution procedure outlined in the previous section, we test the function $cx = 300x_1 + 200x_2$ at each of these extreme points. The values taken on are 0, 10,800, 9000, and 12,000. Thus the maximum weekly profit is $12,000, achieved by producing 30 trucks and 15 automobiles per week.

EXAMPLE 2 A mining company owns two different mines that produce a given kind of ore. The mines are located in different parts of the country and have different production capacities. After crushing, the ore is graded into three classes: high-grade, medium-grade, and low-grade ores. There is some demand for each grade of ore. The mining company has contracted to provide a smelting plant with 12 tons of high-grade, 8 tons of medium-grade, and 24 tons of low-grade ore per week. It costs the company $200 per day to run the first mine and $160 per day to run the second. However, in a day's operation the first mine produces 6 tons of high-grade, 2 tons of medium-grade, and 4 tons of low-grade ore, while the second mine produces daily 2 tons of high-grade, 2 tons of medium-grade, and 12 tons of low-grade ore. How many days a week should each mine be operated in order to fulfill the company's orders most economically?

Before proceeding, we again summarize the problem in the data boxes of Figures 9 and 10. The reader should compare these two figures to see the correspondence between them. We shall make use of these dimensions when we give interpretations of the dual variables in Section 6.

	High-grade Ore HG	Medium-grade Ore MG	Low-grade Ore LG	Cost
Mine 1	$6 \dfrac{\text{tons-HG}}{\text{M1-day}}$	$2 \dfrac{\text{tons-MG}}{\text{M1-day}}$	$4 \dfrac{\text{tons-LG}}{\text{M1-day}}$	$200 \dfrac{\$}{\text{M1-day}}$
Mine 2	$2 \dfrac{\text{tons-HG}}{\text{M2-day}}$	$2 \dfrac{\text{tons-MG}}{\text{M2-day}}$	$12 \dfrac{\text{tons-LG}}{\text{M2-day}}$	$160 \dfrac{\$}{\text{M2-day}}$
Requirements	$12 \dfrac{\text{tons-HG}}{\text{week}}$	$8 \dfrac{\text{tons-MG}}{\text{week}}$	$24 \dfrac{\text{tons-LG}}{\text{week}}$	

Figure 9

	High-grade Ore	Medium-grade Ore	Low-grade Ore	Cost	
Mine 1	6	2	4	200	(per day)
Mine 2	2	2	12	160	(per day)
Requirements	12	8	24		(per week)
	(tons)	(tons)	(tons)	($)	

Figure 10

Let $v = (v_1, v_2)$ be the two-component row vector whose component v_1 gives the number of days per week that mine 1 operates and v_2 gives the number of days per week that mine 2 operates. If we define the quantities

$$A = \begin{pmatrix} 6 & 2 & 4 \\ 2 & 2 & 12 \end{pmatrix}, \quad c = (12, 8, 24), \quad \text{and} \quad b = \begin{pmatrix} 200 \\ 160 \end{pmatrix},$$

which are immediately evident from the data box of Figure 9, we can state the problem above as a minimum problem.

Minimum problem: Determine the vector v so that the weekly operating cost, given by the quantity vb, is a minimum subject to the inequality restraints $vA \geq c$ and $v \geq 0$. The inequality restraints insure that the weekly output requirements are met and the limits on the components of v are not exceeded.

This is a minimum problem of the type discussed in detail in the preceding section. In Figure 11 we have graphed the convex polyhedral set C defined by the inequalities $vA \geq c$.

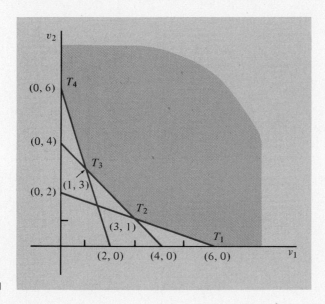

Figure 11

The extreme points of the convex set C are

$$T_1 = (6, 0), \qquad T_2 = (3, 1), \qquad T_3 = (1, 3), \qquad T_4 = (0, 6).$$

Testing the function $vb = 200v_1 + 160v_2$ at each of these extreme points, we see that it takes on the values 1200, 760, 680, and 960, respectively. We see that the minimum operating cost is \$680 per week and it is achieved at T_3—that is, by operating the first mine one day a week and the second mine three days a week.

Observe that if the mines are operated as indicated, then the combined weekly production will be 12 tons of high-grade ore, 8 tons of medium-grade ore, and 40 tons of low-grade ore. In other words, for this solution low-grade ore, is overproduced. If the company has no other demand for the low-grade ore, then it must discard 16 tons of it per week in this minimum-cost solution of its production problem. We shall discuss this point further in Section 6.

EXAMPLE 3 As a variant of Example 2, assume that the cost vector is

$$b = \begin{pmatrix} 160 \\ 200 \end{pmatrix};$$

in other words, the first mine now has a lower daily cost than the second. By the same procedure as above we find that the minimum cost level is again $680 and is achieved by operating the first mine three days a week and the second mine one day a week. In this solution 20 tons of high-grade ore, instead of the required 12 tons, are produced, while the requirements of medium- and low-grade ores are exactly met. Thus 8 tons of high-grade ore must be discarded per week.

EXAMPLE 4 As another variant of Example 2, assume that the cost vector is

$$b = \begin{pmatrix} 200 \\ 200 \end{pmatrix};$$

in other words, both mines have the same production costs. Evaluating the cost function vb at the extreme points of the convex set, we find costs of $1200 on two of the extreme points (T_1 and T_4) and costs of $800 on the other two extreme points (T_2 and T_3). Thus the minimum cost is attained by operating either one of the mines three days a week and the other mine one day a week. But there are other solutions, since if the minimum is taken on at two distinct extreme points it is also taken on at each of the points on the line segment between. Thus any vector v where $1 \leq v_1 \leq 3$, $1 \leq v_2 \leq 3$, and $v_1 + v_2 = 4$ also gives a minimum-cost solution. For example, each mine could operate two days a week.

It can be shown (see Exercise 2) that for any solution v with $1 < v_1 < 3$, $1 < v_2 < 3$, and $v_1 + v_2 = 4$, both high-grade and low-grade ore are overproduced.

EXERCISES

1. In Example 1, assume that profits are $200 per truck and $300 per automobile. What should the factory now produce for maximum profit?

2. In Example 4, show that both high- and low-grade ore are overproduced for solution vectors v with $1 < v_1 < 3$, $1 < v_2 < 3$, and $v_1 + v_2 = 4$.

3. A manufacturer has two machines, M_1 and M_2, which he uses to

manufacture two products, P_1 and P_2. To produce one unit of P_1, three hours of time on M_1 and six hours on M_2 are needed. And to produce one unit of P_2 takes six hours on M_1 and five hours on M_2. Each machine can run a maximum of 2100 hours per year. If the manufacturer sells product P_1 for a net profit of \$40 and P_2 for a net profit of \$50 each, what production mix shall he produce to maximize his total profit?

(a) Set up the data box for the problem, marking the dimensions of all numbers.

(b) Find A, b, and c.

(c) Draw the set of possible production vectors and find the optimum profit point. [Ans. $x^0 = \begin{pmatrix} 100 \\ 300 \end{pmatrix}$ with yearly profit of \$19,000.]

4. Two breakfast cereals, Krix and Kranch, supply varying amounts of vitamin B and iron; these are listed together with one-third of the daily minimum requirements (MDR) in the table below:

Cereal	Vitamin B	Iron
Krix	.15 mg/oz	1.67 mg/oz
Kranch	.10 mg/oz	3.33 mg/oz
$\frac{1}{3}$ MDR	.12 mg/day	2.0 mg/day

Krix costs 8 cents an ounce and Kranch 10 cents an ounce. How can we satisfy $\frac{1}{3}$ MDR at minimum cost?

(a) Let v_1 be the amount of Krix eaten and v_2 the amount of Kranch eaten. Write a minimizing linear programming problem for the above. Set up the data box and find A, b, and c.

(b) Draw the convex set of possible amounts eaten defined by the inequalities in (a).

(c) What is the lowest-cost feasible diet?

[Ans. $v^0 = (.6, .3)$ with cost 7.8 cents.]

5. A farmer owns a 200-acre farm and can plant any combination of two crops I and II. Crop I requires 1 man-day of labor and \$10 of capital for each acre planted, while crop II requires 4 man-days of labor and \$20 of capital for each acre planted. Crop I produces \$40 of net revenue per acre and crop II \$60. The farmer has \$2200 of capital and 320 man-days of labor available for the year. What is the optimal planting strategy? [Ans. $x^0 = \begin{pmatrix} 180 \\ 20 \end{pmatrix}$ with \$8400 revenue.]

6. In Exercise 5 assume that the revenue from crop II is \$90 per acre.

(a) Find the new maximum-revenue scheme, and show that now the best thing for the farmer to do is to leave 30 acres unplanted.

(b) Explain why the farmer should leave part of his land fallow in this case.

7. Suppose that a pound of meat contains 1 unit of carbohydrates, 3 units of vitamins, and 12 units of proteins and costs $1. Suppose also that one pound of cabbage contains 3, 4, and 1 units of these items, respectively, and costs 25 cents per pound. If these are the only foods available and the minimum daily requirements are 8 units of carbohydrates, 19 units of vitamins, and 7 units of protein, what is the minimum-cost diet?   [*Ans.* $v^0 = (.2, 4.6)$ with cost $1.35.]

8. Suppose that the minimum-cost diet found in Exercise 7 is unpalatable. In order to increase its palatability, add a constraint requiring that at least a half pound of meat be eaten, and resolve the problem. How much is the cost of the minimum-cost diet increased owing to this palatability constraint?   [*Ans.* $.24.]

9. In Exercise 8 suppose that we add a different kind of palatability constraint—namely, that at most two pounds of cabbage be eaten. Now how much is the cost of the minimum-cost diet increased?
             [*Ans.* $2.82.]

10. A manufacturer produces two types of bearings, A and B, utilizing three types of machines; lathes, grinders, and drill presses. The machinery requirements for one unit of each product, in hours, are expressed in the following table:

	Machine		
Bearing	Lathe	Grinder	Drill Press
A	.01	.03	.03
B	.02	.01	.015
Weekly machine capacity (hr)	400	450	480

He makes a Profit of 10 cents per type A bearing and 15 cents per type B bearing. What should his weekly production of each bearing be in order to maximize his profits?

$$\left[\textit{Ans. } x = \begin{pmatrix} 8000 \\ 16,000 \end{pmatrix} \text{ with weekly profits of } \$3200. \right]$$

4 THE DUAL PROBLEM

As the examples of the preceding sections have shown, some linear programming problems are maximizing and some are minimizing. Thus we might be interested in maximizing profits, production, or market share—or we might want to minimize costs, completion times, or raw-material usage. We shall show that to each maximizing problem there is a well-defined minimizing problem that uses the same data and whose solution has important mathematical implications concerning the original maximizing problem. Similarly, to each minimizing problem there is a well-defined maximizing problem that uses the same data and is similarly related.

First, we recall that every linear programming problem can be put into one of the two following forms:

$$(1) \qquad \left. \begin{aligned} \text{Maximize} \quad & cx \\ \text{subject to} \quad & Ax \leq b \\ & x \geq 0 \end{aligned} \right\} \text{ the MAXIMUM problem.}$$

or

$$(2) \qquad \left. \begin{aligned} \text{Minimize} \quad & vb \\ \text{subject to} \quad & vA \geq c \\ & v \geq 0 \end{aligned} \right\} \text{ the MINIMUM problem.}$$

If the components of A, b, c are the same, then the two problems (1) and (2) are called *dual linear programming problems*. Every linear programming problem, whether of the maximum or minimum type, has a dual that can be formally stated as above. The dual of a given problem frequently has important economic meaning and always has mathematical significance—see the discussion in Section 6.

To set up a *maximum problem* proceed as follows: Let the variables to be determined be $x_1, \ldots, x_n$; set up the data box as in Figure 12, with the x-variables appearing as labels on the top of the box. It then follows that, taking A, b, and c from the data box, the maximum problem is in form (1) above.

x_1	x_2	$\cdots$	x_n	
a_{11}	a_{12}	$\cdots$	a_{1n}	b_1
a_{21}	a_{22}	$\cdots$	a_{2n}	b_2
$\cdot$	$\cdot$	$\cdots$	$\cdot$	$\cdot$
a_{m1}	a_{m2}	$\cdots$	a_{mn}	b_m
c_1	c_2	$\cdots$	c_n	

Figure 12

To set up a *minimum problem* proceed as follows: Let the variables to be determined by $v_1, \ldots, v_m$; set up the data box as in Figure 13 with the v-variables appearing as labels to the left of the box. It then follows that, taking A, b, and c from the data box, the minimum problem is in form (2) above.

	a_{11}	a_{12}	$\cdots$	a_{1n}	b_1
v_1	a_{11}	a_{12}	$\cdots$	a_{1n}	b_1
v_2	a_{21}	a_{22}	$\cdots$	a_{2n}	b_2
$\cdot$	$\cdot$	$\cdot$	$\cdots$	$\cdot$	$\cdot$
v_m	a_{m1}	a_{m2}	$\cdots$	a_{mn}	b_m
	c_1	c_2	$\cdots$	c_n	

Figure 13

We now make two important observations. First, the dual problem to a maximum problem with data box as in Figure 12 can be obtained by merely labeling the rows $v_1, \ldots, v_m$; and the dual problem to the minimum problem whose data box is in Figure 13 can be obtained by labeling the columns $x_1, \ldots, x_n$. Second, the dimensions of the dual variables in either case can be obtained by dividing the dimensions of the b's or c's by the corresponding a's, as the following examples will make clear. We shall see that the interpretations of the dual variables are easy, once their physical dimensions are determined.

The reader may wonder why we introduce the dual problem instead of concentrating on the original problem alone. The reason is that the simplex method to be discussed later automatically produces the optimum solution to both problems simultaneously. Also, the solution to the dual problem often has important managerial and economic interpretations.

Before we can describe how the simplex method works, we must make a change in the formulation of the dual programs. What we shall do is to add *slack* variables to the inequalities stated in expressions (1) and (2) of this section in such a way as to make them into equations. To see how this is done, consider as an example the system of inequalities

$$-u + 2v \leq 5, \qquad \text{where } u \geq 0 \text{ and } v \geq 0.$$

We now add a new slack variable w and obtain a new system of expressions:

$$-u + 2v + w = 5, \qquad \text{where } u \geq 0, \, v \geq 0, \, w \geq 0.$$

Thus we obtain the equation

$$-u + 2v + w = 5$$

in nonnegative variables. Notice that the new system of expressions is equivalent to the old system, since any solution of the new system that has $w = 0$ represents a case for which $-u + 2v = 5$, and a solution of the new system for which $w > 0$ represents a case for which $-u + 2v < 5$. Moreover, we can write any solution of the old system as a solution of the new system by properly choosing a nonnegative value of w. Thus the truth sets of the two systems are identical.

Now we want to reformulate the constraints of problems (1) and (2). Let y be an m-component vector of *slack variables* y_i, and let f be a number; then (1) is equivalent to

$$
\begin{aligned}
&\text{Maximize} && cx = f \\
\text{(3)} \qquad &\text{subject to} && Ax + y = b, \\
&&& x, y \geq 0.
\end{aligned}
$$

To see this, rewrite the constraint of (3) as follows:

$$\text{(4)} \qquad\qquad\qquad Ax - b = -y;$$

then $y \geq 0$ is equivalent to $-y \leq 0$, and the latter is, from (4), the same as $Ax \leq b$. The number $f = cx$ measures the current value of the objective function of the maximum problem.

Similarly, let u be an n-component row vector of *slack* variables u_j, and let g be a number; then (2) is equivalent to

$$
(5) \qquad \begin{aligned}
\text{Minimize} &\quad vb = g \\
\text{subject to} &\quad vA - u = c, \\
&\quad u, v \geq 0.
\end{aligned}
$$

To see the equivalence rewrite the equality constraint of (5) as

$$
(6) \qquad vA - c = u;
$$

then it is obvious that $u \geq 0$ and $vA \geq c$ are the same. The number $g = vb$ measures the current value of the objective function of the minimizing problem.

Next we show that the pair of dual problems in (3) and (5) can both be represented in the same tableau, and that the tableau can be obtained by extending either of the data boxes in Figure 12 or 13. Consider the (Tucker) tableau, which we shall later call the *initial simplex tableau*, in Figure 14.

	x_1	x_2	$\cdots$	x_n	-1	
v_1	a_{11}	a_{12}	$\cdots$	a_{1n}	b_1	$= -y_1$
v_2	a_{21}	a_{22}	$\cdots$	a_{2n}	b_2	$= -y_2$
$\cdot$	$\cdot$	$\cdot$	$\cdots$	$\cdot$	$\cdot$	$\cdot$
v_m	a_{m1}	a_{m2}	$\cdots$	a_{mn}	b_m	$= -y_m$
-1	c_1	c_2	$\cdots$	c_n	0	$= f$
	$= u_1$	$= u_2$	$\cdots$	$= u_n$	$= g$	

Figure 14

Notice that Figure 14 can be obtained from Figure 12 by adding the 0 entry in the lower right-hand corner, putting variables $v_1, \ldots, v_m$ and -1 along the left margin, putting -1 above the $(n + 1)$st column, marking the right-hand side with $= -y_1, \ldots, = -y_m$, and $= f$, and marking the bottom of the matrix with $= u_1, \ldots, = u_n$, and $= g$. Figure 14 can be obtained in a similar manner from Figure 13. The reason for this labeling is as follows: if we drop the x's and -1 down to the first row of the matrix, multiply by the coefficients there, and set equal to the label on the right, we have

$$
a_{11}x_1 + a_{12}x_2 + \ldots + a_{1n}x_n - b_1 = -y_1,
$$

which is just exactly the first equation of (4). Dropping the labels at the top down to the other rows will give the other equations of (4). Finally, dropping the labels down to the last row gives

$$
c_1 x_1 + c_2 x_2 + \ldots + c_n x_n = f,
$$

which is just the definition of f.

In a similar manner, if we move the labels on the left of Figure 14 into each column of the tableau, multiply, and set equal to the label at the bottom, we have the various equations of (6) together with the definition of g.

EXAMPLE 1 The data box for the automobile/truck example of the last section is shown in Figures 6 and 7; hence its initial simplex tableau is as given in Figure 15.

	x_1	x_2	-1	
v_1	⑤	2	180	$= -y_1$
v_2	3	3	135	$= -y_2$
-1	300	200	0	$= f$
	$= u_1$	$= u_2$	$= g$	

Figure 15

The primal equations for this problem corresponding to (4) are

$$
\begin{aligned}
5x_1 + 2x_2 - 180 &= -y_1, \\
3x_1 + 3x_2 - 135 &= -y_2, \\
300x_1 + 200x_2 &= f.
\end{aligned}
$$

The dual equations for this problem corresponding to (6) are

$$
\begin{aligned}
5v_1 + 3v_2 - 300 &= u_1, \\
2v_1 + 3v_2 - 200 &= u_2, \\
180v_1 + 135v_2 &= g.
\end{aligned}
$$

These are obtained in the manner described above.

EXAMPLE 2 The data box for the mining example of the last section is shown in Figures 9 and 10; hence its initial simplex tableau is as given in Figure 16.

	x_1	x_2	x_3	-1	
v_1	⑥	2	4	200	$= -y_1$
v_2	2	2	12	160	$= -y_2$
-1	12	8	24	0	$= f$
	$= u_1$	$= u_2$	$= u_3$	$= g$	

Figure 16

The primal equations for this problem corresponding to (6) are

$$
\begin{aligned}
6v_1 + 2v_2 - 12 &= u_1, \\
2v_1 + 2v_2 - 8 &= u_2, \\
4v_1 + 12v_2 - 24 &= u_3, \\
200v_1 + 160v_2 &= g,
\end{aligned}
$$

and the dual equations corresponding to (4) are

$$6x_1 + 2x_2 + 4x_3 - 200 = -y_1,$$
$$2x_1 + 2x_2 + 12x_3 - 160 = -y_2,$$
$$12x_1 + 8x_2 + 24x_3 = f.$$

The reader should set up in an analogous way the initial simplex tableaus for Examples 3 and 4 of Section 3.

We next show that from equations (4) and (6) we can immediately derive *Tucker's duality equation:*

(7) $g - f = vy + ux.$

This follows easily since

$$g - f = vb - cx = v(Ax + y) - (vA - u)x = vy + ux,$$

where we used the substitutions $b = Ax + y$ from (4) and $c = vA - u$ from (6).

Nonnegative vectors x, y, u, and v that satisfy (4) and (6) will be called *feasible vectors* for the equality form of the linear programming problem. Note that the duality relation (7) is true for *all* solutions x, y, u, and v satisfying (4) and (6) whether nonnegative or not. However, the following theorem shows that a pair of feasible vectors for one of the problems implies a bound on the objective function of the other problem.

Theorem (a) Let x^0, y^0, and f^0 be *optimal* solutions to maximizing problem (3), and let u, v, and g be *feasible* solutions to the dual minimizing problem (5); then $cx^0 = f^0 \le g = vb$; in other words, for any feasible vector v, the value $g = vb$ is an *upper bound* to the maximum value $f^0 = cx^0$ of the maximizing problem (3).

(b) Let u^0, v^0, and g^0 be *optimal* solutions to the minimizing problem (5), and let x, y, and f be *feasible* solutions to the dual maximizing problem (3); then $v^0 b = g^0 \ge f = cx$; in other words, for any feasible vector x, the value $f = cx$ is a *lower bound* to the minimum value $g^0 = v^0 b$ of the minimizing problem (5).

Proof (a) If u, v, x^0, and y^0 are all nonnegative vectors, then it follows that $vy^0 \ge 0$ and $ux^0 \ge 0$, so that, from (7), we have

$$g - f^0 = vy^0 + ux^0 \ge 0,$$

or, in other words, $g \ge f^0$, as asserted.

The proof of (b) is similar.

We illustrate the theorem by returning to the previous examples.

EXAMPLE 1   If we consider the automobile/truck example whose initial tableau is given
(continued) in Figure 15, we can easily check that the following quantities solve the

primal problem: $x_1 = 10, x_2 = 10, y_1 = 110, y_2 = 75$. These were obtained by selecting arbitrary but not too large values for x_1 and x_2 and then solving for y_1 and y_2. From this feasible solution we calculate $cx = 300 \cdot 10 + 200 \cdot 10 = 3000 + 2000 = 5000$; hence we know that $5000 \leq g^0 = v^0 b$; that is, we have found a lower bound to the optimum value g^0 of the dual minimizing problem.

Similarly, we can select v_1 and v_2 to be fairly large, but otherwise arbitrary, and solve for u_1 and u_2. For instance, $v_1 = 50, v_2 = 40, u_1 = 70$, and $u_2 = 20$ are a feasible choice for these quantities. From them we know that $f^0 = cx^0$ is definitely not greater than $vb = 180 \cdot 50 + 135 \cdot 40 = 9000 + 5400 = 14{,}400$.

Since we know that the optimum value is $f^0 = 12{,}000$, and we will later show that $f^0 = g^0$, we see that, in fact, the lower and upper bounds are correct in this instance. The reader should try several other feasible solutions for this example.

EXAMPLE 2 (continued) Let us check the theorem for the mining example shown in Figure 16. Suppose we choose $x_1 = 20, x_2 = 20, x_3 = 5$, so that $y_1 = 20$ and $y_2 = 20$. We thus obtain the lower bound on g^0 as $cx = 12 \cdot 20 + 8 \cdot 20 + 24 \cdot 5 = 240 + 160 + 120 = 520$.

Similarly, we can choose $v_1 = 2, v_2 = 2$, and correspondingly $u_1 = 4$, $u_2 = 0$, and $u_3 = 8$, so an upper bound for f^0 is $vb = 200 \cdot 2 + 160 \cdot 2 = 720$.

Since the true value is 680, we see that the upper and lower bounds again are correct.

EXERCISES

1. Illustrate the theorem of this section by finding other feasible solutions to the primal and dual problems for the automobile/truck example, and show that the upper and lower bounds so obtained are correct.
2. Repeat Exercise 1 for the mining example.
3. For Example 3 of Section 3:
   (a) Set up and label the initial tableau.
   (b) Write the primal and dual equations.
   (c) Find feasible solutions to the primal equations and determine a bound to the dual problem.
   (d) Find feasible solutions to the dual problem and derive a bound on the primal problem.
4. Repeat Exercise 3 for Exercise 4 of Section 3.
5. Repeat Exercise 3 for Exercise 5 or Section 3.
6. Repeat Exercise 3 for Exercise 7 of Section 3.
7. Repeat Exercise 3 for Exercise 10 of Section 3.
*8. Let x^0 and v^0 be nonnegative vectors such that $f^0 = cx^0 = v^0 b = g^0$, $Ax^0 \leq b$, and $v^0 A \geq c$.

    (a) Show that if x is any other feasible vector, then

$$cx \le v^0 A x \le v^0 b = c x^0,$$

so that x^0 solves the maximum problem.

    (b) Similarly, show that v^0 solves the minimum problem.

    (c) Show that $c x^0 = v^0 b = v^0 A x^0$.

  9. Use (7) to show that if x, y, u, and v are vectors related as in (4) and (6), then $ux \ge 0$ and $vy \ge 0$ imply $g \ge f$. (Note that this is true whether or not $x, y, u,$ and v are nonnegative.)

If x, y, u, and v are vectors related as in (4) and (6), then they are said to have the *complementary slackness property* if and only if

$$ux = 0 \quad \text{and} \quad vy = 0.$$

The remaining exercises refer to this property.

  10. Use (7) to show that if $x, y, u,$ and v satisfy the complementary slackness property, then $g = f$. Is the converse true?

  *11. If $x, y, u,$ and v are nonnegative vectors, show that $g = f$ if and only if they have the complementary slackness property.

  *12. Use Exercises 8, 10, and 11 to show that nonnegative vectors related as in (4) and (6) are optimal if and only if they satisfy the complementary slackness property.

5 THE SIMPLEX METHOD

In Section 3 we solved simple linear programming problems having two variables by sketching convex sets in the plane. To solve such problems in more than two variables by the same method would require visualizing convex sets in more than two dimensions, which is extremely difficult. But fortunately there is an algorithm, called the *simplex algorithm*, that permits us to solve such large-scale linear programming problems without such visualizations. The reader will recall that in Chapter 4 we developed an algorithm for solving simultaneous linear equations that was algebraic (not geometric) in nature and avoided similar visualization problems.

For simplicity we shall make the following two assumptions in the present and next sections:

I. The Nonnegativity Assumption We shall assume $b \ge 0$; that is, every component of b is nonnegative.

II. The Nondegeneracy Assumption The extreme points of the convex set of feasible vectors are each the intersection of *exactly* n bounding hyperplanes, where n is the number of components of the vectors involved.

In Section 7 we shall indicate how these two assumptions can be dropped. We emphasize, however, that for linear programming problems derived from actual applications both assumptions will be satisfied, or else the problem can be reformulated so that they are. Moreover, when codes are written for computers to solve linear programming problems, precautions are taken to insure that these assumptions hold.

We now proceed to describe the simplex method. In the next section we shall discuss reasons why the simplex method works.

After the data box has been set up for either a maximizing or minimizing problem, the simplex method begins with the initial simplex tableau (the Tucker tableau) of Figure 14. Note that it was derived from the data box as described in the previous section. The simplex algorithm will change the initial tableau into a second one, that into a third, and so on, until finally a tableau is obtained that displays the optimum answers to both the primal and dual problems. A typical tableau in this computational process is shown in Figure 17. Note that the variables have been identified as being of two

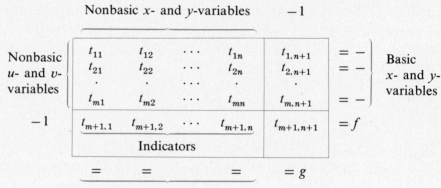

Figure 17   Basic u- and v-variables

kinds: *basic* and *nonbasic*. The basic variables appear on the bottom and right-hand sides of the tableau and the nonbasic variables on the left and top. As we shall see, in any tableau, if we set the nonbasic variables equal to zero, then the corresponding values of the basic variables can be read from the last row and last column of the tableau. The other important thing to note is that the entries of the first n columns of the last row are called *indicators*.

The flow chart in Figure 18 describes how the simplex method works. Look at box 1 in the upper left-hand corner. We see that for the automobile/truck and mining examples of the previous section we have already carried out the directives there: the problems are set up and the initial tableaus formed. We now discuss in detail the rest of the computation for these two examples.

EXAMPLE 1   The initial tableau for the automobile/truck example appears in Figure 15. To solve this problem using the simplex method we go next to box 2 of the flow chart in Figure 18. We note that in the initial simplex tableau of

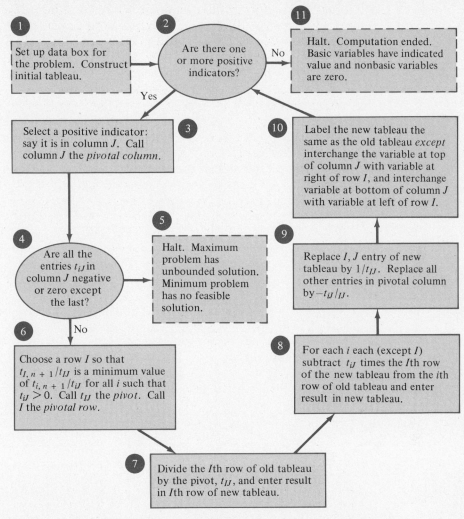

Figure 18   The simplex algorithm for problems with nonnegative righthand sides

Figure 15 there are positive indicators, so the answer to the question in box 2 is "yes." Hence we proceed to box 3, which says, "Select a positive indicator." Suppose we select 300, which makes column 1 the pivotal column and $J = 1$. We now go to box 4 and observe that there are positive entries in column 1, so that the answer to the question there is "no," and we go on to box 6. We must now find the pivotal row. For this we examine the ratios $t_{i,n+1}/t_{i1}$ for $i = 1$ and 2. These ratios are $180/5 = 36$ and $135/3 = 45$. Since the smaller ratio occurs in the first row, we see that the 5 entry in the first column of Figure 15 is the pivot and $I = 1$, so that the first row is pivotal. The pivot is circled in Figure 15.

Next we carry out the directives in boxes 7 and 8 of Figure 18, which construct the rows of the new tableau. In box 7 we find we must divide through the pivotal row of the old tableau by the pivot and insert it in the new tableau (Figure 19). Then we multiply this new row by 3 and subtract

1	$\frac{2}{5}$	36
0	$\frac{9}{5}$	27
0	80	$-10{,}800$

Figure 19

it from the second row of the old tableau to form the second row of the new tableau. In vector form, this computation is

$$-3(1 \quad \tfrac{2}{5} \quad 36) + (3 \quad 3 \quad 135) = (0 \quad \tfrac{9}{5} \quad 27).$$

Similarly, we multiply the new row by 300 and subtract from the third row of the old tableau to form the third row of the new tableau as shown. To complete the new tableau we must replace the pivotal column as described in box 9 of Figure 18; the result is given in Figure 20. Also we must

	y_1	x_2	-1	
u_1	$\frac{1}{5}$	$\frac{2}{5}$	36	$= -x_1$
v_2	$-\frac{3}{5}$	$\left(\frac{9}{5}\right)$	27	$= -y_2$
-1	-60	80	$-10{,}800$	$= f$
	Indicators			
	$= v_1$	$= u_2$	$= g$	

Figure 20

interchange the labels of the variables at both ends of the pivot row with the variables at both ends of the pivot column as described in box 10 of Figure 18. The completed new second tableau appears in Figure 20.

We now find ourselves back at box 2 of the flow chart of Figure 18. Since the 80 in the second column, last row of Figure 20 is positive, the answer to the question in box 2 is "yes," so we go to box 3. Clearly we must choose $J = 2$. The answer to question in box 4 is "no," so we go on to box 6 to choose the pivot. The two ratios to be considered are $36/\tfrac{2}{5} = 90$ and $27/\tfrac{9}{5} = 15$, so that the second row is pivotal and $\tfrac{9}{5}$ (circled in Figure 20) is the new pivot. Carrying out the instructions in boxes 7 and 8 of the flow diagram gives the tableau in Figure 21, and finishing up with boxes 9 and 10 gives the completed third tableau (Figure 22).

$\frac{1}{3}$	0	30
$-\frac{1}{3}$	1	15
$-\frac{100}{3}$	0	$-12{,}000$

Figure 21

	y_1	y_2	-1	
u_1	$\frac{1}{3}$	$-\frac{2}{9}$	30	$= -x_1$
u_2	$-\frac{1}{3}$	$\frac{5}{9}$	15	$= -x_2$
-1	$-\frac{100}{3}$	$-\frac{400}{9}$	$-12{,}000$	$= f$
	$\underbrace{\qquad\qquad\qquad}_{\text{Indicators}}$			
	$= v_1$	$= v_2$	$= g$	

Figure 22

We again find ourselves in box 2 of the flow diagram. But this time we find no positive indicators for the tableau of Figure 22; hence the answer to the question there is "no" and we go to box 11, which says that the computation is ended. The answers to both the primal and dual problems are displayed in the final tableau. To see what they are, we first set the nonbasic variables equal to zero as instructed in box 11 of the flow diagram. Hence we have $u_1 = u_2 = y_1 = y_2 = 0$, since the nonbasic variables appear on the left and top of the final tableau. Knowing that $y_i = 0$ for $i = 1, 2$, we drop the variables at the top of the final tableau down to the first row and multiply, obtaining $-30 = -x_1$ or simply $x_1 = 30$. Dropping these down one row further gives $x_2 = 15$. And dropping them down to the last row gives $f = 12{,}000$, which is the final value of the objective function. Thus the optimal solution vectors to the maximizing problem are:

$$x^0 = \begin{pmatrix} 30 \\ 15 \end{pmatrix}, \qquad y^0 = \begin{pmatrix} 0 \\ 0 \end{pmatrix}, \quad \text{and} \quad f^0 = 12{,}000.$$

Note that this is the same solution that we found in the previous section.

We can also find the optimal solution to the dual problem. (The interpretation of this solution will be given in the next section.) Knowing $u_j = 0$ for $j = 1, 2$, we move the variables on the left of Figure 22 into the first column, multiply, and obtain $v_1 = \frac{100}{3}$. Moving them to the second column gives $v_2 = \frac{400}{9}$, and moving them to the third column gives $g = 12{,}000$, the value of the objective function of the minimizing problem. Hence the optimal solution vectors to the minimizing problem are:

$$v^0 = (\tfrac{100}{3}, \tfrac{400}{3}), \qquad u^0 = (0, 0), \quad \text{and} \quad g^0 = 12{,}000.$$

The reader should substitute x^0 and y^0 into the primal, and v^0 and u^0 into the dual equations written down previously and show that they are satisfied. Note also that $f^0 = v^0 b = cx^0 = g^0$ at an optimum solution. This is always true, and will be discussed further in the next section.

EXAMPLE 2 Let us solve the mining example using the simplex method. The initial tableau is in Figure 16. The first indicator 12 was selected so that the first column is pivotal. The pivot is 6, which is circled in the figure, and was chosen because the two ratios involved are $\frac{100}{3}$, which is smaller than $\frac{160}{2} = 80$, hence the first row is pivotal and the pivot is 6. Carrying out steps 7 through 10 of the flow diagram (Figure 18), we construct the second

	y_1	x_2	x_3	-1	
u_1	$\frac{1}{6}$	$\frac{1}{3}$	$\frac{2}{3}$	$\frac{100}{3}$	$= -x_1$
v_2	$-\frac{1}{3}$	$\boxed{\frac{4}{3}}$	$\frac{32}{3}$	$\frac{280}{3}$	$= -y_2$
-1	-2	4	16	-400	$= f$
		Indicators			
	$= v_1$	$= u_2$	$= u_3$	$= g$	

Figure 23

tableau in Figure 23. There are two positive indicators, and we choose the first one, 4, so that the second column is pivotal. The new pivot is $\frac{4}{3}$, which is circled in the second (pivotal) row. Carrying out the rest of the steps of the flow diagram, we obtain the third tableau (Figure 24). All indicators

	y_1	y_2	x_3	-1	
u_1	$\frac{1}{4}$	$-\frac{1}{4}$	-2	10	$= -x_1$
u_2	$-\frac{1}{4}$	$\frac{3}{4}$	8	70	$= -x_2$
-1	-1	-3	-16	-680	$= f$
		Indicators			
	$= v_1$	$= v_2$	$= u_3$	$= g$	

Figure 24

in this tableau are negative, so the computation is complete. We read off the optimum answers to the primal minimizing problem as

$$v^0 = (1, 3), \qquad u^0 = (0, 0, 16), \quad \text{and} \quad g^0 = 680,$$

and the final minimum operating cost for the mines is \$680 per week. These are the same answers as the graphical procedure gave.

The optimum answers to the dual maximizing problem can also be obtained as

$$x^0 = \begin{pmatrix} 10 \\ 70 \\ 0 \end{pmatrix}, \quad y^0 = \begin{pmatrix} 0 \\ 0 \end{pmatrix}, \quad \text{and} \quad f^0 = 680.$$

Interpretations for these will be given in the next section.

EXAMPLE 3 Our next example illustrates the fact that a given variable may first be basic, become nonbasic, then become basic again, and so on, several times during the course of the simplex computation. Figures 25 through 28 give the necessary tableaus, and the pivots are circled there. There is another way of working this problem that requires only two tableaus. It starts with a pivot in the first column instead of the second (see Exercise 9). This illustrates the rule that it is frequently (but not invariably) better to start the simplex method with a column having the most positive indicator. Note that y_1 started out basic, became nonbasic, then became basic again. And

	x_1	x_2	-1	
v_1	2	①	3	$= -y_1$
v_2	3	1	4	$= -y_2$
-1	17	5	0	$= f$
	$= u_1$	$= u_2$	$= g$	

Figure 25

	x_1	y_1	-1	
u_2	2	1	3	$= -x_2$
v_2	①	-1	1	$= -y_2$
-1	7	-5	-15	$= f$
	$= u_1$	$= v_1$	$= g$	

Figure 26

	y_2	y_1	-1	
u_2	-2	③	1	$= -x_2$
u_1	1	-1	1	$= -x_1$
-1	-7	2	22	$= f$
	$= v_2$	$= v_1$	$= g$	

Figure 27

	y_2	x_2	-1	
v_1	$-\frac{2}{3}$	$\frac{1}{3}$	$\frac{1}{3}$	$= -y_1$
u_1	$\frac{1}{3}$	$\frac{1}{3}$	$\frac{4}{3}$	$= -x_1$
-1	$-\frac{17}{3}$	$-\frac{2}{3}$	$-22\frac{2}{3}$	$= f$
	$= v_2$	$= u_2$	$= g$	

Figure 28

x_2 was initially nonbasic, became basic, and ended up nonbasic. The final optimal answers are:

$$v^0 = (0, \tfrac{17}{3}), \qquad u^0 = (0, \tfrac{2}{3}), \qquad g^0 = 22\tfrac{2}{3},$$

$$x^0 = \begin{pmatrix} \tfrac{4}{3} \\ 0 \end{pmatrix}, \qquad y^0 = \begin{pmatrix} \tfrac{1}{3} \\ 0 \end{pmatrix}, \qquad f^0 = 22\tfrac{2}{3}.$$

EXAMPLE 4 The reader has undoubtedly wondered about box 5 of the flow diagram in Figure 18, since we have not yet ended in it. Actually, if we are solving an applied problem that is correctly formulated so that it has a solution, we shall never end in it. Consider, however, the problem whose initial tableau is in Figure 29. Both the first two columns have positive indicators. If we choose the first one and pivot, we obtain the tableau of Figure 30. Now there is one positive indicator in the second column, so $J = 2$. But

	x_1	x_2	-1	
v_1	-1	1	1	$= -y_1$
v_2	1	-1	1	$= -y_2$
-1	1	1	0	$= f$
	$= u_1$	$= u_2$	$= g$	

Figure 29

	y_2	x_2	-1	
v_1	1	0	2	$= -y_1$
u_1	1	-1	1	$= -x_1$
-1	-1	2	-1	$= g$
	$= v_2$	$= u_2$	$= g$	

Figure 30

the answer to the question in box 4 of Figure 18 is "yes," so we arrive at box 5, which says that the maximum problem has an unbounded solution and the minimum problem has no feasible solution.

To see this let us write the constraints for the maximum problem of Figure 29. They are

$$-x_1 + x_2 \le 1, \qquad x_1 \ge 0,$$
$$x_1 - x_2 \le 1, \qquad x_2 \ge 0.$$

These inequalities are satisfied if x_1 and x_2 are equal and positive. Hence we can make the objective function $f = x_1 + x_2$ as large as we wish. Two constraints of the minimum problem of Figure 29 are

$$-v_1 + v_2 \ge 1,$$
$$v_1 - v_2 \ge 1$$

If we add these, we obtain the contradiction $0 \ge 2$, and hence the minimum problem has no solution.

For practical purposes, however, we can ignore the no-solution possibility, since we will be dealing with well-formulated problems that have solutions.

EXERCISES

1. Use the simplex method to solve Example 3 of Section 3.
2. Use the simplex method to solve Example 4 of Section 3 even though the nondegeneracy hypothesis is not satisfied. Show that there are two ways to proceed, each one leading to a different solution of the minimum problem.
3. Use the simplex method to solve Exercise 3 of Section 3.
4. Use the simplex method to solve Exercise 4 of Section 3.
5. Use the simplex method to solve Exercise 5 of Section 3.
6. Use the simplex method to solve Exercise 6 of Section 3.

7. Use the simplex method to solve Exercise 7 of Section 3.
8. Use the simplex method to solve Exercise 8 of Section 3.
9. Solve the problem in Example 3 by choosing the first pivot in the first column. Show that the answer can be obtained in one step.
10. Use the simplex method to solve Exercise 10 of Section 3.
11. A nut packager has on hand 121 pounds of peanuts and 49 pounds of cashews. He can sell two kinds of mixtures of these nuts: a cheap mix that has 80 percent peanuts and 20 percent cashews, or a party mix that has 30 percent peanuts and 70 percent cashews. If he can sell the party mix at 80 cents a pound and the cheap mix at 50 cents a pound, how many pounds of each mix should he make in order to maximize the amount he can obtain?
[*Ans.* Let x_1 be the number of pounds of party mix and x_2 the number of pounds of the cheap mix. Then the data are

$$A = \begin{pmatrix} .3 & .8 \\ .7 & .2 \end{pmatrix}, \quad b = \begin{pmatrix} 121 \\ 49 \end{pmatrix}, \quad \text{and} \quad c = (80, 50).$$

The packager should make 30 pounds of the party mix and 140 pounds of the cheap mix. His income is \$94.]
12. The operator of all oil refinery can buy light crude oil at \$6 per barrel and heavy crude at \$5 per barrel. The refining process produces the following quantities of gasoline, kerosene, and fuel oil from one barrel of each type of crude:

Type	Gasoline	Kerosene	Fuel Oil
Light crude	.5	.25	.2
Heavy crude	.4	.3	.25

Note that in each case 5 percent of the barrel of crude is lost in the form of gases (which have to be burned) and unusable sludge. During the summer months the operator has contracted to deliver 50,000 barrels of gasoline, 30,000 barrels of kerosene, and 10,000 barrels of fuel oil per month. How many barrels of each type of crude should he process in order to meet his production quotas at minimum possible cost?
13. During the winter months the refinery operator of Exercise 12 contracts to deliver 36,000 barrels of gasoline, 12,000 barrels of kerosene, and 18,000 barrels of fuel oil. What is his optimal winter production plan?
14. In Exercises 12 and 13 show that there is an excess production of at least one of the goods during each time of the year. Discuss practical ways in which this excess production can be used.
15. In the tableau of Figure 16 make the pivot be the 2 entry in the first column rather than the circled 6 entry shown. Show that this leads to a negative value of x_1, and hence explain the reasons in box 6 of Figure 18 for the special choice of the pivot.

6 DUALITY INTERPRETATIONS AND RESULTS

As we saw in the previous section, the simplex method is the same for both maximizing and minimizing problems. The only difference in setting up the two problems is the choice of row or column vectors for the various quantities involved. In either case we ended up with a data box containing a matrix A, a column vector b, and a row vector c. Using these data we stated both a maximizing and a minimizing problem—only one of which initially interested us. The other problem is called the *dual* linear programming problem. The dual of a maximizing problem is a minimizing problem, and vice versa. And the dual of the dual problem is, in either case, the original problem.

We saw that the simplex method solves both the original problem and its dual simultaneously. It is therefore of interest to see what interpretation, if any, can be given to the dual of a linear programming problem. We shall see that we can always give the dual problem mathematical and economic or managerial interpretations that are of considerable interest.

The first step in interpreting the solution to the dual problem is that of determining the dimensions of the variables involved. Recall that in Section 3 we set up for each linear programming problem a data box, and the numbers in the data box had dimensions. We now need to determine the dimensions of the variables of both the primal and dual problems. The following rule tells how to do this.

Rule for Determining Dimensions of Variables

(a) The dimension of x_j is the ratio of the dimension of b_i divided by the dimension of a_{ij} for any i.

(b) The dimension of v_i is the ratio of the dimension of c_j divided by the dimension of a_{ij} for any j.

In working with dimensions we use the rules of ordinary algebra for canceling and so on, as explained earlier in Section 3.

EXAMPLE 1 Let us return to the auto/truck example; its data box is given in Figure 6. We have already found the dimensions of the primal variables x_1 (trucks/week) and x_2 (autos/week). Let us use rule (b) above to determine the dimensions of the dual variables v_1 and v_2. For v_1 we have

$$\text{dimension of } v_1 = (\text{dimension of } c_1)/(\text{dimension } a_{11})$$

$$= \frac{\$}{\text{truck}} \bigg/ \frac{\text{S1-manhr}}{\text{truck}}$$

$$= \frac{\$}{\text{truck}} \cdot \frac{\text{truck}}{\text{S1-manhr}}$$

$$= \frac{\$}{\text{S1-manhr}}.$$

In Exercise 1 the reader is asked to show that we would have obtained the same result if we had divided the dimension of c_2 by the dimension of a_{12}. In the same manner we have

$$\text{dimension of } v_2 = (\text{dimension of } c_1)/(\text{dimension } a_{21})$$

$$= \frac{\$}{\text{truck}} \cdot \frac{\text{truck}}{\text{S2-manhr}}$$

$$= \frac{\$}{\text{S2-manhr}}.$$

Figure 31 summarizes the complete data box for the auto/truck example, indicating the dimensions of all variables and constants.

	$x_1 \dfrac{\text{trucks}}{\text{week}}$	$x_2 \dfrac{\text{autos}}{\text{week}}$	Capacities
$v_1 \dfrac{\$}{\text{S1-manhr}}$	$5 \dfrac{\text{S1-manhr}}{\text{truck}}$	$2 \dfrac{\text{S1-manhr}}{\text{auto}}$	$180 \dfrac{\text{S1-manhr}}{\text{week}}$
$v_2 \dfrac{\$}{\text{S2-manhr}}$	$3 \dfrac{\text{S2-manhr}}{\text{truck}}$	$3 \dfrac{\text{S2-manhr}}{\text{auto}}$	$135 \dfrac{\text{S2-manhr}}{\text{week}}$
Profits	$300 \dfrac{\$}{\text{truck}}$	$200 \dfrac{\$}{\text{auto}}$	

Figure 31

	$x_1 \dfrac{\$}{\text{ton-HG}}$	$x_2 \dfrac{\$}{\text{ton-MG}}$	$x_3 \dfrac{\$}{\text{ton-LG}}$	Costs
$v_1 \dfrac{\text{M1-days}}{\text{week}}$	$6 \dfrac{\text{tons-HG}}{\text{M1-day}}$	$2 \dfrac{\text{tons-MG}}{\text{M1-day}}$	$4 \dfrac{\text{tons-LG}}{\text{M1-day}}$	$200 \dfrac{\$}{\text{M1-day}}$
$v_2 \dfrac{\text{M2-days}}{\text{week}}$	$2 \dfrac{\text{tons-HG}}{\text{M2-day}}$	$2 \dfrac{\text{tons-MG}}{\text{M2-day}}$	$12 \dfrac{\text{tons-LG}}{\text{M2-day}}$	$160 \dfrac{\$}{\text{M2-day}}$
Requirements	$12 \dfrac{\text{tons-HG}}{\text{week}}$	$8 \dfrac{\text{tons-MG}}{\text{week}}$	$24 \dfrac{\text{tons-LG}}{\text{week}}$	

Figure 32

EXAMPLE 2 The data box for the mining example is given in Figure 9. We already know that the dimensions of v_1 and v_2 are mine 1–days/week and mine 2–days/week, respectively. Let us use rule (a) above to find the dimensions of x_1.

$$\text{dimension of } x_1 = (\text{dimension of } b_1)/(\text{dimension of } a_{11})$$

$$= \frac{\$}{\text{M1-day}} \Big/ \frac{\text{tons-Hg}}{\text{M1-day}}$$

$$= \frac{\$}{\text{tons-Hg}}.$$

A similar application of rule (a) gives the dimensions of x_2 and x_3 as $/ton-Mg and $/ton-LG, respectively.

Figure 32 shows the data box for the mining example, indicating dimensions for all variables and constants.

Determining the dimensions of the dual variables is the first step in their interpretation. The next step is to look at the optimal dual solutions for the examples above and give their interpretations.

EXAMPLE 1 (continued)   In Example 1 of Section 5 we found the optimal solution to the auto/truck example to be

$$x^0 = \begin{pmatrix} 30 \\ 15 \end{pmatrix}, \qquad v^0 = (\tfrac{100}{3}, \tfrac{400}{9}), \qquad f^0 = g^0 = 12{,}000.$$

We know that $v_1^0 = \tfrac{100}{3}$ has dimensions $/S1-manhr, which sound like a *value* for shop 1 man-hours. We shall show that this is in fact the case. Suppose we increase the number of shop 1 man-hours from 180 to 183. Our problem is then summarized in the data box of Figure 33, where the dimensions

	x_1	x_2	Capacities
v_1	5	2	183
v_2	3	3	135
Profits	300	200	

Figure 33

are the same as in Figure 31 and are therefore omitted. The reader will be asked to show in Exercise 2 that the optimal solution to this problem is

$$x^0 = \begin{pmatrix} 31 \\ 14 \end{pmatrix} \quad \text{and} \quad v^0 = (\tfrac{100}{3}, \tfrac{400}{9}),$$

with objective value 12,100. Notice that the objective value has increased by 100, which is just three times the dual variable $v_1^0 = \tfrac{100}{3}$. Hence we see that $v_1^0 = 33.33$ is the *imputed value* of an additional hour of shop 1 man-hours. It should be remarked right away that the imputed-value interpretation holds over only a limited range of changes in shop 1 man-hours. Hence we should more properly say that $v_1^0 = 33.33$ is the *imputed value* of an additional hour in shop 1 *provided the dual solution is not changed* by adding this extra capacity.

Note also that the imputed value is determined independently of the *cost* of providing the extra man-hours in shop 1. In order to provide extra man-hours it would be necessary to pay workers overtime and rent additional equipment, or else do subcontracting, or the like. What the optimal dual variables tell us is the cost of providing extra hours in shop 1 should not be more than their imputed value, or else it is not optimal to get them.

In Exercise 3 the reader will be asked to show that the optimal dual variable $v_2^0 = \frac{400}{9} = 44.44$, which has dimensions \$ per shop 2 man-hour, is the imputed value of an additional hour in shop 2 provided the optimal dual solution does not change after the extra time is added. As before, it is the maximum amount one should be willing to pay to obtain the extra time.

EXAMPLE 2
(continued)

In Example 2 of Section 5 we found the optimal solutions to the mining example to be

$$v^0 = (1, 3), \qquad x^0 = \begin{pmatrix} 10 \\ 70 \\ 0 \end{pmatrix}, \quad \text{and} \quad f^0 = g^0 = 680.$$

We know that $x_1^0 = 10$ has dimensions \$ per ton of high-grade ore, which sounds like the *imputed cost* of producing an additional ton of high-grade ore, and we shall show that this is the case. Suppose we increase the requirements for high-grade ore production from 12 to 16 tons. The new data box is shown in Figure 34, the dimensions being the same as in Figure

	x_1	x_2	x_3	Costs
v_1	6	2	4	200
v_2	2	2	12	160
Requirements	16	8	24	

Figure 34

32. In Exercise 4 the reader will be asked to show that the optimal solution to the new problem is

$$v^0 = (2, 2), \qquad x^0 = \begin{pmatrix} 10 \\ 70 \\ 0 \end{pmatrix}, \quad \text{and} \quad f^0 = g^0 = 720.$$

Notice that the costs of production have increased from 680 to 720, which is $4 \cdot x_1^0 = 4 \cdot 10 = 40$. Hence $x_1^0 = 10$ was the per-ton cost of each of the additional 4 units of high-grade ore.

In Exercise 5 you will be asked to show that x_2^0 can be similarly interpreted as the *imputed* or *marginal cost* of producing an additional ton of medium-grade ore, *provided* the additional production does *not* cause a new dual solution to appear.

Now let us look at $x_3^0 = 0$, which has dimension \$ per ton of low-grade ore. What this says is that low-grade ore is free in the sense that producing an additional ton has zero cost. What does this mean? If we look at the slack vector $u^0 = (0, 0, 16)$ found in Section 5, we observe that there is an over-production of low-grade ore by 16 tons beyond the requirements. In other words we have already overproduced, so the additional ton will cost zero to produce since it already exists. However, this is true only within

	x_1	x_2	x_3	Costs
v_1	6	2	4	200
v_2	2	2	12	160
Requirements	12	8	56	

Figure 35

limits. For suppose we change the requirement for low-grade ore to 56 tons, giving the data box of Figure 35. In Exercise 6 the reader will be asked to show that the optimal solution to the problem in Figure 35 is

$$v^0 = (.5, 4.5), \qquad x^0 = \begin{pmatrix} 27.5 \\ 0 \\ 8.75 \end{pmatrix}, \quad \text{and} \quad f^0 = g^0 = 820.$$

Note that we now have a new dual solution, so that the old dual variable $x_3 = 0$ did not hold for the entire range of changes in the requirements for low-grade ore.

Let us try to give general interpretations to a pair of dual linear programming problems. For either problem the matrix A will be called the matrix of technological coefficients, since it indicates how activity vectors are combined into the constraining inequalities. Then we can give different interpretations to the vectors c, b, x, and v, depending on whether our original problem is a maximizing or a minimizing one.

If the original problem is maximizing, we interpret x as the *activity vector*. Then the vector b is interpreted as the *capacity-constraint vector*, whose components give the amounts of the various "scarce resources" that can be demanded by a given activity vector. The vector c is the *profit* vector, whose entries give the unit profits for each component of the activity vector x. Finally, the vector v is the *imputed-value vector*, whose entries give the imputed values of each of the scarce resources that enter into the production process, provided the changes in scarce resources are sufficiently small that the dual solution remains optimal.

If the original problem is minimizing, we interpret v as the *activity vector*. Then c is interpreted as the *requirements vector*, whose components give the minimum amounts of each good that must be produced. The vector b is the *cost vector*, whose entries give the unit costs of each of the activities. Finally, the vector x is the *imputed-cost* vector, whose components give the imputed costs of producing additional amounts of each of the required goods, *provided* the changes in requirements are sufficiently small that the dual solution remains optimal.

Next we shall briefly discuss two important theorems in linear programming. First we restate the dual problems:

The MAXIMUM Problem   *The MINIMUM Problem*

Maximize $cx = f$ Minimize $vb = g$
subject to   (1) $Ax + y = b,$ subject to   (3) $vA - u = c,$
           (2) $x \geq 0, y \geq 0.$ (4) $v \geq 0, u \geq 0.$

Vectors x and y satisfying (1) and (2) and vectors v and u satisfying (3) and (4) are called *feasible vectors*.

In all the examples solved above we found that $f = g$ at the optimum solution. It is no accident that the dual problems share common values. The next theorem, which is the principal theorem of linear programming, shows that this will always happen whenever the problems have solutions.

The Duality Theorem   The maximum problem has as a solution a feasible vector x^0, such that $cx^0 = \max cx$, if and only if the minimum problem has a solution that is a feasible vector v^0, such that $v^0 b = \min vb$. Moreover, the equality $cx^0 = v^0 b$ holds if and only if x^0 and v^0 are solutions to their respective problems.

The duality theorem is extremely powerful, for it says that if one of the problems has a (finite) solution, then the other one necessarily also has a (finite) solution, and both problems share a common value. Another consequence of the theorem is that if one of the problems does *not* have a solution, then neither does the other.

The proof of the duality theorem is beyond the scope of this book, but some parts of it are indicated in Exercises 25 and 26, and in Exercise 8 of Section 4. We saw an example of a linear programming problem without a solution in Example 4 in Section 5. Another example is in Exercise 27.

The duality theorem states that $g^0 = f^0$ at the optimum solution. Applying this to Tucker's duality equation [(7) in Section 4], we obtain:

$$(5) \qquad\qquad 0 = g^0 - f^0 = v^0 y^0 + u^0 x^0.$$

However, since v^0, y^0, u^0, and x^0 are all feasible optimal vectors, they are, in particular, nonnegative. Hence $v^0 y^0 \geq 0$ and $u^0 x^0 \geq 0$. But the only way that two nonnegative numbers can add up to zero is for both of them to be zero. Therefore

$$(6) \qquad\qquad\qquad v^0 y^0 = 0,$$

$$(7) \qquad\qquad\qquad u^0 x^0 = 0.$$

If we now simply restate (6) and (7), we obtain the following important theorem:

The Complementary Slackness Theorem

(A) For each i, *either* $v_i^0 = 0$ or $y_i^0 = b_i - \sum_{j=1}^{n} a_{ij}x_j^0 = 0$.

(B) For each j, *either* $x_j^0 = 0$ or $u_j^0 = \sum_{i=1}^{m} v_i^0 a_{ij} - c_j = 0$.

Proof The proof of this theorem is simple because (6) says that the sum of the products $v_i^0 y_i^0$ must equal zero, but each term of the product is nonnegative so each product must itself be zero, which gives (A). The proof of (B) follows similarly from (7).

EXAMPLE 2 (continued) From the final tableau in Figure 24 of the previous section we found that the complete solution to the mining problem to be

$$v^0 = (1, 3), \qquad u^0 = (0, 0, 16), \qquad x^0 = \begin{pmatrix} 10 \\ 70 \\ 0 \end{pmatrix}, \qquad y^0 = \begin{pmatrix} 0 \\ 0 \end{pmatrix}.$$

We see that since $u_3^0 = 16$—that is, in the optimal solution low-grade ore is overproduced—the imputed cost of low-grade ore must be zero; and it is, since $x_3^0 = 0$. Also, since both v_1^0 and v_2^0 are positive, both components of y^0 must be zero, which they are. The reader should state the other consequences of the complementary slackness theorem for this example.

Let us conclude by discussing the reasons for the various steps of the simplex method. If we always think of the nonbasic variables, which appear at the left and on the top of the tableaus (see Figures 14 and 17), as being set equal to zero, then in the initial tableau of Figure 14 we see the initial solution vectors

(8) $\qquad x = 0, \qquad y = b, \qquad v = 0, \quad \text{and} \quad u = -c.$

Since we have assumed $b \geq 0$, we see that the first three vectors are non-negative, but u is nonnegative only if c was initially nonpositive. In the latter case the initial tableau is optimal (see Exercise 11). Since this is not normally the case, there is usually at least one positive indicator, so that the first answer to the question in box 2 of Figure 18 is "yes." Thus we must go around the loop and carry out at least one pivot. As we do so, the simplex method systematically changes the tableau in order to make u into a non-negative vector without destroying the nonnegativeness of x, y, or v, and also keeping $f = cx = vb = g$ at all times.

In step 6 of Figure 18 the pivot was chosen in order to have the smallest ratio $t_{I,n+1}/t_{IJ}$ so that no current x_i or y_j should become negative. The reader may verify that if the pivot is chosen not to have this property, then some such variable is made negative (see Exercise 15 of the preceding section).

The nondegeneracy assumption made in Section 4 can be used to show (see Exercise 25) that on each pivot step the value of the current f will actually increase. In Exercise 26 you will be asked to show that at most a finite number of pivot steps can be made. Hence, if the problem has a solution, we must arrive in a finite number of steps at a tableau having all positive indicators. At each step the current solution in a tableau satisfies equations (1), (2), and (3) above, and when all indicators are positive we have also satisfied (4), so that $v \geq 0$ and $u \geq 0$. By the duality theorem, if we have found x^0, y^0, v^0, and u^0 satisfying (1)–(4) and also $f^0 = cx^0 = v^0b = g^0$, then an optimum solution to the programming problem has been found.

EXERCISES

1. In Example 1 show that the same answer for the dimension of v_1 can be obtained by dividing the dimension of c_2 by the dimension of a_{12}.

2. Show that the vectors

$$x^0 = \begin{pmatrix} 31 \\ 14 \end{pmatrix} \quad \text{and} \quad v^0 = (\tfrac{100}{3}, \tfrac{400}{9})$$

solve the problem in Figure 33. [*Hint:* Substitute into the primal and dual problems.]

3. (a) Use the optimal solution to the automobile/truck problem in Figure 31 to predict how the objective function, which measures profit, will change if the capacity of shop 2 is changed from 135 to 144 man-hours per week.

   (b) Solve the problem in Figure 31 with the 135 changed to 144 and use its solution to show that your prediction in (a) was correct.

$$[\textit{Ans. Profit } 12{,}400, \ x^0 = \begin{pmatrix} 28 \\ 20 \end{pmatrix}, v^0 = (\tfrac{100}{3}, \tfrac{400}{9}).]$$

4. Show that the solution to the mining example in Figure 34 is

$$v = (2, 2), \qquad x^0 \text{ as before}, \qquad f = g = 720.$$

5. (a) Use the solution to Exercise 4 to predict what will happen in the mining problem if the requirement for medium-grade ore is increased from 8 to 10.

   (b) Solve the mining problem in Figure 34 with the 8 replaced by 10 and show that your prediction in (a) was correct.
   [*Ans.* $v^0 = (1.5, 3.5)$, x^0 as before, $f = g = 860$.]

6. Show that the solution to the problem in Figure 35 is

$$v^0 = (.5, 4.5), \qquad x^0 = \begin{pmatrix} 27.5 \\ 0 \\ 8.75 \end{pmatrix}, \qquad f = g = 820.$$

Interpret the solution.

7. In the automobile/truck example of Figure 31, suppose that the manufacturer can subcontract up to 18 of either shop 1 or shop 2 man-hours at $38 per hour. What is his optimal action? [*Hint:* You can answer this question without solving a linear programming problem.]

8. In the mining example of Figure 32 suppose the mining owner can sell 10 more tons of medium-grade ore at $55 per ton. Should he do so?

9. Consider again the general interpretation of a maximizing problem in which x is an activity vector, b the capacity-constraint vector, and c the profit vector. Let v^0 be the optimum dual solution vector. Discuss the following managerial interpretation of the components v_i^0 of v^0. "Additional amounts of scarce resource i should be acquired only if its cost is less than the component v_i^0 that gives the imputed value of an additional (sufficiently small) quantity."

10. Consider again the general interpretation of a minimizing problem in which v is the activity vector, c the requirements vector, and b the cost vector. Let x^0 be the optimum dual solution vector. Discuss the following managerial interpretations of the components x_i^0 of x. "Additional amounts of the jth good should be produced only if they can be sold with gross profit at least as large as the component x_j^0, which gives the imputed cost of producing an additional (sufficiently small) quantity."

11. Consider the dual maximum and minimum problems in equality form as expressed above. If $c \leq 0$, prove that the intial solution (8) is optimal. [*Hint:* Use the duality theorem.]

12-20. For each of Exercises 1-9 of Section 3 carry out the following steps:
   (a) Find the dimensions of the dual variables.
   (b) Set up the initial tableau with the dimensions of all variables and numbers indicated.
   (c) Read the answers to both primal and dual problems from the final tableau.
   (d) Interpret the dual solutions for the specific problems in each case.
   (e) State the complementary slackness theorem for each problem and interpret.

21-24. Rework Exercises 11-13 of Section 5 using steps (a)-(e) of Exercises 12-20, above.

*25. The assumption of nondegeneracy stated in Section 5 can be shown to be equivalent to the following: At no time in the pivoting process of the simplex method are any of the entries in the first m rows of the last column of the tableau ever zero. Use this fact to show that on each pivot step the value of $f = cx$ *increases.*

*26. Show that there are only a finite number of ways that the components of the x- and y-vectors can be used to label the top and right-hand side of the various tableaus during the pivoting process.

Use the result of Exercise 25 to show that no tableau can ever be repeated in the course of solving a nondegenerate problem by the simplex method. Hence, conclude that the simplex method described in Figure 18 must stop in a finite number of steps with the optimal solution to the linear programming problem, or else with proof that the problem has no finite solution.

27. Use the flow diagram of Figure 18 to show that the problem whose initial tableau is

-1	1	4
2	-4	8
2	3	0

does not have a solution. Verify algebraically and geometrically the statements in box 5 of that flow diagram.

*7 EQUALITY CONSTRAINTS AND THE GENERAL SIMPLEX METHOD

In this (optional) section we shall discuss the removal of the nonnegativity and nondegeneracy assumptions that we imposed at the beginning of Section 5 on linear programming problems. As stated there, most problems will automatically satisfy these assumptions. If not, they can usually be changed so that they do. We illustrate the latter first.

EXAMPLE 1 Consider again the automobile/truck example of Figure 6. Suppose we add the managerial constraint that at least 20 automobiles should be produced —perhaps because we have orders for them. The inequality that will do this is $x_2 \geq 20$, but it is a $\geq$ inequality instead of a $\leq$ inequality as is required for a maximizing problem. Multiplying through by -1 gives $-x_3 \leq -20$. Hence the maximizing problem is

$$\begin{array}{rl} \text{Maximize} & 300x_1 + 200x_2 \\ \text{subject to} & 5x_1 + 2x_2 \leq 180, \\ & 3x_1 + 3x_2 \leq 135, \\ & -x_2 \leq -20, \\ & x_1, x_2 \geq 0. \end{array}$$

(1)

We see that the b vector is

$$b = \begin{pmatrix} 180 \\ 135 \\ -20 \end{pmatrix},$$

(2)

which does not satisfy the nonnegativity assumption. However, let us set up the initial tableau and see what we can do with it. It is shown in Figure 36. Notice that in the third row where the -20 entry is, there is also a -1.

	x_1	x_2	-1	
v_1	5	2	180	$= -y_1$
v_2	3	3	135	$= -y_2$
v_3	0	$\boxed{-1}$	-20	$= -y_3$
-1	300	200	0	$= f$
	$= u_1$	$= u_2$	$= g$	

Figure 36

If we were to pivot on the -1, using the usual rules as given in Figure 18, we could change the -20 into a $+20$. Carrying out this pivot operation gives the tableau of Figure 37, which *has* a positive b vector. Hence we

	x_1	y_3	-1	
v_1	5	2	140	$= -y_1$
v_2	③	3	75	$= -y_2$
v_3	0	1	20	$= -x_2$
-1	300	200	-4000	$= f$
	$= u_1$	$= v_3$	$= g$	

Figure 37

can now proceed in the usual way. Choosing the most positive indicator, which is 300, we determine that the pivot should be the 3 circled in the first column. Carrying out the rest of the pivot steps as in Figure 18 gives the tableau in Figure 38. Since all indicators there are negative, we have

	y_2	y_3	-1	
v_1	$-\frac{5}{3}$	-3	65	$= -y_1$
u_1	$\frac{1}{3}$	1	25	$= -x_1$
u_2	0	1	20	$= -x_2$
-1	-100	-100	$-11{,}500$	$= f$
	$= v_2$	$= v_3$	$= g$	

Figure 38

determined the optimal solution, namely

$$x^0 = \begin{pmatrix} 25 \\ 20 \end{pmatrix}, \qquad v^0 = (0, 100, 100), \quad \text{and} \quad f^0 = g^0 = 11{,}500.$$

In other words, the optimum decision now is to produce 25 trucks and 20 automobiles for a gross profit of \$11,500. Notice that the gross profit has gone down, which is not surprising since we are satisfying an additional constraint. Notice also that the dual solution indicates that for each automobile less that we require to be made, an additional \$100 profit can be realized. This follows because $v_3^0 = \$100$, indicating that if we increase the right-hand side of the third constraint by 1, that is, change -20 to -19, then the profit should increase by $100. Notice also that the imputed value of shop 1 man-hours has gone to zero! This is because $y_1 = 65$, indicating that we are not using all of the shop 1 man-hours. Also the imputed value of shop 2 man-hours has jumped from $44.44 to $100 per hour, which indicates that shop 2 has become a more important "bottleneck" in the production process.

The previous example shows one way of deriving a problem that has negative b vector coefficients—namely, by imposing a $\leq$ constraint with positive right-hand side on the maximizing problem. Another way is to impose an equality constraint. For example, consider the equation

$$\text{(3)} \qquad 2x_1 + 5x_2 - 7x_3 = 12.$$

We can replace it by the two inequalities

$$\text{(4)} \qquad 2x_1 + 5x_2 - 7x_3 \leq 12 \quad \text{and} \quad 2x_1 + 5x_2 - 7x_3 \geq 12,$$

but the second of these is a $\geq$ constraint. We can change it into a $\leq$ constraint by multiplying by a -1, obtaining

$$\text{(5)} \qquad 2x_1 + 5x_2 - 7x_3 \leq 12 \quad \text{and} \quad -2x_1 - 5x_2 + 7x_3 \leq -12$$

as a pair of $\leq$ inequalities that are equivalent to the single equality (3).

When solving simple problems such as in Example 1 by hand it is usually quite easy to see how to pivot on negative numbers in the tableau in such a way that the problem becomes one having nonnegative right-hand sides. However, for large problems, and particularly for computing-machine computation, it is necessary to have a set of rules that will always work, without depending upon the ingenuity of the user. Such an algorithm is presented in Figure 39. It is usually called "phase I" of the simplex method, and what it does is to put the tableau in the standard form so that the flow diagram of Figure 18 can be applied. We illustrate it with an example.

EXAMPLE 2   Consider the linear programming problem

$$\text{(6)} \qquad \begin{array}{ll} \text{Maximize} & 2x_1 + x_2 \\ \text{subject to} & x_1 + x_2 \leq 20, \\ & x_1 + 2x_2 = 30, \\ & x_1, x_2 \geq 0. \end{array}$$

The set of feasible x-vectors is the line segment between the points $\begin{pmatrix} 0 \\ 15 \end{pmatrix}$ and $\begin{pmatrix} 10 \\ 10 \end{pmatrix}$ shown darkened in Figure 40. In order to solve (6) we replace the equality constraint by a pair of inequalities and obtain the problem:

$$\text{(7)} \qquad \begin{array}{ll} \text{Maximize} & 2x_1 + x_2 \\ \text{subject to} & x_1 + x_2 \leq 20, \\ & x_1 + 2x_2 \leq 30, \\ & -x_1 - 2x_2 \leq -30, \\ & x_1, x_2 \geq 0. \end{array}$$

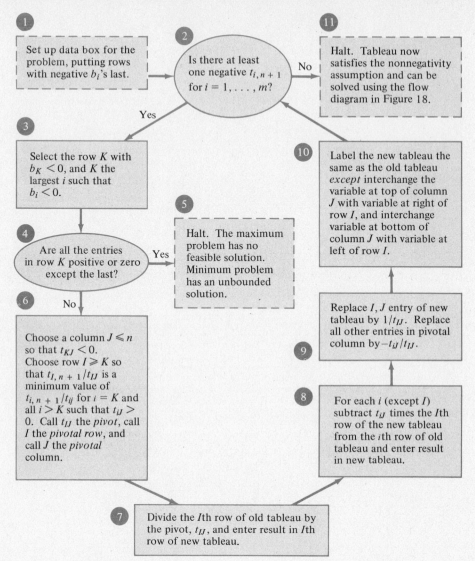

1

Set up data box for the problem, putting rows with negative b_i's last.

2

Is there at least one negative $t_{i, n+1}$ for $i = 1, \ldots, m$?

No

11

Halt. Tableau now satisfies the nonnegativity assumption and can be solved using the flow diagram in Figure 18.

Yes

3

Select the row K with $b_K < 0$, and K the largest i such that $b_i < 0$.

10

Label the new tableau the same as the old tableau *except* interchange the variable at top of column J with variable at right of row I, and interchange variable at bottom of column J with variable at left of row I.

5

Halt. The maximum problem has no feasible solution. Minimum problem has an unbounded solution.

4

Are all the entries in row K positive or zero except the last?

Yes

6

No

Choose a column $J \leqslant n$ so that $t_{KJ} < 0$. Choose row $I \geqslant K$ so that $t_{I, n+1}/t_{IJ}$ is a minimum value of $t_{i, n+1}/t_{ij}$ for $i = K$ and all $i > K$ such that $t_{ij} > 0$. Call t_{IJ} the *pivot*, call I the *pivotal row*, and call J the *pivotal column*.

Replace I, J entry of new tableau by $1/t_{IJ}$. Replace all other entries in pivotal column by $-t_{iJ}/t_{IJ}$.

9

8

For each i (except I) subtract t_{iJ} times the Ith row of the new tableau from the ith row of old tableau and enter result in new tableau.

7

Divide the Ith row of old tableau by the pivot, t_{IJ}, and enter result in Ith row of new tableau.

Figure 39

Thus we obtain a problem that does not satisfy the nonnegativity assumption.

Let us solve the problem by following the flow diagram of Figure 39. We set up the initial tableau with the negative b_i's last as instructed in box 1 of that figure. The initial tableau is given in Figure 41. The answer to the question in box 2 of Figure 39 is "yes," so we go to box 3, where we must choose $K = 3$. The answer to the question in box 4 is "no," so we go on to box 6. Since both entries in the first two columns of the third row of Figure 41 are negative, J can be either 1 or 2; we choose $J = 1$. Then the ratio rule in box 6 gives $I = 3$. Carrying out the pivot steps in boxes 7–10 of Figure 39 gives the next tableau shown in Figure 42. Notice

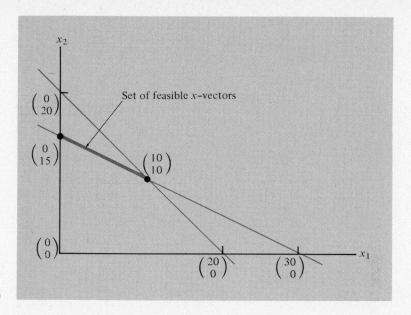

Figure 40

that a new negative has appeared in the third column of the first row! So the answer to the question in box 2 of Figure 39 is again "yes," and we must go around the main loop of the flow diagram again. We find that

	x_1	x_2	-1	
v_1	1	1	20	$= -y_1$
v_2	1	2	30	$= -y_2$
v_3	⊝1	-2	-30	$= -y_3$
-1	2	1	0	$= f$
	$= u_1$	$= u_2$	$= g$	

Figure 41

$K = 1$ and $J = 2$ are the only possible choices, and these give $I = 1$, so that we must pivot on the -1 circled in the first row of Figure 42. After

	y_3	x_2	-1	
v_1	1	⊝1	-10	$= -y_1$
v_2	1	0	0	$= -y_2$
u_1	-1	2	30	$= -x_1$
-1	2	-3	-60	$= f$
	$= v_3$	$= u_2$	$= g$	

Figure 42

pivoting, the new tableau is as shown in Figure 43. Since both indicators are negative, we have obtained the optimal solution without further pivoting.

	y_3	y_1	-1	
u_2	-1	-1	10	$= -x_2$
v_2	1	0	0	$= -y_2$
u_1	1	2	10	$= -x_1$
-1	-1	-3	-30	$= f$
	$= v_2$	$= v_1$	$= g$	

Figure 43

It is

$$x^0 = \begin{pmatrix} 10 \\ 10 \end{pmatrix}, \qquad v^0 = (3, 0, 1), \quad \text{and} \quad f^0 = g^0 = 30.$$

The reader should locate the solution on the diagram of Figure 40.

The last topic of this section is the question of removing the nondegeneracy assumption stated in Section 5. A complete discussion of the problem is beyond the scope of this book, but an interested reader may wish to refer to one of the more advanced texts listed at the end of this chapter. We shall indicate the essential ideas here, however. An example will suffice for this purpose.

EXAMPLE 3 Consider the problem:

$$
\begin{array}{ll}
\text{Maximize} & x_1 + x_2 \\
\text{subject to} & x_1 \qquad \le 4, \\
& \qquad x_2 \le 4, \\
& 2x_1 + x_2 \le 8, \\
& x_1, x_2 \ge 0.
\end{array}
$$

(8)

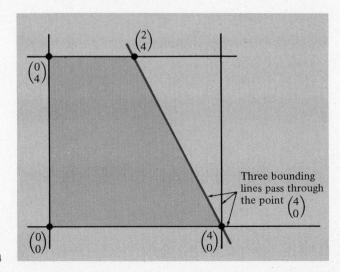

Figure 44

The set of feasible x-vectors is shown shaded in Figure 44. Notice that the set has four extreme points and that each is the intersection of exactly two bounding lines *except* for the point $\begin{pmatrix} 4 \\ 0 \end{pmatrix}$, which has three bounding lines through it. We shall show that this can lead to the appearance of a zero in the b area of the tableau after some pivoting, and when this happens it is possible to pivot without improving the objective function. The initial tableau for the problem is given in Figure 45.

	x_1	x_2	-1	
v_1	①	0	4	$= -y_1$
v_2	0	1	4	$= -y_2$
v_3	2	1	8	$= -y_3$
-1	1	1	0	$= g$
	$= u_1$	$= u_2$	$= g$	

Figure 45

Since both indicators are positive, suppose we choose the first one. The minimum-ratio rule then selects the first row to be pivotal, and we pivot on the one circled. (Note that we could also pivot on the 2 in the third row, first column, and the results will be similar; see Exercise 11.) The new tableau is given in Figure 46. Notice that a zero did appear in the third

	y_1	x_2	-1	
u_1	1	0	4	$= -x_1$
v_2	0	1	4	$= -y_2$
v_3	-2	①	$0 + \epsilon$	$= -y_3$
-1	-1	1	-4	$= f$
	$= v_1$	$= u_2$	$= g$	

Figure 46

row, third column, of Figure 46. In order to make it into something positive a small amount ϵ is added to it. This is called a *perturbation*. Geometrically it corresponds in Figure 44 to moving the line $2x_1 + x_2 = 8$ parallel to itself upward slightly. This makes the extreme point $\begin{pmatrix} 4 \\ 0 \end{pmatrix}$ have just two bounding lines through it, and adds a new extreme point $\begin{pmatrix} 4 \\ \epsilon \end{pmatrix}$ nearby. We will find it on the next iteration. The second column has a positive indicator, and the minimum-ratio rule selects the third row to be pivotal and 1 the pivot, circled in Figure 46. The new tableau is given in Figure 47.

Now we observe that column 1 has a positive indicator, so we must still

	y_1	y_3	-1	
u_1	1	0	4	$= -x_1$
v_2	②	-1	$4 - \epsilon$	$= -y_2$
u_2	-2	1	$0 + \epsilon$	$= -x_2$
-1	1	-1	$-4 - \epsilon$	$= f$
	$= v_1$	$= v_3$	$= g$	

Figure 47

	y_2	y_3	-1	
u_1	$-\tfrac{1}{2}$	$-\tfrac{1}{2}$	$2 + (\tfrac{\epsilon}{2})$	$= -x_1$
v_1	1	$-\tfrac{1}{2}$	$2 - (\tfrac{\epsilon}{2})$	$= -y_1$
u_2	-1	0	4	$= -x_2$
-1	$-\tfrac{1}{2}$	$-\tfrac{1}{2}$	$-6 - (\tfrac{\epsilon}{2})$	$= f$
	$= v_2$	$= v_3$	$= g$	

Figure 48

pivot again. The ratio rule selects as pivot the 2 in the first column, circled in Figure 47. The next tableau is given in Figure 48.

Since both indicators in Figure 48 are negative, we have the optimal solution. Notice that if we replace ϵ by 0 we still have an optimal tableau, hence our perturbation did not affect the original problem enough to change the solution, which is

$$x^0 = \begin{pmatrix} 2 \\ 4 \end{pmatrix}, \qquad v^0 = (0, \tfrac{1}{2}, \tfrac{1}{2}), \quad \text{and} \quad f^0 = g^0 = 6.$$

Actually, if we had ignored the 0 in the last column of Figure 47 and just gone ahead with the simplex method as given in Figure 18, we would have arrived at the same solution without difficulty. But notice that in going from tableau 46 to 47 we then would not have increased the objective function f at all. It can happen with larger problems that the computation could go from one tableau to the next several times in a row without changing f, and after a finite number of pivots return to a tableau constructed earlier. From then on the computational process will go through the same sequence of tableaus indefinitely without changing f. This is called *cycling*. Actually it rarely happens in practice. The smallest known example in which it can occur has seven variables. For small problems that can be worked by hand it never occurs.

There are several ways of avoiding cycling for computer codes that handle large problems. One way is the process of perturbation illustrated above. There only one 0 was found and it was made positive by adding $+\epsilon$ to it. If a second zero were found, then $+\epsilon^2$ would be added; and if a third were found, then $+\epsilon^3$ would be added; and so on. The final tableau will then have numbers plus polynomials in ϵ in the last column. By selecting

ϵ *not* to be equal to any of the finite number of zeros of these polynomials and also very small, we can prove that there always is a perturbation of the components of the b-vectors that will avoid cycling, and that has the same solution as the original problem when ϵ is replaced by 0 in the final tableau.

Still another (practical) way of avoiding cycling is the following. Whenever a zero is about to appear in a tableau, there will be more than one choice of pivotal row in box 6 of the flow diagram of Figure 18. This can be seen in Figure 45, in which, given the pivotal column $J = 1$, we can choose *either $I = 1$ or $I = 3$* when applying the test. Suppose now we choose between these two at random, instead of always choosing the first one. It can be shown that if this method is used to "break ties" when selecting pivotal rows, then the simplex method will not cycle with probability 1. For practical purposes this provides an adequate safeguard against the very rare possibility of cycling in computations.

EXERCISES

1. Write pairs of $\leq$ inequalities that are equivalent to each of the following $=$ constraints:
    (a) $12x_1 + 3x_2 - 7x_3 = 15$.
    (b) $3x_1 - 2x_2 + 4x_3 = 0$ and $-4x_1 + x_2 - 2x_3 = 7$.

2. Consider the mining example (Example 2 of Section 3) again with the additional constraint that exactly 16 tons of high-grade ore should be produced per week. Show that the tableau has a nonnegative b-vector.

3. Show that a minimizing problem with $b \geq 0$ can always be solved using Figure 18 regardless of the form of the additional constraints that may be imposed on the minimizing problem.

4. In Example 1 of Section 3 show that the additional constraint $x_1 \leq 15$ can be imposed and the problem solved using Figure 18.

5. Show that a maximizing problem with only $\leq$ constraints and positive b-vector can be solved using Figure 18 regardless of how many additional $\leq$ constraints are added, as long as the right-hand sides of such additional constraints are nonnegative.

6. Use the results of Exercises 3–5 to show that the phase I computation of Figure 39 is needed only when a $\leq$ constraint with negative right-hand side is added to the maximizing problem.

7. Apply the phase I simplex method of Figure 39 to the following examples.
    (a) Maximize $2x_1 + x_2$
         subject to $\quad x_1 + x_2 \leq 10$,
         $\quad\quad\quad\quad x_1 + x_2 \geq 6$,
         $\quad\quad\quad\quad x_1 \quad\quad \leq 8$,
         $\quad\quad\quad\quad x_1, x_2 \geq 0$.
    (b) Maximize x_1
         subject to $\quad x_1 \quad\quad\quad \geq 2$,
         $\quad\quad\quad\quad\quad\quad x_2 \geq 3$,
         $\quad\quad\quad 3x_1 + 2x_2 \leq 24$.

8. Apply the phase I computation to the problem whose initial tableau is given by

1	1	20
-1	-2	-50
2	1	0

and show that the computation ends up in box 5 of Figure 39. Draw the constraint sets of the primal and dual problems and give a geometric interpretation to the statements in box 5 of Figure 39.

*9. Show in general that if the computation of Figure 39 ends up in box 5, then the statements given there are correct.

*10. Show that phase I is needed if and only if $x = 0$ is *not* a feasible vector for the maximizing problem.

11. Start with Figure 45 and carry out pivoting steps, starting with the pivot in the third row, first column. Show that equivalent results are obtained.

12. Show that even if we do not add $+\epsilon$ in the third row, third column, of Figure 46, the simplex method will yield the correct solution.

13. Add the constraint $-x_1 + x_2 \leq 4$ to the problem in (8) and show that no matter which column is chosen for the first pivot, a 0 is still produced in the b-vector after one pivot. Show that the simplex method still works.

*14. (a) Show that the phase I simplex method will eventually make the last inequality with negative right-hand side into one with positive (or zero) right-hand side without making the right-hand sides of later inequalities negative.

(b) Show that in a finite number of steps all negative right-hand sides will be made nonnegative, or else the computation will end up in box 5 of the flow diagram in Figure 39.

8 STRICTLY DETERMINED GAMES

In Sections 1–7 we discussed linear programming problems that involve *optimization*—that is, the maximization or minimization of a (linear) function subject to linear constraints. In order to optimize a function it is necessary to control all relevant variables.

Game theory considers situations in which there are two (or more) persons, each of whom controls some but not all the variables necessary to determine the outcome(s) of a certain event. Depending upon which event actually occurs, the players receive various payments. If for each possible event the algebraic sum of payments to all players is zero, the game is called *zero-sum;* otherwise it is *nonzero-sum.* Usually the players will not agree as to which event should occur, so that their objectives in the game are different. In the case of a matrix game, which is a two-person zero-sum game in which one player loses what the other wins, game theory provides a solution. The solution is based on the principle that each player tries to choose his course of action so that, regardless of what his opponent does, he can assure himself of a certain minimum amount. Matrix games are discussed in Sections 8 through 11. We shall not discuss nonzero-sum games in this chapter. We refer an interested reader to the suggested readings at the end of the chapter for treatments of this important class of games.

Most recreational games such as ticktacktoe, checkers, backgammon, chess, poker, bridge, and other card or board games can be viewed as games of strategy. On the other hand, such gambling games as dice, roulette, and so on are not (as usually formulated) games of strategy, since a person playing one of these games is merely "betting against the odds."

In this and the following sections we shall formulate simple games that illustrate the theory and are amenable to computation. We shall base these games on applications in business situations and on recreational games.

EXAMPLE 1 Two stores, R and C, are planning to locate in one of two towns. As in Figure 49, town 1 has 60 percent of the population while town 2 has 40 percent. If both stores locate in the same town they will split the total business of both towns equally, but if they locate in different towns each will get the business of that town. Where should each store locate?

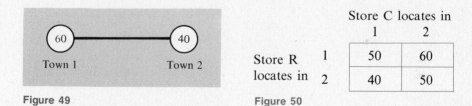

Figure 49

Store C locates in

		1	2
Store R	1	50	60
locates in	2	40	50

Figure 50

Clearly this is a game situation, since each store can control where it locates but cannot control at all where its competitor locates. Each store has two possible "strategies": "locate in town 1" and "locate in town 2." Let us list all possible outcomes for each store employing each of its strategies. The result is given in the *payoff matrix* of Figure 50. The entries of the matrix represent the percentages of business that store R gets in each case. They can also be interpreted as the percentage *losses* of business by C for each case. If both stores locate in town 1 or both in town 2, each gets 50 percent of the business, hence the entries on the main diagonal are 50. If store *R* locates in town 1 and C in 2, then R gets 60 percent of the business as indicated in entry in row 1 and column 2. (This entry also indicates that C *loses* 60 percent.) Similarly, if *R* locates in 2 and C in 1, then R gets 40 percent (and C loses 40 percent) as indicated in row 2 and column 1.

How should the players play the matrix game in Figure 50? It is easy to see that store R should prefer to locate in town 1 because, regardless of what C does, R can assure himself of 10 percent more business in town 1 than in town 2. Similarly, store C also prefers to locate in town 1 because he will lose 10 percent less business—that is, gain 10 percent more business—in town 1 than in 2. Hence optimal strategies are for each store to locate in town 1; that is, R chooses row 1 and C chooses column 1 in Figure 50. The value of the game is 50, representing the percentage of the business that R gets.

In Example 1 we started with an applied situation and derived from it a matrix game. Actually, we can interpret any matrix as a game, as the following definition shows.

Definition   Let G be an $m \times n$ matrix with entries g_{ij} for $i = 1, \ldots, m$ and $j = 1, \ldots, n$. Then G can be interpreted as the *payoff matrix* of the following matrix game: player R (the *row* player) chooses any row i, and simultaneously player C (the *column* player) chooses any column j; the outcome of the game is that C pays to R an amount equal to g_{ij}. (If $g_{ij} < 0$, then this should be interpreted as R paying C an amount equal to $-g_{ij}$.)

EXAMPLE 2   Consider the matrix in Figure 51 as a game. Thus, if R chooses row 1 and C chooses column 1, then C pays 5 units to R; if R chooses row 1 and C

C Chooses

		1	2
R Chooses	1	5	-10
	2	2	0

Figure 51

chooses column 2, then R pays 10 units to C; and so on. How should the players play this game?

Player R would like to get the 5 payoff, and is tempted to play row 1. However, player C clearly prefers to play column 2, since each entry in it is lower than the corresponding entry in column 1. And since player R realizes this, he will play row 2 to avoid the -10 payoff. The optimal strategies then are "play row 2" for R, and "play column 2" for C. The value of the game is $g_{22} = 0$.

The solutions in the first two examples have the following in common. In each case the value is an entry that is the minimum of its row and the maximum of its column. Such an entry is called a *saddle value*. When such a saddle value exists, it is always the value of the game, and the game is strictly determined. To see this, consider any game G with an entry $g_{ij} = v$ which is a saddle value. Then, since v is the minimum of row i, R can by playing row i assure that he will win at least v. And since v is the maximum of column j, C by playing column j can assure that R will not win more than v. This justifies the definition:

Definition Consider a matrix game with payoff matrix G. Entry g_{ij} is said to be a *saddle value* of G if g_{ij} is simultaneously the *minimum* of the ith row and the *maximum* of the jth column. If matrix game G has a saddle value, it is said to be *strictly determined*, and *optimal strategies* for it are:

For player R: "Choose a row that contains a saddle value."
For player C: "Choose a column that contains a saddle value."

The *value* of the game is $v = g_{ij}$, where g_{ij} is any saddle-value entry. The game is *fair* if its value is zero.

In order to justify this definition it must be shown that if there are two or more saddle values then they are all equal. A proof of this fact is outlined in Exercise 10. The next example illustrates it.

EXAMPLE 3   Let us consider an extension of Example 1 in which the stores R and C are trying to locate in one of the three towns in Figure 52. We shall assume that if both stores locate in the same town they split all business equally, but if they locate in different towns then all the business in the town that

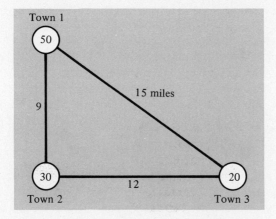

Figure 52

doesn't have a store will go to the *closer* of the two stores. The percentages of people in each town are marked in the circles. The distances between the towns are marked on the lines connecting them.

The payoff matrix for the resulting game is shown in Figure 53. In Exercise 13 the reader is asked to check that these entries are correct.

Each of the four 50 entries in the 2×2 matrix in the upper left-hand corner of Figure 53 is a saddle value of the matrix, since each is simultaneously the minimum of its row and maximum of its column. Note that

Store C locates in

	1	2	3
1	50	50	80
2	50	50	80
3	20	20	50

Store R locates in

Figure 53

the 50 entry in the lower right-hand corner is *not* a saddle value. Hence the game is strictly determined, and optimal strategies are:

For store R: "Locate in either town 1 or town 2."
For store C: "Locate in either town 1 or town 2."

In a real-life location problem one might want to take into account not only present populations of cities, but also rate of population growth. In Exercise 14 the reader is asked to criticize the above strategies from this point of view.

Instead of the somewhat indefinite description of the optimal strategy for player R as "Locate in either town 1 or 2," we can employ the following device: since we don't care which town we locate in, we can just flip a coin, or use any other chance device, and on the basis of the outcome make the choice between the towns. So we can also use the following strategy: "Select one of the numbers 1 or 2 by means of a random device with arbitrary probabilities for each outcome, and locate in the corresponding town." This strategy is also optimal.

Note that if we multiply the matrix in Figure 53 on the left by the vector $(1, 0, 0)$, we get the first row; hence we shall use this vector to represent the strategy "Locate in town 1" for store R. Similarly, the strategy "Locate in town 2" is represented by the vector $(0, 1, 0)$, since multiplying the matrix on the left by it gives the second row. Then the vector

$$(a, 1 - a, 0) = a(1, 0, 0) + (1 - a)(0, 1, 0) \quad \text{for} \quad 0 \leq a \leq 1$$

represents the strategy "Choose row 1 with probability a and row 2 with probability $1 - a$."

Similarly, for store C, the column vectors

$$\begin{pmatrix} 1 \\ 0 \\ 0 \end{pmatrix}, \quad \begin{pmatrix} 0 \\ 1 \\ 0 \end{pmatrix}, \quad \text{and} \quad \begin{pmatrix} a \\ 1 - a \\ 0 \end{pmatrix} \quad \text{for} \quad 0 \leq a \leq 1$$

represents the strategies "Locate in town 1," "Locate in town 2," and "Locate in town 1 with probability a and in town 2 with probability $1 - a$," respectively.

EXAMPLE 4 Consider the game G whose matrix is in Figure 54. It is not hard to see that the game is strictly determined with value 1, and there are four saddle

Player C

1	5	1	7
-2	8	0	-9
1	12	1	3

Player R

Figure 54

values. Optimal strategies are $(1, 0, 0)$ and $(0, 0, 1)$ for player R, and

$$\begin{pmatrix} 1 \\ 0 \\ 0 \\ 0 \end{pmatrix} \text{ and } \begin{pmatrix} 0 \\ 0 \\ 1 \\ 0 \end{pmatrix}$$

for player C. The four ways we can pair optimal strategies for player R with those for player C give the four saddle values. Besides the optimal strategies above we have their convex combinations

$$a(1, 0, 0) + (1 - a)(0, 0, 1) = (a, 0, 1 - a),$$

which is optimal for R for any a satisfying $0 \leq a \leq 1$, and

$$a\begin{pmatrix} 1 \\ 0 \\ 0 \\ 0 \end{pmatrix} + (1 - a)\begin{pmatrix} 0 \\ 1 \\ 0 \\ 0 \end{pmatrix} = \begin{pmatrix} a \\ 0 \\ 1 - a \\ 0 \end{pmatrix},$$

which is optimal for player C for any a in the same range.

As the reader may have already found out for himself, not all matrix games are strictly determined. For instance, the two games shown in Figure 55 are not strictly determined. The solution of such games will be discussed in succeeding sections.

0	1
2	0

(a)

5	-2	3
-5	0	7
3	4	-1

(b)

Figure 55

EXERCISES

1. Determine which of the games given below are strictly determined and which are fair. When the game is strictly determined, find optimal strategies for each player.

(a)

0	2
−1	4

(b)

5	0
0	2

(c)

3	1
4	0

(d)

1	−1
−1	1

(e)

3	1
−4	0

(f)

0	4
0	2

(g)

7	0
0	0

(h)

0	0
0	−7

(i)

0	0
0	0

(j)

1	1
1	1

[*Partial Ans.* (a) Strictly determined and fair; R play row 1, C play column 1; (b) nonstrictly determined; (e) strictly determined but not fair; R play row 1, C play column 2; (j) strictly determined but not fair; both players can use any strategy.]

2. Find the value and all optimal strategies for the following games:

(a)

15	2	−3
6	5	7
−7	4	0

(b)

5	2	−1	−1
1	1	0	1
3	0	−3	7

(c)

0	5	6	−3
1	−1	2	3
1	2	3	4
−1	0	7	5

(d)

1	−12	6
0	−4	1
3	−7	2
3	−4	2
−5	−4	7

[*Ans.* (a) $v = 5$; $(0, 1, 0)$; $\begin{pmatrix} 0 \\ 1 \\ 0 \end{pmatrix}$; (d) $(0, a, 0, 1 - a, 0)$, $\begin{pmatrix} 0 \\ 1 \\ 0 \end{pmatrix}$, $v = -4$.]

3. Find the values of and all optimal strategies for the following games:

(a)

5	10	6	5
5	7	8	5
0	5	6	5

(b)

-2	0	-1
-5	7	8

(c)

0	0	1	0
1	0	0	0
1	0	1	0

(d)

3	2	3
6	2	7
5	1	4

$$[\textit{Ans.}\ (a)\ v = 5;\ (a, 1 - a, 0);\ \begin{pmatrix} a \\ 0 \\ 0 \\ 1 - a \end{pmatrix};\ (d)\ v = 2;\ (a, 1 - a, 0);\ \begin{pmatrix} 0 \\ 1 \\ 0 \end{pmatrix}.]$$

4. Each of two players shows one or two fingers (simultaneously) and C pays to R a sum equal to the total number of fingers shown. Write the game matrix. Show that the game is strictly determined, and find the value and optimal strategies.

5. Each of two players shows one or two fingers (simultaneously) and C pays to R an amount equal to the total number of fingers shown, while R pays to C an amount equal to the product of the numbers of fingers shown. Construct the game matrix (the entries will be the net gain of R), and find the value and the optimal strategies.
    [*Ans.* $v = 1$, R must show one finger, C may show one or two.]

6. Show that a strictly determined game is fair if and only if there is a zero entry such that all entries in its row are nonnegative and all entries in its column are nonpositive.

7. Consider the game

$$G = \begin{array}{|c|c|} \hline 2 & 5 \\ \hline -1 & a \\ \hline \end{array}$$

    (a) Show that G is strictly determined regardless of the value of a.
    (b) Find the value of G.   [*Ans.* 2.]
    (c) Find optimal strategies for each player.
    (d) If $a = 1,000,000$, obviously R would like to get it as his payoff. Is there any way he can assure himself of obtaining it? What would happen to him if he tried to obtain it?
    (e) Show that the value of the game is the most that R can assure for himself.

8. Consider the matrix game

$$G = \begin{array}{|c|c|} \hline a & a \\ \hline c & d \\ \hline \end{array}$$

Show that G is strictly determined for every set of values for a, c, and d. Show that the same result is true if two entries in a given column are equal.

9. Find necessary and sufficient conditions that the game

$$G = \begin{array}{|c|c|} \hline a & 0 \\ \hline 0 & b \\ \hline \end{array}$$

should be strictly determined. [*Hint:* These will be expressed in terms of relations among the numbers a and b and the number zero.]

10. **(a)** Show that if there are two saddle values in the same row, then they are equal.

(b) Show that if there are two saddle values in the same column, then they are equal.

(c) If g_{ij} and g_{hk} are saddle values in different rows and columns, show that $g_{ij} = g_{ik}$. Also show $g_{ik} = g_{hk}$.

(d) Prove that $g_{ij} = g_{hk}$.

11. Two companies, one large and one small, manufacturing the same product, wish to build a new store in one of four towns located on a given highway. If we regard the total population of the four towns as 100 percent, the distribution of population and distances between towns are as shown:

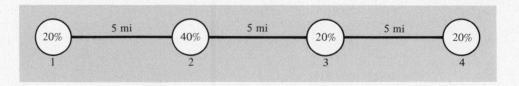

Assume that if the large company's store is nearer a town, it will capture 80 percent of the business; if both stores are equally distant, then the large company will capture 60 percent of the business; and if the small store is nearer, then the large company will capture 40 percent of the business.

(a) Set up the matrix of the game.

(b) Test for dominated rows and columns, that is, rows or columns that will never be used by a player who plays optimally.

(c) Find optimal strategies and the value of the game and interpret your results.

[*Ans.* Both companies should locate in town 2; the large company captures 60 percent of the business.]

12. Rework Exercise 11 if the percentages of business captured by the large company are 90, 75, and 60, respectively.

13. Show that the entries in Figure 53 are correct.

14. In the store location of Example 3 how do the optimal strategies change if the population of town 1 becomes 51 percent and the population of town 2 becomes 29 percent of the total? How might they change if town 2 is growing much faster than town 1?

15. Show that the following game is always strictly determined for non-negative a and any values of the parameters b, c, d, and e.

$2a$	a	$3a$
b	$-a$	c
d	$-2a$	e

16. For what values of a is the following game strictly determined?

[*Ans.* $-1 \leq a \leq 2$.]

a	6	2
-1	a	-7
-2	4	a

9   MATRIX GAMES

As we saw in the numerical examples of the previous section, some matrix games are nonstrictly determined; that is, they have no entry that is simultaneously a row minimum and a column maximum. We can characterize nonstrictly determined 2×2 matrix games as follows:

Theorem   The matrix game

$$G = \begin{array}{|c|c|} \hline a & b \\ \hline c & d \\ \hline \end{array}$$

is nonstrictly determined if and only if one of the following two conditions is satisfied:

   (i) $a < b$, $a < c$, $d < b$, and $d < c$.
  (ii) $a > b$, $a > c$, $d > b$, and $d > c$.

(These equations mean that the two entries on one diagonal of the matrix must each be greater than each of the two entries on the other diagonal.)

Proof If either of the conditions (i) or (ii) holds, it is easy to check that no entry of the matrix is simultaneously the minimum of the row and the maximum of the column in which it occurs; hence the game is not strictly determined.

To prove the other half of the theorem, recall that, by Exercise 8 of the last section, if two of the entries in the same row or the same column of G are equal, the game is strictly determined; hence we can assume that no two entries in the same row or the same column are equal. Suppose now that $a < b$; then $a < c$ or else a is a row minimum and a column maximum; then also $c > d$ or else c is a row minimum and a column maximum; then also $d < b$ or else d is a row minimum and a column maximum. Hence the assumption $a < b$ leads to case (i) above.

In a similar manner the assumption $a > b$ leads to case (ii). This completes the proof of the theorem.

EXAMPLE 1 Jones and Smith play the following game: Jones conceals either a \$1 or a \$2 bill in his hand; Smith guesses 1 or 2, winning the bill if he guesses the number. If we make Jones player R (the row player) and Smith player C, the matrix of the game is as in Figure 56. Because the game satisfies condition (i) in the theorem above, the game is nonstrictly determined. Later we shall solve it.

		Player C Smith guesses	
		1	2
Player R Jones chooses	\$1 bill	-1	0
	\$2 bill	0	-2

Figure 56

EXAMPLE 2 Mr. Sub works for Mr. Super and frequently must advise him on the acceptability of certain projects. Whenever Mr. Sub can make a clear judgment about a given project, he does so honestly. But when he has no reason to either accept or reject a given project, he tries to agree with Mr. Super. If he manages to agree with him he gives himself 10 points; if he is unfavorable when his boss is favorable, he credits himself with 0 points; but when he is favorable and his boss is unfavorable (the worst case), he loses 50 points. The matrix of the game is given in Figure 57. Since the matrix in Figure 57 satisfies condition (ii) of the theorem, it is not strictly determined.

How should one play a nonstrictly determined game? We must first convince ourselves that no single choice is clearly optimal for either player.

Player C
Mr. Super's opinion

		Favorable	Unfavorable
Player R Mr. Sub's	Favorable	10	−50
opinion	Unfavorable	0	10

Figure 57

In Example 1, R would like to get one of the 0 payoffs. But if he always chooses $1 and C finds this out, C can win $1 by guessing 1. And if R always chooses $2, then C can win $2 by guessing 2. Similarly, if C always guesses 1 or always guesses 2, and R finds this out, then R can always get 0. So our first result is that each player must, in some way, prevent the other player from finding out which choice of alternatives he is going to make.

We also note that for a single play of a nonstrictly determined 2×2 game there is no difference between the two strategies, as long as one's strategy is not guessed by the opponent. Let us now consider several plays of the game. What should R do? Clearly, he should not choose the same row all the time, or C will be able to notice and profit by it. Rather, R should choose sometimes one row, sometimes the other. Our key question then is "How often should R choose each of his alternatives?" In Example 1 it seems reasonable that player R (Jones) should choose the $1 bill about twice as often as the $2 bill, because his losses, if Smith guesses correctly, are half as much. (We shall see later that this strategy is, indeed, optimal.) In what order should he do this? For instance, should he select the $1 bill twice in a row and then the $2 bill? That is dangerous, because if player C (Smith) notices the pattern, he can gain by knowing just what R will do next. Thus we see that R should choose the $1 bill two-thirds of the time, but according to some unguessable pattern. The only safe way of doing this is to play it two-thirds of the time at random. He could, for instance, roll a die (without letting C see it) and choose the $1 if 1 through 4 turns up, the $2 if 5 or 6 turns up. Then his opponent cannot guess what the actual decision will be, since R himself won't know it. We conclude that a rational way of playing is for each player to *mix* his strategies, selecting sometimes one, sometimes the other; and these strategies should be selected at random, according to certain fixed ratios (probabilities) of selecting each.

By a *mixed strategy* in a 2×2 game for player R we shall mean a command of the form "Play row 1 with probability p_1 and play row 2 with probability p_2," where we assume that $p_1 \geq 0$ and $p_2 \geq 0$ and $p_1 + p_2 = 1$. Similarly, a mixed strategy for player C is a command of the form "Play column 1 with probability q_1 and play column 2 with probability q_2," where $q_1 \geq 0$, $q_2 \geq 0$, and $q_1 + q_2 = 1$. A mixed-strategy vector for player R is the probability row vector (p_1, p_2), and a mixed-strategy vector for player C is the probability column vector $\begin{pmatrix} q_1 \\ q_2 \end{pmatrix}$.

Examples of mixed strategies are $(\frac{1}{2}, \frac{1}{2})$ and $\begin{pmatrix} \frac{1}{5} \\ \frac{4}{5} \end{pmatrix}$. The reader may wonder how a player could actually play one of these strategies. The mixed strategy $(\frac{1}{2}, \frac{1}{2})$ is easy to realize, since it can be realized by flipping a coin and choosing one alternative if heads turns up and the other alternative if tails turns up. The mixed strategy $\begin{pmatrix} \frac{1}{5} \\ \frac{4}{5} \end{pmatrix}$ is more difficult to realize, since no chance device in common use gives these probabilities. However, suppose a pointer is constructed with a card that is $\frac{4}{5}$ shaded and $\frac{1}{5}$ unshaded, as in Figure 58,

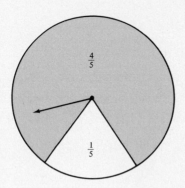

Figure 58

and C simply spins the pointer (without letting R see it, of course!). Then, if the pointer stops on the unshaded part he plays the first column, and if it stops on the shaded part he plays the second column, thus realizing the desired strategy. By varying the proportion of shaded area on the card, other mixed strategies can conveniently be realized. An equally effective and less mechanical device for realizing a given mixed strategy is to use a table of random digits. For the strategy $\begin{pmatrix} \frac{1}{5} \\ \frac{4}{5} \end{pmatrix}$, for example, we could let the digits 0 and 1 represent a play of column 1, and the remaining digits a play of column 2.

We now want to define what we shall mean by a solution to an $m \times n$ matrix game.

Definition Let G be an $m \times n$ matrix with entries g_{ij}. An m-component row vector p is a *mixed-strategy vector* for player R if it is a probability vector; similarly, an n-component column vector q is a *mixed-strategy vector for C* if it is a probability vector. (Recall from Chapter 4 that a probability vector is one with nonnegative entries whose sum is 1.) Let v be a number, let e be an m-component row vector all of whose entries are 1, and let f be an n-component column vector all of whose entries are 1. It follows that the vectors ve and vf are

$$ve = \underbrace{(v, v, \ldots, v)}_{m \text{ components}} \quad \text{and} \quad vf = \left.\begin{pmatrix} v \\ v \\ \vdots \\ v \end{pmatrix}\right\} n \text{ components}$$

Then v is the *value* of the matrix game G and p^0 and q^0 are *optimal strategies* for the players if and only if the following inequalities hold:

(1) $p^0 G \geq ve,$

(2) $Gq^0 \leq vf.$

EXAMPLE 3   In Example 1 of the previous section we had the matrix:

$$G = \begin{pmatrix} 50 & 60 \\ 40 & 50 \end{pmatrix}.$$

We found that the value of this game was $v = 50$ and that optimal strategies were for R to choose row 1, which corresponds to the mixed-strategy vector $p^0 = (1, 0)$, and for C to choose column 1, which corresponds to the mixed-strategy vector $q^0 = \begin{pmatrix} 1 \\ 0 \end{pmatrix}$. Carrying out the calculations in (1) and (2), we have

$$p^0 G = (1, 0) \begin{pmatrix} 50 & 60 \\ 40 & 50 \end{pmatrix} = (50, 60) \geq (50, 50) = 50(1, 1) = ve$$

and

$$Gq^0 = \begin{pmatrix} 50 & 60 \\ 40 & 50 \end{pmatrix}\begin{pmatrix} 1 \\ 0 \end{pmatrix} = \begin{pmatrix} 50 \\ 40 \end{pmatrix} \leq \begin{pmatrix} 50 \\ 50 \end{pmatrix} = 50 \begin{pmatrix} 1 \\ 1 \end{pmatrix} = vf.$$

In a similar manner the solutions to Examples 2, 3, and 4 of Section 8 can be shown to satisfy the definition above (see Exercises 5, 6, and 7). In Exercise 16 you will be asked to show that optimal strategies to any strictly determined game satisfy the definition above.

Let us return now to the nonstrictly determined 2×2 game. Consider the nonstrictly determined game

$$G = \quad \begin{array}{|c|c|} \hline a & b \\ \hline c & d \\ \hline \end{array}$$

Having argued, as above, that the players should use mixed strategies in playing a nonstrictly determined game, it is still necessary to decide how to choose an optimal mixed strategy.

If R chooses a mixed strategy $p = (p_1, p_2)$ and (independently) C chooses a mixed strategy $q = \begin{pmatrix} q_1 \\ q_2 \end{pmatrix}$, then player R obtains the payoff a with probability p_1q_1; he obtains the payoff b with probability p_1q_2; he obtains c with probability p_2q_1; and he obtains d with probability p_2q_2; hence his mathematical expectation (see Chapter 3, Section 11) is given by the expression

$$ap_1q_1 + bp_1q_2 + cp_2q_1 + dp_2q_2.$$

By a similar computation, one can show that player C's expectation is the negative of this expression.

To justify this definition we must show that if v, p^0, q^0 exist for G, each player can guarantee himself an expectation of v. Let q be any strategy for C. Multiplying (1) on the right by q, we get

$$p^0 G q \geq (v, v)q = v,$$

which shows that, regardless of how C plays, R can assure himself of an expectation of at least v. Similarly, let p be any strategy vector for R. Multiplying (2) on the left by p, we obtain

$$pGq^0 \leq p \begin{pmatrix} v \\ v \end{pmatrix} = v,$$

which shows that, regardless of how R plays, C can assure himself of an expectation of at most v. It is in this sense that p^0 and q^0 are optimal. It follows further that, if both players play optimally, then R's expectation is exactly v and C's expectation is exactly v. Hence we call v the (expected) *value* of the game.

We must now see whether there are strategies p^0 and q^0 for the game G. For complicated games the finding of optimal strategies will be discussed in Section 11. For a 2×2 nonstrictly determined game the following formulas provide the solution:

$$(3) \qquad\qquad p_1^0 = \frac{d - c}{a + d - b - c},$$

$$(4) \qquad\qquad p_2^0 = \frac{a - b}{a + d - b - c},$$

$$(5) \qquad\qquad q_1^0 = \frac{d - b}{a + d - b - c},$$

$$(6) \qquad\qquad q_2^0 = \frac{a - c}{a + d - b - c},$$

$$(7) \qquad\qquad v = \frac{ad - bc}{a + d - b - c}.$$

It is an easy matter to verify (see Exercise 12) that formulas (3)–(7) satisfy conditions (1)–(2). Actually, the inequalities in (1) and (2) become equalities in this simple case, a fact that is not true in general for nonstrictly determined games of larger size.

The denominator in each formula is the difference between the sums of the entries on the two diagonals. Since, for a nonstrictly determined game, the entries on one diagonal must be larger than those on the other, the denominator cannot be zero.

Let us use these formulas to solve the examples mentioned earlier.

EXAMPLE 1 (continued) Applying formulas (3)–(7) to the matrix in Figure 56, we have

$$p_1^0 = \frac{-2 - 0}{-1 - 2 - 0 - 0} = \frac{2}{3}, \qquad p_2^0 = \frac{-1 - 0}{-3} = \frac{1}{3},$$

$$q_1^0 = \frac{-2 - 0}{-3} = \frac{2}{3}, \qquad q_2^0 = \frac{-1 - 0}{-3} = \frac{1}{3}, \qquad v = \frac{(-1)(-2) - 0}{-3} = -\frac{2}{3}.$$

Thus the game is biased in favor of player C, since $v = -\frac{2}{3}$, and optimal strategies are

$$p^0 = (\tfrac{2}{3}, \tfrac{1}{3}) \quad \text{and} \quad q^0 = \begin{pmatrix} \tfrac{2}{3} \\ \tfrac{1}{3} \end{pmatrix}.$$

Both Jones and Smith should select their first alternative two-thirds of the time, according to some random pattern.

EXAMPLE 2 (continued) Let us apply the formulas (3)–(7) to the matrix in Figure 57. We obtain

$$a + d - c - b = 10 + 10 - 0 + 50 = 70,$$

so that:

$$p_1^0 = \frac{10 - 0}{70} = \frac{1}{7}, \qquad p_2^0 = \frac{10 + 50}{70} = \frac{6}{7},$$

$$q_1^0 = \frac{10 + 50}{70} = \frac{6}{7}, \qquad q_2^0 = \frac{10 - 0}{70} = \frac{1}{7}, \qquad v = \frac{10 \cdot 10 - 0}{70} = \frac{10}{7}.$$

Notice that the game is biased in favor of Mr. Sub, not his boss Mr. Super! Also Mr. Sub's optimal strategy is to have an *unfavorable* opinion 6 out of 7 times, while Mr. Super's optimal strategy is to have a *favorable* opinion 6 out of 7 times! Thus, if this game is at all realistic, a subordinate should be much more critical than his superior when judging situations in which there is no clear-cut reason to either accept or reject a project. The conclusion is based on game-theory analysis, not on the two persons' relative ages, experience, and so on.

We conclude this section by proving three theorems that characterize the value and optimal strategies of a game.

Theorem If G is a matrix game that has a value and optimal strategies, then the value of the game is unique.

Proof Suppose that v and w are two different values for the game G. Then let p^0 and q^0 be optimal mixed-strategy vectors associated with the value v such that

(a) $$p^0 G \geq ve,$$

(b) $$G q^0 \leq vf.$$

Similarly, let p^1 and q^1 be optimal mixed-strategy vectors associated with the value w such that

(c) $$p^1 G \geq we,$$

(d) $$G q^1 \leq wf.$$

If we now multiply (a) on the right by q^1, we get $p^0 G q^1 \geq (ve)q^1 = v$. In the same way, multiplying (d) on the left by p^0 gives $p^0 G q^1 \leq w$. The two inequalities just obtained show that $w \geq v$.

Next we multiply (b) on the left by p^1 and (c) on the right by q^0, obtaining $v \geq p^1 G q^0$ and $p^1 G q^0 \geq w$, which together imply that $v \geq w$.

Finally we see that $v \leq w$ and $v \geq w$ imply together that $v = w$—that is, the value of the game is unique.

Theorem If G is a matrix game with value v and optimal strategies p^0 and q^0, then $v = p^0 G q^0$.

Proof By definition v, p^0, and q^0 satisfy

$$p^0 G \geq ve \quad \text{and} \quad G q^0 \leq vf.$$

Multiplying the first of these inequalities on the right by q^0, we get $p^0 G q^0 \geq v$. Similarly, multiplying the second inequality on the left by p^0, we obtain $p^0 G q^0 \leq v$. These two inequalities together imply that $v = p^0 G q^0$, concluding the proof.

The theorems just proved are important because they permit us to interpret the *value* of a game as an *expected value* (see Chapter 3, Section 11). Briefly the interpretation is the following: If the game G is played repeatedly and if each time it is played player R uses the mixed strategy p^0 and player C uses the mixed strategy q^0, then the value v of G is the expected value of the game for R. The law of large numbers implies that, if the number *of plays of* G is sufficiently large, then the average value of R's winnings will (with high probability) be arbitrarily close to the value v of the game G.

As an example, let G be the matrix of the game of matching pennies:

$$G = \begin{array}{|c|c|} \hline 1 & -1 \\ \hline -1 & 1 \\ \hline \end{array}$$

Using the formulas above, we find that optimal strategies in this game are for R to choose each row with probability $\frac{1}{2}$ and for C to choose each column with probability $\frac{1}{2}$. The value of G is zero. Notice that the only two payoffs that result from a single play of the game are $+1$ and -1, neither of which is equal to the value of the game. However, if the game is played repeatedly, the average value of R's payoffs will approach zero, which is the value of the game.

Theorem If G is a game with value v and optimal strategies p^0 and q^0, then v is the largest expectation that R can assure for himself. Similarly, v is the smallest expectation that C can assure for himself.

Proof Let p be any mixed-strategy vector of R and let q^0 be an optimal strategy for C; then multiply the equation $Gq^0 \leq vf$ on the left by p, obtaining $pGq^0 \leq v$. The latter equation shows that, if C plays optimally, the most that R can assure for himself is v. Now let p^0 be optimal for R; then, for every $q, p^0Gq \geq v$, so that R can actually assure himself of an expection of v. The proof of the other statement of the theorem is similar.

The theorem above gives an intuitive justification to the definition of value and optimal strategies for a game. Thus the value is the "best" that a player can assure himself, and optimal strategies are the means of assuring this "best."

EXERCISES

1. Find the optimal strategies for each player and the values of the following games:

(a)

1	2
3	4

(b)

1	0
−1	2

(c)

2	3
1	4

(d)

15	3
−1	2

(e)

7	−6
5	8

(f)

3	15
−1	10

[*Ans.* (a) $v = 3$; $(0, 1)$; $\binom{1}{0}$;   (b) $v = \frac{1}{2}$; $(\frac{3}{4}, \frac{1}{4})$; $\binom{\frac{1}{2}}{\frac{1}{2}}$;

(d) $v = 3$; $(1, 0)$; $\binom{0}{1}$;   (e) $v = \frac{43}{8}$; $(\frac{3}{16}, \frac{13}{16})$; $\binom{\frac{7}{8}}{\frac{1}{8}}$.]

2. Set up the ordinary game of matching pennies as a matrix game. Find its value and optimal strategies. How are the optimal strategies realized in practice by players of this game?

3. A version of two-finger Morra is played as follows: Each player holds up either one or two fingers; if the sum of the number of fingers shown is even, player R gets the sum, and if the sum is odd, player C gets it.
    (a) Show that the game matrix is

Player C

	1	2
1	2	−3
2	−3	4

Player R

(b) Find optimal strategies for each player and the value of the game.

$$[\textit{Ans. } (\tfrac{7}{12}, \tfrac{5}{12}), \begin{pmatrix} \tfrac{7}{12} \\ \tfrac{5}{12} \end{pmatrix}, v = -\tfrac{1}{12}.]$$

4. Rework Exercise 3 if player C gets the even sum and player R gets the odd sum.

5. Let G be the matrix in Figure 51 described in Example 2 of Section 8. With $v = 0$, $p^0 = (0, 1)$, and $q^0 = \begin{pmatrix} 0 \\ 1 \end{pmatrix}$, show that formulas (1) and (2) are satisfied.

6. Show that the strategies derived in Example 3 of Section 8 satisfy formulas (1) and (2).

7. Show that the strategies derived in Example 4 of Section 8 satisfy formulas (1) and (2).

8. If

$$G = \begin{array}{|c|c|} \hline a & b \\ \hline c & d \\ \hline \end{array}$$

is nonstrictly determined, prove that it is fair if and only if $ad = bc$.

9. In formulas (3)–(7) prove that $p_1 > 0, p_2 > 0, q_1 > 0$, and $q_2 > 0$. Must v be greater than zero?

10. Find necessary and sufficient conditions that the game

$$G = \begin{array}{|c|c|} \hline a & 0 \\ \hline 0 & b \\ \hline \end{array}$$

be nonstrictly determined. Find optimal strategies for each player and the value of G, if it is nonstrictly determined.
    [*Ans. a* and *b* must be both positive or both negative. $p_1 = b/(a + b)$; $p_2 = a/(a + b)$; $q_1 = b/(a + b)$; $q_2 = a/(a + b)$; $v = ab/(a + b)$.]

11. Suppose that player R tries to find C in one of three towns X, Y, and Z. The distance between X and Y is five miles, the distance between Y and Z is five miles, and the distance between Z and X is ten miles. Assume that R and C can each go to one and only one of the three towns and that if they both go to the same town R "catches" C; otherwise C "escapes." Credit R with ten points if he catches C, and credit C with a number of points equal to the number of miles he is away from R if he escapes.

(a) Set up the game matrix.

(b) Show that both players have the same optimal strategy, namely, to go to towns X and Z with equal probabilities and to go to town Y with probability $\frac{1}{4}$.

(c) Find the value of the game.

12. Verify that formulas (3)–(7) satisfy conditions (1) and (2).

13. Consider the (symmetric) game whose matrix is

$$G = \begin{array}{|c|c|c|}
\hline
0 & -a & -b \\
\hline
a & 0 & -c \\
\hline
b & c & 0 \\
\hline
\end{array}$$

(a) If a and b are both positive or both negative, show that G is strictly determined.

(b) If b and c are both positive or both negative, show that G is strictly determined.

(c) If $a > 0$, $b < 0$, and $c > 0$, show that an optimal strategy for player R is given by

$$\left(\frac{c}{a - b + c}, \ \frac{-b}{a - b + c}, \ \frac{a}{a - b + c} \right).$$

(d) In part (c) find an optimal strategy for player C.

(e) If $a < 0$, $b > 0$, and $c < 0$, show that the strategy given in (c) is optimal for R. What is an optimal strategy for player C?

(f) Prove that the value of the game is always zero.

14. In a well-known children's game each player says "stone" or "scissors" or "paper." If one says "stone" and the other "scissors," then the former wins a penny. Similarly, "scissors" beats "paper," and "paper" beats "stone." If the two players name the same item, then the game is a tie.

(a) Set up the game matrix.

(b) Use the results of Exercise 13 to solve the game.

15. In Exercise 14 let us suppose that the payments are different in different cases. Suppose that when "stone breaks scissors" the payment is one cent; when "scissors cut paper" the payment is two cents; and when "paper covers stone" the payment is three cents.

    (a) Set up the game matrix.

    (b) Use the results of Exercise 13 to solve the game.

$$[\textit{Ans. } \tfrac{1}{3} \text{ "stone," } \tfrac{1}{2} \text{ "scissors," } \tfrac{1}{6} \text{ "paper"}; v = 0.]$$

16. A strictly determined $m \times n$ matrix game G contains a saddle entry g_{ij} that is simultaneously the minimum of row i and the maximum of column j.

    (a) Show that by rearranging rows and columns (if necessary) we can assume that g_{11} is a saddle value.

    (b) Let $v = g_{11}$ and p^0 and q^0 be probability vectors with first component equal to 1 and all other components equal to 0. Show that these quantities satisfy (1) and (2).

17. Verify that the strategies $p^0 = (\tfrac{1}{3}, \tfrac{1}{3}, \tfrac{1}{3})$ and

$$q^0 = \begin{pmatrix} \tfrac{1}{3} \\ \tfrac{1}{3} \\ \tfrac{1}{3} \end{pmatrix}$$

are optimal in the game G whose matrix is

$$G = \begin{array}{|c|c|c|} \hline 1 & 0 & 0 \\ \hline 0 & 1 & 0 \\ \hline 0 & 0 & 1 \\ \hline \end{array}$$

What is the value of the game?

18. Generalize the result of Exercise 16 to the game G whose matrix is the $n \times n$ identity matrix.

19. Consider the following game:

$$G = \begin{array}{|c|c|c|} \hline a & 0 & 0 \\ \hline 0 & b & 0 \\ \hline 0 & 0 & c \\ \hline \end{array}$$

    (a) If a, b, and c are not all of the same sign, show that the game is strictly determined with value zero.

    (b) If a, b, and c are all of the same sign, show that the vector

$$\left(\frac{bc}{ab + bc + ca}, \frac{ca}{ab + bc + ca}, \frac{ab}{ab + bc + ca} \right)$$

is an optimal strategy for player R.

    (c) Find player C's optimal strategy for case b.

    (d) Find the value of the game for case b, and show that it is positive if a, b, and c are all positive, and negative if they are all negative.

20. Suppose that the entries of a matrix game are rewritten in new units (e.g., dollars instead of cents). Show that the monetary value of the game has not changed.

21. Consider the game of matching pennies whose matrix is

1	−1
−1	1

If the entries of the matrix represent gains or losses of one penny, would you be willing to play the game at least once? If the entries represent gains or losses of one dollar, would you be willing to play the game at least once? If they represent gains or losses of one million dollars, would you play the game at least once? In each of these cases show that the value is zero and optimal strategies are the same. Discuss the practical application of the theory of games in the light of this example.

10　SOLVING MATRIX GAMES BY A GEOMETRIC METHOD

In Section 8 we found that a strictly determined game of any size could be solved almost by inspection. In Section 9 we found formulas for solving nonstrictly determined 2×2 games. In Section 11 we shall discuss the application of the simplex method to solve arbitrary $m \times n$ matrix games. In the present section we shall discuss special matrix games in which one of the players has just two strategies, and we shall find that a simple geometric method suffices to solve such games rather easily.

EXAMPLE 1 Suppose that Jones conceals one of the following four bills in his hand: a $1 or a $2 United States bill or a $1 or a $2 Canadian bill. Smith guesses either "United States" or "Canadian" and gets the bill if his guess is correct. We assume that a Canadian dollar has the same real value as a United States dollar. The matrix of the game is the following:

			Smith guesses	
			U.S.	Can.
Jones chooses	U.S.	$1	−1	0
		$2	−2	0
	Can.	$1	0	−1
		$2	0	−2

It is obvious that Jones should always choose the $1 bill of either country rather than the $2 bill, since by doing so he may cut his losses and will never increase them. This can be observed in the matrix above, since every entry in the second row is less than or equal to the corresponding entry in the first row, and every entry in the fourth row is less than or equal to the corresponding entry in the third row. In effect we can eliminate the second and fourth rows and reduce the game to the following 2×2 matrix game:

		Smith guesses	
		U.S.	Can.
Jones	U.S. $1	-1	0
chooses	Can. $1	0	-1

The new matrix game is nonstrictly determined with optimal strategies $(\frac{1}{2}, \frac{1}{2})$ for Jones and $\begin{pmatrix} \frac{1}{2} \\ \frac{1}{2} \end{pmatrix}$ for Smith. The value of the game is $-\frac{1}{2}$, which means that Smith should be willing to pay 50 cents to play it.

Definition Let A be an $m \times n$ matrix game. We shall say that row i *dominates* row h if every entry in row i is as large as or larger than the corresponding entry in row h. Similarly, we shall say that column j *dominates* column k if every entry in column j is as small as or smaller than the corresponding entry in column k.

Any dominated row or column can be omitted from the matrix game without materially affecting its solution. In the original matrix of Example 1 above, we see that row 1 dominates row 2, and also that row 3 dominates row 4.

EXAMPLE 2 Consider the game whose matrix is:

$$G = \begin{array}{|c|c|c|c|} \hline 1 & 0 & -1 & 0 \\ \hline -3 & -2 & 1 & 2 \\ \hline \end{array}$$

Observe that column 2 and column 3 each dominate column 4; that is, player C should never play the last column. Thus the game can be reduced to the following 2×3 game:

$$G' = \begin{array}{|c|c|c|} \hline 1 & 0 & -1 \\ \hline -3 & -2 & 1 \\ \hline \end{array}$$

No further rows or columns can be omitted because of domination; hence we must introduce a new technique for the solution of this game.

Suppose that player R announces he is going to use the mixed strategy $p = (p_1, p_2)$. Using the relation $p_1 = 1 - p_2$, we can write this as $p = (1 - p_2, p_2)$. Assume for the moment that player C knows R will use this strategy. Then he can compute his expected payment y from choosing each of his alternatives in G' as follows:

If he chooses column 1:

$$y = 1 \cdot p_1 - 3 \cdot p_2 = (1 - p_2) - 3p_2 = 1 - 4p_2.$$

If he chooses column 2:

$$y = 0 \cdot p_1 - 2 \cdot p_2 = -2p_2.$$

If he chooses column 3:

$$y = -1 \cdot p_1 + 1 \cdot p_2 = -(1 - p_2) + p_2 = -1 + 2p_2.$$

Notice that each of these expectations expresses y as a linear function of p_2. Hence the graphs of these expectations will be a straight line in each case. Since we have the restriction $0 \le p_2 \le 1$, we are interested only in the part of the line for which p_2 satisfies the restriction. In Figure 59 we

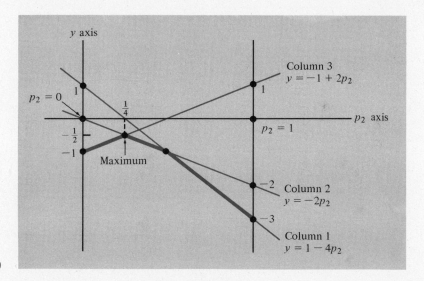

Figure 59

have shown p_2 plotted on the horizontal axis and y on the vertical axis. We have also drawn the vertical line at $p_2 = 1$. The graphs of each of the lines above are shown. Observe that the ordinates of each line when $p_2 = 0$ are just the entries in the first row of G', and the ordinates of each line when $p_2 = 1$ are just the entries in the second row. Since we can easily find these two distinct points on each line, it is easy to draw them.

We now can analyze what C will do. For each value of p_2 that completely determines R's mixed strategy $p = (1 - p_2, p_2)$, player C will minimize his own expectation—that is, he will choose the lowest of the three lines plotted in Figure 59. For each p_2 the lowest line has been drawn in heavily, resulting in the broken-line function shown in the figure. Now R is the maximizing player, so he will try to get the maximum of this function. By visual inspection this obviously occurs at the intersection of the lines corresponding to column 2 and column 3, when $p_2 = \frac{1}{4}$ and the "height" of this function at that point is $-\frac{1}{2}$. From the figure it is clear that $-\frac{1}{2}$ is the maximum R can assure himself, and he can obtain this by using the strategy $p = (\frac{3}{4}, \frac{1}{4})$ corresponding to $p_2 = \frac{1}{4}$. We can find optimal strategies for player C by considering the 2×2 subgame of G (and G') consisting of the second and third columns:

$$G'' = \begin{array}{|c|c|} \hline 0 & -1 \\ \hline -2 & 1 \\ \hline \end{array}$$

Applying the formulas of the preceding section, we obtain as optimal strategies:

$$p^0 = (\tfrac{3}{4}, \tfrac{1}{4}), \qquad q^0 = \begin{pmatrix} \tfrac{1}{2} \\ \tfrac{1}{2} \end{pmatrix}, \qquad v = -\tfrac{1}{2}.$$

We can extend q^0 to an optimal strategy for player C in G by adding two zero entries thus:

$$q^0 = \begin{pmatrix} 0 \\ \tfrac{1}{2} \\ \tfrac{1}{2} \\ 0 \end{pmatrix}.$$

Player R's strategy and the value remain the same, as the reader can easily verify.

EXAMPLE 3   We have already seen examples where a player has more than one optimal strategy. The game whose matrix is

$$G = \begin{array}{|c|c|c|} \hline 3 & 1 & 0 \\ \hline 0 & 1 & 3 \\ \hline \end{array}$$

is another example. To carry out the same kind of analysis as before, assume that R chooses $p = (p_1, p_2) = (1 - p_2, p_2)$. Then

If C chooses column 1: $y = 3(1 - p_2) = 3 - 3p_2$.
If C chooses column 2: $y = (1 - p_2) + p_2 = 1$.
If C chooses column 3: $y = 3p_2$.

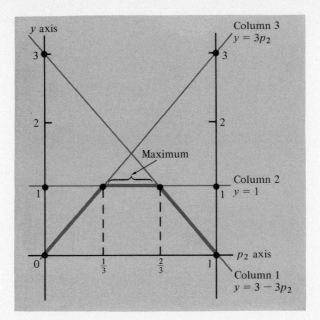

Figure 60

The graphs of these three functions are shown in Figure 60, and the minimum of the three is shown darkened. Since the darkened graph has a flat area on the top, the entire flat area represents the maximum of the function. The endpoints of the flat area are $(\frac{2}{3}, \frac{1}{3})$ and $(\frac{1}{3}, \frac{2}{3})$, and the intervening points that are convex combinations of these, such as

$$a(\tfrac{2}{3}, \tfrac{1}{3}) + (1 - a)(\tfrac{1}{3}, \tfrac{2}{3}) = \tfrac{1}{3}(a + 1, 2 - a),$$

are also optimal strategies, as the reader can verify by inspection. The unique optimal strategy for the column player is to choose the second column, so $q^0 = \begin{pmatrix} 0 \\ 1 \\ 0 \end{pmatrix}$. Of course, $v = 1$.

Theorem The set of optimal strategies for either player in a matrix game is a convex set. That is, if p^0 and r^0 are optimal for player R, then $ap^0 + (1 - a)r^0$ is also optimal for him, for any a in the range $0 \le a \le 1$. Similarly, if q^0 and s^0 are optimal for player C, then so is $aq^0 + (1 - a)s^0$ for a in the same range.

We shall not give a formal proof of the theorem here, but it is clearly illustrated in Figure 60. In the next section we shall show that a matrix game is equivalent to a linear programming problem, and then the theorem becomes a consequence of the corresponding theorem in linear programming.

EXAMPLE 4   So far we have illustrated cases in which the row player had just two strategies and the column player had three or more. A similar method works to solve games in which the column player has just two strategies and the row player has more. Consider the game whose matrix is

$$G = \begin{array}{|c|c|} \hline 6 & -1 \\ \hline 0 & 4 \\ \hline 4 & 3 \\ \hline \end{array}$$

Suppose we reverse the analysis above and assume that the column player selects a mixed strategy

$$q = \binom{q_1}{q_2} = \binom{1 - q_2}{q_2}$$

and then considers what action R will take. Again there are three choices:

If he chooses row 1: $y = 6q_1 - q_2 = 6(1 - q_2) - q_2 = 6 - 7q_2.$
If he chooses row 2: $y = 4q_2.$
If he chooses row 3: $y = 4q_1 + 3q_2 = 4(1 - q_2) + 3q_2 = 4 - q_2.$

In each case y is the expectation that player R has for each choice. Since he is the maximizing player, he will want to maximize his expectation. In Figure 61 we have shown the three straight lines corresponding to each of

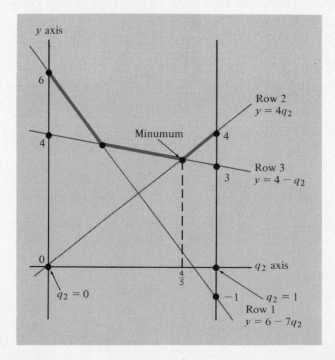

Figure 61

these expectations and have darkened the *maximum* of each of these. Player C will want to choose the smallest value on the darkened broken-line function marked in the figure. Since it corresponds to $p_2 = \frac{4}{5}$, the corresponding optimal strategy for the column player is $\begin{pmatrix} \frac{1}{5} \\ \frac{4}{5} \end{pmatrix}$.

To find the corresponding optimal strategy for the row player we consider the 2×2 in the last two rows of the matrix:

0	4
4	3

Using the formulas of the previous section, we have optimal strategies:

$$p^0 = (\tfrac{1}{5}, \tfrac{4}{5}), \qquad q^0 = \begin{pmatrix} \frac{1}{5} \\ \frac{4}{5} \end{pmatrix}, \qquad v = \tfrac{16}{5}.$$

We can extend the optimal row strategy to one optimal for the original game by adding a zero. Thus

$$p^0 = (0, \tfrac{1}{5}, \tfrac{4}{5})$$

is optimal in the game G originally stated.

By using graph paper and a ruler, the reader will be able to solve in a similar manner other games in which one of the players has just two strategies. In principle the graphical method could be extended to larger games, but it is difficult to draw three-dimensional graphs and impossible to draw four- and higher-dimensional graphs, so that this idea has limited usefulness.

The geometric ideas presented in this section are useful conceptually. For instance, the following theorem is intuitively obvious from the geometric point of view.

Theorem Let G be an $m \times n$ matrix game with value v; let E be the $m \times n$ matrix each of whose entries is 1; and let k be *any* constant. Then the game $G + kE$ has value $v + k$, and every strategy optimal in the game G is also optimal in the game $G + kE$. (Note that the game $G + kE$ is obtained from the game G by adding the number k to each entry in G.)

If we apply this theorem to any of the previous examples, its truth is clear, since adding k to each entry in G merely moves all the lines in each graph up or down by the same amount. Hence the locations of the optimum points are unchanged, and the value is changed by the amount k.

One consequence of this theorem is the fact that a matrix game G can be replaced by an equivalent game all of whose entries are positive and whose value is positive. One simply chooses a sufficiently large k and forms the game $G + kE$. We shall use this fact in the next section.

EXERCISES

1. Solve the following games:

(a)

3	0
−2	3
7	5

$[Ans.\ v = 5;\ (0, 0, 1);\ \binom{0}{1}.]$

(b)

10	5	4	6
18	3	3	4

(c)

1	0	2
0	3	2

$[Ans.\ v = \frac{3}{4};\ (\frac{3}{4}, \frac{1}{4});\ \begin{pmatrix} \frac{3}{4} \\ \frac{1}{4} \\ 0 \end{pmatrix}.]$

(d)

0	2
1	3
−1	0
2	0

(e)

1	2	3
4	2	1

$[An\ ans.\ v = 2;\ (\frac{3}{5}, \frac{2}{5});\ \begin{pmatrix} 0 \\ 1 \\ 0 \end{pmatrix}.]$

(f)

1	0	1	1	2
0	−1	−2	−3	−10

2. Solve the following games:

(a)

0	15
8	0
−10	20
10	12

(b)

−1	−2	0	−3	−4
−2	1	0	2	5

(c)

−1	5	−1	−2	8	10
3	−6	0	8	−9	−8

$$[An\ ans.\ v = -\tfrac{1}{2};\ (\tfrac{1}{2}, \tfrac{1}{2});\ \begin{pmatrix} 0 \\ \tfrac{1}{12} \\ \tfrac{11}{12} \\ 0 \\ 0 \\ 0 \end{pmatrix}.]$$

3. Solve the game

1	2	3
3	2	1

Since there is more than one optimal strategy for C, find a range of optimal strategies for him.

4. Consider the game whose matrix is

13	−7
3	8
−1	14
9	−1

   (a) Find player C's optimal strategy by graphical means.
   (b) Show that there are six possible subgames that can be chosen by player R.
   (c) Of the six possible subgames show that two are strictly determined and do not give optimal strategies in the original game.
   (d) Show that the other four subgames have solutions that can be extended to optimal strategies in the original game.

$$[Ans.\ (\tfrac{1}{5}, \tfrac{4}{5}, 0, 0),\ (\tfrac{3}{7}, 0, \tfrac{4}{7}, 0),\ (0, 0, \tfrac{2}{5}, \tfrac{3}{5}),\ (0, \tfrac{2}{3}, 0, \tfrac{1}{3}).]$$

5. Suppose that Jones conceals in his hand one, two, three, or four silver dollars and Smith guesses "even" or "odd." If Smith's guess is correct, he wins the amount that Jones holds; otherwise he must pay Jones this amount. Set up the corresponding matrix game and find an optimal strategy for each player in which he puts positive weight on all his (pure) strategies. Is the game fair?

6. Consider the following game: Player R announces "one" or "two"; then, independently of each other, both players write down one of these two numbers. If the sum of the three numbers so obtained is odd,

C pays R the odd sum in dollars; if the sum of the three numbers is even, R pays C the even sum in dollars.

(a) What are the strategies of R? [*Hint:* He has four strategies.]

(b) What are the strategies of C? [*Hint:* We must consider what C does after "one" is announced or after a "two." Hence he has four strategies.]

(c) Write down the matrix for the game.

(d) Restrict player R to announcing "two," and allow for C only those strategies where his number does not depend on the announced number. Solve the resulting 2×2 game.

(e) Extend the above mixed strategies to the original game, and show that they are optimal.

(f) Is the game favorable to R? If so, by how much?

7. Answer the same questions as in Exercise 6 if R gets the even sum and C gets the odd sum [except that, in part (d), restrict R to announce "one"]. Which game is more favorable for R? Could you have predicted this without the use of game theory?

8. Two players play five-finger Morra by extending from one to five fingers: If the sum of the number of fingers is even, R gets one, while if the sum is odd, C gets one. Suppose that each player shows only one or two fingers. Show that the resulting game is like matching pennies. Show that the optimal strategies for this game, when extended, are optimal in the whole game.

9. A version of three-finger Morra is played as follows: Each player shows from one to three fingers; R always pays C an amount equal to the number of fingers that C shows; if C shows exactly one more or two fewer fingers than R, then C pays R a positive amount x (where x is independent of the number of fingers shown).

(a) Set up the game matrix for arbitrary x's.

(b) If $x = \frac{1}{2}$, show that the game is strictly determined. Find the value.
[*Ans. $v = -\frac{5}{2}$.*]

(c) If $x = 2$, show that there is a pair of optimal strategies in which the first player shows one or two fingers and the second player shows two or three fingers. [*Hint:* Use domination.] Find the value.
[*Ans. $v = -\frac{3}{2}$.*]

(d) If $x = 6$, show that an optimal strategy for R is to use the mixed strategy, $(\frac{1}{3}, \frac{1}{2}, \frac{1}{6})$. Show that the optimal mixed strategy for C is to choose his three strategies each with probability $\frac{1}{3}$. Find the value of the game.

10. Another version of three-finger Morra goes as follows: Each player shows from one to three fingers; if the sum of the number of fingers is even, then R gets an amount equal to the number of fingers that C shows: if the sum is odd, C gets an amount equal to the number of fingers that R shows.

(a) Set up the game matrix.

(b) Reduce the game to a 2×2 matrix game.

    (c) Find optimal strategies for each player and show that the game is fair.

11. Consider the game:

a	b
c	d

    (a) Draw the graph of expectations for the row player when $a = b$ and prove graphically that the game is strictly determined.

    (b) Draw the same graph when $a > b, a > c, d > b, d > c$, and show that the game is nonstrictly determined.

    (c) Draw the same graph when $a < b, a < c, d < b, d < c$, and show that the game is nonstrictly determined.

    (d) Draw graphs to illustrate cases in which (b) and (c) do not hold and show that the resulting game is strictly determined.

12. Consider the game of Exercise 11 with the same amount k added to each matrix entry. Show graphically that the value of the game is changed by k and that optimal strategies are the same in both games.

The remaining exercises refer to the *product payoff game* (due to A. W. Tucker). Two sets, S and T, are given, each set containing at least one positive and at least one negative number (but no zeros). Player R selects a number s from set S, and player C selects a number t from set T. The payoff is st.

13. Set up the game for the sets $S = \{1, -1, 2\}$ and $T = \{1, -3, 2, -4\}$.

[*Ans.*

1	-3	2	-4
-1	3	-2	4
2	-6	4	-8

.]

14. Consider the following mixed strategy for either player: "Choose a positive number p and a negative number n with probabilities $-n/(p - n)$ and $p/(p - n)$, respectively." Assume that R uses this strategy.

    (a) If C chooses a positive number, show that the expected payoff to R is 0.

    (b) If C chooses a negative number, show that the expected payoff to R is 0.

15. Rework Exercise 14 with R and C interchanged.

16. Use the results of Exercises 14 and 15 to show that the game is fair, and that the strategy quoted in Exercise 14 is optimal for either player.

17. Find all strategies of the kind indicated in Exercise 14 for both players for the game of Exercise 13.

        [*Partial ans.* For R they are $(\frac{1}{2}, \frac{1}{2}, 0)$ and $(0, \frac{2}{3}, \frac{1}{3})$.]

18. By subtracting 10 from each entry, show that the following game is derived from a product payoff game, and find all strategies like those in Exercise 14 for both players. What is the value of the game?

11	7	12	6
9	13	8	14
12	4	14	2

[*Hint:* Use Exercises 13 and 17 and the last theorem.]

19. If a player in the product payoff game has *m* positive and *n* negative numbers in his set, show that he has *mn* strategies like those in Exercise 14.

11 THE SIMPLEX METHOD FOR SOLVING MATRIX GAMES

We have so far restricted our attention to examples of matrix games that were simple enough to be solved by unformalized computations. However, games of realistic size frequently lead to very large matrices for which these simple techniques are not adequate. A clue to a general technique may be found in the fact that the row player is a maximizing player while the column player is a minimizing player. Hence the problems they are trying to solve sound somewhat like the dual linear programming problems of Section 4. So if a matrix game can be formulated as a linear programming problem, it can be solved by the simplex method discussed in Section 5.

There are several ways of showing that a matrix game is equivalent to a linear program. We choose a very simple approach here, based on the fact, stated in Section 10, that every matrix game is equivalent to one in which all entries are positive and hence whose value is positive.

Besides finding an equivalent linear programming problem, we shall give a proof, based on the duality theorem of linear programming, that every matrix game has a solution. And we shall present a simplex format suitable for the solution of any matrix game.

Let G be an $m \times n$ matrix game and let E be the $m \times n$ matrix all of whose entries are 1's. The second theorem of Section 10 states that G and $G + kE$ have the same optimal strategies, and the value of the second game is k plus the value of the first game. Hence if we start with any game G we can replace it by a game G' all of whose entries are positive, and which has the same optimal strategies. For instance, to get G' we could add 1 minus the most negative entry in G to every entry in G.

Thus without loss of generality we let G be a positive matrix game. We also let e be the n-component row vector all of whose entries are 1's, and let f be the m-component column vector all of whose entries are 1's. Let z be an m-component row vector and x an n-component column vector.

We now consider the following dual linear programming problems:

$$(1) \quad \begin{cases} \text{Minimize } zf \\ \text{subject to:} \\ \\ zG \geq e \\ z \geq 0 \end{cases} \qquad \begin{cases} \text{Maximize } ex \\ \text{subject to:} \\ \\ Gx \leq f \\ x \geq 0. \end{cases}$$

Note that $x = 0$ satisfies the constraints of the maximizing problem; also, because the entries of G and f are positive, there is at least one nonzero x vector that will satisfy these constraints. Moreover, the set of feasible x vectors is bounded. Because of these facts, and because e has all positive entries, the maximizing problem has solution x^0 such that $ex^0 > 0$. Hence, by the duality theorem, the minimum problem has a solution x^0 and

$$t = z^0 G x^0 = z^0 f = e x^0 > 0.$$

We now set

$$p^0 = \frac{z^0}{t}, \qquad q^0 = \frac{x^0}{t}, \quad \text{and} \quad v = \frac{1}{t},$$

and observe that p^0 and q^0 are probability vectors.

It is easy to see that p^0 is an optimal strategy for player R in G, since x^0 satisfies the constraints of the minimizing problem, and hence

$$p^0 G = \frac{z^0 G}{t} \geq \frac{e}{t} = ve.$$

In Exercise 1 the reader is asked to show similarly that $Gq^0 \leq vf$.

We summarize these results in the following theorem:

Theorem   (a) Solving the matrix game G with positive entries can be accomplished by solving the dual linear programming problems (1).

(b) Every matrix game has at least one solution; solutions to such games can be found by the simplex method.

Actually, it is not necessary that the matrix game be positive in order that the simplex method work. It is enough that its value be positive. However, in Exercise 3 the reader is asked to work a specific example for which the linear programming problem as described above has no solution if applied to a game with zero value.

Before proceeding to specific examples, let us outline the procedure to be followed in setting up a matrix game for solution by the simplex method.

1. Set up the matrix of the game.
2. Check to see whether the game is strictly determined; if so, the solution is already obtained.
3. Check for row and column dominance and remove dominated rows and columns.

4. Make certain that the value of the game is positive. It is sufficient for this to add 1 minus the most negative matrix entry to every entry of the matrix. Let k be the amount added, if any, to each matrix entry.

5. Let G be the matrix of the resulting game; suppose it is $m \times n$. Construct the following matrix tableau:

G	f
e	0

6. Carry out the steps of the simplex algorithm until all indicators are nonpositive. Determine the solutions z^0 and x^0 to the dual linear programming problems, and let $t = z^0 f = e x^0$. We know $t > 0$.

7. The solutions to the original matrix game are given by

$$p^0 = \frac{z^0}{t}, \qquad q^0 = \frac{x^0}{t} \quad \text{and} \quad v = \frac{1}{t} - k.$$

(If dominated rows or columns were removed from the game, the strategy vectors may have to be extended by the addition of some zero components.)

EXAMPLE 1 We know that the matching-pennies game is fair—that is, it has value zero. To make its value positive, we add $k = 2$ to each matrix entry, yielding the following game:

3	1
1	3

Obviously this game is not strictly determined and it does not have dominated rows or columns. We set up the simplex tableau and solve it as shown in Figure 62(a)–(c). (Note that we have called the variables on the left z_1 and z_2 instead of v_1 and v_2, since we are now using v for the value of the game.) From the final tableau in Figure 62(c) we can see that the value of the game is 2 (the reciprocal of $t = \frac{1}{2}$), so that the value of the matching-pennies game is 0, which we know already. Also, optimal strategies are

$$p^0 = \frac{z^0}{t} = (\tfrac{1}{2}, \tfrac{1}{2}) \quad \text{and} \quad q^0 = \frac{x^0}{t} = \begin{pmatrix} \tfrac{1}{2} \\ \tfrac{1}{2} \end{pmatrix},$$

which we had discovered earlier.

EXAMPLE 2 Let us solve the two-finger Morra game of Exercise 3 of Section 9. To convert the game into one with positive value let us add 3 to each entry of the matrix,

	x_1	x_2	-1	
z_1	③	1	1	$= -y_1$
z_2	1	3	1	$= -y_2$
-1	1	1	0	$= f$
	$= u_1$	$= u_2$	$= g$	

(a)

	y_1	x_2	-1	
u_1	$\frac{1}{3}$	$\frac{1}{3}$	$\frac{1}{3}$	$= -x_1$
z_2	$-\frac{1}{3}$	$⑧/3$	$\frac{2}{3}$	$= -y_2$
-1	$-\frac{1}{3}$	$\frac{2}{3}$	$\frac{1}{3}$	$= f$
	$= z_1$	$= u_2$	$= g$	

(b)

	y_1	y_2	-1	
u_1	$\frac{3}{8}$	$-\frac{1}{3}$	$\frac{1}{4}$	$= -x_1$
u_2	$-\frac{1}{3}$	$\frac{3}{8}$	$\frac{1}{4}$	$= -x_2$
-1	$-\frac{1}{4}$	$-\frac{1}{4}$	$\frac{1}{2}$	$= f$
	$= z_1$	$= z_2$	$= g$	

Figure 62   (c)

noting that this will give two zeros in the resulting game matrix. These zeros will simplify the simplex calculations. The game matrix now is

5	0
0	7

Figure 63(a)–(c) shows the initial and two subsequent simplex tableaus. The value of the game, from Figure 63(c), is $\frac{35}{12}$, which means that the value of the original game is $\frac{35}{12} - 3 = -\frac{1}{12}$. Optimal strategies agree with the answer stated in Exercise 3, Section 9.

EXAMPLE 3   Consider the following game: R and C simultaneously display 1, 2, or 3 pennies. If both show the same number of pennies, no money is exchanged; but if they show different numbers of pennies, R gets odd sums and C gets

	x_1	x_2	-1	
z_1	⑤	0	1	$= -y_1$
z_2	0	7	1	$= -y_2$
-1	1	1	0	$= f$
	$= u_1$	$= u_2$	$= g$	

(a)

	y_1	x_2	-1	
u_1	$\frac{1}{5}$	0	$\frac{1}{5}$	$= -x_1$
z_2	0	⑦	1	$= -y_2$
-1	$-\frac{1}{5}$	1	$\frac{1}{5}$	$= f$
	$= z_1$	$= u_2$	$= g$	

(b)

	y_1	y_2	-1	
u_1	$\frac{1}{5}$	0	$\frac{1}{5}$	$= -x_1$
u_2	0	$\frac{1}{7}$	$\frac{1}{7}$	$= -x_2$
-1	$-\frac{1}{5}$	$-\frac{1}{7}$	$\frac{12}{35}$	$= f$
	$= z_1$	$= z_2$	$= g$	

Figure 63   (c)

even sums. The matrix of the game is

			C shows	
		1	2	3
	1	0	3	-4
R shows	2	3	0	5
	3	-4	5	0

Since the second row has all nonnegative entries, the game is, if anything, in R's favor. And if R plays the first two rows with equal weight, his expectation is positive. Hence the value of the game is positive, and we do not have to add anything to the matrix entries. The simplex calculations needed to solve the game are shown in Figure 64(a)–(d). From this we see that the value of the game is $1/t = \frac{10}{7}$, and that optimal strategies are

$$p^0 = \frac{z^0}{t} = (\tfrac{5}{14}, \tfrac{4}{7}, \tfrac{1}{14}) \quad \text{and} \quad q^0 = \frac{x^0}{t} = \begin{pmatrix} \frac{5}{14} \\ \frac{4}{7} \\ \frac{1}{14} \end{pmatrix}.$$

	x_1	x_2	x_3	-1	
z_1	0	3	-4	1	$= -y_1$
z_2	③	0	5	1	$= -y_2$
z_3	-4	5	0	1	$= -y_3$
-1	1	1	1	0	$= f$
	$= u_1$	$= u_2$	$= u_3$	$= g$	

(a)

	y_2	x_2	x_3	-1	
z_1	0	③	-4	1	$= -y_1$
u_1	$\frac{1}{3}$	0	$\frac{5}{3}$	$\frac{1}{3}$	$= -x_1$
z_3	$\frac{4}{3}$	5	$\frac{20}{3}$	$\frac{7}{3}$	$= -y_3$
-1	$-\frac{1}{3}$	1	$\frac{2}{3}$	$\frac{1}{3}$	$= f$
	$= z_2$	$= u_2$	$= u_3$	$= g$	

(b)

	y_2	y_1	x_3	-1	
u_2	0	$\frac{1}{3}$	$-\frac{4}{3}$	$\frac{1}{3}$	$= -x_2$
u_1	$\frac{1}{3}$	0	$\frac{5}{3}$	$\frac{1}{3}$	$= -x_1$
z_3	$\frac{4}{3}$	$-\frac{5}{3}$	㊵	$\frac{1}{3}$	$= -y_3$
-1	$-\frac{1}{3}$	$-\frac{1}{3}$	$\frac{2}{3}$	$\frac{2}{3}$	$= f$
	$= z_2$	$= z_1$	$= u_3$	$= g$	

(c)

	y_2	y_1	y_3	-1	
u_2	$\frac{2}{15}$	$\frac{1}{6}$	$\frac{1}{10}$	$\frac{2}{5}$	$= -x_2$
u_1	$\frac{1}{6}$	$\frac{5}{24}$	$-\frac{1}{8}$	$\frac{1}{4}$	$= -x_1$
u_3	$\frac{1}{10}$	$-\frac{1}{8}$	$\frac{3}{40}$	$\frac{1}{20}$	$= -x_3$
-1	$-\frac{2}{5}$	$-\frac{1}{4}$	$-\frac{1}{20}$	$\frac{7}{10}$	$= f$
	$= z_2$	$= z_1$	$= z_3$	$= g$	

(d)

Figure 64

The reader should check that these strategies do solve the game.

The examples just solved could have been worked directly, without the use of the simplex method. However, the simplex method works just as well for much larger games for which there is no easy direct method.

EXERCISES

1. If $q^0 = x^0/t$, where x^0 solves the maximum problem stated in (1), and $t = ex^0$, show that q^0 is an optimal strategy for player C in the matrix game G.

2. Solve the following games by the simplex method.

(a)

1	0	3
−2	3	0
−4	5	−6

(b)

−2	3	0	5	−6
3	−4	5	0	7
−4	5	−6	7	0

3. Consider the matching-pennies game with matrix

$$G = \begin{array}{|c|c|} \hline 1 & -1 \\ \hline -1 & 1 \\ \hline \end{array}$$

(a) Substitute it directly into the simplex format described in rule (5) above, and show that the simplex method breaks down.

(b) Consider the linear programming problem defined in (1) with this G and show directly that it has no solution.

4. Use the simplex method to derive formulas (3)–(7) of Section 9 for optimal strategies in a nonstrictly determined 2×2 game.

5. Rework Exercise 19 of Section 9 using the simplex method.

6. Rework Exercise 13 of Section 9 using the simplex method.

7. A passenger on a Mississippi riverboat was approached by a flashily dressed stranger (the gambler) who offered to play the following game: "You take a red ace and a black deuce and I'll take a red deuce and a black trey; we will simultaneously show one of the cards; if the colors don't match you pay me and if the colors match I'll pay you; moreover if you play the red ace we will exchange the difference of the numbers on the cards; but if you play the black deuce we will exchange the sum of the numbers. Since you will pay me with $2 or $4 if you lose and I will pay you either $1 or $5 if I lose, the game is obviously fair." Set up and solve the matrix game using the simplex method. Show that the game is not fair. Find the optimal strategies.
[*Partial ans.* The gambler will win an average of 25 cents per game.]

8. Consider the following game: R chooses 0 or 1 and reveals his choice to C; C chooses 0 or 1, but does not reveal his choice to R; R then chooses 0 or 1 a second time. The sum of the three numbers chosen is computed and R receives odd sums while C receives even sums.

(a) Show that R has four strategies: 00, 01, 10, 11.

(b) Show that C has four strategies: (1) always choose 0, (2) choose the same as R, (3) choose opposite to R, (4) always choose 1.

(c) Show that the payoff matrix is

	(1)	(2)	(3)	(4)
00	0	0	1	1
01	1	1	-2	-2
10	1	-2	1	-2
11	-2	3	-2	3

(d) Solve the game by the simplex method, finding its value and optimal strategies.

$$[Ans.\ p^0 = (\tfrac{3}{4}, \tfrac{1}{4}, 0, 0),\ q^0 = \begin{pmatrix} \tfrac{3}{10} \\ \tfrac{9}{20} \\ \tfrac{1}{4} \\ 0 \end{pmatrix},\ v = \tfrac{1}{4}.]$$

9. Rework Exercise 8 assuming that the players choose 1 or 2 each time.

10. *The Silent Duel.* Two duelists each have a pistol that contains a single bullet and is equipped with a silencer. They advance toward each other in N steps, and each may fire at his opponent at the end of each step. Neither knows whether his opponent has fired, and each has but one shot in the game. The probability that a player will hit his opponent if he fires after moving k steps is k/N. A player gets 1 if he kills his opponent without being killed himself, -1 if he gets killed without killing his opponent, and 0 otherwise. Each player has N strategies corresponding to firing after steps $1, 2, \ldots, N$. Let i be the strategy chosen by R and let j be the strategy chosen by C.

(a) If $i < j$, show that the expected payoff to R is given by

$$\frac{N(i - j) + ij}{N^2}.$$

(b) If $i > j$, show that the expected payoff to R is given by

$$\frac{N(i - j) - ij}{N^2}.$$

(c) If $i = j$, show that the expected payoff to R is 0.

11. In Exercise 10, prove that the game is strictly determined and fair for $N = 2, 3$, and 4. Show that the optimal strategy for $N = 3, 4$ is to fire at the end of the second step in each case. For $N = 2$, show that any strategy is optimal.

12. In Exercise 10, show that the game is nonstrictly determined and fair for $N = 5$, and find the optimal strategies.
[*Ans.* $p^0 = (0, \tfrac{5}{11}, \tfrac{5}{11}, 0, \tfrac{1}{11})$, and q^0 is the column vector having the same components.]

13. A *symmetric matrix game* G is one for which $g_{ij} = -g_{ji}$ for i, $j = 1, 2, \ldots, n$. In other words, for every payment from C to R there is an equal payment from R to C. Show that every symmetric game is fair. [*Hint:* Show that if x^0 is optimal for R, then the column vector y with $y_k = x_k^0$ for $k = 1, \ldots, n$ is optimal for C. From this deduce that the value of the game is zero.]

14. Use Exercise 13 to show that the silent duel is fair for every N.

15. Consider a matrix game G with positive value in which the first row strictly dominates the second row. Show that in the simplex algorithm no entry in the second row will ever be chosen as a pivot in the first step.

16. Consider a matrix game G with positive value in which the first column dominates the second column. Show that if the pivot is chosen in the first column, after the end of the first simplex calculation the indicator for the second column will be nonnegative.

12 COMPUTER APPLICATIONS

The simplex method is ideal for solving linear programming problems, but it is difficult to carry it out by manual calculations. Actually, the method was designed for computers, and we shall show how to program it in BASIC.

The program LP follows Figure 18 closely. It starts with a DIM statement that allows a matrix A of 20 rows and 20 columns, and hence a 21×21 tableau. In the body of the program lines 100–1199 correspond to the 11 boxes in the figure, with each box starting at a new multiple of 100. Thus, for example, box 6 corresponds to the block of instructions starting at line 600. The remainder of the program prints answers and contains the DATA.

███ LP

```
10   DIM T(21,21),M(20,4),X(20),Y(20),U(20),V(20)
20
100  READ M,N
110  MAT READ T(M+1,N+1)
120  FOR J = 1 TO N
130  LET M(J,1) = M(J,3) = J
140  NEXT J
150  FOR I = 1 TO M
160  LET M(I,2) = M(I,4) = -I
170  NEXT I
180
200  FOR J = 1 TO N
210  IF T(M+1,J) > 1E-6 THEN 300
220  NEXT J
230  GOTO 1100
240
300  REM   J IS THE PIVOTAL COLUMN
310
400  FOR I = 1 TO M
```

```
410 IF T(I,J) > 1E-6 THEN 600
420 NEXT I
430
500 PRINT "MAXIMUM PROBLEM HAS UNBOUNDED SOLUTION."
510 PRINT "MINIMUM PROBLEM HAS NO SOLUTION."
520 GOTO 1999
530
600 LET M1 = 1E30
610 FOR I = 1 TO M
620 IF T(I,J) < 1E-6 THEN 680
630 LET Q = T(I,N+1)/T(I,J)
640 IF Q >= M1 THEN 680
650 LET M1 = Q
660 LET I1 = I
680 NEXT I
690 LET I = I1
699
700 LET C = T(I,J)
710 FOR J1 = 1 TO N+1
715 IF J1 = J THEN 730
720 LET T(I,J1) = T(I,J1)/C
730 NEXT J1
740
800 FOR I1 = 1 TO M+1
810 IF I1 = I THEN 860
820 LET C = T(I1,J)
830 FOR J1 = 1 TO N+1
835 IF J1 = J THEN 850
840 LET T(I1,J1) = T(I1,J1) - C*T(I,J1)
850 NEXT J1
860 NEXT I1
870
900 LET C = T(I,J)
910 LET T(I,J) = 1/C
920 FOR I1 = 1 TO M+1
930 IF I1 = I THEN 970
940 LET T(I1,J) = -T(I1,J)/C
970 NEXT I1
980

1000 LET A = M(J,1)
1010 LET M(J,1) = M(I,2)
1020 LET M(I,2) = A
1030 LET A = M(J,3)
1040 LET M(J,3) = M(I,4)
1050 LET M(I,4) = A
1060 GOTO 200
1070
1100 MAT X = ZER(N)
1105 MAT Y = ZER(M)
1110 MAT U = ZER(N)
1115 MAT V = ZER(M)
```

```
1120 FOR I = 1 TO M
1125 LET A = T(I,N+1)
1130 LET S = M(I,2)
1135 IF S<0 THEN 1150
1140 LET X(S) = A
1145 GOTO 1155
1150 LET Y(-S) = A
1155 NEXT I
1160 FOR J = 1 TO N
1165 LET A = -T(M+1,J)
1170 LET S = M(J,3)
1175 IF S<0 THEN 1190
1180 LET U(S) = A
1185 GOTO 1195
1190 LET V(-S) = A
1195 NEXT J
1199
1210 PRINT "VALUE = "; -T(M+1,N+1)
1220 PRINT "X = ";
1230 MAT PRINT X;
1240 PRINT "Y = ";
1250 MAT PRINT Y;
1260 PRINT "U = ";
1270 MAT PRINT U;
1280 PRINT "V = ";
1290 MAT PRINT V;
1299
1900 DATA 2,3
1910 DATA 6,2,4,200
1911 DATA 2,2,12,160
1912 DATA 12,8,24,0
1920
1999 END

READY

RUN

LP

VALUE =  680.
X =
 10.  70.  0
Y =
 0  0
U =
 0  0  16.
V =
 1.  3.

0.279 SEC.
READY
```

Since the flow diagram is, in effect, an explanation of the program, only a few comments are necessary. We have used only one tableau T, and hence the changes are made within the tableau, rather than copying it over. This is possible as long as we are careful in boxes 7 and 8 not to change the entries of the pivotal column. Then the original entries are still available for box 9. Also, in testing for positive entries we have elected to check whether the entry is greater than 10^{-6}, to avoid round-off errors.

The only major change from Figure 18 to the program LP is the matrix M. We have to keep track of where the various variables are placed around the margin of the tableau. The matrix M has four columns, corresponding to the four margins. The first column keeps track of the variables on top, the second column of the right side, the third of the bottom, and the fourth of the left-side margin. In each case the entries are the subscripts of the variables, except that negative entries indicate that we have y or v rather than x or u. For example, if $M(3,2) = 1$, then in the third row the right-hand marginal is x_1; while if $M(3,2) = -1$, then it is y_1. Similarly, if $M(1,3) = 4$, then the first variable on the bottom is u_4, while a -4 would indicate v_4.

The DATA in LP is taken from Example 2 in Section 5, and the RUN shows the results previously obtained. By changing the DATA we work out two other previous examples: LP2 corresponds to Example 3, and LP3 to Example 4—which has no solution.

```
1900  DATA  2,2
1910  DATA  2,1,3
1911  DATA  3,1,4
1912  DATA  17,5,0

READY

RUN

LP2

VALUE  =    22.6667
X =
 1.33333    0
Y =
 0.333333   0
U =
 0   0.666667
V =
 0   5.66667

0.242 SEC.
READY
```

```
1900  DATA 2,2
1910  DATA -1,1,1
1911  DATA 1,-1,1
1912  DATA 1,1,0

READY

RUN
```

███ LP3

```
MAXIMUM PROBLEM HAS UNBOUNDED SOLUTION.
MINIMUM PROBLEM HAS NO SOLUTION.

0.226 SEC.
READY
```

To show the power of the computerized simplex method we need a larger example. The program **LP4** solves the following maximum problem. The

```
1900  DATA 6,3
1910  DATA .8,.5,.3,82
1911  DATA .15,.2,.2,30
1912  DATA .05,.2,.2,30
1913  DATA 0,.05,.15,16
1914  DATA 0,.05,.1,10
1915  DATA 0,0,.05,4
1916  DATA 25,40,75,0

READY

RUN
```

███ LP4

```
VALUE =  8600.
X =
 40.  40.  80
Y =
 6.  0  4.  2.  0  0
U =
 0  0  0
V =
 0  166.667  0  0  133.333  566.667

0.314 SEC.
READY
```

Tasty Nut Company packages three kinds of boxes of mixed nuts. Each box contains a pound of nuts, according to the following rules:

Cheap mix:　　　80% peanuts, 15% almonds, 5% cashews.
Medium mix:　　50% peanuts, 20% almonds, 20% cashews, 5% walnuts, 5% hazelnuts.
Fancy mix:　　　30% peanuts, 20% almonds, 20% cashews, 15% walnuts, 10% hazelnuts, 5% Brazil nuts.

The manufacturer has on hand 82 lb of peanuts, 30 lb almonds, 30 lb cashews, 16 lb walnuts, 10 lb hazelnuts, and 4 lb Brazil nuts. If he makes a profit of 25 cents on the simple mix, 40 cents on the medium mix, and 75 cents on the fancy mix, how much of each should he package? The program LP4 contains the appropriate tableau and solves the problem. We find a value of 8600, i.e., a profit of $86. From the vector X we note that the optimal solution is to package 40 lb each of the two cheaper mixes, and 80 lb of the fancy mix. From Y we note that we shall have left over 6 lb of peanuts and smaller amounts of cashews and walnuts. The vector V is particularly interesting. It imputes to almonds, hazelnuts, and Brazil nuts per pound values of $1\frac{2}{3}$, $1\frac{1}{3}$, and $5\frac{2}{3}$, respectively. This makes it very tempting to buy more Brazil nuts.

The program LP5 differs from LP4 only in adding $\frac{1}{2}$ lb of Brazil nuts to the stock. We note that the profit has increased by one-half of the imputed

```
1915 DATA 0,0,.05,4.5
RUN

LP5

VALUE =    8883.33
X =
 53.3333   20.   90
Y =
 2.33333   0   5.33333   1.5   0   0
U =
 0   0   0
V =
 0   166.667   0   0   133.333   566.667

0.356 SEC.
READY
```

value of $5\frac{2}{3}$, which is what we would expect from adding $\frac{1}{2}$ lb. It is interesting to note that so small a change in the inventory results in the drastic change in the optimal production schedule.

The program LP6 illustrates the fact that the interpretation of imputed

```
1915 DATA 0,0,.05,5
RUN
```

■ LP6

```
VALUE =   9125
X =
 65.   0  100.
Y =
  0   0.25   6.75   1   0   2.89557 E-8
U =
  0   8.4375   0
V =
 31.25   0   0   0   656.25   0

0.331 SEC.
READY
```

values is correct only as long as the nature of the solution does not change. It differs from the original **LP4** by adding one full pound of Brazil nuts. However, the profit goes up only $5\frac{1}{4}$, less than the imputed value. We find an explanation for this by noting that now peanuts have become a critical commodity instead of Brazil nuts. And we no longer produce the medium mix. The nature of the dual solution changes somewhere between 4.5 and 5 lb of Brazil nuts, and hence the imputed value holds for only part of the change.

We next consider some computer applications to the solution of matrix games. The program **STRICT** tests whether a given matrix game is strictly determined, and if it is, it finds the saddle values. We first read the game matrix. Then we set **V** to an incorrect value. If during the computation we discover a saddle value, we shall then know the value of the game and reset **V**. If **V** is not reset during the program, then we shall know that the game is not strictly determined.

The strategy of the program is to look at every entry in the matrix to see whether it is a saddle value. We start the double loop, which will run through all rows and all columns, at line 100. At line 150 we ignore the entry if it is different from the value of the game. However, if we have not yet found the value of the game this test is inapplicable, and that is the reason for line 140. In the loop at lines 210–230 we reject the entry if there is a smaller entry on the same row. In the loop at lines 260–280 we reject it if there is a larger entry in the same column. If it passes both of these tests, it is a saddle value. At lines 310–330 we set **V** to the correct value, print the saddle value, and go on to the next entry. At lines 610–630 we either print the value of the game or we indicate that the game is not strictly determined.

The data for the first **RUN** is from Example 3 in Section 8. This is a

■ STRICT

```
10 READ M,N
20 MAT READ G(M,N)
30 LET V = -99999
40
100 REM  LOOK AT EVERY ENTRY
110 FOR I = 1 TO M
120 FOR J = 1 TO N
130 LET V1 = G(I,J)
140 IF V = -99999 THEN 200
150 IF V1 <> V THEN 400
160
200 REM  IS IT A ROW MIN
210 FOR J1 = 1 TO N
220 IF G(I,J1) < V1 THEN 400
230 NEXT J1
240
250 REM  IS IT A COLUMN MAX
260 FOR I1 = 1 TO M
270 IF G(I1,J) > V1 THEN 400
280 NEXT I1
290
300 REM  IT IS A SADDLE
310 LET V = V1
320 PRINT "ROW";I;"- COLUMN";J;"IS A SADDLE"
330 GOTO 500
340
400 REM  NOT A SADDLE, IGNORE
410
500 REM  NEXT ENTRY
510 NEXT J
520 NEXT I
530
600 REM  IS IT STRICTLY DETERMINED
610 IF V = -99999 THEN 650
620 PRINT "STRICTLY DETERMINED. VALUE =";V
630 GOTO 999
650 PRINT "NOT STRICTLY DETERMINED."
660
900 DATA 3,3
910 DATA 50,50,80
911 DATA 50,50,80
912 DATA 20,20,50
999 END
READY
```

```
RUN

STRICT

ROW 1 - COLUMN 1 IS A SADDLE
ROW 1 - COLUMN 2 IS A SADDLE
ROW 2 - COLUMN 1 IS A SADDLE
ROW 2 - COLUMN 2 IS A SADDLE
STRICTLY DETERMINED. VALUE = 50

0.125 SEC.
READY

900 DATA 2,2
910 DATA 0,1
911 DATA 2,0
RUN

STRICT

NOT STRICTLY DETERMINED.

0.110 SEC.
READY
```

strictly determined game. For the second RUN we have chosen the example of Figure 55(a), which is not a strictly determined game.

The most interesting computer application to games is modifying the program LP to apply to matrix games. If in our DATA we have the enlarged game matrix, including a last column and last row of all 1's (except for a zero in the lower right-hand corner), then we know from Section 11 that we may apply the simplex method directly. The only change necessary to our program LP is to modify the output, since the value is $1/t$, and the vectors X and V have to be multiplied by this value. In the program GAME

GAME

```
1200 LET T = -T(M+1,N+1)
1210 PRINT "VALUE = ";1/T
1220 PRINT "STRATEGY FOR R:";
1230 MAT V = (1/T)*V
1240 MAT PRINT V;
1250 PRINT "STRATEGY FOR C:";
1260 MAT X = (1/T)*X
1270 MAT PRINT X;
```

```
1299
1900 DATA 3,3
1910 DATA 0,3,-4,1
1911 DATA 3,0,5,1
1912 DATA -4,5,0,1
1913 DATA 1,1,1,0
1920
1999 END
READY

RUN

GAME

VALUE =  1.42857
STRATEGY FOR R:
 0.357143   0.571429   7.14286 E-2
STRATEGY FOR C:
 0.357143   0.571429   7.14286 E-2

0.269 SEC.
READY
```

we show only the modifications we make, starting with line 1200. As our example we have used Example 3 of Section 11. We obtain the same results as in the text.

A computer version of the simplex method allows one to solve both very large linear programming problems and very large matrix games.

EXERCISES

Only Exercises 5–12 require the use of a computer.

1. Modify the program LP so that it will print the current tableau after each iteration. Be sure to print the variables in the margins.
2. In the RUN of LP5, for the optimal solution $X(1) = 53.3333$, what should the manufacturer do if he produces only one-pound boxes?
3. The program GAME works only if the value is positive. Modify it so that if there are any negative entries it will add a sufficiently large positive number to all entries. [*Hint:* If you do this, the value of the game changes.]
4. Describe an alternate strategy for the program STRICT. Which do you think is faster?
5. Use LP to solve the tableaus in Figures 34 and 35 (Section 6).
6. Use LP to solve Exercises 12, 13, and 14 in Section 5.
7. How does the optimal strategy of the Tasty Nut Company change if

the profits on the three kinds of mixes are 30, 50, and 90 cents, respectively? [*Ans.* It does not change.]

8. Redo Exercise 7 for profits of
(a) 20, 30, and 40 cents.
(b) 25, 40, and 40 cents.

9. Use STRICT on the games in Exercise 2 of Section 8.

10. Use STRICT on the games in Exercise 3 of Section 8.

11. Try an alternate program for STRICT (see Exercise 4) to see whether it is faster.

12. Try the program of Exercise 3 on the following game:

3	−1	0
−11	0	5
0	−7	7
8	3	−9

SUGGESTED READING

Bellman, R., and Blackwell, D. "Red Dog, Blackjack, Poker." *Scientific American* 184 (1951): 44–47.

Charnes, A., and Cooper, W. W. *Management Models and Industrial Applications of Linear Programming.* New York: John Wiley, 1961. 2 vols.

Dantzig, G. B. *Linear Programming and Extensions.* Princeton, N.J.: Princeton University Press, 1963.

Gale, David. *The Theory of Linear Economic Models.* New York: McGraw-Hill, 1960.

Gaver, D., and Thompson, G. L. *Programming and Probability Models in Operations Research.* Monterey, Calif.: Brooks/Cole, 1973.

Hillier, F. S., and Lieberman, G. J. *Introduction to Operations Research.* San Francisco: Holden-Day, 1967.

Kuhn, H. W., and Tucker, A. W. "Theory of Games." *Encyclopaedia Britannica.* Chicago: William Benton, 1973 edition.

Luce, R. Duncan, and Raiffa, Howard. *Games and Decisions: Introduction and Critical Survey.* New York: John Wiley, 1957.

MacDonald, J. *Strategy in Poker, Business, and War.* New York: Norton, 1950.

McKinsey, J. C. C. *Introduction to the Theory of Games.* New York: McGraw-Hill, 1952.

Morgenstern, Oskar. "The Theory of Games." *Scientific American.* 180 (1950): 294–308.

Rapoport, Anatol. *Fights, Games, and Debates.* Ann Arbor: University of Michigan Press, 1960.

Shubik, Martin. *Strategy and Market Structure.* New York: John Wiley, 1959.

Spivey, W. A., and Thrall, R. M. *Linear Optimization.* New York: Holt, Rinehart and Winston, 1970.

Thompson, G. L. "Game Theory." *McGraw-Hill Encyclopedia of Science and Technology.* New York: McGraw-Hill, 1971.

Tucker, A. W. "Combinatorial Algebra of Matrix Games and Linear Programming," in E. F. Beckenbach, ed., *Applied Combinatorial Mathematics.* New York: John Wiley, 1064. Pp 320–47.

Von Neumann, J., and Morgenstern, Oskar. *Theory of Games and Economic Behavior.* 3rd ed. Princeton, N.J.: Princeton University Press, 1953. Chapter I.

Wagner, H. M. *Principles of Operations Research with Applications to Managerial Decisions.* Englewood Cliffs, N.J.: Prentice-Hall, 1969.

Williams, J. D. *The Compleat Strategyst.* Rev. ed. New York: McGraw-Hill, 1966.

Applications to the
Behavioral and
Managerial Sciences

1 COMMUNICATION AND SOCIOMETRIC MATRICES

Matrices having only the entries 0 and 1 are useful in the analysis of graphs and networks. We shall not attempt to give a complete treatment of the subject here, but merely illustrate some of its more interesting applications.

A *communication network* consists of a set of people, $A_1, A_2, \ldots, A_n$, such that between some pairs of persons there is a communication link. Such a link may be either one-way or two-way. A two-way communication link might be made by telephone or radio, and a one-way link by sending a messenger, lighting a signal light, setting off an explosion, etc. We shall use the symbol $\gg$ to indicate the latter sort of connection; thus $A_i \gg A_j$ shall mean that individual A_i can communicate with individual A_j (in that direction). The only requirement that we put on the symbol is:

(i) It is false that $A_i \gg A_i$ for any i; that is, an individual cannot (or need not) communicate with himself.

It is convenient to use *directed graphs* to represent communication networks. Two such graphs are drawn in Figure 1. Individuals are represented on the graph as (lettered) points and a communication relation between two individuals as a directed line segment (line segment with an arrow) connecting the two individuals.

We can also represent communication networks by means of square matrices C having only 0 and 1 entries, which we call *communication matrices*. The entry in the ith row and jth column of C is equal to 1 if A_i can communicate with A_j (in that direction) and otherwise equal to 0. Thus

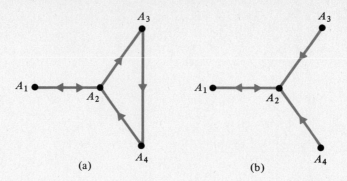

Figure 1   (a)   (b)

the communication matrices corresponding to the communication networks of Figure 1 are shown in Figure 2.

$$C = \begin{pmatrix} 0 & 1 & 0 & 0 \\ 1 & 0 & 1 & 0 \\ 0 & 0 & 0 & 1 \\ 0 & 1 & 0 & 0 \end{pmatrix} \qquad C = \begin{pmatrix} 0 & 1 & 0 & 0 \\ 1 & 0 & 0 & 0 \\ 0 & 1 & 0 & 0 \\ 0 & 1 & 0 & 0 \end{pmatrix}$$

Figure 2   (a)   (b)

Notice that the diagonal entries of the matrices in Figure 2 are all equal to 0. This is true in general for a communication matrix, since the matrix restatement of condition (i) is:

(i)   For all i, $c_{ii} = 0$.

It is not hard to see that any matrix having only 0 and 1 entries, and with all zeros down the main diagonal, is the communication matrix of some network.

By a *dominance relation** we shall mean a special kind of communication relation in which, besides (i), the following condition holds:

(ii)   For each pair i, j, with $i \neq j$, either $A_i \gg A_j$ or $A_j \gg A_i$, but not both; that is, in every pair of individuals, there is exactly one who is dominant.

It has been observed that in the pecking order of chickens a dominance relation holds. Also, in the play of one round of a round-robin contest among athletic teams, if ties are not allowed (as in baseball), then a dominance relation holds.

The reader may have been surprised that we did not assume that if $A_i \gg A_j$ and $A_j \gg A_k$ then $A_i \gg A_k$. This is the so-called transitive law for relations.

---

*Recently dominance relations have been called *tournaments*. See the paper by H. A. David in the Suggested Readings at the end of the chapter.

A moment's reflection shows that the transitive law need not hold for dominance relations. Thus if team A beats team B and team B beats team C (in football, say), then we cannot assume that team A will necessarily beat team C. In every football season there are instances in which "upsets" occur.

Dominance relations may also be depicted by means of directed graphs. Two such are shown in Figure 3. The graph in Figure 3(a) represents the situation in which A_1 dominates A_2, A_2 dominates A_3, and A_3 dominates A_1. Similary, the graph in Figure 3(b) represents the situation in which A_1

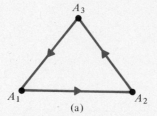

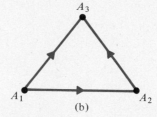

Figure 3   (a)   (b)

dominates A_2 and A_3, and A_2 dominates A_3. These graphs represent the two essentially different dominance relations that are possible among three individuals (see Exercise 1).

Dominance relations may also be defined by means of matrices, called *dominance matrices,* defined as for communication matrices. In Figure 4 we have shown the two dominance matrices corresponding to the directed graphs of Figure 3.

$$D = \begin{pmatrix} 0 & 1 & 0 \\ 0 & 0 & 1 \\ 1 & 0 & 0 \end{pmatrix} \qquad D = \begin{pmatrix} 0 & 1 & 1 \\ 0 & 0 & 1 \\ 0 & 0 & 0 \end{pmatrix}$$

Figure 4   (a)   (b)

Since a dominance matrix is derived from a dominance relation, we can investigate the effects of conditions (i) and (ii) above on the entries in the matrix. Condition (i) simply means that all entries on the main diagonal (the one which slants downward to the right) of the matrix must be zero. Condition (ii) means that, whenever an entry above the main diagonal of the matrix is 1, the corresponding entry of the matrix which is placed symmetrically to it through the main diagonal is 0, and vice versa. To state these conditions more precisely, suppose that there are n individuals, and let D be a dominance matrix with entries d_{ij}.

Then the conditions above are:

(i) $d_{ii} = 0$ for $i = 1, 2, \ldots, n$.
(ii) If $i \neq j$, then $d_{ij} = 1$ if and only if $d_{ji} = 0$.

Every dominance relation is also a communication relation; hence we shall concentrate on the latter, and what we say about them will also be true for the former.

Since a communication matrix C is square, we can compute its powers, C^2, C^3, etc. Let $E = C^2$, and consider the entry in the ith row and jth column of E. It is

$$e_{ij} = c_{i1}c_{1j} + c_{i2}c_{2j} + \ldots + c_{in}c_{nj}.$$

Now a term of the form $c_{ik}c_{kj}$ can be nonzero only if both factors are nonzero, that is, only if both factors are equal to 1. But if $c_{ik} = 1$, then individual A_i communicates with A_k; and if $c_{kj} = 1$, then individual A_k communicates with A_j. In other words, $A_i \gg A_k \gg A_j$. We shall call a communication of this kind a *two-stage communication*. (To keep ideas straight, let us call $A_i \gg A_j$ a *one-stage* communication.) We can now see that the entry e_{ij} gives the total number of two-stage communication paths there are between A_i and A_j (in that direction). For example, let C be the matrix

$$C = \begin{pmatrix} 0 & 1 & 1 & 1 \\ 0 & 0 & 1 & 1 \\ 0 & 0 & 0 & 1 \\ 0 & 0 & 0 & 0 \end{pmatrix}.$$

Then C^2 is the matrix

$$C^2 = \begin{pmatrix} 0 & 0 & 1 & 2 \\ 0 & 0 & 0 & 1 \\ 0 & 0 & 0 & 0 \\ 0 & 0 & 0 & 0 \end{pmatrix}.$$

Thus we see that in this example A_1 has one two-stage communication path with A_3 and two two-stage communications with A_4; similarly, A_2 has one two-stage communication with A_4. These can be written down explicitly as

$$A_1 \gg A_2 \gg A_3,$$
$$A_1 \gg A_2 \gg A_4,$$
$$A_1 \gg A_3 \gg A_4,$$
$$A_2 \gg A_3 \gg A_4.$$

The directed graph for this (dominance) situation is given in Figure 5. The reader should trace out on the graph of Figure 5 the two-stage communication paths given above.

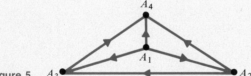

Figure 5

Theorem Let a communication network of n individuals be such that, for every pair of individuals, at least one can communicate in one stage with the other. Then there is at least one person who can communicate with every other person in either one or two stages. Similarly, there is at least one person who can be communicated with in one or two stages by every other person.

Stated in matrix language, the above theorem is: Let C be the communication matrix for the network described above; then there is at least one row of $S = C + C^2$ which has all its elements nonzero, except possibly the entry on the main diagonal. Similarly, there is at least one column having this property.

Notice that every dominance relation satisfies the hypotheses of the theorem, but there are communication networks, not dominance relations, that also satisfy these hypotheses.

Proof We shall prove only the first statement, since the proof of the second is analogous.

First we shall prove the following statement: If A_1 cannot communicate in either one or two stages with A_i, where $i \neq 1$, then A_i can communicate in one stage with at least one more person than can A_1. We prove this in two steps. First by the hypothesis of the theorem, we see that:

(a) If it is false that $A_1 \gg A_i$, then $A_i \gg A_1$.

Second we can prove that:

(b) Suppose that for all k it is false that $A_1 \gg A_k \gg A_i$; it follows that, if $A_1 \gg A_k$, then also $A_i \gg A_k$.

For if $A_1 \gg A_k$, it is false that $A_k \gg A_i$, hence, by the hypothesis of the theorem, it is true that $A_i \gg A_k$.

Now (b) says that every one-stage communication possible for A_1 is also possible for A_i. From this and (a), it then follows that A_i can make at least one more (one-stage) communication than can A_1.

We now return to the proof of the theorem. Let $r_1, r_2, \ldots, r_n$ be the row sums of the matrix C. By renaming the individuals, if necessary, we can assume that the largest row sum is r_1, that is, $r_1 \geq r_k$ for $k = 1, 2, \ldots, n$. We shall show that A_1 can communicate with everyone else in one or two stages. (The proof is based on the indirect method.) Suppose, on the contrary, that there is an individual A_i, where $i > 1$, with whom A_1 cannot so communicate. By the statement proved above, A_i can communicate in one stage with at least one more person than A_1 can. But this implies that $r_i > r_1$, which contradicts the fact that we have named the individuals so that $r_1 \geq r_i$. This contradiction establishes the theorem.

An additional conclusion which can be made from the proof of the theorem is that the individual or individuals having the *largest* row sum in the matrix C can communicate with everyone else in one or two stages. Similarly, the individuals having the *largest* column sum can be communicated with by everyone in one or two stages.

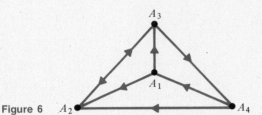

Figure 6

The network shown in Figure 6 satisfies the hypothesis of the theorem, hence its conclusion. The communication matrix for this network is

$$\begin{pmatrix} 0 & 1 & 1 & 0 \\ 0 & 0 & 1 & 0 \\ 0 & 1 & 0 & 1 \\ 1 & 1 & 0 & 0 \end{pmatrix}.$$

Here the maximum row sum of 2 occurs in the first, third, and fourth rows, so that A_1, A_3, and A_4 can communicate with everyone else in one or two stages. (Find the necessary communication paths in Figure 6.) However, it requires three stages for A_2 to communicate with A_1. The maximum sum of 3 occurs in the second column, so that A_2 can be communicated with by everyone else in one or two stages (actually one stage is enough). It happens also that A_3 and A_4 can also be communicated with in one or two stages; however, as observed above, A_1 cannot be.

Neither of the networks in Figure 1 satisfies the hypothesis of the theorem. It happens that the network in Figure 1(a) does satisfy the conclusion of the theorem, while the network in Figure 1(b) does not. (See Exercise 7.)

As a final application of dominance matrices, we shall define the power of an individual. By the *power* of an individual in a dominance situation we mean the total number of one-stage and two-stage dominances which he can exert. Since the total number of one-stage dominances exerted by A_i is the sum of the entries in the ith row of the matrix D, and the total number of two-stage dominances exerted by A_i is the sum of the entries in the ith row of the matrix D^2, we see that the power of A_i can be expressed as follows:

The power of A_i is the sum of the entries in the ith row of the matrix $S = D + D^2$.

In the example of Figure 7 it is easy to check that the powers of the various individuals are the following:

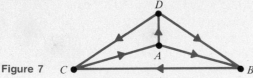

Figure 7

The power of A is 5.
The power of B is 2.
The power of C is 3.
The power of D is 4.

EXAMPLE   (Athletic contest). The idea of the power of an individual can be used to judge athletic events. For example, the result of a single round of a round-robin athletic event results in the following data:

Team A beats teams B and D.
Team B beats team C.
Team C beats team A.
Team D beats teams C and B.

Then it is easy to check that this is precisely the dominance situation shown in Figure 7. By the analysis given above we can rate the teams in the following order according to their respective powers: A, D, C, and B.

It should be remarked that the above definition of the power of an individual is not the only one possible. In Exercise 13 we suggest another definition of power which gives different results. Before using one or the other of these definitions, a sociologist should examine them carefully to see which (if either) fits his needs.

EXERCISES

1. Show that there are only two essentially different pecking orders possible among three chickens, namely, those given in Figure 3. [*Hint:* Use directed graphs.]

2. Find the dominance matrices D corresponding to the following directed graphs:

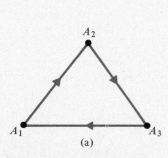

(a)

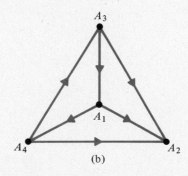

(b)

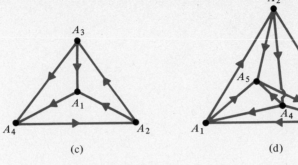

(c)   (d)

$$[Ans. \ (b) \begin{pmatrix} 0 & 1 & 0 & 1 \\ 0 & 0 & 0 & 0 \\ 1 & 1 & 0 & 0 \\ 0 & 1 & 1 & 0 \end{pmatrix}.]$$

3. Compute the matrices D^2 and $S = D + D^2$ and determine the powers of each of the individuals in the examples of Exercise 2.

$$[Ans. \ (b) \ D^2 = \begin{pmatrix} 0 & 1 & 1 & 0 \\ 0 & 0 & 0 & 0 \\ 0 & 1 & 0 & 1 \\ 1 & 1 & 0 & 0 \end{pmatrix}; \ S = \begin{pmatrix} 0 & 2 & 1 & 1 \\ 0 & 0 & 0 & 0 \\ 1 & 2 & 0 & 1 \\ 1 & 2 & 1 & 0 \end{pmatrix}; \ 4, 0, 4, 4.]$$

4. Find the communication matrices for the following communication networks:

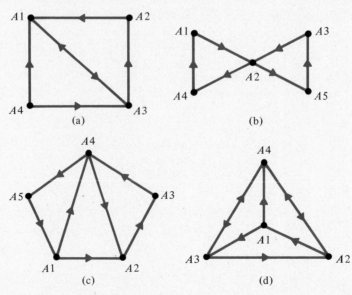

(a)   (b)

(c)   (d)

$$[Ans. \ (a) \begin{pmatrix} 0 & 0 & 1 & 0 \\ 1 & 0 & 0 & 0 \\ 1 & 1 & 0 & 0 \\ 1 & 0 & 1 & 0 \end{pmatrix}.]$$

5. Draw the directed graphs corresponding to the following communi-
    cation matrices:

    (a) $\begin{pmatrix} 0 & 1 & 1 \\ 0 & 0 & 1 \\ 1 & 1 & 0 \end{pmatrix}$.

    (b) $\begin{pmatrix} 0 & 1 & 0 & 1 \\ 1 & 0 & 0 & 1 \\ 0 & 0 & 0 & 1 \\ 1 & 1 & 1 & 0 \end{pmatrix}$.

    (c) $\begin{pmatrix} 0 & 1 & 0 & 1 \\ 1 & 0 & 1 & 0 \\ 1 & 0 & 0 & 1 \\ 0 & 1 & 1 & 0 \end{pmatrix}$.

    (d) $\begin{pmatrix} 0 & 0 & 0 & 0 \\ 0 & 0 & 0 & 1 \\ 1 & 0 & 0 & 0 \\ 0 & 0 & 1 & 0 \end{pmatrix}$.

6. Which of the communication networks whose matrices are given in
    Exercise 5 satisfy the hypothesis of the theorem of this section?
    [*Ans.* (a) and (c).]

7. Show that the network in Figure 1(a) satisfies the conclusion of the
    theorem, while the network in Figure 1(b) does not.

8. By computing the matrix S in each case, find the persons who can
    communicate with everyone else in one or two stages and those who
    can be communicated with in one or two stages, for the communication
    matrices in Exercise 5. (In some cases such persons need not exist.)
    [*Ans.* (a) Everyone; (b) everyone; (d) neither type of person exists.]

9. Find all the essentially different pecking orders that are possible among
    four chickens.   [*Ans.* There are four essentially different ones.]

10. If C is any communication matrix, give the interpretation of the entries
    in the columns of the matrix $S = C + C^2$. Also give the interpretation
    for the column sums of S.

11. Find all communication networks among three individuals which
    satisfy the hypothesis of the theorem of this section. How many of
    these are essentially different?   [*Ans.* There are seven.]

12. A round-robin tennis match among four people has produced the
    following results.

    Smith has beaten Brown and Jones.
    Jones has beaten Brown.
    Taylor has beaten Smith, Brown, and Jones.

    By finding the powers of each player, rank them into first, second, third,
    and fourth places. Does this ranking agree with your intuition?
    [*Ans.* Taylor has power = 6, Smith has power = 3, Jones has power =
    1, and Brown has power = 0.]

13. Let the power$_1$ of an individual be the power as defined in the text
    above. Define a new power, called power$_2$, of an individual as follows:
    If D is the dominance matrix for a group of n individuals, then the
    power$_2$ of A_i is the sum of the ith row of the matrix

$$S' = D + \tfrac{1}{2}D^2.$$

Find the power$_2$ of each of the teams in the athletic contest example in the text. Show that the power$_2$ of an individual team need not equal its power$_1$. Comment on the result.

14. Find the power$_2$ of the players in Exercise 12. Discuss its relation with the power$_1$ of each of the players.
[*Ans.* Taylor has power$_2 = \frac{9}{2}$, Smith has power$_2 = \frac{5}{2}$, Jones has power$_2 = 1$, Brown has power$_2 = 0$.]

15. If C is a communication matrix, give an interpretation for the entries of the matrix C^3. Do the same for the matrix C^4.
[*Ans.* The entry in the ith row and the jth column of C^3 gives the number of three-stage communications from i to j; the same entry of C^4 gives the number of four-stage communications from i to j.]

16. If C is a communication matrix, give an interpretation for the entries of the matrix $S = C + C^2 + C^3 + \ldots + C^m$.

17. Prove the second statement of the theorem of the present section.

18. Prove that the following statement is true: In a communication network involving three individuals, it is possible for a message starting from any person to get to any other person if and only if the following condition is satisfied: each individual can send a message to at least one person and can receive a message from at least one person.

19. Show that the matrix form of the condition in Exercise 18 is: Every row and column of the communication matrix must have at least one nonzero entry.

20. Is the statement in Exercise 18 true for a communication network involving two individuals? For four or more individuals?
[*Ans.* Yes; no.]

2 EQUIVALENCE CLASSES IN COMMUNICATION NETWORKS

When considering communication networks, it becomes obvious that the various members of the network play different roles. Some members can only send messages, some can only receive them, and others can both send and receive. Subsets of members are also important. We shall consider subsets of members having the following two properties: (a) every member of the subset can both send and receive messages (not necessarily in one step) to and from every other member in the subset; and (b) the subset having property (a) is as large as possible. We shall show that it is possible to partition the set of all people in the network into subsets (called equivalence classes) having these two properties, and that between such equivalence classes there is at most a one-way communication link. We then apply our results to three different problems: (i) putting any nonnegative matrix into canonical form; (ii) the classification of states in a Markov chain; and (iii) the solution of an archeological problem.

As in the previous section, let $A_1, \ldots, A_n$, be the members of the communication network. We define a relation R between some pairs of these members as follows: Let $A_i R A_j$ mean "A_i can send a message to A_j (in that direction and not necessarily in one step) or else $i = j$." Then it is easy to show that the relation R has the following two properties:

(1) $A_i R A_i$ for every i.   (Reflexive axiom)
(2) $A_i R A_j$ and $A_j R A_k$ imply $A_i R A_k$.   (Transitive axiom)

To see this, note that property (1) follows from the definition of R, and (2) follows since if A_i can send a message to A_j and A_j can send a message to A_k, then A_i can send a message to A_k by routing it through A_j.

If S is *any* set and R is *any* relation defined for members of S that satisfies axioms (1) and (2), then R is called a *weak ordering* on S.

We next define another relation on the states of the network. Let $A_i T A_j$ hold if and only if $(A_i R A_j) \wedge (A_j R A_i)$; that is $A_i T A_j$ holds if and only if "A_i has a two-way communication with A_j or else $i = j$." It is easy to show that the relation T has the following three properties:

(3) $A_i T A_i$.   (Reflexive axiom)
(4) $A_i T A_j$ if and only if $A_j T A_i$.   (Symmetric axiom)
(5) $A_i T A_j$ and $A_j T A_k$ imply $A_i T A_k$.   (Transitive axiom)

In Exercise 1 the reader is asked to establish these three axioms.

If S is any set and T is any relation defined for members of S that satisfies axioms (3), (4), and (5), then T is called an *equivalence relation* on S. The principal result about equivalence relations defined over a set S is that they partition S into equivalence classes.

Definition   We say that A_i and A_j are *equivalent* if $A_i T A_j$. For any A_i the *equivalence class* E_i that it determines is the truth set of the statement $A_i T A_k$, i.e., it is the set of all A_k such that $A_i T A_k$ is true.

Theorem 1   The equivalence classes of T partition S, the set of members of the communication network.

Proof   We must show that every member A_i of S belongs to one and only one equivalence class. Let S' be the equivalence class of A_i. Since $A_i T A_i$ [from (3) above], we know that A_i belongs to S', which shows that A_i belongs to some equivalence class, and also that S' is not empty.

Now let A_i and A_j be any two members of S, and let S' and S'', respectively, be their equivalence classes. We shall show that either $S' \cap S'' = \mathcal{E}$ or else $S' = S''$. If $S' \cap S'' = \mathcal{E}$, then we are done. Hence suppose that there is an element X of S in $S' \cap S''$. Since X is in S', we have $A_i T X$; and since X is in S'', we have $A_j T X$. Using (4) we have $X T A_j$. But, by virtue of transitivity (5), $A_i T X$ and $X T A_j$ imply $A_i T A_j$; hence A_j is in S'. Let Y be any element in S'' so that $A_j T Y$. Using transitivity again, we have $A_i T A_j$ and $A_j T Y$, so that Y is in S'. We have thus shown that every element of

S'' is in S', i.e., $S'' \subset S'$. In the same manner, one can show that $S' \subset S''$. Hence $S' = S''$.

Since we have shown that every member of S belongs to an equivalence class, and that every pair of equivalence classes are either identical or else disjoint, we have shown that they partition S, completing the proof of the theorem.

We now define a relation R on the equivalence classes of S. Namely, we let $S'RS''$ mean, "either $S' = S''$ or else some member of S' can send a message to some member of S''." We leave it to the reader in Exercise 6 to show that R is a weak ordering of the set of equivalence classes of S.

Theorem 2 Let S' and S'' be two equivalence classes; then, if $S'RS''$, it is false that $S''RS'$. In other words, at most one-way communication is possible between equivalence classes.

Proof Suppose on the contrary, that S' and S'' are two equivalence classes such that $S'RS''$ and $S''RS'$. Then there is an element X in S' that can communicate with some element Y in S''; and there is an element Z in S'' that can communicate with some element U in S'. Since Y and Z are in S'', two-way communication is possible between them; and since X and U are in S', they also have two-way communication. Hence Y can communicate with Z, Z can communicate with U, and U can communicate with X. Therefore X and Y are in the same equivalence class, contradicting the assumption that they were in different (and hence disjoint) equivalence classes. This completes the proof.

For applications it is important to be able to find the equivalence classes for a given communication network. We develop an iterative method that constructs the following sets:

(6) T_k, the set of states that A_k can *send* a message *to* (not necessarily in one step).

(7) F_k, the set of states that A_k can *receive* a message *from* (not necessarily in one step).

(8) E_k, the equivalence class of A_k.

It is easily seen (see Exercise 7) that $E_k = T_k \cap F_k$, so that we develop a step-by-step method for constructing the sets T_k and F_k. We illustrate the method with an example.

EXAMPLE 1 We wish to get in contact with five alumni of a certain college, but do not know all their addresses. However, we have information of the form "Jones knows where Brown is," "Smith knows where Doe is," etc. We summarize this information in the communication matrix of Figure 8. In that figure for $i \neq j$ we put 1 in the i,jth entry if the ith person knows where the jth one is. What is the smallest number of people that we must contact in order to send a message to all of them?

$$
\begin{array}{c}
\phantom{\text{Brown}} \quad \text{Brown} \quad \text{Jones} \quad \text{Smith} \quad \text{Adams} \quad \text{Doe} \\
\begin{array}{c}
\text{Brown} \\
\text{Jones} \\
\text{Smith} \\
\text{Adams} \\
\text{Doe}
\end{array}
\left(
\begin{array}{ccccc}
0 & 0 & 0 & 0 & 0 \\
1 & 0 & 0 & 1 & 0 \\
0 & 0 & 0 & 0 & 1 \\
0 & 1 & 1 & 0 & 0 \\
0 & 0 & 0 & 0 & 0
\end{array}
\right)
\end{array}
$$

Figure 8

In order to solve this problem we first find the "send-to" lists for each person. We start by listing all the persons a person can contact in zero or one steps; these data come directly out of the communication matrix. These people form the "first-stage approximation" to the "send-to" lists. Next we go down the list of persons and add to each one's "send-to" list all the people who can be contacted by people already on his first-stage approximate "send-to" list. The results are the "second-stage approximation to the send-to" lists. We continue this process, step by step, until for the first time we go through the list and do not add any member to any person's "send-to" list. We then have the actual "send-to" sets for each person, since going through the process again would not change any list. The computations for the example in Figure 8 are shown in Figure 9.

Person	Zero- or One-Stage Communication	Send-to List
1 Brown	1	1
2 Jones	1, 2, 4	1, 2, 4, **3, 5**
3 Smith	3, 5	3, 5
4 Adams	2, 3, 4	2, 3, 4, **1, 5**
5 Doe	5	5

Figure 9

The first-stage approximation to the "send-to" list is shown in the second column of Figure 9. On the first pass through the list we add 3 to Jones's list, which is indicated by boldface in the third column. We also add 1 and 5 to Adams' list, also indicated by boldface numerals. On the next pass through the computation we add 5 to Jones's list and make no other changes. The next pass through the computation produces no further changes so that the final lists shown in the third column of Figure 9 is the complete "send-to" list for each person.

We see that we have solved the problem posed above, for by contacting either Jones or Adams, we can relay a message to each of the five alumni members.

Let us go further and find the "receive-from" lists and the equivalence classes for each person in the network. The "receive-from" lists are easy, for we simply go down the "send-to" list and if we find member k on the ith person's "send-to" list, we put i on the kth person's "receive-from" list.

Person	Send-to List	Receive-from List	Equivalence Class
1 Brown	1	1, 2, 4	$\{1\}$
2 Jones	1, 2, 4, 3, 5	2, 4	$\{2, 4\}$
3 Smith	3, 5	2, 3, 4	$\{3\}$
4 Adams	2, 3, 4, 1, 5	2, 4	$\{2, 4\}$
5 Doe	5	2, 3, 4, 5	$\{5\}$

Figure 10

And we compute the equivalence classes from the relationship $E_k = T_k \cap F_k$. These computations are shown in Figure 10.

It is interesting to draw the graph of the weak-ordering relation R on the equivalence classes. To find the graph we simply check whether one-way communication is possible between each pair of equivalence classes. Then we connect two equivalence classes in the graph if such one-way communication is possible and if there is no intermediate class in the communication path. The graph of the weak-ordering relation for the matrix of Figure 8 is shown in Figure 11. Note that equivalence class $\{2, 4\}$ can communicate

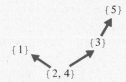

Figure 11

directly to $\{1\}$ and $\{3\}$ and to $\{5\}$ through $\{3\}$. This graph shows very clearly the fact, noted above, that in order to contact all members of the group it is sufficient to contact either member of the equivalence class $\{2, 4\}$.

We can use the weak ordering of equivalence classes to put the matrix of Figure 8 in a canonical form, which is characterized by the following definition:

Definition Let C be any communication matrix, and let S', S'', ..., be the equivalence classes of its states. Then by a *canonical form* of C we shall mean a reordering of the rows and columns of C so that the following two properties are satisfied:

(i) Members of a given equivalence class are listed next to each other.
(ii) No equivalence class S' is listed until all classes S'' "above" it in the graph of the equivalence classes have already been listed; i.e., S' is not listed until all classes such that $S'RS''$ have already been listed.

EXAMPLE 1 We illustrate the above definition in terms of the matrix A of Figure 8.
(continued) Using the weak ordering diagram of Figure 11, we see that the following

listing of the states (row indices) of A will satisfy the definition: 1, 5, 3, 2, 4. The resulting matrix is shown in Figure 12. In that figure dotted lines appear along the main diagonal, indicating the equivalence classes. Note that above the main diagonal blocks the only entries are zeros. Matrices having this property are called *block-triangular*.

		Brown	Doe	Smith	Jones	Adams
1	Brown	0	0	0	0	0
5	Doe	0	0	0	0	0
3	Smith	0	1	0	0	0
2	Jones	1	0	0	0	1
4	Adams	0	0	1	1	0

Figure 12

The same kind of canonical form is possible for *any* nonnegative matrix A, if we let $C(A)$ be the communication matrix derived from A be putting zeros on the main diagonal, and replacing positive off-diagonal entries by ones. We discuss this for Markov chain transition matrices. When the matrix under consideration is the transition matrix of a Markov chain, the classification of the states is extremely important in the study of the behavior of the chain, as the following definition indicates:

Definition Let P be the transition matrix of a Markov chain, and let $C(P)$ be the matrix obtained from P by replacing each diagonal entry by 0 and replacing each positive off-diagonal entry by 1. Let $S', S'', \ldots$ be the equivalence classes of the states of $C(P)$; then:

(i)   The maximal equivalence classes—that is, those classes that cannot send to other classes—are called *ergodic sets*. Members of ergodic sets are called *ergodic states*. If an ergodic set contains a single state, that state is an *absorbing state*.

(ii) All equivalence classes that can send messages to other classes are called *transient sets*. Members of transient sets are called *transient states*.

EXAMPLE 2   Consider the transition matrix

$$P = \begin{pmatrix} 0 & 0 & 1 & 0 & 0 \\ 0 & \frac{1}{2} & \frac{1}{4} & \frac{1}{4} & 0 \\ 1 & 0 & 0 & 0 & 0 \\ 0 & 0 & 0 & 1 & 0 \\ 0 & 0 & \frac{1}{3} & 0 & \frac{2}{3} \end{pmatrix}.$$

Changing the diagonal entries to zeros and the positive off-diagonal entries to ones gives

$$
C(P) = \begin{array}{c} \\ 1 \\ 2 \\ 3 \\ 4 \\ 5 \end{array}
\begin{array}{c} \begin{array}{ccccc} 1 & 2 & 3 & 4 & 5 \end{array} \\
\begin{pmatrix}
0 & 0 & 1 & 0 & 0 \\
0 & 0 & 1 & 1 & 0 \\
1 & 0 & 0 & 0 & 0 \\
0 & 0 & 0 & 0 & 0 \\
0 & 0 & 1 & 0 & 0
\end{pmatrix}
\end{array}.
$$

In Exercise 8 the reader will be asked to show that the equivalence classes of $C(P)$ are $\{4\}$, $\{1,3\}$, $\{5\}$, and $\{2\}$. Moreover, the graph of the weak-ordering relation on these classes is as shown in Figure 13. As before, the

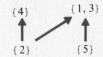

Figure 13

graph is obtained by checking whether one-way communication is possible between each pair of equivalence classes. From this diagram and the above definition we see that $\{4\}$ and $\{1,3\}$ are ergodic sets and that $\{4\}$ is an absorbing state; also, $\{2\}$ and $\{5\}$ are transient sets. A canonical form of the matrix found by listing the states in the order $4, 1, 3, 5, 2$ is

$$
P = \begin{pmatrix}
1 & 0 & 0 & 0 & 0 \\
0 & 0 & 1 & 0 & 0 \\
0 & 1 & 0 & 0 & 0 \\
0 & 0 & \frac{1}{3} & \frac{2}{3} & 0 \\
\frac{1}{4} & 0 & \frac{1}{4} & 0 & \frac{1}{2}
\end{pmatrix}.
$$

Note again that it is block-triangular, as indicated by the dotted lines. There are other orders in which to list the states, which lead to slightly different canonical forms for the matrix (see Exercise 9).

We conclude this section with an application of the above theory to an archeological problem.

EXAMPLE 3 Recent archeological investigations in Asia Minor, between the Mediterranean and Black Seas, have disclosed the existence of an ancient Assyrian civilization dating back to at least the nineteenth century B.C. This civilization came to light when peasants working in fields turned up clay tablets having written inscriptions. Upon being translated, these tablets turned out to be letters written between merchants located at various cities and towns of the ancient civilization. The letters contained the name of the sender, the name of the receiver, and an order to buy, sell, or transport goods, to pay money, etc. But the *date* of the letter was not included. In addition, merchants in different villages sometimes had the same name, and the location of the merchant was not always made clear in each of the letters. More than 2500 such tablets have been discovered; their contents give rise to two different problems. The first problem is to try to order the merchants according to their chronological dates. A second problem is to try to determine when the same name refers to more than one person. By studying the communication network that can be set up from the data of the tablets, we shall illustrate with small examples methods of trying to get partial answers to these questions.

$$
\begin{array}{c}
\begin{array}{cccccccccc} 1 & 2 & 3 & 4 & 5 & 6 & 7 & 8 & 9 & 10 \end{array} \\
\begin{array}{c} 1 \\ 2 \\ 3 \\ 4 \\ 5 \\ 6 \\ 7 \\ 8 \\ 9 \\ 10 \end{array}
\begin{pmatrix}
0 & 0 & 0 & 0 & 0 & 1 & 0 & 0 & 0 & 0 \\
0 & 0 & 1 & 0 & 1 & 0 & 0 & 0 & 0 & 0 \\
0 & 1 & 0 & 0 & 1 & 1 & 0 & 0 & 0 & 0 \\
0 & 0 & 0 & 0 & 0 & 0 & 0 & 1 & 0 & 1 \\
0 & 1 & 1 & 0 & 0 & 0 & 0 & 0 & 0 & 0 \\
0 & 0 & 0 & 0 & 0 & 0 & 0 & 0 & 0 & 0 \\
0 & 0 & 0 & 0 & 0 & 0 & 0 & 1 & 0 & 0 \\
0 & 0 & 1 & 0 & 0 & 0 & 0 & 0 & 1 & 0 \\
0 & 0 & 0 & 0 & 0 & 0 & 1 & 0 & 0 & 0 \\
1 & 0 & 0 & 0 & 0 & 0 & 0 & 0 & 0 & 0
\end{pmatrix}
\end{array}
$$

Figure 14

To illustrate an approach to the first problem, suppose that we set up a (hypothetical) communication matrix for a group of ten merchants, as indicated in the matrix of Figure 14. In that matrix an entry of 1 is made in the i,jth entry if merchant i sent a letter to merchant j. Carrying out the same analysis as in Example 1, we find the equivalence classes to be $\{6\}$, $\{1, 10\}$, $\{2, 3, 5\}$, $\{7, 8, 9\}$, and $\{4\}$. The graph of the weak-ordering relation on these classes is shown in Figure 15. It was determined, as before,

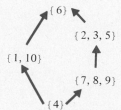

Figure 15

by seeing whether there is one-way communication between each pair of equivalence classes. It is clear that members of a given equivalence class are contemporaries. But it is not clear which of the equivalence classes is earlier, merely from the one-way communication between them. However, further analysis of the content of the messages might help to establish this. For instance, if one of the messages exchanged among merchants 7, 8, and 9 were related to one of the messages exchanged among merchants 2, 3, and 5, then it would be reasonable to assume that they are all contemporaries. We see that here is a case in which mathematics, although it cannot furnish the complete answer to the problem, can indicate directions in which to search for more information.

To illustrate the second problem mentioned above, we use some actual data (see p. 865 of the Gardin–Garelli reference listed at the end of the chapter) summarized in the communication matrix of Figure 16. The matrix is symmetric, indicating that either there is a two-way (direct) communication between two individuals or else no (direct) communication at all. All the merchants belong to the same equivalence class, so that the previous analysis does not shed any light on their relative dates, except that they are all contemporaries. But is it possible that some names really stand for two different individuals? No definite answer can be provided to this question, but some indications can be provided by finding the *cliques* in the communication network.

		1	2	3	4	5	6	7	8	9	10
1	ASSUR-TAB	0	1	0	0	0	0	0	1	0	1
2	PUSHU-KIN	1	0	1	1	1	1	0	1	1	0
3	LAQIPUM	0	1	0	1	0	1	0	1	1	0
4	AMUR-ISHTAR	0	1	1	0	1	1	1	1	1	1
5	ASSUR-TAKLAKU	0	1	0	1	0	1	0	0	0	1
6	ASSUR-NA'DA	0	1	1	1	1	0	1	0	0	0
7	ASSUR-IMITTI	0	0	0	1	0	1	0	0	0	0
8	IM(I)D-ILUM	1	1	1	1	0	0	0	0	1	0
9	HINA	0	1	1	1	0	0	0	1	0	0
10	TARAM-KUBIM	1	0	0	1	1	0	0	0	0	0

Figure 16

Definition A *clique* of a communication network is a subset C of individuals containing at least three members, with the following two properties:

(i) Every pair of members of the clique has two-way communication.

(ii) The subset C is as large as possible with every pair of members having property (i).

The problem of finding all cliques has been solved but is too lengthy to describe here. We content ourselves with listing all the maximal cliques for the data of Figure 16. They are

$$\{1,2,8\}, \quad \{2,3,4,6\}, \quad \{2,3,4,8,9\}, \quad \{2,4,5,6\}, \quad \{4,5,10\}, \quad \{4,6,7\}.$$

From this list we can derive the frequency with which each merchant occurs in a clique, as shown in Figure 17. From that table it is evident that merchants 2(Pushu-Kin) and 4(Amur-Ishtar) occur most frequently in

Merchant	1	2	3	4	5	6	7	8	9	10
Number of times in a clique	1	4	2	4	1	3	1	2	1	0

Figure 17

cliques, and hence these names are most likely to be homonyms for two different people. Here again, mathematics does not completely solve the problem, but merely indicates the direction in which to look for further evidence.

The above calculations, though oversimplified, are illustrative of the kinds of calculations that must be done in order to study the complete communication network revealed by the 2500 tablets so far found at the archeological site.

EXERCISES

1. Show that the relation T satisfies properties (3), (4), and (5).

2. Show that the relation "$\geq$" is a weak-ordering relation on the set of integers. [*Hint:* Show that $x \geq y$, for x and y integers, satisfies (1) and (2).]

3. Show that the relation "$=$" is an equivalence relation on the set of all rational numbers (fractions). What are the equivalence classes it determines?

4. Let x and y be any two words and let xRy mean "Word x occurs no later than word y in the dictionary." Show that R is a weak order on the set of words.

5. Let x and y be people and let xTy mean "x is the same height as y." Show that T is an equivalence relation. What are the equivalence classes it determines? Show that the relation "at least as tall as" is a weak-ordering relation on these equivalence classes.

6. Let R and T be the relations defined in the text; let S', S'', $\ldots$ be the equivalence classes determined by T; and let $S'RS''$ be as defined in the text. Show that R satisfies properties (1) and (2)—that is, it is a weak ordering on the set of equivalence classes.

7. Let E_k, T_k, and F_k be as defined in the text. Show that $E_k = T_k \cap F_k$.

8. Find the equivalence classes of the communication matrix given in Example 2.

9. Show that there are ten different canonical forms for the transition matrix of Example 2.

10. Show that if A can communicate with B in a communication network having n persons, then it must be possible to do this in not more than $n - 1$ steps.

11. Suppose that there are six different individuals each of whom knows the location of certain others. This information is summarized in the following communication matrix:

$$
\begin{array}{c}
 \\
1 \\
2 \\
3 \\
4 \\
5 \\
6
\end{array}
\begin{array}{c}
\begin{array}{cccccc}
1 & 2 & 3 & 4 & 5 & 6
\end{array} \\
\begin{pmatrix}
0 & 0 & 0 & 0 & 0 & 0 \\
1 & 0 & 0 & 0 & 1 & 0 \\
0 & 0 & 0 & 0 & 0 & 1 \\
0 & 1 & 0 & 0 & 0 & 1 \\
1 & 0 & 0 & 0 & 0 & 0 \\
0 & 0 & 0 & 1 & 1 & 0
\end{pmatrix}
\end{array}
$$

(a) Find the equivalence classes of T.

(b) Draw the graph of the weak ordering relation on the equivalence classes.

(c) Suppose you know where 3 is and you want to find out where 1 is. What is the shortest communication path from 3 to 1?

[*Partial ans.* It has length 3.]

(d) What is the longest such communication path?

[*Partial ans.* It has length 5.]

12. Classify each of the states of the Markov chain whose transition matrix is given below, and put the matrix into a canonical form. [*Hint:* Use some of the results of Exercise 11.]

$$\begin{pmatrix} 1 & 0 & 0 & 0 & 0 & 0 \\ \frac{1}{2} & 0 & 0 & 0 & \frac{1}{2} & 0 \\ 0 & 0 & 0 & 0 & 0 & 1 \\ 0 & \frac{3}{4} & 0 & 0 & 0 & \frac{1}{4} \\ \frac{2}{5} & 0 & 0 & 0 & \frac{3}{5} & 0 \\ 0 & 0 & 0 & \frac{1}{3} & \frac{1}{3} & \frac{1}{3} \end{pmatrix}$$

[*Ans.* One canonical form is

$$\begin{pmatrix} 1 & 0 & 0 & 0 & 0 & 0 \\ \frac{2}{5} & \frac{3}{5} & 0 & 0 & 0 & 0 \\ \frac{1}{2} & \frac{1}{2} & 0 & 0 & 0 & 0 \\ 0 & 0 & \frac{3}{4} & 0 & \frac{1}{4} & 0 \\ 0 & \frac{1}{3} & 0 & \frac{1}{3} & \frac{1}{3} & 0 \\ 0 & 0 & 0 & 0 & 1 & 0 \end{pmatrix};$$

state 1 is absorbing; all other states are transient.]

13. If a matrix M can be put into the form

$$M = \begin{pmatrix} A & 0 \\ B & C \end{pmatrix},$$

where 0 is the zero matrix, then M is said to be *reducible* or *decomposable*. If A and C are square and nonsingular show that

$$M^{-1} = \begin{pmatrix} A^{-1} & 0 \\ -C^{-1}BA^{-1} & C^{-1} \end{pmatrix}.$$

14. Use the results of Exercise 13 to show how a canonical form of a nonnegative matrix can be used to simplify the work of finding its inverse.

15. (a) Show that the Markov chain in Exercise 12 is an absorbing Markov chain.

(b) Find the matrix Q in canonical form. Show that the matrix $I - Q$ is block-triangular.

(c) Use the results of Exercises 13 and 14 to find $N = (I - Q)^{-1}$.

[*Ans.* With the canonical form of the answer to Exercise 12, the inverse is

$$
N = (I - Q)^{-1} = \begin{pmatrix} \frac{5}{2} & 0 & 0 & 0 & 0 \\ \frac{5}{4} & 1 & 0 & 0 & 0 \\ \frac{10}{7} & \frac{6}{7} & \frac{8}{7} & \frac{3}{7} & 0 \\ \frac{55}{28} & \frac{3}{7} & \frac{4}{7} & \frac{12}{7} & 0 \\ \frac{55}{28} & \frac{3}{7} & \frac{4}{7} & \frac{12}{7} & 1 \end{pmatrix} .]
$$

16. Draw the graph of a three-person clique. Also that of a four-person clique. Describe the graph of a clique containing n persons ($n \geq 3$).
17. Verify that the cliques given in Example 3 satisfy the two properties given in the definition of a clique.
18. Let C_1 and C_2 be any two *distinct* cliques of the same communication network.
    (a) Show by examples that $C_1 \cap C_2$ may or may not be empty.
    (b) Prove that the sets $C_1 - C_2$ and $C_2 - C_1$ are *never* empty.

3 STOCHASTIC PROCESSES IN GENETICS

The simplest type of inheritance of traits in animals occurs when a trait is governed by a pair of genes, each of which may be of two types, say G and g. An individual may have a GG combination or Gg (which is genetically the same as gG) or gg. Very often the GG and Gg types are indistinguishable in appearance, and then we say that the G gene *dominates* the g gene. An individual is called *dominant* if he has GG genes, *recessive* if he has gg, and *hybrid* with a Gg mixture.

In the mating of two animals, the offspring inherits one gene of the pair from each parent, and the basic assumption of genetics is that these genes are selected at random, independently of each other. This assumption determines the probability of every type of offspring. Thus the offspring of two dominant parents must be dominant, of two recessive parents must be recessive, and of one dominant and one recessive parent must be hybrid. In the mating of a dominant and a hybrid animal, the offspring must get a G gene from the former and has probability $\frac{1}{2}$ for getting G or g from the latter, hence the probabilities are even for getting a dominant or a hybrid offspring. Again in the mating of a recessive and a hybrid, there is an even chance of getting either a recessive or a hybrid. In the mating of two hybrids, the offspring has probability $\frac{1}{2}$ for getting a G or a g from each parent. Hence the probabilities are $\frac{1}{4}$ for GG, $\frac{1}{2}$ for Gg, and $\frac{1}{4}$ for gg.

EXAMPLE 1 Let us consider a process of continued crossings. We start with an individual of unknown genetic character, and cross it with a hybrid. The offspring is again crossed with a hybrid, etc. The resulting process is a Markov chain. The states are "dominant," "hybrid," and "recessive." The transition probabilities are

$$
\begin{array}{c}
\begin{array}{ccc} D & H & R \end{array} \\
P = \begin{array}{c} D \\ H \\ R \end{array}
\begin{pmatrix}
\frac{1}{2} & \frac{1}{2} & 0 \\
\frac{1}{4} & \frac{1}{2} & \frac{1}{4} \\
0 & \frac{1}{2} & \frac{1}{2}
\end{pmatrix}
\end{array}
$$

(1)

as can be seen from the previous paragraph. The matrix P^2 has all entries positive (see Exercise 1), hence we know from Chapter 4, Section 7, that there is a unique fixed-point probability vector, i.e., a vector p such that $pP = p$. By solving three equations, we find the fixed vector to be $p = (\frac{1}{4}, \frac{1}{2}, \frac{1}{4})$. Hence, no matter what type the original animal was, after repeated crossing we have probability nearly $\frac{1}{4}$ of having a dominant, $\frac{1}{2}$ of having a hybrid, and $\frac{1}{4}$ of having a recessive offspring.

In Example 1 we may ask a more difficult question. Suppose that we have a regular matrix P (as in Example 1), with states $a_1, \ldots, a_n$. The process keeps going through all the states. If we are in a_i, how long, on the average, will it take for the process to return to a_i? We can even ask the more general question of how long, on the average, it takes to go from a_i to a_j.

The average here is taken in the sense of an expected value. There is a probability p_1 that we reach a_j for the first time in one step, p_2 that we reach it first in two steps, etc. The expected value is $p_1 \cdot 1 + p_2 \cdot 2 + \ldots$ (see Chapter 3, Section 11). This, in general, requires a difficult computation. However, there is a much simpler way of finding the expected values. Let the expected number of steps required to go from state a_i to a_j be m_{ij}. How can we go from a_i to a_j? We go from a_i to a_k with probability p_{ik} in one step. If $k = j$, we are there. If $k \neq j$, it takes an average of m_{kj} steps more to get to a_j. Hence m_{ij} is equal to 1 plus the sum of $p_{ik}m_{kj}$ for all $k \neq j$. To state this as a matrix equation we define the matrix $\bar{M}$ to be the matrix M but with all the diagonal entries m_{ii} being replaced by 0; also, let C be the square matrix having all entries equal to 1. Then the equations for m_{ij} can be written in matrix form as

(2) $$ M = P\bar{M} + C. $$

To see that this is so let us concentrate on the i,jth entry of equation (2). On the left-hand side it is m_{ij}. On the right-hand side it is the i,jth entry of $P\bar{M}$ which is the sum of all products $p_{ik}m_{kj}$ for $k \neq j$ (since the main diagonal of $\bar{M}$ is zero) plus the i,jth entry in C, which is 1. This is the same as before. Let us now multiply (2) by w, the fixed vector of P. Recalling that w is a probability vector we obtain

(3) $$ wM = w\bar{M} + (1, \ldots, 1) $$

or

(4) $$ w(M - \bar{M}) = (1, \ldots, 1). $$

But all components of $M - \bar{M}$ except the diagonal ones are 0. Hence our equation simply states that $w_i m_{ii} = 1$ for each i. This tells us that $m_{ii} = 1/w_i$. *The average time it takes to return from a_i to a_i is the reciprocal of limiting probability of being in a_i.* In Example 1 this means that if we have a dominant offspring we shall have another dominant in an average of four steps, after a hybrid we have another hybrid in an average of two steps, and a recessive follows a recessive on the average in four steps.

EXAMPLE 2 A more interesting, and also more complex, process is obtained by crossing a given population with itself, and then crossing the offspring with offspring, etc. Let us suppose that our population has a fraction d of dominants, h hybrids, and r recessives. Then $d + h + r = 1$. If the population is very large and they are mated at random, then (by the law of large numbers) we can expect d^2 to be the fraction of matings in which both parents are dominant, $2dh$ the fraction of mating a dominant with a hybrid, etc. The tree of logical possibilities with branch probabilities marked on it is shown in Figure 18. We use it to compute the fraction of each type. To do this we simply add together the path weights of the paths ending in D, in H,

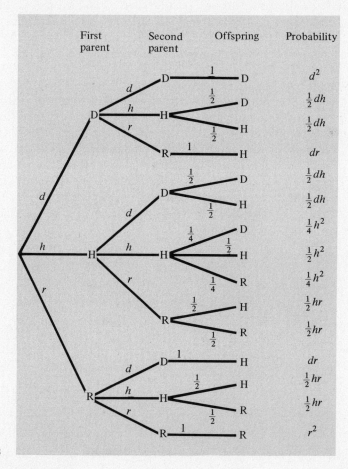

Figure 18

and in R. The results are:

D: $\quad d^2 + 2 \cdot \frac{1}{2}dh + \frac{1}{4}h^2 = d^2 + dh + \frac{1}{4}h^2$

H: $\quad 2 \cdot \frac{1}{2}dh + 2dr + \frac{1}{2}h^2 + 2 \cdot \frac{1}{2}hr = dh + rh + 2dr + \frac{1}{2}h^2$

R: $\quad \frac{1}{4}h^2 + 2 \cdot \frac{1}{2}hr + r^2 = r^2 + hr + \frac{1}{4}h^2$.

If we represent the fractions in a given generation by a row vector, the process may be thought of as a transformation T which changes a row vector into another row vector.

$$(5) \quad (d, h, r) \cdot T = (d^2 + dh + \tfrac{1}{4}h^2, dh + rh + 2dr + \tfrac{1}{2}h^2, r^2 + rh + \tfrac{1}{4}h^2).$$

The trouble is that (see Exercise 2) the transformation T is not linear. Nevertheless, we know that after n crossings the distribution will be $(d, h, r)T^n$, so that, if we can get a simple formula for T^n, we can describe the results simply. And here luck is with us.

Let us compute T^2, i.e., find what happens if we apply twice the transformation specified above. The first generation of offspring is distributed according to the formula (5). We now take the first component on the right side as d, the second as h, and the third as r, and compute $d^2 + dh + \frac{1}{4}h^2$, etc. Here we find to our surprise that $T^2 = T$. Hence $T^n = T$.

This means that $(d, h, r)T = (d, h, r)T^n$, which in turn means that the distribution after many generations is the same as in the first generation of offspring. Hence we say that the process reaches an *equilibrium* in one step. It must, however, be remembered that our fractions are only approximate, and are a good approximation only for very large populations.

For the geneticist, this result is very interesting. It shows that, in a population in which no mutations occur and selection does not take place, "evolution" is all over in a single generation.

To the mathematician the process is interesting since it is an example of a quadratic transformation, a transformation more complex than the linear ones we have heretofore studied.

The next two examples give applications of absorbing Markov chains to genetics.

EXAMPLE 3 If we keep crossing the offspring with a dominant animal, the result is quite different. The transition matrix is easily found to be

$$(6) \qquad P' = \begin{matrix} & \begin{matrix} D & H & R \end{matrix} \\ \begin{matrix} D \\ H \\ R \end{matrix} & \begin{pmatrix} 1 & 0 & 0 \\ \frac{1}{2} & \frac{1}{2} & 0 \\ 0 & 1 & 0 \end{pmatrix} \end{matrix}.$$

This is an absorbing Markov chain with one absorbing state, D. Using the results of Chapter 4, Section 8, we have

$$Q' = \begin{pmatrix} \frac{1}{2} & 0 \\ 1 & 0 \end{pmatrix}, \qquad R' = \begin{pmatrix} \frac{1}{2} \\ 0 \end{pmatrix},$$

so that

$$I - Q' = \begin{pmatrix} \frac{1}{2} & 0 \\ -1 & 1 \end{pmatrix}$$

and

$$N' = \begin{pmatrix} 2 & 0 \\ 2 & 1 \end{pmatrix}.$$

The absorption probabilities are

$$B = N'R' = \begin{pmatrix} 2 & 0 \\ 2 & 1 \end{pmatrix}\begin{pmatrix} \frac{1}{2} \\ 0 \end{pmatrix} = \begin{pmatrix} 1 \\ 1 \end{pmatrix},$$

as was to be expected, since there is only one absorbing state. This means that if we keep crossing the population with dominants, then after sufficiently many crossings we can expect only dominants. The mean number of steps to absorption are found by

$$t = N'c = \begin{pmatrix} 2 & 0 \\ 2 & 1 \end{pmatrix}\begin{pmatrix} 1 \\ 1 \end{pmatrix} = \begin{pmatrix} 2 \\ 3 \end{pmatrix}$$

Hence we expect the process to be absorbed in two steps starting from state H, and three steps starting from state R.

EXAMPLE 4   Let us construct a more complicated example of an absorbing Markov chain. We start with two animals of opposite sex, cross them, select two of their offspring of opposite sex and cross those, etc. To simplify the example we shall assume that the trait under consideration is independent of sex.

Here a state is determined by a pair of animals. Hence the states of our process will be: $a_1 = (D, D)$, $a_2 = (D, H)$, $a_3 = (D, R)$, $a_4 = (H, H)$, $a_5 = (H, R)$, and $a_6 = (R, R)$. Clearly, states a_1 and a_6 are absorbing, since if we cross two dominants or two recessives we must get one of the same type. The rest of the transition probabilities are easy to find. We illustrate their calculation in terms of state a_2. When the process is in this state, one parent has GG genes, the other Gg. Hence the probability of a dominant offspring or a hybrid offspring is $\frac{1}{2}$ for each. Then the probability of transition to a_1 (selection of two dominants) is $\frac{1}{4}$, the transition to a_2 is $\frac{1}{2}$, and to a_4 is $\frac{1}{4}$. The complete transition matrix is (listing the absorbing states first)

$$P'' = \begin{array}{c} \\ a_1 \\ a_6 \\ a_2 \\ a_3 \\ a_4 \\ a_5 \end{array}\begin{array}{c} \begin{array}{cccccc} a_1 & a_6 & a_2 & a_3 & a_4 & a_5 \end{array} \\ \begin{pmatrix} 1 & 0 & 0 & 0 & 0 & 0 \\ 0 & 1 & 0 & 0 & 0 & 0 \\ \frac{1}{4} & 0 & \frac{1}{2} & 0 & \frac{1}{4} & 0 \\ 0 & 0 & 0 & 0 & 1 & 0 \\ \frac{1}{16} & \frac{1}{16} & \frac{1}{4} & \frac{1}{8} & \frac{1}{4} & \frac{1}{4} \\ 0 & \frac{1}{4} & 0 & 0 & \frac{1}{4} & \frac{1}{2} \end{pmatrix} \end{array}.$$

Calculating the fundamental quantities for an absorbing chain, we obtain

$$Q'' = \begin{array}{c} \\ a_2 \\ a_3 \\ a_4 \\ a_5 \end{array} \begin{pmatrix} \overset{a_2}{\frac{1}{2}} & \overset{a_3}{0} & \overset{a_4}{\frac{1}{4}} & \overset{a_5}{0} \\ 0 & 0 & 1 & 0 \\ \frac{1}{4} & \frac{1}{8} & \frac{1}{4} & \frac{1}{4} \\ 0 & 0 & \frac{1}{4} & \frac{1}{2} \end{pmatrix}, \qquad R'' = \begin{pmatrix} \frac{1}{4} & 0 \\ 0 & 0 \\ \frac{1}{16} & \frac{1}{16} \\ 0 & \frac{1}{4} \end{pmatrix},$$

and

$$I - Q'' = \begin{pmatrix} \frac{1}{2} & 0 & -\frac{1}{4} & 0 \\ 0 & 1 & -1 & 0 \\ -\frac{1}{4} & -\frac{1}{8} & \frac{3}{4} & -\frac{1}{4} \\ 0 & 0 & -\frac{1}{4} & \frac{1}{2} \end{pmatrix},$$

and

$$N'' = (I - Q'')^{-1} = \begin{pmatrix} \frac{8}{3} & \frac{1}{6} & \frac{4}{3} & \frac{2}{3} \\ \frac{4}{3} & \frac{4}{3} & \frac{8}{3} & \frac{4}{3} \\ \frac{4}{3} & \frac{1}{3} & \frac{8}{3} & \frac{4}{3} \\ \frac{2}{3} & \frac{1}{6} & \frac{4}{3} & \frac{8}{3} \end{pmatrix}.$$

The absorption probabilities are found to be

$$B'' = N''R'' = \begin{pmatrix} \frac{3}{4} & \frac{1}{4} \\ \frac{1}{2} & \frac{1}{2} \\ \frac{1}{2} & \frac{1}{2} \\ \frac{1}{4} & \frac{3}{4} \end{pmatrix}.$$

The genetic interpretation of absorption is that after a large number of inbreedings either the G gene or the g gene must disappear. It is also interesting to note that the probability of ending up entirely with G genes, if we start from a given state, is equal to the proportion of G genes in this state.

The mean number of steps to absorption is

$$t = N'' \begin{pmatrix} 1 \\ 1 \\ 1 \\ 1 \end{pmatrix} = \begin{pmatrix} 4\frac{5}{6} \\ 6\frac{2}{3} \\ 5\frac{5}{3} \\ 4\frac{5}{6} \end{pmatrix}.$$

Hence we see that, if we start in a state other than (D, D) or (R, R), we can expect to reach one of these states in about five or six steps. The exact expected times are given by the entries of t. The matrix N'' provides more detailed information, namely how many times we can expect to have offspring of the types $(D, H), (D, R), (H, H)$, and (H, R), starting from a given nonabsorbing state. And the matrix B'' gives the probabilities of ending up in a_1 or a_6. These quantities jointly give us an excellent description of what we can expect of our process.

EXERCISES

1. From matrix (1) compute P^2, P^3, P^4, and P^5. Verify that $P^2 > 0$ and that the powers approach the expected form (see Chapter 4, Section 7).

2. Compute T^2 by taking the first component of (5) as d, the second as h, the third as r, and substituting into the formula (5). Making use of the fact that $d + h + r = 1$, show that $T^2 = T$.

3. A fixed point of T is a vector such that $(d, h, r)T = (d, h, r)$. Write the conditions that such a vector must satisfy, and give three examples of such fixed vectors. What is the genetic meaning of such a distribution?   [*Ans.* For example, $(\frac{1}{9}, \frac{4}{9}, \frac{4}{9})$.]

4. In the matrix P the second row is equal to the fixed-point vector. What significance does this have?

5. For Example 1 write the matrix M with unknown entries m_{ij}. Write M by replacing m_{11}, m_{22}, and m_{33} by zeros. Then solve the nine simultaneous equations given by (3), to find the m_{ij}. Check that $m_{ii} = 1/w_i$.   [*Ans.* $m_{11} = 4, m_{12} = 2, m_{13} = 8$.]

6. From the definition of a stochastic matrix (Chapter 4, Section 7), prove that $PC = C$.

7. Prove that, if P is a regular $n \times n$ stochastic matrix having column sums equal to 1, then it takes an average of n steps to return from any state to itself. (See Chapter 4, Section 7, Exercise 8.)

8. It is raining in the Land of Oz. In how many days can the Wizard of Oz expect to go on a picnic? (See Chapter 4, Section 7, Exercise 12.)   [*Ans.* 4.]

Exercises 9–14 develop a simpler method of treating the nonlinear transformation T, in the text above.

9. Let p be the ratio of G genes in the population, and $q = 1 - p$ the ratio of g genes. Express p and q in terms of d, h, and r.
                    [*Ans.* $p = d + \frac{1}{2}h, q = r + \frac{1}{2}h$.]

10. Suppose that we take all the genes in the population, mix them thoroughly, and select a pair at random for each offspring. Show, using the result of Exercise 9, that the resulting distribution of dominant, hybrid, and recessive individuals is precisely that given in formula (5).
                    [*Ans.* $(d, h, r) \cdot T = (p^2, 2pq, q^2)$.]

11. If we write $(d, h, r) \cdot T = (d', h', r')$, show, using the result of Exercise 10, that $h'^2 = 4d'r'$.

12. Show that for equilibrium it is necessary that $h^2 = 4dr$.

13. Show that if $h^2 = 4dr$, then $p^2 = d, q^2 = r$, and $2pq = h$. Hence show that this condition is also sufficient for equilibrium.

14. Use the results of Exercises 11–13 to show that the population reaches equilibrium in one generation.

15. Prove that in an absorbing Markov chain
    (a) The probability of reaching a given absorbing state is independent of the starting state if and only if there is only one absorbing state.

    (b)   The expected time for reaching an absorbing state is independent of the starting state if and only if every state is absorbing.

16. Suppose that hybrids have a high mortality rate; say that half of the hybrids die before maturity, while only a negligible number of dominants and recessives die before maturity.

    (a)   In Example 4 above, modify the matrix P'' to apply to this situation.

    (b)   What are the absorbing states?

    (c)   Verify that it is an absorbing chain.

    (d)   Find the vectors d representing the probabilities of absorption in the various absorbing states.

$$\left[\textit{Ans. For } a_1, d = \begin{pmatrix} 1 \\ 0 \\ \frac{9}{10} \\ \frac{1}{2} \\ \frac{1}{2} \\ \frac{1}{10} \end{pmatrix}.\right]$$

    (e)   Find N, and interpret.

    (f)   Find t, and interpret.
$$\left[\textit{Ans. } t = \begin{pmatrix} \frac{65}{26} \\ \frac{117}{26} \\ \frac{91}{26} \\ \frac{65}{26} \end{pmatrix}.\right]$$

The remaining problems concern the inheritance of color blindness, which is a sex-linked characteristic. There is a pair of genes, C and S, of which the former tends to produce color blindness, the latter normal vision. The S gene is dominant. But a man has only one gene, and if this is C, he is color-blind. A man inherits one of his mother's two genes, while a woman inherits one gene from each parent. Thus a man may be of type C or S, while a woman may be of type CC or CS or SS. We shall study a process of inbreeding similar to that of Example 4.

17. List the states of the chain. [*Hint:* There are six.]

18. Compute the transition probabilities.

19. Show that the chain is absorbing, and interpret the absorbing states. [*Ans.* In one, the S gene disappears; in the other, the C gene is lost.]

20. Prove that the probability of absorption in the state having only C genes, if we start in a given state, is equal to the proportion of C genes in that state.

21. Find N, and interpret.

22. Find t, and interpret.

$$\left[\textit{Ans. } \begin{pmatrix} 5 \\ 6 \\ 6 \\ 6 \\ 5 \end{pmatrix}\right.; \text{ if we start with both } C \text{ and } S \text{ genes, we can expect one of}$$

these to disappear in five or six crossings.]

4 MARRIAGE RULES IN PRIMITIVE SOCIETIES

In some primitive societies there are rigid rules as to when marriages are permissible. These rules are designed to prevent very close relatives from marrying. The rules can be given precise mathematical formulation in terms of permutation matrices. Our discussion is based, in part, on the work of André Weil and Robert R. Bush.

The marriage rules found in these societies are characterized by the following axioms:

Axiom 1. Each member of the society is assigned a marriage type.
Axiom 2. Two individuals are permitted to marry only if they are of the same marriage type.
Axiom 3. The type of an individual is determined by the individual's sex and by the type of his parents.
Axiom 4. Two boys (or two girls) whose parents are of different types will themselves be of different types.
Axiom 5. The rule as to whether a man is allowed to marry a female relative of a given kind depends only on the kind of relationship.
Axiom 6. In particular, no man is allowed to marry his sister.
Axiom 7. For any two individuals it is permissible for some of their descendants to intermarry.

EXAMPLE   Let us suppose that there are three marriage types, t_1, t_2, t_3. Two parents in a given family must be of the same type, since only then are they allowed to marry. Thus there are only three logical possibilities for marriages. For each case we have to state what the type of a son or a daughter will be:

Type of both parents	Type of their son	Type of their daughter
t_1	t_2	t_3
t_2	t_3	t_1
t_3	t_1	t_2

We must verify that all the axioms are satisfied. Some of the axioms are easy to check, others are harder to verify. We shall prove a general theorem which will show that this rule satisfies all the axioms.

In order to give a complete treatment to this problem, we must have a simple systematic method of representing relationships. For this we use family trees, as drawn by anthropologists. The following symbols are commonly used.

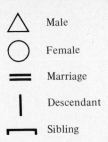

△   Male

○   Female

══   Marriage

│   Descendant

└─┐   Sibling

In Figure 19 we draw four family trees, representing the four kinds of first-cousin relationships between a man and a woman.

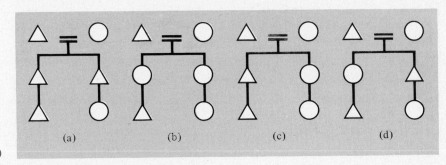

(a)   (b)   (c)   (d)

Figure 19

EXAMPLE (continued)   Does our rule allow marriage between a man and his father's brother's daughter? This is the relationship in Figure 19(a). There are three possible types for the original couple (the grandparents), and in Figure 20, we work out the three cases. We find in each case that the man and woman are

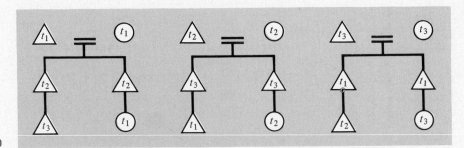

Figure 20

of different type; hence such marriages are *never* allowed. Can a man marry his mother's brother's daughter? This is the relationship in Figure 19(d). The three cases for this relationship are found in Figure 21. We find that such marriages are *always* allowed.

We are now ready to give the rules a mathematical formulation. The society chooses a number, say n, of marriage types (Axiom 1). We call these $t_1, t_2, \ldots, t_n$. Our rule has two parts, one concerning sons, one concerning

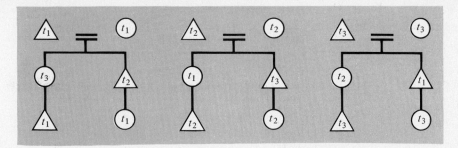

Figure 21

daughters. Let us consider the marriage type of sons. The parents must be of the same marriage type (Axiom 2). We must assign to a boy a type which depends only on the common type of his parents (Axiom 3). If his parents are of type t_i, he will be of type t_j. Furthermore, if some other boy has parents of a type different from t_i, then the boy will be of type different from t_j (Axiom 4). This defines a *permutation* of the marriage types (see Chapter 2, Section 4). The type of a son is obtained from the type of his parents by a permutation specified by the rule of the society. We shall find it convenient to represent these permutations by means of special permutation matrices.

Definition A *permutation matrix* is a square matrix having exactly one 1 in each row and each column, and having zeroes in all other entries.

As examples, consider the following permutation matrices:

$$A = \begin{pmatrix} 0 & 1 \\ 1 & 0 \end{pmatrix}, \qquad B = \begin{pmatrix} 0 & 1 & 0 \\ 0 & 0 & 1 \\ 1 & 0 & 0 \end{pmatrix}, \qquad C = \begin{pmatrix} 1 & 0 & 0 \\ 0 & 1 & 0 \\ 0 & 0 & 1 \end{pmatrix},$$

$$D = \begin{pmatrix} 0 & 1 & 0 & 0 \\ 1 & 0 & 0 & 0 \\ 0 & 0 & 1 & 0 \\ 0 & 0 & 0 & 1 \end{pmatrix}.$$

Suppose that $n = 3$ and $t = (t_1, t_2, t_3)$ is the vector of marriage types and that under the son relation this type vector is sent into the vector (t_3, t_1, t_2). We can represent this as

$$(t_1, t_2, t_3) \begin{pmatrix} 0 & 1 & 0 \\ 0 & 0 & 1 \\ 1 & 0 & 0 \end{pmatrix} = (t_3, t_1, t_2).$$

The following rule can be used for constructing the permutation matrix of a given permutation: If the permutation sends t_i into t_j, then make the entry in the jth row and ith column of the permutation matrix P equal to 1, and make all other entries in the ith column equal to 0.

It can easily be shown that every permutation matrix P is nonsingular and also that $P^{-1} = P'$, where P' is the *transpose*—that is, the matrix obtained by interchanging the rows and columns of P. A proof of this fact is sketched in Exercise 3. In particular note that P^{-1} is itself a permutation matrix.

Let n be fixed and consider the set of all $n \times n$ permutation matrices. Since there are $n!$ permutations, it can be shown that there are $n!$ permutation matrices. Note that the identity matrix I is in the set. We have just seen that if P is in the set, so is its inverse P^{-1}. Now consider two permutation matrices P and Q. In Exercise 4 you are asked to show that their product PQ is also a permutation matrix. Finally, if P, Q, and R are permutation matrices, then they obey the associative law $P(QR) = (PQ)R$, since the operation of matrix multiplication obeys this law.

Definition A set of objects forms a *group* (with respect to multiplication) if

- **(i)** The product of two elements of the set is always an element of the set.
- **(ii)** There is an identity element I in the set such that for every A, $IA = AI = A$.
- **(iii)** For every A in the set there is an element A^{-1} in the set such that $AA^{-1} = A^{-1}A = I$.
- **(iv)** For every A, B, C in the set, $A(BC) = (AB)C$.

By the remarks just above the definition it follows that the set of all $n \times n$ permutation matrices forms a group.

A nonempty subset of a group that satisfies the definition of a group is called a *subgroup*. We shall be particularly interested in subgroups of the permutation group that consist of powers of a single matrix A or powers and products of powers of two permutation matrices A and B. These are called subgroups generated by A, or by the two elements A and B. (See Exercises 5 and 6.)

To return to the marriage rules, suppose that for each marriage type t_i of the parents we determine the marriage type t_j of the son. This determines a permutation of marriage types which we shall represent by an $n \times n$ permutation matrix S. By a similar argument we arrive at the permutation matrix D giving the marriage types of daughters.

We have shown that the mathematical form of the first four axioms is to introduce the row vector t and the two permutation matrices S and D. The last three axioms restrict the choice of S and D. This will be considered in the next section.

We have repeatedly seen how the vector and matrix notation allows us to replace a series of equations by a single one. In the present problem this notation allows us to work out a given kind of relationship for *all* marriage types in a single diagram. As a matter of fact, this can be done without knowing how many types there are in the given society, or knowing what the rules are. Let us illustrate this in terms of Figure 21. The couple at the top of the tree is of a given type, represented by our vector t. Their son is of type tS, their daughter of type tD. Then the son of a son is of type tSS, the son's daughter is of type tSD, etc. We arrive at the single vector diagram of Figure 22. If in this figure we take t to have three

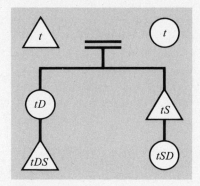

Figure 22

components, then the diagram is a shorthand for the three diagrams of Figure 21.

EXAMPLE
(continued)

Our t vector is (t_1, t_2, t_3) and

$$D = \begin{pmatrix} 0 & 1 & 0 \\ 0 & 0 & 1 \\ 1 & 0 & 0 \end{pmatrix}, \qquad S = \begin{pmatrix} 0 & 0 & 1 \\ 1 & 0 & 0 \\ 0 & 1 & 0 \end{pmatrix}.$$

We know from Figure 21 that a man is always allowed to marry his mother's brother's daughter. Can we see this in Figure 22? The marriage will always be permitted if tDS always equals tSD, which is equivalent to the matrix equation $DS = SD$. It so happens for our S and D that this equation is correct. But we can see more from Figure 22. No matter how many types there are, this kind of marriage will be permitted if and only if $SD = DS$, i.e., if the two matrices commute.

We have now seen one example of how the nature of S and D determines which kinds of relatives are allowed to marry. This question will be the subject of the next section.

EXERCISES

1. Show that the rule for constructing a permutation matrix to represent a permutation is correct.

2. Use the rule to find the permutation matrices for the following permutations:

    (a) (t_1, t_2, t_3) is sent into (t_2, t_3, t_1).

    (b) (t_1, t_2, t_3, t_4) is sent into (t_4, t_3, t_2, t_1).

    (c) (t_1, t_2) is sent into (t_1, t_2).

    (d) $(t_1, t_2, t_3, t_4, t_5)$ is sent into $(t_2, t_4, t_1, t_2, t_5)$.

3. (a) Find the permutation matrix corresponding to the permutation that sends (t_2, t_3, t_1) into (t_1, t_2, t_3).

    (b) Show that the answer to part (a) is the inverse matrix to the answer you got in Exercise 2(a).

    (c) Show that the answer you got in part (a) is the transposed matrix of the answer you got in 2(a).

    (d) In general, show that if P is a permutation matrix then $P^{-1} = P'$.

4. Let P and Q be two permutation matrices. Use the fact that each matrix has exactly one 1 and all the rest zeroes in each row and column to prove that the product PQ is also a permutation matrix.

5. Let A be an $n \times n$ permutation matrix and consider the powers $A, A^2, A^3, \ldots, A^k, \ldots$.

    (a) Use the fact that there are $n!$ permutation matrices to show that not all powers of A can be different.

    (b) If $A^k = A^{k+j}$, multiply on the left by A^{-1} repeatedly to show that $I = A^j$.

    (c) Show that the permutation matrices $I, A, \ldots, A^{j-1}$ form a subgroup, called the *subgroup generated by A*.

6. Let A and B be two permutation matrices. Consider the set of *all* products of powers of the matrices, such as $A^3 B^5 A B^{-2}$. Follow the following steps to show that this set is a group.

    (a) Show that the product of two such matrices is again a product of powers.

    (b) Show that the identity matrix can be written as a product of powers.

    (c) Show that the inverse of such a matrix is again a product of powers. [*Hint:* E.g., $(A^3 B^{-2})^{-1} = B^2 A^{-3}$.]

    (d) Property (iv) is true for matrices in general.

7. In the marriage example in the text above, verify that the rule satisfies Axioms 1, 3, and 4.

8. In the example above, verify that the matrices S and D given represent the rule given.

9. Construct a diagram for the brother-sister relationship.

10. Using the diagram of Exercise 9, show that, in the above example, brother-sister marriages are never permitted.

11. Find the condition on S and D that would always allow brother-sister marriages.   [*Ans. S = D*.]

In the *Kariera* society there are four marriage types, assigned according to the following rules:

Parent type	Son type	Daughter type
t_1	t_3	t_4
t_2	t_4	t_3
t_3	t_1	t_2
t_4	t_2	t_1

Exercises 12–17 refer to this society.

12. Find the t, S, and D of the Kariera society.

13. Show that brother-sister marriages are never allowed in the Kariera society.

14. Show that S and D commute. What does this tell us about first-cousin marriages in the Kariera society?

15. Show that first cousins of the kinds in Figure 19(a) and (b) are never allowed to marry in the Kariera society.

16. Show that first cousins of the kind in Figure 19(c) are always allowed to marry in the Kariera society.

17. Find the group generated by S and D of the Kariera society.

In the *Tarau* society there are also four marriage types. A son is of the same type as his parents. A daughter's type is given by:

Parent type	Daughter type
t_1	t_4
t_2	t_1
t_3	t_2
t_4	t_3

Exercises 18–23 refer to this society.

18. Find the t, S, and D of the Tarau society.

19. Show that brother-sister marriages are never allowed in the Tarau society.

20. Show that S and D commute. What does this tell us about first-cousin marriages in the Tarau society?

21. Show that first cousins of the kinds in Figures 19(a) and (b) are never allowed to marry in the Tarau society.

22. Show that first cousins of the kind in Figure 19(c) are never allowed to marry in the Tarau society.

23. Find the group generated by S and D of the Tarau society.

5 THE CHOICE OF MARRIAGE RULES

In the last section we saw that the marriage rules of a primitive society are determined by the vector t and the matrices S and D. The axioms make no mention of the number of types, and indeed, we shall find that we can have any number of types, as long as $n > 1$. But we shall find that the choices of S and D are severely limited. This shows that the rules of existing primitive societies required considerable ingenuity for their construction.

We must now consider the last three axioms. For Axiom 5 we need a simple way of describing a kind of relationship. The family tree is our basic tool, but we want to replace the family tree by a suitable matrix.

Let us consider Figure 22. Instead of starting with the grandparents and finding the types of the grandson and the granddaughter, we could start with the grandson, work up to the grandparents, and then down to the granddaughter. For this we must consider how we work "up." If a parent is of type t, the son is of type tS. Hence, if the son is of type t, then the parent is of type tS^{-1}. Similarly, if a daughter has type t, her parents have type tD^{-1}. In Figure 23 we find the new version of Figure 22.

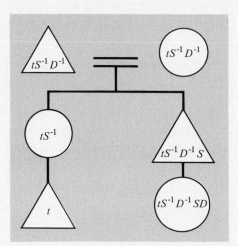

Figure 23

It is easily seen that we can follow this procedure for any relationship. Given a kind of relationship, it determines a matrix M such that if the male of the relationship is of type t, then the female is of type tM. From Figure 23 we see that for "mother's brother's daughter" $M = S^{-1}D^{-1}SD$. We shall speak of M as the *matrix of the relationship*. These matrices are all products of S, D, and their inverses; hence each matrix is an element of the group generated by S and D.

Let us consider Axiom 5. Given any kind of relationship between a man and a woman, we form the matrix of the relationship M. The man will be permitted to marry this relation of his if and only if his type is the same as hers, i.e., if a certain component of t is the same as the corresponding component of tM. This means that this component is left unchanged by the permutation M, which proves our first theorem.

Theorem 1 A man is allowed to marry a female relative of a certain kind if and only if his marriage type is not changed by M.

We know that the permutation I leaves every element fixed. We shall also be interested in permutations that do not leave any element fixed, and we shall call them *complete permutations* (see Chapter 3, Section 4).

A second result now follows from Theorem 1.

Theorem 2 Marriage between relatives of a given kind is always permitted if $M = I$, and is never permitted if M is a complete permutation.

Theorem 3 Axiom 5 requires that in the group generated by S and D every element except I is a complete permutation.

Proof The axiom states that for a given relationship the marriage must always be allowed or must never be allowed. Hence the matrix of every relationship must either be I or a complete permutation matrix. The matrices are elements of the group generated by S and D. And given any element of this group, which can be written as a product of S's and D's, we can draw a family tree having this matrix. Hence the matrices of relationships are all the elements of the group. This means that all the elements of the group, other than the identity, must be complete permutations. This completes the proof.

Theorem 4 Axiom 6 requires that $S^{-1}D$ be a complete permutation.

This theorem is an immediate consequence of the fact that the matrix of the brother-sister relationship is $S^{-1}D$.

Theorem 5 Axiom 7 requires that for every i and j there be a permutation in the group which carries t_i into t_j.

Proof Let us choose two individuals, one of type t_i and one of type t_j. There must be a descendant of the former who can marry a descendant of the latter. Hence the two descendants must have the same type. This means that we have permutations M_1 and M_2 such that t_i is carried by M_1 into the same type as t_j by M_2. Then $M_1M_2^{-1}$ carries t_i into t_j. Hence the theorem follows.

We have now translated Axioms 5–7 into the following three conditions on S and D: (1) The group generated by S and D consists of I and of complete permutations. (2) $S^{-1}D$ is a complete permutation. (3) For every pair of types there is a permutation in the group that carries one type into the other.

Definition   A permutation group is called *regular* if (a) it is complete, i.e., every element of the group other than I is a complete permutation, and if (b) for every pair from among the n objects there is a permutation in the group that carries one into the other.

Basic Theorem   To satisfy the axioms we must choose two different $n \times n$ permutation matrices S and D which generate a regular permutation group.

Proof   Conditions (1) and (3) above state precisely that the group generated by S and D be regular. In a regular group every element other than I is a complete permutation; hence condition (2) requires only that $S^{-1}D$ be different from I. Since $S^{-1}D = I$ is equivalent to $D = S$, we need only require that $D \neq S$. This completes the proof.

It is important to be able to recognize regular permutation groups. Here we are helped by a very simple, well-known theorem: A subgroup of the group of permutations of degree n is regular if and only if it has n elements and is complete.

This leads to a relatively simple procedure. We choose n. Then we must pick a group of $n \times n$ permutation matrices which has n elements and is complete, and select two different elements which generate the group. This is always possible if $n > 1$ (see Exercise 11). One of these is chosen as S and one as D. Since there are not very many regular permutation groups for any n, the choice is very limited.

EXAMPLE   Let us find all possibilities for a society having four marriage types. First of all we must find the regular subgroups of the symmetric group of degree 4, i.e., the groups of permutations on four objects that have four elements and are complete.

Among these we find cyclic groups. Any two of these groups have the same structure and hence lead to equivalent rules. Let us suppose that we choose the permutation group generated by

$$P = \begin{pmatrix} 0 & 1 & 0 & 0 \\ 0 & 0 & 1 & 0 \\ 0 & 0 & 0 & 1 \\ 1 & 0 & 0 & 0 \end{pmatrix}.$$

The group consists of P, P^2, P^3, and I. Either P or P^3 generates the group, and they play analogous roles. We may therefore assume that P is one of the two permutations chosen. This allows us (P, P^2), (P, P^3), and (P, I) as possibilities. We must still ask which is S and which is D. In the second case it makes no difference, since P and P^3 play analogous roles in the group, but there is a difference in the other two cases. This leads to five possibilities:

1. $S = P,$ $\qquad D = P^2$
2. $S = P^2,$ $\qquad D = P$
3. $S = P,$ $\qquad D = P^3$
4. $S = P,$ $\qquad D = I$
5. $S = I,$ $\qquad D = P$. This is the Tarau society; see Exercises 18–23 of Section 4.

There is only one noncyclic complete subgroup with four elements, consisting of I and the three permutations which interchange two pairs of elements. In this group we have essentially only one case, since all three permutations play the same role.

6. The Kariera society. (See Exercises 12–17 after the last section.)

Two of these six possibilities are actually exemplified in known primitive societies.

EXERCISES

1. Figure 23 shows the matrix of one of the first-cousin relations. Find the matrices of the other three first-cousin relationships.
2. Prove that marriage between relations of a certain kind is permitted if and only if the matrix of the relation is I.
3. Use the result of Exercise 2 to prove that no society allows the marriage between cousins of the types in Figure 19(a) and (b).
4. Which of the six rules described above (in the example) allow marriage between a man and his father's sister's daughter? [*Ans.* 3, 6.]
5. Show that all six rules given in the example above allow marriages between a man and his mother's brother's daughter.
6. There are eight kinds of second-cousin relationships between a man and a woman. Draw their family trees.
7. Find the matrices of the eight second-cousin relationships.
8. Are there any second-cousin relationships for which marriage is forbidden by all possible rules? [*Ans.* Yes.]
9. Test the second-cousin relationships (other than those found in Exercise 8) for each of the six rules given in the example above.
10. For n objects, consider the permutation that carries object number i into position $i + 1$, except that the last object is put into first place. Show that the cyclic group generated by this permutation is regular.
11. Use the result of Exercise 10 to show that a society can have any number of marriage types, as long as the number is greater than one.
12. In the example of Section 4, prove that S and D generate a regular permutation group.
13. Prove that the following matrices lead to a rule satisfying all axioms.

$$S = \begin{pmatrix} 0 & 1 & 0 & 0 & 0 & 0 \\ 0 & 0 & 1 & 0 & 0 & 0 \\ 1 & 0 & 0 & 0 & 0 & 0 \\ 0 & 0 & 0 & 0 & 1 & 0 \\ 0 & 0 & 0 & 0 & 0 & 1 \\ 0 & 0 & 0 & 1 & 0 & 0 \end{pmatrix}, \quad D = \begin{pmatrix} 0 & 0 & 0 & 1 & 0 & 0 \\ 0 & 0 & 0 & 0 & 0 & 1 \\ 0 & 0 & 0 & 0 & 1 & 0 \\ 1 & 0 & 0 & 0 & 0 & 0 \\ 0 & 0 & 1 & 0 & 0 & 0 \\ 0 & 1 & 0 & 0 & 0 & 0 \end{pmatrix}.$$

14.   Prove that the rule given in Exercise 13 allows no first-cousin marriages.

6 EXAMPLES FROM ECONOMICS AND FINANCE

Markov-chain models are probabilistic in nature. However, it turns out that sometimes the mathematics used to analyze them can also be used in analyzing deterministic models. In the present section we shall discuss two deterministic models that can be solved by imbedding them in absorbing Markov chains.

In what we are going to do the question of whether a given Markov chain is absorbing is crucial. Hence we need an algorithm for determing the answer to this question. Such an algorithm is given in Figure 24. The proof that the algorithm works is given in Exercises 1 and 2.

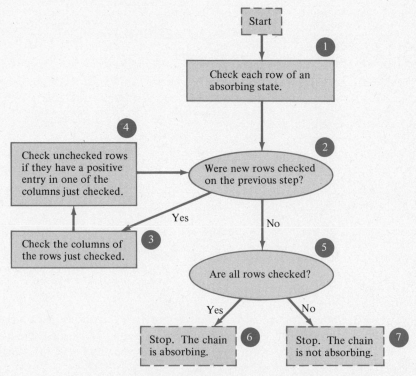

Figure 24   Flow diagram for testing to see whether a Markov chain is absorbing

EXAMPLE 1   Apply the method in Figure 24 to the transition matrix

$$P = \begin{pmatrix} 1 & 0 & 0 & 0 \\ 0 & 0 & \frac{1}{3} & \frac{2}{3} \\ \frac{1}{2} & \frac{1}{2} & 0 & 0 \\ 0 & 0 & 1 & 0 \end{pmatrix}.$$

We carry out the checking process indicated by the algorithm, marking the checks in the order in which they were made. We obtain

$$\begin{array}{cccc} \overset{1}{\checkmark} & \overset{3}{\checkmark} & \overset{2}{\checkmark} & \overset{3}{\checkmark} \\ \end{array}$$

$$\begin{array}{c} 1\checkmark \\ 3\checkmark \\ 2\checkmark \\ 3\checkmark \end{array} \begin{pmatrix} 1 & 0 & 0 & 0 \\ 0 & 0 & \frac{1}{3} & \frac{2}{3} \\ \frac{1}{2} & \frac{1}{2} & 0 & 0 \\ 0 & 0 & 1 & 0 \end{pmatrix}.$$

Since all rows are checked, the Markov chain is absorbing. The reader should find the paths from each state to the absorbing state. The numbers of the checks will help in this regard (see Exercise 3).

EXAMPLE 2   Let us apply the method of Figure 24 to the transition matrix

$$P' = \begin{pmatrix} 1 & 0 & 0 & 0 \\ 0 & \frac{1}{3} & 0 & \frac{2}{3} \\ \frac{1}{2} & 0 & \frac{1}{2} & 0 \\ 0 & \frac{3}{4} & 0 & \frac{1}{4} \end{pmatrix}.$$

The checks produced by the algorithm are

$$\begin{array}{cc} \overset{1}{\checkmark} & \overset{2}{\checkmark} \\ \end{array}$$

$$\begin{array}{c} 1\checkmark \\ \\ 2\checkmark \\ \\ \end{array} \begin{pmatrix} 1 & 0 & 0 & 0 \\ 0 & \frac{1}{3} & 0 & \frac{2}{3} \\ \frac{1}{2} & 0 & \frac{1}{2} & 0 \\ 0 & \frac{3}{4} & 0 & \frac{1}{4} \end{pmatrix}.$$

Here, since not all the rows are checked, the Markov chain whose transition matrix is P' is not absorbing. The reader should check that the states $\{2, 4\}$ form a closed set, in the sense that it is impossible to leave them once entered. In particular it is impossible to go from either of these states to the absorbing state (1), so that the chain is not absorbing.

We now consider our first important applied example.

EXAMPLE 3   *The Open Leontief Model.* Consider an economy with r industries and each industry produces just one kind of good. These industries are interconnected in the sense that each must buy a nonnegative amount of the other industries' products in order to operate. Let q_{ij} be the dollar amount of the output of industry j that must be purchased by industry i in order to produce \$1 of its own goods. Let Q be the $r \times r$ matrix with entries q_{ij}. By definition we have

$$(1) \qquad\qquad\qquad Q \geq 0.$$

It is not hard to see that for fixed i the sum $q_{i1} + \ldots + q_{ir}$ gives the total cost of the inputs needed by industry i in order to produce \$1 worth of output. Clearly it makes sense to require that $q_{i1} + \ldots + q_{ir} \leq 1$; that is, the total value of the inputs going into a dollar's worth of output must be less than or equal to a dollar. For obvious reasons we shall call the ith industry *profitable* if the strict inequality holds, and *profitless* if the equality holds. In order to rule out unprofitable industries we require

$$(2) \qquad\qquad\qquad Qf \leq f,$$

where f is the r-component column vector of all 1's.

Suppose now that the total economy is to be run so that a vector $d = (d_1, \ldots, d_r)$ of goods can be supplied for consumption. Here d_j is the amount of good j to be consumed. At what levels shall we run each industry in order to supply total demand? Let x_i be the level at which industry i is to be run. To make economic sense, $x_i \geq 0$. Then $x = (x_1, \ldots, x_r)$ is the *activity vector* for the industries, and $x \geq 0$. The jth component of xQ is $x_1 q_{1j} + \ldots + x_r q_{rj}$, and this is the total output of industry j demanded by all the other industries when the economy uses the activity vector x. In the same manner one can see that xQ is the vector of internal demands when the economy uses the activity vector x.

Now the vector x must be chosen so as to provide the sum of the internal plus the external demand. That is,

$$(3) \qquad\qquad\qquad x = xQ + d.$$

Equation (3) implies

$$(4) \qquad\qquad\qquad x(I - Q) = d.$$

If the matrix $(I - Q)$ has a nonnegative inverse, we can solve for (4) as

$$(5) \qquad\qquad\qquad x = d(I - Q)^{-1},$$

and the result will be economically meaningful. If this inverse does not exist or if it has negative entries, then there will be some kinds of outside demand vectors d for which there is no nonnegative solution activity vector x.

Thus we need conditions on the matrix Q that $(I - Q)$ have a nonnegative inverse. Here we apply the theory of absorbing Markov chains. We imbed the matrix Q into a Markov chain P having $r + 1$ states as follows:

$$(6) \qquad\qquad\qquad P = \left(\begin{array}{c|c} 1 & 0 \\ \hline R & Q \end{array} \right),$$

where the first state is absorbing, and R is an $r \times 1$ matrix with components $r_i = 1 - (q_{i1} + \ldots + q_{ir})$ for $i = 1, \ldots, r$. (We label the first state 0.) We now apply the flow diagram of Figure 24, but marking only state 0 when in box 1 of the flow diagram. If we end up in box 6, we know that P is an absorbing Markov chain with fundamental matrix $N = (I - Q)^{-1}$. And the fundamental matrix is nonnegative. If we end up in box 7 of Figure 24, it can be shown (see Exercise 5) that $I - Q$ is singular and has no inverse. Hence in this case there is no economic solution to the economy as it stands.

We summarize our results in a theorem:

Theorem Let Q be the input matrix of an open Leontief economy satisfying (1) and (2); then equation (3) can be solved for all demand vectors d if and only if the Markov chain P of (6) is an absorbing chain.

EXAMPLE 3
(continued)

As an example, suppose that there are three industries and

(7)
$$Q = \begin{pmatrix} 0 & \frac{1}{2} & 0 \\ \frac{1}{3} & \frac{1}{3} & \frac{1}{3} \\ \frac{1}{6} & 0 & \frac{1}{2} \end{pmatrix}.$$

Then the Markov chain P is given by

(8)
$$P = \left(\begin{array}{c|ccc} 1 & 0 & 0 & 0 \\ \hline \frac{1}{2} & 0 & \frac{1}{2} & 0 \\ 0 & \frac{1}{3} & \frac{1}{3} & \frac{1}{3} \\ \frac{1}{3} & \frac{1}{6} & 0 & \frac{1}{2} \end{array} \right)$$

Applying the algorithm of Figure 24, we easily find that the Markov chain is absorbing. Hence $(I - Q)^{-1}$ exists. It is

(9)
$$(I - Q)^{-1} = \begin{pmatrix} 1 & -\frac{1}{2} & 0 \\ -\frac{1}{3} & \frac{2}{3} & -\frac{1}{3} \\ -\frac{1}{6} & 0 & \frac{1}{2} \end{pmatrix}^{-1} = \begin{pmatrix} \frac{3}{2} & \frac{9}{8} & \frac{3}{4} \\ 1 & \frac{9}{4} & \frac{3}{2} \\ \frac{1}{2} & \frac{3}{8} & \frac{9}{4} \end{pmatrix}$$

Thus for a demand vector $d = (400, 200, 300)$ we have activity vector

(10)
$$x = d(I - Q)^{-1} = (400, 200, 300) \begin{pmatrix} \frac{3}{2} & \frac{9}{8} & \frac{3}{4} \\ 1 & \frac{9}{4} & \frac{3}{2} \\ \frac{1}{2} & \frac{3}{8} & \frac{9}{4} \end{pmatrix}$$

$$= (950, 1012.5, 1275),$$

so that $950 worth of output must be produced by industry 1, $1012.50 worth of output by industry 2, and $1275 worth of output by industry 3 in order that consumptions of $400, $200, and $300 of each (respective) industry's output may be realized.

EXAMPLE 4

A Cost-Accounting Model. Consider a company that has r departments. It has adopted accounting conventions such that if department i performs services for department j then it charges a fraction q_{ij} of its costs to department j. It requires $q_{ii} = 0$, since it does not make sense for a department to charge costs to itself. It also requires $q_{ij} \geq 0$, so that (1) holds. No department is permitted to charge more than 100 percent of its costs to other departments, so that $q_{i1} + \ldots + q_{ir} \leq 1$, and (2) holds as well. Departments for which the equality holds are called *service departments,* since they charge away all of their costs, and departments for which the inequality holds are *profit centers,* since they actually pay some of their costs. Let d_i be the dollar amount of external costs charged to department i by outside firms, and let $d = (d_1, \ldots, d_r)$ be the corresponding vector. Finally, let x_i be the total costs assigned to department i and let $x = (x_1, \ldots, x_r)$ be the corresponding vector.

Since the costs assigned to a department must be the sum of the internally charged costs plus the external costs, it is easy to see by the same kind of analysis as for the Leontief model that equation (3) must be satisfied by the x's. Therefore we have the same problem as before of determining whether the inverse of $(I - Q)$ exists. The same solution technique of imbedding the matrix Q in a Markov chain and using Figure 24 to see if it is absorbing provides the solution technique.

It is remarkable that from two quite different interpretations in the Leontief input-output model and the cost-accounting model we have arrived at exactly the same mathematical model and corresponding solution technique.

EXAMPLE 4 (continued) As a numerical example, consider the matrix

$$Q = \begin{pmatrix} 0 & 0 & 0 & 0 & 0 \\ 0 & 0 & 0 & 0 & 0 \\ \frac{1}{2} & 0 & 0 & \frac{1}{3} & \frac{1}{6} \\ \frac{1}{4} & \frac{1}{4} & \frac{1}{4} & 0 & \frac{1}{4} \\ 0 & \frac{1}{3} & \frac{1}{3} & \frac{1}{3} & 0 \end{pmatrix}.$$

Here the first two departments are profit centers, since they do not charge any of their costs to other departments of the company. The last three departments are service centers, since they charge off all their costs to other departments. It is easy to show that the Markov chain P obtained by (6) is absorbing, hence $(I - Q)^{-1}$ exists. A computer gave the following values for this inverse:

$$(I - Q)^{-1} = \begin{pmatrix} 1 & 0 & 0 & 0 & 0 \\ 0 & 1 & 0 & 0 & 0 \\ -\frac{1}{2} & 0 & 1 & -\frac{1}{3} & -\frac{1}{6} \\ -\frac{1}{4} & -\frac{1}{4} & -\frac{1}{4} & 1 & -\frac{1}{4} \\ 0 & -\frac{1}{3} & -\frac{1}{3} & -\frac{1}{3} & 1 \end{pmatrix}^{-1}$$

$$= \begin{pmatrix} 1 & 0 & 0 & 0 & 0 \\ 0 & 1 & 0 & 0 & 0 \\ .7547 & .2453 & 1.2453 & .5283 & .3396 \\ .5472 & .4528 & .4528 & 1.2830 & .3962 \\ .4340 & .5660 & .5660 & .6038 & 1.2453 \end{pmatrix}.$$

If we assume that $d_i = 10,000$ for $i = 1, \ldots, 5$—that is, each department incurs outside expenses of \$10,000—then from (5) we find that

$$x = (27{,}359 \quad 22{,}641 \quad 22{,}641 \quad 24{,}151 \quad 19{,}811).$$

Notice that the sum of the costs of the first two departments, which are profit centers, is \$27,359 + \$22,641 = \$50,000. In other words, the profit centers end up paying all the outside costs. This is always true (see Exercise 7).

EXERCISES

1. In Figure 24 show that each time we check a new row when we are in box 4 of the flow diagram, there is a way of getting from state i to an absorbing state. Hence show that if we end up in box 6, the chain is absorbing.

2. In Figure 24 show that if we end up in box 7, there is at least one state that cannot reach an absorbing state.

3. In Example 1 show that if we number each check as it is made, then the numbers on the rows are equal to 1 plus the minimum number of steps required to go from that state to an absorbing state.

4. Apply the flow diagram of Figure 24 to the following examples of Markov chains to see if they are absorbing.

   (a) $\begin{pmatrix} 0 & 1 & 0 \\ 1 & 0 & 0 \\ 0 & 1 & 0 \end{pmatrix}$

   (b) $\begin{pmatrix} \frac{1}{2} & 0 & \frac{1}{2} & 0 \\ \frac{1}{4} & 0 & \frac{1}{4} & \frac{1}{2} \\ 0 & 0 & 1 & 0 \\ 0 & \frac{1}{2} & 0 & \frac{1}{2} \end{pmatrix}$

   (c) $\begin{pmatrix} 0 & \frac{1}{2} & \frac{1}{2} \\ 1 & 0 & 0 \\ 1 & 0 & 0 \end{pmatrix}$

   (d) $\begin{pmatrix} 1 & 0 & 0 & 0 \\ 0 & \frac{1}{2} & \frac{1}{2} & 0 \\ 0 & 0 & 0 & 1 \\ \frac{1}{2} & \frac{1}{2} & 0 & 0 \end{pmatrix}$

5. Assume that we started with an $r \times r$ matrix Q satisfying (1) and (2), defined the Markov chain P as in (6), and applied the flow diagram of Figure 24, ending up in box 7.

   (a) Let $h_i = 0$ when i is a checked row and $h_i = 1$ when i is an unchecked row. Let h be the r-component column vector with components h_i. Show that $h \neq 0$ and $h \geq 0$.

   (b) Show that $Qh \geq h$, and hence that $(I - Q)h \leq 0$.

   (c) If $(I - Q)^{-1}$ exists, use (b) to show that $h \leq 0$.

   (d) Use (a) and (c) to prove that $(I - Q)^{-1}$ does not exist.

6. Let Q and d be as given below for Leontief input-output models. When possible, solve for x as in (5).

   (a) $$Q = \begin{pmatrix} \frac{1}{2} & 0 & \frac{1}{2} \\ \frac{1}{4} & 0 & \frac{1}{4} \\ 0 & \frac{1}{2} & 0 \end{pmatrix}, \qquad d = (5000, 8000, 2000).$$

(b)
$$Q = \begin{pmatrix} 0 & \frac{1}{2} & \frac{1}{2} \\ \frac{1}{2} & 0 & \frac{1}{2} \\ \frac{1}{2} & \frac{1}{2} & 0 \end{pmatrix}, \qquad d = (100, 500, 300).$$

(c)
$$Q = \begin{pmatrix} 0 & 1 & 0 \\ 0 & 0 & 1 \\ \frac{1}{2} & 0 & 0 \end{pmatrix}, \qquad d = (1000, 2000, 3000).$$

7. In the cost-accounting model of Example 4, show that no service center can pay any outside cost. Use this to show that the profit centers must ultimately pay all outside costs.

8. Let Q and d be as given below for cost-accounting models. When possible, solve for x as in (5).

(a)
$$Q = \begin{pmatrix} 0 & \frac{1}{2} & \frac{1}{4} \\ \frac{1}{3} & 0 & \frac{1}{3} \\ 1 & 0 & 0 \end{pmatrix}, \qquad d = (200, 500, 700).$$

(b)
$$Q = \begin{pmatrix} 0 & 1 & 0 \\ \frac{1}{2} & 0 & \frac{1}{2} \\ \frac{2}{3} & \frac{1}{3} & 0 \end{pmatrix}, \qquad d = (3000, 7000, 5000).$$

(c)
$$Q = \begin{pmatrix} 0 & \frac{1}{5} & \frac{3}{5} \\ \frac{1}{6} & 0 & \frac{1}{3} \\ \frac{1}{6} & \frac{2}{3} & 0 \end{pmatrix}, \qquad d = (1000, 1000, 1000).$$

7 OPTIMAL HARVESTING OF DEER

Linear programming models have frequently been used to solve production problems in industry such as determining optimal production schedules and making oil refinery operating decisions. More recently such models have been applied to the solution of local, state, and federal governmental decision problems. We illustrate here the latter type.

Consider a county located in an eastern state that has a large proportion of forested areas, and hence a large deer population. Every year the county forest service has to set the length of both the *regular deer season*, when only mature males may be killed, and the *unrestricted deer season*, during which any deer except a fawn may be killed. In making these decisions the service has conflicting objectives. If it makes the hunting seasons long it will attract many hunters, who will spend large amounts of money in the county and thus please local businessmen. But if the season is too long, then too many deer will be taken in a given year and the stock will be depleted for the next year's hunting. The forest service must also take into account the local property owners whose land is walked over by the hunters. On the one hand, the owners would like to keep the deer population low, since during the winter the deer eat the new growth on small trees, thus killing the trees. But the property owners also dislike the idea of hunters walking in the woods shooting at moving targets.

Still other considerations are involved in the presence of the deer and the hunting season. For instance, every year in the county there are numerous accidents involving cars hitting deer on the roads. Also, during the hunting season there are numerous hunting accidents. Finally, if the deer population is permitted to become too large, then many will starve because of a limited food supply.

Every year the forest service makes a survey of the deer population and estimates the numbers of (a) *mature males* and (b) *other deer* (mature females and yearlings and fawns of both sexes). It then weighs the above factors and sets the number of days for the regular hunting season and for the unrestricted hunting season. Let us set up a linear programming model for the decision problem.

Suppose that for each day of the regular deer-hunting season 150 mature male deer are killed and hunters spend $18,000 in the county for hunting licenses, motels, meals, gasoline, hunting equipment, etc. Also suppose that for each day of the unrestricted hunting season 85 mature males and 400 other kinds of deer are killed and hunters spend $20,000. Let us also assume that during a year a mature male will cause $5 worth of damage to young trees and that other kinds of deer will cause $2 worth of damage.

The annual deer survey has revealed that there are 12,000 mature males and 33,600 other kinds of deer within the county limits. The service wants to leave at least 10,000 mature males and at least 27,000 of other kinds of deer as breeding stock for next year's season. Also, the service has set an upper limit of 5 days for the unrestricted hunting season because of pressure from a local ecological society. How shall it determine the number of days for each season in order to maximize the difference between the revenues to local businessmen and the damage done to the woodlands by the deer?

To set the problem up as a linear programming problem we first define four variables:

x_1 is the number of days of the regular hunting season.
x_2 is the number of days of the unrestricted hunting season.
x_3 is the number of mature males remaining after both seasons.
x_4 is the number of other deer remaining after both seasons.

We then set up the initial tableau of the linear program as in Figure 25. Let us check whether this captures the essence of the problem described above. The third constraint is just the upper bound on the unrestricted

x_1	x_2	x_3	x_4	
150	85	1	0	$= 12{,}000$
0	400	0	1	$= 33{,}600$
0	1	0	0	≤ 5
0	0	1	0	$\geq 10{,}000$
0	0	0	1	$\geq 27{,}000$
18,000	20,000	-5	-2	

Figure 25

hunting season mentioned above. The fourth and fifth $\geq$ constraints are the lower bounds on the remaining mature males and other kinds of deer at the end of both hunting seasons. The first constraint is a kind of "accounting equation" that accounts for the total number of mature males (12,000) as those killed in each of the seasons plus the number remaining (x_3). The second constraint similarly accounts for the number of other deer.

The linear programming problem of Figure 25 is so simple that we can solve it by inspection (see Exercises 2 and 3). The optimal primal and dual solutions are on the top and to the left of the tableau in Figure 26. The reader should check that the indicated primal and dual solutions are feasible and produce the same objective function values. By an extension of the duality theorem to the case of mixed constraints this will guarantee that the solutions are optimal (see Exercise 1).

	10.5	5	10,000	31,600	
120	150	85	1	0	= 12,000
−2	0	400	0	1	= 33,600
10,600	0	1	0	0	≤ 5
−125	0	0	1	0	≥ 10,000
0	0	0	0	1	≥ 27,000
	18,000	20,000	−5	−2	$175,800

Figure 26

The answer indicates that there should be a regular hunting season of 10.5 days, which could be accomplished by starting it at noon on a given day and ending at sundown 10 days later. Also, there should be an unrestricted hunting season of 5 days. At the end of the seasons there will be 10,000 mature males and 31,600 other kinds of deer remaining to provide hunting for the next season. The total net income to the county is $175,800.

The dual solution variables provide very interesting information. It is easy to see that the first dual variable v_1 indicates that a mature male deer has an imputed value of $120. And the third dual variable v_3 indicates that the imputed value of each day of the unrestricted hunting season is $10,600. The interpretations of the other dual variables are indicated in Exercise 4.

Notice that in the solution indicated in Figure 26 there are just 10,000 mature males remaining at the end of the season (the lower bound), while there are 31,600 other kinds of deer remaining, which is a considerably greater number than the lower bound of 27,000. Perhaps this bound should be raised.

But there is a still more serious criticism of the solution and the problem formulation. Namely, it does not take into account the dynamic factors in the changes of the deer population from one year to the next. Thus we know that there will be 10,000 mature males and 31,600 other kinds of deer at the end of the hunting season, but between that date and the beginning of next year's hunting season there will be changes in these numbers due

to births, deaths, and aging of the deer population. We extend the model
to include these factors next.

As part of its annual survey the forest service estimates that about 1 out
of 8 mature males dies from natural causes such as old age, disease, pred-
ators, etc., during the entire year. About 9 percent of the other deer population become mature males during the year. And the other deer population
increases by about 3 percent each year, even after removing from it the
yearling males that mature during the year. These changes are summarized
in the matrix of Figure 27.

This \ Next   Mature   Other
year \ year   Males   Deer

Mature
Males $\begin{pmatrix} .88 & 0 \\ \\ .09 & 1.03 \end{pmatrix}$
Other
Figure 27   Deer

We can use the data of Figure 27 to make predictions as to the numbers
of mature males and other deer who will be alive next year, given the
number alive at the end of the present hunting season.

We now set up a two-year optimal harvesting linear program as shown
in Figure 28. Variables x_1, x_2, x_3, and x_4 are defined as before for the first

x_1	x_2	x_3	x_4	x_5	x_6	x_7	x_8	
150	85	1	0	0	0	0	0	$= 12{,}000$
0	400	0	1	0	0	0	0	$= 33{,}600$
0	1	0	0	0	0	0	0	≤ 5
0	0	1	0	0	0	0	0	$\geq 10{,}000$
0	0	0	1	0	0	0	0	$\geq 27{,}000$
0	0	$-.88$	$-.09$	150	85	1	0	$= 0$
0	0	0	-1.03	0	400	0	1	$= 0$
0	0	0	0	0	1	0	0	≤ 5
0	0	0	0	0	0	1	0	$\geq 10{,}000$
0	0	0	0	0	0	0	1	$\geq 27{,}000$
1	0	0	0	0	0	0	0	$= 0$
18,000	20,000	-5	-2	18,000	20,000	-5	-2	

Figure 28

year, and variables x_5, x_6, x_7, and x_8 are the corresponding variables for
the second year. Similarly, the first five constraints indicate restrictions for
the first year just like those in Figure 25, and the next five constraints indicate
the corresponding constraints for the second year. Note that in columns
3 and 4 of constraints 6 and 7 the numbers of Figure 27 appear but with
negative signs, and with the matrix transposed. Also, the right-hand sides

of constraints 6 and 7 are zeroes. In effect, what the minus signs on the coefficients do is to make predictions from the values of x_3 and x_4 as to the numbers of each of the kinds of deer that will be alive for the next season. In Exercise 5 you are asked to give a detailed explanation of these constraints.

The final constraint forces $x_1 = x_5$, i.e., the same number of regular hunting days both years. Unless the county follows this policy, it will receive many complaints.

The optimal primal solution to the problem in Figure 28 is

$$x = (9.24 \quad 5 \quad 10,189 \quad 31,600 \quad 9.24 \quad 5 \quad 10,000 \quad 30,548).$$

Note that the solution for the first year has changed. The number of regular hunting days is reduced from 10.5 to 9.24. As a result, more than 10,000 mature males are left (see x_3). Also, we note from the values of x_4 and x_8 that the numbers of other kinds of deer are decreasing. Thus it is likely that the number of unrestricted hunting days should be reduced from 5 to 4; this would permit a somewhat longer regular hunting season each year.

The transpose of the optimal dual solution (rounded) is

$$v^{TR} = (110 \quad 7.7 \quad 7,610 \quad 0 \quad 0 \quad 130 \quad -2 \quad 9,723 \quad -135 \quad 0 \quad 1,548).$$

Here the last five dual variables are the same as in Figure 26, but the first five are different. Exercise 7 asks for interpretations of these variables. The value to the county over two years is \$307,310. This is less than twice the value we found for the first year (see Exercise 8).

It is obvious that this model could be extended to cover three years or even longer, which might be particularly useful when planning long-range changes in the deer population.

Although the above model is an extremely simplified version of a governmental decision-making problem, it brings out some of the essential features: in making its decision the public agency (in this case the forest service) has to consider the benefits (in this case added revenues to the county) versus the costs (the negative features of the deer hunting). We have illustrated one kind of cost-benefit calculation commonly carried out by the decision makers. It should be emphasized that there are many other kinds of cost-benefit analyses that are used.

EXERCISES

1. (a) Check that the solution for x_1, x_2, x_3, and x_4 shown in Figure 26 is feasible.
    (b) Check that the dual solution v_1, v_2, v_3, v_4, and v_5 shown in Figure 26 is feasible.
    (c) Show that both solutions—in (a) and (b)—give the same objective value, and that nonnegative v-values correspond to $\leq$ constraints, and nonpositive v-values to $\geq$ constraints. (Either may occur

for $=$ constraints.) An extension of the duality theorem will then guarantee that the solutions are optimal.

2. Solve the problem in Figure 25 by carrying out the following steps:

  (a) Show that the most attractive variable to increase from 0 is x_2. Show that it can be set equal to its upper bound of 5 without destroying feasibility.

  (b) Show that if $x_2 = 5$, then $x_4 = 31,600$.

  (c) Show that x_3 may be set equal to 10,000, thus satisfying constraint 4.

  (d) With $x_2 = 5$ and $x_3 = 10,000$, show that $x_1 = 10.5$.

3. By carrying out a series of steps similar to those outlined in Exercise 2, solve for the dual solution to the problem in Figure 25.

4. For each of the dual variables in Figure 26 find their physical dimensions and give their economic interpretations.

5. Consider the problem in Figure 28. Assume that x_3 and x_4 have been determined and write the equations corresponding to constraints 5 and 6. Move the terms involving x_3 and x_4 to the right-hand side and show that these terms give the predictions as to the numbers of mature males and other deer that will be alive at the beginning of the second year's hunting seasons.

6. Check that the x- and v-vectors given are feasible for the problem in Figure 28. Show that they are optimal.

7. Find the dimensions of the optimal dual variables for the problem in Figure 28 and give their economic interpretations.

8. Explain why the value in the two-year model is less than twice the value for the single-year model.

8 KNAPSACK AND SEQUENCING PROBLEMS

In Section 7 of Chapter 2 we discussed combinatorial decision problems. We continue the discussion here and introduce the so-called *branch-and-bound method* for solving such problems.

Recall that a combinatorial decision problem is one of choosing the most desirable element from a finite set of possibilities. The branch-and-bound technique is a way of solving such problems that (usually) does not involve enumerating all the elements of the finite possibility set. We shall not try to give a formal description of branch-and-bound methods, but merely illustrate them in terms of examples.

EXAMPLE 1 *The Knapsack Problem.* You are going on a camping trip and are considering taking five different items with you. To help decide which ones to take, you have attached a *value* to each item indicating how strongly you want to take that item. These values and the (physical) weights of the various items are listed in the table of Figure 29. The last column of the table lists the items' value-to-weight ratios. Notice that the items are listed in decreas-

Item	Value	Weight	Value/Weight
1	72	30 pounds	2.4
2	65	28 pounds	2.32
3	52	23 pounds	2.26
4	38	19 pounds	2.00
5	30	16 pounds	1.88

Figure 29

ing order of this ratio. Thus the first item has the greatest value per pound, item 2 has the next greatest value per pound, and so on.

Adding up all the items you find (to your horror) that the total weight is 116 pounds. Since you are willing to carry at most 65 pounds you must choose a subset of the items to take with you. You quickly calculate that there $2^5 = 32$ subsets to consider. How can you find the best one?

Here the combinatorial decision problem is clear. A proper subset is *feasible* if its total weight is less than or equal to 65 pounds. The *value of the subset* is the sum of the values of its elements. We want to select the feasible subset with largest value.

This problem, which finds numerous applications in many other forms, has been dubbed a *knapsack problem* from the above rather frivolous illustration.

One way of solving the problem is to list all proper subsets, eliminate those that are not feasible, calculate the values of those that are feasible, and select the one whose value is greatest. Clearly this is a lengthy procedure; it would be even longer if there were, say, 20 items under consideration, for then there would be over a million proper subsets to generate!

The branch-and-bound method is a way of finding the best subset without (usually) having to enumerate all possible subsets. In Figure 30 we have drawn a tree diagram of the computation of the branch-and-bound solution to our problem. Each node of the tree below "Start" represents a decision either to take or not to take a given item. Any path going from "Start" to a given decision node represents a series of decisions. The first node on the path indicates whether or not item 1 is to be included; the second node on the path indicates whether or not item 2 is to be included, etc. Above and to the right of each decision node is a number representing the *upper bound* to the maximum value of any subset which can be chosen so as to agree with the decisions on the path from "Start" to that decision node.

Let us describe how the upper bounds are calculated. For instance, consider the decision "Take 1" (just below and to the right of "Start"). Having made this decision, we know that we have achieved a value of 72 plus whatever else can be obtained from later decisions. We now go down the list of possible items in decreasing order of value-to-weight ratio and assume that we can take them, including (if possible) a fractional part of the last item. In the present case, in addition to 1 we can take all of item

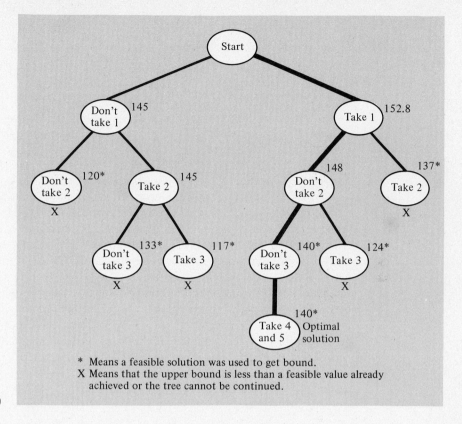

* Means a feasible solution was used to get bound.
X Means that the upper bound is less than a feasible value already
    achieved or the tree cannot be continued.

Figure 30

2; these two items add up to 58 pounds, leaving 7 more pounds, so we take $\frac{7}{23}$ of item 3. Thus our upper bound is $72 + 65 + 15.8 = 152.8$ for the decision. Of course, this value can't be achieved in practice because (we assume that) we can't physically take $\frac{7}{23}$ of item 3. But no subset that includes item 1 can have a greater value (see Exercise 1).

Upper bounds marked with an asterisk indicate that they were calculated using a feasible solution. For instance, the "Take 2" decision branching out from the "Take 1" decision indicates that we have decided to take items 1 and 2, whose weight totals 58 pounds, and to stop there. (Since each of the remaining items weighs more than 7 pounds, none of them can be included in a feasible solution.) Hence the asterisk shows that the set of decisions "Take 1" and "Take 2"—and no other items—is feasible, and the figure indicates an upper bound of 137.

Finally, note that in Figure 30 an X appears below some of the decisions. What this means is that the tree does not need to be continued further because the upper bound is less than a bound already achieved. Thus the branch ending in the "Don't Take 2" node need not be continued further, since its upper bound of 120 is lower than the upper bound of 137 already calculated.

Thus the optimal decision is indicated by the decision path:

Start—Take 1—Don't Take 2—Don't Take 3—Take 4 and 5

which is darkened in Figure 30. This means that you should take just items 1, 4, and 5 on the trip, giving a total weight of 65 and the maximum value of 140.

Examination of Figure 30 indicates that the branch-and-bound process actually evaluated only 6 of the 30 possible proper subsets. The other possible subsets have been *implicitly* evaluated by means of the bounding rules. Thus the branch-and-bound procedure requires considerably less work to find the solution than does the complete enumeration method.

In the previous problem we were trying to find the most valuable subset of a five-element set. In the sequencing problem to be described next we have the problem of finding the least costly permutation of a set of four elements. Again the branch-and-bound procedure will allow us to find the solution with less work than by enumerating all the possible permutations.

EXAMPLE 2 *A Sequencing Problem.* A manufacturer wants to make four different items on a single machine. If the machine has just completed item i and is to be used for item j next, a setup cost c_{ij} is incurred (the area around the machine must be cleaned up, a machinist must reset the machine to produce item j, etc.). The matrix of setup costs is as indicated in Figure 31. (The

		To			
		1	2	3	4
	1	—	10	18	6
From	2	10	—	5	15
	3	18	8	—	13
	4	6	12	9	—

Figure 31

costs c_{ii}, are indicated by dashes and not defined, since a given job will never be assigned to follow itself.) Notice that sometimes the setup cost of going from item i to item j is the same as the setup cost of going from j to i—for instance, $c_{k1} = c_{1k}$ for $k = 2, 3, 4$. But in other cases this is not so—for instance, $c_{23} = 5$ while $c_{32} = 8$.

The combinatorial decision problem is: In what order shall the manufacturer sequence the jobs to be produced on the machine in order to minimize the total setup time?

Since there are four items there are $4! = 24$ possible sequences. We could, of course, enumerate each of these and choose one that minimizes total setup cost. This is practical with four items, but with, say, ten items there would be $10! = 3,628,800$ permutations to enumerate, which would be possible only with a very fast computer. And for 20 items the enumeration of all 20! permutations is even beyond the capability of contemporary computers.

The branch-and-bound method can be applied to solve the problem, however—at least for a moderate number of items. For the example of Figure 31, the branch-and-bound tree is shown in Figure 32. Notice that on the first step the node of the tree has four branches (corresponding to starting with each one of the items). On the second step the nodes have three branches, on the third step at most two branches, etc.

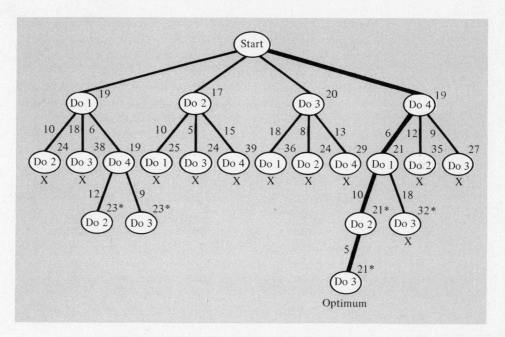

Figure 32

The numbers marked above and to the right of each decision are now *lower bounds* on the total setup cost, since our problem is to minimize this quantity. Those lower bounds marked with an asterisk were computed using feasible permutations, and the other lower bounds were calculated with permutations that are not necessarily feasible. Let us illustrate with the "Do 1" choice at the left of the second stage of choices. If we decide to "Do 1" first, then we shall *not* use any of the numbers in the first column of Figure 31, and we *must* use one number from the first row of Figure 31. Let's assume that we can use the smallest number in the first row, which is 6. To find the rest of the sequence we are now reduced to the 3 × 3 matrix in Figure 33(a), from which we must choose exactly two numbers. Without

	2	3	4
2	—	5	15
3	8	—	13
4	12	9	—

(a)

	1	3	4
1	—	18	6
3	18	—	13
4	6	9	—

(b)

	1	2	4
1	—	10	6
2	10	—	15
4	6	12	—

(c)

	1	2	3
1	—	10	18
2	10	—	5
3	18	8	—

(d)

Figure 33

worrying about feasibility let's assume that we can get the two smallest numbers in Figure 33(a), which are 5 and 8. The sum of these three numbers is $6 + 5 + 8 = 19$, which is the lower bound marked on the second-level "Do 1" decision node. The other lower bounds for the second stage of the tree are calculated using Figures 33(b)–(d). Note that on the third stage of the decision tree we have marked on those branches of the tree the actual setup costs corresponding to the actual decision representing the sequence so far determined. These numbers are used in finding the third-stage lower bounds. As in the previous example, some nodes are marked with an X, indicating that the bound at that node is inferior to a bound already achieved, so that further search on that branch is unnecessary.

When the decision tree is completed it is found that the optimal sequence is to produce the items in the order 4, 1, 2, 3 and that the total setup cost for this sequence is 21. This optimal decision path is darkened in Figure 32. Comparing this value with the lower bounds on some of the terminated branches makes it clear that there is considerable cost saving by finding and using the optimal sequence rather than just choosing a production sequence at random.

In the examples above we have used the so-called "search in breadth" technique for selecting nodes to evaluate, since we found bounds for all decisions on the same level. There is another technique called "search in depth" in which we first go all the way down one path through the tree and actually construct a feasible solution, hopefully with a good bound. In many cases the latter technique has proved to be the better of the two. It is illustrated in the exercises.

EXERCISES

1. In Example 1 use the fact that the items are listed in order of decreasing value/weight ratio to demonstrate that the upper bound calculation insures a true upper bound being found.

2. Solve the knapsack problem whose data is given by the following table:

Item	Value	Weight
1	70	30
2	61	27
3	54	25
4	40	20
5	31	18
6	25	15

The maximum weight to be carried is again 65 pounds.

3. Show that all the upper bounds in Figure 30 are correctly determined.

4. You have $18 to spend on clothes, and have set up the following table of the kinds of clothes you want to buy with their values and costs:

Item(s)	Value	Cost
1 Shirt	15	$ 6.50
2 Shirts	25	12.00
1 Tie	10	4.50
2 Ties	18	8.00
1 Pr. Socks	5	1.25
2 Pr. Socks	8	2.25

Use the branch-and-bound method to determine your optimal set of purchases. (This is an example of what in economics is called a *budget problem*.)

5. Show that the bounds indicated in Figure 32 are correct.

6. Work the four-item sequencing problem with the following data:

	1	2	3	4
1	—	7	11	4
2	8	—	12	7
3	6	13	—	12
4	9	5	4	—

7. In Figure 30 assume that you are doing a "search in depth" by following at each level only the alternative with the greatest upper bound. How does the tree of the branch-and-bound method change?

8. In Figure 32 assume that you are doing a "search in depth" by following at each level only the alternative with the smallest lower bound. How does the tree of the branch-and-bound method change?

SUGGESTED READING

David, H. A. "Tournaments and Paired Comparisons." *Biometrika* 46 (1959): 139–149.

Gardin, J. C., et P. Garelli. "Étude des établissments assyriens en Cappadoce par ordinateurs." *Annales Economies, Sociétés, Civilisations* 16 (1969): 837–876.

Gaver, Donald P. and Gerald L. Thompson, *Programming and Probability Models in Operations Research.* Monterey, Calif.: Brooks Cole, 1973.

Harary, F., R. Z. Norman, and C. C. Cartwright. *Structural Models.* New York: Wiley, 1965.

Kemeny, John G., and J. Laurie Snell. *Finite Markov Chains.* Princeton, N.J.: Van Nostrand, 1960.

Moon, J. W. *Topics on Tournaments.* New York: Holt, Rinehart and Winston, Inc., 1968.

Weil, André. "Sur l'Étude de Certains Types de Lois de Marriage (Système Murngin)." in Appendice à la Première Partie, *Les Structures Elementaire de la Parente.* by Claude Levi-Strauss. Paris: Presses Universitaires de France, 1949, pp. 278–285.

Wilson, R. J. *Introduction to Graph Theory.* New York: Academic Press, 1972.

Index